The Heritage-scape

The Heritage-scape

UNESCO, World Heritage, and Tourism

MICHAEL A. DI GIOVINE

LEXINGTON BOOKS

A division of
ROWMAN & LITTLEFIELD PUBLISHERS, INC.
Lanham • Boulder • New York • Toronto • Plymouth, UK

LEXINGTON BOOKS

A division of Rowman & Littlefield Publishers, Inc.
A wholly owned subsidiary of The Rowman & Littlefield Publishing Group, Inc.
4501 Forbes Boulevard, Suite 200
Lanham, MD 20706

Estover Road
Plymouth PL6 7PY
United Kingdom

British Library Cataloguing in Publication Information Available

Library of Congress Cataloging-in-Publication Data

Di Giovine, Michael A.
  The heritage-scape : UNESCO, world heritage, and tourism / Michael A. Di Giovine.
    p. cm.
  Includes bibliographical references and index.
  ISBN-13: 978-0-7391-1434-6 (cloth : alk. paper)
  ISBN-10: 0-7391-1434-4 (cloth : alk. paper)
  ISBN-13: 978-0-7391-1435-3 (pbk. : alk. paper)
  ISBN-10: 0-7391-1435-2 (pbk. : alk. paper)
  eISBN-13: 978-0-7391-3144-2
  eISBN-10: 0-7391-3144-3
  1. World Heritage areas. 2. Heritage tourism. 3. Unesco. 4. Peace-building. I. Title.
  G140.5.D54 2009
  338.4'791—dc22

                                                                    2008031214

Printed in the United States of America

♾ The paper used in this publication meets the minimum requirements of American
National Standard for Information Sciences—Permanence of Paper for Printed Library
Materials, ANSI/NISO Z39.48–1992.

For Laura, my favorite travel companion

TABLE OF CONTENTS

INTRODUCTION

TRAVELING ACROSS STONES THAT SPEAK

I grew up in a World Heritage site. At least, that is what I tell people. I say "grew up" because many of the formative experiences I enjoyed at the threshold of young adulthood can be traced to the summers I spent, from grade school onwards, in the central Italian town of Urbino. Envisioned by its Renaissance rulers to be a *città ideale*—an "ideal city," perfect in material and social composition—Urbino was built up on the remains of a Roman outpost through the vision of the Montefeltro dukes, who commissioned the finest architects, artists and writers of the time; Piero della Francesca, Luciano Laureana, Paolo Uccello and Giovanni Santi, Raphael Sanzio's father, all lived and worked in the hill town. Urbino became the paragon of princely courts, and as the setting for Baldassare Castiglione's classic narrative, *The Courtier*, it has been henceforth branded in the Italian mind as the epitome of Italian Renaissance refinement and rebirth. Because of these virtues, these important contributions to not only the heritage of the Italian people—whatever and whoever that may be exactly—but to the heritage of the World as we know it, the United Nations' Education, Scientific and Cultural Organization (UNESCO) determined that Urbino possesses universal cultural value, and the entire city was designated a World Heritage site in November 1998.

Each time I set foot on its cobblestoned streets, the city spoke with increasing clarity to me about universalities in an intensely personal way. Before I had ever visited Urbino, I was but a boy, an adolescent born and raised in suburban New Jersey, slowly discovering his own significance, his own heritage. My identity had been formed through a perception of my own Italian-American heritage that incorporated oft-competing notions of "Italian-ness" from our family's traditions, an American education, and the American media's idealized representations of Italy. It was a perception fusing the Leaning Tower, the *tarantella*, baked ziti and mandolin music. As I physically and emotionally experienced Urbino from day to day and year to year—soaking in the vistas, touching the red

1

brick buildings, tasting the different cuisines—a more complex awareness emerged of not only how subjective the notion of "heritage" is, but also how different expectations and perceptions of authenticity intermingle to create meaningful identity transformations. It also emphasized the unperceived power of places to create and shape identity. And so I say I "grew up," for those summers allowed me to develop and complexify my "Italian" identity, expectations and perceptions.

In young adulthood, I grew up once again at the hands of World Heritage sites—but this time they had no traditional linkage to my lineage or ethnic heritage. After graduating college, I began organizing educational, cultural tours for members of museums, alumni associations and other non-profit organizations. The aim was to deepen the travelers' knowledge and appreciation of the destination, while fostering a sense of community that bonded the individual members who had often come from different parts of the country and enjoyed different outlooks on the world. My intimate knowledge of Italy landed me the job, and my passion for Southeast Asia, coupled with a fortuitous restructuring of the position, brought Vietnam[1] and Cambodia into my purview, as well. These places were just coming into the mass cultural tourism market, but I had visited them earlier with some college friends, back when the primary reaction from family, friends and even industry colleagues was still skepticism and fear. Their awareness of the region was undoubtedly colored by 1980s-era war movies; they would ask in all seriousness why we would want to visit such a dangerous, pitiful place, so full of bad memories. Admittedly, we were also unsure of what we would encounter, but we were fascinated with the prospect of adventure, and this exotic yet eerily familiar destination provided us with tingles of excitement and of trepidation.

Upon arriving in Saigon for the first time in 2001, foreignness smacked me squarely in the face like the seemingly suffocating heat accompanying it. But as I toured diverse sites such as Huế and Hội An, swiftly I began to cultivate a deep appreciation for this foreign culture, for these foreign-looking places. Returning to the United States and to the office, I regaled my colleagues with tales of my interactions with these precious places, and I produced mounds of photographs to show them. I insisted that we begin operating tours to Vietnam and also Cambodia—another country whose name would still send shivers down people's spines. Newspapers had just ceased to publish articles of bones unearthed from the Killing Fields, and news of Cambodia's World Heritage site, Angkor Wat, began to trickle in from backpackers. Likewise, Bill Clinton and John McCain had recently visited Ha Noi, Colin Powell was departing for a State visit,[2] and travel magazines were beginning to write about the colonial exoticism and adventure that awaited the brave Americans who would return to Vietnam. I was fortunate that a few of our clients also were intrigued by the idea, and I began designing and accompanying these tours. My clients were diverse in demographic, provenance and composition; they ranged mainly from middle-aged to elderly. Passengers came from Birmingham, Alabama; Oakland, California; Lexington, Virginia; Chicago, Illinois; Washington, DC; and from Newark, New Jersey. Although the groups' agendas differed—some focused on retracing Vietnam War battles, others art buying, and still others discount shopping—we nevertheless visited many of the same places— Hội An, Huế, Hạ Long Bay, Angkor Wat. And despite their very divergent interests, the travelers seemed to pull different, but equally insightful, meaning from these places. They grew in appreciation of the sites, and so did I.

It was no surprise to me that these destinations were World Heritage sites. They all had the ability to inspire a range of meanings deep in the cores of most travelers. They could each speak fluently and coherently to disparate visitors. They educated and they enlightened. They broke staid stereotypes engrained in travelers' memories of Điện Biên Phủ, Khe Sanh and the Killing Fields, of Ho Chi Minh and Pol Pot, of the struggles between Communism and Capitalism. Deeper understandings of the people, the land, the culture, and the different ways we all make meaning of our surroundings were imparted. Some people promised to return, some vowed to donate money for preservation, and someone even offered to sponsor a Phnom Penh resident's emigration to America (against her protestations). It was clear that, although these places had previously been unknown, foreign, and imbued with negative connotations, they spoke with equal valor and equal voice to diverse sets of visitors.

And they spoke to me, too. Every interaction with these natural and cultural sites, alone or with different groups of fellow travelers, imparted to me a deeper appreciation of the world's diversity. I internalized them, and attributed new meanings to them that were ever the more robust, detailed, and digested. I committed each site to memory; as I returned time and again, my mind would not only juxtapose experience against experience at the same location, but location against location. In my mind, my own history became linked with the life history of those sites, and of those cultures for which the places acted as durable containers. Diversity became familiar, and as it grew more familiar, my understandings of these places played against the understandings I cultivated about places of my own ethnic origins. And so I grew up again. I grew to make meaning, however limited it may be, of the great complexities of one's heritage, and of the possibility of uniting within one's being a wealth of disparate manifestations of cultural diversity.

This book was born of such experiences. As I logged more trips to Southeast Asia, I endeavored to know more about UNESCO's elusive designation, and I found that my travelers did, too. Many had never even heard of UNESCO, an understandable admission by those living in the United States, where the intergovernmental organization is not as active as it is in Europe or in developing countries. Although many knew very little about UNESCO's politics, processes or objectives—in this or any of its myriad other educational or scientific initiatives—the "World Heritage" title it bestows upon these local places was easily comprehensible nonetheless. What is interesting from an analytical standpoint is the changing conceptual meaning placed on these designations by visitors. My travelers would attest to being able to recognize the "universal value" of these monuments even if they were unaware of UNESCO's ostensibly "objective" and "scientific" criteria or reasoning. And the more seasoned travelers began to take notice of the designation as they moved from site to site within a tour itinerary, and from tour to subsequent tour over their traveling careers. They began to formulate deeper understanding of the title's meaning as they began creating their own mental World Heritage lists based on their travels. And preconceived notions about the horrors and the strife of these lands began to be supplanted by nebulous expectations of the "cultural value" of these nation-states. The value of these places were not approached as esoteric, understandable only to the locals or to professional ethnographers, but to the lay traveler. And as they returned home, these new perceptions were conveyed to others; they were passed on orally from person to person, visually in a number of new museum exhibitions such as those at the Meridian House in Washington, DC or at New York's famed American Museum of Natural History,[3] and textually in the form of travel articles, tourism books and trip brochures.

This is not simply a qualitative assertion. In the dark days of post-9/11 travel—marked by airline bankruptcies, airport security inconveniences, exorbitant fuel surcharges, worldwide economic recession, jittery passengers and even multiple terrorist bombings in Indonesia—Western and Asian travelers to the region have increased at a consistent annual rate of over 5.25%, according to statistics from the United Nation's World Tourism Organization (UNWTO).[4] In the decade between 1995 and 2005, the number of tourists to Vietnam and its World Heritage sites increased from 1,351,000 to 2,972,000 at an annual rate of 9.2%. Cambodia has enjoyed an equally stunning increase in visitors, from 220,000 incoming visitors in 1995 to 1,055,000, at an average rate of 19% per year, primarily concentrated at the World Heritage site of Angkor Archaeological Park. In the last few years, however, this percentage has increased dramatically, and tour operators in the region are unflappingly optimistic that the trend will continue; in 2003, 10,577,000 internationals visited Cambodia, while the following year, this number increased 33% to 15,703,000.[5] These numbers reflect the wildly momentous change in how they are perceived by the Western public—from a painful place of war and genocide to a luxurious cultural site in the course of but a few years. Public and private donations are flowing in to help document and protect these designated sites, art collectors are noticing the creative contemporary aesthetic scene, and even cookbooks on the regions' cuisine have become bestsellers in American bookstores. Thanks, in part, to the large increase in tourism, international investment is at an all-time high, and infrastructural development is booming.

In the same five-year span, construction began on a number of new superhighways intended to cross international borders to maximize tourist flow between Thailand, Cambodia, Laos, and Vietnam;[6] and the once-gravelly Ho Chi Minh trail running along the Lao border is being converted into a major roadway linking the north and the south of Vietnam, coinciding with major new initiatives to draw Vietnam war veterans to the major battlefields the thoroughfare crosses. The Association of Southeast Asian Nations (ASEAN), of which both Vietnam and Cambodia are a part, plans to complete an international railway linking Malaysia, Singapore, Thailand, Cambodia, Vietnam, Laos and China. Short-term, inter-ASEAN visa requirements have recently been dropped, allowing locals from any of these nations to freely and more spontaneously visit their neighboring countries for tourist purposes. The pre-war airbases built by the French and Americans (which were used for commercial flights at the inception of post-war tourism in the affected countries) have been torn down, and new, modern airports—architectural works of art in their own right—have been constructed in Saigon, Phnom Penh and Siem Reap. "Tourist police" now patrol the streets of Saigon as well as the ruins of Mỹ Sơn and Angkor, dealing a significant blow to black-market looting (though this problem persists). And with the help of international experts and funding, World Heritage sites from Angkor Wat to Huế's Imperial City have been preserved, protected and, in some cases, rebuilt entirely. For these readily recognizable reasons, UNESCO considers its World Heritage initiative the organization's crowning achievement in furthering its ambitious objective of creating "peace in the minds of men."

The Theoretical Perspective

Intended for social scientists studying placemaking strategies, professionals engaged in the management and promotion of these touristic destinations, and the occasional enlightened traveler interested in learning more about the World Heritage sites he may encounter as he follows an itinerary interspersed with these UNESCO-designated properties, this book explores UNESCO's World Heritage program in light of its atypical assertion that concrete peace can be achieved through such a seemingly simple and ethereal designation. I contend that the designation is more than merely a change in nomenclature or an empty titular reward, but rather the key element in a more ambitious placemaking strategy designed to rearrange the geopolitical landscape into a reconceptualization of the world.

Applying anthropologist Arjun Appadurai's theory that globalization produces a series of amorphous -*scapes* that spread across the world,[7] I have termed UNESCO's newly ordered social structure the *heritage-scape*. My arguments constructing this model of UNESCO's World Heritage endeavor is based on close readings of UNESCO documents and texts, as well as on roughly eight years of heritage and tourism research (including extended participation within the tourism industry). However, while I argue—sometimes quite forcefully—that the heritage-scape is a real social structure which creates real material effects on a globally distributed population in accordance with UNESCO's long-term goals, this is my own theoretical model and not UNESCO's. UNESCO does not use the term, nor does it explicitly state that it intends to reorder the geo-political system in its quest to foster "peace in the minds of men."

As I conceptualize the heritage-scape, UNESCO's World Heritage Program is geared predominantly to oft-mobile tourists—temporarily situated "outsiders" who can bring their own unique understandings of "culture" and "cultural diversity" to the site, experience a transformative encounter, and return to their home like secular missionaries, spreading their newfound knowledge of the site in relation to cultural diversity. Concerned with the meaning-making processes of UNESCO's World Heritage claims as they are encountered by primarily Western tourists, it is clearly out of the scope of this book to discuss indigenous reception to the heritage-scape, or to provide a "bottom-up" ethnographic analysis of how locals perceive of heritage claims and touristic processes, though some detail is offered. However, this book does not aim to be "top-down" in its analysis of these two coinciding phenomena, either. That is, it does not posit that UNESCO, tourism providers and heritage managers form a "superstructure"—a political class of people or institutions who impose upon subordinates prescribed ways of acting and who ensure control over all means of production, tangible and intangible.[8] Marx defines a superstructure when he writes:

> The ideas of the ruling class are in every epoch the ruling ideas: i.e., the class which is the ruling material force of society, is at the same time its ruling intellectual force. The class which has the means of material production at its disposal, has control at the same time over the means of mental production, so that thereby, generally speaking, the ideas of those who lack the means of mental production are subject to it. The ruling ideas are nothing more than the ideal

expression of the dominant material relationships, the dominant material relationships grasped as ideas.[9]

At first glance, it can certainly appear that UNESCO, as a global and intergovernmental organization composed itself of the "united nations" who make up the designating World Heritage Committee, can fit the category of a superstructure. This seems especially salient when one limits his studies of World Heritage solely to documentary evidence produced by UNESCO. These publications—written in part as internal manifestos and in part as awareness-raising public relations endeavors—dictate appropriate action (peace through appreciation of diversity) by mediating between ideas and material cultural resources.

Tourism, too, is often conceptualized as a "superstructure," insofar as the "tourist-generating end of the touristic processes" is concerned, speculates Dennison Nash. Likening touristic production to other "superstructural phenomena" such as religion, myth and art, Nash contends that "tourism is a superstructural or expressive manifestation of some society and that it is capable of acting back upon the more essential aspects of a society that brought it into being."[10] In another work, he offers an argument for the consideration of "tourism as a form of imperialism" in much the same way that UNESCO's World Heritage program is imperialist in its basic endeavor to expand a particular society's interests abroad. These interests—be they economic, religious, political or something else—can be "imposed on or adopted by an alien society," establishing "evolving intersocietal transactions, marked by the ebb and flow of power."[11] Nash's offering is indeed helpful; it aids in conceptualizing the ephemeral and multifarious processes of touristic visitation in a comprehensible way.

However widespread such conceptualizations of heritage or touristic processes are, I believe they paint too limited a picture of the complexities of both movements for a number of reasons. The first is the empirical. When one delves behind the rhetoric of UNESCO, he will find that there is little "means of production" that UNESCO controls. As I will attempt to show, UNESCO has no legal jurisdiction over the material site itself and exerts itself through socially coercive power. Though a World Heritage site is supposed to be protected by the world community, under normal circumstances it is directly managed by the nation in whose political boundaries it is located. It is also subject to multiple re-presentations in a variety of contexts. Thus, the site spirals through the world in embodied and disembodied re-presentations of itself.

The second argument rests on the limitation of applying Marx's sociopolitical idea to UNESCO. UNESCO's World Heritage Convention is not a political monolith; it is composed of a variety of diplomatic representatives from across the political spectrum, but it also necessitates very real material and intellectual contributions from private and non-profit entities. All of these "stake-holders"—as many are wont to call them—have different concerns, and are involved in different operations.

Tourism, likewise, is far too multifaceted to be lumped as a political mono-lith. Although eminent tourism scholars of the past have argued that the tourism industry dupes visitors by effectively creating a smokescreen-like re-presentation of places, this is a very one-dimensional analysis of tourism that minimizes the agency of tourists themselves. It also de-emphasizes the very real *in situ* interactions between "hosts" and "guests" that often occur at the destination, which Mary Louise Pratt calls the "contact zone." Pratt uses this term to "invoke the spatial and temporal copresence of subjects previously separated by geographic and historical disjunctures, and whose trajectories now intersect";[12] in this way she spatializes what Marshall Sahlins calls the "structure of the conjuncture"[13]—which, as I will argue—is integral to creating the type of "unity in diversity" that the heritage-scape endeavors to do.

But in this pervasive conceptualization of tourism as imperialistic, tourists are portrayed as lacking fundamental knowledge of the destination and seeking "pseudo-events,"[14] or as being unwittingly deceived by the tourist industry's superficial "staged authenticity."[15] But drawing on the contributions of Valene Smith, Nelson Graburn and John Urry, I posit that tourism is a particular form of interaction that visitors voluntarily engage in for the purpose of experiencing a formative change in their life.[16] As this book argues, tourists do have a significant amount of power in shaping the destination and its varying re-presentations. Before they ever "tour," they are influenced by, and influence, the circulation of ideas about the site itself. The same can be said of indigenous "hosts" who, in many circumstances, are privy to the same circulation of re-presentations and actively (yet differently) engage in shaping subsequent iterations of them.

Thus follows the third reason against a superstructural argument: it is difficult to posit that the World Heritage Convention or the tourism industry represent the "ruling class of ideas." One look at the protracted negotiations that exist in UNESCO's designating process, management procedures, and tourism, reveal that there are no clear dominant ideas about how a site reveals its "universal value"—both before and after its listing. Nor is there a dominant idea of how to enforce whatever contextualization is ultimately embraced. The very notion of what these processes are and what they are meant to do are fluid and shifting; they move between the minds of men and constantly re-frame themselves. These processes work dialectically with the memories of individuals who interact with them, producing meanings that are far too varied to identify with any precision.

The theoretical foundation of this book is that both the heritage-scape and tourism—however locally instantiated they both may be—are the result of

Bourdieuian fields of production.[17] Drawing on Pierre Bourdieu, I define the *field of heritage production* and the *field of touristic production* as multi-layered, global social structures wherein individuals struggle and negotiated to create, define, and promote formative encounters with place. The ultimate result of the field of heritage production, I argue, is the World Heritage List. The end product of the field of touristic production, however, is much more varied and depends upon the site itself. These two fields intersect to form the heritage-scape—an amorphous and conceptual "place" populated by those peoples who temporarily, voluntarily, and perspectively interact with World Heritage sites. Thus, this book looks at the meaning-making processes of local, national and non-governmental levels of these two fields to create the heritage-scape. That is to say, the ultimate aim of this book is not to look at the meanings locals attribute to a World Heritage site—constrained by the place's designation or not—but rather to look at the ways in which tourists, managers, experts and politicians are moved to create, impart, and remember a site's disparate meanings.

Outline of the Book

By means of introduction to this conceptual argument, chapter 1 begins the book by directing the spotlight on the "main characters" of both heritage and tourism discourses: the monuments themselves. Chapter 1 asserts that monuments, through their perceived authenticity, are indeed social actors, which mediate between multiple agents to create enduring claims of community. Monuments are multifaceted mediators for the construction of an "imagined community," in the famous words of Benedict Anderson.[18] By focusing on the monuments themselves, it is possible to trace the relationships they have with different theoretical issues associated with the heritage and tourism processes—concepts such as narrativity, authenticity, re-presentationality and mediation. This focus also allows me to trace the relationships these monuments have with the relevant heritage and tourism producers—UNESCO, Advisory Bodies, politicians, preservationists, site managers, the tourism industry and the tourists themselves. This also reveals the very interconnectivity of the fields of heritage and tourism production; they converge uniquely at each site, yet exist in the global milieu. Thus, most importantly, this chapter summarizes the concept of the heritage-scape, an authentic social structure constructed through the juxtaposition of unrelated, but similarly designated, World Heritage sites, whose ultimate goal is to produce "peace in the minds of men."

Theorizing that placemaking is a social and material process mediated by memory, chapter 2 examines how UNESCO appropriates tangible monuments to create an amorphous "heritage-scape," to borrow a neologism from Arjun Appadurai,[19] which exists not in the material world but in the "minds of men." This understanding of how places are conceptually made has roots in the writings of Benedict Anderson and his protégées.[20] A historical analysis of the World Heritage program's development is also undertaken, further underscoring the assertion offered in chapter 1 that the overarching concepts of "universal value" and "world heritage" are themselves amorphous, products of negotiation, and constantly re-framing themselves.

Utilizing social memory theory as offered by Maurice Halbwachs and John Connerton, which sees the remembering of intangible narrative claims as paramount in social endeavors,[21] chapter 3 expounds on the heritage-scape's unique meta-narrative of "unity in diversity." This claim is all-important for the ultimate construction of "peace in the minds of men," for UNESCO contends that it is the divisive quality of diversity, revealed through the manipulation of the site's life-historical narrative, which is the root of worldwide strife. By unifying diversity, or, rather, by totalizing differences, individuals interacting with these sites can come to appreciate and celebrate diversity.

To do so, however, individuals must first interact with World Heritage sites, fully aware of their universally valorized status. Building on chapter 1's argument that tourism is the optimal manner of interacting with the heritage-scape, chapter 4 delves more deeply into the theory that tourism is itself a structured form of meaning-making that compels and constrains the perspectives with which visitors approach, and understand, these monuments. Tourism is often linked to heritage in a one-to-one relationship by scholars and industry professionals alike; one of the most convincing arguments can be found in Barbara Kirshenblatt-Gimblett's book, *Destination Heritage*. Kirshenblatt-Gimblett attributes a somewhat causal relationship to the two, stating:

> Heritage and tourism are collaborative industries, heritage converting locations into destinations and tourism making them economically viable as exhibits of themselves. . . . Once sites, buildings, objects, technologies, or ways of life can no longer sustain themselves as they formerly did, they "survive"—they are made economically viable—as representations of themselves."[22]

This is indeed true at least some of the time, but much of the criticism about a destination's inappropriate or "pseudo" representationality[23] levied at tourists and the industry that supports them inadequately considers tourism as an overly monetary and monolithic entity. I therefore offer an alternative definition of tourism—one that is rooted in cultural, rather than overly economic or political.

Combining the now well-trod explanations of tourism by scholars such as Valene Smith, Nelson Graburn, John Urry and Lucy Lippard, I define tourism in the first chapter as a temporary, voluntary and perspectival *ritual interaction* that an individual chooses to undergo to experience a change in his daily life—often to heighten one's sense of place, refocus the mind, and maybe even reinforce identity. In this chapter, I attempt to unpack this definition more fully, revealing the multiplicity of actors within this field of touristic production. Guiding this chapter's organizational framework is Graburn's classic conceptualization of tourism as a structured ritual.[24] The chapter is therefore divided into the three phases of a ritual and discusses the (albeit loose) forms and sets of practices associated with each stage. I hope to show that, as a distinct web of meaning—or a "way of seeing," to appropriate Svetlana Alpers' description of museum interactions—tourism can be undertaken by locals and foreigners alike, irrespective of constraints such as social status, economic mobility, cultural outlook or educational level. Understood in this manner, tourism thus satisfies UNESCO's universalizing appeal, as well as its objective to peacefully bond disparate peoples under a unified conception of place that knows no territorial bounds. The work of heritage and tourism producers, as well as other professional and lay persons who have interacted with particular World Heritage sites in the past, foster a number of competing re-presentations that work their way into the ritual stages of tourism. There is no easily identifiable one-to-one causal relationship, nor a simple co-construction of meaning, but rather a dialectical process of continual remembering and re-presentation that frame and re-frame the individualized meanings made of these sites by its singular touristic interactants throughout the process, from initial separation, to his or her liminal interaction with the place, all of the way through the final reaggregation phase. Indeed, I argue, there is almost no "ultimate" meaning made by one individual about a particular World Heritage site—at least, it is exceptionally difficult to ascertain—for it continues to reshape itself in the tourist's memory as he embarks upon another encounter with an entirely different World Heritage site.

Turning once again to the places themselves, chapter 5 then looks at the production of World Heritage sites. The meta-narrative of "unity in diversity" is ultimately a discourse about the monuments' relationships to each other, as well as to individual tourists. This claim, therefore, allows localities to be transformed into World Heritage sites through a museological process whereby the monument is isolated from its original context and recontextualized; chapter 5 reveals the transformative ritual these sites undergo. Because the heritage-scape is intangible in nature, existing with varying clarity and precision "in the minds of men," it is presented illustratively through the lens of Vietnam and Cambodia's World Heritage sites as of June 2008. Although there is talk that both

Vietnam and Cambodia will have sites added in the upcoming years, there are currently five World Heritage sites currently recognized in Vietnam—the two "natural" sites of Hạ Long Bay and Phong Nha-Kẻ Bàng National Park, and the three "cultural" sites of Hội An, Mỹ Sơn and Huế. Until recently, Cambodia counted only one—the vast Angkor Archaeological Park, which consists of some five thousand built structures, the most famous of which is Angkor Wat.

Noting that this ritual process is part of a Bourdieuian field of heritage production, chapter 6 looks in more detail to the states-parties who originally offer up their site for universal recognition. Questioning the reasons why a state-party would willingly offer up their important local heritage site to the scrutiny of UNESCO and its alternative geopolitical construction, this chapter also explores some of the tangible political implications a World Heritage designation brings, and offers some interpretation of how the "unity in diversity" narrative imbues some of these Southeast Asian World Heritage sites. While the World Heritage Convention contractually obliges nation-states to offer their properties to the world, the "intergovernmental" nature of UNESCO—and thus of this field of heritage production—allows nation-states to manipulate the ways in which their places are symbolically contextualized. In particular, I argue that States-parties can subvert the "unity in diversity" meta-narrative through the strategic employment of UNESCO's Enlightenment-era categorization scheme of natural and cultural sites.

The management decisions also impact the meanings of the sites, especially when they are "living" towns such as Hạ Long's Cửa Vạn fishing village or Hội An. "Museumification" is a common risk. Because this is a particularly prevalent concern for heritage managers, the brief chapter 7 is devoted entirely to tracing the process of museumification at Hội An. As I hope it will show, museumification is but one of a wide variety of unintended outcomes that is necessarily produced through the intersection of these two fields of production.

While museumification is often a gradual and unintended process brought on by the confluence of diverse position-taking actors within these fields of production, other outcomes are strategically intended by site managers. In chapter 8, I utilize the metaphor of a "stage" for the heritage-scape (after all, the traditional geopolitical configuration of nations is often called the "world stage") to argue that site managers can dictate the roles their World Heritage sites play to a touristic audience. In particular, they can be featured front-stage or shift to the background as a mere setting or prop for some other activity. These positional shifts are common in touristic interactions with World Heritage sites and, I argue, greatly impact the meanings made of "unity in diversity."

As localities become ideal manifestations of "unity in diversity," and are juxtaposed against other unrelated but similarly designated properties when they are inscribed on the World Heritage List, these individual sites are also imbued with a greater sense of "value," since they are understood to authoritatively and emotionally speak to the present about the past, giving direction to the future. Such valorization is recognized for its potential to help develop economic infrastructure, preserve heritage properties, and, above all, raise awareness of the country's "universal value." *Value* is a contested term, but one that is integral to a multiplicity of actors. Chapter 9 defines value in terms of authenticity, as UNESCO does; it reveals that these sites are considered valuable because of their perceived intransience. Monuments are thought to resist the damaging onward movement of time. Since they are valuable material links to the past in the present, it is natural, so I argue, that the World Heritage movement would become so closely aligned with the cause of historic preservation. The bulk of this chapter explores the notion of historic preservation and the concrete ways in which UNESCO promotes their undertaking.

Yet unintended consequences always arise, and chapter 10 utilizes the Angkor Archaeological Park as a case study to illustrate some of the problematics of international preservation at such a local site. Again, while the some thoughts are offered about possible meanings that could be attributed by tourists to locals, their histories and their cultures through the mediation of this vast World Heritage site, it does not aim to describe the meanings of the site attributed by these indigenous users, just as it does not purport to offer meanings made by the tourists. Rather, since tourists are deeply divergent in their attitudes, expectations and perceptions—and indeed, there is not one kind of tourism but a multiplicity of tourisms that all share a similar meaning-making structure—the commentary is concerned with the processes at work which stimulate such potential meanings.

While the peaceful, "imagined community" of the heritage-scape gains materiality through touristic interactions with the place, the heritage-scape is built upon all kinds of experiences with these individual World Heritage sites and their multitudinous re-presentations. Following the previous chapters' concerns with the ways World Heritage sites are re-presented *in situ*, chapter 11 explores the other ways in which these sites re-present themselves in contexts disembodied from their physical situatedness. I unpack the categories of re-presentation offered in the first chapter: *Fragmentary re-presentations* are disembodied physical pieces of the authentic monument that are contextualized in museums, Worlds Fairs, and other "exhibitionary complexes,"[25] and are thought to have as much power to re-present the place as the site does *in situ*. Ethnical considerations aside, fragmentary re-presentations are effective means of diffusing the heritage-scape, for they are easily moved, and afford individuals who do not have the means or awareness of the original site to commune with the site in another geographic area. In addition to their authentic physical link with the sites of which they were once a part, their relationship with many of the same sets of actors who collaborate in the heritage-scape's field of production—namely, the epistemic communities of academic experts, museum professionals, and conservators, among others—grants a measure of control over their contextualization, although this has historically not always been the case.

Reproducible re-presentations, on the other hand, are completely separate from the site itself and, owing to their ability to be relatively unchecked in their replication, often create and replicate narratives that are incompatible or conflicting with UNESCO's. Reproducible re-presentations take a number of sensory forms: from textual (travel accounts, fictional books, weblogs of an individual's travels) to visual (photography, artistic and cinematographic), and both together—a phenomenon particularly emphasized here. The site itself thus performs a double mediation: it first mediates between the society and the individual reproducer *in situ*, and then its re-presentation mediates between the site and individual consumer. Focus is given to digital media sources, for the Internet is especially conducive to inexpensive, simultaneous and juxtapositional reproducibility across the world. It can ultimately foster forms of "virtual tourism," which are embodied interactions like traditional tourism, yet the interactions are not with the authentic site itself but with the re-contextualized re-presentation on the computer screen. To illustrate a way that the virtual tourist can literally travel across the heritage-scape of World Heritage sites in the context of his own home, a survey analysis of Angkor's re-presentations is conducted through Google's database. As it will become clear from both this survey and the discussion of other reproducible re-presentations, especially cinema, intertextuality may inform the possible meanings made of the site—and thus of the heritage-scape.

Addressing the "future of the heritage-scape," I next offer a concluding summary of the major themes of the book, focusing especially on UNESCO's peacemaking claim. Though the heritage-scape is an ephemeral conception of an "imagined community," it impacts the material world in multiple ways, paving the way, perhaps, for a more peaceful future. The chapter has a future-oriented bent, as it offers a number of thoughts on the trajectory of the designation process—what sites may be considered in the future and what sites, as the heritage-scape presently stands, will not. Since the "Cairns Decision," which asserted the need for more heritage sites in underrepresented regions of the world,[26] change may certainly be afoot in the interpretation of UNESCO's conceptually nebulous typologies used to determine "universal value." In particular, modernity is becoming conceptualized as heritage, a point revealed in the ground-breaking designation of the Sydney Opera House in 2007. The case of the Sydney Opera

House is interesting on a number of levels, one of which is the designation's expected potential to materially help the site. Though it is not in need of restoration as Angkor Wat does, it is conceived as a means to "restore" the architect's original plans, which were not carried out during its construction. As an aesthetically and historically "modern" site, its designation—the first of its kind— may open the way for the designation of other novel places constructed in the contemporary era, such as Frank Gehry's Guggenheim in Bilbao, Mies van der Rohe's "International" style architecture in Germany, or "Prairie School" places of Frank Lloyd Wright in the Midwestern United States. The focus on contemporary works as "heritage" may open the way for "new" cultures—such as Australian and North American ones, whose properties are primarily designated as "natural" sites—to vary their World Heritage listings. It may also induce developing countries to attempt greater representation by creating new "monuments" rather than designating traditional ones. Thus, the temporal gap between the past and the present—which today is mediated by the very idea of heritage, the existence of the past in the present—may incrementally close, with extreme consequences for the distant future of the heritage-scape. In the future, perhaps everything may be designated heritage—everything and anything can be an outstanding example of universal value; appreciating everything might just be the means to creating a lasting peace.

Methodology

This rather populist reading of UNESCO's work—which, it should be noted, is carried out almost unwittingly by the nation-states themselves—is founded on complementary methodologies of documentary analysis and ethnographic fieldwork. Because UNESCO's placemaking activity is directed to lay people of all interests and walks of life—the wealthy American retirees and the young Australian backpackers, international preservationists and museum professionals, food critics and art aficionados, armchair travelers and Internet surfers, groups of Chinese and French, Italians and Koreans, foreigners and natives alike yearning to understand the broader cultural significance of local sites—I felt that it was important to begin by analyzing what UNESCO says publicly about itself. Written and visual tools that are made available for public consumption—much of which UNESCO makes readily accessible at the World Heritage Centre's website, http://whc.unesco.org—were preferred over behind-the-scenes accounts of politicking at the World Heritage Centre's headquarters in Paris or at the People's Committee for Information and Culture in Ha Noi, although some juicy bits have been included in anecdotal form, as well. As mentioned above, such documentary sources are not treated as the unadulterated expositors of historical reality that can be used to explain true and underlying meaning of UNESCO, the heritage-scape, or individual World Heritage sites. Indeed, though the term "universal" often comes up, like most (if not all) contemporary anthropologists, I do not assume all persons are alike and that the "culture" to which they are ascribed, either by themselves or by outsiders, is a homogenous whole—although, for the sake of succinctness, I may speak of the cultures of "locals," "foreigners," "tourists," "Cambodians," "French colonials" and the like in such problematically generalized terms. Contemporary anthropology grants that culture, as a totalizing "web of meaning that we ourselves have spun"[27] is as unique from webstrand to webstrand as it is from person to person. Thus, I treat these documents as ethnographic evidence in their own right, which can be analyzed not for their true meaning, but as rhetorical vehicles that shape individuals' meaning-making processes.

I also treat the tangible World Heritage sites in the same vein, as another type of ethnographic text that can be "read" for possible ways in which they inspire and shape individuals' subjective meaning of the heritage-scape. Particular emphasis has thus been placed on the (often changing) semiotics of the individual sites themselves, as documented during multiple periods of fieldwork from 2001 through 2006. Placemaking theory as it is applied here emphasizes the strong role that material, ritual encounters with the site plays in formulating meaningful remembered narratives; what one sees, smells, and feels, both individually and collectively—as well as what strikes him with wonder and what resonates with his expectations—impacts his awareness and understanding of the place. These World Heritage sites can therefore be considered figuratively as "texts" in the vein of Clifford Geertz, whose method of semiotic analysis understood tangible and intangible cultural forms as unwritten, yet nevertheless meaningful, documents that can be read, interpreted and analyzed.[28] Focusing on the visual and experiential dynamics of these highly charged places also recognizes that many of those who interact with World Heritage sites—both locals and foreign travelers—may not read UNESCO's written documents.

Indeed, these sites can also be considered "texts" in a more literal sense. Since UNESCO plays a regulatory role in how these sites are chosen, presented and preserved, these aesthetic components can be read as additional forms of documentary evidence. The *World Heritage Convention*, the program's foundational document, was predicated on the deliverable of identifying and preserving for perpetuity these monuments to universal culture. In the decades since UNESCO's initiative began, thousands of expert conservationists, archaeologists, anthropologists, geologists, historians and preservationists, have joined a multitude of politicians, educators and donors, in an effort to pinpoint the authenticity and integrity of each tangible site. The presence of such elements will make or break a designation. Even after the site is elevated to World Heritage status, UNESCO and its affiliated experts will continue to make recommendations on its management, both structurally and representationally; threats to strip a designation have also been leveled when site managers or the State party acts against their recommendations or the interest of the heritage-scape. Most often these threats suffice (or are ignored, with no noticeable effects); however, sometimes a site is even removed from the heritage-scape as Oman's Oryx Sanctuary was in 2007.

Similar to my universalist caveat in the preceding paragraph, I hasten to add that the perspective of the analyzer in any semiotic analysis undoubtedly will color his well-meaning interpretation. As Talal Asad contends, even the most eminent of anthropologists such as Geertz have problematically universalized the reading of signs; it is a misconception to think that one culture's symbols can be interpreted using the lens of another culture.[29] Indeed, symbols themselves are representative cultural constructs; the same physical symbol may not have the same meaning across cultures. Although I may not repeat the requisite caveats whenever semiotics is invoked, I do wish to reaffirm that my intention is not to reveal any "true" meaning of these World Heritage sites or their particular architectonics, but rather to simply point out possible features that may contribute to shifts in the way places are understood particularly by "Western" or "Westernized" visitors (categories containing most North Americans, Europeans, Australian/New Zealanders, and to which we may also add Japanese, South African, some Latin Americans and others). However, reading these sites as UNESCO-produced "texts" (both figuratively and literally) also permits a level of Western-infused semiotic reading, which I specifically link to a rather untraditional ethnographic undertaking. Unlike more common ethnographies, which are geographically bounded or somehow delimited by demographics or population, I am conducting a form of "global ethnography"—that is, I examine what I view as a distinct, global cultural form to which these sites-as-texts pertain. This is the culture of the heritage-scape, which is not geo-socially bounded, yet which espouses its own processes and webs of meaning with certain distinctive characteristics that make it global.[30] UNESCO's creations—individual World Heritage sites in the micro sense, and the heritage-scape in the macro—are each individual, symbolic indicators of a new world order predicated on claims of "unity in diversity"—a global "culture of cultures"[31] that UNESCO attempts to generate.

Furthermore, UNESCO is predominantly a Western cultural construction; along with its parent, the United Nations, the organization was originally founded by Allied forces before the end of World War II with a decidedly post-Enlightenment philosophical bent, despite some more contemporary (yet on the whole futile) attempts to modify this over-arching perspective. The social space of the heritage-scape, therefore, shares in this Western Enlightenment tradition although it is composed of distinct localities around the world which may not. Thus, in analyzing the meaning-making processes themselves, I utilize decidedly Western anthropological, art historical and even philosophical perspectives—especially (but not limited to) concerning the definition of monumentality, authenticity, heritage, transience and historic preservation, the understood "power" of these monumental sites to evoke resonance and wonder, the purpose of cultural institutions such as museums, and tourists' dual yearning for education or enlightenment. Though other cultures may share some common strains of thought, by no means should they be read as philosophies espoused by Vietnamese or Cambodians—although globalization has certainly made these Western modes of thought diffuse. Rather, they should be read as perspectives at the foundation of the heritage-scape, which inexorably color the local meanings these individual places have as World Heritage sites.

Another caveat. There is always an element of subjectivity and arbitrariness in selection and categorization processes, and the reader may question why, for example, I excluded from in-depth analysis the numerous other Asian World Heritage sites from Thailand, China, Indonesia or, at the very least, Laos—the third and most often overlooked country that was a part of former French Indochina. Conversely, the reader can also question the seemingly capricious analytical interlinking of these very different sites from two very different, yet neighboring, countries. Although the cultural and political systems in these two countries are indeed quite different—and both have had such a long history of aggression towards each other that a certain level of deeply ingrained animosity seems to fester among them still—both countries emerged on the tourist market at relatively the same time. By this, I do indeed mean the current tourism market, which sees both of these countries in a post-colonial context. However, I hasten to add that tourism in these two countries is also historically linked, as I argue in chapter 1.

By the time the École Françes d'Estrême Orient was founded in Saigon in 1901 to study predominantly the "Indian" influenced Khmer and Cham sites in Cambodia and Annam (Central Vietnam), colonial Grand Tour-goers had already begun to make secular "pilgrimages" to these Indochinese sites—to use a term employed by tourism commentators from the colonial travel writer Pierre Loti to the contemporary anthropologist Nelson Graburn.[32] Indeed, the very (re)discovery of Angkor by Henri Mouhot in 1860 can be seen as a product of early expeditionary tourism in both of these two present-day nation-states. A relatively obscure naturalist who could not secure a grant from the French government, Mouhot funded his voyage through personal connections, and had great flexibility in planning an exploration that followed his own personal interests—interests that were piqued by previously published accounts by European explorers and missionaries such as Charles-Emile Bouillevaux, a French Jesuit priest who came to Cambodia from the southern Vietnamese protectorate of Cochin China in 1850. In his seminal historical account, author Bruno Dagens gives Bouillevaux the dubious title of Angkor's "The First Tourist."[33] Utilizing my own definition of tourism as outlined below, I would argue that there had been many other secular tourists to the Angkorian monuments before Bouillevaux, including the thirteenth-century Chinese emissary Cho Ta-Kuan, but Dagens' assertion is helpful in making the point that Mouhot, like the French Jesuit before him, was a tourist whose itinerary combined the disparate regions of Vietnam and Cambodia that I utilize in this text. Mouhot's desire to replicate, in part, the touristic experience of Bouillevaux—but tailoring it to include botanical exploration—was indeed his true impetus for the trip. Destinations in the voyage that Mouhot recounted would subsequently be subsumed under the French colonial political unit known as the *Union Indochinoise*, or *Indochine*; he toured Annam (Central Vietnam), Cambodia and Angkor, which at the time was under Thai control. After exploring the Angkorian ruins in Siam, he headed up the Mekong to Laos, where he was struck with malaria while visiting Luang Prabang—which is also a World Heritage site today. He died in present-day Laos only a year after discovering Angkor; he is still entombed there. Published posthumously in serial form in an early travel magazine *Tour du Monde*, his journal—which juxtaposed these regions in one literary unit—not only raised awareness of Angkor and these other sites, but helped form an Indochinese travel itinerary which, in subsequent decades, many would recreate.[34]

The formation of the École Françes d'Estrême Orient, which compiled archaeological documentation and created museum exhibitions featuring material culture from these regions, also aided in creating a touristic conception of heritage tourism linking Cambodia and Vietnam. Though the EFEO was founded in Saigon, France's flagship city in the southern Vietnamese colony then called Cochin China—and moved to Ha Noi in the protectorate of Tonkin shortly thereafter—by French presidential decree, it was charged with studying "that part of Indochina which owed 'its monuments, its customs and its culture to India'"[35]—that is, Cambodia and the cities of Champa which dotted the central Vietnamese coastal protectorate of Annam. Though it was founded as a research institution akin to those formed in Rome, Athens and Cairo,[36] and was officially changed with conserving the monuments of Angkor, as soon as the temple complex was politically ceded to Cambodia from Siam in 1907, it was charged with "improving [sic] access and accommodation for visitors."[37] This was indeed portentous, for that year would see a marked increase in visitors to Angkor. Like today's visitors, they were often global tourists—either wealthy independent travelers seeking to check off another interesting place on their worldwide lists, or members of the French Legion on leave from their posts in the protectorates of present-day Vietnam. The secular pilgrim Pierre Loti, himself a French naval officer, visited Angkor during a two-week shore leave from Saigon in 1901; as he only stayed two days at the site, his journal stands more as a record of his voyage up the Mekong through Cochin China, Phnom Penh in Cambodia and up to Siam, who claimed Angkor at the time.[38] French colonial agents were not the only ones who visited Angkor and the Vietnamese protectorates together in one itinerary; the British writer Grace Thompson Seton published her evocatively entitled vacation memoir, *Poison Arrows: Strange Journey with an Opium Dreamer through Annam, Cambodia, Siam and the Lotus Isle of Bali, illustrated with maps and many photographs taken by the author* in 1938.[39] Indeed, for both the Southeast Asia-stationed colonials and the Grand Tour "globetrotters," a visit to Angkor most often coupled a visit to Phnom Penh, Saigon or, later, Ha Noi and Đà Nẵng—not to mention the Thai hinterlands that lay outside of Siem Reap province. By the 1920s, tour operators worked in the region, advertising trips to visit the Angkorian relics in Indochina, facilitating such excursions, and—one can imagine—pressing for improved visitor infrastructure and accommodations—much like they do today.

In the present-day context, both Cambodia and Vietnam have quantitatively enjoyed the largest annual percentage increases of tourism, and qualitatively, in my observations as a tour operator, these two countries have benefited from the most marked of changes in cultural perceptions. In addition, they are often included together as one unit in visitors' itineraries to Southeast Asia—and in the same order, such that tourists who are strangers to one another will find that they cross paths multiple times during the course of their trips. Backpackers and other independent travelers seem especially wont to begin a conversation with each other by asking "are you going the Northern route or the Southern route?"—meaning, "are you working your way up from Saigon to Ha Noi, or are you starting in Ha Noi and working your way down the coast?" Depending on the type of traveler and the route taken, a bus, boat or plane trip to Angkor is often tagged onto the beginning or end of these itineraries, with or without the inclusion of the Cambodian capital of Phnom Penh. While Vietnam requires visas to be purchased in advance, Cambodia allows for visas to be purchased immediately at border crossings, to capitalize on this dynamic. Locals in Cambodia will likewise start conversations with travelers by asking if they came from Bangkok or Saigon (especially when monetary transactions are concerned; they often readily accept Thai baht but not Vietnamese đong, and prefer U.S. dollars even over the Cambodian riel)—further emphasizing that, either way,

Cambodia as a tourist destination still has not yet reached "independent" status, but rather continues to be pulled along the tourist track by more popular places.

I also hasten to note that the increase in tourism and general awareness of these sites will also change the way their narratives are articulated and marketed to diverse constituencies, the manner in which they are preserved and the increasingly more cutting-edge technologies used for this purpose, and the approach to solving site management problems that are unique to every tourist site; in subsequent chapters I have tried to illustrate the some of the changes that have already occurred over the last decade. Furthermore, the successes attributed to World Heritage endeavors in these two countries will undoubtedly lead to the addition of several new sites. Indeed, after this book had gone into production, Cambodia achieved the long-awaited designation of the contested Preah Vihear, sparking a rather troubling response from Thailand; I have added just a few analytical remarks about this development in the conclusion. These points should in no way diminish the relevancy, illustrative properties, or analytic qualities of my rather arbitrary selection of World Heritage sites. Rather, it should further underscore the unique nature of the heritage-scape as amorphous, constantly evolving, and ever deepening in meaning and in articulating its meta-narrative claim.

While these six Southeast Asian sites are intended here to be the primary exemplars of the heritage-scape, the reader will also note a number of additional well-known World Heritage sites from around the world are also referenced. This is done to reinforce the understanding that the heritage-scape is both cohesive and juxtapositional in nature, that even the most unrelated of cultural and natural sites become related within the heritage-scape. Indeed, when conceptualizing World Heritage, it is absolutely imperative to consider the concept of interrelatedness. Divergent from most local or national heritage discourses, *World Heritage* always espouses a narrative of "unity in diversity." That is, it seeks, through discourse but also through practice, to create commonality amongst even the most disparate of forms. This creates a dialectic of discourses and practices between members of these fields of production, the sites, and their representations. Each World Heritage site gains deeper meaning and descriptiveness as it is integrated side by side with others on the World Heritage List, and across the whole of the heritage-scape.

In addition to documentary and semiotic analyses, I also conducted traditional ethnographic fieldwork among predominantly American tourists and locals working in the tourism industry. Ethnography afforded the possibility of documenting the ways in which various constituencies of primary interest to the diffusion of the heritage-scape interacted with individual sites. During the period between 2001 and 2004, this was undertaken more informally while working as a tour operator, and it focused mainly on participant observation from the alternating standpoints of a tourist and a travel professional. I believe that the latter, in fact, provides a rare yet valuable "behind-the-scenes" look at the touristic field of production by revealing how these sites are interpreted and presented for consumption from a professional standpoint—a perspective rarely taken in academic texts. Foreign tour operators and sponsoring organizations, in-country "land operators" composed of domestic and foreign professionals, and local tour guides, curators, artists and site managers all have a hand in dialectically shaping the meaning UNESCO initially offers to diverse tourist cultures, which all have different needs, interests and expectations; to this end, I have also included my insights on the touristic production side—primarily in chapters 1 and 4. Formal ethnographic fieldwork was undertaken in the summer of 2006 from the perspective of an anthropologist independent of professional affiliations in the tourist sector. In addition to semiotic analysis of the sites and direct participant observation once again, this entailed a wide range of semi-structured interviews with a variety of informants whose expertise or vocations place them in regular contact with these sites, or who have a significant hand in the way they are subsequently contextualized, managed and presented to the general public. UNESCO representatives, local governmental officials, site managers, tour operators, curators, guides, and travelers were asked a series of standard, open-ended questions concerning their perception of the sites, their understanding of UNESCO and its works, the impact of the designation, the importance (or lack thereof) of tourism for broader infrastructural development, and, where appropriate, the history of the designation or preservation efforts.

Acknowledgements

I am especially grateful to these informants for their candor, openness to critique their own efforts, and willingness to discuss often-sensitive information. For these reasons, I cannot name them all here, but I would like to publicly acknowledge a number of colleagues who have been truly insightful in providing guidance, facilitating these meetings, and offering constructive suggestions to my own analysis, which, I believe, have shaped the resulting work for the better. My gratitude is extended to Edle Tenden, Programme Coordinator for Culture at UNESCO-Vietnam's head office in Ha Noi, Philippe Peycam at the Centre for Khmer Studies in Cambodia, and Alan Kolata at the University of Chicago. Much of the theoretical basis for this work was developed and shaped with the help of several professors at the University of Chicago, including Michael Dietler, Karin Knorr-Cetina, Morris Fred, Raymond Fogelson, Neil Harris, Mark Lycett, Amahl Bishara, Peter Homans and Bert Cohler. I am especially grateful to Michael Dietler, John MacAloon, and to my colleague Kevin Caffrey, for their thorough and thoughtful consideration during the initial stages of this project. Their constructive comments and helpful pointers were invaluable. My colleague and good friend Robert Pennoyer was also extremely helpful in educating me in current theories of information technologies and society. Amahl Bishara and a coterie of colleagues at a number of conferences in the United States and the United Kingdom were also helpful in providing their thoughts as I worked on chapter 1, which I hope provides an introductory summary of the major themes in this book. I am also grateful for commentary on this manuscript by both Johanna Schoss and an anonymous peer reviewer; the text is far stronger because of their thoughtful and in-depth notes. Lastly, I would like to particularly thank Raymond Fogelson for his guidance, insight and faith in my abilities to write this so early in my career.

During the final editing phase of this manuscript, I was the grateful recipient of several small grants from the University of Chicago, which aided me immensely. The Doolittle-Harrison Fellowship, issued by the Division of the Social Sciences, provided me with much appreciated writing and editing time. Valuable opportunities to "test" my theories through the participation in a number of conferences in late 2007 was made possible through an award from the Department of Anthropology's Marion R. & Adolph J. Lichtstern Fund, as well as a travel grant from the Committee on Southern Asian Studies (COSAS) at the University of Chicago.

In Southeast Asia, I am very appreciative of the time and attention to my work that was given to me by Mr. Trần Kỳ Phương, former curator of the Đà Nẵng Museum of Champa Sculpture, whose devotion to the preservation of Cham artifacts and to the cultivation and dissemination of academic study throughout the decades have made a significant mark on the World Heritage site of Mỹ Sơn. My thanks also are extended to professors Nguyễn Huu Thong, Mai Khắc Ứng and Gerd Albrecht for their instruction. Their academic and professional insights in the field were invaluable in supplementing my own research. Peter Murray from the Saigon office of Trails of Indochina has been an especially helpful source for his broad perspective on the changing dynamics of tourism since Vietnam opened its market. Finally, I am ever grateful to Professor Phan Thuận An, and his daughter, Phan Thuận Thao, whose work at the Huế Relics Conservation Center has been integral in raising awareness of Vietnam's first World Heritage site and the recent designation of its royal music by UNESCO as a work of intangible heritage. As they extended their hospitality to me over the years, I came to appreciate their strong dedication to this initiative, a factor that shaped my desire to explore more deeply the meaning and effects behind World Heritage properties in Vietnam and Cambodia.

I must also acknowledge a few of the many guides I have had the pleasure of working with in Cambodia and Vietnam over the years, who have not only shed great light onto the ways in which World Heritage designations are understood and presented from a local's standpoint, but who have been tireless in their work to make these places "all things to all people"—emotionally and epistemologically accessible to a variety of diverse constituencies. They have also been of great personal assistance in immersing me deeper in their cultures, suggesting destinations, and in bridging the linguistic and cultural gaps. *Aw kohn* to Chen Sokhoeun, and *cảm ơn* to Pham Van Anh and Viet Nguyễn.

I am extremely grateful for the generous support provided by John Tue Nguyễn and his staff at Trails of Indochina, and to Marissa Castro at Singapore Airlines. They were invaluable in helping to maximize my various experiences in Southeast Asia, and I am pleased to count them as great colleagues and friends. I also benefited from the time I spent working at the Council on Foreign Relations, which placed me in contact with a number of current and past governmental and United Nations officials. A very special acknowledgement must also be given to Kennie Ann Laney-Lupton, Director of International Seminar Design, Inc., where I spent some of my most formative years. I was fortunate to have made my initial observations on tourism and heritage, encountered a wide array of World Heritage sites, and experienced the multifaceted travel industry while working with her. She has provided me with great opportunities, and an invaluable chance to grow professionally, academically and personally.

At Lexington Books, I sincerely thank my valued editors, Erin Hill-Parks, Patrick Dillon and Michael Wiles for their faith, support and wise counsel throughout every stage of this process, from proposal to publication. I am also very appreciative of the superb cover design efforts of Cynthia De Ieso, who was able to admirably translate my theoretical notions of the heritage-scape into accessible pictorial form on the front cover. A warm expression of gratitude must also be extended to Hildreth England, David Vaccaro and Marissa Di Giovine for their critical eye in reviewing several parts of this work back in 2005.

My deepest gratitude goes to my family. Without their love, encouragement and support, none of this would have been possible. I thank my parents, Donald and Maria Di Giovine, and my sister Marissa, for providing me with so many gifts, especially an open and inquisitive mind, and a deep appreciation for education, culture, heritage and travel. I especially thank my wife, Laura, who has not only shown unconditional support to me in my endeavors, but who has also taken an active role in assisting me throughout this process. In addition to her superlative editing skills, she has always been my best travel companion, and I cherish all of our experiences, at home and abroad.

CHAPTER ONE

MEDIATING WORLD HERITAGE:
AUTHENTICITY AND FIELDS OF PRODUCTION
IN TOURISM AND HERITAGE

Monuments are a unique and varied form of media. Etymologically stemming from the Latin verb *monere* (to remind), the term *monument* has been defined in a number of different ways, with differing degrees of precision and foci, but all seem to hearken back to this notion of reminding, of stimulating in the memory some story of an object or experience. To wit, Merriam-Webster's dictionary defines a *monument* as: "a lasting evidence, reminder, or example of someone or something notable or great: a distinguished person"; "a memorial stone or a building erected in remembrance of a person or event;" and "an identifying mark." Be they structures or inscribed markers to memorialize, historically significant objects venerated for their temporal endurance, or lasting vestiges of something notable, all of these vernacular definitions include notions of spatiality and temporality in a way that combine to stir up some sort of remembrance of the past, leading scholars such as Susan Alcock and others to describe monuments as "places, structures or objects deliberately designed, or later agreed, to provoke memories."[1] These objects then, are not passive and inanimate symbols, but active forms of mediation, which William Mazzarella defines as a process "by which a given social dispensation produces and reproduces itself in and through a particular set of media."[2] Through the medium of monumentality, society renders itself concretely "imaginable and intelligible" to its individual members in a communicative procedure that is simultaneously constitutive[3] and representative of the society's cultural values and belief systems,[4] consequently binding its individual adherents together in a discrete "imagined community."[5]

Since a monumental structure is often fixed in its spatiality and therefore marks the very landscape within which it is found, it is often integral to a community's placemaking strategy, fostering "deep attachments . . . [and] profound emotional legitimacy"[6] for those who see themselves as a part of its environment. That is, a narrative is created that links the individual with society through the selective employment of the monument's own story of its life history.[7] Such narratives are not "historical" fact, however, but rather highly selective, ideological claims about the community and its connection with the site, conceptions often built around arbitrary yet clearly demarcated boundaries that gain precision when defined in binary opposition to each other.[8] As Henri LeFebvre states, "Monumentality . . . always embodies and imposes a clearly intelligible message. Monumental buildings mask the power and the arbitrariness of power beneath signs and surfaces which claim to express collective will and collective thought."[9] Imbued with narrative claims predicated on the notion of cultural possession, therefore, the monument becomes a pivotal mediator between those who can claim physical, historical or cultural ownership over the site and those who cannot—often setting into motion protracted conflicts as disparate groups vie for physical and ideological possession of the site.

In its most universal sense—to use an anthropologically tabooed term—placemaking is a social and material process, one that is mediated by memory. It is a social process in that it actively draws upon previously held conceptions of customs, beliefs, values and worldviews—those immaterial "webs of significances" spun by a society over time, which Clifford Geertz, borrowing from Max Weber, defined as "culture."[10] Yet as collective memory theorists such as Maurice Halbwachs and others have argued, for these intangible beliefs to be viable—for cultural systems to be meaningfully used, remembered and perpetuated by a society, they must be sedimented in concrete—that is, material and monumental—form.[11]

The issue of the site's authenticity, therefore, features prominently into the monumental media form. *Authenticity* is itself a highly contested word; it is employed in a variety of venues and is endowed with a multiplicity of meanings. Yet this term is always intimately associated with the notion of the monument or object's singular and ineffable life history. Famously writing about the "Work of Art in the Age of Mechanical Reproduction," Walter Benjamin's definition is telling: it is the object's "presence in time and space, its unique existence at the place where it happens to be." Its "unique existence," Benjamin writes, is "determined [by] the history to which it was subject throughout the time of its existence. This includes the changes which it may have suffered in physical condition over the years, as well as the various changes in its ownership."[12] In addition to its physical presence, it is also conceptual, a disembodied discourse about the monument that moves between the minds of men. "The authenticity of an object is the essence of all that is transmissible from its beginning, ranging from substantive duration to its testimony to the history which it has experienced," Benjamin continues.[13] "Authenticity" animates objects, making them as real an actor as any other social being;[14] it conveys the sense that the monument not only has a life history, but a life—a life which follows a biological conception of linear time, and subject to the same constructive and destructive forces of history and society.[15] The object is born when the artist or constructor distinctively puts his brush to the canvas or the chisel to the stone; it is modified both physically and conceptually as it carries on its existence, whether it is physically passed from person to person like a conch in a Trobriander *kula*, or if one passes through it, like a monumental archway in the center of an ancient city; and like all other biological things, is transient and will eventually, even inevitably, turn to dust. It thus moves through time—if not space, as well—impacting and interacting with other objects, human or otherwise. And in that auratic interaction,[16] both life histories will contextualize the event; they will be called upon, indexed, and experienced by both parties with durable longevity.

Authenticity, therefore, is that animate quality of even the most inanimate of objects—its soul or *hau*, which always is conscious of its origin, and often longs for a return.[17] There is as much a spatial materiality to this conception as there is a temporal one; the object is embedded in the fabric of history and the tradition of human-object interaction that congeals into a vital kernel of life,[18] surrounding the entire experience of its existence like an "aura."[19] It is the object's core identity, and, much as a diasporic community member is cognizant of (and frequently wishes for a return to) his motherland, so too may the authentic object associate itself with (and may be perceived to long for) its place of conception. Such an idea is integral to the monumental media form, for, in speaking about it as an authentic object, one is immediately granting a measure of agency to the object itself. Rendered a subject—at least conceptually—it is no longer inanimate, but impacts others as it indexes the moments of its own life. A monument is a social being, mediating between other social beings. Intersecting with the authentic object's life history are individual and collective histories, which follow a similar linear temporality but which each have their own unique history of birth, development and inevitable death. The life history of the discrete, authentic monument intersects with that of a discrete, authentic human only in one time and space per interaction, but it lives on. Just as the interaction may continue to exist in the memory of the human participant, so too does the interaction with the human participant inevitably modify and complexify the object's own life history.

As a medium, the authentic object is therefore not simply indexical, but constitutive as well. As Mazzarella points out, the "aura" provides the human with an initial motivation for interaction with such an object—to commune with its authenticity, to link oneself with the time and space which is imbued deeply in the essence of the object. And in so doing, the object, through its aura, actually touches the human before he tangibly interacts with the object itself. Thus, the authenticity of the object is able to reference a time and space that is distanced from the actual time and space of the particular interaction. In so doing, it actualizes the life history of the image—it renders the inanimate object animate in the minds of the human participants such that they can really believe, and even imagine, the monument existing and interacting with others outside their discrete experience with it. It becomes as real an actor as any of the participants involved. Mazzarella quotes an explicit passage from Benjamin's essay on Baudelaire to illustrate this point:

> Experience of the aura thus rests on the transportation of a response common in human relationships to the relationship between the inanimate or natural object and man. The person we look at, or who feels he is being looked at, looks at us in turn. To perceive the aura of the object we look at means to invest it with the ability to look at us in return.[20]

One particularly notable example of this phenomenon can be found in the complex of monuments in the Angkor Archaeological Park, a sprawling four hundred-square kilometer UNESCO-designated World Heritage site containing the archaeological remains of over six hundred years of the Khmer empire at its height, from roughly the ninth to the fifteenth centuries. Since the construction of Phnom Bakheng by King Yasovarman, who moved the Khmer capital to the region of Angkor in the ninth century, the monumental temples in today's Angkor Archaeological Park have featured prominently in many political regimes' placemaking strategies. Articulating claims that his capital was the spiritual, political, cosmological and astronomical center of the Hindu world, the twelfth century Khmer king Suryavarman II created the great Angkor Wat, unquestionably the most detailed, precisely designed and aesthetically refined structure the ancient Khmers produced.[21] His artisans bestowed two awe-inspiring features to Angkor Wat: a number of bas relief series tracing scenes from the *Mahābhārata*, *Rāmāyana* and Khmer political history, and a towering statue of Vishnu, most likely symbolizing the king himself. Attempting to destroy Khmer authority in greater Southeast Asia, the Hindu kingdom of Champa, with their capital at Vijaya, halfway between the present-day central Vietnamese cities of Da Nang and Nha Trang, staged an unprecedented attack on the area, reducing many of the wooden structures surrounding Angkor Wat to ashes.[22]

Fifteen years later, Jayavarman VII, arguably the most powerful ruler in Khmer history, defeated the Chams in a naval battle upon Angkor's Tonle Sap Lake. As the exiled son of Dharanindravarman II, Suryavarman II's ineffective successor, Jayavarman VII asserted his power, and that of his lineage, through a remarkably ambitious religious and urban revitalization program. He built a new city in stone called Angkor Thom with three vast Mahayana Buddhist monastic complexes adorned with monumental Buddhist statuaries in the likenesses of himself and his parents, constructed Buddhist rest houses and hospitals, and even modified Hindu bas reliefs on Angkor Wat itself to reflect Khmer Buddhist tropes. Politically, he extended the borders of his sprawling empire into the Mekong Delta in present-day Vietnam and through the Khorat Plateau in present-day Thailand. Commissioning an impressive network of laterite roadways that stretched across his vast domain, Jayavarman VII ensured that all roads quite literally led to Angkor.[23] These efforts produced a contextual shift in Angkor Wat's narrative claim, as it now contributed to the constitution of Jayavarman VII's personal vision of a Khmer Buddhist society ruled by a divinely compassionate God-King who materially ensures the well-being of his subjects.[24]

Revelatory of such monuments' powerful—and even menacing—mediating capacities, Jayavarman VII's constructions moved some of his Hindu subjects to iconoclastic action upon the king's death, as a great social backlash to his grueling revitalization campaign ensued. Though Jayavarman VII was tolerant of Hinduism, in the thirteenth century citizens rose up, perhaps with the instigation of the Khmer king,[25] and defaced over 45,000 Buddhist images along 5.1 miles of walls around Jayavarman VII's monasteries. They also converted many bas-reliefs of Buddhas into images of Hindu ascetics or *linga*,[26] much in the same way Jayavarman VII converted Hindu images into Buddhist ones.[27] This was, according to Michael Coe, a display of iconoclasm that not only "staggers the imagination," but was "not to be matched until the entry of Mehmet II into Constantinople in 1453."[28]

It also moved the Thai armies of Ayutthaya, who in the fifteenth century captured the Khmer capital for the exposition of their own political and material claims as the pre-eminent force in Southeast Asia. A series of Thai invasions in the fifteenth century saw the Khmer settlements sacked, looted and partially destroyed, though not entirely abandoned. The area fell into Thai control, and Angkor Wat shifted in religious orientation again, this time to the Thai's Theravada form of Buddhism, which Cambodians today still follow.[29] Performing their capture of Khmer power, the Thais brought back to their capital a number of *linga*, Hindu symbols of Shiva and fertility, which Jayavarman VII himself had pillaged from the Cham capital of Vijaya. As Charles F. Keyes asserts in his famed monograph on Southeast Asia, temples housing *linga* and statues of the *Bodhisattva* were monuments "of the same significance. They were architectural models of the cosmic order that served to harmonize the human world with cosmic reality."[30]

The movement of these pieces to Ayutthaya was important, for not only did these objects provide concrete evidence of their conquest, they transferred the legitimacy of Khmer power to the Thai. Not simply a means to secure "valuable" economic commodities, the act of plundering is a well-documented form of performing ownership claims, and has been central to what Ronald Inden calls "imperial formation" throughout history.[31] Such a performance of power renders these monumental fragments mediators between the vanquished and the victorious, creating in very material ways this narrative of possession so integral to the spatial construction of identity. They became *fragmentary re-presentations*, parts of the authentic monument which nevertheless have the same capacity to re-present at home these placemaking claims with the same level of authority as the original place simultaneously does *in situ*. The efficacy of fragmentary representations—like that of the monuments from which they were taken—lies in the perception of their authenticity. Because they shared the same point of origin and life history as the original, they are believed to be of the same mediatory potency as the original structure from which they came. Thus, authenticity in this case can be considered as the viewer's perception of the secular sacredness of an artifact, whose value is attributed based on its temporal permanence—its "aura." Since this value is a quality attributed to the object externally from a subjective actor and is not an intrinsic natural quality, it cannot be reduced or fragmented even when the object is split from something larger; the object possesses the same amount of authenticity as its place of origin, and can preserve this authenticity even if the original structure from which it was taken has succored to oblivion. As Emile Durkheim noted:

> When a sacred being is subdivided, it remains wholly equal to itself in each of its parts. In other words, from the standpoint of religious thought, the part equals the whole; the part has the same powers and the same efficacy. A fragment of a relic has the same virtues as the whole relic. . . . [I]f the virtues the thing is deemed to have are not intrinsic to it, if they come to it from certain feelings that it calls to mind and symbolizes (even though such feelings originate outside it), *it can play an evocative role whether it is whole or not, since in that role it does not need specific dimensions*. Since the part evokes the whole, it also evokes the same feelings as the whole. A mere scrap of the flag represents the country as much as the flag itself; moreover, it is sacred in the same right and to the same degree.[32]

Stemming from the legitimizing power of these fragmentary re-presentations, by the seventeenth century the Thai rulers had constructed a compelling narrative claim contending that the former Khmer capital was a creation of the first Ayutthayan king—one that still generates great controversy today[33]—and erected replicas of Angkor Wat in Thailand.[34]

Hearing Portuguese, Spanish and, later, French Jesuits' piecemeal accounts of a mysterious "lost" city in the Kampuchean jungles that seemed as unbelievable as "Plato's *Atlantis* or of his *Republic*,"[35] the French explorer-cum-naturalist Henri Mouhot "discovered" the temples two centuries later, in 1860. "There are few things that can stir such melancholy feelings as the sight of places that were once the scene of some glorious or pleasurable event, but which are now deserted," Mouhot wrote of these collapsed constructions strangled by thick, twisting trunks of banyan trees.[36] In part because of their impressive monumental scale and in part because of their dire need of restoration that the West could provide, the temples of Angkor factored prominently into colonial claims legitimizing the "necessary" formation of French Indochina. While the Khmer and Thai relied heavily on the mediating ability of these monumental structures to resonate in form and function with preexisting religious and political narratives of the region, the French explorers coming a few centuries later relied heavily on the sensation of wonder these structures evoked to mediate between their colonial endeavors in Indochina and their society at home.[37] The thrill of discovery, the foreignness of the built structural forms, the unusual display of natural power, and the surprising vestigial display of "civilization" in a place previously thought to be primitive and barbaric, all contributed to the formation of Orientalist narrative claims that saw Western Europeans as heirs to the luminous torch of "civilization." *Lux ex Oriente*, as the narrative goes;[38] the "light from the East" has been extinguished there in Kampuchea, but through the colonial efforts of the French, it can once again be brought back to the heirs of the Khmer.

And they brought Angkor back to France, too. Just as Jayavarman VII "carried home all the linga" from the Chams he defeated, which the Thais subsequently took to Ayutthaya and the Burmese later took to Mandalay, so too did French explorers carry off lintels, kingly statues and devotional images. Exhibited alongside plaster reproductions during the numerous World's Fairs that marked the Western colonial era, these fragmentary re-presentations were able to not only provide concrete evidence to the French people of the fruits of the colonial endeavor, but as physical objects from a different place and time, they were able to mediate between individuals in France and the colonial experience in the mysteriously faraway Kampuchean jungles. Museums were also created to house the disparate fragments collected from Cambodia, Vietnam and Laos. As theorists from Carol Duncan and Tony Bennett have argued, since the foundation of the Louvre, state-operated museum spaces themselves serve as an authorizing voice of the society, juxtaposing often unrelated collections of objects

and artifacts under a single roof, imbuing them with a single nationalistic narrative claim.[39] Through the physical museum space itself, these Khmer objects,
juxtaposed with artifacts taken from the various other Vietnamese and Laotian
protectorates which made up French Indochina, were thus literally enveloped by
the nation-state, lending conceptual coherence to the very idea of a unified *Indochine*. Such a narrative was performed most unabashedly during the Universal
Expositions held in Paris and Colonial Exhibition in Marseilles at the end of the
nineteenth and early twentieth centuries. A product of Western political and
technological advances of the mid-nineteenth century and early twentieth century, the Universal Expositions and World's Fairs that regularly emerged on the
international stage were events in which the industrialized Western countries
competitively played out their geopolitical power struggles not through arms and
armaments, but through "a congratulatory orgy of ethnocentrism," as Raymond
Fogelson writes.[40] Western countries marched out their finest in cutting-age
technologies and simultaneously juxtaposed them with the primitive relics of
their colonial subjects. Like museums, they were thus representational spaces
employing tangible cultural forms spatially to promote their own conceptions of
place and society.

These fragments not only performed claims of imperial power and colonial
nation-building, but they revealed the second prong of the French narrative
claim: that of France's role as heirs to, and protectors of, civilization. While
these objects had been left to rot in the oppressive elements by the barbaric descendents of their own constructors, they were now rescued by the French, who
cut them free from the stranglehold of nature and the neglect of their own people. They were carried off to the cities—some to Phnom Penh, but many of the
most valuable to Paris—where they were cleaned, preserved, studied, documented and then systematically displayed in buildings designated explicitly for
them. These museums, then, were venues revealing the value of the École Françes d'Estrême Orient (EFEO), whose experts worked tirelessly and often in
good faith to excavate, research and preserve Khmer material culture; while one
should not be quick to question the scholars' ideological intentions in the work
they had done, on the whole their praiseworthy efforts can nevertheless be seen
as implicitly performing their colonial Orientalist narrative.[41] Indeed, a central
element in Edward Said's theory of Orientalism is that it is subtle and pervasive,
often unintentionally informing one's understanding and portrayal of the Oriental Other in binary opposition to himself and his cosmology.[42] Through the effort
of the EFEO, therefore, these objects were seen as rescued from the stranglehold
of nature and restored to their rightful location in the new place in which civilization had settled. These objects actively performed the white man's burden;

they were safeguarded by the French on behalf of their undeserving and feeble heirs, who through ignorance or barbarism had carelessly left them to ruin.

Mediating the Heritage-scape

In today's rapidly globalizing world, the imperative to harness this ideologically charged media form for peaceful cultural coexistence is most pronounced in the United Nations Educational, Scientific and Cultural Organization (UNESCO)'s World Heritage Programme, a unique global placemaking endeavor fostering "peace in the minds of men" through a ritual reappropriation of tangible monuments, which are juxtaposed against one another to create a worldwide imagined community called the *heritage-scape*. Central to UNESCO's enterprise is the designation of these cultural properties as "World Heritage sites," a process that, on the surface, may appear to be an empty gesture, endowed perhaps with potent symbolism but a passive and impotent political performance nonetheless. Such a cynical viewpoint, however, inherently overlooks these monuments' capacities as powerful mediators, which, in very material terms, create, articulate, and replicate a society's situated sense of community. Noting that throughout history, wars have always originated in some part through local suspicions or ignorance of other peoples at the individual level, the Preamble to UNESCO's Constitution posits that people's identities are problematically based on traditional territorial conceptions[43]—conceptions of an imagined community that are constructed and promulgated through these highly emotionally charged monumental media. UNESCO's goal of creating lasting peace in the world, then, includes a fundamental reworking of the international geopolitical system, but in a way that is not achieved through physical conquest. Rather, it is accomplished by reordering individuals' sense of place the world over—so that no longer do they base their identities on conflictual territorial distinctions predicated on narratives of possession, but on the recognition and celebration of diversity at the individual level. The Preamble to UNESCO's Constitution expresses the organization's objective concerning the "construction" and subsequent "diffusion" of "intellectual and moral solidarity of mankind" in the "minds of men":

> The Governments of the States Parties to this Constitution on behalf of their peoples declare:
> - That since wars begin in the minds of men, it is in the minds of men that the defenses of peace must be constructed;
> - That ignorance of each other's ways and lives has been a common cause, throughout the history of mankind, of that suspicion and mistrust between

the peoples of the world through which their differences have all too often broken into war; . . .

- That the wide diffusion of culture, and the education of humanity for justice and liberty and peace are indispensable to the dignity of man and constitute a sacred duty which all the nations must fulfill in a spirit of mutual assistance and concern;
- That a peace based exclusively upon the political and economic arrangements of governments would not be a peace which could secure the unanimous, lasting and sincere support of the peoples of the world, and that the peace must therefore be founded, if it is not to fail, upon the intellectual and moral solidarity of mankind.[44]

Monuments once again play a mediatory role in creating the sense of community "in the minds of men." While following in the imperial tradition of reappropriating monumentality, pivoting monumental meanings to present new claims of place and identity, UNESCO's claim is not imperial in nature, however; it is not predicated on territoriality but on the common recognition and identification with the world's shared cultural heritage. Similar to authenticity, the term *heritage* is a powerful yet vague word that is concerned with an object's life history. Unlike authenticity per se, however, heritage is a specific narrative claim about the object's ability to temporally mediate between an individual's lineage and the society's history as a whole. If society is, as Durkheim states, *sui generis*, wherein individuals are born into it and die out of it,[45] heritage is a narrative that allows an individual to transcend his immediate past and present to connect with his predecessors, whom he often feels to be unknown yet intimately a part of. The remarks of Koïchiro Matsura, UNESCO's Director General, are telling in this regard: "To value heritage in all its dimensions, to care for it as a treasure bequeathed to us by our ancestors, to recognize it is our duty to transmit it intact to our children, is a sign of wisdom."[46] An authentic object of cultural heritage, therefore, is a movement-inducing medium that not only indexes the link between an individual and his culture, but constructively conjoins the two.

If a heritage object connects an individual with the socio-cultural milieu from which he came, UNESCO's *World* Heritage objects are intended to transcend the temporal and spatial situatedness of one culture's heritage claims:

What makes the concept of World Heritage exceptional is its universal application. World Heritage sites belong to all the peoples of the world, irrespective of the territory on which they are located. . . . How does a World Heritage site differ from a site of national heritage? The key lies in the words 'outstanding universal value' . . . Sites selected for World Heritage listing are approved on the basis of their merits as the best possible examples of the [world's] cultural and natural heritage. The World Heritage List draws attention to the wealth and diversity of Earth's cultural and natural heritage.[47]

This sentiment had been canonized in UNESCO's *Budapest Declaration on World Heritage*, which, while "encouraging [sic] countries that have not yet joined the Convention to do so at the earliest opportunity, as well as with other related international heritage protection instruments," states in no uncertain terms that the "properties on the World Heritage List are assets held in trust to pass on to generations of the future as their rightful inheritance."[48]

As both of these citations reveal, the concept of World Heritage underscores a seemingly incompatible dualism: On one hand, it clearly recognizes the multiplicity of distinct cultural and natural forms, and therefore of the very differences that often lead to the worlds' conflicts; on the other hand, it purports that there exists some sort of universal cultural form that can be empirically located, and unanimously recognized. Yet taken together, it seems that UNESCO is defining a world system based on the structural unity of difference, a "culture of cultures" as Marshall Sahlins famously remarked.[49]

"Unity in diversity" is thus UNESCO's rallying cry, the narrative claim behind the heritage-scape. Unity lies in the collective understanding that diversity exists outside one's known social and natural environment. "Every society known to history is a global society, every culture is a cosmological order; and in thus including the universe within its own cultural scheme . . . the people accord beings and things beyond their immediate community a definite place in its reproduction," Sahlins writes.[50] This is not to say that the group and the Other conceptualize themselves in the same way, or even are aware of how the other thinks of them. Nor does it assert that a group believes that it has complete knowledge of the greater world. Rather, Sahlens contends, all act with the understanding that there is a continuation of a world outside their conceptual and material boundaries that may impact them. Proclaiming UNESCO's *Universal Declaration on Cultural Diversity*, passed just months before the September 11, 2001 terrorist attacks, Matsura echoes Sahlins' sentiments, asserting that "each [individual] must acknowledge not only otherness in all its forms, but also the plurality of his or her own identity, within societies that are themselves plural."[51]

For UNESCO, as for Sahlins, "Culture" can thus be perceived as a process of totalizing differences. Such a project is not merely translating a cacophony of seemingly chaotic and unintelligible forms into one group's scientifically classificatory language, but integrating it into an ever-deepening, over-arching structure that is never fixed, always moving. UNESCO's Director-General later re-marked:

> Diversity and culture are fundamentally interrelated: culture is diversity, an in-finite tapestry of distinctions, nuance and change; a relentless return to all that exists in order to render it both new and the same, to understand it and bring it to life. Culture is, by nature, diversity. Yet, for that same reason, it gives diver-sity a dimension that surpasses and envelops it. Diversity per se does not exist; it is even, in the absence of culture, incomprehensible, and everything looks the same to anyone lacking cultural depth. Diversity is constructed by culture. Cul-ture is what shapes it, gives it scope and meaning. Diversity is essentially cul-tural, just as culture is diversity.[52]

UNESCO's project of tangibly totalizing differences, therefore, is not merely translating a cacophony of seemingly chaotic and unintelligible forms into one group's cultural language, but integrating it into an ever-deepening, over-arching structure that is never fixed, always moving. This is the *heritage-scape*, the social space of an imagined community linked together by their common appreciation and identification with cultural diversity. Like other communities, that of the heritage-scape gains materiality through these material monumental media, who index and perform the new meta-narrative claim of "unity in diver-sity."

A monument previously mediating between individuals and their society is conceptually converted into a medium of global reach through a complex and ritual process. It first undergoes a separation phase wherein it is de-contextualized, isolated from its original context and examined as an object in its own right. Next, it enters into liminal status, where it is evaluated and ideal-ized. Finally, it is re-aggregated into a new social context, joining hundreds of other unrelated but similarly valorized World Heritage sites as another mediator in the service of the heritage-scape. This is a lengthy procedure, one that takes years to complete and involves a great number of stakeholders from the local, national, international and nongovernmental levels engaged in a Bourdieuian struggle of positions and position-taking that marks a field of production.[53] In-deed, just as Howard Becker and Pierre Bourdieu assert that a work of art is not merely the work of one painter, but rather "the result of the co-ordinated activi-ties of all the people whose co-operation is necessary in order that the work should occur as it does,"[54] so too is a World Heritage site the result of a pro-tracted and institutionalized[55] series of interactions between objective sets of social relations with their own historical trajectory, expertise, and realm of au-thority, who struggle within and amongst themselves to define the place's World

Heritage narrative. It is through this institutionalized field of production that a site previously of local interest can become an internationally recognized site of universal value. To appropriate a remark by Bourdieu, the World Heritage site "is an object which exists as such only by virtue of the (collective) belief which knows and acknowledges it" as a World Heritage site."[56]

At one level is the State-party, the political organization which, by economically contributing to the World Heritage Centre, UNESCO and the United Nations, is afforded the opportunity to nominate a monument in its territory for consideration. The site itself is, of course, most often a product of a much longer, socially and historically situated process of contested monumental mediation; Angkor is a case in point. This nomination consists of formally inscribing the site on a country-specific Tentative List, a "wish list" of places within the country that the nation believes would, or should, make a valuable contribution to the heritage-scape. This effectively isolates the site from its original environmental context; it holds it up as an object to be considered apart from its physical, social or political interrelationships. Juxtaposing it with other similarly decoupled natural and cultural "nominations" within the country effectively serves to change its meaning and the very context of its use and import; it becomes not a cultural monument, but a "nomination," thereby setting into motion an entirely different series of actions and interactions. It becomes an object open to scrutiny, to evaluation. This is integral to any Bourdieuian field of production, as he contends that "the production of discourse (critical, historical, etc.) about the work . . . is one of the conditions of production of the work."[57] Although the heritage-scape, as a real social structure predicated on the narrative of "unity in diversity," is innately subversive to the authority of the nation-state, which is built on conflict-inducing narrative claims of difference, nation-states do not recognize this long-term and idyllic goal. Rather, actively engaged with the process from the very beginning, they recognize the dual "benefits" of the Programme, which ritually perform international *communitas* while simultaneously raising the social capital of their country on the world stage, subsequently serving as a "catalyst" for a variety of material improvements:

> The overarching benefit of ratifying the World Heritage Convention is that of belonging to an international community of appreciation and concern for universally significant properties that embody a world of outstanding examples of cultural diversity and natural wealth. . . . The prestige that comes from being a member of the Convention and having sites inscribed on the World Heritage List often serves as a catalyst to raising awareness for heritage preservation."[58]

Upon being nominated for consideration, the site enters its liminal period; it is "betwixt and between" statuses[59]—thoroughly decoupled from its original context, poked and prodded in an attempt to locate its kernel of "universal value," and then evaluated on its representative qualities—but not yet designated as a World Heritage site. Professional and regional specialists from non-profit "Advisory Bodies" work with experts, site managers, and political representatives at the local and national levels to compile all of the monument's necessary biographical information, and to asses the mechanisms in place to preserve it from environmental and tourism pressures. Sites that are to be nominated under criteria specific to the natural world are examined by experts under the aegis of the World Conservation Union, or IUCN. Places that are nominated as "cultural sites" benefit from the expertise of ICOMOS, the International Council of Monuments and Sites, whose coterie of professional conservators and regional specialists work with experts, site managers, and political representatives at the local and national levels to compile all necessary biographical information on the life history of the monument, and to analyze the site's environmental and tourist management structures. If the monument or site is in need of preservation management or expert assistance in this regard, a third advisory body, the International Centre for the Study of the Preservation and Restoration of Cultural Property (ICCROM) is also engaged. At the heart of these evaluative measures, these Advisory Bodies ascertain the site's authenticity—the ability to speak to the present and the future about a common world-historical past.

In the final stage of this liminal period, the property is specifically idealized by comparing it against UNESCO's predetermined set of typologies, whose conceptual amorphism allows for its applicability in a variety of settings across the world. To become a World Heritage site, a place must be determined to:

(i)   represent a masterpiece of human creative genius; or

(ii) exhibit an important interchange of human values, over a span of time or within a cultural area of the world, on developments in architecture or technology, monumental arts, town-planning or landscape design; or

(iii) bear a unique or at least exceptional testimony to a cultural tradition or to a civilization which is living or which has disappeared; or

(iv) be an outstanding example of a type of building or architectural or technological ensemble or landscape which illustrates (a) significant stage(s) in human history; or

(v)   be an outstanding example of a traditional human settlement or land-use which is representative of a culture (or cultures), especially when it has become vulnerable under the impact of irreversible change; or

(vi) be directly or tangibly associated with events or living traditions, with ideas, or with outstanding universal significance (a criterion applied only in exceptional circumstances, and together with other criteria).[60]

Thus, a place is inscribed as a World Heritage site not because it *is* something, but rather because it is *representative* or exemplary of something that can be understood, in part, through touristic interactions with the place. That "something" is also necessarily vague, determinable by the nominating agency and UNESCO themselves; it can be *an important interchange of human values, testimony to a cultural tradition*, or a *type of building or landscape*. The conceptual amorphousness of these typologies almost guarantees a decidedly unique interpretation of what aesthetics, values, traditions or tangible forms demonstrate World Heritage status for each individual site. Yet as the nominating field determines how the site fits into the above typologies, it really redefines the object, producing an idealized mediator, or a quintessential material embodiment, of those virtues UNESCO's criteria seek.

Once this documentation is compiled into the site's official File at the World Heritage Centre, the property is ready for its final evaluation by the Intergovernmental Committee for the Protection of the World Cultural and Natural Heritage—or "World Heritage Committee," as it is called. Once a year, the World Heritage Committee meets to evaluate some thirty nominations whose Files are completed. Convening for a week-long session, the Committee is composed of representatives from twenty one State-Parties who are elected for a six-year term by the General Assembly. Also in attendance, but who cannot vote, are representatives from the Advisory Bodies who helped to compile the Files, representatives from the State-Party from whom a monument under consideration comes, and any other representatives from those countries who are members of UNESCO or the United Nations (but who may or may not have signed the World Heritage Convention). Based on the contents of the File, and upon considering the technical evaluation compiled by the Advisory Bodies, the Committee votes to inscribe, reject or withhold judgment on the site. In the first twenty years of the Convention, a full sixty percent of properties nominated were inscribed, according to a millennium's-end assessment by UNESCO.[61]

Declaring a monument a World Heritage site also entails confirming the particular wording of its narrative claim—that is, the way in which its particular authentic self satisfies and reveals its "outstanding universal value." As the textual wording is exceptionally important, it is often subject to politicking as all parties involved struggle in the Bourdieuian sense to determine the specific wording of its narrative. Most often it conforms to the narrative constructed in the Advisory Body's technical recommendation, which itself was a product of

discourses and position-taking struggles between local, state and nongovernmental actors, mediated by the "disposition" of the individual representative
agents involved.[62]

Because World Heritage sites and their individual narrative claims are ultimately products of evaluation and negotiation within a Bourdieuian field of production, unintended consequences often arise. Using much of ICOMOS' wording, the World Heritage Committee designated the Angkor Archaeological Park
on the basis of the following reasoning:

Criterion i:	The Angkor complex represents the entire range of Khmer art from the 9th to the 14th centuries, and includes a number of indisputable artistic masterpieces (eg Angkor Vat, the Bayon, Banteay Srei).
Criterion ii:	The influence of Khmer art, as developed at Angkor was a profound one over much of south-east Asia and played a fun- damental role in its distinctive evolution.
Criterion iii:	The Khmer Empire of the 9th–14th centuries encompassed much of south-east Asia and played a formative role in the political and cultural development of the region. All that re- mains of that civilization is its rich heritage of cult structures in brick and stone.
Criterion iv:	Khmer architecture evolved largely from that of the Indian sub-continent, from which it soon became clearly distinct as it developed its own special characteristics, some independently evolved and others acquired from neighboring cultural tradi- tions. The result was a new artistic horizon in oriental art and architecture.[63]

Such wording is telling, for it constructs a narrative that oscillates between one
valorizing the Khmer empire (and that of its heir, today's Kingdom of Cambodia)
as profoundly influential producers of cultural masterpieces (*criteria i* and *ii*),
and another espousing more Orientalist claims of a civilization that moved from
East to West; it "evolved" from India, "developed" in the region, and was left to
nature, leaving only "remains of . . . cult structures in brick and stone" (*criteria
iii* and *iv*). UNESCO further defined this complex as "a geographical region, an
archaeological site and a cultural concept,"[64] highlighting both Khmer culture
and the strength of nature over primitivity as co-contributors to the site's "universal value." Designated as Angkor Archaeological Park, its title also reveals this
discursive oscillation between the historical focus of archaeology and the leisure-
oriented activities of a park, a natural playground.

This narrative is not simply conceptual, but materially manifests itself in the
manner in which the site is subsequently conserved and packaged for touristic

consumption. In Angkor's case, edifices are alternatively "restored" or "preserved." While these two terms are utilized somewhat interchangeably in the general field of historic preservation, instantiated within the Angkor Archaeological Park, they produce the same two conflicting narratives, which the visitor to Angkor must problematically negotiate. Sites such as Angkor Wat and the Bayon can be considered "restored"—that is, they were cleared of the jungle's stranglehold and partially reconstructed as they are imagined to have appeared for its intended use by the host society—thereby espousing a narrative that valorizes Khmer culture. However, other sites such as Ta Prohm and Preah Khan have been "preserved" in the true sense of the term—they have been cleaned and reinforced, but have been left largely as the French discovered them, vestiges of cultural forms suffocated by the tendrils of nature.

Ethnographic research conducted through group tours from 2002–2006 reveal that the methods of preservation implicitly inform the manner in which tourists interact with these structures. For sites such as Angkor Wat and the Bayon, tours are structured by the monument's original architecture and architectonics. As a consequence, guides pause before cleaned bas reliefs and reconstructed statuary to discuss the history, artistry and mythology of the Khmer people, pointing out depictions of deities and daily life processes, and answering cultural questions elicited from these experiences. This process stands in marked differentiation to the same groups' excursions to the "preserved" sites of Ta Prohm or Preah Khan, where guides often allow their visitors to wander at leisure over, under and through the disarray of collapsed ceilings, crumbled walls and cluttered causeways. Scrambling atop the jumbled stones of these temples, visitors literally are able to "walk all over" Khmer culture. Like the pop icons Indiana Jones and Lara Croft, one can easily re-experience the colonials' power over primitivity, and travelogues from the 1920s to today have extolled the wonder of discovery, the freedom of control over the ruins, and the liberation of communing with nature and primitivism.[65]

Once designated, these discrete World Heritage sites are inscribed together on the World Heritage List, which inserts them as nodes on a newly ordered heritage landscape that exists above and beyond the world's traditional boundaries. While, for example, Angkor's specific narrative is a bifurcated one based on cultural diffusion and domination, through its juxtaposition with monuments from across the world who share its celebratory title, Angkor is imbued with UNESCO's meta-narrative claim of "unity in diversity." Thus the *heritage-scape* is not simply a mosaic of aggregate individual sites, a network of specially-delineated destinations with their own local social relations, but rather, it is a unique place with its own social context that is constantly evolving and expanding as UNESCO continues its activities, integrating increasingly more places, objects and now even intangible customs within its nebulous boundaries.[66] Characterized by tangible geographic World Heritage sites that are decoupled from local individuals and the nation-states in which they reside, the *heritage-scape* exists above and beyond international borders; it has roots in the physical world yet exists apart from it, primarily in the "minds of men." In the heritage-scape, the imagined boundaries are neither clearly defined nor fixed; rather, they are amorphous and dynamic,[67] ever changing and expanding both outwardly (as sites in new regions of the world are inscribed) and inwardly (as new sites within previously represented regions continue to be added). And with each new discrete addition to the heritage-scape, which deepens and complexifies the very notion of "unity in diversity," the heritage-scape continues to expand conceptually as well.

These World Heritage sites, therefore, serve as bridges and conduits between the physical world and the ephemeral heritage-scape, mediating between individuals who live in and are informed by traditional geopolitics and the nebulously multicultural social system of the heritage-scape. One question remains, however, of the most practical nature: If these monuments are truly mediatory links between these two social realms, what kind of non-local person can utilize them, and how? How and for whom can a singularly authentic site in Cambodia effectively mediate between an individual in North America and the heritage-scape? Indeed, UNESCO cannot carry off all of the proverbial *linga* of the heritage-scape, as the Khmer, Thai, Burmese and French did to mediate between their citizens and the distant society that produced the medium; it is physically and ideologically impossible.[68] Rather, UNESCO must harness the global flows of international travelers to interact with the authentic monuments *in situ*.

The Field of Touristic Production and the Heritage-scape

Tourism is the ideal form of interaction with UNESCO's monumental mediators, for its "deep structure" closely resembles that of the heritage-scape. As the world's largest and fastest growing industry,[69] tourism's reach is indicative of the same globalizing forces on which UNESCO relies for the creation of a worldwide imagined community. Tourism harnesses the capitalistic ethos of the "modern" world system,[70] yet, like the heritage-scape, it subtly inverts it. To borrow an observation from Barbara Kirshenblatt-Gimblett, tourism is the largest export industry in the world but exports none of its tangible goods. Rather, it exports its consumers, who travel to the destination to purchase their tourist products,[71] which range from the souvenirs to the hotel experience to interaction with the World Heritage site itself. Most importantly, like that of the heritage-scape, touristic cultures are at once collective and individuated; they are predicated on the communion with monumental mediators which transcend geopolitical boundaries and act directly on the "minds of men."

These World Heritage sites cannot be effectively consumed by the heritage-scape's intended audience—that is, the individual members of the international community—without the work of another field of production, operating independently yet concentrically with the World Heritage Convention. This is the touristic field, and although its products are significantly more varied than the monolithic heritage-scape,[72] it nevertheless packages and produces "destinations" whose stars are World Heritage sites. Places are created as "destinations" through a similar Bourdieuian process of positioning, packaging and politicking that marks the heritage-scape's field of production.

While tourism takes many forms, based in part on which actors are involved in the planning process, the example of an institution-sponsored "group tour"—of the kind in which this author was involved and from which most ethnographic data in this research was obtained—includes the most levels of position-taking organizations to shape the touristic experience. Institution-sponsored group tours are highly specialized packaged tours that are sold or otherwise marketed by a sponsoring organization (such as a university alumni association, museum, garden club, etc.) to its membership or constituency. It is sometimes subsumed under the category of "incentive tourism," a similarly packaged group tour that is usually given for free or at a reduced cost by a corporation, conference organizer, national tourism organization or travel agency or as a reward or incentive for excellent work. The corporation does not need to be affiliated in any way with the cultural sector or with professional tourism; what makes these tours possible is quantity: the third-party tourism professionals who design these tours on behalf of the sponsoring entity are able to discount the price of the tour incrementally as the number of travelers increases. In all of these forms of group tours, it is clear that the first level of the field of production is the sponsoring agency. They are the original clients of the tourism sector; they determine which tours are most desirable, and they offer them (sometimes directly and sometimes indirectly, through marketers) to their constituencies.

The next level is the tour operator itself. A tour operator is an organized group of tourism professionals who research a destination, design the itinerary, arrange the day-to-day operations of the tour, and often provide a "tour director" to ensure that everything operates smoothly *in situ* for the duration of the tour. Most often, these journeys are sold to consumers as a "package tour"—that is, all tour arrangements are bundled together, with the traveler paying one price for the entire trip. The price of each package tour is dependent on different types of "inclusions," or prepaid itinerary features ranging from coach excursions and meals to accommodations and airfare. Those who furnish these services are called "providers," and range from commercial airline companies to self-employed tour guides, hoteliers to restaurateurs. Often the tour operator purchases these inclusions in bulk from local providers at a reduced rate based on the commercial or personal history a tour operator has with them. On their end, local providers are often eager to increase the quantity of sales and market reduced rates to these travel professionals, often at a discount of ten percent or more. The discount itself is almost always the product of negotiation, regardless of whether the provider is a large corporate chain or a small family-owned business. This also serves to keep a package tour relatively affordable, since tour operators, like their travel agent counterparts, make their profit on this percentage reduction. There is therefore a symbiotic relationship between the local provider, the tour operator and the consumer: the provider quantitatively increases his sales, the tour operator is able to compete with those who book directly with a provider while still making a profit, and the consumer pays relatively the same price as he would if he arranged the tour himself. Indeed, in the experience of this author, a majority of consumers cite the convenience of pre-paid, pre-arranged travel as a primary motivation of the purchase of a packaged tour.

Like the narrative of a World Heritage site, the specific itinerary that is purchased by touristic consumers is a product of negotiation between a number of interested parties. The aforementioned pricing struggles between a local provider and tour operator plays a fundamental part, for the outcomes will constrain or facilitate the inclusion of components in the itinerary. There have been many a time, in this writer's own experience, that the cost of a desired inclusion was deemed too high to include in a particular itinerary; hotels, as the largest single cost in a typical tour (outside of the airfare), are often the culprit. In this case, either a substitute for a high-priced hotel is found, or, should a particularly expensive hotel be regarded as a selling point of a tour, other potential inclusions—such as the quantity of meals or number of courses in a particular dinner—will be eliminated or reduced. The inclusion of "private visits"—specially arranged touristic experiences such as curator-led museum tours, exclusive receptions held in unique venues, or meetings with local artists, politicians or nobility who do not often offer their services to traditional travelers—is also a product of this commercial-cum-personal negotiating struggle. Such Bourdieuian struggles work both ways to shape the ultimate outcome of a packaged tour experience; while high-priced inclusions may constrain that which an operator can offer in a particular itinerary, inclusions that are regarded as a good deal will be used again and again in new tours to future clients.

In addition to pricing struggles between a local provider and a tour operator, the group tour operator who does not sell directly to individual travelers but who works through a sponsoring institution also must negotiate with its client—the aforementioned corporation, cultural institution, or member-based organization. Before such a tour is ever marketed to the public, it must be approved by the sponsor, and often the potential client solicits an itinerary from a variety of competing operators. Thus seeking to differentiate itself in this competition, an operator will creatively construct a marketing package around its itinerary; the itinerary is sent to a potential client as a detailed brochure or proposal written in "travelese"—the descriptive style of a travelogue or tour book—and endowed with beautiful images of the proposed destination. Potential clients have attested to selecting a particular company's itinerary based on the aesthetic qualities of its proposal when competing operators are on equal footing.[73] A "tour highlights" summary may also be included, which extols the various "special visits" the operator could provide that the lay client, lacking specific knowledge of the unique offerings of the destination or the operator's connections and special relationships with the destination's tourism providers, could not organize on its own. The sponsoring organization often has a distinct "feel" for the tour in mind as well, and may also have a list of sites or private visits it believes its members would like. When ultimately confirming an itinerary to be marketed under the organization's name, timing, distance, price and types of visits will come into play as the operator—possessing macroscopic knowledge of the destination and general tourist desires—negotiates with the sponsoring organization, who is more knowledgeable about its specific members' cost thresholds, expectations and familiarity with the tour's theme. Thus, it is in this level of interaction that the touristic field of production takes its most notable shape: it is clearly a form of positioning and position-taking, as both sides attempt to "read" the expectations, desires and constraints of the other to produce a satisfying itinerary.

This process most closely resembles that part of UNESCO's ritual process wherein a State Party struggles with Advisory Bodies and the World Heritage Committee to define a particular site's overarching narrative and the typologies for which it will be associated. Like a World Heritage site, these package tours often are publicized with a distinct narrative that is closely aligned with the sponsoring organization's own meta-narrative claims as revealed in its mission statement and the perceived interests of its members; as with any claim utilizing such monumental mediators, certain parts of the destination's life history are highlighted while other parts are "forgotten" when describing sites on an itinerary, so that a coherent theme of the tour emerges and is emphasized. Thus, tours featuring the same excursions but sponsored by different clients will emphasize different parts of the destinations' discourses to create sometimes vastly different narratives. In the case of tours to the highly popular Italian region of Tuscany—which feature the same excursions to hill towns, vineyards for wine tastings, and private receptions in garden villas—an art museum may draw on specific artistic or literary connections, an alumni association might emphasize the historical and World Heritage aspects of the same places, and a horticultural group might highlight garden design or intriguing botany included in its visits. All will attempt to accentuate particular connections the organization has with the destination: a museum who owns a particular Renaissance painter's work will specifically highlight the museums and sites associated with the same artist; vineyards or villas owned by families connected with a university will be emphasized for that organization's alumni association tour; and American garden groups will call attention to the prominent gardens upon which their own green spaces were modeled. More specifically, for example, Jesuit Catholic universities may feature tours with such thematic titles as "In the Footsteps of St. Ignatius" that highlight the Jesuit presence in the same hill towns, churches and museums as those included in itineraries for Jewish groups, which may emphasize the historical presence—or absence—of Jews in these same destinations, as Naomi Leite reveals in her study of the construction of "Jewish Portugal."[74]

Lastly, the tour's narrative will also incorporate some reference to luxury; this is a commercial endeavor, after all. The narrative of luxury will meet the demands of potential travelers and color expectations for the trip; it thus must be carefully crafted for each group to which the tour is marketed. Inexpensive garden tours open to the general public or active horticulturalists who can get "down and dirty" often emphasize the authentic rustic charm of the various visits. An identical itinerary may then be marketed for high donors or administrators from the same institution, but would emphasize the luxury of the accommodations, the sumptuousness of the meals, and the exclusivity of the private visits.[75] The case of tours to Cambodia and Vietnam offers a particular salient example of these assertions. Because of their relatively recent emergence on the tourism circuit, "typical" itineraries linking these two countries do not vary much; both feature excursions to the same World Heritage sites, museums, cafes, restaurants and landscapes, and often in the same order of visitation, but their narratives vary greatly depending on the sponsoring organization's thematic niche and its target demographic. One university alumni association led by a professor of American history marketed its tour as a historical exploration of the Vietnam War and the horrors of the Khmer Rouge, one major art museum advertised its tour as an exploration of Vietnamese and Khmer contemporary art, a smaller museum sold its tour as an exploration of authentic Southeast Asian "crafts" (as opposed to fine art), and still another marketed its tour with a decidedly archaeological bent. Still others advertised their tour with romanticized narratives of the "phantasmic"[76] luxury of colonial Indochina, emphasizing visits made famous in Graham Greene novels and the 1992 French film *Indochine*.

Although tour operators are often involved with their destinations independently for many years—and indeed, a number specialize in only a few select locations throughout the world—they are also influenced by another important level in this touristic field of production. National, international, and corporate culture industries, of which UNESCO can be considered a part, also dialectically influences tour operators' itineraries and offerings in a number of ways. Heritage and culture industries create and disseminate re-presentations of their destinations, as the examples of package tour narratives reveal. In the last decade, the Malaysian Tourist Promotion Board, an arm of the country's Ministry of Culture, Arts and Tourism, published advertisements in prominent travel magazines with the tagline "Malaysia—Simply Asia" to underscore a claim that the nation-state is the quintessential Asian destination. As part of its long-running "Yokso! Japan" ("Welcome! Japan") campaign, the Japan National Tourist Organization (JNTO) will hold special "Visit Japan" weeks throughout the low-seasons of the year. Through such awareness-raising activities, these national ministries construct and reinforce claims about their sites for potential tourists. World Heritage discourses often mark such claims; they can be found on print advertisements and are often featured prominently on national tourist board websites. For its part, UNESCO is immensely concerned with the proper promotion of its World Heritage sites, and offers guidelines nation-states must agree to follow when packaging a World Heritage site for touristic consumption; should they renege on this tacit agreement on responsible conservation and representation of their World Heritage site, UNESCO has the right to de-list a site. Most importantly, UNESCO disburses small grants from the World Heritage Fund—to which all nation-states must contribute—that are earmarked not for direct conservation use, but primarily for educational and promotional means. In this way, UNESCO's specific World Heritage discourse can inform both touristic producers and consumers with ease.

Often these same regional, governmental or corporate marketing agencies will also work as mediators between the operator and locals. Through participation in industry-wide conferences, private meetings with operators and travel agents, and sponsorship of "familiarization" (or "FAM") tours for tourism professionals, they work to raise awareness of the destination's conductivity to tourism and its unique attributes for those in the travel industry. Familiarization tours are a particularly interesting example of the ways in which these governmental agencies directly intersect with touristic production. FAMs are free or low-cost tours sponsored by a country or region's Ministry of Tourism or Culture, an airline (most often state-run airlines, such as Alitalia, Singapore Air, British Airways or Japan Airlines), or a large local operator. They are offered specifically to travel agents, tour operators, travel writers, photographers, and sometimes to tour operators' potential clients (such as the membership director of well-known museums). In this case, the governmental agency becomes both the sponsoring organization and the tour operator itself to reveal a new potential itinerary that could be replicated by the actual sponsoring organizations and tour operators.

FAMS are usually small in participant number and exceedingly luxurious, marked by first-class travel, five-star accommodations, sumptuous feasts and private visits with famous locals—all designed to reveal the best the destination has to offer. They are affordable because local providers "donate" their services for the imagined future benefits of the promotion. Ironically enough, many of these tours cannot be replicated on a practical basis, for many of the private visits either cannot or will not accommodate larger group tours, let alone the fact that the ideal tour's cost to consumers would far exceed the pricing threshold of even the wealthiest group travelers.[77] Yet the long-term benefits of a FAM extend beyond these base considerations; they ultimately serve to raise awareness of the safety, tourability and "universal value" of local destinations—notions that indeed inform tourism professionals and tourists alike. Tour operators are especially inclined to market a region or destination promoted in a FAM, for they have tested first-hand the experiences offered in the itinerary. And while responsible travel writers certainly conduct their own, anonymous excursions to a destination, informal conversations with journalists on these FAMs reveal that a number of magazine articles have especially been informed—at least in the earliest stages—by the awareness-raising activities of these tourism and heritage ministries, if not by the inclusion of a writer on a FAM itself. Once again, World Heritage discourses feature prominently in these tours.

Linking Heritage and Tourism

The connection between discourses of heritage and tourism is not merely a present-day phenomenon, though today's globalization of markets and infrastructures certainly have created a uniquely "modern" linkage. Rather, this linkage can be historically traced to a number of early societies, both in the East and the West.

In an intriguing article entitled "Walking in Memphis," British Egyptologist Steven Snape reveals the deep connection between conceptions of heritage, tourism and conservation in ancient Egypt. By the time of Ramses II in the Nineteenth Dynasty (1303 BC–1213 BC)—the famous pharaoh to whom the World Heritage site of Abu Simbel is dedicated—the ancient Egyptian city of Memphis, long the burial ground of the pharaohs of the Old Kingdom (2650 BC–

2175 BC), had in the course of almost two millennia ceased to be a religious center, and its monuments fell into decay. Ramses' son, the high priest of Ptah named Khaemwese, "driven by his sense of identity, responsibility and respect for the monuments of the past," set upon an ambitious conservation project—one of the first of its kind—to restore and preserve these sites that were considered so important to "his cultural background." In particular, he re-cased the exterior of a number of pyramids, and erected monumental "restoration texts"[78] that followed a similar formula to the one he created for the pyramid of King Unas of Dynasty Five, at Saqqara:

> His majesty decreed an announcement:
>
> It is a High Priest [of Ptah], the sem-priest, Prince Khaemwese who has perpetuated the name of King Unas. For his (i.e., Unas') name was not found on the face on his pyramid. Prince Khaemwese greatly wished to restore the monuments of the Kings of Upper and Lower Egypt because of what they had done, the strength of which (i.e., the pyramids themselves), was falling into decay.[79]

These dedicatory remarks indicate not only a prevalent appreciation by New Kingdom individuals for what could only be described as Egyptian "heritage,"[80] but also the conceptualization that these monuments needed interpretative placards to inform visitors of their narratives. According to Snape, latter was not merely an empty symbolic endeavor, but reflected a growing culture of tourism that occurred in Ramses II's time.

In addition to these interpretative inscriptions, Snape points out, two other important indicators reveal the existence of private, touristic interactions with these heritage properties: the erection of contemporary monumental statuary and graffiti on older monuments. Snape interprets the former initiative as an endeavor to allow better visitor access to religious structures built by Ramses II, in essence granting the possibility of touristic experiences with these newly constructed places. Traditionally, pyramids—the burial tombs for Egyptian pharaohs—were loci of religious participatory activity conducted only by elite, specialist priests; private individuals—including mobile secular elites and common citizens—had little interactive place at these cult sites save as spectators at "major processional festivals."[81] However, one of Ramses II's "innovations" was the building of colossal statues of the king outside of the pyramids and temples he erected at the time. Such an endeavor encouraged visitation and, though nevertheless in limited measure, a greatly enhanced level of participation where "ordinary people" could interact with what was within.[82] In essence, they became secondary mediators for the monumental mediators that were the Nineteenth Dynasty temples themselves, for the expressed purpose of individual and perhaps non-priest-regulated religious tourism.

However, the excavation of ink graffiti dating to the New Kingdom (Ramses II's era) on Old Kingdom temple walls also indicates that pure tourism to Egyptian heritage sites occurred. Snape provides the example of the pyramid attributed to the "wise king" Sneferu, the founder of the Fourth Dynasty, who reigned from 2613 BC–2589 BC. Located at Meidum, the southern end of a cluster of Old Kingdom pyramids, the cult rituals inside this site had "long since ceased," but was turned into a touristic destination, "an obvious place for casual, but respectful, visitors to express, through ink graffiti written on the walls of the mortuary temple itself, their admiration for the pyramid and for its builder":[83]

> Year 41 of the reign of King Tuthmosis (III). The scribe Aakheperkaraseneb, son of Amenmensu the scribe and lector-priest came here to see the beautiful temple of King Sneferu.

> He found it as though heaven were within it, when the sun god is rising in it. He exclaimed "Heaven rains with fresh frankincense and drops incense upon the roof of the temple of King Sneferu!"[84]

This is not an isolated occurrence or one relegated only to the priestly elite, argues Snape, who provides a number of graffiti dated to the reign of Ramses II on the step pyramid of the Third Dynasty pharaoh Djoser (reigning roughly around 2650 BC) at the Memphite site of Saqqara. Important to the heritage context through which New Kingdom visitors approached it, Djoser was understood as the first stone-using king, and this pyramid today is thought to be the "most ancient of pyramids."[85] In one graffito, an elite group of tourists writes:

> Year 47, 2nd month of Winter, Day 25. The treasury-scribe Hednakht, son of Tjenro and Twosret, came to take a stroll and enjoy himself in the West of Memphis, along with his brother Panakht, scribe of the vizier.

> He said: "O all you gods of the West of Memphis and glorified dead, may you grant a full lifetime in serving your good pleasure, with a goodly burial after a happy old age, like yourself."[86]

Both Hednakht and Aakheperkaraseneb attest to having undergone a transcendental touristic encounter; as with any touristic interaction, theirs were both predicated on seeing the beautiful temple for their own personal enjoyment of their heritage, of interacting with it not in a prescribed cultic way, but through a very individuated "tourist gaze," to use John Urry's famous expression.[87] Like the modern visitor's requisite sunrise visit to Angkor, Aakheperkaraseneb wanted to experience the temple in a particular time of day, and the result—echoing so many tourist responses to this experience at Angkor—was illuminating.

Notions combining heritage and travel can be found in some of the greatest epic poems of the Western canon, as well. The *Epic of Gilgamesh*, Homer's *Odyssey* and Virgil's *Aeneid* are only three of the many literary examples wherein the protagonist is a tourist traveling across the heritage landscape of his own culture's cosmology. Such touristic re-presentations of heritage had distinctly material effects; arguing that poetry "is a private statement, yet at the end it raises a public value," Stephen Owen points out that Homer's travel depictions induced Alexander the Great to conquest.[88] And in the contemporary era, one of the most sensational effects of the Homeric epics was Heinrich Schliemann's discovery of ancient Troy. Like so many young men of his time, Schliemann had read the Homeric travel poetry of Odysseus and the Trojan War, and a particularly striking painting of a burning Troy remained in his memory for his entire life; after his father read Homer to him at age eight, he supposedly announced his intention to one day discover the lost city. After making a fortune in the Indigo trade, he retired at age thirty-six and learned archaeological methods in the hopes of identifying the site of Homeric Troy, despite encountering skepticism about the very veracity of the mythological city's existence. He traveled Ottoman Greece and Anatolia, and conducted a series of digs that eventually produced the remains of this famed city (as well as hitherto unknown Minoan Crete). Though he is today considered the "modern discoverer of prehistoric Greece," his sensationalized discovery of Troy is credited with popularizing the discipline of archaeology; as Glyn Edwin Daniel remarks:

> It has been said that "every person of culture and education lived through the drama of discovering Troy." Schliemann became a symbol not only of the new archaeological scholarship of the second half of the 19th century but also of the romance and excitement of archaeology.[89]

The confluence of heritage and tourism is not simply a Western phenomenon; the greatest of T'ang Chinese lyric poetry can be considered touristic interpretations of the poets' understandings of their natural and cultural heritage, and the particular instances of their interactions with such sites. Unequivocally stating that "Chinese and Japanese traditions carry within them the most sensitive, mind-deepening poetry of the natural world ever written by civilized people," Gary Snyder points out that such lyric depictions of a culture's heritage locales were direct results of a traveling—and actively touring—culture:

China is wide. Travel was mostly on foot, maybe with a packhorse, sometimes also riding a horse. In the lowlands a network of canals provided channels for slow-moving passenger boats as well as freight barges. Travelers moved by boat on the big rivers, slowly and laboriously upstream, pulled by men on shore, and swiftly and boisterously back down. Boats sailed across the lakes and slow-moving lower river reaches. Horse and ox carts moved men and materials in the alluvial plains and rolling hills. In the mountains and deserts, long caravans of pack animals moved the goods of empire. Government officials were accustomed to traveling weeks or even months to a new appointment, with their whole family. Buddhist monks and Taoist wanders had a tradition of freely walking for months or years on end. . . . Travelers' prose or rhymed-rose descriptions of landscapes were ingenious in evoking the complexity of gorges and mountains. Regional geographies with detailed accounts of local biomes were encouraged.

While the poetic products of this touring culture have oft been analyzed for their religious sensitivity, within these works there is also a deeply engrained notion of heritage—of the complex interplay between transience and permanence, of the recognition in the present of one's ancestral claims to the land, and, most importantly, of the author's transcendence from the present into the past. Suffice one extremely well-known example—often titled "Deer Park" in English translations—by the famous eighth-century poet Wang Wei, a one-time government official, monk and recluse:

> Empty mountain devoid of people
> But words of ancestors echo
> Light breathes through the deep forest
> Illuminating patina-colored moss above[90]

This brief poem captures perfectly the intersection of tourism and heritage. The author is traveling up a deserted mountain, where nothing but emptiness can be felt—it is a void, a site where no society seems to exist. Moss patinas the unmolested trees, and basks in the sun's warm rays; the place—or rather, its empty quality—is the actor. It is important to note that the Buddhist concept of emptiness[91] is a positive term—it is conceptualized by T'ang culture as a potential for an illuminative rebirth, rather than as the evidence of decadence that so marked French colonial musings at the empty Angkorian structures a millennium later. Wang Wei further underscores this by contrasting the living with the dead— unknown ancestors and the known self. The mountain is pure nature, defined in opposition to "culture." Yet a culture of nature is still there—echoing throughout this fertile void are the memories of the ancestors who have long since left society and have become one with Creation. Their presence echoes throughout the landscape, mediated by the emptiness of the venue itself. This is the heritage concept at its most refined. And through the author's touristic activity, through this potent way of perceiving the mountain, Wang Wei is able to tangibly sense their presence, communing at once with them, and with the long temporal trajectory of life itself.

With regards to Angkor as a monumental mediator, the historical connection between heritage, conservation and tourism is extremely pronounced in the years of French activity in its Indochinese Protectorates, from Mouhot's "discovery" of the Khmer temple complex onward. Mouhot, a French naturalist who was "barely known at the time and had failed in his first grant application to the French government," was what the current travel industry would call today an *FIT*, or "free and independent traveler"; though he received some funding from the Royal Geographical Society of Britain, which came about through his marriage to an Englishwoman, his own personal curiosity and desire to travel to this heretofore unknown region in Southeast Asia to document the flora and fauna was the true impetus for the trip. Though interpreted nowadays as a voyage of exploration and discovery, the original copy of his journal was published after his death in the Grand Tour serial appropriately named *Tour du Monde*. This trend of coupling independent tourism with academic exploration would continue, culminating in the formation of the École Françes d'Estrême-Orient in 1901.

The École Françes d'Estrême Orient, which was officially changed with conserving the monuments of Angkor, played a dual role in the academic promulgation of heritage discourses and conservation activities, and the promotion of tourism to Angkor. In less than a decade, a notable tourist culture within these regions was already developing in which many of the most prominent figures in colonial Angkorian history were involved. When Angkor was 'repatriated' to Cambodia in 1907, the EFEO quickly proposed to "improve access and accommodation for visitors" and to "ensure conservation and upkeep of the buildings," according to Bruno Dagens.[92] Motivated "by neither profit nor politics, but by a romantic and often deeply personal fascination with Angkor"[93]—certainly touristic attributes—the *Société d'Angkor pour la conservation des monuments anciens d'Indochine*, or *The Angkor Society for the Conservation of Ancient Monuments of Indochina*, was founded in 1907 by a group of archaeologists in Paris who themselves had previously toured Angkor. By October of the same year, this society was recognized by both the EFEO and the French Ministry of Public Education "as a potential catalyst for a flow of tourists towards Angkor."[94]

Indeed, according to Dagens, the year 1907 saw some two hundred colonial tourists in the span of three months who came from Saigon or Phnom Penh to

Angkor in an arduous land-and-river journey up the Mekong.[95] To manage such a flow of tourists and archaeologists, the EFEO appointed Jean Commaille as its first curator in Angkor in 1908—a member of the French Foreign Legion who had first come to Angkor as a tourist in 1893 to paint the ruins.[96] In 1908 he drew up a map of the Angkorian complex that identified the major known buildings, and most likely served as a preliminary tourist itinerary to the ruins; Commaille would subsequently publish a tourist guidebook to these sites based on this map, selectively identifying in a "sketch plan of the Angkor complex"[97] Angkor Wat, Angkor Thom, Ta Prohm and Preah Khan—the same blockbuster sites included on touristic itineraries today. By the 1920s, travel companies were promoting "excursions to Angkor's ruins;"[98] a direct road from Saigon and Phnom Penh was also in the process of being built, and tourists—who were "either colonials or, increasingly, globetrotters for whom Angkor had become an obligatory stopover"—came by flat-bottom boat, car, elephant, horse, "or the incommodious cart, whose comfort had not improved with the roads."[99] And in 1925, Angkor was officially opened as a "park"—a touristic categorization that remains in the site's World Heritage nomenclature today.

Though tourism to Cambodia in the colonial era certainly differed from that of the "modern" era—at least at the level of travel and comfort—it is clear that the development of Angkor as a touristic park complemented the infrastructural development necessary for the construction of Angkor as an archaeological heritage site. In particular, both were global developments; they not only imported professional experts and lay explorers from afar, but they implemented a series of discourses, structures and institutions to facilitate such international flows of visitors. As Penny Edwards contends, the EFEO was created to mirror the prestigious French research institutions studying Mediterranean archaeology in places as disparate as Cairo, Rome and Athens;[100] all of these schools employed the same institutional structure of curators, conservators and expert contributors, who all came from the same academic institutions and disciplines in France despite the differences in cultures in which they eventually worked. As many of those who explored these regions were members of the French Foreign Legion, they were therefore employed by the same central government, were subject to the same procedural rules and regulations, and their travel arrangements processed in the same way. Likewise, the touristic experiences of Vietnamese and indigenous Cambodians who would be employed as guides, translators, assistants and servants—though clearly not at the same social status as their colonial overlords, charged with different tasks than their leaders, and certainly differently informed by their own cultures—nonetheless were constrained by these same procedures and infrastructures in the same way.[101] All of these factors served to homogenize difference among potential touristic cultures, providing a similar experience at Angkor for what is ultimately a vastly disparate grouping of colonial individuals.

Today, the social structures and institutions that serve to homogenize difference among cultures of tourists resemble, and often share, the structures on which UNESCO relies for the creation of the heritage-scape. In particular, the interrelatedness of governments caused by their participation in varied intergovernmental organizations such as UNESCO has produced a number of structural similarities in the physical operations of the "modern" nation-states, which John Meyer has called "global infrastructures."[102] For example, though the nations participating in the United Nations, UNESCO, and its subsidiary World Heritage Convention are a mix of large and small kingdoms, republics, commonwealths, theocracies and totalitarian regimes which span the political spectrum from fascist to socialist, in order to interact with each other they have been forced to create political categories which correspond to one another. The construction of common "global infrastructures" is an effort at translation between nations of diverse political systems; it does not mean that each operates in the same way, have the same clout at home, or even share the same objectives. To participate in UNESCO's specific World Heritage Convention, for example, each State Party must have a diplomatic representative to the on-going[103] Convention who may or may not be the same as its representative to UNESCO. While the U.S. representative to UNESCO is a temporary political appointee and falls under jurisdiction of the State Department, until recently the permanent Cambodian representative was Prince Sihamoni, who left UNESCO in 2005 to assume the throne as Cambodia's current king. Their power, lineage, expectations and duration of time spent in the position were completely different.

Other global infrastructures must also be in place to ensure a smooth operation. A Treasury Department of some sort must also be in place to fulfill the obligatory disbursements required of membership in these organizations. To coordinate the preparation of a site's nomination File, including the organization of site visits by UNESCO's expert Advisory Bodies, some sort of Ministry of Culture, Information and/or Tourism must be in place. For the United States, which does not have such a department, the role is played alternatively between the Department of State (who coordinates relations with UNESCO) and the Department of the Interior, whose subsidiary—the National Parks Service—constructs its own lists of potential World Heritage sites and coordinates regional heritage managers and the U.S. Committee to ICOMOS to complete individual nomination Files. According to the National Parks Service, the Secretary of the Interior, "through the National Parks Service, is responsible for identifying and nominating U.S. sites to the list. The Service's Office of International Affairs provides staff support for U.S. participation in the World Heritage Convention."[104] Indeed, such a Ministry is also required for coordinating the eventual flow of tourists once the site is designated. The U.S. Secretary of the Interior is thus a political appointee charged with affecting the environmental policies of the political party, maintaining the natural and cultural resources of the nation-state, and managing the national narrative claims with which they can be consumed, but is also charged with determining which national sites are of potential global import. On the local level, the Advisory Bodies specifically evaluate the site on the prospects of their management, upkeep and preservation; offices must be in place to ensure this is followed through. This ethos impacts the very site itself, as infrastructural elements conducive to mass visitation— regardless of tourists' places of origin—are put into place: roads are paved, an entrance is designed, a ticket booth is erected, restrooms are installed and trash cans are strategically positioned. If there is demand, and space permits, gift shops, restaurants, interpretative signage, galleries or museums are erected nearby as well.

Although tourism is inherently different from culture to culture—and locals in Cambodia and Vietnam are especially wont to discuss the differing touristic attitudes of Koreans, Chinese, Americans and Japanese—it is likewise standardized through a similar system of global infrastructures. On the most basic level, tourism outside of one's home country requires the procurement of various documentary rites of passage, both institutional ones such as identification cards, passports, visas, and practical, individual ones such as phone cards and foreign currencies. It also requires an internationalized understanding of air, train, car or boat travel. These transportation industries are themselves fairly standardized from country to country; all commercial air travel requires an airport, which is given a discrete internationally recognized airport code by the International Air Transport Association (IATA), a trade association representing two hundred and forty commercial airlines, or 94% of all passenger and cargo air traffic.[105] An airport also boasts a number of standard features, such as some sort of ticket booth or check-in desk, as baggage drop-off and pick-up areas, a departure and arrival gate. If it is an international airport, there will be a customs desk, immigration bureau and passport check, and a security office. Furthermore, the standardization of security features in airports worldwide are increasingly being influenced by the United States' Federal Aviation Administration (FAA) (and, after September 11, 2007, the newly formed Transportation Security Administration (TSA)). On the practical level, airports often have restrooms, a waiting area near the gate, "duty free" shops selling a mix of local products and heavily taxed international goods such as alcohol and tobacco, and food stands. Particularly telling of this global standardization, international airports, like the tourist destinations themselves, will mark all of these areas with symbols, both pictorial and linguistic, that are determined to be universally understandable, and often are situated in places of touristic contact. That is, there are always easy to identify drawings utilizing common tropes for even the most uncommon of messages.[106] And mirroring the ubiquitously global nature of the Internet, online travel sites such as Orbitz (www.obitz.com) and TripAdvisor (www.tripadvisor.com) have introduced web-pages wherein international travelers can post comments on their experiences with their travel to, and at, tourist destinations—including "real-time updates from fellow travelers about airport security lines, traffic, parking and more."[107] All of these infrastructures mediate between the vast diversity of individuals, the heritage destinations they chose to visit, and the social structure of international tourism.

Finally, despite widely varying differences in habits, cultural understandings, and appreciation of diversity among groups of international visitors, contemporary tourism at its most fundamental level has a common cultural ethos and ritual structure. At its root tourism is always a voluntary, temporary and perspectival interaction with place, one that is conceived of as an intentional 'break' or a 'change of pace' from the everydayness of life,[108] and therefore is deliberately planned and enacted with the understanding that the interaction is transformative in some way. As a voluntary phenomenon, tourism differs substantially from other types of movement such as forced migration; people travel as tourists because of some personal desire or disposition, not because an outside hegemonic presence forces it upon them. Tourists travel from 'home' to a destination, and, unlike émigrés, they return 'home' again. Since it is voluntary, the actor understands that he exerts some level of determinate agency over the interaction. That is, he cultivates a series of expectations and perspectives regarding the encounter, starting from the most basic: he always has some knowledge that his activity is fleeting; barring the rare unforeseen incident such as a debilitating illness or a catastrophic event, there is always the prospect of returning home, or of extending one's stay, though it may not be practical or economically viable.

Tourism is therefore the converse of a local interaction, wherein the individual enjoys repeated encounters with the same place over an extended period of time. Because time at a particular destination is limited, the tourist is in search of idealized destinations that can simultaneously reveal that which is unusual or distinct from his own quotidian existence, and also meaningfully mediate between the individual and this Otherworldly society. Local interactions are considered permanent, unchanging, and directly impacting the person's life at the most mundane level, such that the person feels intimately connected with the place—at least for the duration of the experience. For locals, the site often takes on a personality of its own that is clearly defined and intimately understood, and which is linked to a complexity and proclivity of distinct and overlapping memories such that it is internalized within one's very being. The local feels he "knows" the site as he does his very self. In a very subtle way is one emotionally connected to it, which, because of its commonness, causes not the broad and distinctly perceptible psychological effects of resonance and wonder, but rather provides a continuum of more microcosmic emotions that ebb and flow, moment by moment, in everyday life.

Local interaction produces deep and contextual, yet rigidly situated, understandings of a single place, while tourism does not. But what quality the touristic interaction forfeits in understanding the complexities and intricacies of the microcosmic, he often makes up for in quantity of different touristic interactions. Taken together, touristic experiences are intended to be brief, yet transformative and often multi-sited, in an effort to deepen one's understandings of the macrocosmic world in which he is a part. Thus, the socially structured tourist perception of space is similar to that of the heritage-scape, as both are inherently juxtapositional in nature. That is, perceived touristic space is a collection of discrete tourist encounters that the individual had experienced throughout his lifetime. Just as the heritage-scape is not simply an aggregate of multiple isolated sites, but rather is more than the sum of its parts, so too is touristic space exponentially deepened with the integration of a new destination experience in the tourist's mind. Such an addition complexifies his idea of the world system and his place in it.

Reproducible Re-presentations as Mediators

The title "World Heritage site" not only allows for disparate properties to be conceptually compared to one another, but it is also a compelling statement of value about the site itself, one that is intended to "raise awareness" of the site's existence,[109] and to pique the interest of potential tourists. Yet these monuments cannot accomplish this alone; they are made "viable," Kirshenblatt-Gimblett remarks, "as re-presentations of themselves."[110] That is, while on the interactive level, the monument serves to render material an immaterial social community, and thus mediates between touristic individuals in the tangible world of conflictual geopolitics and the imaginary world of the heritage-scape, to be effective in this awareness-raising endeavor they must also allow for the dissemination of their own self-images, which mediate between the potential tourist and themselves. Thus, to raise awareness of the heritage-scape, discrete World Heritage sites are forced to perform a double mediation: the World Heritage site first acts as a medium between the potential tourist and itself through its image form, and then, through *in situ* interaction with the tourist, the authentic monument can mediate between the individual and the heritage-scape.

To achieve this secondary mediating capacity, the monument's stakeholders employ a variety of *reproducible re-presentations,* mass media forms that can re-present the site, with a measure of simultaneity, to different constituencies across the world. Furthermore, monuments can be presented in the "front stage" as objects of a viewer's gaze, or relegated to the "backstage" where it serves as a background to some other representation. Some of the most common front stage re-presentations are found in literary travel accounts from the Grand Tour era, such as those associated with Mouhot's journey; as descriptive documentary accounts of the unique Khmer structures, they positioned Angkor at the center of their narratives. Indeed, the monuments of Angkor have a deep historical connection with these literary reproducible re-presentations. The re-presentations contributed to subsequent travel (both physical and "armchair") to the site, which, in turn, produced new re-presentations that sometimes were further removed in accuracy from the original; revelatory of the dialectical mediatory capacity of such monumental media, Angkor has thus both served to create, and be re-created by, these re-presentations. The earliest documentation of the Khmer temple complex that heretofore exists, in fact, is a well-known Chinese account of the city dating from 1296. In his book, *Memorials on the Customs of Cambodia*, Chinese diplomat Chou Ta-kuan discusses the year he spent as an emissary to the once-vassal "barbarian" kingdom China called Chenla, describing in evocative detail the "walled city" of Angkor Thom, the royal buildings, neighboring temples and even the homes of Khmer commoners. He also described the customs of the people, their interactions with the Chinese population, and the occasional public rituals of the royal family.[111] Such detailed depictions of Chenla may have certainly contributed to constructing an imagined linkage between the Chinese "Middle Kingdom" and its peripheral vassals to the south.

Beginning in the seventeenth century, Japanese merchants had also been active in Cambodia, Thailand and Annam, and there is documentation that pilgrims to Japan had visited Angkor. In particular, an untitled map of Angkor Wat was created in the early 1600s by a pilgrim who thought he had visited the Indian city of Magadha (present-day Bihar), the "cradle of Buddhism." As Dagens muses, this pilgrim must have "heard so much" of the monastery from "the old Chinese texts" and, "spurred on by his faith, he would have had no difficulty recognizing [it]."[112] In this case, reproducible re-presentations of Angkor, before and after this particular pilgrim's cartographic rendering, served as mediators that both indexed and constructed an imagined religious community that extended beyond the borders of China and Japan, into both India and Cambodia.

The broadening of a religious community's boundaries was also a primary factor in the creation of early Western literary accounts of Angkor. At the inception of the Western Age of Exploration, Portuguese and, subsequently, Spanish Jesuit and Capuchin missionaries and traders stationed in Malacca and Manila respectively, visited Cambodia. Though they did not leave a lasting influence over the area, they did fill "chapters of books and entire volumes . . . devoted to the country, and Angkor Thom duly figured in these accounts." As Dagens notes, "Soldiers of fortune and traders were not writers, but their stories got around, and missionaries often sent their superiors detailed letters" in which they expressed both "admiration and disbelief" at the Angkorian capital city, which one called "an exceptional phenomenon which may be regarded as one of the Wonders of the World."[113] Though they did not captivate the European as much as Mouhot's serialized travel memoir did later, the writing of another priest, Fr. Charles-Emile Bouillevaux, perhaps was seminal in reaching the right person. Bouillevaux's *Voyage dans l'Indo-Chinese 1848-1856* was published in 1858, was most likely read by Mouhot, who credits a contemporary English work on Thailand as providing the impetus of his desire to document plant life. He set out for Indochina the same year as Bouillevaux's book was published, and aided by a missionary, followed his same itinerary as Bouillevaux to Angkor.[114] The publication of Mouhot's voyage represented the first in a long line of block-buster literary works to strike at the French imagination, raising awareness of the existence of the site and motivating travel, providing evidence of civilizational decline and the need for heritage conservation, and constructing imagined notions of both Indochinese community and greater French civilization.

What was most effective about Mouhot's account, argues Dagens, was the multiple forms of re-presentationality that the writer employed. In addition to heartfelt descriptions of the temples, Mouhot included some of the first sketches and paintings of the temples. Acknowledging that he knew "nothing" about architecture or archaeology, Mouhot adorned his depictions of Angkorian monuments with elements from the natural world—trees, grasses, weeds, blue skies, and very dark Primitives—the latter perhaps to provide a sense of scale, Edwards muses.[115] Importantly, these images—which, it should be remembered, were drawn by a naturalist and not an archaeologist—set the stage for the ways in which Angkor would subsequently be depicted. Dagens points out that the first French version of his publication edited many of Mouhot's "minutely detailed descriptions" in favor of "a number of remarkable engravings"[116] made by prominent artists such as Sabatier, Boucort, Rousseau, Thérond, Beaumont, Hanet, Lange and Catenaccis.[117] Finally, "armchair travelers" were able to have a clear idea of these strange Khmer pyramids, despite the fact that these secondary engravings were fanciful interpretative re-presentations of Mouhot's own re-presentations and bore little relation to what Mouhot had seen. Edwards points out that these pictorial re-presentations reinforced the message that the Khmers were a vanished race, and allowed Angkor to enter "*l'imaginaire fran-çaise* as an emblem of the fate awaiting empires—and civilizations—in decline."[118] Shortly thereafter, John Thompson—a pioneering Victorian-era photographer and travel writer—became the first person to photograph Angkor. As one of the first photographers of the Far East, Thompson spent ten years pictorially documenting Asia, and had read Chou Ta-kuan. Upon returning to Britain, he presented his photographs and sketches of Angkor Wat to an architectural historian, who was familiar with the accounts of Mouhot and French explorer Doudart de Lagrée (which was edited in 1873 by his second-in-command, Francis Garnier).

Though Thompson's images fell into the hands of a professional academic, images of Angkor began to be replicated, and re-presented for ulterior purposes. Juxtaposing images of ruined temples with elements of flora, fauna and savages, the barrage of interpretative re-presented Angkorian re-presentations sedimented the pervasive Orientalist narrative of a civilization lost to the jungle—of which "all that remains are cult objects in brick and stone," to borrow UNESCO's official description of the temples. Like images of Angkor today, they did not simply present passively what existed in Southeast Asia, but were used as backstage re-presentations to promote many other things, from touristic enterprises to watches and cars. In these reproducible re-presentations, Angkor takes a backstage, providing an intertextual context of heritage and durability against the transient movement of time. The car company Lincoln, for example, compares the durable craftsmanship of the car, in the foreground, to that of Angkor peering out from a background of strangler fig tendrils that partially cover an imaginative depiction of a face from Bayon, but are parted in the center as a stage curtain to reveal a pink pineapple spire from Angkor Wat. A similar advertisement articulates the durability of the structure in the face of nature even more clearly, stating "Angkor defies the centuries, the Rolls watch counts them."[119] Indeed, Panivong Norindr argues

Graphic art, from colonial propaganda posters to trade signs, contributed rather effectively to the idea of an exotic Inodochina along with publicizing their goods and services. They promoted products such as tea from the Compagnie Coloniale; coal from the Hongay coal mines . . . as well as travel, with such companies as the prominent Messageries Maritimes and Air France. These iconic representations restyled Indochina in glossy colors and inviting terms. For instance, one slogan proclaims: "Young people, go to the colonies, fortune awaits you." They thus transformed the Indochinese colony into an alluring and commodified object, a familiar icon or sign to be desired or possessed. The power these iconographic lures exerted on the French is difficult to measure accurately. Their enduring impact, however (only superseded by the emergence of the moving image), should not be underestimated.[120]

Today, film and digital imagery has produced a wide range of subtle and creative reproducible re-presentations that position World Heritage sites backstage to some other action, as Angkor Wat and Ta Prohm were in the 2001 Angelina Jolie blockbuster film *Tomb Raider*. According to informants, Cambodian site managers were drawn to the project not because of the direct revenue they would receive from Hollywood—producers paid the Kingdom a paltry rate of $18,000 per day for less than a month of disruptive filming—but because of the awareness the blockbuster film would generate.[121] And it certainly succeeded;[122] Ta Prohm, that lovely temple ruin frozen in the grasp of nature, had since the colonial era been the site of fantasy, inspiration and the thrill of excitement, and today, a visit here amongst the twisting trees and collapsed constructions literally impels visitors to indulge in imaginary expeditions ala Indiana Jones or Lara Croft. While this sentiment is best enjoyed when it is empty of massive groups of tourists, parts of this rambling structure have invariably become congested with visitors vying with and locals dressed in cheap "native" costumes to photograph themselves before a distorted doorway covered in strangler fig tendrils, which was fleetingly featured in the film.

As *Tomb Raider* reveals, while the reproducible re-presentation is a powerful medium that generates both meaning and socially meaningful activity across a broad spectrum of time and space, its defining characteristic is an extremely low level of physical interactivity with its object—the destination—and thus begs a reconsideration of the hegemony of authenticity for being the exclusive authoritative voice of truthful representation. In this medium, the authentic materiality of the fragmentary re-presentation—those proverbial *linga* carted across Southeast Asia and to Europe, which still maintain their kernel of authenticity—ceases to exist, evaporating into the ephermerality of the digital world. As Joanna Sassoon states, "digital images are produced without the intermediaries of film, paper or chemicals and as such 'never acquire the burden of being originals because they do not pass through the material phase' (Bruce 1994:17)."[123] This opening statement is telling, for it relegates the original—the "authentic"—to the status of a mere intermediary, a filter through which the final digitalized product passes, and which can only serve to lower the quality, precision or, curiously, the visual authority of the final product. After all, as Sassoon, Berger and even Benjamin points out, "the very principle" of this media form is that the "resulting image is not unique, but on the contrary infinitely reproducible."[124] The advent of technology that immediately capture an image digitally is therefore seen by some as a step forward, for it jumps over this intermediary step altogether, allowing a particular image to be immediately able to be infinitely (re)produced, manipulated and re-presented. Although the loss of auratic "authenticity," which only comes from a material original, brings up questions of fidelity and authenticity of a digital image, Sassoon asserts that digitization's removal of the original actually encourages a more pointed shift from "thinking about the complexity of the material object to viewing the visual surface of the image."[125] Thus, authenticity is actively re-positioned from the material form of the World Heritage site to the subject content of its re-presentation.[126]

While reproductions such as travel literature, paintings, panoramas, maps and plaster casts have since antiquity been commissioned to mediate or otherwise raise awareness of distant people, places and objects,[127] reproducible re-presentations are products of today's Benjaminian era of mechanical reproduction and the cornerstone of current mass-mediating mechanisms such as the Internet. Like the museum is to fragmentary re-presentations, the Internet today can be considered the storehouse and exhibition space for these "virtual" re-presentations of World Heritage sites. While the museum is fixed in one location, however, the Internet as a digital and replicable entity exists "virtually" in what William Gibson famously called *cyberspace*. Citing commentaries by both Phillip Agre and David Hakken, Samuel Wilson and Leighton Peterson note that though Gibson's neologism seems to suggest that the Internet is a hallucinatory space set apart from the world,[128] in actuality it is deeply embedded in the traditional social world and thus has real social meaning.[129] Their contention underscores the alternative and ephemeral spatiality the Internet seems to create through reordering traditional temporal and physical boundaries in much the same way the heritage-scape does. Thus, re-producible representations of World Heritage sites have the mediatory capacity to bridge the Internet's own cultural communities with that of the social world,[130] in much the same way that the authentic site itself links the same social world with that of the heritage-scape.

Indeed, many describe the Internet in utopian terms as the great democratic equalizer, which can disseminate equal amounts of re-presentations across the world irrespective of geographical boundaries and with relative cost-effectiveness. It is therefore imbued with the same powerful narrative claims of "unity in diversity," of the potentiality to create meaningful social changes in the minds of individuals that may even impact the broader community. In particular, Daniel Miller and Don Slater contend that it in developing and developed countries alike, the Internet simultaneously serves as a venue for "expansive realization" and of "expansive potential"—that is, it is both a means through which one can enact idealized claims about himself or his culture in the present, as well as a trigger for envisaging possibilities of transcending the mundane world.[131] Both of these notions come into play in the realm of tourism. On one level, potential tourists can utilize the Internet's capacity for "expansive realization" of their touristic desires by providing the necessary awareness-raising information and practical services required in their preparations. With the mere click of a computer mouse, a cacophony of images and information concerning both the physical site and its tourist infrastructure (i.e., hotels, airport information, entrance fees, visitation hours, etc.) can be accessed. On the other level, one's notion of the Internet's "expansive potential" is a powerful motivation in its own right for expanding his understanding of the depth and breadth of the world's cultural diversity through virtual tourism. 'Armchair travelers' seeking the same sorts of transcendent or formative temporary escapes as on-site tourists can voluntarily glide across a cyberspace juxtaposing digitalized re-presentations of various World Heritage sites, creating their own imagined understandings of the heritage-scape in the comfort of their own homes.

If tourism can be defined as temporary, voluntary, ritualized and perspectival, image search mechanisms are conducive to armchair tourism like never before. Despite the altruistic exultations of the Internet's power to foster parity, there are marked differences between these two forms of mediated touristic interactions, which are both embodied yet in divergent ways. A tourist exploring Angkor *in situ* will be met with an entirely different mix of sensations than the virtual tourist—sensations that extend beyond discourses of materiality and virtuality. Moving across the Park in the heat of the Cambodian sun, kicking up the yellow Cambodian dust, the tourist may be enveloped in the distinctive smells of incense and fish sauce wafting almost rhythmically to the din of temple bells and *tuk tuk* motorbikes. A cacophony of languages emanating from the throngs of tourists pushing their way through the Angkorian temples mix with the chants of faithful locals and the cries of children selling their wares. The movement of the armchair tourist, however, is done in a more sedentary fashion; with a click of a mouse one is instantaneously transported to the image reproduction, eschewing bus rides across the park and long hikes to the summit of Angkor's temple mounts. The clanging of distant Buddhist bells are substituted by the rhythmic tapping of a computer keyboard, the bark of a dog or the sound of a radio or television. These images are illuminated by the computer screen, a desk lamp or an overhead light, rather than the gleam of the midday Southeast Asian sun. All such sensations serve to tame the transcendent foreignness so integral to the traditional tourist experience, producing meaningful changes that reterritorialize the Angkor Archaeological Park.

There are, of course, great epistemological differences between these two touristic practices which problematically recontextualize the meaning of these sites, and therefore the heritage-scape's meta-narrative claim of "unity in diver-

sity." While the World Heritage site is created through a heavily institutionalized and authorized field of production, which ensures a relatively precise narrative contextualization specific to the heritage-scape's claim, reproducible re-
presentations can be copied and disseminated with alacrity, precision, and detail
by those outside the authority of these UNESCO-identified stakeholders. As
composed entirely of digital reproductions, the images and messages offered by
these World Heritage re-presentations, as well as the identity of the person sending them, can of course be manipulated in subtle ways. Without that basic kernel
of traditional authenticity that the original possesses, there are no assurances that
these re-presentations are accurate depictions except for the trust the viewer puts
in the source's motives. The fictional *Tomb Raider* film, which utilizes a backstage representation of Angkor to problematically promote pillaging the World
Heritage site for profit, is just the tip of the iceberg.

The online search itself powerfully recontextualizes these images in often
competing ways. One can take an example of a "typical" search for images of
Angkor Wat on the popular search engine Google. The *Google Image Search*, a
powerful, ubiquitous and free Internet site that can almost instantly locate numerous different images of a particular thing a viewer wants to see, can essentially produce individually-defined digital collections of images culled from
virtually all public websites the world over. This impromptu digital archiving
adds another layer of mediation to the life history of the authentic World Heritage site itself, which is already secondarily re-presented through its own image
on an "authentic" digital photograph. Like most other "digital collections," what
is lost now is most of the social biography of the particular image itself—not
only the materiality of the image, but the date of its 'birth,' the series of contexts
it passed through, but even, in some cases, the author and the meaning he intended the image to convey. In short, these databases de-contextualize and de-
historicize the digital image, only to put them neatly and transparently, and un-
complicatedly[132] into the searcher's own context, which he formed when he
specified the parameters of his search.

Those searching the Google image banks can rapidly draw up an entire itinerary of individually de-territorialized place-images that gain coherence in the
unique, contextual logic of the searcher. Temporally conflating the total touristic
experience of the heritage-scape, the Internet image surfer can flit across Angkor
Wat, the Great Wall of China, Machu Picchu, the Leaning Tower of Pisa and the
Statue of Liberty in either one search (if the user types all of these names into
the search field), or in one quick series of searches (if the user searches for each
individual site in one sitting). In addition, search results are predicated on the
searcher's titular parameters—if he is interested in seeing "Angkor Wat" rather
than "Angkor Archaeological Park," he will type these words in and a different

set of images will emerge on the screen, along with the number of different images located, and speed it took for the Google program to complete the search ("Angkor Wat" yielded "about 1,760 images" in "0.18 seconds"). Despite the authority that one gives to the "objective" Google search program, the titling is done by each photographer, often with their own mistakes or imprecisions. Sites will be spelled differently (or even wrong), and will only pop up when a searcher inadvertently types that particular spelling; a search for "Angkor Watt" brings up an entirely different set of photographs, owing to the fact that many people, especially Europeans, spell it this way.[133] Thus, the very experience of visualizing these sites is constrained by the linguistic selection of both the searcher and the person who originally posted the image.

The image itself can also be labeled wrong; in the original search, the seventh image was of Ta Prohm, created by King Jayavarman VII one hundred years later than King Suryavarman II's Angkor Wat; in the search "Angkor Watt," the second, fourth and sixth photos (from three different websites) are all of the Bayon, the central temple in King Jayavarman VII's "Great City." The searches also feature a diversity of perspectives on what it is to be "Angkor Wat"—the first is a view of the complex via helicopter, the second and third are the stereotypical view of the pinecone-shaped complex from the main gate; the fourth and fifth are NASA satellite images of the complex, the sixth is a "sunset view" from the pineconed tower down into the complex below; the seventh is a different temple (Ta Prohm), the eighth and ninth are views just off the side of the main thoroughfare, and the tenth is a map of Cambodia with "Angkor Wat" marked with a dot.[134] Like the databases that Sassoon describes, there is minimal captioning save the title of the image with the searcher's words in bold (i.e., the seventh image says "Sunset over Angkor Wat," with the name of the site in boldface), the size of the "original" digital image on the website in which Google found it, and the address of the website's homepage.[135] There is nothing about the author or institution; the website's address, in fact, serves as the artist's signature, authenticating it as best it can.

Yet it is not only a signature, but an invitation,[136] and a simple click on the address or the image brings you to the website in which it was found, although it is still contained within the Google search webpage. If he so wishes, one can click a link, located above the "original" website in the Google webpage, that says "See full sized image" and gives the actual webpage in which it is located on the host's site.[137] The host's webpage, to which Google initially directed the searcher, re-contextualizes the image from the way the searcher intended, to the way the 'original' user intended. Many times images of tourist destinations are found on blogs and private websites, and a click on the seventh photo brings one to a website that is imminently exemplary of "armchair tourism"—it is the webpage of possibly an amateur photographer-traveler, who offers up his images "for desktop wallpaper or screensaver," and even provides a digitized signature from (ostensibly) his own hand, authenticating his work in the traditional manner. One can scroll down a veritable database of images from many prominent tourist destinations, such as "classic view of Machu Picchu," "birds in flight in the Amazon," "thatched houses in Thailand," and others. The viewer is explicitly allowed to pull as many images out from their juxtaposition on the website and re-juxtapose them in his own computer's digital photo bank. Being digital, the image can then be re-named, manipulated by cropping or even "photoshopping"[138] portions of the content, and then posted on the searcher's own website as a new image, ready for another virtual tourist to access it in a Google search. All this is possible without ever visiting the authentic place or authentically snapping the picture; it is done simply in the convenience of one's armchair.

Conclusion: Traveling Across Stones that Speak

Playing on individuals' memories and senses, World Heritage sites in all of their re-presentational forms are powerful media for the production and dissemination of meaning. Though historically and even physically embedded firmly in indigenous contexts, these monuments are more than merely local; they are able to speak to visitors in a personal way, connecting with them, deepening their sense of self, and calling them to action. World Heritage sites inspire. They inspire creativity, long-distance and armchair travel, philanthropy and forays into imaginative realms of possible identities. At their core, they are potent mediators, constructing a cohesive sense of community by bridging individuals with a variety of competing societies who claim narrative possession of the site. Through its World Heritage Programme, UNESCO capitalizes on the monumental media form's capacity to pivot in meanings for the production of an alternative social system predicated not on the conflictual identity claims of division so often utilized in the traditional geopolitical world, but rather on the peace-inducing unity that comes with universal recognition of the value of diversity. By fostering touristic interaction with a variety of valorized World Heritage sites, a conceptualization of the heritage-scape is created "in the minds of men," which exists above and beyond these traditional territorial boundaries. Yet an examination of how these monuments act as mediators reveals that they are strongly contextual and inherently re-presentational, able to articulate competing claims and to produce unintended social consequences simultaneously. These stones speak in meaningful ways indeed, yet how they are presented—both in form and in practice—will ultimately determine their message.

CHAPTER TWO

THE HERITAGE-SCAPE:
UNESCO's GLOBALIZING ENDEAVOR

This is not a story about Southeast Asia. Or, rather, this is not *only* a story about Southeast Asia, but of the greater context in which lie those nations' World Heritage sites, designated by the United Nations' Educational, Scientific and Cultural Organization (UNESCO). Though historically and even physically embedded firmly in indigenous contexts, these monuments are somehow more than merely local; they are able to speak to visitors in a personal way, connecting with them, deepening their sense of self, and calling them to action. World Heritage sites inspire. They inspire creativity, as indicated by the wealth of poetry, painting and photographic images artfully composed by sightseers, and subsequently found on Internet weblogs, foreign bookstores and local art fairs across the world.[1] They inspire long-distance travel off-the-beaten track, convincing tourists to leave behind their conventional and often prejudicial notions about particular countries and to embrace encounters with diversity on foreign soil. They inspire the imagination, as visitors playing out fantasies of being archaeologists or colonial explorers attest amid their clamorings over ancient cobblestone walkways, across mountain passages and through archaeological excavations. They inspire philanthropy and development, with nation-states and new non-profit organizations from both the East and the West donating resources and experts to preservation and human rights causes.[2] Such actions are telling, for they indicate individual, personal responses to seemingly local and removed causes. Somehow, singular World Heritage sites seem to truly be one with the world; they are viewed as global.

While many things inspire action—an event, a piece of artwork, a person or a moral tenet—the sense of place is perhaps most inspirational of all. Events, works of art and interpersonal interactions are all inexorably bound to places, lending them distinctive materiality and contextual pertinence. Even intangible forces of inspiration, such as religious and moral doctrines, or "cultural" worldviews, must be linked to the tangible in order to inspire meaningful action, as sociologist Maurice Halbwachs has illustrated,[3] and are often tangibly associated with specific instances, interactions, sermons or objects found in places, as well.[4] Everything, so to speak, has its place. And well it should. Places are distinguished from mere spaces, anonymous and undifferentiated. They are lived spaces—spaces that have distinctive and marked social meanings. "People actively give their physical environments meanings," attest Michael Parker Pearson and Colin Richards,[5] echoing geographer Phillip Wagoner's definition of *place* as a "locus of meaningful human dialogue, social and physical: place as a potential for action."[6] When spaces become places, they have names, their life histories are socially traceable, they contain activity, and they connote past experiences and inspire new ones. Culture—that nebulous "web of meanings" as Max Weber and Clifford Geertz have both elegantly described it,[7] is rendered tangible and saddled with meaning through its connection with material places. Yet dialectically, a place does not exist *a priori*, but rather is created and imbued with meaning of its own precisely through such socially mediated elements. The process by which individuals and societies differentiate, shape or create a marked place from mere conceptual space can be termed *placemaking*.

World Heritage sites are places. They are differentiated, they have known narratives, and they inspire action. Whether they are "cultural" or "natural"—as UNESCO categorizes them—they are still places, they are still socially differentiated, and they still have separate and highly localized life histories. What is novel about them is the way in which, through little more than giving a different title to them—one of "*World* Heritage"—their significances and the actions these meanings give seem to change. World Heritage sites are places, but they are *made* places. Though inexorably bound to the local, they are imbued with global meaning through UNESCO's designation. And as UNESCO categorizes each one in juxtaposition to another, they are part of a unique global order—one that extends far beyond the mere proximate setting in which they are found— they are linked to other similar disparate places, and dialectically impact and are impacted by them. In short, they form the nodes on a newly ordered heritage landscape that exists above and beyond the world's traditional boundaries. Thus, World Heritage sites are places, they are made places, and they make up a new, extensive and cohesive global place. This new global map, which this book calls a *heritage-scape*, is not simply a mosaic of aggregate individual sites, nor a network of specially-delineated destinations with their own local social relations, but, rather, it is a unique place with its own social context that is constantly evolving and expanding as UNESCO continues its activities, integrating more and more places, objects and now even intangible customs within its nebulous boundaries.[8] Thus, World Heritage sites are not undifferentiated spaces, nor are they simply localized sites. They are a specific kind of place, with a specific kind of social context—one that is both *global* and *monumental*. To understand how this can be, one must examine these two terms in further detail.

World Heritage is a *global* phenomenon. Even for the uninitiated—for those who only briefly have come into contact with a "World Heritage site" unknowing of the complex multinational and bureaucratic procedures that accompany such designations—it is clear by the place's honorific title that it is a product of globalization. Though the places may be found alone in the deep of a jungle, or casually amid a bustling local street, each one is revealingly called a *World* Heritage site—not a religious heritage site, not an ethnic heritage site, not a national heritage site, not even a regional heritage site, although such nomenclatures exist elsewhere in a variety of forms and usages throughout the world. As locally embedded or as foreign as they may seem to the visitor, this lexicon attests that World Heritage sites are "social facts" stemming from an emerging, globalizing society. More materially, they all share several common elements regardless of their actual geographic orientation or original local uses they may have. In particular, they all boast a global tourist infrastructure that may include ticket counters and gift shops, museums or galleries, published maps and guidebooks. They also share discursive features commonly associated with globalization. Alongside local languages or standing alone, most of this material is published in English, the era's *de facto* global language—and many (especially in Southeast Asia) are also translated into French, the literal *lingua franca* of the previous era. Symbols and pictograms commonly featured in such global arenas as airports, hospitals and museums are also employed to inform or instruct proper action; of the former, pictures for "man," "woman," "toilet," and "food" are most common, while the latter ranges from the standard "no cameras," "be quiet" and "no smoking" to "no squatting with your feet on top of the toilet seat" as one visual sign instructed locals at a ladies' outhouse near Ta Prohm.

Too often globalizing enterprises are viewed through Marxist or Foucaultian lenses as contentious phenomena that increase wealth and power discrepancies, exacerbate geopolitical tensions, or cause a frightening loss of "authenticity" in local cultures. Indeed, the term "globalization" has been used and misused by such a multiplicity of agents that it has become rather passé, leading some to question the concept as merely an "intellectual fad,"[9] akin to the equally banal idiom "post-modern." Frequently neglected in these arguments is the recognition of its fundamental potential to create a cultural consciousness of its own, and, as such, to demarcate a specific sense of place that can blur the distinctions between local and global. Explicating this notion is Roland Robertson's understanding of globalization as, in its purest sense, a phenomenon that both compresses the world and its societal structures, as Anthony Giddens contends, but additionally intensifies a *consciousness* of the world as a more cohesive, interrelated whole.[10] Individual agency, as opposed to the agency of sovereign nation-states, is a key component in this theory; no longer are people bound to traditional territorial conceptions of themselves, whereby their identities are formed only through the physical, spatial relationships they enjoy on a daily basis within a town or country's neatly delimited political borders. Rather, globalization allows geographic constraints on socio-cultural relationships to recede in the minds of individuals. By eliminating traditional boundaries and reordering time and space, this phenomenon can alter individual identities to include conceptions of a more global self.

Born from the wreckage of the world's warring nation-states in the first half of the twentieth century, the United Nations (UN) and its Educational, Scientific and Cultural affiliate, UNESCO, were founded with such global ideals in mind. Indeed, United States president Franklin Delano Roosevelt gave the organization its title of "United Nations" in 1942 to emphasize the unified and global geopolitical nature of the twenty-six Allied nation-states in combating the Axis threat in specific localities across the world during World War II. Though at the height of wartime conflict, education ministers from the European nation-states united against the fascist powers met in London that same year to search for "ways and means to reconstruct their systems of education once peace was restored."[11] This meeting, called the Conference of Allied Ministers of Education (CAME), which swiftly took on a "universal note" and came to include the full array of Allied states, is generally regarded as the precursor to the present-day UNESCO. Indeed, shortly after World War II ended, a United Nations Conference for the Establishment of an Educational and Cultural Organization (ECO/CONF) took place as CAME had recommended several years before. From November 1–16, 1945, representatives of forty-four countries met in London to establish a non-traditional method of fostering "a genuine culture of peace" to prevent the outbreak of another world war.[12] Within a year, the governments of twenty countries from North and South America, Africa, Europe, Asia and Oceana officially ratified UNESCO's Constitution, which came into force on November 4, 1946. Its first General Conference was held in Paris later that month.

Noting that throughout history, wars have always originated in some part through local suspicions or ignorance of other peoples at the individual level,[13] UNESCO posits that people's identities are problematically based on traditional territorial conceptions—conceptions often built around arbitrary yet clearly demarcated boundaries that gain precision when defined in binary opposition to each other. UNESCO's goal of creating a peace in the world, then, includes a fundamental reworking of the international system that downplays war-prone national interests. It requires the construction of a new sense of place among individuals—one based not on divisive geopolitical territorial distinctions, but rather bound by the recognition and celebration of diversity at the individual level. The Preamble to UNESCO's Constitution expresses the organization's objective concerning the "construction" and subsequent "diffusion" of "intellectual and moral solidarity of mankind" in the "minds of men":

> The Governments of the States Parties to this Constitution on behalf of their peoples declare:
> - That since wars begin in the minds of men, it is in the minds of men that the defenses of peace must be constructed;
> - That ignorance of each other's ways and lives has been a common cause, throughout the history of mankind, of that suspicion and mistrust between the peoples of the world through which their differences have all too often broken into war; . . .
> - That the wide diffusion of culture, and the education of humanity for justice and liberty and peace are indispensable to the dignity of man and constitute a sacred duty which all the nations must fulfill in a spirit of mutual assistance and concern;
> - That a peace based exclusively upon the political and economic arrangements of governments would not be a peace which could secure the unanimous, lasting and sincere support of the peoples of the world, and that the peace must therefore be founded, if it is not to fail, upon the intellectual and moral solidarity of mankind.[14]

Though this "intergovernmental" institution is composed of representatives from sovereign nation-states, and considers their existence as a foundational element of the world's political system, its stated mission as outlined in its Constitution—to establish "intellectual and moral solidarity of mankind"— illustrates that the creation of more global selves in the myriad minds of the world's individuals is fundamental to UNESCO's peacemaking cause. No doubt an unofficial product of the Marshall Plan and of the pressing need to reconstruct and re-educate post-World War II societies, UNESCO was engaged in rebuilding educational institutions and sponsoring joint research projects in European and Asian countries suffering intellectual and "cultural" devastation.[15] Early in the next decade, the mission was elaborated to include the construction of educational facilities in rural Latin American and the Caribbean countries, and in the 1960s the multi-tiered *Addis Ababa Plan for Vast Expansion of Education in Africa* was signed, providing both short-term and long-term strategies for educational development in the impoverished and largely illiterate populations within the African continent.[16] In addition to physically constructing facilities aimed to systematically educate individuals in a globally recognized and

uniform manner, UNESCO concurrently sponsored a number of scientific studies to break down commonly held antagonistic cultural barriers. Emerging from
the terrible World War II-era xenophobia and subsequent holocausts against
Jewish and minority peoples in Europe and the Chinese and Koreans in Asia, the
United Nation's founding charter boldly proclaimed its support and advocacy
for human rights for all "without discrimination as to race, sex, language, or
religion," and followed this up with the passing of the *United Nation's Universal Declaration of Human Rights* on December 10, 1948, which was to be applied "without distinction of any kind, such as race, color, sex, language, religion, political or other opinion, national or social origin, property, birth or other
status."[17] More tangibly, UNESCO sponsored research studies and funded the
dissemination of scientifically sound, objective data concerning genetics and
issues of race. In a 2001 address to the UNESCO-sponsored World Conference
to End Racism, Pierre Sané, Assistant Director-General for Social and Human
Sciences (and, up until April of that year, the longtime Secretary-General of
Amnesty International) states that:

> Since 1948, UNESCO initiated a programme which, through the dissemination
> of scientific facts, established the fallacious nature of racist theories. The re-
> sults of the work of eminent experts convened by UNESCO were summarized
> in four statements on the question of race. These statements elucidated the
> genesis of theories of racial superiority. They emphasized that the biological
> differentiation of races does not exist and that the obvious differences between
> populations living in different geographical areas of the world should be attrib-
> uted to the interaction of historical, economic, political, social and cultural fac-
> tors rather than biological ones.[18]

Yet, as Mr. Sané pointed out just over a week before the September 11,
2001 terrorist attacks on the United States, "racism and xenophobia still continue to infect all societies around the globe"; the proclivity of peoples to define
themselves in opposition to others has "hardly vanished," but has "not only survived the scientific deconstruction of the concept of 'race' but even seem to be
gaining ground in most parts of the world. In the age of globalisation, this situation may seem paradoxical."[19]

Indeed, although the groundwork may have been laid in creating such solidarity among individuals across the world through the formation of UNESCO
and its initial work in post-World War II reconstruction, the decades that followed perhaps underscored that a more fundamental placemaking strategy was
needed. By the early 1970s, the Cold War had effectively divided the UN Security Council and the world, creating once more an alarming sense of place predicated on national alliances defined in binary opposition to each other. This di-

vide played out in Vietnam, Laos and Cambodia—embroiling the United States army in protracted warfare against Soviet-supported Communists—and would manifest itself at the end of the decade in Afghanistan, where the Soviet Union's army would become similarly entangled in war against United States supported Mujahideen. Coupled with this fracture among nation-states was the threat of terrorism, which emerged in a variety of forms in Europe and the Middle East. With airline and cruise ship hijackings around the Mediterranean Sea, kidnapping and bloodshed at the 1972 Munich Olympics, civil rights struggles and assassinations in the United States, revolutions in Asia, Africa and the Middle East, and "Red Brigade" train bombings, kidnapping and murders in Italy, individual agency in the struggle to dictate conceptions of place was underscored over and above the strength and authority of powerful nation-states.

The concept of designating and protecting the well-being of places determined to be of World Heritage was born of such recent global tragedies. Convening in Paris for its seventeenth session, representatives of UNESCO's member-states passed a formal declaration creating the World Heritage Convention on November 16, 1972—twenty-seven years to the day after UNESCO itself was founded. Perhaps more tellingly, this program was created just a month after the Palestinian guerrilla organization, Black September—as part of their own violent placemaking effort—terrorized the Olympic Games, which itself stood as a symbol of worldwide geopolitical unity. Confronting this struggle over the control of place by individuals, UNESCO's World Heritage Convention sought to create a new policy, one that could more effectively foster this "culture of peace" as outlined in the United Nations' foundational documents. That the current civil rights and revolutionary struggles of the 1970s were controlled by individuals and small groups, rather than by powerful allied nations as in the previous World Wars, only further underscored the UN's assessment twenty years' prior that an "intellectual solidarity" at the individual level would be the means to achieving this goal, as the World Heritage Convention's Mission Statement so eloquently attests:

> For this specialized UN agency, it is not enough to build classrooms in devastated countries or to publish scientific breakthroughs. Education, science, culture and communication are the means to a far more ambitious goal: to build peace in the minds of men."[20]

The World Heritage Convention swiftly grew to be one of the most visible departments under the United Nations' Educational, Scientific and Cultural Organization. Charged with identifying and protecting sites deemed to be of importance to the history and culture of the human race, its formational documents posit a more precise placemaking focus, one based on mutual ownership and communal celebration of those tangible places regarded as integral to the identities of individuals and societies throughout the world:

- *Noting* that the cultural heritage and the natural heritage are increasingly threatened with destruction not only by the traditional causes of decay, but also by changing social and economic conditions which aggravate the situation with even more formidable phenomena of damage or destruction,
- *Considering* that deterioration or disappearance of any item of the cultural or natural heritage constitutes a harmful impoverishment of the heritage of all the nations of the world,
- *Considering* that protection of this heritage at the national level often remains incomplete because of the scale of the resources which it requires and of the insufficient economic, scientific, and technological resources of the country where the property to be protected is situated,
- *Recalling* that the Constitution of the Organization provides that it will maintain, increase, and diffuse knowledge by assuring the conservation and protection of the world's heritage, and recommending to the nations concerned the necessary international conventions,
- *Considering* that the existing international conventions, recommendations and resolutions concerning cultural and natural property demonstrate the importance, for all the peoples of the world, of safeguarding this unique and irreplaceable property, to whatever people it may belong,
- *Considering* that parts of the cultural or natural heritage are of outstanding interest and therefore need to be preserved as part of the world heritage of mankind as a whole,
- *Considering* that, in view of the magnitude and gravity of the new dangers threatening them, it is incumbent on the international community as a whole to participate in the protection of the cultural and natural heritage of outstanding universal value, by the granting of collective assistance which, although not taking the place of action by the State concerned, will serve as an efficient complement thereto,
- *Considering* that it is essential for this purpose to adopt new provisions in the form of a convention establishing an effective system of collective protection of the cultural and natural heritage of outstanding universal value, organized on a permanent basis and in accordance with modern scientific methods,
- *Having decided,* at its sixteenth session, that this question should be made the subject of an international convention,

Adopts this sixteenth day of November 1972 this Convention.[21]

Emerging from such worldwide socio-economic turmoil, as well as the struggles of communities striving to carve out their own autonomous localities,

UNESCO's World Heritage Convention notes the primacy of place as integral in the formation of individual identities. Many of these places are contested sites with meanings that are contentious in nature, a point made clear in the Resolution's first line, which states that cultural and natural heritage are "increasingly threatened with destruction not only by the traditional causes of decay, but also by changing social and economic conditions which aggravate the situation with even more formidable phenomena of damage or destruction." Thus UNESCO reveals the social reality that, while places form loci of community coalescence, it is often within a cycle of hostility, antagonism, and violent destructiveness as one group, defining itself in opposition to another, seeks to destroy the other's tangible locus of solidarity. In this vein, safeguarding is therefore an important element when confronting placemaking strategies, for without tangible places, it is more difficult for a community to come together and prosper. Although it discusses safeguarding such properties in lofty and neutral terms, this important foundational text also conveys an intelligent grasp of the inherent subjectivity of these "unique" places, revealing that UNESCO and its World Heritage Convention deftly wish to twist their preexisting nationalistic connotations into a more unified, global understanding of their value and significance. Like Durkheimian sociologists looking for "social facts" in the form of legislation and resolutions, the Convention bases its assessment of the importance of local places in the formation of solidarity on "existing international conventions, recommendations and resolutions concerning cultural and natural property." To the Convention, these international events "demonstrate the importance"—not for simply the local groups to which they pertain, but "for all the peoples of the world, of safeguarding this unique and irreplaceable property, to whatever people it may belong . . . to mankind as a whole." The creation of World Heritage sites then, is part of a distinctive *placemaking* endeavor—one that strives to rework territorial conceptions in the minds of its global populous through the promotion of new and universally understood intellectual and cultural conceptualization of the world.

UNESCO was not the first to espouse an approach to placemaking predicated on a deeper understanding of its inhabitants' identity that includes diverse historical and cultural forms of which they were not a part. As Benedict Anderson illustrates in his seminal work, *Imagined Communities*, nationalistic enterprises themselves successfully utilize the same sort of homogenizing consciousness amongst their inhabitants for the purpose of creating a cohesive national identity, despite great variations in religion, history and worldviews. He contends that such communities are "inventions of the [sic] imagination," which are based on tangible "cultural artifacts" akin to those monuments in this heritage-scape.[22] Salient to the topic of UNESCO's world heritage endeavors, Anderson illustrates how tangible vestiges of peoples past can create "deep attachments. . . [and] profound emotional legitimacy,"[23] creating a sense of commonality, and of community. Himself an historian of Southeast Asia, Anderson was most concerned with "social change [and] transformed consciousness" in the region, specifically how nationalistic movements such as those in Vietnam and Cambodia could impart upon disparate peoples not only a cohesive collective identity with cultural forms not historically one's own, but also the willingness to "be ready to die" for this fractiously disparate, yet imaginatively monocultural group.[24] But Anderson is quick to mention that his notion of an imagined community is not simply localized to one type of community or one time period but can be applied across a broad spectrum of groups. Indeed, he contends that "all communities larger than primordial villages of face-to-face contact . . . are imagined"; it is simply the ways in which they remember and make meaning of the cultural artifacts in light of the (re)contextualizing narrative claims with which these relics are imbued.[25] Thus, the same imagined placemaking process that Anderson demonstrates for towns, regions and nation-states can be applied to the entirety of the world.

The task of creating a "homogenizing" sense of place, however, puts UNESCO in a predicament, for it problematizes the role of the sovereign nation-state in the international system. At one end of the spectrum, such placemaking strategies are often conflictual. As Anderson and other theorists have shown, nationalistic movements often rely on the very production of difference to create solidarity among its citizenry—a concept evident in the actions of the Axis powers, which provided the driving force for the creation of UNESCO. The United Nations' goal is to create peace, not conflict, amongst its disparate and sovereign members, even as these member-states may continue to rely on polarizing political rhetoric, and thus UNESCO must balance itself on a fine line of neutrality and understanding. More importantly, the organization must ultimately create a new sense of place without relying on the traditional insider-outsider strategies that its very members utilize in their own placemaking endeavors.

At the other end of the spectrum, it must be remembered that the United Nations is not as "nongovernmental" as it claims to be. The United Nations is already composed of these nation-states; the organization is, after all, named the "United *Nations*," not "United *Peoples*" of the world. To destroy or usurp the geopolitical authority of the nation-state would be to significantly change the mission and the composition of the organization itself, even as it strives to create a new place at the expense of individual nationalistic enterprises. No doubt such an obvious undermining of the nation-state's power would also be met with extreme reluctance, much stronger than that which the League of Nations suffered during its formation a few decades earlier. This is likewise true for its subsidiary organization, UNESCO, and its initiative, The World Heritage Convention—both of which fall under the United Nations, but which require secondary and tertiary memberships of the nation-state. It is not only conceivable, but a political reality, that a nation could join one and not the other.

To use a Western example, Italy joined UNESCO in 1948, seven years before being admitted to the United Nations in 1955.[26] Although Italy was an active foundational member of the UNESCO, currently boasts the most World Heritage sites, and is today one of the largest contributors to its World Heritage initiatives, the Italian government purposefully did not ratify the World Heritage Convention until June of 1978. Even then, Italy waited years to allow UNESCO's designation of its major World Heritage Sites—much to the chagrin of the Convention's members, who desired the prestige that would come to their newly compiled World Heritage List through a swift addition of the famed Italian cities and complexes such as Milan's Santa Maria delle Grazie and its *Last Supper* (1979), Rome (1980), Florence (1982) and Venice (1987).

Vietnam's affiliation with these organizations is even more complicated. Although the present-day Socialist Republic of Vietnam was admitted to the United Nations in 1977, its history with UNESCO began in the 1950s, when the country was still transitioning from a partitioned colonial enterprise to a free and independent state. The Imperial City of Huế had been the site of intense combat between French troops and the liberating forces, and Vietnamese leaders urged UNESCO-affiliated architectural experts to assess the damage. The signing of the Geneva Accords in 1956, which ended the First Indochina War and imposed a temporary partition between Ho Chi Minh's Communist Northern forces and pro-Western South Vietnam, placed Huế under Southern rule. According to Phan Thuận An, UNESCO representatives finally came to the town to assess the integrity of the imperial structures, and assisted in restoration efforts. Yet the nation was plunged into war again, this time with the Americans, and by 1975, the Republic of South Vietnam was no more. By the next year, 1976, the new Socialist Republic of Vietnam joined UNESCO; the following year it was officially was admitted to the United Nations. However, it took almost ten years for Vietnam to sign onto the World Heritage Convention; it officially joined on Monday October 19, 1987.

Complicating this further is the fact that, because of the United Nations' non-conflictual political formation, it relies not only on the cooperation, but also on the monetary donations, of these very nation-states for its actual existence. UNESCO, therefore, cannot create peace through an actual restructuring of the world's economic, political or ethnic boundaries—there exists too great a possibility for contention and, truly, for a collapse in its very organization. Rather, this placemaking endeavor must be predicated on an imaginative remapping of the globe in each person's consciousness. It relies on the cooperation of nation-states while simultaneously striving to conceptually weaken and blur their borders. It must be rooted in the physical and socio-cultural world—the global system of independent nation-states—but must exist above it, "in the minds of men." It must reference the preexisting histories, narratives and worldviews upon which nation-states were founded, but must make them speak directly and equally to all the world's citizenry.

With such a focus on the intersection between the ephemeral imagination and the tangible world, UNESCO's unique placemaking strategy is thus an exercise in *monumental mediation*. As chapter 1 revealed, monumental mediation is the specific employment of both the authentic cultural or natural media form and the memorialized memory of its life history, for the purpose of linking an individual interactant with the greater social system that lays claim to the site. That monuments are preeminent cultural tools for creating a communal sense of place is well documented. Grandiose statues of the Caesars and even larger commemorative columns were found across the far reaches of the Roman Empire. Across Christendom, illustrious monks and noble patrons plastered the floors of Romanesque churches with mosaics adorned in commonly understood symbols, erected evocative statuary of the Tridentine God and his saints, and commissioned scintillating stained glass in Gothic cathedrals. Similarly, dotting the landscape of the Buddhist world are soaring stupas and awe-inspiring pagodas; though built around a minuscule and solitary ash of the Enlightened One, they pierce the skies and can often be seen for miles around. Cenotaphs, markers and imposing mausoleums litter the town squares and empty battlefields of Europe, reminding those who pass before them of the history in which their footsteps follow, and in which they may share.

Monuments also evoke memories and create meaning even when not erected in the same geographic location to which they refer, a point integral to understanding the universal efficacy and global applicability of World Heritage sites. Washington, DC's National Mall, for example, is dotted with an array of imposing and emotionally charged memorials and museums constructed in remembrance of past presidents, ethnic groups, and heroic wartime sacrifices. These monumental places on the Mall evoke memories of significance to the country's "national memory" despite the fact that many of these personalities never set foot on Washington's expansive parkland, and that many of these memorialized events occurred outside the country itself—in places such as Iwo Jima, Vietnam and Korea, where a majority of Americans have never even visited. Recently, emotionally and ideologically charged debates have been raging on how best to construct commemorative representations for preserving the memory of Native Americans, African-Americans, World War II veterans and the victims of the September 11, 2001 terrorist attacks on New York City's World Trade Center.

The Khmer, Cham and Vietnamese were all "memorial cultures,"[27] as evidenced by the remains of detailed historical bas reliefs and precisely inscribed stela. At Angkor, the powerful king Jayavarman VII erected great stelae in each of his temples precisely listing his religious beliefs, lineage, his parents' histories and the historical events leading up to the dedication of each edifice. Additionally, the amount of wealth bestowed upon each temple and its caretakers were carefully documented in stone. Contemporarily, the Cham kings practiced the same process, and Mỹ Sơn's detailed stelae collected at the beginning of the twentieth century by French archaeologists have provided great insight into the history and culture of that ancient civilization. The caves of Phong Nha-Kẻ Bàng also contain Cham inscriptions. Even after their integration, the Chams continued this practice; of particular note is the evolving inscription at the doorway of the great Po Klong Girai tower near the coastal town of Phan Rang, which provides dates and detailed descriptions of the temple's restoration efforts throughout the centuries.

The ruling Vietnamese elite, too, were historically concerned with leaving stone markers for posterity. One excellent example of literal memorial markers can be found in Ha Noi's Temple of Literature (Văn Miếu). Known as Vietnam's oldest university, the Temple of Literature had been the center of civil service instruction for aspiring mandarins from its creation by an emperor of the Lý Dynasty in the early eleventh century until 1910. In 1484, the famed Confucian emperor of the Lê Dynasty, Lê Thánh Tông, began a tradition of inscribing the names of newly graduated mandarins upon immense *stelae* chiseled out of large granite tortoise statues. The tortoise—itself a symbol of longevity—conveyed to onlookers that the inscribed names would be forever passed down to subsequent generations. They would be remembered even after they, and the Emperor they served, passed on. This prospect could also prove distasteful to an emperor when a mandarin falls out of his favor; the ex-mandarin's name would summarily be chiseled out of the list, leaving biting scratch marks—literally empty holes in the stelae—for all generations to see. Even today, the visitor gazing at the collection of these immense tortoise-borne stelae will notice that almost every graduating class had at least one deposed mandarin, the identities of these unfortunate ex-bureaucrats lost forever to history. Today, the memorializing Temple of Literature is itself memorialized on the backs of 100,000 Đong banknotes.

Monuments need not be created as such, however; often they are designated after their construction. Driving past particularly tortuous stretches of roadways in the United States and in Europe, for example, one may find flowers, photographs, and personal items left behind by relatives of car-accident victims, transforming these seemingly innocuous patches of earth into spontaneous monuments that strike at the viewer's imagination. Catholic pilgrims travel great distances to the loci of Marian apparitions—even to those such as Garabandal, Spain; and Medjugorje, Bosnia; which have not been recognized by the Vatican as verified sites of divine transubstantiation[28]—to pay homage to the memory of divinity and to reinforce the sense of community among the multinational faithful. Most salient to the discourse of World Heritage sites, ruins and archaeological excavations of places once created for entirely different local uses are often left by communities in their un-reconstructed forms as remembering devices of the tragedy that befell them and, by extension, the community as a whole. For example, behind the Catholic basilica in rural Benevento, a southern Italian town that endured Allied air raids during the Second World War, stands the shell of a bombed-out building; although it has never officially been declared a World Heritage site like Hiroshima's UNESCO-designated A-bomb Dome, it nevertheless is regarded by locals as an equally potent, collective remembering device for the tragedy that occurred in the last years of the war. It remains to this day unaltered despite extensive renovations and historic reconstructions of the buildings around it.[29]

And so too, are World Heritage sites these types of monuments—created for one use, but designated after the fact to be tangibly representative of the memories of a broader world community. These particular designations are carried out systematically by analyzing the place's historical, aesthetic and compositional qualities against a series of criteria established by the 1972 World Heritage Convention. To review, they must:

(i)   Represent a masterpiece of human creative genius; or
(ii) Exhibit an important interchange of human values, over a span of time or within a cultural area of the world, on developments in architecture or technology, monumental arts, town-planning or landscape design; or
(iii) Bear a unique or at least exceptional testimony to a cultural tradition or to a civilization which is living or which has disappeared; or
(iv) Be an outstanding example of a type of building or architectural or technological ensemble or landscape which illustrates (a) significant stage(s) in human history; or
(v)   Be an outstanding example of a traditional human settlement or land-use which is representative of a culture (or cultures), especially when it has become vulnerable under the impact of irreversible change; or
(vi) Be directly or tangibly associated with events or living traditions, with ideas, or with outstanding universal significance (a criterion applied only in exceptional circumstances, and together with other criteria).[30]

The ancient Hebrew military fortress of Masada, destroyed two thousand years ago by the Romans, is an oft-cited illustration of a place whose memorialized meanings have shifted as different cultures re-contextualized and re-appropriated it.[31] In her book *Recovered Roots*, an exploration of the formation of contemporary Israeli identity, Yael Zerubavel conducts a thorough textual analysis of Masada's long history of changing memorialized meanings. According to both Zerubavel and UNESCO-affiliated experts, records indicate that the edifice was originally a lavish and fortified Roman villa, hewn from the rocky mountains overlooking the Dead Sea and the desert of Judea for King Herod in the first century BC. Because of its solid composition and large proportions, it was soon converted into a fortress by the Romans, and was taken by the Hebrew rebels in their final—and futile—struggle for independence from the Empire before the Diaspora. Indeed, despite their defeat by Emperor Titus in AD 70, the chronicler Josephus notes that a contingent of Jewish rebels remained in the fortress and utilized it as a line of defense against the Roman Imperial army for two more years, until the Emperor's army laid siege to it. Rather than succumbing to the Romans, Josephus notes that the last Jewish rebels holed up inside committed mass suicide, preferring to die free by their own sword than to be enslaved.[32]

Despite the existence of records—two Roman chronicles concerning the physical site exist, as well as a Medieval account of the defeat by the historian Jossipon—Masada was almost completely forgotten in popular Jewish culture during the two millennia of the Diaspora, perhaps because suicide is taboo in Jewish culture, as Zerubavel suggests.[33] Certainly a source of embarrassment and a symbol of ultimate Jewish defeat, Masada was not positively memorialized, but rather forgotten by the majority of European Jewish lay-persons who did not readily have access to Josephus' documents. Adding to this "forgetting" was the physical loss of the site, as forces hostile to Medieval Westerners took control over the land and, not sharing in the same memory of the site's meaning, let the desert sands wash over it.

Yet in the second half of the nineteenth century, nascent Zionists attempting to unite a people and to justify a subsequent socialist occupation of Palestine recovered the memory, so to speak. Josephus' account was rediscovered and translated into Hebrew in 1862, leading to a wealth of poetic interpretations.[34] But rather than portray it in the commonly held symbolic understanding of the site, these interpretations re-presented the narrative in a manner that stressed various particularities of Israeli national ideology. As the last physical holdout of the Jewish rebels, it became understood as a symbol of land reclamation; as a container for the defiant final struggle for freedom against the Romans before

the Diaspora, it is also repackaged as a symbol of defiance and ultimate liberation. Already packaged in the Israeli national memory, the narrative found its
monument when the actual site was unintentionally discovered in 1932 by a
German archaeologist who was excavating remains of Roman encampments.[35]

Today, the ruins are a destination of national pilgrimage for Jewish youths
from around the world.[36] These pilgrimages are called *tiyulim*, which are special
hikes "designed to promote an emotional attachment to the land of Israel
through the cultivation of knowledge of its landscapes, its fauna and flora, as
well as its history."[37] This is a specialized and highly charged form of knowledge which in Hebrew is called *yedi'at ha'aretz. Yedi'at ha'aretz* can be considered "knowledge of one's native country," or *Heimatkunde* in German.[38] As a
major venue for these cultural walks, Masada stands as a symbol of unity in a
common memorializing ritual. Though Masada was neither created explicitly to
be a monument, nor was it recognized as such for almost two millennia, today it
is a material manifestation of the ideological claims of the Israeli nation-state,
itself engaged in an ongoing, violently contested battle over the definition of
place and its active nationalistic placemaking efforts.

But designated as one of Israel's first World Heritage sites by UNESCO in
2001, its meaning has changed once again, subtly converting the numerous and
contentious meanings into a more universally applicable symbol.[39] First, rather
than symbolizing Israeli land reclamation, UNESCO cites its purely archaeological value as evidence of Roman architecture and ingenuity:

> Criterion iv: The palace of Herod the Great at Masada is an outstanding ex-
> ample of a luxurious villa of the Early Roman Empire, whilst the
> camps and other fortifications that encircle the monument con-
> stitute the finest and most complete Roman siege works to have
> survived to the present day.

Since Masada was nominated by the internationally recognized nation-state
within which it is physically situated, UNESCO cannot but reference Masada as
a site of extreme importance to the Israeli people. But since land reclamation
and the ideology of Jewish "liberation" is certainly a contentious issue in the
Middle East today (as well as for the Middle Eastern nation-states who are also
signatories to, and active participants in, the World Heritage Convention), the
World Heritage Convention subtly repackages the site's link to the Jewish people:

> Criterion iii: Masada is a symbol of the ancient Jewish kingdom of Israel, of
> its violent destruction in the later 1st century CE, and of the sub-
> sequent Diaspora.

In this criterion, Masada is a symbol of history, not of contemporary life; it references the "ancient Jewish kingdom of Israel" not the modern Israeli state. Indeed, this criterion references three historical periods in the Jewish past for which the fortress is representative—the ancient Biblical kingdom, its well-documented end, and the Diaspora. Notably absent is the current, post-Diaspora period—the period of liberation from the Diaspora, to which Masada's narrative potently speaks today. The criterion speaks of a Jewish kingdom which was violently destroyed in the first century; it avoids describing the connection it has with any present-day Jewish state. Finally, the act of defiance itself—of the deadly struggle for control over a place, which is ongoing today—is also referenced in the final criteria, although once again homogenized:

> Criterion vi: The tragic events during the last days of the Jewish refugees who occupied the fortress and palace of Masada make it a symbol both of Jewish cultural identity and, more universally, of the continuing human struggle between oppression and liberty.

Deftly, UNESCO injects universal applicability to Masada's nationalistic symbolism. Calling it first a "fortress and a palace," the description allows for a wider range of interpretative applications—it can reference the Romans, the ancient world, or military struggles. Because of the "tragic events" that took place within the edifice's walls in a particular historical timeframe, UNESCO concedes that it is a "symbol" of "Jewish cultural identity," but, it should be noted, UNESCO does not state that it references *Israeli* or *Israeli national* identity. Furthermore, while conceding this important symbolic link to the Jewish people—albeit culturally, and not nationally—it also is a "symbol . . . more universally, of the continuing human struggle between oppression and liberty." Such struggles are not limited to the first century AD or to the twentieth century, but are "continuing" throughout time; such struggles are not limited to the Jewish people, but to "human[ity]." Indeed, marked universality of these words evokes images and memories of other diasporas and other historic struggles across the world in the subjective minds of those who interpret the phrase; depending on the political and historical understandings of its interpreters, it could reference Armenians, Tibetans, Native Americans, or, perhaps somewhat paradoxically, today's Palestinians.

Masada is not alone in being a place whose historical interpretation has changed as UNESCO memorializes it. By their very nature, all World Heritage sites are primarily potent monuments, intended to invoke subjective remembrances and provoke individual imagination, despite any previous practical usage they may have had before their nomination. Although not all are literally described as "monuments" proper—UNESCO officially divides them first into sites of "natural heritage" and sites of "cultural heritage," with the latter being sub-divided into the rather arbitrary categories of "monuments," "groups of buildings," and "sites"[40]—all World Heritage sites nevertheless are considered monumental because UNESCO recognizes them not for their current social usages, but rather for their representational properties. That is, they are designated precisely to stir the viewer's memory and the imagination. They evoke and contain some type of remembrances, some type of meaning, regardless of whether they were intentionally created as monuments or, like Masada, they were designated after the fact.

Indeed, Vietnam and Cambodia's World Heritage sites straddle these two aspects of monumentality, with some being monumental constructions from the start, and others being designated after the end of their intended use. The central Vietnamese port town of Hội An, for example, is small, living city—full of residents and businesses, a continuing and contemporary center for social, cultural and economic exchange despite its retention of "traditional" forms of material culture and lifeways. It was designated as a World Heritage site precisely because of such traditional values and aesthetics, as ICOMOS states:

> Hội An Ancient Town is an exceptionally well-preserved example of a South-East Asian trading port dating from the 15th to the 19th century. Its buildings and its street plan reflect the influences, both indigenous and foreign, that have combined to produce this unique heritage site.

> *Criterion (ii)*: Hội An is an outstanding material manifestation of the fusion of cultures over time in an international commercial port.
> *Criterion (v)*: Hội An is an exceptionally well preserved example of a traditional Asian trading port.[41]

Although Criterion ii mentions some sort of ongoing, continually evolving culture of Hội An's people "over time," the greater description centers not on the people today, but rather on the representational properties of the city as a greater symbol of what Vietnam was during the period of initial cultural exchange between the East and the West. The dates mentioned are telling: Hội An is an "exceptionally well-preserved example" of a particular kind of town that can be rather precisely dated as existing only between the fifteenth and the nineteenth centuries. All of the "influences" that contributed to such a notable "fusion of cultures over time" seem to have occurred within this specific period, and ostensibly not afterwards. Of course, when this official description was written in 1999, UNESCO officials must have turned a blind eye towards the various late-French colonial and Soviet-style constructions, the contemporary Socialist billboards, bicycles and motorbikes, electric wires crisscrossing the streets, and the unseemly television antennae jutting from nearly every home.[42] Regardless of the many anachronistic aspects found in this World Heritage site, UNESCO's precise focus on past temporality, on a "traditional" form of "Asian" port that ostensibly does not exist anymore, and on the "unique" melding of "indigenous and foreign" aesthetics all stir the mind, begging the viewer to imaginatively remember how Vietnam used to be through this "exceptionally well-preserved" and living material manifestation.

Angkor Wat, as well as most other temples in the Angkor Archaeological Park, interestingly straddles both aspects of World Heritage monumentality. While his primary intent in building the colossal temple remains unclear, undoubtedly Suryavarman II originally constructed the great temple as a particular type of monument; through its designation by UNESCO it was converted into a very different type. Archaeologists agree that it was built to be a Vaishnavist Hindu temple[43] by Suryavarman II (who reigned from 1113–c. 1150) but, pointing to the Khmer king's subsequent internment inside the vast edifice, some experts still contend that it was primarily intended to be a monument to the king from its onset. It is generally agreed that the immense sculpture of Vishnu at the heart of Angkor was in the image of Suryavarman II, thereby imbuing his temporal claim as a god-king akin to the god-king Rama of the *Rāmāyana*.[44] Based on the artistry of the construction, the inclusion of numerous bas reliefs memorializing mythical battles (especially from the *Mahābhārata*) and contemporary events, its proportions and striking cosmological features, however, it is clear that it was intended to be monumental. That is, like the soaring Gothic cathedrals of Western Europe, it was intended to evoke in the minds of its contemporaries images, memories and remembered religious stories—if not only about Suryavarman as a god-king, then about the Khmer people and their relationship to the Triune divinity.

Like Masada, however, Angkor Wat's meaning changed numerous times over the course of its life. The next great king, Jayavarman VII, who began his reign approximately in 1181 and continued until about 1215, converted to Mahāyāna Buddhism and, constructed some of the greatest and most intriguing monumental temples and monasteries in the Angkor Archaeological Park—and indeed, throughout Southeast Asia. Tolerant of Hinduism, through contextual framing he infused the great Angkor Wat with Buddhist undertones. Interested in melding the two iconographies, he did not deface or destroy the old icons and bas reliefs, but created a multitude of imposing Buddhist temples replete with Buddhist, or Hindu-Buddhist, images. But shortly after the king's death, Hinduism resurged for a brief yet destructive time, as violent masses set out to change the meaning of these edifices back again. Buddhist images were literally de-faced—rows of Buddhist bas reliefs can be seen today with what looks to be scribbles scratched over their faces. Where possible, some edited the bas reliefs; into an image of the Buddha seated in lotus position they carved a propped leg, thereby changing its symbolism to that of Vishnu, Angkor Wat's first patron deity. But often this was not easily done, and images were chiseled, chipped or smashed out of their niches, leaving patterns of holes and gruff scratches along many of Jayavarman's temples. This iconoclasm—which literally means "break-ing of icons"—was deliberately meant to erase the Buddha from Khmer collec-tive memory, not solely in the present, but more importantly, for posterity.

Yet Angkor Wat continued to serve as a powerful remembering device for Buddhists, even after the area was depopulated. Bruno Dagens reveals that Japanese pilgrims in the seventeenth century had even come upon Angkor, sub-sequently sketching a map of its layout that today can be found in Tokyo.[45] In addition to being a sacred remembering device, Angkor was considered such a monument to power and majesty that a variety of conquering peoples, such as the Thais and the French, wanted to transport it as best they could into their capitol cities, precisely to remind their subjects and citizens of their own impor-tance and authority. Rama IV, a Thai king who reigned in Bangkok from 1851 to 1868, placed a large model of Angkor Wat on display outside of the Grand Palace's Temple of the Emerald Buddha for his subjects to see; Cambodia was still a vassal state at the time, although his successor, Rama V, would be forced to cede the land to French Indochina in 1907. The French colonials themselves performed a similar activity, creating an immense model of Angkor Wat in the Trocadéro for the Paris World's Fair of 1937. Even today, it is a locus of both religious devotion and touristic visitation; resonating with the faithful and strik-ing wonder in the minds of its visitors.

Thus, Angkor Wat was always a monument, always a remembering device. But what memories it urged the viewer to call forth was strongly predicated on the socio-political context in which it contemporaneously found itself. It could remind viewers of the power of Vishnu, of the grandeur of the Khmers under Suryavarman II or Jayavarman VII, of the extreme beneficence of Vishnu or the Enlightened One, or of imperial ideologies of the conquerors and the conquered. Yet as a World Heritage site, UNESCO calls upon all of these aspects, but si-multaneously contextualizes them in a new way, such that it speaks neutrally to all peoples of the world:

> Angkor is one of the most important archaeological sites in South-East Asia.
> Stretching over some 400 sq. km, including forested area, Angkor Archaeo-
> logical Park contains the magnificent remains of the different capitals of the

Khmer Empire, from the 9th to the 15th century. These include the famous Temple of Angkor Wat and, at Angkor Thom, the Bayon Temple with its countless sculptural decorations. UNESCO has set up a wide-ranging programme to safeguard this symbolic site and its surroundings.[46]

Like that of Hội An, UNESCO's description of Angkor is temporally contained with exactness and precision. It is first and foremost an extremely important "archaeological site," an often problematic term that suggests ossification rather than a continually evolving living history, which this monument enjoys. Further underscoring fixity over continuity, in the vein of the last century's hair-splitting Processualist archaeologists, the site exists within a mapped out, measured and delimited boundary spanning "some 400 sq. km." and precisely "includes [sic] forested area" as well as "magnificent remains." Being an "archaeological site" of "remains" swallowed by the forest, rather than a locus of living devotional and cultural continuity, certainly strikes at the mind in a particular way, as contemporaries interpreting these words today undoubtedly call forth in their memories of similarly described "archaeological" locations, such as the intriguing pyramids in Egypt, the ruins of the Roman forum, or the Incan city of Machu Picchu supposedly abandoned atop a forested mountain. Finally, the memory-inducing "pastness" of Angkor Wat is reinforced a third time as UNESCO dates the place between the ninth and the fifteenth centuries, once again ignoring the importance Angkor played in other periods of time and for other peoples.

And yet by continually focusing on the "pastness" of individual sites, regardless of where they are located or what kinds of usage they enjoy today, UNESCO creates places of global monumentality that are understandable not simply to the locals, but to all peoples. UNESCO's World Heritage Convention boils down the winding and disparate lifeways of its monuments into an easily understood period in a vague "past"—removed from any individual's ability to identify with them as living sites, or sites that have a particular value in the present. Although there is a wealth of anthropological data contending that different societies have radically different understandings of the "past" and of "history," the "pastness" of these sites—as conveyed in UNESCO's efforts to antiquate their monuments either by attributing dates to them, or by describing them with commonly used words such as "heritage," "traditional," "archaeological" and "remains,"—is nevertheless a dynamic that provides global applicability. All people have a past, regardless of the role it plays in their daily contemporary lives. Likewise, all of these sites have a past—but unlike people of today, who are living and continually creating new experiences and new pasts on a daily basis, these sites are all monuments, "preserved" in a fixed and, immutable past, albeit imaginatively reconsidered. Like the "traditional cultures" or "heritage" of the peoples to which they pertain, they are valued for their representational properties and the memories they produce, not for the usage they enjoy now. The World Heritage Convention is globally applicable precisely because of its imprecision, and with such vague wording and rough calendrical estimates, it is open to a wide variety of interpretation. It is an imprecise but rather universally understandable temporality not entirely removed from the peoples of today. This is the first way UNESCO makes it "universal"—it removes much, if not all, of the spatial, temporal, or living connection one might have with the land.

Furthermore, by distilling a particular monument in a way common to all of the other monuments, it allows for individuals—especially tourists—to interpret each one in relatively the same way, regardless of the site's specific history or cultural relevance. The commonality of UNESCO's descriptive terminology to convey this pastness provides an added level of universality. "Traditional," for example, means different things when attributed to different sites. When attributed to Hội An, described as a "traditional Asian trading port," it means something entirely different than when the word is attributed to, say, Venice as a traditional northern Italian port. But because both are categorized as World Heritage sites and described with the same lexicon, UNESCO juxtaposes them, allows them to be understood in the same way. And yet the term also means different things to different people. A Native American will have different memories associated with tradition than a Russian or a Japanese person will have. Different remembrances will provide subtly different interpretative meanings, but each individual will call forth their own memories of the term to make meaning of both of these disparate sites in a cohesive way. Despite the sometimes contentious, anachronistic or imprecise lexicon with which UNESCO utilizes to underscore the value of World Heritage sites, it is clear that these sites are individual forms of universal monuments. With such a designation, each are intended to be universally applicable devices for remembering, bringing to the viewer's mind some notion, feeling, or inkling of time past—a time that is part historical, part imagined, but always a product in some way of the greater social situation in which the globally-oriented viewer finds himself. Regardless of where they are located, or where their visitors come from, World Heritage sites touch people at the individual level, in their minds, evoking the memory and stirring the imagination.

The stones that make up these monuments are not idle stones. They are a rallying cry of a community, be it heterogeneous or, as is often the case, cast across disparate lands. These stones speak: they stoke the individual memories of a collectivity of viewers, and they issue call to action. When juxtaposed against one another—when considered together as each equally representative of a same, unifying narrative—they form the building blocks of a cohesive and expansive place. Predicated on the construction of World Heritage sites—physical places of local interest recontextualized into sites of imaginative universal value—this place is termed the *heritage-scape*.

The Geography of the Heritage-scape

The heritage-scape can be conceived as a topographical representation of UNESCO's reordered world, a method of mapping the World Heritage List. As a conceptual model of the United Nation's placemaking efforts, the choice of its title is not arbitrary; Michael Parker Pearson and Colin Richards assert that a name is a "cultural artifact" that transforms "undifferentiated space" into a "delimited place"—a place that resonates with narrative claims by virtue of its titular associations.[47] This particular idiom, *heritage-scape*, has been chosen for its two potent terms, each of which suggest a veritable litany of narrative associations and ideological claims.

Heritage is a powerful word in its own right, for it is at once extraordinarily suggestive and ideologically charged, but simultaneously vague enough to be applied to nearly everything across any space and time. It is a word whose significance changes with its myriad invocations, designations or legislations. Depending on its usage, heritage can determine personal property, explicate unknown qualities, foster patriotism among disparate peoples, become a tourist destination, exacerbate geopolitical tensions, or call for help in the form of preservation, among other usages. In the words of Lord Martin Charteris of Amisfield, the former Chairman of the British National Heritage Memorial Fund, heritage can mean "anything you want."[48] Though the apparent flippancy of this assertion had been highly criticized, it illustrates the inherently contextual nature of the term, whose significance changes according to the broader social milieu in which it is invoked; it can be understood as a conceptual memorialization of a specific ideological claim about the past, and a group's particular relationship to it in the present and the future. Heritage fits into UNESCO's embrace of globalization precisely for this reason: though it clearly refers to past time, it knows no definitive spatial or temporal bounds, but rather can be applied across a wide variety of social contexts with equal ease.

As a temporal allusion, heritage first refers back to some common, imagined time—a timeframe from which all individuals who subscribe to the particular heritage claim can supposedly trace their divergent lineages. Important in this rather universalistic, communal understanding of temporality is that "heritage time" is left unspecified and open to interpretation, rather than calendarically bounded. It cannot be traced back to a particular moment in history, despite the fact that it may be referring to a specific monument whose construction can, indeed, be precisely dated. The "heritage of Cambodia" as visibly articulated in the World Heritage site of Angkor Wat is not simply traced back to its construction in the twelfth century. Rather, it calls forth a deeper temporal lineage that references not only this kingly action, but also the mythological joining of various tribes into the Khmer people, the advent of Hinduism in the region from India, and thus, the Hindu-Indic creation myths. It also represents its subsequent usage as a monumental mausoleum for the king, as well as its conversion into a vast Buddhist temple whose use in this capacity extends to this day, and, later still, as a legitimizing tool for conquering French colonials.

Likewise, the "heritage of Vietnam" as evidenced by the Imperial Purple City, part of the UNESCO World Heritage Complex of Huế Monuments, cannot simply be traced back to 1804 when the first Nguyễn emperor Gia Long proclaimed an independent country and began construction of his new palace in accordance to the divinations of his geomancers. Rather, it references all of those stories and myths that differentiate the Viet people from their Indic and Chinese neighbors, the development and borrowing of uniquely "Vietnamese" worldviews and cultural forms, and the gradual southward movement of Viet territory. Nor can the inestimable natural heritage of the nature preserve-cum-World Heritage site of Hạ Long Bay be traced back to a precise date or timeframe in the Paleolithic era when erosion and shifting tectonic plates created vast outcroppings of karst pillars in the South China Sea, nor in Vietnamese mythology when a large sleeping dragon supposedly "descended into the sea" after helping the Viet people found a new nation.[49] Rather, it is also evocative of the great and diversified power of nature to create unique spaces that inspire human interactions across the globe.

Yet even these references to diverse historical periods in the lifespan of the heritage monument are not fixed, but rather are intensely subjective, varying based on the previous knowledge and memory of the individuals that interpret the site. The "heritage of Vietnam" as conveyed through the monumentality of Huế's Imperial City can only reference the Viet people's historical southward movement, for example, for those who already know or come into contact with this narrative, and can attribute it to the site itself. Likewise, conveyed through the spectacular site of karst pillars in the emerald waters at Hạ Long Bay, heritage can only be representative of the gods' primordial blessing of the Viet people to those who are aware of the creation myth, and who are able to apply it to the site. Such varied forms of contact between the tangible site and the remembered narrative claims applied to it can come in the form of history books, references by tour guides and tour directors, or perhaps in a museum or placard at the site itself.

Thus, the unique temporal understanding of heritage does not simply reference some vague time in the past, but also simultaneously talks of the individual's time in which he or she is living; it concurrently references the present and the future based on the individual memories of the people who contemporaneously come into contact with it. Angkor Wat as a site of local and national import is the heritage of the Cambodian people—the people living in the land now, as well as their progeny. Its image on the Cambodian national flag underscores this point: today, at this very moment, the monument of Angkor Wat speaks of the people who march under it, who pledge allegiance to it, and who will create new citizens under its banner in the future. As a *World* Heritage site, the population to whom it references expands, ostensibly to encompass the whole of the world, but nonetheless still references the same temporality. The World Heritage site of Angkor speaks about the people of the world today, and their descendents of tomorrow. Today, the world's population shares in the cultural legacy that Angkor Wat illustrates; it is the responsibility of the world's citizenry to ensure its existence for the benefit of future generations.

"Heritage time" therefore, is a compressed time—in the globalization terminology of Anthony Giddens—or, as Benedict Anderson calls it, a time of "simultaneity of past and future in an instantaneous present."[50] The monument to which "heritage" is attributed speaks of an idealized time that is not simply traced back to a particular point in the past, pinpointed to some neatly delimited present or projected into a specific date in the future. Rather, it is filtered through ongoing and iterative social relations, allowing the present imagination to conceptualize the past and the future, in all of the vagaries to which it refers.

The Nature of the -*scape*

If *heritage* represents the sense of idealized temporality in UNESCO's global placemaking scheme, the suffix -*scape* conversely represents the sense of idealized spatiality that UNESCO also strives to attain. The idiom -*scape* immediately brings to this model both a potent list of associations as well as a suggestive framework with which one can create a compelling visual representation. For Arjun Appadurai, from whom this neologism is borrowed,[51] the suffix offers a framework for mapping the "new global cultural economy [as] a complex, overlapping, disjunctive order that can no longer be understood in terms of existing center-periphery models."[52] Although critics of his ideas point to a number of imprecisions in this theory, this particular description of a -scape is quite salient in conceptualizing UNESCO's global form of place. Appadurai's -scape essentially refers to a place wherein power structures are markedly de-localized. In such a place, there is no one capital, no one focus or bounded central area from which those inside can dictate policy to the rest of the public, or can define themselves in opposition to those outside. This delocalization of determinate power structures, furthermore, contributes to a -scape's overall amorphism and weakly bounded nature. Such a notion is not difficult to conceptualize; one need only to examine social relations in systems where individuals possess more autonomy than those who are rigidly controlled by a central authoritative power, such as modern-day terrorism networks or America during the somewhat mythical age of pioneers in the last century. What is so famously difficult in the early years of the twenty-first century and its "War on Terror" is the unbound-edness of terrorist networks, spurred on by its decentralized power structure. Although much is not known about these venomous and secretive organizations, experts in the field point to individuals' relative autonomy in increasing the geo-graphic reach of terrorism in the world today. Although the nations' political leaders are quick to pinpoint principal organizers and heads of various "cells," it is becoming increasingly evident, based on the continued popping up of "new" leaders, groups and cells, that these politicians are applying their own terminol-ogy to a geopolitical reality that differs from their own. The very efficacy of this present-day terrorist organization in enlarging their sphere is precisely its lack of centrality or borders. Much in line with Appadurai's definition of a -scape as a type of place that does not subscribe to central-periphery models, the decentral-ized agents of terrorism are famously known in popular culture as people whose insider-outsider identities are blurred; outwardly they look like insiders but in-wardly they act like enemy outsiders.

A more historical and well-studied example of this can also be found in the geographic expansion of the United States during the era of Manifest Destiny. As the pioneers pushed westward, loosely supported by the central government in Washington, DC, but nevertheless quite autonomous in deciding their direc-tions and spread, the borders of territories were constantly in flux. Although armed skirmishes erupted, outposts built, and contracts negotiated with neighboring countries and Native American groups, the boundedness of the Western reaches of America was quite amorphous, porous and unsolidified, pre-cisely because of this lack of effective determinate authority structures on both sides. The boundaries of the United States and the land contained therein were not so easily or unanimously recognized, despite any connotations otherwise listed in American elementary school Social Studies textbooks. Yet the inaccu-racy, unpredictability and this asystematic non-fixity that can be observed in the geographic spread of terrorism or Manifest Destiny lends itself to greater idealization, and to a greater notion of its expansiveness. Without precise maps, quantifiable acreages and firm borders that would determine what is "inside" the place as opposed to what lies "outside," the geographic reach is contested. It is open to interpretation and the application of ideological narrative claims that cannot easily be disproved. Both the effective recruiting speeches extolling and often embellishing the amorphous spread of terrorism, as well as the American myth of "Manifest Destiny" are such narrative claims, which, perhaps through extensive study in hindsight might be negated, but as experienced contemporarily seem to be as truthful as any other claim.

Evoking notions of expansiveness, idealization, and amorphism, the term -scape conveys this sense of a deterritorialized, or, at the least, a loosely demarcated, space where notions of "insiders" and "outsiders" are blurred. Visual imagery of these -scapes is often called upon in artistic representations of place, as exemplified by Romantic-era panoramas, or landscapes, intended to portray an idealized setting that seemingly has no boundaries yet may still be rooted in geographic reality. Indeed, in the era of the Grand Tour, panoramas of far-away lands were often created and published to benefit the majority of the citizenry who did not have the means or continence to travel such long distances. Placed in nineteenth-century museums, these panoramas were integral to recreating the places from which the collection came, in the broadest, most idealized and universally applicable terms. They included all of the "important" or "relevant" sites of interest, filtering out the rest, as guidebooks and tour accompaniers do at tourist sites and World Heritage monuments today.

At Hué, for example, the UNESCO-designated monuments are not localized in one clearly bounded area, as they are at the 164,000 acre Angkor Archaeological Park, but rather spread across 400 square miles of diverse terrain—a mixture of vivaciously urban and bucolically rural settlements in and around dense jungles, flowing waterways, and soaring mountains. Yet visitors simply hop on a bus or "Dragon Boat" that, in the span of twenty minutes to one hour, can take them from one monument to another with nary a word about the non-tourist areas they will invariably pass. Yet emblazoned in the travelers' minds, the first site carries across this filtered decontextualized area to the next site, creating a memory of the two monuments juxtaposed in one single place called "Hué" where they imaginatively exist in close proximity to each other. Visually filtering out parts of the real land and the real life experiences in these areas, panoramas worked in the same way as guides do at Hué today. They were thought to be "virtual grand tours," akin to the films and photographs seen in the cinemas and web sites in today's "age of mechanical reproduction"[53]—as effective as actually being at the destination. As one early nineteenth-century commentator remarked in *Blackwood's Magazine*:

Panoramas are among the happiest contrivances for saving time and expense in this age of contrivances. What cost a couple of hundred pounds and half year a century ago, now costs a shilling and a summary manner. . . . The mountain or the sea, the classic vale of the ancient city, is transported to us on the wings of the wind. . . . [54]

Yet even before Walter Benjamin would question the inherent manipulation of the authentic at the hands of mechanical reproduction, panoramas were decried by some museum directors as romanticized and not inauthentic. They saw significant difference between communing with the physical place and these panoramas; much in the same way as some contemporary theorists consider the embodied tourism experience to be a mere "pseudo-event," inauthentic in relation to experiencing the place on a daily basis, so too did these critics consider the "virtual" panoramic travel experience in relation to partaking in the Grand Tour. These criticisms arose precisely because panoramas depicted a romanticized ideal of a particular destination, often leaving out aspects of the greater social world that are integral to truly defining the place. They were socially filtered, rather than naturally depicted. In short, panoramas—these artistic representations of -scapes—allowed for too much imagination, too much idealization, at the expense of the reality of "being there."

But just because panoramas fell out of favor as tools of object-based epistemology does not mean that the term -scape has fallen out of favor, as well. On the contrary, coupling the suffix with a reference such as *land-*, *sea-*, or even *heritage-*, as this book does, is a common occurrence. In the musical realm, contemporary New Age artist Michael Jones has entitled a number of albums with some version of -scape; from the late 1980s onwards, his piano opuses have been called *Seascapes*, *Sunscapes*, and *Pianoscapes*, musically depicting romantic notions of the oceanic flow of the world's energy in a pianistic form of placemaking. And when this chapter was first written, a popular series of American stamps titled "Cloudscapes" had been in circulation, depicting fifteen different ideal types of meteorological phenomena, complete with their scientific nomenclature, courtesy of a collaborative effort with The Weather Channel, American Meteorological Society and the National Weather Service. The choice of utilizing the suffix -scape in the title of these stamps was not arbitrary. As the United States Postal Service's press release conveys in its headline, *"Reach for the Sky and Collect Stamps!" With Cloudscapes,* the title of this philatelic series was selected precisely to evoke this sense of limitless possibility for enjoyment and education that the hobby can provide. [55]

More importantly, these precisely categorized, yet idealized philatelic cloud forms were chosen to adorn the stamps for both aesthetic and epistemological purposes. In a way, they resemble, on a miniature scale, the panoramas published in travelogues and placed in museums by Grand Tour-goers, which were seen as exemplary teaching tools for those who could not travel to foreign lands. These images of typical cloud forms also serve as Weberian "ideal types"— abstract models distilled from real data sets but idealized to provide "artificial simplicity" and exemplary status, since a perfect example—instances that represent all of the possible characteristics of the object or phenomenon studied—"is seldom found in history."[56] Max Weber reasons that tangible reality cannot truly be modeled or reproduced by any scientific system of analysis, since no theoretical model can ever accurately capture the disparate and diverse nature of social or natural phenomena. The theoretical "ideal type" is thus a human construct, a subjective attempt employed to better understand and approximate reality such that each instance of diversion from this norm can be highlighted and examined. It is a hybridization of the best, most accurate or most exemplary features of a category found through systematic social scientific investigation of multiple cases; the ideal type

> is formed by the one-sided accentuation of one or more points of view and by the synthesis of a great many diffuse, discrete, more or less present and occasionally absent *concrete individual* phenomena, which are arranged according to those one-sidedly emphasized viewpoints into a unified *analytical* construct.[57]

Despite his rather obtuse definition of an "ideal type," Weber provides a very astute understanding of how ephemeral knowledge is conveyed through the use of tangible objects or places. To fully grasp a complex historical place such as Rome without being there, or a stratospheric phenomenon such as a cirrus cloud formation without extensive study aided by precise scientific instruments, an abstract conceptual model must be created from a real example by emphasizing certain aspects deemed epistemologically important for the concept, and likewise de-emphasizing those features that may prove to be difficult to the overall narrative claim about the object or site. An epistemic abstraction of reality, a -scape, then, can be conceived as such an idealized type of place, one that emphasizes claims to amorphism, expansiveness and idealization.

Even today, the most prominent usage of the term -scape remains the idiom *landscape*, perhaps because it is the most clearly evocative of the suffix's connotation of idealized spatiality. Indeed, a "landscape" is not simply land; it is not simply a piece of territory. Affixing the suffix "-scape" to the prefix "land," it

becomes an idealized version of a territorial space, the depiction of land mediated by the creator and his or her remembered interpretation of place. The Win-
nipeg Art Gallery's online art exhibition entitled "Panoramas: The North American Landscape in Art" may have described the art-historical term "landscape"
best when its curator wrote:

> Landscape, being largely a representation of nature, is constructed through our
> imagination. This process gradually forms collective, continuously mutating
> memories, which constitute the biography of each of our countries. . . . Land-
> scapes reflect a powerful convergence of physical processes and cultural mean-
> ing. Works of landscape art, therefore, represent more than a scene or a view of
> nature—they are often portraits of the social face of our world. Artists are keen
> observers of the processes of cultural change that become imprinted on the
> land."[58]

As evidenced by its usage in art history, "landscape" references a particular
genre of painting, one made famous not solely by the dilettante panorama
sketchers of the Grand Tour, but by renowned Chinese, European and American
artists of various epochs. A sign of cultural refinement, the flawless execution of
pen-and-ink landscapes by Chinese literati such as Li Sixun and his son Li
Zhaodao, who created these works from the Tang period onward, were human
"expressions of the cosmos" according to art historian Roann Barris,[59] their subjectivity epitomized by the phrases *wo you*—"to dream of traveling in bed"—
and *chang shen*—"to let the spirit unfold." Although today the study of these
works are categorized under "art history," the executers of Chinese landscape
paintings were not considered artists; the skillful visual rendering of one's un-
folding natural spirit was thought to be a requisite ability for all literati, who
would perform and compete against each other as a source of entertainment at
courtly parties and social gatherings. Thus, being able to idealize an image of
nature was itself a prime method for idealizing not only nature, but also the very
cultural capital of the literati.

Centuries later and in another part of the world, Romantic artists such as
Jean-Auguste-Dominique Ingres and Claude Delacroix in France, and Joseph
Turner and John Constable in Britain, would create vast pictorial landscapes—
or, as in the case of Turner, of shipwreck-obsessed seascapes—characterized by
their astute conveyance of human emotion, as well as by their originality in conveying nature's "uncontrollable power, unpredictability, and potential for cataclysmic extremes."[60] Indeed, Romantic landscapes do not depict simply a snap-
shot of nature, but the individualism of the artist as a mediatory filter for an
interpretation and depiction of nature. Preferring to execute grandiose sketches,
John Constable, in fact, characterized his genre's work as "nothing but one state

of mind—that which you were in at the time."[61] French Impressionists such as Van Gogh and Gauguin would carry this tradition in a new stylistic direction, underscoring the subjectivity of the artist even further while continuing to bring idealized images of far-away lands to Europeans, often concentrating on exotic Tahitian-scapes like Gauguin did or poignantly nostalgic landscapes of flowery fields or haystacks as Van Gogh would.

In early nineteenth century America, the expansiveness of the continent's natural territory contributed to the emergence of landscape as the preeminent art form in the young United States, rising to prominence largely through the work of Thomas Cole and his Hudson River School. Painting at the inception of the era of Manifest Destiny, Cole and his compatriots believed that the careful examination of the land would lead to enlightenment and a greater connection with the divine; their detailed visual depictions of idealized creeks, impressive mountains and mossy stones conveyed not topographical exactness but an almost moralistic expansiveness of God's natural gifts, which, easily recontextualized into a patriotic narrative claim of "Manifest Destiny," translated into the moral right of the United States' imagined claims of limitless national expansion. While Americans moved Westward, hacking the forests and cutting the country with iron railroads as George Inness' *The Lackawanna Valley* depicts, immense panoramas by artists such as Thomas Moran were integral in bringing idealized and beautified images of nature to the attention of East Coast Americans. Moran's landscapes—his striking and idealized depictions of the American West, which were painted on a monumental scale to approximate the live experience—were instrumental in the establishment of Yellowstone as the first national park in 1872,[62] which is considered the precursor to today's World Heritage establishment. Thus, the idealizing force of the -scape has, for a century longer than UNESCO has been in existence, been raising awareness for imagined heritage.

Art is not the only genre that utilizes the term *landscape*. In gardening—or, officially, "landscape design"—the term also connotes an idealizing form of placemaking at an even more reductive, more material level. According to garden historian and royal landscape designer Penelope Hobhouse, the act of "landscaping" is the tangible altering of the natural world to achieve a socially mediated, idealized form of nature. From their very origins in ancient China, Assyria and Medieval Europe, gardens, yards and even "urban landscapes" are not simply collections of plants growing happenstance within a particular plot of land, but rather are all man-made, often painstakingly designed, implemented and embellished over time. Like the painters' landscapes, they are material manifestations of intensely imaginative conceptions of the natural world. A product of concentrated social action, they emerge from man's desire to exert control over

wild nature—to convert, as the Renaissance humanists thought, nature into culture—the flawed into the ideal.[63] Even today, the part-time high school land-
scaper working to earn extra cash in suburban America participates in turning
the land into a landscape; he helps his clients realize their personal desire to perfect the slice of the natural world that falls within their property line, in accordance with their own imagined notions of what constitutes an ideal plot of land.
All of his responsibilities lie in manually manipulating the land. Among other
similar tasks, he plants bushes where previously there were none, removes unsightly weeds growing naturally in flowerbeds, rakes fallen leaves rather than
leaving them to decompose naturally, throws down aromatic mulch to stave off
unwanted insects and shoots, dusts the earth with chemicals to either encourage
or inhibit growth, and mows the lawn into a seamless, perfected carpet of green.
In short, he -scapes the land.

The idealizing form of placemaking that the suffix -scape connotes may
have reached its creative apex in a recently approved plan for the redevelopment
of the Fresh Kills Landfill, ambitiously entitled *Fresh Kills Lifescape*. Located
in Staten Island, NY, Fresh Kills was one of New York City's primary landfills
until it reached capacity. The final resting place for much of the unusable remains of the World Trade Center, which was destroyed in the September 11,
2001 terrorist attack on New York City, it is regarded by many as a sacred site.
In seeking a redevelopment plan to turn "Landfill into Landscape," the city
commission necessarily sought out plans that referenced vibrancy, a symbolic
rising up from the ashes of waste and destruction. Thus the winning design firm
entitled its plan "Fresh Kills Lifescape." Coupling the word *life* with the suffix
-scape, this firm clearly wishes to characterize their redeveloped plot of land not
simply as a living site, but one that is idealized, that is more than simply living
on a day-to-day basis, like other places. With roots in the sacred ashes of the
World Trade Center, the life that emerges from the landfill is -scaped: it is meticulously controlled and idealized, set apart from daily life. Indeed, the redevelopment firm projects a narrative claim that "recognizes humanity as a symbioti-
cally evolving, globally interconnected, and technological *system*."[64]
Underscoring that "Lifescape is not a loose metaphor or representation—it is a
functioning reality, an autopoietic agent," the landscape architects provide a 30-
year projected timeline, where every new phase is titled with a different -scape
that connotes an idealized progression from burial to redemption; it moves from
"moundscape" (first year) to "openscape" (sixth year) to "eventscape" (twenty
years), and, finally "lifescape" (thirty years).[65] That the company's winning proposal was introduced to the greater public as a temporary art exhibit in New
York's newly re-opened Museum of Modern Art (MoMA) further underscores
the artistic and imaginatively mediated quality of this application of a -scape.

Regardless of the genre in which they are found or the practical message they are meant to convey, the disparate uses of the suffix -scape have one commonality. The different forms of landscapes, seascapes, cloudscapes and even "lifescapes" all seem to conjure up romanticized images of a world of distant horizons, which, with a little imagination on the part of the viewer, may seem to expand onward forever.[66]

My conceptualization of the *heritage-scape* draws upon all of these evocative connotations. Characterized by tangible geographic World Heritage sites that are decoupled from local individuals and the nation-states in which they reside, the heritage-scape exists above and beyond international boundaries. This act of decoupling and re-inserting is underscored by UNESCO's terminology; once a site is designated, it is "inscribed" onto a World Heritage List, not simply written or recorded. Thus, the heritage-scape has roots in the physical world yet exists apart from it, primarily in the "minds of men." As Appadurai points out, the suffix -scape suggests a decidedly shapeless nature, characteristic of the heritage-scape, which is "fundamentally fractal, that is, as possessing no Euclidean boundaries, structures or regularities."[67] In the heritage-scape, the imagined boundaries are neither clearly defined nor fixed; rather, they are amorphous and dynamic, ever changing and expanding in three separate dimensions—outwardly, inwardly and conceptually. Relatively fluid, the geographic expansiveness of the heritage-scape is subject to the places that are continually added to this new global place, and is also impacted by the constant flow of people who come into contact with a World Heritage site and then return home.

Qualities of the Heritage-scape

The heritage-scape is *outwardly expansive*. That is, though it is not traditionally bounded with fixed borders and confines that could lend one to concretely identify its "inside" and "outside," it nevertheless enjoys an approximate maximum extent that rises and recedes like the tide on a beachfront. While the confines of the heritage-scape are therefore fluid and dynamic, relying on the dialectical process of social interaction with heritage monuments, a rough calculation of its maximum spread can be gained by analyzing the introduction of new World Heritage sites in previously un-represented parts of the world. Adding new World Heritage properties at the heritage-scape's confines, UNESCO effectively integrates entirely new geographies to this new form of place, and extends its scope across new geopolitical borders.

Analyzing the pattern of sites designated since the project's inception, one can veritably visualize this tide-like flow of the heritage-scape's boundaries. In

1978, the first year of the World Heritage Convention's designations, there were twelve sites in a relatively compact area whose maximum extent differed from the Roman Empire's only in its inclusion of select sites in North and northern South America. To the south, the heritage-scape touched North Africa (Ethiopia and Senegal) and Northern South America (Ecuador); Eastern Europe (Poland) represented its easternmost stretch, while Northern Europe (Germany) and North America (Canada) represented its northern confines, and natural sites in the landlocked areas of Western United States (Wyoming, Arizona) provided its westernmost points.

Reflecting additional signatories to the World Heritage Convention, 47 new World Heritage sites were added the next year, but its borders only increased slightly southward in Africa (Tanzania and Ghana), northward into Scandinavia (Norway), and eastward into the Middle East (Syria, Iran) and Southwestern Asia (Nepal). With the exception of Nepal, a decade after the World Heritage Convention had been signed, effectively signaling the beginning of UNESCO's placemaking efforts, Asia had not been touched, nor had the heritage-scape reached the numerous islands in the Pacific Ocean. In fact, it only reached East Asia, as represented by sites in China, Japan and Korea, as late as 1987 when numerous renowned Chinese sites, such as the Great Wall, the sacred mountain of Tian Shan, Beijing's Forbidden City and Emperor Qin's burial place in Xian were integrated. Likewise, the heritage-scape reached Southeast Asia only when the ancient Thai cities of Sukhothai and Ayutthaya were integrated in 1991; it reached Southeast Asia's eastern shores when Hué was designated in 1993, despite the fact that Vietnam had been a signatory of the World Heritage Convention since 1987. Finally, it reached Oceana in 1990 when two New Zealand national parks were designated as natural World Heritage sites, with Australian sites beginning their integration the next year. Although such a quantitative analysis does not identify the specific reach of the heritage-scape, it is useful only insofar as to provide a roughly conceptualized idea of its continual outward expansion.

Because of the political and intergovernmental nature of the World Heritage Convention, such expansiveness is predicated on the participation of nation-states. Although quantitatively evident, it would be unfair to assert that the heritage-scape's expansion was at first a product of a concerted effort to reify Western culture. Rather, it is better understood as a reflection of the World Heritage Convention's political culture; the nation-states who saw the value in "world heritage" as a concept were the first to benefit from it. Indeed, as an entity composed first and foremostly of nation-states who offer up their cultural and natural sites for integration in this alternative geographic rendering, the primary impetus for the heritage-scape's outward expansiveness comes when a

World Heritage site is designated within the geopolitical confines of a new nation. For example, Italy joined the World Heritage Convention on June 28, 1978, with its nature preserve in the Dolomite Mountains the first site designated soon thereafter. Politically reticent to give up its famed cultural properties-cum-tourist destinations to UNESCO's World Heritage designations, Italian monuments located in Milan and in Rome were nominated later, followed by Florence and, almost eight years later, Venice and the "Leaning Tower" of Pisa were finally designated. Across this time period, one can conceptualize the heritage-scape expanding southward down the Italian peninsula from France, Austria and Germany, whose territories had already been subsumed by the heritage-scape a number of years beforehand. The sovereign theocratic nation of The Holy See (Vatican City), located in Rome, joined the convention four years later, and once again one can visualize the spread of the heritage-scape to include the whole of its territory, which was designated as one complex World Heritage site in 1982. The heritage-scape reached Southeast Asia in 1987 with Thailand and Vietnam joining the Convention in September and October, respectively. Cambodia was admitted as a member-state to the Convention in 1991, with Angkor becoming a node on the -scape in 1992.

Indeed, as of this writing, there are 878 properties in 145 nation-states (50 of which are transboundary) inscribed in the World Heritage List, and with an increasing number of locations around the world threatened by strife and war, it seems that UNESCO will only increase the heritage-scape's reach. Every year, in fact, an average of thirty-two new sites are added to the heritage-scape,[68] increasing not only its diversity, but also its size and shapeless form as it grows to include areas of the world that had previously been untouched or underrepresented in this amorphously global place. In a concerted effort to expand the heritage-scape's boundaries, UNESCO has undertaken an aggressive program to integrate sites "underrepresented" in both geographic location and type. In 1994, a *Global Strategy for a Representative World Heritage List* was adopted to

> make it more balanced and reflective of our cultural diversity. By broadening the definition of World Heritage, the List encouraged underrepresented parts of the world, notably Africa, the Arab region and the Pacific, to nominate more sites—especially in categories which were not yet fully represented on the List such as cultural landscapes, itineraries and industrial heritage, not to mention natural sites such as deserts, coastal regions and small islands.[69]

As it expands both inwardly and outwardly over time, the heritage-scape "loses all semblance of isomorphism" as local geographies are freed from the "shackles of highly localized, boundary-oriented, holistic, primordialist images of form and substance."[70]

Yet the outwardly expansive boundaries are not so geographically fixed; they are not so easily measurable simply by plotting out the addition of sites on a map of the world. Rather, fundamental to the notion of the heritage-scape as a distinct form of place that exists in the imagination of individuals, it is predicated on the ebb and flow of people in geographic proximity to each other. Like Anderson's "imagined community," the heritage-scape too exists primarily in the minds of people who identify with its narrative claim, regardless of how locally they reside or where at which monumental node they interact. It is for this reason that the heritage-scape cannot be so easily bounded, but rather its ever-extending confines are always amorphous, changing and rather fluid. Indeed, the metaphor of a seashore is a good way to conceptualize the heritage-scape's expansiveness. The bulk of the heritage-scape can be likened to the sea, seemingly limitless, expansive, but always pushing its tidal confines farther onto the shore. Yet its breakers—those last waves before the water hits the land—do not break right at the edge of the tide, but rather earlier, churning and foaming, letting the water mix, trickle and flow with less strength and volume to reach its maximum extent. The people who come into contact with the heritage-scape spread like these trickling waters farther out from its maximum fixed geographic extent. They are the UN and governmental workers who become engaged in the work of the World Heritage Convention and call upon memories of their past fieldwork experiences for their present task. They are the tourists who visit a World Heritage site and return home with a deeper conception of world cultural diversity and how they fit in such claims. They are the preservationists, journalists and travel writers called to labor at a particular site, bringing expertise cultivated elsewhere. They are the students, newspaper readers, and social contacts of all of these individuals who hear about World Heritage and begin to conceptualize the heritage-scape without even visiting one of its monuments.[71] And as these individuals become concentrated into epistemic communities, the heritage-scape expands and deepens, forming puddles and expanding into tide pools. It is possible that they may eventually dry up—as these individuals may "forget" or reposition their understanding of the heritage-scape—yet like the laws of erosion they most likely will expand, forming puddles and tide pools, pushing their confines outward into lakes eventually melding with the sea. Like islands and atolls, areas untouched by notions of World Heritage yet surrounded by the heritage-scape will also come to be subsumed.

Similar to the erosion of peninsulas and the subsuming of island atolls wrought by the oceans and seas of the physical earth, this "subsuming" of dry areas between pockets of the amorphous heritage-scape can be categorized as a quality of *inward expansiveness*. UNESCO's World Heritage Convention does not stop its placemaking activity within countries and regions currently occupied by the heritage-scape, but continues to solicit nominations for World Heritage designation from areas already represented, already within its nebulous boundaries. To continue using the Western example of Italy as an illustration, the boot-shaped peninsula enjoys a rich history of World Heritage additions even after the first of its cultural properties became integrated into the heritage-scape; beginning with one in 1979 and two more in 1980, it now boasts forty-one World Heritage sites, the bulk of which have been designated only in the last decade. While Cambodia has maintained only one site since 1992, in the same short time period, Vietnam boasts five. Thus, the heritage-scape increases the "depth" of its coverage inside its shifting territories, much in the same way that seventeenth-century maps of the New World were "deepened" and clarified through subsequent exploration. While the cartographers of several centuries ago were aware of North America's maximum geographic extent, huge swaths of their renderings of the mainland were left blank, for they simply did not know of anything existing between the oceans. But by the nineteenth century, as a greater number of landforms, peoples and structures were "unblackboxed," the maps reflected this more precise consciousness of the land.

The same is true of the heritage-scape; most of the globe is represented in varying degrees in UNESCO's cartography, yet every year new sites are inscribed from within its nebulous boundaries, continually intensifying one's understanding of cultural diversity. Although, for example, a nation such as Italy may enjoy a multitude of World Heritage designations throughout its regions and territories, UNESCO continues to designate more sites, this time in closer proximity with each other. Tuscany, that Italian region for centuries so beloved by tourists, artists and writers, persists in enjoying more designations. Added to the World Heritage sites of Florence and Pisa came the medieval towns of Siena (1995) and San Gimignano (1990), approximately an hour's drive from the Renaissance capitals. Later came the "ideal city" of Pienza (1996), another hour's drive from Siena. And in 2004, the Val d'Orcia countryside around Pienza was added as a "natural site," adding more density to the heritage-scape in this area of the world. While Cambodia has been slow to add new World Heritage sites—owing in part to the transitional socio-political climate of the country as well as the difficulties associated with the massive crush of tourism at Angkor—Vietnam, like Italy, continues to add new places to the heritage-scape. After Huế became the first Vietnamese World Heritage site in 1993, nearby Hội An and Mỹ Sơn were added in 1999. Hạ Long Bay was first inscribed in 1994 then expanded and re-inscribed in 2000, while Phong Nha-Kẻ Bàng was designated in 2003. Although they exist in relative proximity to each other within the same nation-state, all are conceptualized as speaking to different histories and cultural qualities.

Conversely, the possibility that a World Heritage site can lose its designation should be noted as well. Appalled by the theme of the film, UNESCO threatened Cambodian authorities with this possibility after Angelina Jolie's *Tomb Raider* was allowed to be filmed at Angkor Wat and the monastery of Ta Prohm.[72] At the low rental price of USD $18,000 a day for less than a month of shooting, perhaps the World Heritage Committee was also disappointed with the low profit such physically and intellectually damaging work raised. Developing countries are not the only nations upon whom this threat is leveled; in their push for modernization and industrial development, European states, especially in the east, have threatened the artistic or structural integrity of their World Heritage sites. During the annual World Heritage Committee meeting in Vilnius, Lithuania on July 11, 2006, the Committee even leveled this threat against Germany. The municipal government of the former East German city of Dresden had been planning to build a bridge over the Elbe River within the 11-mile stretch of land designated a World Heritage site in 2004 for its aesthetic blending of Baroque architecture and natural beauty. The Committee preemptively inscribed the site on its "short list" of World Heritage in Danger "with a view to also consider, in a prudent manner, delisting the site from the World Heritage List in 2007 if the plans are carried through."[73] This threat was enough; on July 21, 2006—just ten days after the announcement—the city government intervened, halting plans to build the bridge. Citing a Referendum wherein citizens had voted for the bridge construction, the regional government sued the city, and courts ruled in favor of the Saxony regional government.[74] At its meeting in Christchurch, New Zealand in 2007, UNESCO conceded that the "judicial process has been exhausted."[75] Nevertheless, a number of alternatives had been suggested earlier in the year that might keep Dresden on the List, while still constructing a motorway. But the outlook looks grim for Dresden: In its 2007 World Heritage Committee meeting, UNESCO also decided to de-list the site as soon as ground was broken and if such an alternative could not be found.[76] To add teeth to the argument, the same Committee also de-listed its first site: Oman's Oryx Sanctuary, citing the government's poor conservation efforts (most of the animals had died) and oil drilling on World Heritage land.

This inward expansiveness in the form of nominating additional World Heritage sites from within the heritage-scape and its political member-states is complemented by another unique action. UNESCO also "deepens" or "complexifies" the scope of previously designated World Heritage sites by subsequently adding onto them. Called "Extensions," such action attaches more monuments to a particular, preexisting World Heritage site. Extensions come in a variety of forms. Some are clarifications or technical additions to a World Heritage site, as is the case with South Africa's Fossil Hominid Sites of Sterkfontein, Swartkrans, Kromdraai and Environs, first designated a World Heritage site in 1998. This site was extended in 2005 to specifically include The Taung Skull Fossil Site and the "many archaeological caves" of the Makapan Valley, both of which already fell within the boundaries of the 1998 designation but whose names had not specifically been mentioned in the original designation. As this South African example illustrates, many extensions come from within the nation-state, although, unlike the Fossil Hominid Sites of Sterkfontein, Swartkrans, Kromdraai and Environs, most expand their territorial reach. In 2005, for example, India's Darjeeling Himalaya Railway World Heritage site (designated in 1998) was expanded to include the stretch of land occupied by the Nilgiri Mountain Railway, for UNESCO determined the latter to be a further example of the criteria the Darjeeling railway illustrates. As is often, but not always, the case when such an addition is made, an extension requires a change in the name of the World Heritage site itself. Indeed, the name change is a noticeable signal of UNESCO's ongoing complexifying action. Upon the addition of the Nilgiri Mountain Railway to that of Darjeeling, the site's nomenclature was changed to the Mountain Railways of India World Heritage site, reflecting a deeper, more precise understanding of the characteristics and diversity it illustrates.

Although indicative of a complexifying endeavor, the act of changing a World Heritage site's name does not simply add meaning to the site, but it also serves to subtract other connotations that may not fit in with the overall narrative claims about the site. The colonial Darjeeling Railway Company was reified to a certain extent over other colonial for-profit railway companies when it enjoyed inclusion in the Indian World Heritage site's nomenclature, despite the fact that, in hindsight, other companies—such as the recently included Nilgiri Mountain Railway—employed the same remarkable feats of engineering[77] and served the same notable functions. Yet including the name Darjeeling Railway in the World Heritage title elevated not only the company that constructed it above other companies, but it also elevated the region of Darjeeling and the societies found within, over those of the other regions that similar trains touched. Indeed, the common characteristic of both mountain railway systems is their strong impact on the local cultures they affected; an official tourism website for the "Hill Railways of India" states that

> no other railway system in the world is as ineluctably interwoven with the lives of the peoples it serves. DHR [The Darjeeling Railway System] has been part of the Darjeeling landscape for over a hundred years and is central to the hill economy of the region. The railway was instrumental in attracting people from neighbouring Sikkim, Nepal, West Bengal and even as far away as Tibet, mak-

ing Kurseong, a wayside town, a true entrepot of eclectic cultures. . . . [Like-wise, the Nilgiri Railway] derives its charm from its natural setting. It is a trek-ker's paradise. . . . To quote a south Indian railway spokesman in 1935: "those engineers must have been lovers of nature when they decided on the align-ment."[78]

UNESCO likewise underscores the social and natural significance of both systems when it states that the railways were

> highly significant in facilitating population movement and the social-economic development in the British colonial era. . . . [They are] outstanding examples of the interchange of values on developments in technology, and the impact of in-novative transportation system on the social and economic development of a multicultural region, which was to serve as a model for similar developments in many parts of the world.

Based on such an intricate interweaving of people, geographies, and techno-logical innovation that are representative of both places, favoring one area over another does not seem to be in line with the unifying mission of the heritage-scape. Thus, shifting its title to "The Mountain Railways of India," essentially "forgets" the Darjeeling Railway, or, at the least, lessens its importance, restor-ing the balance in value between that of Darjeeling and that of Nilgiri. Thus, despite the erasure of one aspect of the World Heritage site, this forgetting actu-ally improves the overall message, efficacy and unifying ability of the World Heritage site. It is in this way that David Lowenthal's seemingly cynical asser-tion rings true: "What heritage does not highlight it often hides . . . heritage is enhanced by erasure."[79]

Indicative of UNESCO's globalizing endeavors, the World Heritage Con-vention may also choose to create an Extension to a site that falls within the borders of another nation-state, as is the case with the newly created "Frontiers of the Roman Empire" World Heritage site, a 2005 Extension to Hadrian's Wall, the United Kingdom's longtime World Heritage site. According to the official informational website for Hadrian's Wall, found in the English countryside, the remnants of the famed Roman partition, called a *limes*, was designated a World Heritage site in 1987 for its "complexity and high level of survival as the most elaborate of all the frontier works of the Roman Empire."[80] Although when it was designated, UNESCO and its affiliate, ICOMOS, stated that "No other en-semble from the Roman Empire illustrates as ambitious and coherent a system of defensive constructions perfected by engineers over the course of several generations,"[81] UNESCO added the Upper German-Raetian Limes to the site in a concerted effort to form a major transnational World Heritage Site, freshly dubbed the "Frontiers of the Roman Empire." As its new name attests, such an Extension complexifies the meaning of Hadrian's Wall and the other "Roman limes," as its official description attests:

> The site consists of sections of the border line of the Roman Empire at its greatest extent in the 2nd century A.D., part of what is known as the "Roman Limes". All together, the Limes stretched over 5,000 kms from the Atlantic coast of northern Britain, through Europe to the Black Sea, and from there to the Red Sea and across North Africa to the Atlantic coast. Vestiges in this site include remains of the ramparts, walls and ditches, watchtowers, forts, and civilian settlements, which accommodated tradesmen, craftsmen and others who serviced the military.[82]

The description of this new site, which includes references to North Africa, French and Spanish coastal areas, Eastern Europe and the Middle East, uniquely reveals the heritage-scape's transnational intent as embodied in a singular World Heritage site. Although no additional Roman limes from these other regions had been specifically added to the Frontiers of the Roman Empire site as of its designation, it is clear that UNESCO intends to include them in subsequent Extensions. Indeed, according to a press release by the United Kingdom's Department of Culture, Media and Sport, the designation is understood as

> the second phase of a possibly wider, phased, serial transnational nomination to encompass remains of the Roman Frontiers around the Mediterranean region. Hadrian's Wall is regarded by both governments as the first part of the new transnational site and to reflect this, the World Heritage Committee has agreed to change its name to Frontiers of the Roman Empire: Hadrian's Wall.[83]

Such highly publicized transnational cooperation is truly indicative of the peacefully unifying intention of UNESCO in the creation of a heritage-scape. It also enacts the heritage-scape's nature as transcending national boundaries, of existing above and beyond traditional geographic borders.

It should also be noted that 2005 experienced a record number of such Extensions, which were previously relatively few and far between. Perhaps this is indicative of a relatively comprehensive spread of the heritage-scape across the globe, especially when considering that its maximum extent is not simply calculated by the proximity of World Heritage sites at its confines, but rather by the amount of people who have come into contact with the -scape. Indeed, with tourism and media allowing for large amounts of the world's population to come into contact with World Heritage sites, thereby expanding the extent of the heritage-scape, perhaps Extensions—this form of "inward expansion" is the new trend in UNESCO's designations. Rather than complexifying the inner body of the heritage-scape through the creation of many new World Heritage properties, perhaps it is wiser to transregionally and even transnationally extend the reaches of those sites previously understood to be of World Heritage.

Despite the political composition of the World Heritage Convention, which, in turn, imparts an equally political bent on its designating procedures, the heritage-scape by its very nature as oriented towards individuals considers the representation of diverse geographic regions to be of greater importance in its efforts at expansion. The *Global Strategy* as outlined by UNESCO makes no reference to underrepresented nations, but rather to *underrepresented parts of the world*,[84] notably Africa, the Arab Region and the Pacific." Indeed, the document's introduction also underscores a regional focus by attesting that "the World Heritage List lacked balance in the type of inscribed properties and in the geographical areas of the world that were represented. Among the 410 properties, 304 were cultural sites and only 90 were natural and 16 mixed, while the vast majority is located in developed regions of the world, notably in Europe."[85]

As late as 2004, in fact, the World Heritage Committee reviewed the Strategy's implementation, once again conducting a series of analyses through their associated agencies, ICOMOS and IUCN. Both of these analyses were "carried out on regional, chronological, geographical and thematic bases in order to evaluate the progress of the Global Strategy." This type of review, predicated on the analysis of multiple World Heritage sites in a particular region, is not new or unique to the Global Strategy, but is the common method of grouping and analyzing the coherence of the heritage-scape at a more micro level. While World Heritage sites in developed areas such as Europe or North America are not often subjected to this kind of intensive review, UNESCO often scrutinizes the ongoing preservation activities in developing countries such as Cambodia or Vietnam on a regional basis, rather than simply on a national level.

As outlined in Article 29 of the World Heritage Convention, nation-states are "invited" to submit "periodic reports" on the status of the implementation of the World Heritage Convention's guidelines and on the State of the Conservation of World Heritage properties by the "person(s) directly in charge of the property's management."[86] However, this regulation had only begun to be enforced in 1997 as more sites from developing countries have been integrated into the heritage-scape, and, indeed, seems to be voluntary on the part of the nation-state. Indeed, the benefit to conducting such a costly and time-consuming analysis is dubious, and depends on the quantity of World Heritage sites in a country, as well as the quality of the conservation work conducted by the nation at these places. The cynic would be wont to point out that nation-states who are not fulfilling their predetermined functions in preserving their monuments would not wish to bring attention to this fact, since UNESCO always reserves the right to revoke a World Heritage designation. But on a less pessimistic level, there are a number of other practical issues that would preclude a nation from compiling these reports. First, since the state of preservation, as well as the individual preservation plans, are thoroughly analyzed for each site before its designation, most are not deemed to be in need of periodic updates. Second, if UNESCO does designate a World Heritage site that is in dire need of preservation, the monument is inscribed on a secondary list called "World Heritage in Danger" which requires the place to be subject to regular and concentrated scrutiny. Third, developing nations—for whom this procedure is most prominently directed—usually benefit from direct aid from the World Heritage Fund and from its associated historic preservation agencies. Because they are directly utilizing UNESCO's resources, periodic updates on the progress of individual monuments' conservation activities are already required. In addition, most developing nations only enjoy a few World Heritage designations; it is likely that each of these are already scrutinized on an individual level.

But in addition to these practical reasons, which may preclude UNESCO from analyzing World Heritage sites from a national point of view, the World Heritage Convention's regional focus serves an even more important function when considering the overall placemaking endeavor of the heritage-scape. Designating and analyzing World Heritage sites from a regional standpoint reinforces the deterritorialization of the site from its original nation-state, allowing for it to be contextualized in a way that de-emphasizes traditional territorial boundaries that often are integral in creating contention and disunity. The Angkor Archaeological Park is an excellent example, for throughout its history, multiple peoples residing today in a diversity of nation-states have fought against one another for control of the potently symbolic structures. Although created by the Khmer, the Chams, Thais and even the French have all staked authoritative claims to its possession. Such claims are deeply rooted in the collective memories of these people, and have not been easily broken, even after the area was ceded back to Cambodia from Thailand in the nineteenth century, even after the fall of French Indochina, and even after its recent designation as a World Heritage site lying in Cambodia's territory. Indeed, such deep-seeded contention over the cultural possession of the site, which fosters not only disunity amongst ethnic groups but also the potential for violence, was evident as recently as January 29, 2003, when rumors circulated in Phnom Penh that Thai actress Suwanan Kongying supposedly made an off-the-cuff remark that Angkor Wat belonged to neighboring Thailand, an assertion that the actress later denied saying. Perpetuated by the powerful former Khmer Rouge member-turned-Prime Minister, Hun Sen, who said the Thai actress was "not even worth a few blades of grass" that grow around Angkor's temples, mobs took to the street, burning the Thai embassy, the ambassador's residence and Thai-owned businesses such as the Royal Phnom Penh Hotel in the Cambodian capital, causing flight cancellations, a temporary de-normalization of relations between the two countries, a disruption in tourism, and an estimated $46.8 million dollars in damage. Though less violent, mobs took to the Bangkok streets in reaction, protesting in front of the Cambodian embassy, burning Cambodian flags and stomping on pictures of the Cambodian king, prompting Suthichai Yoon to write in *The Nation*, "Until that dark ugly night of January 29, the Thai psyche simply refused to absorb the hard, cold fact that we were considered a new breed of imperialist. . . . We thought since they use our mobile phone service, watch our TV soap operas and consume our instant noodles, they must really love all things Thai.[87]

UNESCO's regional focus therefore is a unifying action in line with the overall mission of the heritage-scape. Downplaying heated ideologies of possession by nation-states in favor of more basic geographic notions, it challenges traditional territorial conceptions of a place by juxtaposing a contentious site such as Angkor Wat with sites in neighboring countries such as Thailand, Vietnam and Laos. Such a change in perception comes from how the individual site is contextualized in the heritage-scape, and UNESCO understands that this change emerges first and foremost from how the site's managers articulate such universalizing claims. Conducting regional analyses is an opportunity for such authorities to join together and to cultivate such universal understandings. In a 2003 report on *The State of World Heritage in the Asia-Pacific Region*, for example, the "benefits and lessons learnt"[88] of such a regional examination are recognized as "numerous."[89] Stating that the "Asia-Pacific Region presents many challenges, with immense diversity in terms of geography, ethnicity and culture, as well as disparity in terms of wealth and development," the examination was "instrumental in providing a global vision" in terms of identifying "World Heritage values, heritage legislation, management and monitoring challenges, educational and promotional activities, the use of new technologies, and partnerships for conservation." It also provided "stronger knowledge of the *World Heritage Convention*, its *Operational Guidelines* and its reporting mechanisms."[90]

Along with the *Global Strategy for a Representative World Heritage List*, these regional studies attest to the primary fact that the heritage-scape is an entity predicated on the identities and changing conceptions of place by individuals residing in diverse geographic areas. As such, imagined boundaries are not the only elements of the heritage-scape characterized by dynamic and expansive amorphism; the heritage-scape must also be *conceptually amorphous* to allow for the seamless applicability of a multitude of very different spaces within its nebulous boundaries. What constitutes the very notion of a World Heritage site is always subject to debate and interpretation; UNESCO's 1972 *World Heritage Convention* provides a list of possible sites ranging from human constructions to natural landforms, whose only common link appears to be the vague assertion that all are of "outstanding universal value." Article I identifies a number of disparate possibilities for "cultural sites":

- Monuments: architectural works, works of monumental sculpture and painting, elements or structures of an archaeological nature, inscriptions, cave dwellings and combinations of features, which are of *outstanding universal value* from the point of view of history, art or science;
- Groups of buildings: groups of separate or connected buildings which, because of their architecture, their homogeneity or their place in the landscape, are of *outstanding universal value* from the point of view of history, art or science;
- Sites: works of man or the combined works of nature and man, and areas including archaeological sites which are of *outstanding universal value* from the historical, aesthetic, ethnological or anthropological point of view.[91]

Article II similarly describes "natural sites" as:

- Natural features consisting of physical and biological formations or groups of such formations, which are *of outstanding universal value* from the aesthetic or scientific point of view;
- Geological and physiographical formations and precisely delineated areas which constitute the habitat of threatened species of animals and plants of *outstanding universal value* from the point of view of science or conservation;
- Natural sites or precisely delineated natural areas *of outstanding universal value* from the point of view of science, conservation or natural beauty.[92]

Like the "cultural sites" before them, these natural sites are recognized once again for their intrinsic "outstanding universal value" towards aesthetics, (scientific) research, or conservation. Yet when examined in detail, this nature / culture dichotomy seems to be a system of categorization fraught with difficulties and inconsistencies, for it incorrectly assumes that these spaces are examples of "naked life," untouched by human hands and therefore meant to be separated from humanity—or at least from society—and preserved on its own. Theoretically, the understanding that places can be either cultural or natural—that is, either touched or untouched by humanity—is a problematic one for placemaking strategy in general.

Although the World Heritage Convention's foundational document makes no reference to it, as early as 1979 the World Heritage Committee tacitly realized that such a nature-culture dichotomy was problematic, as nominations were crossing categories and typologies. That year, the World Heritage List's categorization was expanded to include a third delineation—that of a "Mixed Site"—which fuses both natural landforms and cultural constructions. Today, there are twenty three of such sites, whose designation were determined in practice through what P. J. Fowler calls a "straightforward numerical, almost formulaic equation along the lines of '2 natural criteria + 2 cultural criteria = a World Heritage 'mixed site'."[93] Yet perhaps because no mention of a "mixed site" per se exists in the World Heritage Convention's charter, and because there was "dissatisfaction" with its nomenclature or connotations, Fowler compiled an in-depth documentation of what UNESCO has grown to call a "cultural landscape," published for UNESCO in 2003. Fowler examines this term, which was inserted into the third definition of a "cultural site" in the early 1990s, in what amounts to a systematic approach to find the basis for "mixed site" designations in the World Heritage Convention's charter:

> Cultural landscapes represent the 'combined works of nature and man' designated in Article 1 of the World Heritage Convention. They are 'illustrative of the evolution of human society and settlement over time, under the influence of the physical constraints and/or opportunities presented by their natural environment and of successive social, economic and cultural forces, both external and internal. They should be selected on the basis both of their outstanding universal value and of their representativity in terms of a clearly defined geo-cultural region and also for their capacity to illustrate the essential and distinct cultural elements of such regions' (para. 36) . . . 'The term "cultural landscape" embraces a diversity of manifestations of the interaction between humankind and its natural environment' (para. 37).[94]

Fowler continues with a "classic" quote from Carl O. Sauer, the famed cultural geographer: "The cultural landscape is fashioned from a natural landscape by a culture group. Culture is the agent, the natural area the medium, the cultural landscape the result."[95]

A fusion of nature and culture, the presence of mixed sites further underscores the subjective and intensely interpretative qualities of these definitions. Indeed, Fowler calls it an "intellectually flaccid idea" that is "meaningless" to seriously quantify,[96] for it illustrates the fact that all places are socially mediated, value is not intrinsic, and that to be a place of any "value" to people, there must always be some sort of interrelationship. Indeed, by highlighting "value" as the common thread that runs throughout each of these categories, UNESCO illustrates the heritage-scape's primary feature as intensely social and socially

mediated. Buildings and monuments, geological formations or biological phenomena do not possess inherent value; they are ascribed value by individuals. It
is based on perception—a body of remembered knowledge concerning its understood features, scarcity and symbolisms. Yet these perceptions, of course, are
always highly interpretative.

In addition to this blurring of the cultural and the natural in tangible World
Heritage sites, UNESCO recently added another conceptually amorphous concept to the mix, further complexifying the meaning and interpretative potential
of World Heritage. Passed in 2003, The *Convention for the Safeguarding of the
Intangible Cultural Heritage* ultimately produced a new List and a new set of
ritualized processes that seeks to reify immaterial cultural expressions.[97] With
this activity, the already conceptually amorphous term "world heritage" is further deepened; not only is it somehow materially evident tangible cultural and
natural places, now it can be discerned from ephemeral "social practices" and
performances—such as poetry, song, rituals, "knowledge," myths and folklore—
across various spaces and moments in time:

> The "intangible cultural heritage" means the practices, representations, expres-
> sions, knowledge, skills—as well as the instruments, objects, artefacts and cul-
> tural spaces associated therewith—that communities, groups and, in some
> cases, individuals recognize as part of their cultural heritage. This intangible
> cultural heritage, transmitted from generation to generation, is constantly recre-
> ated by communities and groups in response to their environment, their interac-
> tion with nature and their history, and provides them with a sense of identity
> and continuity, thus promoting respect for cultural diversity and human creativ-
> ity. . . .
>
> The "intangible cultural heritage", as defined in paragraph 1 above, is mani-
> fested inter alia in the following domains:
> (a) oral traditions and expressions, including language as a vehicle of the
>   intangible cultural heritage;
> (b) performing arts;
> (c) social practices, rituals and festive events;
> (d) knowledge and practices concerning nature and the universe;
> (e) traditional craftsmanship.[98]

As Barbara Kirshenblatt-Gimblett points out, such a designation, focuses on
the "traditions themselves" as opposed to the material objects these traditions,
and therefore "entailed a shift from artifacts . . . to people, . . . their knowledge
and skills."[99] In essence, UNESCO's new designation highlights not the material
products of culture, but culture, in all of its immaterial webs of significances,
itself. Such a notion firmly underscores the heritage-scape's primary goal: to

create a place predicated not on traditionally bounded territories, but on the celebration and universal identification of culture at the individual level. Expanding the definition of World Heritage to include "living culture"—the one thing all groups possess, and the one thing that UNESCO wishes to celebrate equally amongst all societies—broadens the possibility of finding value in anything, tangible or not, as Kirshenblatt-Gimblett notes, and she calls on Cullen Murphy's cynical article for the *Atlantic Monthly* for an evocative illustration. Describing Alfonso Pecoraro Scanio's well-publicized and ultimately successful crusade to declare pizza a Masterpiece of World Heritage,[100] Murphy provides a list of other potential candidates for "intangible heritage" designations— candidates, it could be argued, that are even more universal in nature, such as "the white lie, the weekend, and the passive voice."[101]

But less cynically and more materially, including intangible instances of "living culture" as another, even more amorphously conceptual, building block of the heritage-scape broadens, too, the possibility of determining the "universal value" of any *place*. After all, these intangible practices endow an otherwise "empty" space with definition and significance; UNESCO even defines "intangible cultural heritage" as societies' "interaction with nature and their history." It is the very intangibility of worldviews and cultural perspectives that turn a physical space into a delimited place. Dialectically, it is a delimited place—the tangible locus of meaningful interaction—that likewise determines these very worldviews and cultural perspectives that UNESCO dubs "intangible cultural heritage," and which, they even point out, "provides them with a sense of identity and continuity." The creation of a new sense of identity, a new sense of temporal and spatial continuity in the minds of individuals across the globe, is the very purpose of the heritage-scape.

By formally establishing the concept of "intangible heritage," UNESCO comes full-circle, creating a cohesive heritage-scape that fuses the ephemeral and tangible expressions of culture. And indeed, true to form, now World Heritage sites can be interpreted as a mixture of all three kinds of world heritages, where tangible cultural and natural formations meld with intangible and living practice. Such is the case for the Angkor Archaeological Park, which UNESCO calls "a geographical region, an archaeological site and a cultural concept."[102] Not only is Angkor valued for its unique and influential material constructions, but for its ongoing living nature. It is a park—a vast and dynamic container of temple complexes, natural formations and cultural practices that expand over a vast distance and cover a broad period of use and disuse all fuse together in a representation of "outstanding universal value."

The heritage-scape is a useful model of UNESCO's globalization process because it affords the possibility of referencing actual geographic elements to illustrate its phenomenology. Indeed, at its core are tangible, albeit deterritorialized, places that are subsequently reintegrated into a new world system. The *deterritorialization* that occurs when such local places become World Heritage sites is what Anthony Giddens calls a "disembedding," or, a "lifting out of social relations from local contexts of interaction and their restructuring across indefinite spans of time and space."[103] It decouples traditional actors from geographic boundaries and recontextualizes them in a new environment whereby they are understood in relation to one another. Though each individual site may have been deterritorialized, they are not simply singular "decontextualized cultural capital" as heritage theorists such as Celia Lury have written; they are not blank slates to be gazed at in purely some aesthetic manner, devoid of discursive assumptions, value judgments or ideological claims.[104] Rather, to paraphrase Phillip Fischer, they will always possess a distinct set of traits that are dependent upon the "social scripts" in which they are found.[105] Indeed, UNESCO's meta-narrative claim, which points to some type of measurable "universal value" embodied within each distinct cultural manifestation, provides a necessary contextual framework whereby each site gains meaning from, and is understood in relation to, one another. The following chapter will explore this "social script"— this idealizing narrative articulation of the "universal value" evident in the heritage-scape's individual monuments—in greater detail.

CHAPTER THREE

UNITY IN DIVERSITY:
THE HERITAGE-SCAPE'S META-NARRATIVE CLAIM

Places are not simply physicalities. That is, places are more than merely the sum of their material characteristics; they encompass more than just their volume; they are seen beyond their aesthetic features. Places are also social. They are spaces imbued with meaning that extend from the material world and into the ephemeral realms of individual and collective memories. Socially agreed upon connotations, ideas, symbols, titles and meanings permeate places. As geographer Henri LeFebvre states, a place "underpins not only durable spatial arrangements but also representational spaces and their attendant imagery and mythic narratives"[1]—those webs of significance "which we ourselves have spun," in the words of Clifford Geertz.[2] According to Geertz, a group's culture consists of these overlapping, networked "webs of meaning," which themselves are ephemeral but are materially manifested through tangible structures and experiential rituals. Likening a society's culture to an "ensemble of texts,"[3] Geertz further highlights the fact that meaning is generated through a network of narrative understandings; as *texts*, culture can be perceived as overlapping interpretative accounts that are consistently modifying and reinterpreting themselves throughout time. These narratives are not historical fact, but rather actively selective ideological claims. Textually expressed in narrative form and materially manifested through monumentality, such claims are indeed the most important quality for the creation of Anderson's "imagined community"[4]—a community, which, despite disparate origins of its members, is cohesive through remembered understandings in the minds of collectivities. Such a community operates in the same fashion as the community that UNESCO wishes to construct within the parameters of its heritage-scape.

The heritage-scape is composed of such places. Be they natural landforms recognized for their beauty, biodiversity or mythic imagery; religious or civic spaces imbued with claims of power or legitimacy; or public structures expressly built for monumental expositions, each forms a locus of community that exists in the contemporary imagination of one or more social groups. Unifying these groups who are imaginatively congealed around singular places imbued with individual narrative claims, the heritage-scape requires an overarching meta-narrative claim to conceptually create a coherent sense of place amongst a complexity of often competing individual narratives spread across expansive swaths of space and even time. Mediated by memory, this understanding then inspires action between individuals and the place. Thus, although each monument may have its own divergent life history, when it is recontextualized with other like monuments under the heritage-scape's unifying meta-narrative, it becomes an ideal material manifestation of a carefully considered claim about the "universal value" of the world's cultural diversity. Such conceptual narratives are essential for ultimately constructing UNESCO's new sense of place "in the minds of men," as Halbwachs contends:

> The memory of groups contains many truths, notions, ideas and general propositions . . . but if a truth is to be settled in the memory of a group it needs to be presented in the concrete form of an event, of a personality or of a locality. . . . [In order for] these recollections to prosper and in time to be combined, they had to become saddled with images of persons and places, and to take on those traits that characterize a recollection and that are allowed to last. As to the facts, they become more prominent, and some of them gained salience in comparison to others.[5]

When they are remembered, narratives convert intangible notions, outlooks, truths and facts alike into meaning. It is this meaning that inspires human action. Indeed, sociologists such as James Wertsch have pointed to the "omnipresence and importance of narrative in human activity."[6] Calling Man a "story-telling animal," Alisdair MacIntyre demonstrates that identity is formed not simply through actual, physical experiences that occur within one's lifetime, but through the narratives made of them in one's memory. Authorship, however, is not essential; while these narratives can certainly be constructed through lived instances, these stories can also have been passed down generationally or transmitted horizontally from person to person. MacIntyre states that "there is no way to give us an understanding of any society, including our own, except through the stock of stories which constitute its initial dramatic resources."[7]

In the mind, nothing becomes something when a narrative is affixed to it; abstraction is concreted when it is inserted into a narrative. "Knowing" someone, for example, connotes that there has been a shared experience, a shared interaction, a shared narrative, with another person; "not knowing" somebody, on the other hand, indicates that the person's name makes no sense—it provides no narrative connection; it has no meaning. In most languages, the phrase "knowing of" someone exists as a midpoint between the two—here, no direct narrative experience is shared between the two people, but nevertheless one can draw forth from his memory some bits of related narrative in which the name was imbedded. There is some recognition, some meaning, albeit vague.

The same is true of placemaking. Pearson and Richards' eloquent statement is worth repeating here: "Through the cultural artifact of a name, undifferentiated space is transformed into marked and delimited place. Stories and tales may be attached to such places, making them resonate with history and experience."[8] A name etched into a tomb stone, a plaque denoting a famous person "slept here," or the title denoting to which saint a cathedral is dedicated, all immediately imbue an unknown space with a host of narrative claims and imagined imagery in an extraordinarily succinct manner.

For example, happening upon a mildly reflective, black granite slab sunken into a tree-lined ditch in Washington, DC's National Mall, an uninformed American tourist may very well pass it by with but a cursory look at its unusual aesthetic characteristics. Even if the visitor pauses up-close to note the numerous tiny names carefully imprinted upon the almost undulating stone, he still may not recognize its monumental value. Perhaps he would assign another, officially incorrect, meaning to the structure based on prior encounters with large commemorative plaques listing the names of benefactors to museums or public buildings—those often ostentatious commemorative signs immortalizing major donors who funded the restoration of a church, the construction of a museum, or the beautification of a park. As is especially the case with tourists, often the names, however significant they might be in some local or historical context, are completely foreign; they have no narrative meaning, and thus do not impart any added meaning to the site. How many people simply pass these by, with nary a second glance? Despite the good that came from these patrons' charity, the existence of the overlooked plaque would not change the overall experience of the site they helped to create. But if the visitor to this place notes and comprehends the name of the monument—the Vietnam Veterans Memorial—may suddenly change the place's significance in his mind. Images—perhaps burnt in the consciousness from actual combat experience, or perhaps created by living through such a time of turmoil and reading the newspaper's listing of the day's fallen, or perhaps seared in the mind after watching bloody cinematic depictions of the Vietnam War such as *Full Metal Jacket*, *Platoon* or *Apocalypse Now*—flow from the memory, commingling with the sights, sounds and even smells of the place. Imbuing the plain, granite memorial with evocative narrative claims, the title significantly alters the experience and the understanding of the site. It adds meaning.

Similarly, affixing the title "World Heritage site" also contributes to the meaning of the place. These three simple words immediately bring forth in the mind potent ideas, connotations and notions. Each of these words spark multiple memories and understandings that are at once collective and singular. To English speakers, for example, the word "World" has distinctive literal meaning. But in addition to common dictionary meanings, the actual imagery attached to this seemingly innocuous word varies vastly from person to person; one can think of textbook photographs, sketched panoramas, "natural" landforms or "cultural" constructions, or satellite imagery. The word may call forth particularly significant rememberings attached to news articles, romance novels, television documentaries, fictional films, evocative editorials or expressed political ideologies. Individuals could also affix certain personal encounters to the term as well, such as those garnered from leisure travel, anthropological fieldwork, international business, or wartime service. The same can be said for the words "heritage" and "site," as well. Yet when all of these words are put together, the meaning of this idiom does not simply become the sum of the three, but rather an expression of its own. It will also gain further remembered meaning when unique monumental natural and cultural sites become mentally linked to the term. Since there is an increasing variety of contexts in which one finds this title—from traveling to working in historic preservation, from reading literature extolling the virtues of a site to reading critical editorials concerning the ill effects of UNESCO's work— the meaning of UNESCO's title varies as much in complexity and connotation as the individuals who come to understand it. Therefore, the title garners a separate meaning that is distinctive from any other, which draws from the collective and singular understandings of each individual word, and also the title itself. The site to which the title refers, therefore, becomes imbued with such a dialectical formulation of meaning as well.

For example, the ancient Cham sanctuary of Mỹ Sơn, in its current state of disarray, might resemble a blackened pile of rubble to the most callous or unaware of travelers. Many of its lintels, statuary and aesthetic riches have been stripped from their physical location and placed in museums such as Đà Nẵng's Cham Museum or Paris' Musée Guimet, or sold to private collectors for display in their homes. What was left was seriously damaged by violent bombings during the Vietnam War. Considered so aesthetically un-evocative, or perhaps so undifferentiated from other structures seriously damaged during Vietnam's numerous wars in the contemporary era, most "cultural" tour operators did not even offer excursions to the site, reserving it as a locus for only the most adventurous of backpackers who wish to recreate an arduous journey of colonial discovery. For the latter, the allure of Mỹ Sơn was predicated more on the state of its ruins, located deep in the jungle confines of Vietnam and Laos, accessible only by motorbike or jeep over a rocky and unpaved road. Before its designation as a World Heritage site in 1999, Vietnamese tour operators would remark to their American travel planners that it was "not worth the trip." Yet this perception has been altered through a change in Mỹ Sơn's appellation. Now that it is deemed a World Heritage site, a whole host of other narrative claims and corresponding imagery can—and are—applied. People who have encountered the striking World Heritage sites of Stonehenge, Angkor Wat, Machu Picchu or even Venice now relate to Mỹ Sơn not as a primitive pile of damaged or pilfered rubble, but as akin to these other great loci of cultural innovation, worthy of celebration, interaction and study. Their desire to visit it increases, and the value of the experience of communing with such a World Heritage site is augmented. As a number of countries scramble to restore the crumbling edifices, academic research into Mỹ Sơn's design, use and traditional significances has begun anew, after a century hiatus. Simply through its new title, its meaning has changed. And this new meaning, in turn, has inspired new forms of meaningful interaction.

This consciousness, this memory, is fundamental in how action is determined and meaning is made of future situations. Wertsch states that

> a great deal of thinking, speaking and other forms of action are fundamentally shaped by narratives. We are especially "story-telling animals" when it comes to recounting and interpreting our own and others' actions—the motives that lie behind them, the settings in which they occur, the outcomes they produce, and so forth.[9]

Paul Connerton also illustrates this point at the most elemental level:

> More fundamentally, it is that in all modes of experience we always base our particular experiences on a prior context in order to ensure that they are intelligible at all; that prior to any single experience, our mind is already predisposed with a framework of outlines, of typical shapes of experienced objects. To perceive an object or act upon it is to locate it within this system of expectations. The world of the percipient, defined in terms of temporal experience, is an organized body of expectations based on recollection.[10]

Over time, more events will occur in a person's life based on these actions, and therefore an ever-increasing collection of memories will deepen one's consciousness. Scientists agree with this assessment, stating that every perceived experience enters into the mind through a series of synapses; as psychologist

George Johnson states, "in a matter of seconds, new circuits are formed that can change forever the way you think about the world."[11] Simply reading these words, just like simply looking at a World Heritage site or gazing out the window, builds upon the previous understandings of the world at least in some small way.

Yet while the physical processes in the brain might build upon each other, Connerton's above-mentioned comment is important—memory is used to frame and make meaning of current experiences. Thus, it is important to note that memory is not simply a cumulative, concretized thing but

> a process in which a new experience is first perceived, evaluated, and then made meaningful within a preexisting context. . . . [One] person's memory at work, [entails] not just accessing and reproducing stored memories in some mechanical manner but actively recollecting, in the literal sense of "re-collecting" and thus selecting and emending, his past experience.[12]

Essential to memory's iterative process is its active selectivity, whereby previous understandings frame the way in which the individual makes meaning and remembers new events. In the course of the life history of the monument, the current collective understanding about the site will undoubtedly underscore certain aspects of its total history that adhere to the over-arching collective narrative claim, and simultaneously de-emphasize those factual occurrences that are problematic to the same claim. Indeed, Yael Zerubavel states,

> a dual process of 'recovery' thus takes place at one and the same time: while some aspects of the past are uncovered or shift from the margins to the center of our historical consciousness, other aspects of the past are marginalized or fade into oblivion. Any remembrance thus entails its own forgetfulness, as the two are interwoven in the process of producing the commemorative narratives."[13]

Framing each World Heritage site in such a way as to underscore its particular universal value, the heritage-scape's meta-narrative often seeks to "forget" or underplay contentious aspects of the place's own life-history and attendant narrative claims—elements often marked with tragedy, cultural intolerance or conflict—which would undercut the heritage-scape's unifying, peacemaking ideals. Indeed, out of the almost one thousand World Heritage sites, there are but a handful of "negative World Heritage sites"—monuments designated specifically as exemplars of the destructive nature of war and cultural intolerance, such as the Auschwitz concentration camp (designated in 1978), Hiroshima's Genbaku "A-Bomb" Dome (designated in 1996), and, most recently, the empty spaces where Afghanistan's Bamiyan Buddhas once stood (designated in 2003).[14] Even in these examples, however, there is a marked attempt to put a unifying spin on the narrative by downplaying the specifics of battle in favor of generalities concerning humankind and the need to create world peace.

Indeed, until the recent designation of the Bamiyan Valley, these negative World Heritage sites were already framed within the narrative context of a World War—a conflict that supposedly subsumed all people throughout the world—rather than in specific contexts of genocide or of conflicts between singular nation-states. The fact that Afghanistan's Bamiyan Buddhas, which were long recognized as symbols of the commingling of cultures across the historic Silk Road, were designated after the September 11, 2001 terrorist attacks rendered terrorism a "global epidemic" that required all nations to conduct a global "war on terror," only furthers this assertion.[15] Indeed, at UNESCO's Thirty-first General Conference on September 12, 2001—just one day after the terrorist attacks on the World Trade Center and exactly six months after the Buddhas' destruction—UNESCO's Director-General called the Taliban's act a "crime against the common heritage of humanity."[16]

Describing Auschwitz, the infamous Nazi concentration camp, as "the symbol of humanity's cruelty to its fellow human beings in the 20th century," UNESCO inscribed the property as Poland's first World Heritage site in 1979. It was based only on criterion *vi*, which requires a site "to be directly or tangibly associated with events or living traditions, with ideas, or with beliefs, with artistic and literary works of outstanding universal significance," although the World Heritage Committee expressly states that this criterion "should preferably be used in conjunction with other criteria." Calling Auschwitz "the largest cemetery in the world: 4 million persons of all nationalities (sent from 24 different countries, and among these, so many Jews), were systematically starved, tortured and assassinated," ICOMOS justifies the "outstanding universal significance" of the deadly events that took place within its walls as "one of the greatest crimes . . . against humanity," and thus applicable for designation:

> vi. Auschwitz-Birkenau, monument to the martyrdom and resistance of millions of men, women and children, is not a historical museum in the usual sense of the word; it bears irrefutable and concrete witness to one of the greatest crimes which has been perpetrated against humanity; the example, by excellence, which undeniably elucidated an essential aspect of that historical phenomenon which is Hitlerism. The Museum of Auschwitz-Birkenau, through its numerous activities (films, lectures, publications, expositions, etc...) [sic] has brought to the public the political, historical and psychological processes rise the establishment and utilisation of the extermination camps of the Third Reich

[sic]. Moreover, its organizers are in hope that this project, supported by such terrible proof, will contribute to the maintenance of world peace.[17]

It would be easy, no doubt, to level the blame squarely on fascism and its collaborators in general, the Nazi party, or Hitler; after all, the perpetrators can fall into one of these categories. Like so many of today's films, museums and literature, it would be likewise easy to contextualize their horrific actions as per-petuated against the Jewish people, for they were the greatest majority of the victims. While still acknowledging these, ICOMOS nevertheless downplays the specifics in favor of the universal significance. It is a "monument"—a "remem-bering device"—to the martyrdom of "men, women and children," rather than to specific kinds of people. Likewise, it bears witness to the horrific crime "against humanity," not against Europeans, non-Germans, or Jews. Finally, ICOMOS also notes the sentiments expressed by the site's curators that it will "contribute to the maintenance of *world* peace."

As a World Heritage site, Hiroshima's Genbaku Dome imparts similar uni-versalized sentiments, both in UNESCO's documentation and in on-site visits. The only surviving structure of the United State's atomic attack on the industrial Japanese city in 1945, which killed not only Japanese nationals but numerous conscripted Korean prisoners, the "A-Bomb" Dome was preserved as aestheti-cally close to how it looked in the immediate aftermath of the American raid. However, perhaps in typical Japanese fashion, there is no reference whatsoever to either of these countries or its leaders whose direct actions led to such de-struction, but rather only to a "tragic Situation" pertaining to "mankind," and the need to eliminate "all" such weapons "on earth":

> Firstly, the Hiroshima Peace Memorial, Genbaku Dome, stands as a permanent witness to the terrible disaster that occurred when the atomic bomb was used as a weapon for the first time in the history of mankind. Secondly, the Dome itself is the only building in existence that can convey directly a physical image of the tragic Situation immediately after the bombing. Thirdly, the Dome has be-come a universal monument for all mankind, symbolizing the hope for Perpet-ual peace and the ultimate elimination of ail nuclear weapons on earth.[18]

Stating that the actual building possesses "no aesthetic or architectural sig-nificance," ICOMOS nevertheless outlines a meticulous, three paragraph history of the monument from its proposal in 1910, its design in 1914 by the Czech ar-chitect Jan Letzel, its renaming in 1933 and finally its ultimate destruction "when the first atomic bomb exploded over Hiroshima." Although it includes the precise date and time, and specifies the number of casualties—"8:15 AM on 6 August 1945, causing the deaths of 140,000 people"—it makes no mention of whom these aggressors or victims were. Rather, it focuses on the worldwide effects of the bomb, as well as the peace that supposedly followed:

> The overriding Significance of the Dome lies in what it represents: the building has no aesthetic or architectural significance per se. Its mute remains symbolize on the one hand the ultimate in human destruction but on the other they communicate a message of hope for a continuation in perpetuity of the worldwide Peace that the atomic bomb blasts of August 1945 ushered in.[19]

Yet illustrative of the inherently conflictual nature of such a war site, both China and the United States issued statements questioning the appropriateness of such a designation. The United States, perpetrator of the act, issued the following dissociation:

> The United States is dissociating itself from today's decision to inscribe the Genbaku Dome on the World Heritage List. The United States and Japan are close friends and allies. We cooperate on security, diplomatic, international and economic affairs around the world. Our two countries are tied by deep personal friendships between many Americans and Japanese. Even so, the United States cannot support its friend in this inscription. The United States is concerned about the lack of historical perspective in the nomination of Genbaku Dome. The events antecedent to the United States' use of atomic weapons to end World War II are key to understanding the tragedy of Hiroshima. Any examination of the period leading up to 1945 should be placed in the appropriate historical context. The United States believes the inscription of war sites outside the scope of the Convention. We urge the Committee to address the question of the suitability of war sites for the World Heritage List.[20]

Site managers at Hiroshima nevertheless attempt to convey a universalized, non-conflicting sentiment in line with UNESCO's verbiage. While the museum features extraordinarily poignant artifacts—including numerous photographs, melted glass, deformed children's' toys and even a staircase with a silhouetted imprint that naturally occurred when a person, unexpectedly sitting on the steps, was instantaneously vaporized in the attack—it steers as clear as possible from placing blame on, or from mourning, specific groups. Even its exhibit on the events that lead up to the dropping of the bomb, which naturally mentioned the Japanese Imperial Army's conflict with Korea, China and the United States, as well as the American response, the inventors of the bomb, and the Enola Gay aircraft that dropped it, is decidedly non-conflictual and always refers back to the overriding meta-narrative of world peace and the need to eliminate all such weapons from the earth. To the astute observer, it certainly seemed as if the memorial and the museum were "re-writing" the memory a bit, reframing it in a global perspective and effectively downplaying the specific circle of violent causes-and-effects between the Japanese and the Americans that so often bog down memorials of the type.

But memory is an individual and procuessual phenomenon that requires time and new experiences to rewrite, as I realized when accompanying a group of American senior citizens to Hiroshima in April 2001. Most, if not all, lived through World War II and brought to the site their memories of not only the American attack on Hiroshima, but the Japanese attack on Pearl Harbor—which was not mentioned in the exhibit. While many were affected by the sheer horror of the violence and poignantly were grasped by the universality of the message, a number of widows whose husbands either fought on the Pacific Front or who served in Japan as occupying forces immediately after Emperor Hirohito's surrender angrily accosted me. Calling the visit "inappropriate," some asked, "Why do they have to make us feel so bad? It was their fault; they deserved it," or, "they attacked Pearl Harbor first," or "it saved millions of American lives." Clearly the individual memories of living through the experience and loving people whose lives were intimately connected with the dropping of the bomb were quite more vivid, such that they were used to frame and make meaning of the site in a way that ignored the alternative narrative claims conveyed by UNESCO and the site's managers. Although UNESCO and the curators left out the "whodunit" to foster a sense of universal blame, remembering that the American military—and, by extension, their husbands and friends—dropped the bomb in retaliation for the Japanese atrocities committed during the war, the widows inserted these remembered facts into UNESCO's blank space, making meaning of it in their own way. The discrepancies between what UNESCO did not say and what they remembered were also the root of these visitors' strong and negative reactions; only did they insert their own identities into the narrative of "who dropped the bomb," but they expected the Japanese to apologetically take more of the blame for the events leading up to the attack. Similarly, these women most likely had not ever committed the images of Hiroshima's aftermath to memory—but rather of the celebrations in America of the peace that quickly followed, or of the horrors of Pearl Harbor's and Iwo Jima's aftermaths—the realization that the Japanese suffered as well was too striking.

Yet for those who did not benefit from having such vivid memories and strong remembered experiential connections, the universalizing and peace-inspiring narrative claims were very effective in conveying the heritage-scape's mission: to create a unifying peace in the minds of men. Large groups of tourists from around the world flock to Hiroshima even though it takes hours from Kyoto, the nearest major "tourist city" in Western Japan. Many of them wait silently to personally ring the Peace Bell hanging in view of the A-Bomb Dome.

World Leaders, too, pay homage to the hopes of peace in often highly ritualized and ceremonious visits to the memorialized place. And inspired by the now-mythological story of Sadako Sasaki, a child who tried to fold a thousand origami cranes (*senbazuru*)[21] to cure the deadly cancer she developed from the fall-out, school children from around the world continue to mail origami cranes to Hiroshima, which are hung on the Children's Memorial. So many are sent in her memory that the site's curators must ritually remove and burn them once a week to make space for the next wave of paper birds.

As visitors' reactions at Hiroshima reveal, these negative World Heritage sites are emotionally charged, and inspire sometimes conflicting associations of guilt. While Japan, a United States ally, is careful in its mitigation of guilt claims, politics surrounding Poland and Germany would produce an intriguing change in Auschwitz's nomenclature. Eager to distance itself from the guilt surrounding the Nazi concentration camp's atrocities, which was first directed towards Polish nationals, the Republic of Poland argued at the 2006 World Heritage Committee meeting in Vilnius, Lithuania that the site should change its name "in order to promote adequate historical understanding of its creation"[22]—that is, to clearly separate the site's host country from the regime that perpetuated Auschwitz's crimes. At the next annual meeting in Christchurch, New Zealand in June 2007, the World Heritage Committee granted Poland's request to change the name of this World Heritage site from "Auschwitz Concentration Camp" to "Auschwitz Birkenau: German Nazi Concentration and Extermination Camp (1940–1945)." Unlike the negative World Heritage sites of Bamiyon or Hiroshima, which do not in their titles mention the perpetrators, such a subtle rewording places blame on the specific party who committed the atrocities. In a revised "Statement of Significance," which accompanied the name change, the World Heritage Committee also noted the victims with specificity:

> Auschwitz-Birkenau was the principal and most notorious of the six concentration and extermination camps established by Nazi Germany to implement its Final Solution policy which had as its aim the mass murder of the Jewish people in Europe. Built in Poland under Nazi German occupation initially as a concentration camp for Poles and later for Soviet prisoners of war, it soon became a prison for a number of other nationalities. Between the years 1942–1944 it became the main mass extermination camp where Jews were tortured and killed for their so-called racial origins. In addition to the mass murder of well over a million Jewish men, women and children, and tens of thousands of Polish victims, Auschwitz also served as a camp for the racial murder of thousands of Roma and Sinti and prisoners of several European nationalities. [23]

While the universalizing justification remains inherent for Auschwitz, such a concentrated effort at specificity may serve to discursively diminish its appeal to "unity in diversity," rendering it an example of a contained historical moment.

When evaluating the rationale for the designation of Vietnam and Cambodia's World Heritage Sites, this "forgetting" of several portions of each place's total life histories is evident, albeit, in some cases, more subtle than others. In the case of historic Hội An, a multicultural trading port that welcomed representatives from both the East and the West over the course of its existence, the historic commingling of various, and often contentious, cultures into a seemingly seamless polity appears to lend itself well to UNESCO's "universality" claim. One can simply walk the dusty streets of this small town and pass a Cantonese meeting house, a home of a Vietnamese artisanal family, a French colonial mansion, and a vermillion Japanese covered bridge all in the course of but a few minutes, recognizing those elements in UNESCO's designation to be clearly evident:

> *Criterion ii:*   Hoi An is an outstanding material manifestation of the fusion of
> cultures over time in an international commercial port.
>
> *Criterion v:*   Hoi An is an exceptionally well preserved example of a tradi-
> tional Asian trading port.[24]

However, upon a more subtle walking tour—one in which American tour operators are especially loathe to allow their visitors to take—Hội An's visitor might happen into the present community's small public museum aptly named the "Hội An Museum" in their English-language brochures. Hội An *Museum*— the *museum* of the town of Hội An. The ever-so-unimaginative, yet carefully chosen name, seems to conjure up expectations of UNESCO's universalist claim in much the same way the pleasant stroll down its quaint streets do. And indeed, upon entering the small and nondescript edifice, these expectations are swiftly met. A single room displays elements from the community's recent history, including photographs, tools and Imari-style, white-and-blue pottery left from either Japanese or Portuguese traders. The narrative claim of peaceful coexistence amongst differing cultural groups seems quite in order, until a representative of the museum will undoubtedly ask if the visitor has seen the room upstairs. Motioning to a staircase so narrow it seems to be a ladder, half with a smirk and half with knowing pride, the representative urges the visitor upward, where he is met with a similarly nondescript room. The contents in this room, however, is striking in its anti-American feel. Glass cases, lined with photographs of the brave men and women of the village who fought a secret, yet bloody, resistance to the American imperialists, display the tools of the Viet

Minh opposition coupled with captured American weaponry. Tales, carefully written in English for the benefit of Western visitors, extol the virtues of Viet Cong spies and of those allied with Ho Chi Minh's northern forces in the "American War." Suddenly the visitor does not seem quite as accepted into the "universalism" claim that this museum—as the official "Hội An Museum" of the Hội An World Heritage Site—is supposed to espouse. Yet a visit to this museum is extremely worthwhile, for only here exists the unfiltered feelings of many contemporary Hội An residents—residents who, by simply being who they are in the place they are in, have contributed to the life history of this monumental town and, in essence, guided it to World Heritage status.

The United States' war in Vietnam is certainly something that UNESCO's non-conflictual, peace-making narrative claim is eager to forget, for its devastating impact is still felt on both sides of the Pacific, and still colors individuals' understanding of the significances of these places and of these cultures. The horrors incurred in the "American War" are even more materially manifested in a visit to Huế, not more than a two-hour drive from Hội An up through the stunningly beautiful Hải Vân Pass. According to the advisory body, ICOMOS, the imperial capitol of Vietnam's last ruling dynasty, Huế City, as a World Heritage Site is representative of the monumental power and authority of not only an autonomous Vietnamese people, but also of a flourishing "Eastern feudal capital" like that in Beijing, Nanjing, Kyoto, and other similar places:

> *Criterion iii:*   Hue represents an outstanding demonstration of the power of the
> vanished Vietnamese feudal empire at its apogee in the early
> 19th century.
> *Criterion iv:*   The complex of Hue monuments is an outstanding example of
> an eastern feudal capital.[25]

On paper, Huế and its Imperial Purple City sounds romantically mysterious and exotic, with visions of grandiose Mandarin-style imperial buildings on par with its prototype, Beijing's imposing Forbidden City. Indeed, arriving by either land or river at its expansive plaza surrounded on one end by an imposing Citadel boasting the tallest flagpole in the country and an equally large Imperial gate on the other, one expects the experience to mirror these expectations. Passing through the thick-walled, imperial Ngọ Môn Gate, the visitor even has the opportunity to climb to its top, where he is greeted at one end by a picturesque view of the plaza, the Citadel, the lovely Perfume River (Hương Giang), and a regal red-and-yellow-starred flag flapping defiantly in the wind from the 37-meter high flag tower, dubbed the "King's Knight" by foreigners. At the other end, the visitor can see an equally vast interior plaza, striking in its size and proportion, extending from a wide lotus-filled moat to the Palace of Supreme Harmony, or Điện Thái Hòa. Because of the length of the piazza and because this view is bordered by the greenery of dense trees as far as the eye can see, the viewer cannot see how far into the horizon the palace extends, or what other regal buildings might delight him. Eagerly, he walks down the gate past placards extolling the virtuous history of the city, over the placid moat on the Trung Đạo Bridge, up a series of stairs, across the wide square and into the strangely Oriental building.

He is once again contented. Darkness fills the room and incense fills the nostrils as the visitor is met with the sight of a long throne room, its low ceiling held up by eighty thick pilasters lacquered a deep red. Velvet museum ropes corner off the elevated throne, which the Emperor used during state occasions to receive homage from his mandarins,, but nevertheless the visitor can see its elegant gildings. After exploring the spacious throne room, he walks towards the light streaming in from a door at the right hand side. In the center of this narrow room, which opens to the Forbidden Purple City outside, stands a scale model of the entire complex—or, rather, how it looked at the height of the Nguyễn dynasty—further enticing the visitor with the expectation of exploring an extensive and wonder-filled complex of imperial buildings. Sunlight streams in from the narrow doorway, revealing two immense bronze urns, beckoning him to continue his exploration.

Stepping outside into the light, however, he is met with a surprise: vast emptiness.

The visitor realizes that the Forbidden Purple City was almost completely destroyed during the Tet Offensive in 1968. Unexpectedly attacking the South Vietnamese city, Ho Chi Minh's Communist forces defiantly raised their flag from the Citadel's tower, overthrew Huế's government, and implemented a detailed and pre-planned house-to-house search to round up all suspected South Vietnamese loyalists. In the twenty five days that Communists ruled Huế—the only city to be held by Ho Chi Minh's forces for over a few days—more than three thousand merchants, Catholic priests, Buddhist monks, government officials, intellectuals and travelers were summarily shot, clubbed to death or buried alive. But the violence had just begun. In an attempt to dislodge Ho Chi Minh's forces, South Vietnamese aerial units dropped bombs on Huế for over ten days, leveling whole blocks and forcing the Viet Cong into retreat inside the Citadel and its Forbidden Purple City, where two-thirds of the civilian population had taken cover. Aided by these devastating air strikes, United States forces shelled the Citadel, and the Viet Cong responded in kind as brutal house-to-house fighting ensued, destroying the city and killing over 10,000 people. And so today, walking out of the Palace and into the plaza, the visitor stands between two immense urns—some of the only objects to survive the bloodshed. His back to the palace, reminiscent of so much past grandeur, he looks forward to the deep emptiness. Bullet holes can still be seen in the crumbled concrete, and scattered about the empty space, a few buildings—mostly in skeletal form—stand blackened as a testimonial to the violent and deadly duplicity that was the Vietnam War.

And yet UNESCO has forgotten this event, monumental if not for its tragic loss of civilian life or of its brother-against-brother narrative, but for the devastating impression it has wrought on a building complex supposedly of such "outstanding universal value." Viewing such bullet-ridden destruction, such nothingness, the symbolism seems fresh and clear, and quite antithetical to UNESCO's claim—especially to the Western visitor who has seen combat footage or even fictitious Hollywood accounts of the Tet Offensive such as that in *Full Metal Jacket*. Despite what the Truman Doctrine espoused or what President Nixon may have said, the Vietnam War, at least for the Vietnamese, was not a global contestation, a worldwide fight against communism. For many Vietnamese, it was another event in a long progression of combat against the Chinese, the Cham, the Khmer, the French, the Japanese and the Americans—certainly not a global event. This is extremely problematic for UNESCO's universalizing claims. And so in its designation and its literature, UNESCO "forgets" this tragic event, one that still is raw and visually evident when experiencing this World Heritage site. Utilizing the expertise of foreign preservationists and local experts alike, UNESCO is also rebuilding the site, brick by brick, from scratch. Returning nearly every year since 2001—when farmers were still tilling the tiled remains of the Forbidden Purple City into vegetable gardens—I have noticed new re-creations slowly rising. The library is rebuilt and now houses a gift shop. The Halls of the Mandarins are freshly painted. Formal gardens are being replanted. Even students from the nearby university stop to talk to Western visitors, trying to practice their English or French in an ultimate sign of cultural interchange. Soon, the World Heritage site will not so readily reveal the scars of its destruction, but will hide its history of violence. Further aided by a narrative that makes no mention of the Tet Offensive, the future visitor will truly be able to see those qualities of "universal value" for which it was designated, overlooking the full truth of its life history. In turn, the monument will also "forget" its pain—at least to the public eye.

Wartime tragedy is not the only theme that the heritage-scape seeks to forget. UNESCO's individual designations also focus on eliminating any type of contentious narrative claims. Since these conflictual and interpretative claims historically occur after the site's construction, UNESCO most often solely focuses on the "universal value" evident at the time of the monument's construction, aiming to forget subsequent events in its complete life-history. Thus, most often these monuments are designated, at least in part, because they are thought to reveal important insights into the culture that constructed it. Indeed, two-thirds of the designating criteria focus on the aesthetic or architectural symbolism of the site. Even though the designations of Masada and Mỹ Sơn touch upon cultural interactivity, for example, they also discuss their architectural relevance. Even Angkor's designation "forgets" the contestation, violence and abandonment that comprised so much of these Cambodian temples' lives. Nothing is said of the Cham army's innovative and unprecedented attack on Angkor, which was a highly notable military feat in the history of Southeast Asia. Furthermore, scarcely a mention is made of the monuments' life-histories after they were almost completely abandoned in the fourteenth century, despite their importance in claims of Thai and French colonial legitimacy in Southeast Asia, and also the unique melding of nature and culture that makes so many of the temples popular to visit today:

> The Angkor complex represents the entire range of Khmer art from the 9th to the 14th centuries, and includes a number of indisputable artistic masterpieces (e.g. Angkor Vat, the Bayon, Banteay Srei).
>
> (i) The influence of Khmer art, as developed at Angkor, was a profound one over much of the south-east Asia and played a fundamental role in its distinctive evolution.
>
> (ii) The Khmer Empire of the 9th-14th centuries encompassed much of Southeast Asia and played a formative role in the political and cultural development of the region. All that remains of that civilization is its rich heritage of cult structures in brick and stone.
>
> (iii) Khmer architecture evolved largely from the Indian sub-continent, from which it soon became clearly distinct as it developed its own special characteristics, some independently evolved and other acquired from neighboring cultural traditions. The result was a new artistic horizon in oriental art and architecture.[26]

Clearly, the "universal value" of these particular Angkorian monuments rests in their exemplary nature of ancient Khmer culture and its role in shaping the region's political, social and artistic "evolution." Despite UNESCO's reasoning, it may still be unclear exactly how these vestiges of the Khmer empire—which are "all that remains of that civilization"—are markers of cultural universality.

The idea that there exists a universalism amongst disparate cultures seems to border dangerously close to the Modernization theories of the past century or so. These theories implicitly draw on the Enlightenment-era conception of human progress as well as Darwinian evolutionary notions of "descent with modi-fication"—that complex creatures evolve from more simplistic organisms over time[27]—and see all peoples in various stages of cultural transformation move towards a more developed, universal and "modern" culture. The extreme exam-ple of such a social evolutionist was Lewis Henry Morgan, who in 1877 pub-lished a treatise on the "Line of Human Progress from Savagery through Barba-rism to Civilization." This title clearly reveals his argument: that all cultures can be conceptualized as sitting on individual rungs of a uni-linear evolutionary lad-der.[28] Theorists the likes of Marx and Engels were quick to pick up on this no-tion, as were "capitalistic" colonials. Modernization proponents, who undertake the perspective "as if there were no concrete relationships between societies, let alone the possibility that over and beyond the phenomenon of societal interac-tion there was a global circumstance *per se*,"[29] propose that all cultures are linked in their desire for social development into a rational, capitalistic form of civilization.[30] In this vein, ethnographers like Morgan would look for similarities among cultures to determine the evolutionary progress of Mankind as a single entity, a single civilization; differences would be considered hierarchically as indicative of the stage of progression in which the culture found itself.

ICOMOS' evaluation of the World Heritage site of Mỹ Sơn seems to con-vey this idea. Out of the five criteria outlined as necessary for UNESCO's World Heritage designation, the advisory body notes only two. However, both of the criteria convey a sense of "cultural interchange," of evolution and cultural commingling:

Criterion ii: The My Son Sanctuary is an exceptional example of cultural in-terchange, with the introduction of the Hindu architecture of the Indian sub-continent into South-East Asia.

Criterion iii: The Champa Kingdom was an important phenomenon in the political and cultural history of South-East Asia, vividly illus-trated by the ruins of My Son.[31]

From ICOMOS' criteria above, it seems that Mỹ Sơn represents a particular phase in the unitary progression of "cultural history of South-East Asia." Crite-ria ii more exactly pinpoints this stage as the point in which Hindu architecture from the Indian sub-continent was introduced into this region, as if it occurred in a particular delimited instance. From the criteria, it seems that the vaguely cohe-sive "South-east Asian" culture was transformed in a synchronic bout of "cul-tural interchange" from an outside source (India), rather than diachronically over time and in accordance with a variety of diverse encounters and experiences. More problematic is the notion of "cultural interchange" utilized here. Though this term conveys a vague sense of give-and-take among different cultural groups, ICOMOS does not reveal what, if anything, the totalized culture of "South-east Asia" could have 'given' the Indian sub-continent in exchange. The exchange appears rather unidirectional. UNESCO seems to clarify this point in a subtle yet revelatory re-writing of ICOMOS's criteria in its official proclamation:

> *Criterion ii*:   The My Son Sanctuary is an exceptional example of cultural in-terchange, with an indigenous society *adapting to external cul-tural influences*, notably the Hindu art and architecture of the Indian sub-continent.
>
> *Criterion iii*:   The Champa Kingdom was an important phenomenon in the po-litical and cultural history of South-East Asia, vividly illustrated by the ruins of My Son.[32]

In their reworking of Mỹ Sơn's criteria for designation, UNESCO qualifies ICOMOS' assertion that the site exemplifies cultural interchange. "Cultural interchange" connotes that there exist two equal groups, mutually engaged in a cultural give-and-take where knowledge, tools and ideas are passed equally from one to another. It implies a melding of various webs of significances, producing two entirely new webs based upon threads introduced by the other. It therefore reveals a conceptualization of the iterative process in which cultures are constantly engaged. However, UNESCO describes it differently, as "an indigenous society adapting to external cultural influences . . . from the Indian sub-continent." Suddenly, this does not sound like interchange at all. Rather, this specification seems quite unidirectional. One society, coming from the Indian sub-continent, imposes its culture upon another. It transfers or transmits—rather than exchanges—ideas and tools disproportionately from one to the other. There is no mutual exchange of webs, no give-and-take, but rather, a stronger outside authority captures the indigenes in its own web of significance—making it more complex than when it started. UNESCO's qualification seems to convey that a stronger, more developed culture requires the weaker to change, lest it perish entirely. To survive, the indigenous society must evolve, much like the tortoises and finches Charles Darwin observed on Galapagos Island. Rather than connoting a continual process of sharing and exchanging, UNESCO's qualifier indicates an evolutionary progression towards some universal culture, which, steamrolling itself through time and space, subsumes and develops all others.

The great German-born American anthropologist Franz Boas had, in fact, argued vehemently against such nineteenth century evolutionists for much of his career on this very point. While evolutionist ethnologists such as Otis Mason and John Wesley Powell suggested, as UNESCO seems to suggest in this case, that culture can be transmitted uni-directionally in accordance to the power or weakness of a particular group on the evolutionary chain towards modernity,[33] Boas points out that all cultures in a given geographic area are products of foreign influences. Conducting fieldwork for the British Association in the U.S. Pacific Northwest between 1888 and 1897, Boas found that the mythologies of two tribes, though diverse in cultural forms and political power, were "not of native growth, but—partly at least—borrowed . . . , being grafted upon mythologies of various tribes."[34] He continues:

> Wherever geographic continuity of the area of distribution of a complex ethnographical phenomenon is found, the laws of probability exclude the theory that in this continuous area the complex phenomenon has arisen independently in various places; but they compel us to assume that the distribution of this phenomenon in its present complex form is due to dissemination, while its composing elements may have originated here and there.[35]

The prominent Boasian expert George Stocking, Jr., summarizes Boas' important contention as combating evolutionist notions on two fronts. First, culture is "simply an accidental accretion of foreign material." Such accretion is not unidirectional, but inevitably dialectical. Second, although Boas renounced the concept of a culture's independent, organic growth, he also argued that culture is a form of "integrated spiritual totality" that "somehow conditioned the form of its elements."[36] Indeed, Boas eloquently summarizes culture's two-fold dynamic when he writes in the same report for the British Association,

> [I]t follows that the mythologies of the various tribes as we find them now are not organic growths, but have gradually developed and obtained their present form by accretion of foreign material. Much of this material must have been adopted ready made, and *has been adapted and changed in form according to the genius of the people who borrowed it.*[37]

Boas' selection of the word "genius" is important. It grants dignity and respect, not to mention agency, to the borrowing culture. Most importantly, it combats the prevalent notion that the "native mind" is somehow less evolved and thus incapable of everyday "genius."[38] Even the least powerful of societies do not sit passively and absorb the cultural forms from another group, but "borrow" them, integrate them, recontextualized them and reshape them. In short, not only does exchange happen, but it is not a forced or passive one, and in the process, the cultures modify each others' borrowed forms in different ways, in accordance to their own needs for continuity and understanding—making them intimately their own.

Unity in Diversity

Like Darwinian evolutionists and Modernization theorists, then, at first glance UNESCO also seems to espouse this notion of some homogeneous cultural progression in which all peoples are engaged to a varying degree. This seems to be especially true in its foundational documents, which not only refer to "culture" in the singular, but also juxtapose it with an equally singular idea of "nature." These documents seem to assert that there is one natural world, and there is likewise one world culture; "natural" or "cultural" forms that are designated as indicative of some heritage of the world would therefore be able to be universally applied. The World Heritage Convention's Mission Statement, in fact, defines the world's "cultural heritage" as those sites deemed to possess some "outstanding universal value":

> What makes the concept of World Heritage exceptional is its universal application. World Heritage sites belong to all the peoples of the world, irrespective of the territory on which they are located. . . . How does a World Heritage site differ from a site of national heritage? The key lies in the words 'outstanding universal value' . . . Sites selected for World Heritage listing are approved on the basis of their merits as the best possible examples of the [world's] cultural and natural heritage.[39]

In its insistence on evaluating tangible cultural artifacts based on the merit of some "universal value," it may seem that UNESCO wishes to draw out similarities between cultures that could comprise one universal culture, perhaps based on these evolutionary notions. Yet analyzing the disparate monuments UNESCO designates as World Heritage sites, in an attempt to ascertain what these "universal values" or similarities could be, only explicit differences emerge.

Cultural difference is the cornerstone of today's commonly accepted ethnographic theories that see not one universal culture, but a plurality of diverse and ever-changing cultures that vary even within a particular society.[40] Each distinct culture represents a perfect example of those "webs of significance" that Clifford Geertz calls "patterns of meanings embodied in symbols"[41] and Victor Turner describes as a society's "total system of meanings."[42] Such symbols—in this case, built structures—inspire action and have their own elaborate systems of meanings that do not necessarily mean the same thing outside their particular cultural context. As an "ensemble of texts, themselves ensembles, which the anthropologist strains to read over the shoulders of those to whom they properly belong,"[43] a culture is dynamic and is richly layered in strata of interpretation.

Yet instead of leading to some master culture, these interpretations can only reveal previously hidden cultural dimensions, which complexify one's understanding of the world's cultural diversity.

UNESCO talks of the world's cultural difference just as much as it talks of the world's cultural universality. The same Mission Statement, in which UNESCO underscores the "universal value" of World Heritage over just national or regional heritage, also discusses the "diversity of mankind's creations." Immediately following the citation: "Sites selected for World Heritage listing are approved on the basis of their merits as the best possible examples of the [world's] cultural and natural heritage," the Mission Statement continues: "the World Heritage List draws attention to the wealth and diversity of Earth's cultural and natural heritage."[44] Diversity of culture is furthermore underscored in the *Universal Declaration of Cultural Diversity* passed immediately after the September 11, 2001 terrorist attacks on the United States. Of interest here is that UNESCO begins to speak of "culture" not in the singular, but in the plural. Arguing against the prevailing rhetoric of a "clash of cultures and of civilizations,"[45] Koïchiro Matsura, the Director-General of UNESCO, stated that the new Declaration

> was an opportunity for States to reaffirm their conviction that intercultural dialogue is the best guarantee of peace and to reject outright the theory of the inevitable clash of cultures and civilizations. Such a wide-ranging instrument is a first for the international community. It raises cultural diversity to the level of "the common heritage of humanity", "as necessary for humankind as biodiversity is for nature" and makes its defense an ethical imperative indissociable from respect for the dignity of the individual. The Declaration aims both to preserve cultural diversity as a living, and thus renewable, treasure that must not be perceived as being unchanging heritage but as a process guaranteeing the survival of humanity; and to prevent segregation and fundamentalism which, in the name of cultural differences, would sanctify those differences and so counter the message of the Universal Declaration of Individual Rights.[46]

Article 1 of the Declaration emphasizes the necessity of global cultural diversity, stating:

> Culture takes diverse forms across time and space. This diversity is embodied in the uniqueness and plurality of the identities of the groups and societies making up humankind. As a source of exchange, innovation and creativity, cultural diversity is as necessary for humankind as biodiversity is for nature. In this sense, it is the common heritage of humanity and should be recognized and affirmed for the benefit of present and future generations.[47]

Article 2 further underscores this idea of cultural plurality with talk of "our increasingly diverse societies," "groups with plural, varied and dynamic cultural identities," and the "reality of cultural diversity." If cultural diversity is not only a reality, but also the common heritage of all humanity, then what is of universal value is the world's marked cultural differences. The sameness of global culture is difference itself.

This idea seems to include a distinctively Saussurian dualism that became the cornerstone of Structuralist theory as articulated by Claude Levi-Strauss during the same time period that UNESCO formulated its concept of World Heritage. While it is criticized by many American cultural anthropologists— Appadurai critiques Structuralism's problematic "ahistorical, formal, binary, mentalist and textualist associations"[48]—a more contemporary version is still the predominant system of analysis in for social anthropologists in Europe, where UNESCO is based. Despite such valid criticisms, its relational concept of bifurcation, which was first formulated by Ferdinand de Saussure, is particularly useful in this case. Through Structural bifurcation, something is defined not by what it is, but by what it is not. A linguist, Saussure pointed out that no word has meaning on its own; there is always present in each word all the synonymous and antithetical terms in relation to which they are all used by speakers. Each word has thus a signifier, which is the immutable universal; and a signified, which is the application of the universal that varies and changes as different peoples use it across time. Levi-Strauss applied this to anthropological thought, claiming that at the heart of every myth across every culture is this structure of commonality and diversity, this signifier and signified, and that each is defined in relation to the other. Thus, although such a notion problematically reifies universal categorization and, for that matter, conceptualizes "culture" as a neatly packaged container that can be divided into such neat categories, one of its virtues lies in this very "concept of difference, a contrastive rather than a substantive property of certain things."[49]

In its foundational documents, UNESCO seems to contend that a place's divisiveness is predicated on conflicting claims of value or ownership with which different communities make to contextualize them. Both the extreme example of World War II and also the episode surrounding Thai-Cambodian claims regarding Angkor reveal the ways in which the same site is employed by diverse groups to deepen differing identities. It makes sense that UNESCO relies on "ahistorical" and "mentalist" concepts of imagined heritage time and place. Like Structuralists, UNESCO is primarily concerned with cultural diversity but recognizes some universality among its articulation "in the minds of men." For UNESCO, cultures may very well be at the root of the deadly contest between peace and war, but they are also at the epicenter of community unification. They are also constructed, cultivated and changing; one must tap into this dynamic to employ culture for the latter, rather than the former.

UNESCO articulates this reasoning through its meta-narrative claim. A simplified version of binary opposition also lies at the core of UNESCO's concept of global culture; here too exists a signifier and a signified—a universality of applicability and a diversity of application—and, most importantly, they are defined in relation to each other. In UNESCO's concept, universality is to diversity as the signifier is to the signified. Cultural universality exists across the globe specifically because the *same sort* of differences exist, and likewise these differences emerge precisely when considering the universality of cultural forms. By taking memories of tangible events and places, which have been packaged in the mind through traditional insider-outsider claims, and turning them on their backs, UNESCO is able to foster the notion that all people find themselves inside an area that is defined by insider-outsider claims. If all individuals realize that they are all the same in that they all define themselves by what they are not, then peace can be created "in the minds of men."

The practical applications of this Structuralist dualism coincide with the placemaking mission of UNESCO as a whole on three levels. It addresses the individual and his or her imagined understandings, individuals' interactions among themselves and with monumental objects, and finally individual sites and their relationships to one another. The narrative claim of "unity in diversity" allows UNESCO to reach beyond collectivities—traditionally understood as either "societies," "civilizations," "cultures" or, more specific to UNESCO, "nations"—and appeal directly to people at the individual level. Individuals are the same inasmuch as they are infinitely diverse. They are also the same in terms of the infinitely diverse experiences and memories they possess. Such a claim allows individuals to ascribe their different meanings, which stem from their different remembered versions of any one narrative truth claim, to sites with equal truthfulness. Conversely, it also provides the realization that one's particular understanding of truth is neither universal, nor is it exclusively correct. There may be no one "correct" interpretation of the value or importance of a potently symbolic monument, but, equally as true, there may be no one "incorrect" version as well. Such an assertion—that everyone's understanding of the truth of a place is mutually diverse—alleviates contentious accusations around monuments such as Angkor. The Thai actress' alleged accusation that Angkor "belongs" to the Thai people, in this case, would be correct—but with the qualification that it equally "belongs" to the Cambodians, to the French, and to every individual in the human race.

UNESCO's claim of "unity in diversity" therefore provides a new social context for these disembedded places, whereby traditional boundaries do not demarcate or regulate ownership. As symbolic and material manifestations of individuals' meaningful activities and understandings, these monuments are ideologically charged, since they are intimately connected with people. Possession—symbolic and material—is always key. But with this unity in diversity claim, if everyone symbolically possesses the site, everyone can lay equal claim to it. No one person, organization or entity can proclaim exclusive ownership over the site, regardless of where individual monuments may reside. UNESCO reinforces this with an added stipulation in the World Heritage Convention, pointing out that

> countries recognize that the sites located on their national territory, and which have been inscribed on the World Heritage List, without prejudice to national sovereignty or ownership, constitute a World Heritage "for whose protection it is the duty of the international community as a whole to cooperate."[50]

Once designated, something that was used or belonged to a specific individual or group in a particular place and time period now is now owned, at least in imagination, by all people across the whole expanse of the earth and throughout the whole expanse of time. Locals do not have exclusive possession—material or imaginative—over a site; they are not the only ones who are allowed to utilize it as a means of creating identity. This concept renders moot the need to assert and argue over the territorial possession of single sites such as Angkor. Now, a site can be the source of community—if only imagined—regardless of whether a person can come into regular contact with it.

Such a narrative claim also adds a further level of interactive applicability, for it precludes the traditional notion that one is required to interact with the site in order for it to contribute to the formation of his identity. One need only remember some image, some re-presentation, of the site in this meta-narrative form, rather than come into contact with it. Indeed, there are a good number of World Heritage sites located in territories relatively inaccessible to certain citizenries—either because of material cost, extreme distances, available time, fear of travel, danger, or political embargos. For instance, United States citizens are not readily able to visit sites located in North Korea, Cuba, Iraq and Libya. Indeed, in today's unfortunate age of global terrorism, Americans are especially wont to travel to North Africa and the Middle East; however, this does not prevent them from identifying with the area's World Heritage sites, just as religious hostility or lack of social mobility did not preclude Medieval Europeans from identifying with them in other time periods, formulating their own "imagined communities" based on the concept of "Western civilization." For example, Westerners rarely are able to visit Libya, yet a number of its World Heritage sites are inscribed in Western collective memory, such as the famous Greek out-post of Cyrene (the origin of the Gospels' Cyrus of Cyrene), which has been a well-known archaeological area since the eighteenth century. Iraq, of course, holds the cities of Ancient Mesopotamia, which American and European school children learn about as the cradle of their Western civilization. And one of the best examples is the World Heritage site of Carthage in Tunisia, which, since antiquity has been regarded as a part of "Western culture." The ability to use these sites, if only to imaginatively identify with them from afar, becomes a right for all, not just for those who constructed them, live near them, or hold their titles.

Finally, the claim of "unity in diversity" can be applied directly to individ-ual sites, as well, affording each site the ability to be contextualized within the heritage-scape with equal ease. Recognizing that these sites are all places, all material manifestations of individuals' meaningful activities—both constructive and interpretative—this claim celebrates the fact that every place can be diverse without reifying their qualities or valorizing one over another. They are diverse in their meanings to individuals, but they are also equally diverse in their mean-ings to each other. This allows each monument—with its own unique life histo-ries, contested narrative claims, and infinite number of meanings—to be contex-tualized with equal ease into the heritage-scape. It precludes one type of claim, one type of monument, and one type of understanding as to its value, to be more applicable than another. UNESCO's "unity in diversity" meta-narrative claim thus serves as the conceptual glue connecting disparate World Heritage sites together within the singular heritage-scape.

Awareness of the heritage-scape's meta-narrative claim can only get one so far, however. Or, rather, remaining deep within the shadowy confines of one's own mind, it does not get one far enough. UNESCO's claim of "unity in diver-sity" can only provide the context for physical action; it is not an end in itself. It is to its audience a Virgilian guide—providing imperfect and subjective infor-mation to shape meaning, encouraging one to delve deeper in the journey to the unknown, and providing comfort to he who bodily engages with the foreign, but bringing him only to the threshold of true understanding. To fully capitalize on the epistemological and enlightening capabilities of these tangible places, to completely bridge the memory's gap between simply knowing of something and verily knowing them, to truly harness the emotional effects of these World Heri-tage sites, one must enjoy another, more physically interactive activity. He must interact materially and mentally with place.[51] Only through these actual, physical interactions can their meaning be fully realized, ultimately fostering peace in the minds of men. The next chapter will examine the ways in which tourism, as a socially structured, ritual form of interaction, can convey the heritage-scape's meta-narrative equally at individual World Heritage sites.

CHAPTER FOUR

TOURISM:
THE HERITAGE-SCAPE'S RITUAL INTERACTION

There are many ways in which people physically interact with tangible places—at least as many as there are variations of each. Yet as chapter 1 argued, the structural similarities between the touristic and heritage fields of production—especially both of their reliance on juxtaposition—renders tourism the optimal form of interaction in the heritage-scape. An understanding of tourism as a structured social form—one that can be empirically analyzed using traditional ethnographic theory and methodology, following Graburn's lead—can reveal the formative value of touristic interactions, and illuminate the underlying ways in which it shapes and constrains World Heritage sites' re-presentationality.

Tourism is by definition a short-term, transitory escape from normal, quotidian interactions. No matter how active, frenetic or physically demanding a particular itinerary may be, tourism is always considered by the practitioner as a time of rest, a time to re-focus the eyes, shift concentration, and delve egoistically into the imagination while still interacting on some social and tangible level with a place. Unlike a local resident, the tourist interacts with place on a temporary and voluntary basis[1] for the expressed purpose of slipping out of the daily obligations of the "ordinary workaday, mundane life, particular work, which includes the workplace, homework and housework," as Nelson Graburn writes.[2] This becomes particularly apropos when tourism is conceived expressedly as a vacation, as one tourist remarked, "To me, a vacation is just to relax. Just put me by a lake, by the water, and just relax and do nothing." When pressed as to why she has to travel to a lake, instead of simply remaining at home to do nothing, the same tourist remarked, "Because at home I see all the work that needs to be done."[3] Thus, tourism is always and consistently a choice—not an obligation—as most business (workplace), academic (homework) or local (housework) interactions necessitate, no matter how enjoyable or rewarding they may be during or after the fact. Being temporary and voluntary also means that anyone can move freely in and out of this form of interaction with relative ease.

Defining tourism primarily as a form of interaction with place, comprehended here in temporal rather than spatial terms, affords the possibility of shifting away from some of the analytical pitfalls that have plagued traditional tourism researchers since Victor Turner defined pilgrims as "literally, persons who go through fields or countries (*per*, through; *ager*, field); they are wanderers, peregrinators, transients, strangers to their lands of passage."[4] Some conceptualize tourism as a system of movement, defined in relation to pilgrimage,[5] but also to emigration, exile and even daily commuting. Undoubtedly occupied with the business of tourism, New Zealand's Ministry of Tourism, for example, provides an overly restrictive definition of a "tourist" that is contingent on this association with movement; they contend that a tourist is "anyone who spends at least one night away from home, no matter what the purpose."[6] Even the United Nations' approved definition of tourism centers on the notion of travel, although it does specify its temporary, leisure nature. It defines tourism as "the activity of persons traveling to and staying in places outside their usual environment for not more than one consecutive year for leisure, business or any other purpose."[7] Indeed, when conceptualizing tourism in the minds of pop culture, notions of "jetlag" and "the jet set" often are associated, along with images of airplanes and locomotives, of cars, campers and cruise ships. Opposing ideals of what constitutes an ultimate "tourist experience" also frequently center on motion and movement, or lack thereof: is it better to trek the Outback, climb Phnom Bakheng on elephant-back, or cruise through the Panama Canal—or is it better to lie motionless beneath a beating sun on a beach in an all-inclusive resort, served *mai tais* by the natives, and soaking languidly in crisp emerald waters? Does one with the means to travel squander time off from work by sitting at home, rather than exploring some far away land?

By focusing on movement, as opposed to the narratively perceived temporal quality of the interaction, the analysis may become mired in economic concerns, since one must then struggle to qualify tourism based on one's capacity to move around, as well as the means by which a person can monetarily support such travel. Class differentiation usually emerges in such analyses, followed by issues of international finance, commodification, and development. Dean MacCannell, regarded as a pioneering voice in the sociological study of tourism, applies a somewhat heavy neo-Marxist analysis in *The Tourist*. Calling his own work a "new theory of the leisure class"[8] within the social framework of the working class,[9] he sees today's form of tourism as a distinct element of the modern / post-modern "international middle class" who "systematically scavenges the earth for new experiences to be woven into a collective, touristic vision of other peoples and other places."[10] Renowned Africanist John Middleton prefaces a book on *The World of the Swahili* by launching into a diatribe against what he sees as rampant commodification of indigenous cultural resources by "culturally illiterate" tourists to illustrate his contention that "tourism is the final form of colonialism."[11] Dutch anthropologist Jon Abbink, who quotes MacCannell and Middleton to illustrate many social scientists' "ambivalence" towards tourism, speaks matter-of-factly of this phenomenon as an "avant-garde of globalization" that "emanates largely from societies that are relatively powerful and wealthy"[12]—thereby underscoring economics as an *a priori* factor of any tourist encounter. Even Barbara Kirshenblatt-Gimblett, whose museological approach to tourism and heritage sites is presented quite even-handedly in her book *Destination Culture*,[13] refers to tourism as "an export industry and one of the world's largest. Unlike other export industries, however, tourism does not export goods for consumption elsewhere. Rather, it imports visitors to consume goods and services locally."[14] The linkage of tourism with consumption and economic commodification is further underscored by her choice of a cover image for her book: a man dressed in Mariachi garb, head covered as if a bandit or hostage, with a message scrawled on his chest: "Please don't discover me!"[15]

Considering its predominance in the contemporary global economy, as well as the multifaceted material outcomes it produces, it is true no practical discourse about tourism can avoid touching on its economic impact. Nor should it avoid this important consideration, either. According to the World Tourism Organization (UNWTO), tourism is both the largest and the fastest-growing industry in the world today, and continues to increase by over 5% per year in a post-September 11, 2001 era wherein terrorism threatens the very fabric of international exchange by promoting fear in non-essential travel and in unknown cultures. Tangible interaction certainly causes tangible outcomes, especially in the confluence of tourism and development. In no uncertain terms does the United Nations underscore this point, writing, "It is recognized that in principle any form of tourism development in a country can reduce poverty."[16] Citing the recent accession of ten new, lesser-developed nation-states into the European Union, Luigi Cabrini, UNWTO Regional Representative for Europe, issued a concluding statement on behalf of delegates at a March 2006 conference in Vilnius, Lithuania, contending that tourism can "play a major role in European integration, at a time when the construction of the European Union is faced with demanding challenges." Pointing out that "the tourism sector is not only a generator of wealth and a major contributor to European GDP, but it is also closely interrelated with other economic and social aspects," the report expressed hope in rural tourism, among others, as a sub-sector expected to play an important part in the development and integration of newer member-states, and emphasized the very social nature of tourism as "a factor of social cohesion" that can contribute to "the fight against exclusion caused by poverty, cultural differences or physical disabilities."[17]

Indeed, the mere arrival of people, regardless of how temporarily or permanently they choose to remain, increases the palpable need for infrastructure to accommodate them. One of the most striking examples of how tourism translates into marked development can be found at the outskirts of the Angkor Archaeological Park. In the course of a few years, Siem Reap has seen a 30% increase in visitors, which has transformed it from a sleepy town into a veritable pleasure place replete with top-of-the-line hotels and resorts set amid lush nursery-grown vegetation. New airports opened in both Phnom Penh and Siem Reap in 2003 and 2006 adorned with beautiful artwork, fountains and sculptures set amid neatly manicured gardens. The airports were complete with modern facilities such as immigration and customs areas, baggage handling facilities, tour bus and taxicab drop-off zones; under an agreement with the IFC signed at the end of that same year, funds were earmarked to subsequently lengthen the runways to accommodate large, international jets rather than smaller connecting planes.[18] Roads such as National Highway 6 connecting the airport and the town six kilometers to the east, was paved, and an electric light system was added shortly thereafter to accommodate evening arrivals. Siem Reap's first traffic light was installed in 2006. In 2005, the number of tourists to Siem Reap surpassed one million people, a point local tour guides and government officials love to include in conversations.[19] Today, even the homepage of the Embassy of the Kingdom of Cambodia in Washington, DC, which features an image of one of the Bayon's "smiles of Angkor" extols this statistic, as a badge of honor:

> Cambodia with its Angkor Temple complex has become one of the main tourist destinations in the world. Last year, there were more than *one million tourists* visiting the country. Compared to 2003, the number of visitors increased at a speeding rate of over than 30%.[20]

This stunning increase awakened Cambodia's neighbors to the possibility of further economic development, as well. Responding to the increase of tourists arriving in Siem Reap to interact with Khmer ruins, the Prime Minister of Thailand, Cambodia's traditional adversary to the west, declared his intention to capitalize on this phenomenon through infrastructure development that would lead to bilateral cooperation between the two countries. In a visit to Thailand's eastern provinces in early 2006, Prime Minister Thaksin Shinawatra announced his dedication to develop needed infrastructure, such as asphalt roads and border marketplaces, in Thailand's Khorat Plateau, rich in monuments attesting to the area's Khmer legacy. In pledging to widen the Trat-Khlong Yai Road into four traffic lanes and to lengthen its reach to the Thai-Cambodian border, Shinawatra attested to his desire to link tourism in his country with attractions in Cambodia and, ultimately, all the way to Vietnam, as well.[21]

Although it creates tangible and measurable change—both for the better and for the worse—tourism is too complex, too multifaceted, too non-localized a phenomenon to be analyzed quantitatively or reduced to mere Western socio-economic assertions, although many of the pioneering experts of this field have fallen into this trap. Considering tourism as a byproduct of global "modernity," experts have drawn the connection between a growing worldwide middle class that can afford the time and expense of engaging in leisure activities.[22] Such economic factors may indeed be valid considerations, but viewed simply as a form of transitory, yet substantive and meaningful, interaction with place, tourism is a much more encompassing spatial interface than an analysis centered on money would project. As a temporary escape, a respite from the daily interaction with place (no matter what that interaction may be), anyone anywhere can be a tourist for a time. To be a tourist, the only requirement is an alternative approach to material interaction, a perspectively different lens through which one makes meaning of his or her surroundings, a different way of seeing[23]—or a "tourist gaze," to use John Urry's now famous term.[24] Tourism manifests itself equally when one travels great distances to exotic lands as it does when he temporarily succumbs to the "lure of the local" in his own hometown, as Lucy Lippard so poetically describes.[25]

Tourism as a Ritual

Because it is centered around this acute desire to experience inward change, tourism is consistently and decidedly a ritual interaction, which van Gennep and, later, Turner, has shown is a temporary yet socially transformative activity that occurs in three prescribed phases: *separation*, *liminality* and *re-aggregation*.[26] Indeed, Graburn has dubbed tourism a "secular ritual" while MacCannell and others have called it a "modern ritual" to underscore the fact that it possesses the fundamental structure and function of this traditional ethnographic concept. Like other rituals described by Hubert and Mauss, van Gennep, and Turner, this change occurs in the same three phases; the tourist first steps out of the daily routine (for example, he takes time off from work), temporarily experiences a modification of his traditional status as time and space is reordered (for example, he wears Bermuda shorts instead of a suit and tie; he indulges in fine dining and long walks on the beach; or, most importantly, he achieves a transcendent or educational communion with a World Heritage site), and then is once again reaggregated into daily life (for example, he returns to the daily grind refreshed and rejuvenated).

As Graburn also points out, often rituals are categorized in accordance with the dual concepts of *rites of passage* and *rites of intensification*.[27] Established by Arnold van Gennep in his seminal work by the same name, rites of passage are defined as "all the ceremonial patterns which accompany a passage from one situation to another or from one cosmic or social world to another."[28] Through these rites, the members of a society are informed of the participant's new status and simultaneously give him their approval; the participants are then instructed to return to their "normal behavior incorporating the added or lost personnel and the added, lost or changed social statuses."[29] There are notable instances wherein tourism also serves as a rite of passage, undertaken to create and / or to indicate a sweeping change in one's social status or conception of "self." These, too, often occur during the slow biological transition to adulthood, and are often marked with the themes of independence, responsibility (often juxtaposed with temporarily heightened irresponsibility), and expansion of one's concept of his or her place in the world or in the family. Boy Scout camping trips or one's first journey to the big city without parental supervision can also be considered some of the few mundane, but important, touristic rites of passage for many "modern," suburban Americans. More prominently, however, are those more complex cross-country or international tours to which MacCannell and others no doubt would attribute as the purview of modern middle and upper classes. Here, too, the participant exerts newfound independence, and negotiates the gray line between this freedom and the responsibility that goes with it; but, perhaps more indicative of middle or upper class values, the expansion of one's concept of his place in the world is translated to a distinctive form of cosmopolitanism or worldliness.

Many Jewish-Americans between the ages of 18 and 26, for example, embark on highly ritualized group tours to Israel, visiting sites of religious, national and world heritage in an effort to "recover their roots" or strengthen their sense of Jewish identity and pride. Trips to Biblical heritage sites such as Jerusalem, the Dead Sea, and the ancient fort of Masada are juxtaposed with a hodgepodge of encounters intended to convey the contemporary Israeli national experience to these diasporic youths. Thus, they also visit the Golan Heights or another such contested area between Israel and its neighbors, enjoy the opportunity to fire an Israeli machinegun, and usually reside for a few nights on a historic *kibbutz*—a socialist settlement camp established at the turn of the twentieth century by the original Zionists who left Europe to claim their ancestral homeland.[30] Synagogues and other non-profit organizations are known to assist in funding this experience to all Jewish-American adolescents, thereby fostering ethno-religious solidarity that transcends class or economic constraints. The Taglit Foundation is one such organization that enjoys trifold funding by the Israeli government, "local Jewish Federations, and private Jewish philanthropists," and is dedicated to providing an all-expenses paid "gift of first time, peer group, educational trips to Israel for Jewish young adults ages 18 to 26 . . . from all over the world." Organizers say that *Taglit* literally means "Birthright Israel," and by funding such an experience, they hope to provide equal opportunity to youths from all over the world to imbibe in their heritage, to make it their own, and to bond with others who similarly are in danger of losing touch with their ancestral homeland. Indicative of the very social nature of this rite of passage, Taglit's website states that its goal is "to diminish the growing division between Israel and Jewish communities around the world; to strengthen the sense of solidarity between Israeli youth and Jewish communities throughout the world; and to promote the idea of a trip to Israel for all Diaspora Jews as a critical part of Jewish life outside of Israel."[31] That is, to foster social solidarity while simultaneously educating those specifically transitioning from childhood to adulthood.

For many young Americans of all ethnicities, the ritual of "studying abroad" is another exemplary rite of passage, especially for those who come from liberal arts universities or institutions that stress international or linguistic perspectives. Often these universities have villas or satellite campuses that teach classes in English, which complement direct-matriculation programs. Despite the ostensible linkage to an academic atmosphere, these university-sponsored study abroad rituals are most often marked by inordinate amounts of travel, either independent or organized. It is commonly understood within the undergraduate travel-abroad community that, for the most part, even professors in those intensive, direct-matriculation programs tend to turn a blind eye towards semi-regular absence when related to travel.[32] In my own experience as an American undergraduate studying abroad at the University of Bologna, even the Italian professors and the students themselves were notably more lenient not only in linguistic ability or knowledge, but also in acceptable behavior and study skills. Absences to travel were tolerated. Students were graded on a separate curve. Most notably, when it was time to undergo the decidedly Italian academic ritual of engaging in an oral final exam, one-on-one with the professor in public, foreign exchange students alone were allowed to conduct their finals in private. Domestic or foreign-born students who were fully matriculated were not able to benefit from this option.

Some programs embrace tourism as an epistemic virtue of the study abroad experience. Gonzaga University, a small, Jesuit school based in Spokane, Washington, poses possibly the most extreme example of this. Its year-long Italy program, which places around one hundred and twenty five students a year in Florence, sponsors optional tours from this home base nearly every weekend. In addition to taking students on in-depth explorations of the country's many cities and hill towns nearly every week, the program's advisor,[33] a spry Italian priest, accompanied students to Oktoberfest in Munich, the Dalmatian coast in Croatia, the unofficial Catholic pilgrimage site of Medjugorje in Bosnia-Herzegovina, where they also viewed the remnants of the recently completed Balkan war, heritage sites in Greece, Bethlehem and Jerusalem for Christmas, Cairo and the Great Pyramids in Egypt for New Year's (in 2001 the latter two destinations have been switched to Turkey; in 2007 students were taken to China instead), and to Mount Kilimanjaro after the completion of the academic year. According to participants, students were encouraged—officially or unofficially—to travel as much as possible even if not participating in these director-led programs. Certainly this was more "touring abroad" than "studying abroad," and indeed, a number of students attest that they felt the focus certainly was on the learning experience garnered through touristic interactions, rather than Italian grammar and history classes.[34] Mimicking the ubiquitous rock music t-shirts advertising a band's "world tour" itinerary on the back, some Gonzaga students distributed their own t-shirts with the dates and locations of each week's tour written on the back. One look at such an ambitious itinerary confirms the true focus of this experience.

Similarly, British youths and their compatriots from Australia, New Zealand and Canada often embark on a requisite "gap year" traveling or living abroad between their graduation from secondary school and the commencement of serious university study. Most often these young men and women—known as "gappers" in Australia—follow the Grand Tour routes of their ancestors, seeing the major sites of Western or Oriental Civilization. They often join other "backpackers," composed in part, by their American counterparts studying abroad, in a frenetic search for the authentic local experience, which they often view as occurring in inexpensive and un-touristy locales. Thus, toting the aptly named *Let's Go* guidebook, compiled by Harvard students who have undergone the same experience, they often travel from hostel to hostel, living out of their backpacks, socializing with and soliciting feedback from local youths and international backpackers, constantly on the search to experience the next hottest place to visit before it is overrun by the hordes of retired tourists. Juxtaposing a genuine interest in expanding their worldliness and knowledge with a cathartic burst of self-indulgence, such tourist interactions are rites of passages transitioning the participants from the blithe irresponsibility of an ignorant childhood to the looming heaviness of the quotidian workaday lifestyle of adulthood.

Yet even in adulthood, tourism is a means by which one seeks change, if just temporarily intermittent and less critically formative. As Graburn contends, tourism in this case serves as a valuable *rite of intensification*—as periodic or cyclical rites that renew the social or natural order.[35] Defined in juxtaposition to van Gennep's rite of passage, a seemingly necessary "critical" phase in one's social and natural life that he must overcome before proceeding onward, Chappell and Coon's rite of intensification is often associated with renewal and rejuvenation, activities that may be less intensely decisive yet nevertheless understood as integral for one's mental or biological health. As Graburn illustrates, tourism, too, "is a ritual expression—individual or societal—of deeply held values about health, freedom, nature and self improvement, a re-creation ritual which parallels pilgrimages (cf. Moore 1980) and other rituals in more traditional, pervasively religious societies."[36] These touristic rituals can be cyclical, punctuating the calendar year in regular intervals and in a socially prescribed fashion, such as the yearly trek "over the river and through the woods to grandmother's house" for a weekend of holiday feasting, or the traditional *Ferragosto* exodus to the beach that Italians and other Europeans take every August, much to the chagrin of American and Asian tourists who arrive in Italy's hill towns to closed shops and quieted cafés.

Valene Smith points out that the tourist also embarks upon a strikingly similar experience, which is by definition undertaken through an individual's conscious decision "for the purpose of experiencing a change" from daily life.[37] This intended change could be a temporary reordering or reprioritizing of obligations, such as when one chooses to lie on a beach for a few days instead of working in a cubicle, or it could be a temporary inversion of societal mores, such as when the college student on a decadent "spring break" embarks on a more uninhibited and unbridled effervescent experience of sensory pleasure that traditionally would be out of the campus' social norms. Change could also be decidedly educational in nature, as when one embarks on a group "study tour" of Renaissance art history in Florence, or a garden tour in the English countryside. The desire for formative change need not be outwardly academic, but rather could manifest itself as simply the desire to experience something new or out of the ordinary—a new culture, a new environment, a new cuisine. Such change could also translate into a reconciliation with one's roots, as when an overseas Vietnamese-American returns to her parents' homeland, or a third-generation Polish-American steps out of her American culture, mentality and way of life and experiences what she perceives as her "heritage" in the land of her ancestors.

The change might also be an emotional one—a chance to experience certain sensations of a religious nature, as when the pilgrim visits a sacred site to commune with the Divine. Historian Rachel Fulton discusses a pilgrimage to Jerusalem undertaken in 1026 by Richard II, duke of Normandy. Richard and his large entourage followed the traditional yet perilous overland route through Eastern Europe to Constantinople and through the Muslim-controlled areas to Jerusalem. As they entered the sacred city on Palm Sunday,

> Richard realized his lifelong desire "to suffer for Christ, to abide with Him, and to be buried [with Him] that he might be granted through Christ to rise again in glory with Him." Richard's site-by-site imitatio Christi was accompanied by great floods of tears. . . . Richard returned home with his companions by way of Antioch, satisfied that he had seen "all of the places of Christ's humanity."[38]

This emotional change can also be seen as an opportunity to release pent-up feelings one might deem inappropriate to daily life, such as when one Vietnam War veteran returned to Đà Nẵng to mourn the loss of his compatriots, having repressed those feelings of grief so many years earlier. Revisiting a place from his lived past, one might also wish to directly manage or embrace nagging feelings of nostalgia, which Roy Schaffer describes as "idealized memories" of the past "in contrast with painful feelings of disappointment in his or her current life,"[39] or, as Svetlana Boym describes it, a "mourning for the impossibility of mythical return, for the loss of an enchanted world with clear borders and values; it could be a secular expression of a spiritual longing, a nostalgia for an absolute, a home that is both physical and spiritual, the edenic unity of time and space before entry into history."[40] Here, tourism plays out this emotional longing in very material terms; it is a type of pilgrimage, which Erik Cohen, inspired by the work of the great mythographer Mircea Eliade, poetically describes as "the quest for the mythical land of pristine existence, of no ignorance or suffering, the primeval centre from which man originally emerged, but eventually lost it."[41]

Whether undertaken individually or within a prescribed group, there is a decidedly communal aspect to all ritual behavior. Although rituals are in fact always evolving and are not as static as the participants believe, their repetitive qualities create a sense of continuity that extends not only across space, but time as well. All participants regardless of when and where they live are drawn together in a *communitas*[42] of those who have undergone the exact same experience. As Victor Turner argues, *communitas* is more than merely a sense of "community"—a term which itself is imbued with a geographical sense of common living.[43] Rather, occurring in the liminal phase of rituals wherein individuated statuses are suspended as individuals pass from one state to another, or from one structure to another, *communitas* is "a spontaneously generated relationship between leveled and equal total and individuated human beings, stripped of structural attributes."[44] Turner also calls *communitas* "anti-structure" to convey the sense that it is an inversion—or, rather, a subversion—of traditional social structure, the "'patterned arrangements of role-sets, status-sets and status-sequences' consciously recognized and regularly operative in a given society and closely bound up with legal and political norms and sanctions."[45] It is the transcendence of traditional boundaries that mark daily social life, a recognition among individuals temporarily stripped of their social trappings that they are all the same. "Communitas is universalistic," Turner writes.[46] At the same time, the structure never passes away; Turner recognizes that "seeking oneness is not . . . to withdraw from multiplicity; it is to eliminate divisiveness, to realize nonduality."[47] In short, it is the creation of unity in diversity.

Thus, this feeling of communal solidarity—of "unity in diversity"—is the embodiment of the imagined community that the heritage-scape wishes to foster. Not only does each individual come to personally internalize and understand UNESCO's narrative by interacting with each World Heritage site, but the structure of the total interaction itself fosters solidarity among all individuals who partake in it. The heritage-scape's unique imagined community is created at a double locus, one spatial and one temporal—at the World Heritage site and through the ritual interaction.

Separation: Planning a Tour, Creating Expectations

The first phase in a ritual is separation. It is here that the participant tangibly demonstrates, for himself and often for onlookers as well, that he is creating a break in the "way things are," and that he will undergo a temporary reordering of his place in space and time that will ultimately lead to an important transformation. The tourist leaves his everyday life, typical social circle, and usual environment, and transfers himself to an-other, unordinary place.

While the transfer is often physical, it must be remembered that tourism is not necessarily predicated on movement, but on a differentiated way of perceiving one's surroundings. Tourism's separation phase therefore disconnects the participant's approach to the place and its meaning; it creates an alternative conception of the intended future interaction, which is separate in meaning from that of an everyday interaction, to one that is more experiential, temporary, and transformative. Thus, it separates a site of "local" interest into a ritual site of touristic value in the participant's mind.

Because this phase is so important for laying the contextual foundation to how the tourist site is ultimately experienced, it often is the longest, most extensive period of the touristic ritual, and begins far earlier than many may believe. In this extended separation period, the participant readies himself intellectually, emotionally and physically for the experience; expectations are created, nurtured and solidified at this point. This is effected through the separation phase's three distinct components, which vary in length and quality in every instance. These components occur somewhat chronologically—as the soon-to-be tourist passes through periods of *decision, preparation* and ultimate *disconnection*—although they frequently overlap as the tourist backtracks, re-evaluates and gathers more information about the destination.

This separation phase begins with a distinct *decision* to approach a site in a certain way, to engage in the "way of seeing" that is particular to tourism. It is a conscious selection of a particular narrative claim, already imbedded in some fashion in the individual's mind, for use in making meaning when encountering the site in this specific future instance. This decision could be formulated in one of two directions, as either a *goal-oriented approach* or a *destination-oriented approach*. On one hand, the participant can select a site based on his desire to experience a break. For example, the person might wish to escape to an undifferentiated tropical island beach, and after speaking to a travel agent or searching online for favorable fares, decide on Antigua instead of Barbados or Bermuda. In this case, the decision originated first from his desire to achieve a certain goal, followed by his selection of the most appropriate method to fulfill such a desire. On the other hand, he may have already been aware of the destination and selected the appropriate method of interacting with it. In this case, he already had the desire to experience the site, and just required a selection of the most appropriate method of interacting with it. These conclusions often present themselves almost immediately; one might wish to visit Montana, and after a quick assessment of the time he could spend there, the effort he wishes to exert, his business and family situations, he decides on a week-long tourist trip, rather than relocating there permanently as a "local."[48] In either paradigm, however, the influence of re-presentations of these sites, and the awareness they foster in each person, plays an integral part.

Permeating all of the decision-making process, from this initial selection of the site onwards through the subsequent information-gathering stage with increasing intensity is the influence of one's personal taste. *Taste* refers to the total body of one's inclinations towards or against something—his likes and dislikes. As Pierre Bourdieu illustrates in *Distinction*, while these preferences may seem so innate that he might believe they are natural inclinations, such as a person's aversion to the flavor of seafood or the sound of heavy metal rock music, they are, in essence, socially mediated. Though one may think he possesses agency to freely choose what he wishes, these choices are really predicated on subtle, deep-seated preferences contextualized by how he perceives himself within a society. People make meaning, Bourdieu argues, by what they think is appropriate based on the social situation from which they approach it. They will then show preference or prejudice towards them based on those meanings. Bourdieu writes:

> Taste classifies, and it classifies the classifier. Social subjects, classified by their classifications, distinguish themselves by the distinctions they make, between the beautiful and the ugly, the distinguished and the vulgar, in which their position in the object's classifications is expressed or betrayed.[49]

Because the ritual of tourism is concerned with personal, interior change upon which one embarks through a conscious decision, taste places an important part. Out of a multiplicity of possible destinations that satisfy his general criteria, one chooses which place to visit largely based on what re-presentation seems most appealing to him. If he were interested in visiting a Caribbean island beach resort, for example, he would undoubtedly encounter a number of islands that fit his basic monetary, time and destination requirements. One re-presentation, however, would present itself as more in line with his taste than the others. Perhaps a valued family member or friend in the same social circle enjoyed his stay at one, or perhaps the place's re-presentations painted a more appealing picture of its luxury, authenticity, decadence or refinement. He will choose a specific beach in which he sees himself visiting, which he finds most appealing and most suited to his particular taste, and which he would like to describe to others in his social circle upon his return. In doing so, consequently, he categorizes himself into a type of tourist.

The professional travel world also categorizes tourists in an effort to create a useful system of measurement upon which they base their pricing and service deliverables. Interestingly, the industry underscores the inherent ritual qualities of tourism by organizing participants based on the level of *communitas* they exhibit. It divides them into two broad categories: those who travel independently, and those who travel in groups. Each possesses different needs and different tastes that are oftentimes articulated in opposition to one another. Independent travelers are dubbed *FIT*s, short for "Free and Independent Travelers."[50] As the name suggests, this type of tourist is much less restricted in terms of pre-arranged structures and group travel. Typically, he does not purchase pre-packed travel itineraries, nor does he pre-pay for anything other than airfare, if applicable, and hotels. Only very infrequently does an FIT pre-arrange other aspects of the tour, except sometimes when it is necessary—such as quickly selling out concert or theatre tickets. He prefers to "pay as you go," and most often organizes his own travel on the spot.

Within the independent traveler community, there are a number of sub-categories, depending on the style of independent travel and the expectations held therein. Characterized by youth—or at least a certain level of physical prowess associated with youthfulness of body and spirit—as well as spontaneity and a distinct taste for all travel that is often unstructured, unadulterated and impulsive, backpackers seem to embody the ideal of being "free and independent" travelers. Typically backpackers eschew any pre-planning of the itinerary—except points of arrival and departure, which is necessary when booking airline or train tickets, or where there is a particularly strong interest—in favor of soliciting information from other backpackers they may meet in hostels, bars or tourist sites. Although often traveling as individuals or in very small groups, they are known to join or otherwise meet up with other backpackers they meet along the way—a spontaneous illustration of the *communitas* this form of tourism fosters. Indeed, this is a community that spans ages, races and cultures, but nevertheless is bound together by a distinctive ideology, a highly visible "backpacker culture" whose social taste is evident even in the choice of guidebooks, accommodations, restaurants and bars.

At the opposite end of the spectrum is the luxury independent traveler. This traveler essentially books an all-inclusive, group tour for himself or his family but is still technically considered an FIT. Some foreign tour operators attribute to him a slightly different nomenclature, *SIT*, or "Semi-Independent Traveler," which indicates the tourist's preference for pre-arranged or semi-pre-arranged tours that are private and personalized. Because of the costly nature of these arrangements—essentially, he is not only paying for all of the inclusions, but also the very personalized service of many people during the planning and the touring process—the traveler often comes from the higher echelons of wealth. A few luxury tour operators specialize in this demanding and selective sub-group. In particular are Abercrombie & Kent, which boasts that they are "internationally recognized as the original luxury travel company,"[51] and Butterfield & Robinson, whose tagline "There's Luxury—and Then There's B&R Luxury."[52] With these taglines, both companies wish to convey their dedication to the high-class taste of their clientele. Yet it should be remembered that tastes also vary by type of destination; while the jet-setting elite may—and do—use these operators for luxury escapes to "typical" European venues, the classist net is cast a little wider for those traveling in developing countries, where the prices are more affordable and the destination dauntingly less familiar. African safaris—the type of tour in which, incidentally, Abercrombie & Kent got its start—are commonly included as such destinations wherein physical, environmental, and legal concerns constrain the freedom that one has to simply "go it alone." Here, even "middle class" individuals, couples or small groups of friends or family can book a private, all-inclusive tour complete with guide, transportation by "luxury" air-conditioned jeep, five-star "tents" complete with beds and sumptuous bedding, and armed escorts to protect them from not simply the animals, but, sadly and more importantly, the locals.

The ritual structure of tourism is most pronounced in a group tour, since it is often a structured event that can endure across iterations. It is planned out beforehand, and, resembling the structure of other rituals, the group tour includes a clear beginning, middle and an end. Because a group package is essentially a commodity that is produced, marketed, vended, and competes against similar packages within a group travel market, these phases are, in turn, standardized by the industry. This standardization should not be viewed as simply a product of multinational corporations that dictate the rules of the game, regulate the players and homogenize the services offered,[53] but also as a general framework for helping disparate tourist sites, and the ritual encounters they inspire, be applicable to everyone in a way that fosters the sentiment of *communitas*. Standardization produces the effect of "unity in diversity" across time and space by controlling the participant's approach to the site. Additionally, group tours innately have a much more pronounced social dynamic, which emphasizes the aspect of *communitas* that is fostered in any ritual interaction. In juxtaposition to FITs, participants in group tours categorize themselves based on the social component of experiencing an unordinary site in communion with others. Generally, there are three different reasons for traveling in a group, all of them related to this social component in some way—socialization, safety and value-addeds.

First, many group travelers—especially those of college and retirement ages—attest to enjoying the social experience of travel; it should be noted that this does not necessarily mean the social experience of engaging with locals at the destination, but rather being immersed in the *communitas* of like-minded people undergoing the same ritual simultaneously. Friendships and bonds are created that last far beyond the end of the trip; stories are numerous of married couples meeting on a tour. This also explains the recent surge in popularity of cruises based on dating groups, such as young professionals, gay and straight singles, and widows and widowers.

Traveling in a group also reinforces *communitas*, and sponsoring group tours, retreats or outings is a strategy utilized by many corporate human resources departments to foster collegiality and a sense of community among large and otherwise disparate workplace bureaucracy. Perhaps a bit more cynically, corporations striving to create a "team" atmosphere while simultaneously trying to boost production, revenue or quality, may also offer what the travel industry calls "group incentive tours." These tours are essentially rewards that management may give to a team for achieving a particular benchmark; tour operators offer these to corporate management at reduced prices, as they are booked by the company in bulk.

The nonprofit world also considers group tours as a means to create the sense of community among their members or donors, who are often spread widely across the country or the world. University alumni associations and museums are the major sponsors of educational and cultural group tours, but church parishes, art clubs, horticultural societies, trade associations, and even member-based think-tanks also organize such touristic rituals. The organization of these tours often falls within the purview of the fundraising department, despite the fact that American laws prohibit the padding of tour costs with compulsory donations to the non-profit organization. Sometimes a modest "office fee" might be included to cover the operational costs incurred by the sponsoring organization (for example, faxes to the tour operator, outreach to members, staff time, and the traditional sponsorship of a "pre-tour" and "post-tour" party), and often the organization requires prospective participants to either become a member or donate at a certain monetary level before being allowed to register for the tour, but whatever direct monetary benefits that these may produce are not the fundraising office's true goal in sponsoring these events. Rather, organizing an enjoyable and formative ritual experience, where self-ascribed members grow closer in *communitas* and simultaneously feel the individual benefits of resonance and wonder translates into long-term investment potential. The logic is clear: individuals inclined to philanthropy will give more to the organization if they feel a part of the community and take pride in the quality and type of programming the institution provides.[54]

Group tours can also serve as valuable tools for fostering political and social change, especially in underrepresentative or minority communities. Celebrity lesbian couple Rosie and Kelli O'Donnell, together with travel professional Gregg Kaminsky, founded R Family Cruises, a child-friendly cruise line for the Lesbian, Gay, Bisexual and Transgender (LGBT) community, with the expressed purpose of forging a stronger sense of *communitas* among those within the demographic who choose to raise families—currently a hot-button political issue in the United States. Regularly scheduled departures of this type of cruise serve as a potent symbol to the rest of the country of not only the existence, but the popularity and solidarity, of this group. It also serves to educate and foster group cohesiveness between those in the community who do not have families and those who do, as one gay writer for the LGBT magazine *Pink* states:

> After attending the most recent R Family Vacations cruise, I discovered both a vacation experience that made a lifelong impression and that the reality of to-day's American gay family was far different than I imagined. . . . My definition of "gay family" was completely broken from the moment guests boarded the magnificent Norwegian Dawn in New York City. Every possible family size was represented from a broad cross-cultural perspective. What surprised me most was the amount of extended family in attendance. Grandparents as well as aunts, uncles, cousins and even family friends came to enjoy this unforgettable week on the high seas. This made the initial passing of the Statue of Liberty from New York harbor an even more profound experience.[55]

Private activists are not the only ones utilizing tourism to further the cause of LGBT families. The Canadian government, which has legalized same-sex marriages, has also joined the international fray. In June 2006, the Canadian Tourism Authority launched a concentrated ad campaign intended to make the country "more of a Mecca for same-sex marriages." This initiative reflects the country's growing popularity within this community, which sees it as a desirable and chic tourist destination; indeed, the widely visited online LGBT website gay.com recently rated Montréal—considered "Canada's gay-tourism leader"—the eighth most romantic city for travel.[56]

Not to be outdone, fundamentalist Christian music conglomerate Premier Productions started their own cruise line in 2003. Premier Christian Cruises' co-owner Roy Morgan said, "We saw a huge niche for family vacations that were clean and wholesome and something more than a week away from home." These music-filled cruises foster fellowship among strangers of a similar faith group, while at the same time promoting Christian recording artists. "It's more than a cruise," Premier's press report advertises. "It's a life-changing, boat-rocking experience that brings people closer together. Spiritual batteries are re-charged. New directions are taken and lives are never the same."[57] In short, it is a pilgrimage without a particular end point.

Second, predicated on the phrase "there's safety in numbers," group travelers also enjoy the benefit of an anthropomorphic safety net. The safety net is especially attractive to infrequent travelers, first time travelers to the destination, those who express strong negative perceptions or prejudices about the destination but still feel compelled to visit, those who feel daunted by the "foreignness" of the written or spoken language and/or the culture, or those who are otherwise unsure of what to expect. Although it seems that criminal entities that target tourists—such as pickpockets or, in extreme cases, organized terrorists—

logically tend to target venues in which large groups gather—such as tourist hotels, public busses and even popular attractions—the group tour is also appealing for many who wish to travel to dangerous, high-risk or otherwise physically unsafe lands, from today's Middle East to the African jungle safaris. These travelers place their trust in the tour operator's selection of guides and other local providers, simply by virtue of being selected by the professional operator, who are seen to possess greater knowledge of the needs of their travelers, and access to the best assortment of possible providers.

This translates into the third perceived benefit of traveling on a group tour—the value added of letting a professional entity, a member of a socially recognized epistemic community, plan one's vacation. The convenience of quickly booking all of the necessities through an agent has been perennially noted by the travel industry since its modern-day foundation by Sir Thomas Cook in the 1840s, and indeed, there has been a significant increase in the percentage of FITs who book air, flight and rental car packages online with the major Internet travel sites in 2006.[58] Indeed, the online booking agency *Travelocity*, located at www.travelocity.com, emphasizes this point in an advertisement released the same day as the U.S. Travel Consumer Survey mentioned above:

<u>Flight + 4 Nights Hotel for $718.00</u>
Going all-inclusive allows you a vacation from greenbacks and plastic because everything is prepaid. That means you can splurge on two desserts with dinner or grab a snorkel mask for a look beneath the waves, you won't have to reach for your cash. It's all paid for. All upfront. Book your All-Inclusive vacation today.[59]

Travelers choosing a group tour, however, perceive a benefit beyond mere convenience. In addition to not needing to worry about "reaching for your cash," there seems to be a valuable knowledge-based safety net, wherein the tourist is assured he will "see everything he needs to." Tour operators are recognized as an epistemic community privy to the most reliable and up-to-date information of a destination and its components. Seen as the experts on the ground, tour operators are afforded the faith and trust that, not only will they know the best ways to keep their groups safe, but they will know and expertly discriminate between which sites, hotels, guides, and restaurants are the "most authentic," "most luxurious," or "most worthwhile to experience." A group tour provides the potential tourist with the added convenience of not having to meticulously research and plan the itinerary himself, with the potential risk of missing something important.

While travel agents specialize in booking the basics—hotels, air and train tickets,—tour operators arranging these group tours specialize in crafting a full morning-to-evening itinerary, a product that aims to be unique among others so as to capture the attention of its potential demographic. The value-added here is the addition of "special visits," called *privates* in the industry, which are supposedly not open to the "average" tourist who would arrange his visit by himself or through a travel agent. Nor are they supposedly open to the average local, either. These privates are a component of the tourism sector to which MacCannell refers as the industry's supposed Goffmanian "back region," wherein paradoxically the foreign tourist enjoys preferential treatment from selected local hosts and entrée into venues that are not even open to locals themselves.[60] They are a backstage performance of local life observed by an audience of tourists; yet these high-end tourists are invited to peek "behind-the-scenes," into the private dressing rooms and boiler rooms barred from the common tourist riff-raff but also from the locals. Examples range from private demonstrations by artisans in their studios to meetings with expert speakers, curators, professors, preservationists, artists and gallery owners; from specially-arranged after-hours entrances to famous or popular tourist attractions, to the ubiquitous meal with aristocracy in their private villas, palaces and gardens, the latter being the most common of all private visits. These privates are often presented to the public as a benefit of the operator's friendly relationships at the destination, as one operator writes:

> Meet the last surviving and little-known Medici. Over tea and biscuits or a meal at her family's palazzo in Florence, this very private woman who prefers not to be named will talk with you about her ancestors' history as prosperous bankers (at one time they were perhaps the wealthiest family in Europe) and patrons of the arts (supporting Brunelleschi, Donatello, and others), in particular the period in the fifteenth century when Cosimo ruled over all of Florence.[61]

Of course, the *Condé Nast Traveler* writer who reported this private visit goes on to show that this experience comes with a hefty price tag: the chance to hear the musings of this lady costs between US$6,000.00 and US$8,400.00, including a donation to her favorite charity. While the extent of operators' prized personal contact list should not be discounted, therefore, the real reason these privates are open to group travelers and not as frequently to single travelers is economic—while the cost they charge for playing the gracious host is often prohibitive for one tourist, divided amongst a group of twenty participants, it is easily digestible.

Tourism may be an influential, edifying and enlightening ritual with positive long-term effects, but it is also a form of *edutainment*,[62] one of a cacophonous glut of possible ways to spend one's limited amount of free time. Coined by National Geographic Society's documentary film producer Bob Heyman, this neologism refers to the production of educational entertainment or entertaining education; it recognizes the choice individuals have to engage in such experiences, and therefore acknowledges the need to render education as enjoyable as possible. Always entered into through a conscious decision, the touristic ritual is imbued with the participant's expectation of an outcome that is oftentimes epistemologically or transcendentally rewarding, but always pleasurable. In an era of long work hours and ubiquitous media flows, tourist sites face unprecedented competition from a variety of sources for the public's leisure activities. A recent Harris Poll[63] that listed the top leisure activities enjoyed by Americans noted that while intellectual pursuits such as reading were at the top (reading was actually number one at 35%), "traveling" registered sixteenth on the list and tied with "sleeping"; both claimed 4% of the responses.

Long ago did the travel industry realize that their destinations must be tailored and marketed to correspond with the expectations of their target constituencies. They are marketed as products to be consumed. Thus, in attempting to deliver on the assumed expectations of a variety of passengers, destinations are "sold" to disparate consumers in a variety of ways, in accordance with their taste. Not only are disparate places categorized together in an effort to appeal to a particular taste—that is, as an "exotic island paradise," an "ancient historical site," a "pristine natural environment," a "luxury get-away," and so on—but the place itself can fall into multiple categories. All the industry must do is highlight different aspects of the place's narrative claim, re-presenting it in various ways to appeal to the assorted constituencies. Vietnam, in fact, is marketed alternatively to backpackers as an authentic country relatively untouched by mass tourism, to wealthy travelers as the luxurious jewel of French colonial Indochina, and to Vietnam War veterans as a place plagued with their painful memories of conflict that must be rectified. And tour operators, both foreign and indigenous, are only too happy to oblige with itineraries that are structurally the same—for example, a typical two week tour with a Saigon-Đà Nẵng-Huế-Ha Noi itinerary—but that emphasize different visits to seemingly make each appear as entirely different experiences to be enjoyed. Yet it is not only the large industry leaders who practice this standardization for their mass market, even the private visits, which explicitly differentiate themselves from the destinations on mass tourism itineraries, have begun to standardize their practices and their offerings. From Italy to Vietnam, owners of private homes, vineyards, gardens, schools and art studios all have begun modeling themselves on each other, imitating their competitors' best practices, and anticipating the already standardized expectations of the particular groups inclined to experience these visits—while at the same time trying to sell themselves in alternative ways to capture a greater diversity of tourist groups. In turn, any of the authentic backstage offerings these private visits supposedly suggest seem a sham to some dispassionate observers, although they are most often relished by the individual participants.

This narrative slight of hand may very well be the root of a famous debate on the tourist industry between Daniel J. Boorstin and Dean MacCannell, which continues among a new generation to this day. Writing in the 1960s with a level of cynicism towards the technological and cultural changes of the era typical for the time, Boorstin criticized a rather universalized idea of a tourist taste for its inauthenticity. He lambasted tourists for cultivating a preference for encounters that only appear exotic or different on the surface, but still maintain all of the preferred characteristics of their traditional lifestyle. Contending that tourists are in search of thinly veiled "pseudo-events," hollow re-presentations that promise all the thrill of changing one's perspective with none of the risks of distasteful unpleasantries associated with interacting with the real thing, he writes:

> The modern tourist now fills his experience with pseudo-events. He has come to expect both more strangeness and more familiarity than the world naturally offers. He has come to believe that he can have a lifetime of adventure in two weeks and all the thrills of risking his life without any real risk at all. He expects that the exotic and the familiar can be made to order: that a nearby vacation spot can give him Old World charm, and also that if he chooses the right accommodations he can have the comforts of home in the heart of Africa. Expecting all this, he demands that it be supplied to him. Having paid for it, he likes to think that he has got his money's worth. He has demanded that the whole world be made a stage for pseudo-events. And there has been no lack of honest and enterprising suppliers who try to give him what he wants, to help him inflate his expectations, and to gratify his insatiable appetite for the impossible.[64]

Addressing Boorstin's skepticism, MacCannell proposes that these vulnerable travelers are essentially duped by the tourist industry's "staged authenticity"[65]—a "staged quality to the proceedings that lends to them an aura of superficiality, albeit a superficiality not always perceived as such by the tourist."[66] Thus, while debunking Boorstin's criticisms of the tourist and his intentions, MacCannell nevertheless agrees that there is a pervasive inauthenticity in tourist encounters. Rather than placing the blame for this on the tourist himself (both he and Boorstin do not grant much agency to individual tourists), he contends that these inauthentic experiences are staged by a large and impersonal industry:

> Touristic consciousness is motivated by its desire for authentic experiences, and the tourist may believe that he is moving in this direction, but often it is very difficult to know for sure if the experience is in fact authentic. It is always

possible that what is taken to be entry into a back region is really entry into a front region that has been totally set up in advance for touristic visitation. In tourist settings, especially in industrial society, it may be necessary to discount the importance, and even the existence, of front and back regions except as ideal poles of touristic experience.[67]

While these experts seem to consider the industry in perhaps an overly harsh light, portraying it as a sort of multinational cabal, there is a solid kernel of truth to these assertions. Places are created, it must be remembered. They are both social and material in nature, just as much a product of tangible interactions as they are intangible narrative understandings. Just as UNESCO creates "unity in diversity" by alternatively "remembering" and "forgetting" parts of a World Heritage site's total life history, so too does the travel industry practice what can be called *standardized diversity*. Standardized diversity stems from the understanding that tourist sites must be differentiated to appeal to diverse groups of people, but they also must have a certain level of universality. This standardization is not only material, but social. This practice standardizes a place's infrastructure to meet the general needs and accessibilities of the broadest possible group of potential travelers, but it also attributes to the place generalized and universalized characteristics that allow it to be easily and organically represented along diverse lines in accordance with the emotional needs and expectations of different potential travelers. In this way, they can truly be "all things for all people" and for all circumstances. These places may certainly be differentiated, but they are also interchangeable.[68]

Thus, at the height of Mad Cow disease, in the months after September 11th, and as SARS and Avian Flu swept over different parts of the world, travelers were able to find places that they perceived were "similar" to the original destination to which they wanted to travel. Fearing Mad Cow disease, those booked on tours of the English countryside went to Tuscany instead; those supposed to be visiting the Pyramids in Egypt detoured to the British Museum after September 11, 2001; those wishing to view Angkor fled the flu by visiting the halls of the Musée Guimet. And even in peacetime, when the well-worn and already visited villas of Tuscany held no more intrigue for some repeat travelers who nevertheless wished to have a similar experience elsewhere in the country, tours of the estates in the Italian Lake District, or in the countryside outside of Milan, Trieste or Palermo, were created. But what is similar between a villa in Trieste and one in Tuscany, or between one in Tuscany and one in England, for that matter? What is similar about the Musée Guimet and Angkor Wat? What is similar about Vietnam and Japan? In the aforementioned cases, these travelers were not ignorant of history, geopolitics and aesthetics—indeed, they viewed themselves as "cultured" enough to recognize the extreme differences between these substitute destinations. Rather, the similarities in the expected, or desired, experiences were the same. For example, aside from those who for very specific, familial purposes wanted to visit the English countryside, it seems that the average tourist registered for these educational group excursions during the Mad Cow scare had the desire, for their voluntary and temporary leisure activity, to visit a European country setting that was well-known, easy to get by in, and safe—both physically and within the American imagination. Indeed, just as Americans are educated extensively in British history, culture, and cuisine, so too is classical and Italian art, history, culture and cuisine embraced comfortably in American society. They saw similar parallels. Portugal, Russia, Scandinavian countries, and even France were harder sells, despite all being untouched by Mad Cow disease. It seems that they just were not similar enough.

"Similar," of course, is an extraordinarily subjective word. Recently in Siena, a traveling companion who had never been to Tuscany remarked that the medieval clock tower atop the town's Palazzo Pubblico "looked like Big Ben."[69] Were one to place these edifices side by side, they would look nothing alike: One is lithe, orange-bricked and battlemented, while the other is thick and gray. One juts out from a large building that is itself attached on both sides to other medieval buildings; the other stands alone. One is seen from the expansive, pedestrianized and ovular Campo Square, while the other is seen from across a busy London street. Yet what is similar is that they are both bell towers, and that they are both foreign. This traveler, who by no means would be considered provincial in outlook, having visited her extended family in southern Italy a number of times, had only been on a purely "tourist trip" to England before, and certainly was struck by the newness of her Tuscan experience; in her mind, its foreignness created a center-periphery perception. Stating that it resembled Big Ben more closely than, say, a public clock in Paterson, New Jersey, she was articulating her perception that it was more like "them" than "us."

Pierre Loti, in the turn-of-the-century travelogue of his pilgrimage to Angkor, also finds himself comparing the Khmer sites to those in the Western canon, despite knowing that Italian artists surely did not create the fine bas-reliefs in Angkor Wat. He writes:

> Without hurrying this time, for no cloud threatens me, I climb the arduous steps which lead, above, to the dwelling of the gods. Oh, the graceful and exquisite carvings scattered in profusion everywhere! These ornamental scrolls, this leaf-work and decorative foliage—how to explain it—resemble those which appeared in France in the time of François I and the Medicis. For a moment one might be tempted to believe, if it were not an impossibility, that the artists of our Renaissance had sought their models on these walls, which, nevertheless, in

their days had been slumbering for three or four centuries, in the midst of forests, quite unsuspected by Europe.[70]

Loti had already been well-traveled by the time he had visited Angkor; in addition to having pursued the traditional "Grand Tour" through Italy and Southern
Europe, he had already seen China and Japan, as well as North Africa. He was
well aware of the regions' divergent histories, as well as the aesthetic differences between European Renaissance artwork and that of South and East Asia.
Yet when making meaning of the stunning decorations at Angkor Wat, he nevertheless drew upon knowledge of "his" artistic heritage to describe "theirs."
Thus, in the heritage-escape, understandings are able to complexify; similarities
and subtleties emerge. "Unity in diversity" becomes a comprehensible concept,
as the mind, glutted with multitudinous strangeness, grows more comfortable
with diversity and its infinite intricacies. Things out of the ordinary nevertheless
become less strange, more familiar. The simplistic, oppositional concept of "difference" gives way to complexified conception of "diversity." And, coupled
with a narrative claim of "World Heritage," these sites resist being considered
foreign at all; "them" gives way to "us."

Based on the quantity and quality of awareness and mediated by taste, these
expectations constantly form and re-form as the participant proceeds through the
separation phase of the touristic ritual. After deciding on the destination, the
would-be tourist next prepares himself for the ritual experience, by performing
two distinct activities. First, he gathers greater and more specified practical information about the site and the ritual experience itself. This process often begins when making the decision, but is brought to fruition only after the decision
has been made. Information can be collected either formally through true research in the library or online, or informally by soliciting the input and thoughts
of his associates—both those who have been to the destination, and those who
have not but possesses some awareness of the locale or its particulars. This also
includes research on the travel and land arrangements—he ascertains whether he
requires additional transportation, accommodations or meals; whether passports
are required or if there are any visa or immigration procedures for which to prepare; what are the departure and arrival times, when can he check in and check
out of the hotel; whether assistance is needed in booking these arrangements;
what are the associated costs; what season is best to visit; or what type of
weather should he anticipate. Once the participant has received enough of the
information—and each person is different in his or her threshold for information
gathering and decision-making—he will then begin to act on them, physically
making the arrangements necessary for fulfilling the ritual. The itinerary is
planned, maybe even written out; the gas tank is filled or the flight is booked;

hotel, restaurant and even museum reservations may be confirmed. Taking into consideration expectations concerning the weather, the physical impact of the journey, the sartorial needs of the trip, length of time that will be spent away from home, and even the amount of assistance in carrying suitcases or the capacity for transporting baggage, he also packs his suitcases accordingly.

With preparations complete, the participant may now embark on the third and final step of the separation process—that of *disconnection*. Although most commonly conceptualized, and indeed manifested, as physical movement from one place to another, disconnection seems a more appropriate term when considering tourism not simply as travel, but as a ritual interaction predicated on a specific way of seeing. Disconnection here denotes the conscious shift in focus from the normalcy of such permanent or semi-permanent interactions to the removed, temporary interaction that is tourism. This shift is clearly evident when effected as a physical movement itself; embarking on a boat or airplane to move across the world, driving in a car or bus to a park or museum, or opening the door to look at one's backyard all are actions that have been cited by experts as evidence of tourism as a ritual endeavor.[71] It is further pronounced in international tours, which begins with a complex procedure of obtaining passports and visas that officially and symbolically grants *temporary* access to this movement away from one's "normal" locality (for example, his "homeland"), and ends after the participant, upon reaching his foreign destination, passes through customs and immigration; the stamp on his passport granting entry into this new, un-normal territory provides the symbolic record of his temporary disconnection. Yet the change in the mind's approach to the local and foreign places alike—from a monotonous way of seeing to a new "tourist gaze"—can also begin with a mere glance of the eyes or a refocus of any of the five senses, without the use of airplanes, passports or visas.

Disconnection also colors expectations, as one weighs the energy, time, and money that are necessary for physical movement. Not only would a glance have significantly less of a long-term impact than the use of an airplane and a hired limousine service, but the expectations of whether the endeavor itself was "worth it" would most likely be much lower. Taste continues to play an important part. For some, traveling with the masses in coach class on an airline is appalling, and more money is spent on a business or first class ticket; expectations then often rise not only as the class of service rises, but often as the price of these higher-class tickets increases. From this author's experience, the passenger's price threshold is related not only to the class of the booking, but also to the distance traveled; passengers hailing from the United States' East Coast expect incrementally more luxury if the price is very high on a trans-Atlantic (European) flight than if it is high on a longer, trans-Pacific or African flight.

Frequent Flier programs, which cultivate loyalty, also play a factor, as people are promised to expect preferential treatment, such as an upgrade or seating in "economy plus"—which because of individual flights' seating capacities often may not materialize as planned. Finally, and most importantly, the specific form of travel may often recall individual sets of images, re-presentations and narratives. These could have been formed through previous experiences; for example, many will talk about how luxurious or how terrible a particular airline is, based on an experience that may have had very little to do with the service or amenities of the airline itself, such as a bad case of turbulence. These can also be formed through previously consumed re-presentations of travel. For example, hearkening back to a somewhat mythological Golden Age of locomotive travel, many may view travel by rail as a "romantic" endeavor, expecting the same romance and luxury as portrayed in films, photos and nineteenth-century lore; certainly the rail industry seeks to capitalize on this, marketing their own rosy re-presentations of this era, despite the fact that today's rail lines are frequently not as luxurious as perhaps they once were. Thus, distance, price, difficulty, taste and imagined narratives associated with the form of travel all contribute to the formation of the expectations lens through which the entire touristic ritual will be approached and experienced.

Expectations are the separation phase's most significant products—and indeed, they remain so throughout the tourist experience—for they lay the very contextual foundation for how a person approaches and views the site. This, in turn, impacts the actions he produces *in situ*, and meaning he will make of the place once he returns to normalcy. Thus, one calls forth memories of past experiences not only to make meaning in the present, but also to anticipate the future. Rachel Fulton eloquently puts this when she writes:

> Phenomenologically . . . the crafting of narrative as lived involves more than just the retrospective emplotment of facts or memories and the discovery within this emplotment of origins or beginnings, patterns of development, characteristic structures, symptoms, and the like (that is, the usual project of history). *It also involves the prospective emplotment of endings*, the projection into the imagined or remembered beginnings and lived middles of human experience of that Solonic conclusion without which it is deemed impossible to judge the happiness, rectitude, or importance of a human life or community of lives, either relatively, in their historical context, or more absolutely, in their moral or cosmological context.[72]

Especially when tourism involves any movement over space, or especially, over time—be it down the street, to a museum, or to an exotic locale, in the present or sometime in the future—it is planned. Even the most spontaneous or swiftest of travel involves expectations, imaginings that anticipate what the future will bring. These expectations are often built upon the desire to live out an imagined idea—the traveler seeking education would expect the interaction to expand his knowledge, the pilgrim would expect an enlightening experience, and the island vacationer would expect relaxation. But predicated on representations, these expectations may emplot an unattainable ending to the imagined story.

Liminality: Interacting with Authenticity

The liminal stage is the pivotal period in any ritual, for it is the core around which the entire event revolves. Liminality is often conceptualized as a sort of timelessness, where calendrical temporality is suspended. Stripped of status and suspended in time, preconceived social conceptualizations of normality is relaxed. Turner describes it as "the liberation of human capacities of cognition, affect, volition, creativity, etc., from the normative constraints incumbent upon occupying a sequence of social statuses."[73]

Achieving the markedly unique sensation of liminality is the expected goal of tourism, its "sacred" crux, as Graburn argues.[74] For the tourist, these places are magical, they are sacred; they are the object of "secular pilgrimages" whether these pilgrimages are lengthy or short, difficult or easy, foreign or local. As a way of seeing, furthermore, even a common, everyday place can be a "sacred" tourist site when gazed upon in this fashion. Thus, one's backyard can equally be the portent of transcendence and education, it can be the center of a ritual creating *communitas* with others near and far. Even van Gennep described the interchangeability of something from profane to sacred, and vice versa, when he discusses the "pivoting of the sacred:"

> The presence of the sacred is variable. Sacredness as an attribute is not absolute; it is brought into play by the nature of particular situations. A man at home, in his tribe, lives in the secular realm; he moves into the realm of the sacred when he goes on a journey and finds himself a foreigner near a camp of strangers . . . thus the "magic circles" pivot, shifting as a person moves from one place in society to another. The categories and concepts which embody them operate in such a way that whoever passes through the various positions of a lifetime one day sees the sacred where before he sees the profane, or vice versa. Such changes of condition do not occur without disturbing the life of society or the individual.[75]

Thus, the sacredness, the magic, which seems an inherent product of the site's authenticity, is actually merely a perception—a way of approaching and viewing that place or object. Claims of authenticity, therefore, are woven subtly into both the place's overall narrative and that of the tourist, which he imposes on the site.

Just as UNESCO takes great pains to verify the supposed authenticity of each of its sites, so too are tour guides and travel articles obsessed with pointing out the "real," "the true" and the "authentic" in every venue and destination. The reason is pragmatic. At considerable expense—if not monetary then at least temporally, as leisure time is limited—tourists escape the quotidian workaday to interact materially with the site. It would come as quite a shock, and indeed, would undoubtedly produce a staggering feeling of unfulfillment, if the site was fake; otherwise the entire escape could be merely a façade. Yet there is a fine line between authenticity of tangibles and authenticity of experience, and "preserved" heritage sites often find themselves negotiating this line. Authenticators are compelled to decide, on a case by case basis, when restoration becomes re-creation. This was an especially charged debate after the Taliban destroyed Afghanistan's Bamiyan Buddhas. Unlike broken pottery or an archaeological remain, this is a site that quite literally vanished into dust; all that is left are empty spaces, holes in the mountains where previously stood immense heritage objects. In that moment of interaction between dynamite and sandstone, a vortex was created where once a portal stood between the past and the present. Their memory still fresh in the collective contemporary mind, one contingent urged reconstruction. Reconstruction was considered not because it was a site of ongoing worship, for the local people were not even Buddhists but Muslims, but because it would restore the tangible evidence of a specific and valued period of history. Reconstruction could not restore the authentic site, but it could restore the authenticity of the experience future visitors would have. Ultimately this plan was abandoned, for recreating the site would be denying the place an important part of its total life history: that of its death.

This anecdote reveals that authenticity of tourist sites pertains not only to the singular, physical object—as in a museum, where these objects remain permanently separated from their physical environments and stand alone—but to their greater surroundings, as well. Yet what constitutes these surroundings, what constitutes the experience of the "original" is quite subjective. Thus, authenticity is not an absolute, but rather a perception based on the narrative understandings each individual utilizes when approaching the site. It varies from person to person and site to site, depending on what each person believes are essential components for providing the physical link between past and present that only an "original" can offer. Thus cultivated beforehand in the mind, the *in situ* perception of authenticity is also always tempered by one's expectations of what he or she previously imagined it would be.

In the liminal phase of the touristic ritual, the participant finds himself "betwixt and between" his previous state of "normalcy" and the future state he expects to grow into upon completion of the total experience. He is as van Gennep states, in a passage from one world to another as if at the threshold of the doorway—in this case, in the doorway between the local and the foreign. He is not quite a local, but nevertheless is found communing with the destination in a more tangible way than before. This between status of the tourist is not simply reflected in the ethereal grayness of the mind, but is manifested materially in the relaxation of common social norms that are afforded to him by the host culture. He is at once subject to the customs, laws and mores of the land, but yet given a pass should he make a mistake. Like the immunity diplomats from foreign embassies enjoy while at their post in another country, the visitor has a sort-of unwritten "tourist immunity" wherein the locals' traditional expectations of decent practice are relaxed for him.

Indicative of this betwixt and between state of being, the relaxation of social norms occurs even within a tourist's host country, not just when he is a foreigner in a different society. Basic learned activities such as spending money within one's means, not stealing, and "looking both ways" when crossing the street suddenly do not seem as obligatory as they would be when at home. Tourists are on vacation—not only from the daily rigmarole, but also from their worries, their budgets, and their traditional social obligations. During April 2006 at the Tidal Basin on the National Mall in Washington, DC, a number of domestic tourists were observed ripping whole cherry blossom boughs off of trees with little regard for their status as federal and historic property—let alone the signage explicitly prohibiting this action. Signs in Cannon Beach, Oregon that forbid climbing on picturesque Haystack Rock, a protected marine garden rising two hundred and thirty-five feet above a sandbar off the coast, are similarly disregarded by vacationers to this beach town; tourists can be observed clambering on the rocky surface, trampling the tidal pools and ripping starfish and sea anemones from their unique habitat. To combat this, a Haystack Rock Awareness Program was created in 1985, which sends "volunteer interpreter and protectionists of the Rock and the life it supports" onto the beach a low tide, when this offense most often occurs.[76]

On the international scene, Vietnam's Hạ Long Bay fares even worse, its slow destruction occurring at the hands of those who paradoxically look to it for material and mythological sustenance. Entrepreneurs sell pieces of their fragile, local ecosystem to souvenir-hungry tourists. They rip seashells and coral from the bay, and even stalagmites from within the islands' caves, to sell on land as natural souvenirs. The destruction has become so widespread and so troublingly overlooked by foreign visitors and those who assist them in their search for take-home tourist treasures, that one edition of *Lonely Planet Vietnam* even writes:

> Dragons aside, the biggest threat to the bay may be from souvenir-hunting tourists. Rare corals and seashells are rapidly being stripped from the seafloor, while stalactites and stalagmites are being broken off from the caves. These items get turned into key rings, paperweights and ashtrays, which are on sale in the local souvenir shops. You might consider the virtue of not buying these items and spending your cash instead on postcards and silk paintings.[77]

Interestingly enough, the writers make no reference of the actual illegality of robbing this UNESCO World Heritage site, nor do they provide any forceful rebuke; rather, they simply make an even-handed suggestion to "consider the virtue" of spending one's money on other forms of souvenirs.

Tourist sites encountered within the liminal period are seen in a different light. They are floating in an ambiguous in-between state, at once a fragile and transient vestige of a culture past and, at the same time, an indestructible structure resisting that very same fragility, enduring endlessly onward into the future. Their status, as well as the tourist's status, is in equal flux. They are encountered by individuals in their own nebulously in-between state, where they are not quite locals intimately associated with the site, nor are they simply a dispassionate outside observer. And the two ambiguous beings collide, often to disastrous consequences. This interaction seems to swirl in an undefined temporality where past, present and future intermingle, where both are wiped of their here-ness and are free to act without consequences towards one another. Though it remains unstated, the tourist nevertheless comprehends the acute transience of this very fleeting interaction, and he needs to grab on, to delay it, and to take back with him some tangible evidence of this unique experience through which he could live and relive the experience again upon his reemergence from the ritual—just as the site itself has etched that interaction upon its very being, keeping, too, a part of the past and carrying a piece of the tourist with it as it persists in its onward movement through time. And stealing from the site becomes nothing more than the acquisition of souvenirs, the innocent yet important practice of bringing home one's memories crystallized into material form.

Hotels bear the brunt of the pilfering of souvenirs, as many guests take not only the complementary soaps and amenities, but also the towels, washcloths, slippers and robes. Although many may try to justify their actions by the fact that money has exchanged hands for their room, this rationalization fails to hold water as they will admit to understanding that the money they paid specifically does not include the towels and other articles. And sometimes their stealing defies even the best rationalization, as in the case of one group tour to Cambodia in early 2004. Having pulled away from the Siem Reap hotel en route to the airport for a flight to Vietnam, bags stowed beneath, the busload of tourists slowly erupted in a commotion from the back of the bus forward. As the din grew louder to include more of the group, this tour director investigated. Holding up the hotel's remote control, one passenger's husband said flatly, "she packed it with the rest of the stuff." She literally packed everything but the kitchen sink, and indeed the group at the back of the bus had been debating whether to tell anyone about it or to simply keep it as a souvenir—most likely to be thrown away shortly thereafter. Indeed, precisely because common norms for safety and acceptable behavior seem relaxed—and dangerously at that—tour directors and guides have often commented that they are less guides and more "babysitters," watching after their passengers, checking their chairs and motorcoach seats for purses and bags undoubtedly left behind, and stopping traffic as the group crosses the street like a pack of lemmings, without looking both ways.

Sometimes, however, the relaxation of social rules for tourists can be seen as a rather dangerous double standard, especially when these rules are written into law, as in a recently passed piece of Malaysian legislation. Although its capital city, Kuala Lumpur, is a multicultural mix of ethnic Chinese, Malay, and Indians, Malaysia is an Islamic state whose legal culture is colored by *sharia* sensibilities. In 2003, police arrested a Malaysian couple of Chinese descent for kissing and holding hands in a park in front of the famed Petronas Towers; in the summer of 2005, Malaysia's highest court upheld this ruling, sentencing the young couple, Ooi Kean Thong, 23 and Siow Ai Wei, 22, to a year in jail and a hefty fine of US$4,200. In response to criticism by human rights activists, Kuala Lumpur's mayor Roslin Hassan assured tourists that they would be exempt from indecency charges if they wish to kiss and hold hands, warning, "We will not harass tourists for kissing in public, but it better not be the passionate kind." Nevertheless, the couple's lawyer, S. Selvam questioned what can be perceived as an unfair and socially damaging double standard, "If locals can be prosecuted for kissing, why not foreign tourists?"[78]

Re-Aggregation: Returning Home, Rectifying Expectations

All of these expectations are evaluated *post hoc* as the participant experiences the third and final phase of the touristic ritual. This reaggregation phase represents the culmination of the entire tourist experience, as the tourist, fresh from his interactions with the destination, re-inserts himself, changed, into what for him is a "normal" state of interaction. While the separation phase was significant for generating the expectations ultimately used to perceive the destination *in situ*, and the liminal phase was integral for fostering the formative and transformative interactions with the place itself, this phase is important for making meaning of the entire experience, which will in turn, be utilized in future interactions by the changed participant. In this last period, the returning tourist attempts to rectify that which he expected he would perceive with that which he actually perceived; in short, he evaluates the expectations cultivated during the separation phase against his perceptions of the authentic site that he actually experienced during the liminal phase. The final result of this reaggregation process is that the experiences garnered in this ritual are committed to memory through the formation of meaningful narratives that are based not solely on objective observations of the site, but rather are colored by the level of satisfaction they have with the experience. Of course, these narratives can—and frequently do—change and deepen as they are played and replayed in the mind, as new information is added, or as they are used to make use of new memories from future reaggregration phases of subsequent touristic rituals.

The possible outcome of this evaluative process is often measured by the level of satisfaction one ultimately has for the experience. This satisfaction is inversely proportional to the size of the "expectations gap"—the disconnect between that which was expected and that which was produced—which exists upon completion of the interactive experience. This gap works both ways, though it is often more apparent when it provides a negative meaning of the place. Often glowing post-tour evaluations state that a trip "exceeded my wildest dreams" or was "more than I had hoped for." In such cases, there is a positive expectations gap, as the expectations were exceeded. When travelers tend to be satisfied, their expectations were generally met.

One very satisfied colleague recounted her favorite travel experience, which occurred as she was leaving Cambodia for Vietnam. Crammed on a bus with friendly locals, the memory of her inspirational interaction with Angkor still fresh in her mind, she said with peace and exuberance that she achieved "travel Nirvana." This was a striking description, and a telling one at that. Although this Buddhist term is conceived somewhat differently between the two great Indo-Chinese strands of the religion—the Theravāda and Mahāyāna traditions—achieving it nevertheless represents the supreme goal of the religion's ritual meditative practice, in much the same way that achieving transformative transcendence or illumination is the tourist's intended objective in the touristic ritual. The Mahāyāna tradition associates Nirvana with *dharma-dhatu*, or "ultimate reality"—a confirmation that one's transcendent or otherwise illuminative perceptions have cut through tourism's staged authenticity and brought the participant into direct contact with the truly authentic, the "really real." Likewise, for the traveler, achieving travel Nirvana seems that he has stepped over the outsider's perspective into the local situation, that he cut through the simulated and the fabricated and touched the authentic, that he truly understands what life is like for the locals—no matter how gritty or difficult—and that it is a perfected experience. However, it is not that one has truly crossed over into the privileged realm of the local, but that his mind has reconciled that which he expected with that which he has actually perceived.

Dissatisfaction with an experience occurs when one's perceptions do not live up to expectations. There are two possibilities for the emergence of this negative expectation gap. The first occurs when a tourist re-visits a site, expecting it to resemble the memory of his prior experience, but is met with an unfavorable experience. Accompanying a renowned garden expert to Palermo, Sicily one recent spring was a heartbreaking experience for this very reason. Walking around together in the famed *Orto Botanico*, one of the Mediterranean's oldest botanic gardens, this author noticed the horticulturalist becoming more and more lethargic and saddened. She suddenly stopped and sat dejected on a bench, tears welling up in her eyes. When asked why she became so depressed, she confided that the garden was not as she remembered it used to be. She had visited the garden a good number of years earlier, and even wrote on it; unfortunately, since the time of her writing, a new custodian had taken over, leaving the large public gardens to wither in neglect. Tree branches littered the dirt pathways, the box hedges were in need of trimming, the greenhouses were very limited, and even the enormous banyan trees for which the garden was famous looked sad, wilted. In the decade since she had visited, the garden had changed without her knowing. And it produced a striking expectation gap that could not be easily rectified.

Second, as Alain de Botton evocatively argues, when constructing expectations, the traveler rarely takes into account the seemingly secondary qualities of the destination.[79] These qualities which had lived in the margins of his imaginings move with striking emphasis to the forefront of his perceptions during the actual tourist encounter, and he perceives a difference. One blogger's great expectations of communing with Hạ Long Bay were completely overshadowed by an experience of being overcharged for a beer by his tour boat operator. Although feeling "ripped off" by the boatmen might seem to have very little direct connection to the Bay's aesthetic or historical qualities, this ancillary experience clearly overshadowed any experience of direct communion with the site itself, and left a negative overall perception of the World Heritage site.

Hotels are often innocuous sites of such an expectation gap, for they are in the unenviable position of serving as both a primary locus of touristic interaction with the place, as well as a refuge from that same place, which one purchases for a price.[80] The tourist's temporary lodging—his "home away from home"—the hotel becomes local while still being foreign, unusual, or at least out of the ordinary. Those who have not anticipated any true differences will therefore naturally expect all of the amenities and comforts as he is accustomed to having at home, and are surprised—sometimes violently upset[81]—when the hotel does not live up to expectations. Amenities are especially important here; often one has expectations of differences between the size, structure and adornments, but neglect to consider the small things, such as hair dryers, body wash, Internet access and toothpaste. Americans expect cotton over terrycloth in their towels; they also expect facecloths. Indeed, facecloths are looked on quizzically in many standard European and Southeast Asian hotels, and many hoteliers this author has spoken with have attested to being taken aback by the sheer volume of unexpected complaints leveled against their establishments if they were not able to produce these small cotton towels; a manager at a prominent five star hotel in Tuscany once confided that they put facecloths in the rooms only when they see they are booked by Americans. And, reacting a bit irrationally to this gap in what she expected and what the hotel delivered, one traveler boasted that she cut up a terrycloth towel into the size of a washcloth when a hotel could not produce one.[82]

While the dissatisfaction with a hotel's amenities most often stems simply from neglecting to consider the accommodation's secondary qualities, the expectation gap is exacerbated when the hotel quite simply does not live up to what the tourist had imagined. This is especially a problem in so-called "historic" hotels across the world, such as the once-renowned grand old hotels such as Saigon's Majestic, Rex, and Grand Hotels that seem to have lived past their primes. Travelers often chose these hotels in a nod to their desire as tourists to experience something out of the ordinary, to commune with the past, to "live like the locals" or to share in the heritage of luxury from a different era. Yet they may neglect to consider the differences in expectations of what constitute luxury between generations. On the other end of the spectrum, new constructions that purport to provide an "authentic" experience of the place—such as the luxurious Grand Hotel d'Angkor or any of the many decadent resorts recently constructed in Siem Reap or outside Hội An—are met with extreme satisfaction because they are constructed with their foreign visitors' expectations in mind. Not only do they provide all of the modern, American amenities that simply did not exist in the historic era of *Indochine*, but their aesthetics are polished and idealized to meet the rather colonial expectations fostered through numerous romanticized re-presentations of what Indochine was supposed to be.

Another secondary characteristic is the smell of the place—something not easily conveyed in a site's fragmentary or reproducible re-presentations. Travelers to the Mekong Delta, for example, often have cultivated expectations based on its numerous re-presentations in fictional Vietnam War films and documentaries—the murky water, the jungle, perhaps even the heat. Yet they are nevertheless taken aback by the pungent smell of *nước mắm*—the ubiquitously consumed fish sauce cultivated in export quantities right in the Delta. While for the Vietnamese *nước mắm* is considered the food of the gods, for some foreign visitors, including the food expert and travel writer Alan Richman, it is thought to be "a condiment unfit for human consumption," "rotted-shrimp paste" that "smelled like a cross between old cheese and cat droppings." Richman, who fought in the Vietnam War, remembered, "the insanely pungent, omnipresent fish sauce . . . had platoons of men diving for cover whenever a Vietnamese got hungry."[83]

A destination's climactic conditions are another area of potential discontent, for this intangible factor is truly perceivable only *in situ*, and is not easily conveyed in imagery. This sentiment is not relegated to merely modern tourists, but can be found in the classic travel accounts during the French colonial period, such as Pierre Loti's famed *A Pilgrimage to Angkor*. Though Loti's 1901 voyage from Saigon to Angkor did not benefit from the modern convenience of air-conditioning, he recorded very similar thoughts about the oppressive nature of the climate, which certainly colored his overall appreciation of the site for which he had pined to visit since childhood. He describes Saigon's climate as such: "A noxious moist heat oppresses the lungs; the air seems to be the vapor of some cauldron in which perfumes are mingled with putrefaction." (9). Just as he anticipated achieving transcendence when reaching Angkor, as he departed Saigon he anticipated a more comfortable climate as he ventured into the jungles. But as he reached My Tho, sixty kilometers southwest of Saigon in the Mekong Delta, he remarks that, although there is "peace and silence" and park-like beauty, "the place would be perfect were it not for this eternal heaviness of the air and these enervating scents."[84] At Phnom Penh, he states that "the air here is already less oppressive than at Saigon, less charged with electricity and moisture. One feels more alive."[85] But after spending a little time there, he laments the morning heat, which is "already oppressive."[86] The heat had a pointed effect on Loti's overall enjoyment of Angkor Wat, which—it should be reiterated—he had dreamed of visiting since he was a little boy. Recounting his first impressions of Angkor Wat, he writes, "the colossal ramparts and the towers that have just appeared to us, like some mirage of the torrid heat, are not the town itself [Angkor Thom], but only Angkor Wat." As he recognized the towers "at once" from "the old picture which had so troubled me once upon a time, on an April evening, in my childhood museum," he writes sadly,

> Yet somehow I do not feel the emotion that I should have expected. It is probably too late in life, and I have seen too many of these remains of the great past, too many temples, too many palaces, too many ruins. Besides it is all so

blurred, as it were, under the glare of the daylight; it is difficult to see because it is too bright. And, above all, midday is drawing near with its lassitude, its invincible somnolence."[87]

Loti's sentiments are indicative of the expectations gap that often plagues tourists, and reveals that the gap between anticipated and actual experiences is a complex composite of many factors. He muses that his lack of enthusiasm could stem from his prior experiences, which dulled his sense of excitement when encountering new temples and exploring new ruins. He seems to suggest that he is "Churched out" as so many American tourists have been overheard remarking in their contemporary European tours.

Weather also plays an inordinate part in fulfilling or disappointing expectations. Very rarely do postcards, guidebooks, or promotional travel materials depict destinations under a gray sky or during a downpour, even if they are representing places—such as Southeast Asia—that regularly enjoy large amounts of rain. This affects one's expectations of the imagery and overall experience, such that the emotions of resonance and wonder, garnered when interacting with the site itself, mix and mingle in the memory with the emotions of the heat, distasteful smells, or other sentiments of disillusionment. For Loti, Saigon is awash in "the customary deluge. Everything is streaming with tepid water," which reminds him that his brother "like so many others of his generation [came here] to absorb the germs of death."[88] Cambodia fares no differently; he laments the rain and curses the "evil dew" that "moistens everything."[89] At one point he remarks, "There has been such an excess of humidity during the night, so heavy a dew, that in spite of the thatched roof everything around me and on me is soaked, as after a shower."[90] Such "eternal humidity," he muses, is also responsible for impeding his enjoyment of Angkor's bas reliefs, which had been turned "a blackish color."[91] Yet it is the rain that truly ruined his enjoyment of Angkor, as this evocative excerpt reveals:

> The rain! A few first drops, astonishingly large and heavy, by way of warning. And then almost at once the general drumming on the leaves, torrents of water which descend in fury. Then through a portico, the overloaded lintel of which is in the form of flames and finials, running to take shelter, I enter at last what must be the sanctuary itself. . . . This, then, is the sanctuary which formerly haunted my childish imagination, which I have only at last reached after many journeyings about the world, in what is already the evening of my wandering life. *It gives me a mournful welcome. I had not foreseen these torrents of rain, this confinement amongst the spiders' webs,* nor my present solitude in the midst of so many phantom gods. . . . *A prisoner here for as long as the storm may last,* I go first of all to a window, instinctively, to get more air, to escape

the odour of the bats. . . . The water can be heard crackling more and more, rushing in a thousand streams.[92]

Present-day tourists fare no better, even when they are closer to home. This author remembers a fateful garden tour of the Italian lake region in an unusually rainy May 2002. Though the group was composed of American gardeners who, to their credit, were used to traipsing in the mud, and they often commented on how much more beautiful flowers are in the rain, after a week it just was too much. Travelers were grouchy and disappointed—they clearly did not anticipate the added hassle of raincoats, of changing multiple times, and of not soaking in the beautiful vistas of the Alpine lakes, which were obscured by the low, gray clouds. To make matters worse, this was a tour of the lake, with a number of planned boat excursions. *Acqua di sopra, acqua di sotto*—water, water everywhere—laughed one guide later; no wonder everyone was so gloomy. The guide then proceeded to recount her own story about a recent group of British golfers on holiday in the Tuscan countryside. It rained every day without fail, but they made the most of it, golfing with umbrellas and ponchos. On one of the last days, they met the guide in Florence for a day's walking tour. Stepping out of the bus and into the rain once again, many were taken completely by surprise, having left their umbrellas back at the hotel outside of town. "But why didn't you bring your umbrellas?" she asked them, knowing they had been outdoors in a consistently rainy Tuscany for a week. One traveler answered, "We didn't think it rains in Florence."

Ultimately, the resolution of these expectation gaps is intensely variable and powerfully personal. Some rectify it by suggesting themselves it simply was not what they expected, despite having cultivated precise ideas in the separation phase. Others call forth their own ethical assumptions to create a positive experience from one that is perceived to be negative, as one elderly Evangelical Christian did on a visit to Phnom Penh.

In addition to the important meaning-making process the reaggregation phase advances, it also cultivates a deepened *communitas* built around UNESCO's claim of unity in diversity. Like the other two ritual phases, the reaggregation phase is equally standardized across tourist genres for both FITs and group tour participants. When it involves formal movement from place to place—especially by air—three equally standardized sub-phases become very distinct, as well. In air travel, the participant first departs the destination to begin his trip home, completing a number of formalities that publicly and legally declare his intention to complete the tourist ritual (a mini separation phase); he then transfers from tourist destination to home, where he is physically "betwixt and between" the tourist destination and what is for him his local place of origin (a mini liminal phase); and, finally, he arrives in his locality to complete formal procedures that legally recognize his return into the society from which he temporarily left (reaggregation). These structures create a final level of *communitas* that is integral to the heritage-scape, as they create solidarity amongst travelers, albeit tenuous, irrespective of the particular heritage site with which they interacted.

In the mini separation phase, the international tourist departs his hotel, either alone or with companions, and arrives at the airport—a homogenous global meeting ground that is sanitized of most indigenous qualities. There are the eateries, the exchange booths, the duty free stands, and the bathrooms. All are marked with universally applied symbols—both pictorial and linguistic. That is, they are always marked with easy to identify drawings, as well as signage in the English language. The traveler must negotiate several ritualized formalities for officially leaving the country and returning home—he checks in at the appropriate airline counter, obtaining a tangible receipt of his seat on the return trip home, and he then hands over his bags filled with the souvenirs, remnants and clothes dirtied from the trip. Afterwards, he passes through immigration and possibly customs, where, with the presentation of his passport, visa and any VAT tax forms, he makes formal his desire to separate from the tourist destination. A stamp by the foreign customs agent over the visa in his passport officially recognizes that his stay has occurred, and that there is no turning back; he transfers to the appropriate terminal and departure gate to wait for his turn to board the vehicle that will physically take him back to his country of origin.

After he has passed through these check-in and immigration proceedings, the traveler enters into a mini liminal sub-phase, as he finds himself and his status, both physically and legally, in flux. Although his legal status reflects it, he has not quite physically departed the country. Yet he has not been recognized by his own country as having arrived, either. In addition, throughout this period he resides in a sanitized space, that of the international airport and, later, the international plane. Both of these are liminal holding spaces, rather undifferentiated from one to another, regardless of the country in which they are found or, in the case of passenger jets, from where they come or go. Finally, the traveler finds himself with very little of his personal effects from his local life or mementos from his touristic experience with him; he has been compelled to check them in before boarding, and is permitted only one small carry-on and one personal bag to take with him on the plane. While in the airport, he is allowed to purchase a certain amount of "duty free" goods, yet these articles also have equally been sanitized of any indigenous qualities; they are themselves in a permanent state of betwixt and between, subject to few regulatory laws and no entry or exit taxes. And if he buys too many, he is often forced to "gate-check" these articles or his carry-on bag, leaving them with the flight attendants until he returns to his country. Even those personal memory devices he manages to physically transport with him on the plane are removed from his presence before he is strapped in place. Upon boarding the flight, he "stows away" any remaining "carry on bags," remanding them out of sight in indistinguishable compartments above him. Not only are all of his possessions effectively out of sight, but they are out of mind as well; he is encouraged to forget about them while traveling—films are shown, food is served, newspapers and in-flight magazines are provided, music is offered with private headphones, and even video games are offered by many carriers for further distraction. Should this not be enough to dissuade him from accessing these personal articles stowed sightless above, he is also warned of the dangers of standing up to access them; not only can his actions inconvenience others around him, or turbulence might throw him around if he stands up, but he must also exercise extreme caution because "contents may have shifted"—a warning repeated to passengers with such severity it would seem that the bags had morphed into something more dangerous during the time they were out of sight. Thus, by the time he is actively transferring from the tourist destination to his own local destination, he has been stripped almost completely naked of all tangible remnants of his touristic ritual, not to be seen again until he finishes the reaggregation phase.

But he is not alone. Joining him at the airport hub are hundreds of other strangers, similarly stripped naked of most physical characteristics that identify the specific touristic experience in which they were engaged. Furthermore, the ritual encounter that airports foster is not only a part of the broader touristic ritual, but also brings together non-tourists engaging in travel for alternative reasons, as well as those who are working on the quotidian level in this global space. In this sanitized, undifferentiated global holding space, all of these individuals mix and mingle, cultivating their own unique form of *communitas* linked by common and ritual behavior. As each participant finds himself in different statuses and at different points within the same multi-locational ritual, each provides different color to this multihued mix. Some are departing, eagerly embarking on their journey, their minds filled with expectations. Some are arriving home, actively rectifying any expectation gap that may have emerged during the touristic ritual, the perceptions of the experience still fresh in their minds. Some are simply in transit, transferring from plane to plane and place of departure and place of arrival, either on their way home or their way to the destination. And some are even in the midst of their tourist vacation, transferring from one destination to another, in between points of the itinerary, their expectations intermingling with their perceptions. Thus, each traveler in this intermingling community brings different levels of expectations, perceptions, and meaningful understandings of the touristic interaction, constructing a deeper understanding of the narrative "unity in diversity," which is infused in the minds of the participants through passive sensory perceptions and active person-to-person interactions alike.

The total reaggregation phase concludes after the participant arrives at his local airport—and how it resembles the foreign one he just left! Here, he makes the formal entry back into his normal, local status. While still on the plane, he fills out a customs declaration and, with his signature and date, swears that what he declared was truthful under penalty of law. Upon disembarkation, he is led through a secure passageway to an immigration processing center. Just as when he arrived in the foreign airport at the commencement of his journey, he is forced to publicly choose whether to be counted as a "foreigner" or a "national." This time he can choose to be a "national," and he moves towards that particular line, where usually an airport greeter meets him with a "welcome home." After waiting in line, the traveler reaches an immigration officer, to whom he formally presents his credentials. The officer examines the passports, the stamps contained inside, and the customs declaration to ensure they coincide; the officer often asks a few questions of the passenger as well. A firm stamp welcomes the weary traveler home, sending him to collect his baggage. He eagerly awaits his suitcases, filled with all of the tangible remnants of his touristic journey—the only true material proof of the change the trip made. If all his bags arrive intact, the traveler has only one more hurdle to overcome—the reconciliation of his new status, as represented materially by his baggage, and his previous status as a local. Material changes in possession is highly regulated; one cannot enter with an excess of valuables, cash, souvenirs or goods such as liquor or tobacco. Nor can he bring in seeds, plants, and many kinds of perishable foods—in short, samples or products of indigenous life that could be consumed outside its context or otherwise propagated in this new environment. If he does have such an excess, or suspects as much, he must "declare" it in customs, or risk being possibly detected and searched. The latter often happens when one returns from more "foreign" or suspect locales, sometimes, it seems, more the product of a customs agent's curiosity to know just what exactly does the destination provide. Once this final point is reconciled, he is granted passage to reaggregate; often there is even a sign warning that there is no turning back once the traveler exists customs. The giant door opens to a roar of the crowd. The traveler, blinking in the light and dazzled by the local life outside the sanitized airport, emerges, blending into the mosaic of his countrymen. And he joins the confluence of individuals—some returning, some departing, and some transferring—and becomes a part of yet another *communitas* of similar travelers, the narrative of "unity in diversity" deepening further still.

Through the ritual interaction of tourism, UNESCO's narrative of "unity in diversity" is actively played out, rendered tangible and given dimension. Participants are compelled to undergo a binding experience that is both highly standardized and social; this experience highlights the cultivation of *communitas* irrespective of the quality, timeframe or location of the actual tourist experience. The form of *communitas* generated is not superficial in nature, but characterized by individual, interior transformation, of which status is only a part. While this experience, like other ritual encounters, may mark a change in the participant's social status—especially when they are linked to coming-of-age rites of passage for "gap year" backpackers—the World Heritage tourist undergoes a more fundamental transformation in the way in which he perceives his place in space and time. Communing with these sites, which themselves have mixed and mingled with other disparate-yet-similarly-identified places, he feels a connection to the past in the present, and to the foreign in the local. And he internalizes it all, broadening his awareness of the bonds between him and the diversity of natural and cultural constructions, of the preexistence of life before his time, and of the continuation of life in previously undifferentiated spaces that existed beyond that which he perceived on a daily basis. He brings this narrative understanding back with him, mixing and mingling the remembered images and narratives with subsequent ones, and sharing them with others as they share theirs with him. And as they do, the heritage-scape ever expands, fostering a global imagined community defined not in opposition to others, nor on nationalistic ideologies or invisible boundary markers, but on the unity in the diversity that exists between the near and the far, the past and the present, the transient and the eternal.

CHAPTER FIVE

CONVERTING LOCAL SPACES
INTO HERITAGE PLACES

The process of disembedding locales and reinserting them into a newly defined heritage-scape follows a procedure akin to that which museums utilize to recontextualize the objects in their possession.[1] The cultural institution of a museum can be metaphorically likened to the heritage-scape, for, like UNESCO's uniquely global place, it is an imagined social script made tangibly comprehensible through the visual isolation and recontextualization of its material objects. This fact gains further credence when considering the historical roots of modern-day national museums, such as Paris' Musée du Louvre, London's National Museum, or even Washington, DC's Smithsonian Institution. The birth of such museums was not only closely linked to the birth of the nation-state as problematized by UNESCO, but, as Carol Duncan demonstrates, these institutions serve as cultural tools for fostering a sense of solidarity amongst a diversity of peoples, social strata, and worldviews in these nascent republics. Likewise, each monumental place in the heritage-scape is first and foremost a distinctive tool in a vast cultural toolkit for cultivating a global "imagined community" centered on the peace-inducing narrative of "unity in diversity."

Echoing that of the heritage-scape, the placemaking enterprise of these nation-states is most clearly evident in museums, especially the first state-sponsored museums that appeared in the nineteenth century, such as the Musée du Louvre and the National Gallery of London. These institutions were, and to a certain extent are to this day, instructive spaces that rely on some form of object-based epistemology. According to historian Steven Conn, "object-based epistemology" is the Enlightenment-era idea that knowledge—specifically that highly nuanced form of information concerning a people and their broader historical-cultural context—can be imparted simply by viewing an object. While "in this epistemology, objects are not precisely transparent, but neither are they hopelessly opaque," narrative claims imbued in the material object are made manifest to both the scholar and the uninitiated alike.[2] Conn likens these objects to an open book—"the stories would reveal themselves,"[3] at least if the person knows how to decipher its language. Illustrating best this point, Conn excerpts a beautiful story from an 1894 article in the *Philadelphia Press* concerning anthropologist Frank Hamilton Cushing, the head of the Smithsonian's Bureau of Ethnology at the time. Touring the University of Pennsylvania's newly opened anthropological museum with a group of journalists, Cushing was asked to demonstrate his "uncanny skill" at "reading stories" that were supposedly contained in the various anthropological objects on display. At an exhibit dealing with Native American tools, Cushing handled a clay pot from Missouri and said:

> We can learn from this bowl more than the maker knew himself. We conclude that this Missouri people came from some forest country where the crested wood-duck was common. This handle is the conventionalized head of that bird. This pattern was originally carved from wood, or made from a gourd. The shape tells that. It was made in a part of the country where the wood was good for carving, and there was not fit bark for making vessels, probably therefore from the northeast. Thus the maker of the lay bowl kept the same pattern long after he perhaps knew why he put the head of a wood-duck for a handle.[4]

Belying this performance of such an ostensibly objective reading of the item is the fact that Dr. Cushing was utilizing the anthropology museum's overarching narrative, coupled with his own remembered encounters with other similar objects, as a jumping-off point for further insight. Had the pot been displayed in an art museum, or had he been an expert in aesthetics, a very different reading could have been offered just as authoritatively. The museum reformer George Brown Goode alludes to such a socially mediated conclusion in an 1889 lecture to the Brooklyn Institute when he remarked that a museum must be "a nursery of living thought."[5] Here then, once again, is another example of Halbwachs' assertions of social memory—one that seems individual and objective, but in actuality is predicated upon common ideas in the living "minds of men" to make meaning of contemporary situations. The sight of this material object *resonated*, in the words of Stephen Greenblatt, with the visitor's preexisting understanding of the world, its history and its cultures. According to Greenblatt,

> The effect of resonance . . . can be achieved by awakening in the viewer a sense of the cultural and historically contingent construction of art objects, the negotiations, exchanges, swerves, exclusions by which certain representational practices come to be set apart from other representational practices that they partially resemble. A resonant exhibition [in a museum] often pulls the viewer away from the celebration of isolated objects and toward a series of implied, only half-visible relationships and questions.[6]

Cushing felt that he could see beyond the bowl to the larger world—a point made clear with his assertion that he knew "more than the maker knew himself." And indeed, he had; he was able to call upon his memory's reflexive dynamic, remembering pieces of information about similar types of objects, remembering the geological composition of the area in which the artifact was found, and remembering perhaps the oral histories he and his colleague collected at the Bureau of Ethnology. From these experiences amassed during his career, meaning had been made in his mind—and, during his site visit to the university's anthropological museum, it had shaped his "reading" of this singular pot's meaning.

Often cited in opposition to the epistemological resonance of museum objects is the notion that museums and the objects contained within cannot provide knowledge, but can nevertheless evoke strong sensations of wonder or transcendence in the minds and imagination of the viewer. Emerging at the beginning of the twentieth century, the notion of a museum artifact as a veritable site of creative thought, rather than that of pure historical instruction, was most fully articulated by the Boston Museum of Fine Arts' Benjamin Ives Gilman in his 1918 influential work, *Museum Ideals of Purpose and Method*. In it, he stressed that the museum's goal should be to provide beautiful works of art that could capture the imagination, allowing for "sacred conversations" and active contemplation—which Duncan identifies as an "imaginative act of identification between viewer and artist."[7] Writing almost a century later, Greenblatt also echoes this notion in his theory on *wonder*, which he defines as the captivating emotional quality of objects, whereby the piece's "arresting sense of uniqueness" allows for the viewer to be transported outside of the confines of the museum, into a new and imaginary world based in his mind. So-called "post-modernists" have also embraced this idea,[8] arguing that in today's scientific age, visitors seek a feeling of transcendence from objects and monuments that they no longer can sense in traditional religious venues. Rather than providing merely a tangible and resonant illustration of previously held concepts and notions, the wondrous object can expand the mind, forming new impression and complexifying preexisting ideas.

Whether the idea of a museum was to foster object-based epistemology as early nineteenth-century institutions wished, or to provide the visitor with a quasi-religious experience as Gilman would first advocate, both of these concepts are potent illustrations of the museum's inherently social context, revealing the complex interplay between tangible artifacts, narrative claims, and the people with whom they come into contact. Calling the museum a "ritual space," Duncan points out that, like other sites of liminality, the museum is "carefully marked off and culturally designated as reserved for a special quality of attention—in this case, contemplation and learning."[9] Museum objects—like the monuments of the heritage-scape—are thus always put "under the pressure of a way of seeing" as Svetlana Alpers notes,[10] ready to be contextualized within a museum-designed narrative framework that could be easily interpreted by their visitors. Indeed, with objects at its core, a museum is defined by its relationship to people, and can be instructive and enlightening when it authoritatively offers up narrative claims to contextualize the objects on display.

Rather than simply being storehouses of object-based information or aesthetic temples for visitors to seek transcendence, museums as a specific type of place are officially charged with reproducing an official narrative. The narrative claim offered by the placemakers themselves, as opposed to the objects, takes center stage. Unlike the private *Wunderkammer* of their predecessors—those richly jumbled "cabinets of curiosities" requisite for an ideal Renaissance court—the original public museums collected and displayed objects in a decided effort to construct a nationalistic social script. Like the "imagined communities" of the nation-state and this heritage-scape, these museums utilized preexisting objects, with their own life histories and disparate social understandings, and contextualized them in a novel way—a way wherein they could be used as tangible illustrations of a unifying narrative claim. The case of Paris' nationally sponsored Louvre is an especially salient example, for as Duncan reveals, it was a primary tool of the new French Republic. Liberating, as it were, private art objects from the throes of the fallen royals, it became a "new kind of public ceremonial space" which

> not only redefined the political identity of its visitors, it also assigned new meanings to the objects it displayed and qualified, obscured, or distorted older ones. Now presented as public property, they became the means through which a new relationship between the individual as a citizen and the state as benefactor could be enacted. But to accomplish their new task, they had to be presented in a new way.[11]

The manner in which the Louvre and, later, other nascent public museums, accomplished this was to organize its collections in a decidedly evolutionary manner, one that utilized their objects for explicating claims of cultural development. Indeed, administrators of the Louvre in 1794 decreed that the museum's goal was to demonstrate to visitors "the progress of art and the degrees of perfection to which it was brought by all those peoples who have successively cultivated it."[12] Chronologically juxtaposing selected artifacts of Egypt, Greece, Rome, the Middle Ages, the Renaissance, and, in a final and authoritative burst of national pride, those of France, its curators could tangibly articulate an ideology of cultural progress that concludes with that of the nation-state, as the objects themselves served to frame and re-frame previously held understandings about the different cultures. Thus, these institutions were less storehouses for relics as they were instructive places that tangibly illustrated a nation's narrative claim through the deployment of processual display tactics, wherein objects deemed to be of value to the "imagined" heritage of the nation-state were juxtaposed in a linear narrative of civilizational progress.

More importantly, museums in their forms and functions utilize a narrative very similar to that of the heritage-scape: "unity in diversity." Not only are they specially delimited places where a plurality of people can come together and ritually enact the same experience, but they symbolically articulate the claim of "unity in diversity" through their collection and selection of the objects on display. The Louvre's collection of ancient archaeological artifacts, antiquities, religious images and secular paintings from disparate peoples and places under one roof render "unity in diversity" tangibly comprehensible. Its traditional chronologically organized layout furthermore dictates that visitors must negotiate a complex series of narrative frames, which serve to actively contextualize and re-contextualize the objects on display much like an individual's memory does. As one progresses through the exhibit, therefore, an iterative memorializing process continues to occur, where memories will be called forth, contextualized by one narrative frame, utilized to make further meaning, and then reframed once again. Even today, as renovations at the Louvre allow visitors for forge their own paths through its rich and diverse collections, they nevertheless encounter the same diversity of cultural artifacts under a unified setting. Thus, the museum's unity in diversity claim—evolutionary or not—becomes a quantifiable truth. The Foucaltian theorist Tony Bennett, drawing on the writings of Stephen Bann and Eileen Hooper-Greenhill,[13] best articulates this notion when he asserts that

> the museum functions as a site in which the figure of 'Man' is reassembled from its fragments. If the dispersal of that figure across what now emerges as a series of separated histories means that Man's unity can no longer be regarded as pre-given, the museum allowed that unity to be reconstituted in the construction of Man as a project to be completed through time. Like all the king's horses and all the king's men, the museum is engaged in a constant historical band-aid exercise in seeking to put back together the badly shattered human subject.[14]

Had he not specifically identified the museum as the subject of his discourse, Bennett could have easily been describing UNESCO and the heritage-scape. While Bennett is alluding to Enlightenment-era "modernization" ideals that saw all cultures in a universal process of development, his attuned verbiage can also be applied to UNESCO's worldview, as it strains to create a unified peace in the fractured global body that is Mankind. As UNESCO's foundational documents convey, the destructive forces of war demonstrated that no longer could the universality of Man be taken as a given, nor the peace that comes from such a universally internalized response. Rather, it has to be recreated in a particularly ritual space that could change notions of identity in the minds of its participants. In the most telling of historical documents, Theodore Low, the educational director of the Metropolitan Museum of Art during World War II, echoes this sentiment when he described the museum's powerful "potential force for good" in 1942:

> No one can deny that museums have powers which are of the utmost importance in any war of ideologies. They have the power to make people see the truth, *the power to make people recognize the importance of the individual as a member of society, and, of equal importance in combating subversive inroads, the power to keep minds happy and healthy.* They have, in short, propaganda powers which should be far more effective in their truth and eternal character than those of the Axis which are based on falsehoods and half-truths. . . . [I]t is clearly apparent that the present job of museums goes far beyond the normal wartime duties. It is the army and navy which will win the war. The museum's task lies in preparation for the peace to come. It is then, in a world which we hope will be more ready to understand the problems of others, from nations down to individuals, and which will be searching for ways to make "peace" a word having real and lasting meaning, that the museum can assume a leadership befitting its position.[15]

Low conveys most politically the orientation of a public museum. Arguing that museums should be more than simply idle storehouses, Low's assertion effectively charged museums to focus on the people, to contextualize objects in ways that would tangibly articulate a peacemaking narrative claim. For Low, the museum in form, structure and presentation would induce the visitor into a particular way of seeing. Conversely, pressuring its material items into a specific way of being seen, the museum was to utilize objects to articulate a well-conceptualized social script.

But the museum as a form of social script does not end with simply the interaction between the visitor and the object, or, rather, the viewer and the viewed. As a whole, it is a particular kind of place—a specially delimited locale, and an exponent of particular ideological claims. It is born from a distinct power structure with its own placemaking strategy not unlike UNESCO's heritage-scape. Without visitors, the objects would not be seen or experienced—yes—but equally important, without a Director and a Board, they would not be funded; without collectors, the objects would not be amassed; without curators, the objects would not be systematically displayed and contextualized. Unlike the private Renaissance *Wunderkammer* or imperial collections, the contemporary museum as a product of such a systematic and placemaking process is imbued with an air of authority that stems not merely from the unsubstantiated claims of power brokers, but is supported by more "modern" and "rational" classification schemes. These power brokers apply ostensibly objective or "scientific" methods that are socially agreed-upon, in an equally alleged uniform fashion. Sir William Henry Flower, the Director of the Natural History Museum in South Kensington, illustrates this when he wrote in 1884:

> First, as I said before, you must have your curator. He must carefully consider the object of the museum, the class and capacities of the persons for whose instruction it is founded, and the space available to carry out this object. He will then divide the subject to be illustrated into groups, and consider their relative proportions, according to which he will plan out the space. Large labels will next be prepared for the principal headings, as the chapters of a book, and smaller ones for the various subdivisions. Certain propositions to be illustrated, either in structure, classification, geographical distribution, geological position, habits, or evolution of the subjects dealt with, will be laid down and reduced to definite and concise language. Lastly will come the illustrative specimens, each of which as procured and prepared will fall into its appropriate place.[16]

Flower's thoughts, which have become the basis for the museum's uniform method of analysis and, more subtly, of placemaking, indicate the complexity and professionalism necessary in creating a convincing sense of place. A group of specific professionals must compose such an instructive arena; these individuals form a particular "epistemic culture," in the words of Karin Knorr-Cetina.[17] This is a group composed of individuals who are socially sanctioned as possessing the knowledge, habits and skill for carrying on a particular type of work. Members of an epistemic culture are linked not by some geographic or ethnic affinity, but through highly specific, often globally circulating knowledge—a knowledge, therefore, that transcends national boundaries. Their role, as accepted by their communities, is to be educated and dedicated in a particular field; in the case of museum or heritage professionals, they are expected to authoritatively devote their energies to closely examining each object, to evaluate their appropriateness within the place's narrative claim, and to articulate the information each piece is to convey within these bounds. Only "lastly" do the "illustrative specimens," once they are "prepared," come into play; the bulk of the important preparatory work is conducted by this epistemic community of professionals[18] who possess highly specialized forms of information that are regarded as authoritative by the greater community who will view the objects. Thus, as Bennett states, the true "epistemic desire" of a museum is the desire to convey "a knowledge of totality"—of unity in diversity—but authoritatively "acquired by means that were, ultimately, secretive and cultic."[19] It is from this institutionalized and "cultic" structure that allows museums to be "given cultural recognition and entitlement to tell a particular story by virtue of their official role as culturally named and framed contexts for the production of discourses about the past," as Tamar Katriel writes.[20]

Being the authoritative voice does not merely mean serving as the keepers of knowledge, but also the creators and arbiters of that very same body of information. An epistemic culture sets the parameters and decides what the "facts" are; they then define and interpret these facts, and mediate where there are disagreements or discrepancies among their individual members should they question certain doctrinal points. This knowledge is subsequently disseminated, albeit incompletely, to the greater society who has recognized their authority. One of the best examples of an epistemic culture, although it is not often referred to as such, is that which is shared by the Roman Catholic College of Cardinals. Throughout history, but most concertedly in the Middle Ages, this international community of knowledge-based authorities set the very terms upon which Christendom's very understanding of life—spiritual, social and material—was based. They define, interpret and arbitrate what constitutes the "correct" understanding of this doctrine; this is evident when recalling the history of disputes and pontifications over the verbiage of the very Nicene Creed which, over 1600 years later, Catholics still recite at Mass, or the acceptability of creating "graven images" to enlighten and educate during periods of Byzantine iconoclasm. This group then disseminates these "facts," and, particular to the medieval Church, even prosecuted those who deviated from these beliefs within the society which recognized the College's authority. They choose a spokesperson—the Pope— who regulates, supports and further mediates among the College. The College also disseminates the teachings in print and from the pulpit and through issuing Papal Bulls, encyclicals, proclamations and theocratic laws.

Today, the term "epistemic culture" is most commonly associated with "global" knowledge communities, such as astrophysicists, biochemists or financial market analysts. Like the College of Cardinals, they are transnational in nature, bound together not through geography, politics or heritage, but rather by the authority given to them on the international level to be the experts in their field. In academia, this often translates into the conferring of a Ph.D., an M.D. or a J.D., while in the commercial sector, this is based more on experience and the firm for which one works; an M.B.A. often serves to establish hierarchies within this system.[21] Through private meetings, conferences and publications in specific trade journals, each community sets the definitions of the facts that society should use when thinking about the particular field.

One recent example particularly parallels the placemaking authority of UNESCO. Founded in 1919, the International Astronomical Union (IAU) is the representation of the epistemic culture of astronomers; like most such scientific communities, it is open to those who have a Ph.D. in the field and are actively researching and publishing. The IAU publishes scientific journals, issues press releases announcing new finds, and generally serves as a perceivable bond between the disparate international body of these scientists.[22] It also determines what constitutes a fact in the universe. Although the community rarely gets much media attention, even when a new solar body is discovered, the IAU's controversial mid-August, 2006 meeting drew passionate responses from not only individual members within the community, but from laypeople outside. At this meeting, the IAU changed the definition of the term "planet" and stripped Pluto, long considered the ninth planet, of its status. "Pluto Voted off the Island," *National Geographic's* tongue-in-cheek headline read, complementing the cacophony of headlines informing the world, "Pluto Not a Planet." Some astronomers and many laypeople "revolted"; Harvard historian and astronomer Owen Gingerich called the decree "a semantic atrocity," and others, like the religious heretics of old, refused to acknowledge it. Recognizing the cultural embeddedness of this nugget of planetary knowledge, some offered forth alternate definitions of a planet precisely to save Pluto from being demoted, but in the end, the prevailing opinion of the community won out:

> The distant, ice-covered world is no longer a true planet, according to a new definition of the term voted on by scientists today. 'Whoa! Pluto's dead,' said astronomer Mike Brown, of the California Institute of Technology in Pasadena, as he watched a Webcast of the vote. 'There are finally, officially, eight planets in the solar system.' In a move that's already generating controversy and will force textbooks to be rewritten, Pluto will now be dubbed a dwarf planet.[23]

Although the process was anthropologically arbitrary—the IAU simply set imaginary parameters and definitions—the changing of the "facts" was recognized and impacted wider society; textbooks the world over will be changed, the approaches to the study of Pluto will differ, and even the semiotic references in art and society most likely will change over time. Moreover, the media coverage received from the proclamation and the outcry it produced on the part of laypeople underscore the authoritative voice with which this small group of scientists have regarding this particular body of knowledge.[24] Had this come from a novelist, an anthropologist, a school teacher or even the Pope, such a proclamation would have been taken with little seriousness.

The members of UNESCO's World Heritage Committee form an epistemic culture. They determine and debate the definition of what constitutes a World

Heritage site, they interpret the World Heritage Convention document, amending it where necessary; they evaluate monuments and decree which places can be World Heritage sites. They do this all in a way similar to Sir William Henry Flower's method stated above.

UNESCO's method of converting local places into heritage spaces, then, follows a decidedly museological procedure that is very much "cultic" or, restated more generously, highly ritualized through professionalization and institutionalization. Eschewing casual nomination and collection techniques of the Wunderkammer for more institutionalized and collaborative processes that utilize a variety of organizations, institutions and individuals, UNESCO creates World Heritage sites that comprise a distinct heritage-scape in an authoritative manner. Like the disparate relics or works of art that become Museum Pieces, so-to-be World Heritage sites are identified, selected, collected, categorized, documented, evaluated, idealized and recontextualized into a unified whole by a socially sanctioned authoritative force.[25] Thus, as they are pulled from their environment, recontextualized, and then reinserted—inescapably changed in meaning—into the environment once again, local places become World Heritage sites through a process that is at once decidedly ritualized, and a little bit "cultic."

The Ritual Process

As chapter 4 described, Turner's ritual process is a socially sanctioned, almost scripted[26] process whereby individuals undergo symbolic yet meaningful transformation. This change is accomplished through three steps, which he identifies as *separation*, *liminality*, and *re-aggregation*. The individual to be transformed first is separated from his preexisting social context; he is often physically removed from the greater community, and may even be invested with markedly distinct clothing or makeup that serves to further symbolically separate himself from others through his outward appearance.

The second stage is that of liminality, wherein the individual is "betwixt and between" the old self and the new. It is in this stage that transformation takes place over time; the time can be as brief or as long as this social script prescribes. In this context, it is important to note that all participants, stripped of their previous statuses or life-histories and undergoing the same ritualized transformation, form a *communitas*, or group based on common humanity and equality rather than on recognized hierarchy. Consciously recognizing that they are undergoing the same experience, irrespective of their previous individual pasts and statuses, the *communitas* cultivates unity in diversity. Indeed, in this liminal phase, the *communitas* finds itself in a "kind of institutional capsule or pocket which contains the germ of future social developments, of societal change," Turner argues.[27] They do not germinate fully, however, until the ritual is finished.

When the transformative rites are completed, the individual can now be authoritatively re-aggregated, or introduced back, into the society that sanctioned such rituals. The individual's outward appearance may or may not be changed, but his meaning within the societal context has. The subject is not the only one who is aware of his changed status; so too do members of his greater community recognize and accept his new social standing. As meaning dictates appropriate action, a change in the individual's meaning indicates a marked change is expected in subsequent interactions.

Although Turner describes rituals in the context of individuals' social status within a community, I argue that it can also be applied to UNESCO's museological procedure of placemaking. Just as an individual is a social being whose identity is constructed through his understanding and memory of his role in society, a place is also an inherently social construct, complete with its own form of life-history, and based on the remembered claims, aesthetic features and the greater socio-geographic context in which it finds itself. Thus a place, too, can undergo a similar conversion ritual, whereby it is separated from its common, contemporarily quotidian understanding and recontextualized through equally socially sanctioned, or institutionalized means.

While the three ritual phases remain essentially the same, I have renamed Turner's terms to more clearly indicate their ultimate objectives. Thus, the separation phase is termed *isolation*, the liminal phase is called *idealization*, and the reintegration phase is labeled *valorization*. I have made these changes to better convey the primary activity undergone by the site during a particular phase. Because in the particular case of the heritage-scape Turner's term "separation" can connote a conflictual conflicting territorial removal that would be both physically misleading as well as unsavory within the context of UNESCO's metanarrative, herein it is described as "isolation." "Isolation" is also a more precise term, for though a place can rarely be physically moved or separated, it can be isolated, both conceptually and in its various re-presentations, from its preexisting context. Indeed, just as the museum pulls the objects out of one spatial and temporal context and puts them in another,[28] so too are fixed monuments effectively pulled out of the traditionally understood socio-cultural environment and recontextualized anew in the heritage-scape by isolating them. In the liminal, second step of the ritual process, the museum object or monumental place is specifically idealized to better representatively match the qualities espoused in the heritage-scape's meta-narrative claim. Finally, re-aggregation into the greater international context is achieved; the object or site is reintroduced to the world as changed in meaning and status. While the an inanimate object is not cognitively aware of the change brought on by the ritual, its new status is, however, recognized and celebrated by the greater human community, which sanctioned the ritual and of which it is now a part. It is valorized—put on a pedestal, so to speak—as being culturally sanctioned to have greater representational, epistemological and transcendental power than its "commonplace" siblings. Despite no material change through a rather secretive designating process, the World Heritage site, similar to a museum object, is authoritatively understood as meaningfully altered in the minds of men. This is because, like the museum, the heritage-scape is an imagined social script, offered up by a culturally accepted power, and made tangibly comprehensible through the isolation and recontextualization of their objects.

Calling on the specialized knowledge and authority of a variety of professionals—socially accepted epistemological-political brokers—UNESCO's institutionalized, ritual procedure is as follows:

I.   ISOLATION ("Separation" phase)

A locality is nominated by the country in which it is located in a lengthy process:

1. The State-party places the locality on a Tentative List with other potential considerations
2. The State-party compiles an individual File on the locality, which contains exhaustive documentation concerning the site (precise geographic coordinates, maps, images, primary source documents, surveys), and a completed, official form categorizing it. The State-party can solicit help from the World Heritage Centre in Paris.
3. The State-party submits the File to the World Heritage Centre, which checks that all documentation is in place.
4. The World Heritage Centre then sends the File off to two advisory bodies:
   i.   FOR CULTURAL SITES: The International Council on Monuments and Sites (ICOMOS)
        FOR NATURAL SITES: The World Conservation Union (IUCN)
        Both conduct on-site research to evaluate the proposed monument and detail the way in which it is and should be managed.
   ii. The International Centre for the Study of the Preservation and Restoration of Cultural Property (ICCROM) provides expert advice on any restoration that is required.
5. The two Advisory Bodies travel to locality and conduct detailed research aimed specifically at the precisely delimited site.

II. IDEALIZATION ("Liminal" phase)

The two Advisory Bodies complete their evaluation, whereby they assign specific typologies to the locality. As these typologies are static and applied to a *communitas* of potential World Heritage sites, they effectively change the place into an idealized material form of the narrative "unity in diversity."

III. VALORIZATION ("Reintegration" phase)

After discussion and voting, the World Heritage Committee designates the locality a World Heritage site through the following process:

1. The evaluation is presented at the yearly meeting of the World Heritage Committee, who examine the nominations based on the technical evaluations.
2. The World Heritage Committee votes to either inscribe or reject a site. In addition, the Committee might vote to withhold judgment, recommending that the State-party implement better site management, collect further documentation, rethink the categorization, or change the physical boundaries of what should be considered the site.
3. The World Heritage Committee inscribes the new World Heritage site's name and geographic location on the World Heritage List, along with all of the other, similarly valorized, places. This list is the tangible rendering of the heritage-scape.[29]

Isolation

The first step in converting a local place to a heritage site rests on *isolation*. For museum objects, this is rendered materially evident and pieces are collected. During the development of museums in the colonial era, objects were often physically pulled out from their environment, either by locals seeking to sell them to foreigners or trade them in symbolic gestures of goodwill, or by Western "robber barons" seeking to acquire what they saw as valuable and exotic riches for exposition in their private collections or for donation to colonial museums. Chipped away from larger structures, pillaged from treasuries, or purchased from bazaars, temples and private homes, the future museum artifact was tangibly and forcibly isolated from the context in which it previously existed.

Though veritably millions of examples abound—from famous ones such as the Parthenon's "Elgin Marbles" now in London's National Museum to relatively unknown ones such as Henry Walters' collection of Thai artifacts now on exhibition at The Walters Museum in Baltimore—one significant anecdote suffices concerning Angkor and the French Indochinese museum. The French explorer-turned-cultural minister, Louis Delaporte, was officially responsible for systematically amassing a collection of what he deemed the finest Indochinese artifacts for the French government to take back to Europe. However it was portrayed to France's citizenry at the time, such a project extended beyond merely objectively educating French nationals; it was a concerted effort to introduce French citizens to the colonial enterprise. Transporting the symbolic and material riches of these conquered lands would provide one tangible illustration of the benefits of such a costly and time-consuming enterprise. While Delaporte was, in effect, plundering cultural property (albeit after securing permission from the king his government supported), it was portrayed as a salvific enterprise, a preservationist's articulation of the colonial "white man's burden." The French believed they "discovered" the last remnants of a civilization lost to the destructive forces of time and nature; they were thus saving it from further neglect and ultimate destruction for the good of scientific research and civilizational preservation. Since the government had already begun to dedicate money and energy into restoring the crumbled temples—in part to perform symbolic acts of benevolence to their Protectorates—they would also "save" some from the locals for the benefit of the French who, through their taxes and conscription, were engaged in this enterprise.

Launching an ambitious and ultimately successful program for their procurement, Delaporte obtained the authorization from the Cambodian king to transport a large quantity of important relics, and engaged the labor of hundreds of locals to help. His actions are immortalized in a series of etchings, depicting hundreds of "natives" in foreign haircuts forging tree-lined rivers with immense statues borne on their bare backs. Such images of the backwardness and primitivity of the natives only contributed to the effectiveness of the colonial narrative, as Europeans could comprehend how such isolation of these sacred objects could be so salvific.

While the heritage-scape does not physically lift a place from its environment like Delaporte's museum object was able to have been, the World Heritage Committee nevertheless begins the recontextualization process by isolating the desired place. Indeed, for both the museum object and the heritage site, the isolating process does not begin with its physical removal from the original context; this is ancillary. Rather, it begins in the very act of selection in the minds of the collector, curator or pillager. Save those pieces commissioned with the specific intention of being looked at or installed in a museum or home, such as Renaissance portraits or modern art instillations, the majority of museum pieces have undergone an initial isolating procedure, as they were originally created for some other purpose and later separated from that context. Medieval triptychs, bronze Buddhas, stone linga, and stained glass that now find their homes in museums across the world stood as talismanic devices for religious veneration, not simply for aesthetic contemplation. Likewise, the arrowheads, textiles, and even Cushing's clay pot that are now found in anthropology institutes were intended for daily use, rather than simply for instructing interested students into the historical roots of a foreign culture; they were instead created for hunting, for clothing, for cooking—and were understood and treated as such by the locals who possessed and utilized them. Yet as soon as they were selected by curators or collectors from within the museum or academic milieu—as soon as they were viewed as something worth collecting, worth removing, transporting, placing in such institutions, and, above all, worth looking at alone, as objects in their own right with their own epistemic properties—they were isolated.

Delaporte, in fact, had isolated these objects long before he engaged native laborers to chip the bas-reliefs from temples or transport large statuary across rivers and jungles. These giant busts were isolated far earlier, before Delaporte even arrived in Angkor or even Indochina. He conducted extensive research, based on texts written by early explorers such as Henri Mouhot, recommendations by French archaeologists working in the area, and documents by French colonial overlords. He drew up plans identifying the ones he wanted, and devised requests for their procurement from the Cambodian king. Arriving in the capital of Phnom Penh some days' journey south of Angkor, he spoke to Khmer officials, including the king and his high ministers, where presumably they further discussed what could and could not be taken out. And finally, arriving on-site, he looked with an isolating gaze himself at the desired object, visually separating it from the environment where it materially found itself. No longer were they considered a part of a larger religious place, whereby their meaning was predicated in part on the surroundings from which they came, but as Delaporte identified the various treasures he wished to take back to France, they became "pieces," "objects," "artifacts," or, even, "art" that were able to speak their meanings without any help from their original home.

Such an assertion is not simply limited to the case of Delaporte and his meticulous pre-pillage-planning. All isolation begins in the mind, through the very act of identifying an object as standing alone, as possessing some intrinsic value that is not predicated on its greater social and natural context. Indeed, isolating the orientation of something indicates that it has some meaning that can be attained by interacting with it alone. Herbert Blumer theorizes that all "symbolic interactionism"—be it among people or aimed at an object—begins with a subtle and often immediate isolation from the complex totality in which the other is found. He notes, "to indicate something is to extricate it from its setting, to hold it apart, to give it meaning, or, in Mead's language, to make it an object—that is to say, anything that an individual indicates to himself [sic]."[30] Underscoring this point, James Cuno, the director of the Art Institute of Chicago, states that the museum experience is the "experience of engaging with works of art, especially in their most fundamental sense—as objects, manufactured things making claims on our close and sustained attention." The same is true with World Heritage sites. Seen to be "resisting the commonplace" like Cuno's museum objects, they are the heritage-scape's primary resource, as they are "re-*sourced*, reoriented, and renewed"[31] in a concerted ritual process that begins with isolation.

A future World Heritage site undergoes a highly ritualized—some would say "politicized"—set of isolating processes. Officially, the first step is the nomination process by the State-party. UNESCO attests to not consider any property for recontextualization as a World Heritage site unless the nation in which it is found has fulfilled a number of procedural requirements: First, the nation is a member of the World Heritage Convention; second, it has paid its annual dues and is a member in good standing; third, it officially "offers up" a place in its sovereign territory to the Committee as a potential site. Furthermore, this third point cannot be satisfied unless the member-state has included it on its Tentative List of sites they think would make appropriate World Heritage sites; has compiled a specific file on the individual site, which includes precise documentation, maps and images; and has engaged the expertise of two nongovernmental organizations who would objectively evaluate the site based on the World Heritage Convention's criteria for inscription and the state of its conservation. The adherence to this protracted and costly procedure is sometimes frustrating, especially to a particular State Party who has dedicated many resources to preparing a site, only to have the Committee either reject its nomination or request further study—both of which happen about once annually. It has also been frustrating to the World Heritage Committee in several instances when its members note that a particular place possesses that certain "universal value" the heritage-scape seeks, but that is held back for consideration by the country to which it politically belongs. Both Angkor and the city of Venice had this problem. While Cambodia was in the midst of a horrific social and political crisis that precluded it from becoming a State Party, no such excuses could be made by Italy. Most likely, the country simply did not want to join the Convention or offer up its well-known national heritage site of Venice as a "World Heritage" site. ICOMOS opens its recommendation for Venice to the World Heritage Committee by citing the nine years of frustration over UNESCO's inability to designate the city because Italy had not joined the Convention:

> The nomination of Venice to the list preceded by nine years the ratification of the World Heritage Convention by Italy. There was some concern about such a delay, which international opinion deemed inexplicable: on several occasions, notably during the discussions which preceded the elaboration of the tentative lists, the Committee expressed the wish for a short-list presentation of the most prestigious cultural properties and cited how paradoxical it was that Venice had not been included on the World Heritage List.[32]

Yet adherence to the procedure of the State-Party "offering up" its monuments for designation serves a number of material and symbolic purposes. It primarily induces nation-states to become collaborators in this new placemaking enterprise, for if the nation would want the valorizing and conserving effects of a World Heritage designation, it must submit to the official protocol of the non-governmental organization. On the more immediate level, this means that it must politically and economically support the ongoing efforts of UNESCO and the World Heritage Convention without regard for the country's specific desires. On the broadest of levels, however, this also induces the nation-state to conform to "modern" procedures and institutions that are requisite for a globally oriented country. Requiring the country to gather its own documentation and draft plans for cultural, infrastructural and tourism management necessitates the creation of specific government-approved experts and officials, such as a Cultural Minister, a Minister of the Interior, or even a Tourism Minister. By virtue of their position, these ministers also are able to benefit from contact with the World Heritage Centre in Paris, or with colleagues from other countries who are engaged with similar work. With such a quantity of tasks, the minister usually forms an entire governmental department or organization to assist him. These networked institutions begin to form a "global infrastructure." As I noted in chapter 1, the concept of global infrastructures as defined by globalization theorist John Meyer "account[s] for a world whose societies, organized as nation-states, are structurally similar in many unexpected dimensions and change in unexpectedly similar ways."[33] The benefits of fostering this global infrastructure are two-fold. First, creating an outward sense of governmental homogeneity fosters an air of authority for the nation-state. At least at the infrastructural level, they are considered to be on par with that of the more important nation-states; they are seen to have the basic foundations of a "modern" government, which translates into a broad, necessary diplomatic accessibility and also a sense of legitimacy. For the specific transformation ritual at hand, this also ensures that the nation-state is equal in the eyes of its State Party peers. Indeed, a ritual must be understood in a similar fashion by all involved, and is only effective if its determining agents are regarded as legitimate sponsors. Second, as Meyer conveys, the presence of global infrastructures within a particular nation-state allows the country to act in ways that are similar to other globalized countries despite vast cultural and economic differences. By fostering a global infrastructure within all of its nation-states, UNESCO is able to assure that each of its members has the same capacity for understanding and subsequently disseminating its universalizing meta-narrative claim in a similar fashion, once the locality is transformed into a World Heritage site.

Furthermore, there is great symbolic importance in having the nation-state—rather than UNESCO—make the initial public overture, for otherwise UNESCO's efforts may be likened to that of Delaporte's colonial pillaging. UNESCO's placemaking strategy is foremostly non-conflictual in policy and

organic in nature; it seeks to impart a peacemaking narrative centered on individuals' and groups' willing celebration of unity in diversity. It cannot allow the
possibility that a designation was strong-armed or forcibly taken. Using Delaporte's case to illustrate a hypothetical situation, one can immediately recognize
the difference in paradigms, had Khmer ministers sailed to France on their own
accord with goodwill gifts of Khmer statuary, rather than having representatives
of France come with its army in tow to "request" such objects.

But more subtly, and more importantly, such an institutionalized procedure
eases such a potent place into isolation, to ensure that it is thoroughly conceptually freed from any prior context and able to begin UNESCO's liminal process
of idealization. First, when the nation becomes a member of the World Heritage
Convention, it is urged to write down a Tentative List of potential World Heritage sites. This is mostly a "wish list" identifying all of those places within the
nation's territory that it would like to have UNESCO consider designating as a
World Heritage site. The list can be as long or as short as the nation wishes, and
can be extended as the nation deems appropriate, but as the World Heritage
Committee determined in its Seventh Session in December 1983, the list is intended to be a "forecast" of a nomination within the time frame of five to ten
years, not immediately. Addressing questions from States-parties regarding the
necessity (and the procedure) of submitting Tentative Lists, the Committee
wrote:

> Tentative lists, as their name implies, do not definitely commit the States nor
> the Committee. They should therefore be treated in a confidential manner.
> Their aim is to enable the Committee and the non-governmental organization
> concerned to carry out comparative and serial studies which are necessary for a
> methodical approach in building up the World Heritage List.[34]

This Tentative List serves as an initial isolation point—it isolates a collectivity
of potential sites within a nation-state, juxtaposing them in a preliminary effort
to tease out those qualities that would make them good candidates. The rather
lengthy time frame provides adequate time to collect all of the necessary documentation concerning each individual site, which further isolates the site.
Documentation includes, but is not limited to, precise coordinates where the
place is located in the world, an official description of the site attesting to its
unique values, maps of the place, and images. Offering specific geographic coordinates locates the place on a map of the globe, delimiting it. In effect, it car-
tographically isolates the place from the greater global context.

Describing the site forces the nation-state to categorize the place in accordance with UNESCO's typologies. First, they are identified as either "cultural"
or "natural" sites by placing a check mark in the appropriate box (both can be

checked as well, conveying that it is a "mixed site"). Second, the drawing up of specific maps, as well as the inclusion of photographs and other images (such as satellite images, infra ray, et al.) serves to delimit the place as tangibly as possible. From now on, the site will be remembered and assessed by those visual images; it visually isolates the place.

Most importantly, specific reasoning is solicited as to its "universal value;" the nation-state is urged to utilize UNESCO's Criteria for Inscription as a guideline, and also to solicit help from the World Heritage Centre in Paris. This textual procedure serves to conceptually isolate the site from its former context, forcing the nation-state to shed prior notions of use-value or social-environmental factors. Though this is often un-recognized, both by the States-Parties and those analyzing UNESCO's endeavors, UNESCO does make this clear in its revised *Operational Guidelines*:

> Outstanding universal value means cultural and/or natural significance which is so exceptional as to transcend national boundaries and to be of common importance for present and future generations of all humanity. As such, the permanent protection of this heritage is of the highest importance to the international community as a whole. The Committee defines the criteria for the inscription of properties on the World Heritage List.[35]

Once all of the documentation is in place, and the World Heritage Centre has reviewed it to ensure it is as complete as possible, the Centre then sends it to two separate Advisory Bodies for evaluation. This engaging of these two outsider advisory bodies—one that assesses the Criteria for Inscription, and the other that assesses the state of conservation (if necessary)—represents the final isolating step. Here, tangibly and performatively, the site is once and for all isolated; it is not only isolated in name, but in practice. It becomes an object of intense scrutiny, a sight to be seen and assessed on its own. It is visually, structurally and qualitatively scrutinized with instruments and with an isolating gaze similar to Urry's "tourist gaze"—"directed to features of landscape and townscape which separate them off from everyday experience."[36] The experts, in essence, take on a tourist gaze; both endeavors "are socially organized" and "systematized as is the gaze of the medic." They are also both contrastive—that is, the objects of both gazes are comparatively assessed and contrasted with other places that are considered different. Finally, both gazes are predicated on "anticipation"—for the tourist gaze, it is an anticipation of something pleasurable; for the expert advisory bodies' gazes, no doubt there is an anticipation of pleasure, but there is also an anticipation of the site's nomination.[37]

The heritage site is privy to this touristic-cum-"museum effect"[38]—this pressurized, isolating tourist gaze— precisely because it is thought to be out of

the mundane—not simply for tourists, but for experts, for the placemakers themselves. As Kirshenblatt-Gimblett remarked, "once it is a sight to be seen, the life
world becomes a museum of itself."[39] Indeed, the site is treated completely as an
object in its own right, like those individual pieces in a museum, isolated from
its "commonplace" application within the social context in which it was previously constructed, ready to be recontextualized alongside places similarly isolated from its disparate "commonplace" social contexts—and assessed as to how
it fares. Angkor Wat, for example, may have originally been a temple constructed for the worship of Vishnu, calling forth myths and symbolisms that
reached across time and space; but in this stage, on file and in the nation's and
the Advisory Bodies' practice, it becomes isolated from that historical-religious
context, and considered a formal object in its own right. Precise dimensions are
given that geographically mark it off from its surroundings, separating what
tangibly constitutes a culturally valuable "Angkor Wat" and what constitutes the
anonymous and culturally invaluable environment around it. Photographs are
taken of its bas reliefs, of its towers and of its moats; the surrounding jungles,
the trees and even the sky are cropped off as best they can. Archaeologists may
excavate to find the precise depth of its extent. ICOMOS examines the "universal" cultural value it is thought to intrinsically possess, which in reality is an
assessment of the monument's proclivity to be effectively imbued with
UNESCO's narrative claim. ICCROM assesses the authenticity of the place itself, the state of preservation it is in, and the ability of the country to be able to
care for this particular piece of material culture in perpetuity.

Idealization

When this is completed, the isolated site begins its second state, that of liminality, where the Advisory Bodies complete the definitive "evaluation." It is here
that the place is in what Turner calls the "betwixt and between" state—already
isolated from its prior social context, but not yet reborn into the world as something new. It possesses "the germ of future social developments, of social
change" that will only grow once the step is completed. Like the extensive
museological procedures conducted by curators when considering which objects
to acquire or display, this step begins with the formal research—scrutiny of its
physical attributes, authentication, the assessment of the appropriate apparatus in
place to handle restoration efforts, the processing of tourists and the staving off
of destructive elements, the analysis of the applicability of UNESCO's placemaking narrative, and the interviews with local curators and preservationists—
and ends with the completion of the formal evaluation to be submitted to the
World Heritage Committee.

Over and above these practical evaluative procedures, this liminal process is intended to conceptually change the object in question from "commonplace" to ideal. In its "commonplace" situation, for example, a chair is a seat on which to rest, but in a museum situation, the chair is reoriented and viewed differently. Within an archaeological or anthropological museum's meta-narrative, it could be telling of a particular stratum of culture—how the people presented themselves, what forms of symbolism was associated with it, what materials were commonly used in the construction of such objects, even how these members sat. Likewise, within an art museum, this same chair would be ideally representative of a particular set of aesthetic elements or artistic innovation, based on its colors, composition, and decoration. Although the material object remains unchanged, based on the categories and typologies applied to it, its meaning and representational ability changes. It becomes idealized.

In this step, UNESCO similarly converts a place from a functional locality that is used in a particular everyday manner in the present time and space, into an "ideal type" of monument that espouses UNESCO's narrative claim of unity in diversity, and exists in heritage time and within the heritage-scape. Idealization is a key element for any epistemological or transcendent object, whether it is found within the walls of an art museum or within the amorphous confines of the heritage-scape, for in both of these entities, it is the object that is illustrative of a claim, not the other way around. As individualistic as the narrative claim can be—and UNESCO's is by nature one of the most celebratory of individual diversity—the object or place is ultimately chosen from amongst an almost infinite amount of tangibles for its aesthetic and conceptual ability to take on the meta-narrative's claim. As expositive elaborators of a narrative claim, therefore, the museum object or heritage-scape site serves as a Weberian "ideal type," bringing aspects of the meta-narrative claim to light in a simplified manner that would be easily comprehensible and consumed by a collectivity of diverse individuals in a uniform fashion. Like Weber's "ideal types,"—"analytical constructs" formed from truths rendered tangible by real events or localities, yet "artificially simplified" and exhibiting "one-sidedly emphasized viewpoints"—a World Heritage site is specifically idealized by comparing it against UNESCO's predetermined set of typologies, whose conceptual amorphism allows for its applicability in a variety of settings across the world. To become a World Heritage site, a place must be determined to:

(i)   represent a masterpiece of human creative genius; or
(ii) exhibit an important interchange of human values, over a span of time or within a cultural area of the world, on developments in architecture or technology, monumental arts, town-planning or landscape design; or

(iii) bear a unique or at least exceptional testimony to a cultural tradition or to a civilization which is living or which has disappeared; or

(iv) be an outstanding example of a type of building or architectural or techno-logical ensemble or landscape which illustrates (a) significant stage(s) in human history; or

(v) be an outstanding example of a traditional human settlement or land-use which is representative of a culture (or cultures), especially when it has be-come vulnerable under the impact of irreversible change; or

(vi) be directly or tangibly associated with events or living traditions, with ideas, or with outstanding universal significance (a criterion applied only in excep-tional circumstances, and together with other criteria).[40]

Thus, as chapter 1 mentions, a place is inscribed as a World Heritage site not because it *is* something, but rather because it *represents, exhibits, bears tes-timony, is an example,* or *is tangibly associated with* something. That "some-thing" is also necessarily vague, determinable by the State-parties, Advisory Bodies and UNESCO themselves; it can be *an important interchange of human values, testimony to a cultural tradition,* or a *type of building or landscape.* With nearly one thousand properties currently comprising of the heritage-scape, there are equally as many distinctly different interpretations of what aesthetics, values, traditions or tangible forms demonstrate World Heritage status. Despite the broad applicability of these criteria, they are nevertheless specifically categori-cal. Defining a locality in such a manner necessarily delimits the place concep-tually; it attributes specific representative qualities while concurrently de-emphasizing or "forgetting" specific aspects of the place's total life history, just as Weber does with his conceptual "ideal types." Thus, as a nominating body determines how the site fits into the above typologies—squeezing the site into predetermined categories—it really redefines the object as an ideal representa-tion, or a quintessential material embodiment, of those virtues UNESCO's crite-ria seek. Such a process inexorably changes the meaning of the place, at least officially. It is up to the subsequent diffusion of this newly re-defined place that will change its meaning in the minds of individuals.

Valorization

The third step completes the ritual process, and corresponds to "reintegration," where the object's new status is publicly confirmed, or valorized. *Valorization* is the process by which the re-contextualizing body—be it a museum or the heritage-scape—adds value to an object by virtue of the fact that it has been spe-cially identified and chosen to exist in a particular collection for a specific rea-son. In the museum, an idealized object is selected from among a variety of

similar items for exposition based on the assessment of its value to best represent the museum's meta-narrative claims. This decision is based on the documentation compiled by the curators and experts. The competitive nature of this
selection process ultimately adds value to the piece. And once selected, it is literally placed on a pedestal or hung on a wall with other unique yet idealized
articles that similarly were selected to best espouse some aspect of the meta-
narrative. With the object's juxtaposition against similarly value-added pieces—
this inclusion in such a highly selective collection—the object is valorized.

The potential World Heritage site is valorized in exactly the same way, although it is inscribed on the heritage-scape, rather than hung on a gallery wall. It
is at this stage that the place has effectively become something different—no
longer is it valued simply in local terms, but now it is recognized by an authoritative, international consortium to truly be of "universal value." To render such
valorization definitive and authoritative in the international political context, it
once again undergoes several bureaucratic procedures. First, a presentation is
made to the World Heritage Committee based on the evaluation compiled by the
two Advisory Bodies. This step essentially analyzes how well-idealized the
monument has become. The Committee then decides whether or not to designate
the place a World Heritage site. Revelatory of the ultimate valorization accomplished in this step, not all localities are automatically accepted, even if they
have undergone the entire idealizing nomination and idealizing evaluative processes. The World Heritage Committee either votes to inscribe a place on the
World Heritage List predicated on certain criteria—which, as the case of Mỹ
Sơn demonstrates, can be re-worked based on the final perspective of this consortium—or they can reject it altogether.

Although the State-party, often in collaboration with the Advisory Bodies,
has the initial voice in delimiting what constitutes its potential World Heritage
site, the World Heritage Committee can also vote to designate a site, but with
modifications to its parameters. In decree 28COM14B of the 2005 World Heritage Convention, for example, the Committee voted to inscribe Italy's Etruscan
Necropolises of Cerveteri and Tarquinia on the World Heritage List on the basis
of cultural criteria *i*, *iii* and *iv*, but redefined its territorial boundaries. While
Italy's nomination envisioned the preexisting archaeological museums in
Cerveteri and Tarquinia to be included as part of the World Heritage site, perhaps because these contemporary institutions cannot truly "represent a masterpiece of human creative genius" (criteria *i*), "bear a unique or at least exceptional testimony to a cultural tradition or to a civilization which is living or
which has disappeared" (criteria *iii)*, or be considered "outstanding example[s]
of a type of building or architectural or technological ensemble or landscape
which illustrates (a) significant stage(s) in human history" (criteria *iv*)—reasons

for which the actual archaeological sites were designated—the Committee rejected these portions with the statement:

> The World Heritage Committee . . . decides not to include the Caerean Archaeological Museum in Cerveteri or the National Archaeological Museum in Tarquinia in the inscription, underlining nevertheless, the extraordinary value of the collections to the understanding of the two necropolises.[41]

Similarly, at the same 2005 convention the United Kingdom wished that an extension be granted to their previously inscribed World Heritage site of St. Kilda. This was not a geographic extension, but rather a conceptual one—the United Kingdom wanted UNESCO to re-recontextualize the property, previously understood as representative of Natural Criteria *iii* and *iv*, as both a natural site additionally falling under Natural Criteria *ii*, as well as a "cultural landscape"—effectively rendering it a "mixed" site. However, in decree 28COM14B.19, the Committee approved only Natural Criteria *ii*, and voted to "Defer [sic] consideration of the cultural values of St. Kilda, United Kingdom, to allow the State Party to undertake a further comparative analysis of relevant relic cultural landscapes."[42]

The Committee also rejects nominations, determining that they do not meet the criteria and thus cannot be idealized in the "unity in diversity" meta-narrative claim of the heritage-scape. Decision 28COM14B.38 of the 2004 World Heritage Convention illustrates this:

> 28 COM 14B.38   The World Heritage Committee,
> 1. Decides not to inscribe the Wine Village Terraces, Cyprus, on the World Heritage List.[43]

At this Convention, in fact, two nominations were outwardly rejected; one was kept confidential to avoid public embarrassment, as the aforementioned citation defining Tentative Lists guaranteed. However, the number of annual "rejections" is much larger than this number, since these presentations are often made in advance of the official Convention and the country often knows the status of the Committee's vote beforehand. In 2004, eight nations withdrew nominations, which included potential sites in Costa Rica, Slovakia, Ecuador, Portugal and the Czech Republic:

> 28 COM 14B.2   The World Heritage Committee,
> 1. Takes note that the following States Parties had requested that their nominations not be examined at the 28th session of the Committee in 2004:
>   • Corcovado National Park and Isla del Caño Biological Reserve (Costa Rica)

- Cajas Lakes and Ruins of Paredones (Ecuador)
- Primeval Forests of Slovakia (Slovakia)
- Ilhas Selvagens (Portugal)
- Rock Cities of the Bohemian Paradise (Czech Republic).[44]

Additionally, UNESCO most often defers its valorizing decision back to the State-party for further review. Sometimes this is necessary from a legal standpoint, as was the case with Panama's proposed World Heritage site of Coiba National Park. Technically, the law which would establish Coiba as a National Park had not yet been passed; not only would this have been problematic for the World Heritage site's official title—what happens if Coiba never becomes a National Park *per se*?—but it would be entirely possible that national politicking would change the dimensions and conceptual dynamics of the natural site. Thus, the Committee deferred deciding on its value "until the new proposed national law establishing the National Park is approved by the President of Panama and a revised, expanded nomination is submitted for examination."[45] A deferral is also procedurally necessary if the Committee had planned to vote on a site, but the evaluation was not ready in time, as was the case with the Paleohabitat of Tarnoc, Hungary. IUCN required more time to bring in outside paleobotanical experts before compiling its exhaustive evaluation. But sometimes this deferral is a way of saving face, with the Committee urging the nation-state to "rethink" the designation and the categories for which it pertains, such as in the case of Azerbaijan's failed attempt to nominate its Gobustan Rock Art Cultural Landscape. Recognizing that the State-party did not make an effective case illustrating the "universal" importance of the site, the Committee deferred the nomination "to allow the State Party to undertake a research and analysis programme for the site, using methodologies which are now emerging in other rock art sites in the region, in order to quantify the site's significance in the wider world context."[46]

With an affirmative vote, the locality is definitively designated as a World Heritage site, and ready to emerge as such to the greater public. In this ritual process, UNESCO and the World Heritage Committee never announce that a place is "designated" a World Heritage site, but rather that it is ceremonially "inscribed" upon what UNESCO understatedly terms the "List." The verbiage is once again telling. While "designation" may suggest a decision that has been made as to a new title, "inscription" seems to convey both a sense of permanency, as well as sacredness. The two, in fact, often go hand in hand. A plaque, intended to be permanent and revelatory, is inscribed. A sacred manuscript is likewise inscribed, rather than simply written or published. There is an air of authority, a sense of timelessness with this word—which corresponds exactly with the heritage-scape's authoritative timelessness and expansive spatiality. Indeed, this official list is the material, textual manifestation of the heritage-scape's cartography, expressing an inventory of the valorized places found within the ephemeral boundaries of the heritage-scape much like a museum's catalogue concisely presents the often vast holdings found within its walls. Like the museum catalogue, it is complete with the same sort of images, historical anecdotes, and evaluative curatorial messages. Most importantly, it is an entity where all of the unique-yet-idealized, valorized holdings can be juxtaposed in one place. Such unification ensures that all of the objects or places are juxtaposed equally against one another, adding equal value to each, irrespective of the socially stratified nations in which they are found. With one inscribed line dedicated to each site, all are equal in value. All are equally indicative of the great unity that exists in the world's cultural and natural diversity.

Like the museum object, when this step is completed, the World Heritage site is fully reintegrated into society, ready for interaction on a daily basis. But idealized and valorized, the site's meaning has inexorably been altered, which, in turn, alters the type of interaction individuals are able to have with it. Possessing added value, individuals will treat it as such; their interaction with it and expectations of its epistemological and emotional potency will inexorably change. This value distinction between a local space and a World Heritage site is perhaps best articulated in ICOMOS' nomination of Venice, when the organization writes, "The least *palazzetto*, which in Venice seems only a minor construction, would constitute the glory of many historic cities."[47] In Venice the "commonplace" locality, the most minor building would be nothing of note; in Venice the World Heritage site, all of its buildings are equally valorized. Even a minor construction is thus valuable enough to be glorified.

Because this value is realized not simply through idealization but through the juxtaposition of World Heritage sites, the overall value of each of the sites increases through the addition of each new property. This, in turn, dialectically serves to increase the total value of the heritage-scape to which the List textually corresponds, as ICOMOS makes clear in recommending Angkor: "There can be no doubt regarding the eligibility of the Angkor complex of monuments for inclusion on the World Heritage List. It has, indeed, been argued, with justification, that their absence devalues the list."[48]

The heritage-scape is one cohesive place composed of an ever-increasing quantity of sites that are themselves ever-increasing in value. As such, its value does not increase in an aggregate fashion as more sites are added to it, but rather exponentially. The heritage-scape is more than simply the sum of its parts. As more unique, idealized material interpretations of UNESCO's "unity in diversity" meta-narrative are integrated, the total complexity of this place, which is imbued with such a claim, increases. This notion is underscored in UNESCO's most recent *Information Kit*, which simplifies the organization's myriad processes and documents for the layperson. Speaking about the *Global Strategy for a Representative World Heritage List*, wherein World Heritage Committee agreed to give preference to "underrepresented" regions of the world, UNESCO states:

> By adopting the Global Strategy, the World Heritage Committee wanted to broaden the definition of World Heritage to better reflect the full spectrum of our world's cultural and natural treasures and to provide a comprehensive framework and operational methodology for implementing the World Heritage Convention . . . Crucial to the Global Strategy are efforts to encourage countries to become States Parties to the Convention, to prepare Tentative Lists and to prepare nominations of properties from categories and regions not currently well-represented on the World Heritage List.[49]

According to this document, the purpose of the Global Strategy is to "broaden the definition of World Heritage" primarily through adding new, diverse sites. The intended effect of this initiative is to provide, on the most basic level, new physical opportunities for visitors and locals alike to interact with the heritage-scape. However, it also has another, more far-reaching effect for the heritage-scape itself. Although the Global Strategy encourages the addition of sites from "categories . . . not currently well-represented," it does not propose to change, add, or alter any of its typologies. Rather, it encourages new sites to find ways to become idealized manifestations of the same narrative claim, in the pre-subscribed manner. Thus, the very "definition" of World Heritage is predicated not on UNESCO's documents, but rather on the totality of the sites that espouse UNESCO's meta-narrative claim. As new sites are added, the very definition of what World Heritage means for each and every site changes. This consequently provides the impetus for constantly integrating more idealized places within its nebulous boundaries, for as each new one is added, the narrative claim's very definition—its very articulation—comes better into focus. And through this ritual procedure, the heritage-scape continues to expand in depth, breadth and complexity.

CHAPTER SIX

POLITICS AND PERSONALITIES
WITHIN THE HERITAGE-SCAPE:
NARRATIVES OF NATURE AND CULTURE IN VIETNAM

Upon close examination, it seems that participation in UNESCO's World Heritage program is a complex and costly endeavor from which states-parties derive very little direct, material benefit. In many ways, the World Heritage Convention is a "pay to play" system. Like a fraternity or exclusive social club, prospective members must demonstrate through tangible—and even ritualized—means their willingness just to be invited to participate; yet after being accepted, the profits do not automatically flow, but rather emerge in direct proportion to what each makes of its membership. And this only gets the member-state to the table. After becoming a participating member in good standing, achieving a designation nevertheless receives years of preparation, documentation, hosting outside experts, and, above all, capital investment at the particular site. Often a great deal of political maneuverings is necessary, both inside the country and among the World Heritage Committee members. Yet despite the dedication of such an admirable amount of time, money and manpower, the direct results are mainly immaterial: a designation on a List posted primarily online, the ability to use UNESCO's logo in the site (at the country's cost and with no assurance that visitors will recognize its meaning), the potential to receive nominal funding for awareness-raising purposes, and, finally, the possibility that tourist guide books and preservation societies will then utilize the new title to indicate the place's heightened value to their constituencies, who, in turn will hopefully visit the site. Finally, although many State-Parties seem not to be aware of it, offering up the state's property to the borderless heritage-scape weakens, if not destroys, the state's ownership over what undoubtedly was, or would be, an important site of national hubris.

All of this is reiterated to indicate the very uncertain, costly and contingent

nature of a nation's participation in this process—three qualities that often mark
a risky political endeavor. And this process is, above all, inherently political in
nature. The nomination, decision and implementation of a site's World Heritage
designation is ultimately made for, and by, politicians—not museum professionals, archaeologists, preservationists, NGOs or tour operators. Nor does the political process begin in Paris, either. The group charged with the responsibility of
restoring, preparing and maintaining each site consists of politicians within the
state-party, as well. In the case of Cambodia, it is the APSARA organization,
which was created by decree of the king in 1995 to serve as a political umbrella
organization overseeing the other governmental ministries who, in varying
ways, work to develop, preserve and maintain the Angkor Archaeological Park.
Even more telling is the political entity which oversees Vietnam's World Heritage activities: the Ministry of Culture and Information, "the key executive arm
for cultural policy in the Socialist Republic of Vietnam."[1] Although the executive branch is located in the capital of Ha Noi, satellite offices are located in
most cities and at every World Heritage site to oversee the minutiae of each cultural property, including the bulk of the preparations necessary for the country's
representative at the World Heritage Committee to offer forth a nomination.
Created in its present state by decree of the Party in 2003, the Ministry is the
government-run organization that oversees not only all issues relating to cultural
heritage, but also owns and manages state-run publishing houses, theaters, tourist sites, the State patent office, "National Creativity Houses" in various cities
across the country, the Cultural Development Import-Export Company, construction companies whose purviews specifically relate to heritage sites, preservation offices, and "ethnic culture" offices that are ostensibly charged with
documenting, preserving and promoting—but also re-contextualizing—the cultural forms of minority ethnic peoples within Vietnam.

It is not surprising, therefore, that a World Heritage designation would be
understood as a politically beneficial tool for articulating, to its citizenry and to
the broader international community, the particular narrative claims of the
nation-state itself. An examination of Cambodia and Vietnam's World Heritage
properties reveals a subtle proclivity to underscore ethnocentric or nationalistic
claims on the part of the political powers that control the individual site. Because of the unusual designation and preservation activities of an unusually active segment of the international community—which I will recount in chapter
9—it is not clear whether the Kingdom of Cambodia is the primary beneficiary
of Angkor's valorized state. But World Heritage designations translate differently in Vietnam, which endeavors to balance often problematic and conflicting
narratives within a universalizing meta-narrative. Through the designation of a
variety of properties that espouse different claims, Vietnam offers forth narra-

tives valorizing the Việt people and the present-day Socialist Republic, often with the (un)intended consequences of marginalizing others who fall outside this rubric. Minority ethnic groups living within the confines of the present-day country, as well as historical enemies of the state such as the Cham, the Chinese and the Western colonialist / "imperialist," are subtly marginalized through the selection of the site, the semantics of the designation itself, and the semiotics of the physical place as it subsequently is preserved and packaged for touristic consumption based on the criteria for which UNESCO recognized it.

Valorizing the Việt

In their quest to document, preserve and appropriate the historic structures of "past" Indochinese cultures within their realm, French colonials imparted the decidedly Western notion of heritage to their Vietnamese counterparts. By the time UNESCO was founded, Vietnamese nationals considered the organization a valuable tool for valorizing the Việt people and therefore their claims to statehood. Even before the French definitively pulled out of Southeast Asia in 1954, civic leaders were appropriating historic places as heritage sites, and soliciting the advice of UNESCO affiliates in an effort to assert their ability to preserve the properties independent of outside assistance.

The period immediately following UNESCO's foundation was a politically transitional one for Vietnam. The capitulation of the Axis Powers in 1945 had freed French Indochina from the rule of Axis-collaborating Vichy France, who had allowed Japan to occupy the country. To many Vietnamese, the defeat of their colonial overlord was perceived *de facto* as the gaining of independence, though that the Allied powers regarded this as its victory over an illegitimate French government. France swiftly reasserted its domination over Indochina, and Vietnam's war for independence was sparked. Because it was not yet recognized in the international sphere as a sovereign state, Vietnam could not join the United Nations; however, citing the need for educational and cultural assistance, "Vietnam," represented by the French-collaborating emperor Bảo Đại (who spent more time in France than in Huế), managed to join UNESCO on July 6, 1951. UNESCO experts trained locals in horticulture and assisted in planting trees in the south. Three years later, the Geneva Accords officially ended the war and temporarily split the country into North and South, with the dividing line at the seventeenth parallel.

According to informants, that the line was drawn here was not arbitrary; it dictated who controlled the former imperial capital of Huế.[2] Ho Chi Minh, in fact, had pushed for the dividing line at the fifteenth parallel, or at the strategic Hải Vân Pass that separated Huế from Đà Nẵng, but Bảo Đại was sympathetic to South Vietnam and insisted on his capital in this region. The United States succeeded, over French insistence, in refusing Bảo Đại's leadership, and moved the capital to Saigon under the control of President Ngô Đình Diệm the following year. In a typically political turn of events, then, Bảo Đại lost his claim to govern South Vietnam, thereby negating the articulated reasoning for including Huế in the territory of the South, but the compromise remained. Nevertheless, it was a welcomed one for the South, for the inclusion of Huế within the country's boundaries transferred great symbolic and political legitimacy onto Diệm's government.

As South Vietnam was pro-Western, membership in UNESCO transferred to Diệm's government. In 1955 the artifacts from the Nguyễn dynasty were consigned to the Huế Museum, which was placed under the authority of the Ministry of Education. The Ministry had been in direct contact with representatives from UNESCO's educational sector, arguably the most active division of UNESCO at the time. For the twenty years the Saigon government existed, it paid for reconstructions and urgent repairs on ninety-five structures, according to ICOMOS.[3] Mr. Phan Thuận An, a member of the Huế Relics Conservation Center, remembers that at the government's behest, UNESCO assisted the municipal government in recommending preservationists to assess the restoration of Huế's damaged properties. The effort was ultimately for naught, as the city was plunged even deeper into chaos and destruction during the "American War" less than a decade later; the 1968 Tet Offensive effectively leveled much of the Imperial City and the emperor's Forbidden Purple City. Phan recalls, however, that UNESCO wanted to remain abreast of the situation and sent an envoy in 1971 and again in 1973. "An American architect for UNESCO, Mr. Martin—Mr. Martin Brown—came to Huế to research the Citadel and the Tombs [to assess] the condition of the restoration, what was left from the Tet Offensive. He proposed a technical report and submitted it to UNESCO. But the war was very severe, very terrible."[4] Nothing could be done.

When Saigon fell in April 1975, the country's membership in UNESCO was transferred *de facto* to the Socialist Republic of Vietnam, and country formally agreed to the membership terms the following year. It was not until 1978 that a second expert was sent from UNESCO. Jean-Pierre Pichard, a French archaeologist specializing in Southeast Asia, spent a month researching the damage in Huế before submitting a report to UNESCO, which led UNESCO to send more experts to Ha Noi and Huế. In 1980, the Vietnamese architect Hoàng Đạo Kính, who was serving as Director of the Ministry of Culture and Information's Department of Conservation, was sent to Romania and Poland for technical training, where he met an architect by the name of Kazimier Kwiatkowski. "Kazim" as the Vietnamese later called him, was the conservator at the *Pracownie Konserwacji Zabytkow* (PKZ)—known in Vietnam by the French title *Ateliers for the Conservation of Cultural Properties of Poland*—and assembled a team to visit Huế and the Cham ruins at Mỹ Sơn. By 1981, an "action plan" for restoring Huế had been put together, and Amadu Amatibo, the Senegalese Director-General of UNESCO at the time, personally flew to the city, where he met Phan. "After two days in Huế, we went to Ha Noi, [where] the Director-General called on the international community to help restore Huế."[5]

There was little support. America and many of its allies had embargoed the country, and limited funding trickled in from Japan, England and Thailand— presumably through private or semi-private donors. For its part, Vietnam was embroiled in an arguably bleaker period of social strife. Since Christmas 1978, Vietnam had been combating the China-backed Khmer Rouge in Cambodia, which sapped political and economic resources that could have gone to the organization or the World Heritage Convention. Exacerbated by the Communist party's reorganization of land and redistribution of rice to the soldiers fighting in Cambodia, a devastating rice famine swept across the country in the early 1980s, killing millions. In Huế, people resorted to taking the wood from the demolished imperial city to use for cooking fire, Phan recalls. Despite the hardship, the municipal government's Center for the Complex of Monuments of Huế took UNESCO's "action plan" for restoring Huế and compiled a preliminary File in preparation for its nomination as a World Heritage site. The File was ready by 1983, said Phan, who, as a member of the Center, had a hand in compiling it.

But Huế had to wait.

In addition to turning their attention to the more pressing material needs of the Vietnamese people at home, the Communist government was not as interested in preserving or designating the former imperial city as a heritage site, national or otherwise. To the government, which had just completed two wars against foreign "imperialists," Huế's narrative was a distasteful mix of imperial "feudalism"—a Marxian mode of production that "ensurfed small peasantry," turning them into slaves[6]—and collusion with Western imperialists, which was indicative of weak national leadership. The destruction of Huế, in fact, had not been entirely the America's fault—it was the Viet Cong who first attacked, went door-to-door in a rampage of destruction, and used the fortress as cover. Furthermore, the Forbidden Purple City had been modeled after Beijing's Forbidden City, and the Chinese were loathed during Vietnam's war with the Khmer Rouge. Huế needed a different narrative—one that was evocative of the positive qualities of the Vietnamese yet separated the Communist government from the embarrassing feudal overtones of the Nguyễn era.

It was clear that, through most of the 1980s, the government did not feel that Huế embodied these values, but as Kazim and his teams of Eastern European worked contemporaneously on the Cham-minority site of Mỹ Sơn, the tiny backwater town of Hội An, and the ruined imperial capital, the qualities to which the Vietnamese government was attracted began to emerge very clearly in Huế's imperial structures. Members of the Center for the Complex of Monuments of Huế were only too eager to point out the power the Citadel's fortifications exuded, and the refined sublimity of its original architecture that rendered it an equal to such Oriental cities as Beijing and Japan's first capital Nara. The presence of Kazim and his teams should also not be discounted, as they were not only responsible for helping to materially preserve the sites, but they also raised awareness of the destination to other Soviet-bloc experts who were advising the Vietnamese government on a range of infrastructural and military affairs. These were the first tourists, and while they treated Ha Noi—and to a lesser degree, Saigon—as working cities, they frequently holidayed in Huế and Đà Nẵng. Tourist revenue increased. The government listened, and issued successive ordinances classifying the site as a Grade AII Historical Property in 1984, 1985 and 1986. At the end of 1989, the government considered Huế to be one of the central sites of tourist development, and it factored prominently into the government's National Platform for Socio-Economic Development 1990-2000.[7] While only fifteen major restoration projects and thirty smaller "urgent repairs" were undertaken during the thirteen-year period between 1975 and 1988, in the two years between 1989 and 1991, the government carried out another fifteen major restoration projects and thirty-five urgent repairs on structures "in imminent danger of collapse."[8] A management plan was devised, and ICOMOS was invited to make another assessment in March 1993. Later that year—exactly a decade after the File had been finished—Huế was designated a World Heritage site.

While it is certainly true that "tourism just may have saved Huế's cultural sites from oblivion," as the *Lonely Planet* guidebook states, Huế' was ultimately embraced by the government as its first World Heritage site, but not exclusively for such a simple reason. Rather, the city's particular history, unique architectural and topographical composition, and narrative malleability enabled it to be contextualized—both textually and physically—in accordance with the needs of the government. First, Huế as an urban center is geopolitically important; in ancient times, the Khmer, Cham and Việt peoples all struggled to control this strategically located outpost. The contemporary period also largely focused on the diplomatic and military struggle to gain control of the city; Ho Chi Minh, Bảo Đại, Ngô Đình Diệm, the French and the Americans all jockeyed for its control, and much blood was spilled in the area. Although the 1968 Tet Offensive was coordinated all around South Vietnam, the most significant, and significantly devastating, battle was at Huế; the Viet Cong held this city longer than any other during the Vietnam War. The celebration of the government's possession of Huế is a celebration of the ultimate victory of the North Vietnamese forces, both in 1968 and in 1975. It reveals, better than any other conquered city, the continuous exhibition of strength and willpower of the "Vietnamese people" as embodied in the Viet Cong. In a particularly ethnographic moment, the authors of *Lonely Planet* recount this anecdote:

> Long after the American War ended, one American veteran is said to have returned to Huế and, upon meeting a former VC officer, commented that the USA never lost a single major battle during the entire war. "You are absolutely correct," the former officer agreed, "but that is irrelevant, is it not?"[9]

Huế, then, is not simply the embodiment of a victorious Viet Cong, the Viet Minh, of Communism or of Ho Chi Minh, but of true nationalism. It became a unique symbol of continuous unity of the people—one that was not forged with the blood of the Viet Cong, or that of the Americans, French, Japanese, Chinese, or whichever aggressor it faced in contemporary history; it was forged through generations of average citizens working under the dynasties of the empire. Although the Nguyễn dynasty did not last as long, nor was as powerful as the other dynasties—the Lý, it should be remembered, repelled the invading Mongol-Chinese, while the Nguyễns capitulated to the French and supported the Americans—the imperial system was itself imbued with a sense of tradition and continuity. The Nguyễns were seen as legitimately authorized by higher powers in the same way their dynastic predecessors were—extending into the mythological period. If executed properly, designating Huế as the nation's first World Heritage site could both symbolically unify the people and valorize the Socialist Republic in the eyes of those at home and abroad. It was a choice to recognize Huế as an ideal representation of the contemporary Vietnamese people—to themselves and the world.

Inherent in this reasoning lurked the danger of overly celebrating the Nguyễn dynasty—especially since the "last emperor" Bảo Đại was still alive in Paris at the time (he died in 1997). Constructing a proper narrative would certainly be a concern when the international milieu is taken into consideration. Not only had Vietnam suffered greatly to prove its strength and independence against many of the same people who would later patronize the World Heritage site, but many Vietnamese brethren themselves had fled overseas. By the 1990s, the *Việt kiều* (a pejorative epithet for "overseas Vietnamese") were not the American-colluding boatpeople—the escaping losers—they may have appeared at the fall of Saigon fifteen years earlier. They wielded more communicative power and were more wealthy than those they left behind. And they demonstrated it—they wrote about it in letters and they regularly sent money back home to help the impoverished family members they left behind. A fine line had to be drawn that would sufficiently abstract the site to speak of the continuity of Vietnamese unity, while at the same time separating the site from the Nguyễn reign. Fortunately for the Communist party, the authorizing voice was not a deity, an emperor, the Western elite or the envied *Việt kiều*—it was the government itself.

Because the State-Party ultimately dictated the terms of the nomination, several measures were taken to achieve this necessary narrative balance. The first was textual. Upon ICOMOS' review of Huế in March 1993, where they worked for three days with Vietnamese officials and consulted the nomination file prepared by the Center for the Complex of Huế Monuments,[10] they gave the following reasons for their recommendation:

> *Criterion iii:* Hue represents an outstanding demonstration of the power of the vanished Vietnamese feudal empire at the apogee in the early 19th century
>
> *Criterion iv:* The complex of Hue monuments is an outstanding example of an eastern feudal capital.[11]

While Criterion *iv* is extremely abstract and fitting for the heritage-scape's meta-narrative claim, the recommendation is balanced out by Criterion *iii*. In this criterion, the distinction between past and present is quite evident, while nevertheless focusing on the abstracted power of the people. First comes the positive attribute: it is representational of power. But it is not simply power of the constructors that the structures demonstrate, but the *active and constructive demonstration of power* of the "empire." In addition to conveying a sense of national pride in its victory, the government's Communist ideology is conveyed through these words, which are indicative of a Marxist archaeological perspective. Such a perspective interprets a regime's power in terms of the labor-power mobilized to create a monumental building by calculating the "means of production" most likely employed: the types of materials, forms of tools utilized, number of people mobilized, and so on.[12] ICOMOS' first sentence introducing the recommendation documents attests to this form of thinking when the authors write,

> The Hue complex represents unique architectural, sculptural and aesthetic achievements and highly creative *labour by the Vietnamese people* over a long

period of time, particularly in monumental arts, town planning and landscape design."[13]

The distancing then begins. This "creative power" refers not to the Nguyễns who planned and commissioned it, but to the Vietnamese people, according to ICOMOS' introduction. Criteria *iii* echoes this, stating that the monuments are evocative of an "empire," rather than of a particular family, dynasty or ruling class; this empire, furthermore, is a *Vietnamese* empire. Thus, it is generalized enough to mean "people," without being so abstracted that it purports to simply represent an "eastern" empire as criterion *iv* describes. It is also specific inasmuch as it is not representative of any empire in the history of Vietnam, but rather "the" empire, though the loathed name of the dynasty ruling this Vietnamese empire is never mentioned. Substituting the name Nguyễn, in fact, is the Communist party's favorite epithet for them: feudal. This was a "feudal Vietnamese empire," a community of ensurfed yet proudly powerful people. Finally, the coup de grace: this feudal empire is "vanished." The Revolution had come; the king had fled to France; a new order supplanted the old order—and nothing is left but the powerful and united people.

Much to the chagrin of the Vietnamese State-Party, the World Heritage Committee struck criterion *iii* from the official 1994 designation, leaving only the bland, yet non-conflicting, reasoning that Huế served as an example of an "eastern feudal capital." Nevertheless, when initially compiling the final version of the File, the State-Party also contextualized the World Heritage site in such a way that would also convey a similar perspective. The Complex of Monuments of Huế is not simply the land within the Citadel, but also includes a number of monuments dispersed throughout the province of Huế. In fact, they can be roughly divided into four major categories: the Imperial Complex (Citadel, Imperial City and Forbidden Purple City), The Royal Tombs, the iconic Thiên Mụ Pagoda, and the Perfume River. The first two are monumental remembering devices of the Nguyễn era, while the second two can be considered living sites, one cultural and one natural. In particular, the Thiên Mụ Pagoda has for centuries stood not only as a symbol of the Nguyễn empire (it was constructed in the early 1600s by the Nguyễn lord), but as an icon of the city itself; it is celebrated in folktales and children's songs. Furthermore, the numerous monuments comprising the first two categories are all in various states of ruins. Half of the categories, therefore, are remembering devices for a "vanquished" and "feudal" episode in the people's history, while the other half represent continuous, living sites.

The living sites are also interesting in their meaning. Thiên Mụ Pagoda, the only living cultural site, is extraordinarily positive in its contextualization; of all the monuments, this is continually described as the eternal "symbol of Huế" in guidebooks, postcards and other travel literature. This is not an accidental occurrence. While the Nguyễn emperors were the feudal oppressors and colonial colluders, the monks of the Thiên Mụ Pagoda were revolutionaries in the true sense of the word. They frequently rose up in protest against the regime of the Catholic President Diệm on multiple occasions in the early 1960s, culminating with the spectacular 1963 self-immolation of its most famous monk, Thích Quảng Đức. He is currently considered a bodhisattva; with his charred heart—which supposedly resisted re-cremation—as proof of his supernatural sainthood. The Austin Westminster sedan that transported him to Saigon on that fateful day remains in an outdoor niche dedicated to the monk's veneration; like the rest of the temple, the car, too, is geographically part of the World Heritage site. Finally, joining the vanquished and the victorious, the vestiges and the living, is the Perfume River (*Hương Giang*)—a symbol of temporal continuity, an eternal life force that flows without ceasing, linking the disparate cultural sites together. The Perfume River is certainly a liminal site, a timeless place whose state is constantly betwixt and between; it is an eminently natural site within the context of a cultural designation, and it has seen the ravishes of time yet withstood it, leaving no outward markings on its placid surface. It renders the entire World Heritage site a vast and vaguely differentiated "cultural landscape."[14]

The separation between the contemporary people's regime and that of the past is also spatially enforced. Unlike Hội An, not all of Huế Province, nor all of the city, are contained in this rather unusual designation; only selected monuments are recognized as part of the World Heritage site. As with every World Heritage site, its total dimensions are precisely delimited, but instead of tracing preexisting urban or provincial political boundaries, these delimitations surround each individual monument in the form of a series of "buffer zones."[15] Multiple buffers are established surrounding each site: the one closest to the site limits the alteration of any part of the landscape—such as deforestation, creating roadways, or erecting residential or commercial building. The next buffers allow for incrementally more landscape manipulation, residential living, and infrastructural development. These spatial limitations restrict not solely the amount of area of the land developed, but also how high buildings can be erected. To protect the continuity of the cultural landscape's authenticity, tall structures are forbidden along the lake and in the sightlines of the various monuments.

Yet Huế continues to grow, not only in wealth and population, but also in sensibility. As more tourists visit, the World Heritage designation continues to be branded on the consciousness of its people, leading to a greater awareness of the "universal importance" of the site. While at first the State-Party needed to separate the bulk of the monuments from the rest of the population, today their narratives are inexorably fusing with those of contemporary Huế. They are be-coming part of urban life, and some of these barriers are beginning to collapse—much to UNESCO's chagrin. "Illegal" residential settlements have sprung up in proximity to a number of monuments. A new roadway is being built within the buffer zone of the Perfume River, which UNESCO condemned in 2004 but later permitted after negotiations in 2005. And in 2006, Huế's first high rise hotel was erected—in the buffer zone along the Perfume River. Outcry has been great, both by preservationists and those in the tourist community. Noting the anachro-nistic structure, guides say this sentiment is shared by the people, as well, but it is unlikely that the building will be torn down. Nor has UNSCO listed this site on the List of World Heritage in Danger as it has for other places whose "heri-tage integrity" is compromised by contemporary building (such as the Dresden Bridge).

Indeed, gone are the days of pillaging the site for firewood, but gone, too, are the days when the government was compelled to keep these places separate, physically and conceptually. This is most clearly manifested in the govern-ment's new outlook on preservation. ICOMOS reveals that at the time of Huế's nomination, the State-Party accepted the UNESCO-recommended plan of action that consisted of:

- Maintaining the complex in its present state, without further deterioration;
- Repairing those monuments in danger of collapse;
- Requesting the continuing contributions from its Plan of Action;
- Increasing research, completing survey and inventory, and making use of display materials to increase revenue from visitors.[16]

In addition, ICOMOS pointed out that of the remaining edifices, "the level of authenticity is overall high, in view of the fact that a large proportion of the original structures are in ruins and that interventions on those that survive have been relatively limited."[17] Today, however, a new plan has been enacted that calls for the actual reconstruction of the Imperial City, including the completely leveled Forbidden Purple City. In 2005, the painted enamels on the bronze en-trance gates were replaced, made anew. In just eight months, the imposing West Gate has also been completely reconstructed; it blends in with the preexisting wall such that one cannot differentiate the old and the new. Also begun in 2005 is an ambitious reconstruction of the complex system of galleries crisscrossing the exterior of the Forbidden Purple City, which were used by the Mandarins to move between administrative buildings within the Imperial City without being subjected to the rain. There are no authentic materials left from the original gal-leries; they have all been reduced to rubble or burned. Yet they are being erected out of fresh wood and plaster, using contemporary tools. As early as 2005, an experience of the place is wholly different from that of years earlier. When the tourist steps out of the Palace of Supreme Harmony, no longer is he confronted by the vast nothingness that shocked so many of his predecessors; the galleries now greet him. In addition, there is a vibrancy and industriousness that now imbues the site; workers are talking, hammers are pounding, industrial plastic sheets covering the naked wood rustle in the wind and rain. This restoration is not simple "preservation"—which is defined by John Sanday, Field Director for the World Monuments Fund's Preah Khan project at Angkor, as the conservation of a structure as it is thought to have appeared in its last traceable state. Here, it is being restored to its imagined original state—complete with fresh paint and stronger foundations. The place is being changed; its recent life history is being erased.

And it will continue to be. According to Phan, the new plan calls for the completion of three more major projects, in addition to the already finished bronze gates and West Gate. The first is this system of galleries. The second are the three major tombs; Minh Mạng's suffers from cracks in its foundations, a number of Tự Đức's private chambers have collapsed in his sprawling villa-like tomb, and Khải Định's poorly constructed concrete edifice has never been substantially renovated. The third major project will be re-landscaping the vast Cơ Hạ Park at the far end of the Imperial City; the pavilions inside will also be reconstructed. Amazingly, although most official records and architectural drafts of these buildings have long since been lost to the destructive forces of the past, they are being "re-created" utilizing the photographs in a 1931 National Geographic article.[18]

It is clear that authenticity—the benchmark of any UNESCO designation—once served as the protective shield that definitively separated the old regime from the new, while ensuring UNESCO's recognition of Vietnam's unity. Now it seems, on the surface, to be a barrier to growth and development—something to be tossed aside. But it can also be read as the manifestation of a confluence of narratives, which have emerged as contemporary citizens integrate the monuments into their daily life. It is indicative of the very living nature of all World Heritage sites—they are not as ossified, as unchanging or as indicative of an irreparably "vanished" people as they might be portrayed. Rather, the sites are just as alive, just as continuous, and just as much a part of the contemporary consciousness of the people as are the urban center, the jungles and the eternal Perfume River.

There is a scale model of the Imperial City and the Forbidden Purple City that has stood at the back exit of the Palace of Supreme Harmony for years. It had always been a mediating site between the materially visible structures and the vast nothingness that lay ahead. It seemed to have been placed there for the tourists as a kind of apology and a kind of exhortation to use one's imagination when continuing to walk among the ruins. *Something once was here, something great*—it seemed to say, and indeed, guides would frequently gather their groups around to explain what once was there. Gazing out at the new gallery in the summer of 2006, Phan pointed to this model. "Soon, all these monuments will be restored, step by step."[19]

Marginalizing Minorities through Cultural Designations

The designation of Mỹ Sơn as a World Heritage site in 1999 can be viewed as the culmination of over a century of research by a small yet dedicated group of archaeologists and experts of the ancient kingdom of Champa. As with the designation of other monumental ruins in former Indochina, the years following its "discovery" by French soldiers at the end of the nineteenth century were marked by intense excavations by the French, who regarded the discovery and preservation of such vestiges of ancient kingdoms to be central to the moral imperative guiding their colonialization enterprises. Mỹ Sơn was an especially important find, for like Angkor, many centuries of architectural and artistic progression was preserved in a relatively compact area. These two components were interlinked, owing to the unique use of Mỹ Sơn as a locus of Cham religiosity.

The Chams have cultivated through the centuries a unique religious fusion of traditional animism, Hinduism influenced from India and the Khmers, Mahāyāna Buddhism from the Chinese and the Vietnamese, and Islam from the Arabs and Malays. Although Mahāyāna Buddhism was introduced into Champa by the Chinese, Hinduism—particularly the worship of Shiva—was the state religion of Champa; according to Champa scholar Po Dharma, Mỹ Sơn had been "the centre for the propagation of Hinduism since the fourth century."[20] By the sixth century, Hindu-animist kings of Champa favored the "beautiful" and strategic location of Mỹ Sơn and almost every one built a new temple there, such that when the capital was moved south from nearby Trà Kiêu in the ninth century, each king nevertheless continued to commission a temple in Mỹ Sơn. Thus, Mỹ Sơn became not as much a center of worship as a locus for performing kingly religious duty. For these reasons, Trần Kỳ Phương, the former curator of the Đà Nẵng Museum of Champa Sculpture, believes that Mỹ Sơn was much more a site for elites, rather than for popular religious worship.[21]

When the Chams moved their kingdom farther south at the end of the ninth century, the Cham rulers modeled their social structure, concept of divine kingship, and devotional practices on Hinduism. This included a rigid class system topped by a god-king who assumes, like Rāmā, the position of father to all.[22] As Dharma states, "in short, the very existence of this Hinduised kingdom . . . depended on the court, which was composed of an aristocratic elite imbued with Sanskrit culture." There was a resurgence of interest in Mỹ Sơn, and some of the most impressive temples were constructed. After the Chams were forced from Angkor by Jayavarman VII in the twelfth century, Mỹ Sơn was occupied by the Khmers. Although they eventually were able to wrest free from Khmer control, this was the beginning of a decline for Champa, and slowly the Vietnamese pushed southward. Buddhism firmly regained primacy by the fifteenth century.[23]

The fifteenth century also saw two important developments that would forever change the history of Mỹ Sơn. The first was a definitive Vietnamese victory over Vijaya, which forced the Cham leaders to abandon the area once and for all; while many of the local people still remained, kingly construction projects forever ceased at Mỹ Sơn. With the Chams' southward movement and the development of international trade routes between Hội An and Malacca in Muslim Malaysia, many of the people converted to a uniquely Southeast Asian form of Islam, which is heavily infused with local animist beliefs and practices. Since there were no kings to look after the upkeep of their ancestors' constructions, and few locals who regarded Mỹ Sơn as a site of popular worship, it was almost entirely abandoned by the local people. In the nineteenth century, Nguyễn emperor Minh Mạng squelched a final Cham uprising; the people were dispersed in two main groups: there are hill-tribes living in the high plateaus of central Vietnam, around Đà Lạt; they speak an Austronesian language. The second are Chams proper, who continue to live in central Vietnam, especially around Phan Thiết. In Vietnam, these Chams number 95,000[24] and many are considered Muslim. Many have also intermarried with ethic Vietnamese; one Đà Nẵng-based Vietnamese informant told me that "all of us are Cham."[25] There are also some 150,000 who have settled in Cambodia.[26]

Because of the recurrent religious and political intersections between the Cham and the Khmer, nineteenth century French archaeologists frequently crossed borders in their studies of the "Indianized States of Southeast Asia"[27]— namely, Angkor and Champa. Although there were earlier French explorers who "discovered" the virtually abandoned Cham structures around Mỹ Sơn, the early twentieth-century archaeologist Henri Parmentier is generally regarded as the first major contributor to raising awareness of Mỹ Sơn to the international community. Shortly after the turn of the century, a young Parmentier began studying the sculpture and bas reliefs of Mỹ Sơn. Also working at the time was Louis Finot, another Frenchman who in 1898 and 1899 studied and transcribed the Sanskrit inscriptions present in Mỹ Sơn. Parmentier and Finot collaborated on a series of articles published in the 1904 edition of the *Bulletin de l'École Française d'Extreme-Orient*, which first introduced Mỹ Sơn to a broader audience. Moved by the volume of artifacts recovered from Mỹ Sơn and Duong Dong and their neglect by the colonial authorities, Parmentier would eventually became the founding father of the Cham Museum in Đà Nẵng, and would publish the first comprehensive *Inventory* of the collection in 1919. By 1934, the French ethnographer and archaeologist, Jean Yves Claeys, began restoration work. This led to broader involvement by the École Française d'Extreme-Orient, which carried out a series of restoration initiatives from 1938 until 1944, including the construction of basic infrastructure needed to access the site, such as a dirt road and a dam to prevent flooding. Nguyễn Xuân Đồng, a conservationist who worked in the 1930s with Claeys and the EFEO in the restoration work, became the first Vietnamese curator of the Parmentier Cham Museum in Đà Nẵng, a position he held from 1937 to his retirement in 1970.[28]

Despite Nguyễn Xuân Đồng's dedication to the monuments of Mỹ Sơn, neither the South nor the North Vietnamese government had much regard for them during the period of unrest in the mid-twentieth century. Like other Cham and Montagnard sites across Vietnam, they were perceived as the vestiges of a foreign "Other," and therefore of little pertinence. Durable and well positioned throughout the jungles, their importance was entirely strategic, and many were converted into *ad hoc* bases by the Viet Cong. As early as April 1947, less than three years since the EFEO had completed basic restoration of the monuments, a French expeditionary force shelled Mỹ Sơn with cannons in an attempt to root out the Vietnamese insurgents hiding there, severely damaging a number of the temples. By 1965 Mỹ Sơn was established as a base for the Viet Cong, and South Vietnamese troops had garrisoned around Cat Tooth Mountain to secure the region. Mines were placed around Mỹ Sơn, and as one modern Vietnamese author mentioned, "Sài Gòn puppet troops, under American support . . . shot at random at various constructions, making many valuable ones crumble."[29] The coup de grace, however, occurred in 1969, when American B-52s heavily bombed the Mỹ Sơn sanctuaries, reducing much of it to rubble. Whereas at the time of Parmentier, some sixty structures were visible, with about half in relatively complete condition, after the conclusion of the war, only about twenty remain. Perhaps the most disastrous loss was that of the temple classified as A1, which was considered one of the most important existent structures. Durable and massive, it withstood fierce bombardment from the air; a sapper team had to come by helicopter to specifically destroy it.[30] Immediately after this travesty at Mỹ Sơn, Nguyễn Xuân Đồng sent a message to his French colleague, Philippe Stern, who was the curator of Indochinese art at the Musée Guimet in Paris and had been responsible for establishing the definitive classification system of

Cham architectural styles.[31] Stern immediately denounced the matter to the White House, moving President Richard Nixon to send a message in January 1970 to the U.S. Commandant in South Vietnam: "The White House desires that, to the extent that is possible, measures be taken to ensure damage to historical monuments is not caused by military operations."[32]

Following the country's reunification, the only significant activity at Mỹ Sơn was an extensive de-mining operation, most likely carried out by former South Vietnamese soldiers who were forced into "Reeducation Camps." During the de-mining operations around Mỹ Sơn in 1977, nine were killed and eleven more were injured.[33] On April 29, 1979, the Ministry of Culture and Information designated the Cham temples in Mỹ Sơn protected cultural relics in Decision 54/VH-QD.[34] With the growth of interest in preserving the nation's cultural heritage in the 1980s and Hoang's participation in training activities in Eastern Europe, eyes turned again to Mỹ Sơn. In 1980, Nguyễn Xuân Đồng accompanied Hoàng Đạo Kính to the PKZ conference in Poland, where he discussed the site and its state of preservation. Among those whose interest he captured was Kazim's, and the Polish architect swiftly flew to Mỹ Sơn, where he would work from 1980 to 1994. Although he consulted in Huế and was credited with "discovering" Hội An, Mỹ Sơn remained Kazim's passion and his primary area of interest. Along with members of the Vietnamese Ministry of Culture and Information, he first studied the remains in central Vietnam. A joint Committee for the Restoration of Champa ruins was then established, and a plan of action was drawn up, which included clearing the debris and naturally growing vegetation at the site; this was carried out from 1990 to 1996.

In 1997, Kazim succumbed to cancer while working on the monuments in Huế. Following his rather unexpected death, the Fondazione Lerici, an Italian institute affiliated with Milan Polytechnic University and Italy's Ministry of Cultural Heritage, prepared a project for comprehensive computerized mapping of the area. Practicing "non-invasive geo-archaeology"[35] and operating both in Italy and abroad, the Fondazione Lerici continues to carry out its 1998 plan in collaboration with UNESCO and the Vietnamese Ministry of Culture. In subsequent years, it has joined French, Japanese and Polish groups in systematically restoring various sites, and is particularly active in the "Group G" monuments. In 1999, both Mỹ Sơn and Hội An would join Huế as Vietnamese World Heritage sites.

As with the monuments of Huế, Mỹ Sơn is imbued with certain narrative strands that were incompatible with Vietnamese nationalism. For this Cham site, the reasoning is much more straightforward. Like the Khmers, the Vietnamese have a long history of conflict with the Cham people, and every century from the tenth to the nineteenth were marked with extensive wars with their neighbors to the north. This even continued into the twentieth century, as Cham minority tribes throughout the Central Highlands and the region near Nha Trang fought on the side of the Americans and the Saigon government. A World Heritage designation needed to once again be abstracted enough to reveal the universal value of a Vietnamese-possessed site while marginalizing the grandeur of the Cham people. This was once again achieved textually and aesthetically at the site itself.

Textual descriptions of Mỹ Sơn by both ICOMOS and UNESCO serve to clearly separate the Cham from the Vietnamese, both temporally and phenomenologically. While this point has been discussed at some length earlier in the book, it is worth pointing out the unique temporality with which UNESCO contextualized the site. In criterion *iii*, UNESCO asserts that Mỹ Sơn serves as an example of a civilization "adapting to external cultural influences, especially . . . from the Indian sub-continent." This refers to the founding of Mỹ Sơn in the fourth century, when the animist kings of Champa began to embrace Shaivism[36] as a state religion, rather than at the height of the Cham empire in the tenth century, when the most important and massive monuments were erected. led by the Lý emperors in Ha Noi, it was in this period that Đai Việt (as Vietnam was called) was defending its lands from the Chinese, while Champa to the south was on the offense, launching a stunning naval attack on the Khmers at Angkor. The importance of the Chams of this era overshadows even the advances of the great Lý dynasty to the north.

The focus on the very pastness of Mỹ Sơn is also important when considering the recent relations between the Cham minorities and the Ha Noi government. By virtue of its near abandonment, as criterion *iii* states, Mỹ Sơn is "vividly illustrative" [sic] of "the Champa Kingdom [which] was an important phenomenon in the political and cultural history of South-East Asia," rather than of the Cham people who continue to exist as minorities in Vietnam today. Yet there are a number of well-preserved Cham religious sites that continue to be loci of active worship today. Indeed, the Cham tower complex of Pô Klong Girai near Phan Rang is an exceptional example of Cham Hindu-animist architecture, albeit on a smaller scale than those of Mỹ Sơn. Constructed at the end of the thirteenth century atop a striking granite plateau, its main tower is dedicated to Shiva, who is represented not only in an exquisite bas relief over the doorway of the main *kalan* or sanctuary, but also inside the vestibule in the form of a *mukha-linga*, a traditional Hindu phallic symbol (*linga*) with a male face painted on it. Most importantly, Pô Klong Girai, which has been recently recognized as a national monument, is the site of national pilgrimage for the Cham people, and hosts the largest processions during the Katê New Year celebrations. These celebrations are today intensely important to the Cham people's maintenance of their own cultural heritage, and honors Cham ancestors, local heroes (many of whom fought against the Việt) and particularly Cham Hindu-animist deities. It is marked with traditional music, clothing and rituals, and in recent years overseas Cham have returned to participate in the festivities.

There is also an inherent anonymity present in the textual descriptions of the individual constructions at Mỹ Sơn, which are still referred to by their French cataloguing codes. Before the French were able to extensively study the numerous Sanskrit inscriptions at each temple, they divided Mỹ Sơn's monuments into ten main groups, lettered A, A', B, C, D, E, F, G, H, K. Individual structures within a particular lettered group are given a number. These lettered groups are delimited geographically rather than strictly by the period in which they were constructed, though the Cham kings of various eras tended to build temples in proximity to those of their recent predecessors. Thanks to subsequent archaeological excavation and the deciphering of Sanskrit stelae, many of the temple names are known. However, these original Cham names are not applied to them, neither in official documents nor in tourist manuals, unlike the edifices at Hội An and Huế—and at Angkor, for that matter. Such a practice suppresses the dissemination of their individual narratives; it restrains the elaboration of their life histories to tourists. On paper, the individual edifices seem ossified, sterile and anonymous—more the product of an empirical experiment or a vast museum catalogue of the vestiges of an unknown culture, rather than living structures of a people who remain alive and active today. The selection of Mỹ Sơn and its accompanying textual descriptions serves to integrate the ancient Champa Kingdom within the heritage-scape's narrative of "unity in diversity," while effectively marginalizing their descendents who are still present. Within the context of the heritage-scape, this World Heritage site defines what the people *were* without discussing who they *are* today. While Mỹ Sơn undoubtedly deserves World Heritage designation, to truly capture the Cham people's role in adding to the heritage-scape's "unity in diversity," it is advisable that it be coupled with a site of continual, active worship such as Pô Klong Girai.

The ossified pastness of Mỹ Sơn is most strongly conveyed in its state of preservation and management, which stands in stark contrast to that of Pô Klong Girai's. While Pô Klong Girai is virtually located at the crossroads of the southern Vietnam highway system—one leading down from the Central Highlands city of Đà Lạt and the other running north from Saigon to Nha Trang, Đà Nẵng, Huế and Ha Noi—until recently Mỹ Sơn was lost in the unforgiving jungles, with only a dirt road traversable by jeep or motorbicycle. The difficulty and the poor infrastructure was traditionally not only a deterrent to visiting Mỹ Sơn, but it served to heighten its very aspect of primitivity. Tourists in the late twentieth and early twenty-first century still can play the part of the French colonial braving the elements to reach a lost city. This sensation does not end when one reaches the holy city, either. Site managers are responsible for cleaning vegetation from the temples—their deep roots can easily damage the mortarless structures—yet saplings and tall grasses seem to be constantly growing on the roofs of these buildings. Such a sight is evocative of Ta Prohm: nature serves to reinforce the constructors' primitivity, and to reveal the culture's very weakness. Like the destructive consort of Shiva,[37] here is "Dame Nature" conquering an already vanquished empire; she literally steps on the heads of the Cham.

Almost more problematic is that the same imagery is constantly used in promotional and expositional materials. This is perpetrated by not only official governmental sources, but by UNESCO and private organizations as well. Book covers and travel guides feature photographs of Mỹ Sơn's patina-covered monuments framed by green weeds in the foreground and verdant mountains in the background; mosses, grasses and saplings grow from virtually every protrusion in the jumble of monuments. This particular presentation of the World Heritage site is even employed in the banner photograph on UNESCO's webpage for Mỹ Sơn: lumps of blackened buildings emerge from the bottom of the photo, obscured of all details by shadows, save the greenery which sprout out of the shadows and are captured by the light. Their verdant hue blends with the greenery of the mountains that fill in the middle of the rectangular-shaped photograph. Above is the blue sky, dotted with white clouds. It is clear that nature is the true focal point of the photograph. This is complemented by a second photograph featured in the body of the explanatory text on the page. This image appears to be of a bas-relif of a stone carving, perhaps a dragon's head, but it is taken at an angle and not entirely close-up. The photograph includes the relief's stone frame, which is covered in white and dark patina. Growing up the left side of the picture is a bright green vine, as if to remind the viewer of the role nature plays in choking these ruins.[38] This stands in stark juxtaposition to the images that illustrate Vietnam's other cultural sites, wherein architecture is the primary focus of the banner images and supplementary photographs.

Indeed, this juxtaposition is most evident on the cover of a Vietnamese-published hardcover picture book of Vietnam's World Heritage sites entitled *Những Di Sản Thế Giới ở Việt Nam: World Heritage in Vietnam*. Published in 2002 and subsequently republished to add Phong Nha-Kẻ Bàng when it was designated a World Heritage site in 2003, the cover features one photograph from each World Heritage site. Each photo is of equal proportion; the 2002 edition, which features four World Heritage sites, arranges the images in a square. To the top left is a picture of Hạ Long Bay, where, interestingly enough, the central focus of the image is a grouping of boats in a floating village; the verdant karst islands seem to blend into a gray background and are partially obscured by the silhouetted mouth of a cave that frames the whole picture, which was obviously taken from inside the cavern. The second photograph, on the top right, is an image from Huế's Imperial City. It features the Nine Dynastic Urns before the Hiển Lâm Pavilion, which was one of the first edifices restored after the war. The foreground is almost completely devoid of any vegetation, and the small landscaped garden that exists in the middle of the plaza can be seen. A large defoliated tree can be seen rising from behind the Pavilion; it is sickly looking and black, and is contorted away from the building as if recoiling in fear. Clearly nature is not the conqueror here. Architecture is at the foreground of the third image at the bottom left; it is a photograph of the rooftops of Hội An. Taken before the electrical wires were buried underground, the melding of contemporary and past culture is imminently evident; between the rooftops one spies a youth riding on a bicycle on the beige clay road. The roofs cover almost the entire photograph, with a thin band of green jungle and a gray sky peeking out. The last photograph, located at the bottom right, seems almost anachronistic. The bottom third of the image is a flat brick pavilion covered over by green grasses, an anonymous building completely obscured in shadow rises to the left. Off-center is a low pile of broken bricks and clay, a bush growing out of it. Surrounding this are various ruined temples of Mỹ Sơn, jumbled and in the background. Once again, grasses and saplings can be seen growing from the roofs. Only one building is relatively intact, but because of its proximity to that black mass in the foreground and its position in the background, it is not the immediate focus of the photograph. Low-hanging white clouds loom overhead, as if to further contain these structures within the grasp of nature.[39]

Such confused imagery and juxtapositional anachronism is indicative of the way in which Mỹ Sơn is presented to outsiders, both those visiting the site and those who merely wish to learn more through print and online media. As a representation of the Cham people, it isolates them from the present day, relegating them to an obscure past—one which conveys both their primitivity and defeat. Its textual description also conveys the sense that the Chams were primitive beings until the influence of outsiders. And in its visual form, wherein nature plays a significant contextual role, it seems the Cham culture has passed on, leaving only jumbled ruins under the tendrils of a conquering nature.

Marginalizing Minorities through Natural Designations

While the pervasiveness of nature over the ruined cultural constructions serve to color the viewer's understanding of the Cham people in the cultural heritage site of Mỹ Sơn, other minority peoples are directly marginalized through their association with so called "natural" sites. According to the World Heritage Convention, World Heritage sites officially fall into one of two categories—cultural or natural. While "cultural" sites are defined by Article I of the Convention in general terms as

- Monuments: architectural works, works of monumental sculpture and painting, elements or structures of an archaeological nature, inscriptions, cave dwellings and combinations of features, which are of *outstanding universal value* from the point of view of history, art or science;
- Groups of buildings: groups of separate or connected buildings which, because of their architecture, their homogeneity or their place in the landscape, are of *outstanding universal value* from the point of view of history, art or science;
- Sites: works of man or the combined works of nature and man, and areas including archaeological sites which are of *outstanding universal value* from the historical, aesthetic, ethnological or anthropological point of view.[40]

Likewise, Article II of the Convention defines natural sites as:

- Natural features consisting of physical and biological formations or groups of such formations, which are *of outstanding universal value* from the aesthetic or scientific point of view;
- Geological and physiographical formations and precisely delineated areas which constitute the habitat of threatened species of animals and plants of *outstanding universal value* from the point of view of science or conservation;
- Natural sites or precisely delineated natural areas *of outstanding universal value* from the point of view of science, conservation or natural beauty.[41]

Like the "cultural sites" before them, UNESCO recognizes natural sites for their intrinsic "outstanding universal value" towards aesthetics, (scientific) research, or conservation. Yet when examined in detail, this nature / culture dichotomy seems to be a system of categorization fraught with difficulties and inconsistencies, for it incorrectly assumes that these spaces are examples of "naked life," untouched by human hands and therefore meant to be separated from humanity—or at least from society—and preserved on their own. Theoretically, the understanding that places can be either cultural or natural—that is, either touched or untouched by humanity—is a problematic one for placemaking strategy in general. As Michael Parker-Pearson and Colin Richards eloquently state, empty space becomes a "place" precisely when it becomes social:

The meanings that are given to places and the spatial order are not fixed or invariant givens but must be invoked in the context of practice and recurrent usage. Meanings adhere to a spatial frame only though the medium of human activity. However, the capacity to reinterpret and change meanings and ideologies is constrained by the already existing spatial order (Moore 1996:186-187). In other words, we make history not as we wish but under circumstances not of our own choosing. The relationship between spatial form and human agency is mediated by meaning. People actively give their physical environments meanings, and then act upon those meanings.[42]

One might think conceptually of *space* in relation to *place*, then, in simplified Kantian terms, as an *a priori* form of sensible intuition that is undifferentiated—a blank slate wherein all recognized places are contained. It is not a humanly empirical concept that is drawn from outer experiences, but tautologically, all outer experiences of place come out of, and take dimensionality from, this all-encompassing blankness. It does not represent things at all, but rather is the representation of the sum of the whole of reality; it is an infinite, singular container in which all experienced things lie in relation to one another.[43] Space becomes a place precisely when it is delimited, thought about, and acted upon; all of these are human actions.

With Immanuel Kant's definition of space, the assertion that all places are inherently tinged with the touch of humanity through the cultural artifact of a place-name[44] provides the very innuendo behind the old philosophical question, "If a tree falls in the woods and nobody hears it, does it make a sound?" This questions the very reality of the tree, the place, and its own activity, should the three complementary elements not be recognized by humanity. The scientific answer to this question is, of course, "Yes"—the breaking of cellular bonds within the wood, the wind rushing through the falling leaves, and the impact between the gravity-driven horticultural being and the firm ground all create distinct distortions in the forms of auditorily-sensed waves that ripple through the firmament. But does it exist to man? The answer is less certain. Without some social recognition, the noting of its very existence, the naming of the object and of the sound—it is just another unknown in the vastness of undifferentiated space. Yet when this undifferentiated space is imbued with these social practices, it becomes a full-fledged place. Such social practices need not be those activities simply contained within the space, such as hiking, logging, eating or building homes, but extend also to the very act of differentiating the place from space. Places are recognized, named, categorized, cartographed, and even changed by communities, regardless of the specific meanings or values assigned to them. Even before these acts, all places are "discovered"; they are experienced for the first time as a specific spatial element. This occurs both for a society noting and delimiting the place for the first time, and also for each individual who comes into contact with this previously unknown and inexperienced area for the first time. In addition to assigning a specific spatiality to a previously undifferentiated space, the act of discovery assigns it temporality and historicity within a linearly conceived framework—that is, it inserts it into a specific point in the socially constructed notion of chronological history. The life histories assigned to so-called "natural" sites—which are thought not to correspond as directly with human cultural movements as do architectural forms—can fall within the broad, culturally subjective categories of history, prehistory or mythology. By assigning it distinct spatial and temporal dynamics, society integrates the place into its ever-more complex webs of meaning; it uses its culture to interpret the sights, sounds, histories and even myths of the site. All of these actions, therefore, imbue the previously undifferentiated space with the social. The places dialectically make some impact on the individuals or groups who recognized and delimited them, and, in return, these same humans make their own imprint on the total life histories of the sites.

This discourse is especially pertinent when discussing UNESCO's "natural" World Heritage sites. By virtue of the nomination and designation process, these natural sites are not wild, undifferentiated spaces but are precisely documented, delimited, bounded and named. Though some transnational natural sites exist, most are contained within the nominating nation's borders. They are therefore imbued, at least tangentially but often much more closely, with the nation-state's own narratives before later being imbued with UNESCO's own claims of outstanding universal value. Most tellingly, they also undergo a very ritual process that turns them into social objects available for "universal" scholarly or touristic consumption. It should be remembered that this process is uniform for both cultural and natural sites: in short, each place must be mapped, studied and analyzed; visitor "management" plans must be drawn up and safeguards are set in place for its conservation in the physical state for which it is recognized. And then all of these measures are scrutinized, considered, debated and, finally, voted on by UNESCO delegates—all in the context of the distinct webs of meaning created for, and by, this social organization itself. In this way, the terminology "natural," as differentiated from "cultural," seems grossly misplaced. Others have also noted as much, and at the end of 2004 UNESCO passed Decision 6 EXT.Com 5.1, which merged the six cultural and four natural criteria into one cohesive set of typologies. A revised *Operational Guidelines for the Implementation of World Heritage Convention* was issued, explaining that a place can now be analyzed for any of these "cultural" or "natural" typologies.[45] In the end, though, this measure is clearly half-hearted; in addition to not eliminating the misnomers from previously designated sites, they continue to require states-parties to categorize their proposed sites through the same excessive categorizations. And UNESCO continues to publicize its new designations this way, too.

These general semantic considerations aside, there are also a number of contingent qualities that emphasize the "cultural" dynamics of Vietnam's two "natural" World Heritage sites, Hạ Long Bay and Phong Nha-Kẻ Bàng. According to the 1994 World Heritage Convention announcement of Hạ Long Bay's designation, the site was recognized for the "outstanding universal value" of its natural elements, and not its cultural ones:

Natural property:

Criterion iii: Outstanding examples representing significant ongoing geological processes, and biological evolution. Ha Long's spectacular combination of seascape and islands is the direct result of orogenic processes. The area is biologically rich, especially in marine species.[46]

IUCN, the advisory body that originally wrote the accepted assessment, did mention its cultural dynamics in its assessment, although it was not offered forth as an additional reason for Hạ Long's nomination, and thus was not included in UNESCO's official declaration:

Cultural property:

Criterion not specified. Hạ Long Bay area contains numerous sites of archaeological interest, indicating occupation from as long ago as 10,000 years. Ha Long was a significant trading area in prehistoric times.[47]

In addition to potential archaeological interest in the site, which IUCN is technically not authorized to assess, the place is also steeped in a web of Vietnamese ethno-national mythology. As the very name of Hạ Long Bay reveals, this place is defined foremostly by mythological references pointing to the origin of the Vietnamese people as pious descendents of deities and protected by dragons. Furthermore, IUCN points out that, among the original 1,600 islands and islets that fell within the original borders of the World Heritage site, "1,000 have been named";[48] the pre-existence of the names of these "islets" further denotes a deep-rooted cultural context to these islands. Historically, it was here that the hated Mongol-Chinese were defeated by the heroic general Trần Hưng Đạo in a great naval battle, securing the country's independence. In modern historicized time, the Bay was also a site of political exile for anti-colonial elements during French occupation, and, as such, it has also been inserted into modern Communist-nationalist mythology. It has also been inserted into international cinematic mythology as a primary setting for the contemporary French blockbuster, *Indochine*, which integrated the visual landscape and the anti-colonialism nationalist myth within its fictional narrative—another form of human interaction that has notably contributed to today's influx of tourists and induced the government to develop the region "very fast, super fast," as the head of UNESCO's Vietnam office has been quoted as saying.[49] Finally, there remains today a significant population of indigenous "boat people" who live in a number of small floating villages—complete with schools, churches and temples—spread across the Bay. All of these factors have combined into what Australia National University anthropologist Amareswar Galla has called an "enormously complicated interaction" between the natural features and "climatic, hydrological and human influences."[50]

It would have been valuable, therefore, for ICOMOS or another advisory body authorized to assess a place's cultural qualities, to have made its own recommendations in subsequent years. Interestingly enough, Vietnam did renominate Hạ Long Bay six years later, but only to add an additional natural criterion, which, according to a Hungarian delegate to the World Heritage Convention, should have been originally included:

> The site is the most extensive and best known example of marine invaded tower karst and one of the most important areas of fengcong and fenglin karst in the world. The size of the area provides sufficient integrity for these large scale geomorphic processes to operate unhindered.[51]

Phong Nha-Kẻ Bàng shares a similar problem with its natural designation, which UNESCO recognized as follows:

> Phong Nha is part of a larger dissected plateau, which also encompasses the Ke Bang and Hin Namno karsts. The limestone is not continuous and demonstrates complex interbedding with shales and sandstones. This, together with the capping of schists and apparent granites has led to a particularly distinctive topography.
> The caves demonstrate discrete episodic sequences of events, leaving behind various levels of fossil passages, formerly buried and now uncovered palaeokarst (karst from previous, perhaps very ancient, periods of solution); evidence of major changes in the routes of underground rivers; changes in the solutional regime; deposition and later re-solution of giant speleothems and unusual features such as sub-aerial stromatolites. The location and form of the caves suggests that they might owe much of their size and morphology to some as yet undetermined implications of the schists and granites which overlay the lime-

stone. On the surface, there is a striking series of landscapes, ranging from deeply dissected ranges and plateaux to an immense polje. There is evidence of at least one period of hydrothermal activity in the evolution of this ancient mature karst system. The plateau is probably one of the finest and most distinctive examples of a complex karst landform in SE Asia.

In summary, Phong Nha displays an impressive amount of evidence of earth's history. It is a site of very great importance for increasing our understanding of the geologic, geomorphic and geo-chronological history of the region.[52]

Despite its intriguing underground rivers and karst caves, lush mountainous landscape, and supposedly untouched paleo-historical evidence that could greatly benefit the geological and "geo-chronological" studies of the region, Phong Nha-Kẻ Bàng also reveals a rich history of human interaction. Like Hạ Long Bay, the name *Phong Nha*, or "the wind's teeth," reveals its connection to a deeper mythology; up to the mid-1970s, the entrance to the famous caverns resembled a jack-o'-lantern-like mouth with sharp, pointed stalactites and stalagmites through which the wind whistled; it was as if the mountains themselves were breathing. That this area was not simply an untouched natural area was also noted by IUCN, which stated as a corollary to the designated site's natural qualities that archaeological evidence points to human occupation in the region from as far back as the Neolithic era. Indeed, there seems to have always been a continuous presence of indigenous people living in the area delimited as the World Heritage site; an old subterranean Cham temple has long been a site of religious pilgrimage, and today is a primary stop for tourists exploring the underground river-caves. There are also two villages at the very center of the World Heritage site in which members of the Arem, Ma Coong and Ruc ethnic groups continue to live. In more contemporary periods, relics were found in Maria Mountain at the north of the park from the reign of King Hàm Nghi, the unfortunate eighth emperor of the Nguyễn dynasty who unsuccessfully fought to maintain autonomy from the French at the turn of the twentieth century. A July 4, 1885 coup had forced him to flee to the mountainous Lao-Vietnamese border region around Phong Nha-Kẻ Bàng, from which he waged guerrilla warfare against the French occupying forces. He was eventually captured, deposed and exiled to Algeria in 1888. The French replaced him with his brother, Emperor Đồng Khánh, who is regarded today as the first true puppet emperor of the French colonial era. Finally, during the Vietnam War, this land was important to North Vietnamese forces. The forests and caves provided valuable shelter for both Communist forces and the local people. They were also utilized by the Viet Cong as garrisons and weapons depots, and the indigenous people hid in Phong

Nha caves to escape allied bombing—which, unfortunately, destroyed the karst teeth at the entrance to Phong Nha for which the caves were named.

This nature-culture dichotomy translates to very real problems in assigning meaning to the indigenous people who live at both of the sites. The division of all life—especially human social life—into either nature or culture is an out-dated conceptualization held over from the Modernization theories of colonial times, which saw all peoples in a universal evolutionary process from the primitive state of nature to modern cultured society. They were at once barely human and uber-human—that is, though they were seen as deficient in mental and cultural capacities, their supposed lack of evolution made them physically and developmentally closer to Man's original natural state. Influenced by the discovery of the New World, European thinkers of the late Renaissance and the Enlightenment frequently extolled the epistemological value of conquering and studying these "noble savages" as a way to rediscover civilized Man's origins. At the end of the sixteenth century, Michel de Montaigne commented on Girolamo Benzoni's account of the newly discovered New World natives:

> These peoples, then, seem to me to be barbarous only in that *they have been hardly fashioned by the mind of man, still remaining close neighbours to their original state of nature. They are still governed by the laws of Nature and are only very slightly bastardized by ours*; but their purity is such that I am sometimes seized with irritation at their having not been discovered earlier, in times when there were men who could have appreciated them better than we do. It irritates me that neither Lycurgus nor Plato had any knowledge of them, for it seems to me that what experience has taught us about those peoples surpasses not only all the descriptions with which poetry has beautifully painted the Age of Gold and all its ingenious fictions about Man's blessed early state, but also the very conceptions and yearnings of philosophy. They could not even imagine a state of nature so simple and so pure as the one we have learned about from experience; they could not even believe that societies of men could be maintained with so little artifice, so little in the way of human solder. . . . How remote from such perfection would Plato find that Republic which he thought up—'viri a diis recentes' [men fresh from the gods].[53]

Through UNESCO's problematic nature-culture dichotomy, the people living in these "natural" sites are differentiated from those living outside this natural state, and are thus subsumed by this narrative of primitivity.

And indeed, both Hạ Long Bay and Phong Nha-Kẻ Bàng contain what Vietnamese informants consider minority peoples, although in different ways. Those living in Phong Nha-Kẻ Bàng are considered "Montagnards," a Vietnamization of the French term for "mountain people" carried over from the colonial period. Taking their cue from the Vietnamese, the French sometimes also called them *moi*, or "ethnic minorities" (*moi* literally translates as "savage"[54] and is today an extremely derogatory term[55])—conquered outsiders whose land and cultures were subsumed by the Vietnamese people as they moved southward. Their varied heritages, as well as their cultural practices, continue to brand them as "minority tribes," who, although legally Vietnamese citizens, do not share fully in the Vietnamese cultural experience. Such separation between the ethnic majority and Montagnard minorities runs deep, and is solidified in popular mythology. Legend has it[56] that Lạc Long Quân—an ancient Dragon King from the southern lowlands—married a beautiful fairy named Âu Cơ who lived in the mountainous regions present-day northern Vietnam. They made their home in these mountains, where they had one hundred sons. The Dragon King, however, grew weary of mountain living and nostalgic for the watery land of his youth, and moved back to the lowlands with half of his sons in tow. These lowland boys became the precursors to the Vietnamese; the eldest son is believed to be Hùng Vương, the first emperor of Lạc Việt, as the country was known at the time. Their brothers, scattered and left behind in the mountains, were the ancestors of the fifty-plus different minority tribes present in Vietnam today.

The idea that these Montagnards present at Phong Nha-Kẻ Bàng were "left behind"—not only by the father of the Việt, but by civilization in general, which, in the case of Vietnamese mythology, has its origins at the sea—is subtly confirmed through the semantics of the designation and related UNESCO and IUCN literature. By virtue of their inclusion "at the core" of the World Heritage site, as IUCN states, the Phong Nha-Kẻ Bàng Montagnards are abstracted from the rest of Vietnamese society, and imbued in the same narrative of primitivity that covers the rest of the "natural" site. Nestled in the middle of a particularly comprehensive documentation of the varieties of unique natural elements in the park, the World Conservation Monitoring Centre, an office within the United Nation's Environmental Programme, even includes a brief blurb about the minorities living in the park, which essentially equates them as yet another ecological dynamic of the natural site:

> The oldest evidence of human occupation of the area are Neolithic axe heads and similar artefacts found in some of the caves. There are some relics of Ham Hghi King, a final King of the Nguyen dynasty before the French colonial period, at the Maria Mountain in the north of the Park. Currently the Arem, Ma Coong and Ruc ethnic groups live in two villages in the core zone of Phong Nha Ke-Bang National Park. Until 1962 these indigenous people lived in the forest in houses made of bamboo and leaves or in the caves, living from forest products and hunting. They used simple tools and their clothes were made from the bark of a toxic forest tree (Antiaris toxicaria) and lianas. Since 1992 the Government of Vietnam has set up two new settlements for these 475 people,

who are the two smallest ethnic groups in Vietnam. These people are familiar with a number of economically valuable species, especially precious timber such as Mun and Hue (Diospyros spp., Dalbergia rimosa), and oil-extraction from species such as Tau (Hopea hainanensis) and many medicinal plants.[57]

In this informational packet, these small minority groups are portrayed not only as vestiges of a people who seemed to have outlived their proper time, but truly as part of the natural site. They are portrayed as noble savages, *Naturvölken* who seem to be more closely linked to nature than they are to civilization. They are backwards hunter-gatherers who, before the intervention of the Vietnamese government, preferred living in trees or in caves, utilizing "simple tools," and clothing themselves with poisonous tree bark. Their knowledge, too, is more closely linked to the natural world than to that of the modern—a primitive understanding of the natural world that seems to have been left behind with these tribes, but lost to today's more technologically and industrially advanced society. Thus, their familiarity with medicinal herbs, as well as with the skills of extraction necessary to tap into nature, are "economically valuable" and worthy of being preserved. And so it is acceptable that these noble primitives were rounded up and forced to live on reservations, for in this manner their way of life can be controlled—the backwards can be either tapped into or eliminated—and they can be objects of conservation and study in their own right. Like the Neolithic artifacts and the ancient karst caverns—which, as one guide stated, reveal "some vestiges from the creation of the earth"—these people, too, can today provide unique insight into prehistoric human life.

Left out of the conservation advisory body's evaluation above was one of the primary reasons that convinced IUCN and UNESCO to grant World Heritage status to Phong Nha-Kẻ Bàng National Park. According to site managers who worked on the File, the Vietnamese government and the World Wildlife Federation—who put pressure on the government—were greatly concerned with the negative environmental impact that these minority groups were creating at the national park, specifically with regards to game hunting. According to IUCN, Phong Nha-Kẻ Bàng is part of the greater Northern Annamites eco-region, which is considered "one of the more important eco-regions of the Indo-Pacific." Besides housing eight hundred and seventy six vascular plant species—thirteen of which are endemic to the park and thirty-six of which are endangered—the area encompassing the World Heritage site also contains five hundred and sixty eight vertebrates, including seven species of indigenous primates. Several "Red Books"—international wildlife catalogues that list vulnerable, rare, threatened, endangered or very rare species of fauna—count around seventy-three important endangered species living in the park and its environs,

including tigers, brown hornbills, Asian Black Bears, the "barking deer" or
Muntjak (*Muntiacus muntjak*), and the *sao la,* also known as the Vu Quang ox
(*Pseudoryx nghetinhensis*), which was thought to have been extinct until they
were re-discovered in Vietnam in 1993. The sao la, in fact, is "an entirely new
genus of cattle," the largest land-dwelling mammal to be discovered since the
gray ox was described in 1937.[58] Sixty-six animal species, in fact, are listed in
the Vietnam Red Book, and twenty-three are featured in the World Red Book.

Game hunting in this area, apart from being a traditional form of subsistence for the Montagnards, is deeply imbedded in the region's society. This was
once tiger-hunting land—and recognized as such by Westerners at the turn of
the century; locals boast that Theodore Roosevelt visited the surrounding Central Highlands area in 1905 in an attempt to quench his insatiable desire for the
pelts of these cats. What is verified is that his sons, Theodore, Jr. and Kermit,
went hunting here in 1929, a few years after their father's death, where they discovered the muntjak, or "barking deer." They named it the *muntjak roosevelto-
rum* and presented a single specimen to Chicago's Field Museum.[59] Furthermore, the earliest known film shot in French Indochina, in fact, was a 1938
silent docudrama that takes place in the highlands of Annam by Marquis Henri
de la Falaise entitled *Kliou the [Killer] Tiger*,[60] which follows a bare-chested
Montagnard boy named Bhat as he hunts a killer tiger terrorizing his village.

The various animals are also perceived to have medicinal qualities by the
local minority peoples. According to advertisements at minority-owned game
restaurants, wild animal meat, priced at less than US$15.00 per kilogram, can
cure gout, asthma and even mental disease.[61] According to one ethnic Vietnamese journalist, Montagnard hunters utilizing traps and traditional tactics often
find their game in U Bò Forest in Quảng Ninh District; and those who hunt with
guns prefer Phù Nhiêu Forest—both of which fall within the World Heritage
site. The captured animals are not simply consumed among the community, but
represented a viable commercial outlet. Each hunter can bring home a monthly
income of around VND 900,000—VND 1,500,000—or between US$50.00 and
US$80.00—by selling their catch to restaurateurs and shop owners, the latter of
which sells much of the meat dried. As late as 2002, the roadway leading to the
entrance of the park was lined with minority-owned restaurants selling traditional game of all sorts, most commonly porcupine, wild boar, deer and civet—
but also endemic species such as monkeys, flecked rabbits and partridges. Endangered tigers, bears and sao la could also be ordered. Locals and the few foreigners who visited the natural park before its designation could bargain among
the hawkers for the best price, and could often pick the particular animal they
wanted, while still alive, from cages at the entrance to the restaurant. "Even the

park rangers couldn't do anything about it; that's why they wanted UNESCO's help," added one guide.[62]

And at first glance, it seems that it worked. The UNESCO preparation process provided a worthy occasion for shutting down many of the most conspicuous minority-owned game restaurants at the site. Although today local restaurants continue to line the entrance route to the World Heritage site, they now sell traditional Vietnamese-style food—at least to the visitors. To further combat this practice, Vietnamese newspapers—owned by the Ministry of Culture and Information, of course—have produced a number of articles, both in Vietnamese and in English, which raise awareness of the plight of these endangered species at the hands of the barbaric restaurants. Finally, the subsequent increase in tourism resulting from Phong Nha-Kẻ Bàng's World Heritage designation has also provided an alternative source of revenue for minority residents, as they have increasingly invested in tourist "dragon boats," similar in style to those on Huế's Perfume River, to ferry visitors in and out of the subterranean karst caverns.

But upon closer examination, it seems that this initiative has done little in the way of truly staving off game hunting. Rather, the tightening of regulations have served to make wild game meat even more of a delicacy, and wild game restaurants operating along the Ho Chi Minh highway outside of the World Heritage site seem to be flourishing. These restaurants operate "under the support and ignorance of state cadres," states Leo Botrill from Flora and Fauna International (FFI). "In some cases, villages and commune officials are the wild animal traders. In Quy Dat Town, there is a policeman who is also the owner of a restaurant that sells wild animal meat."[63] Indeed, wild game restaurants in villages such as Quy Dat continue to flourish; one such institution boasts such a high volume of business that it has two roads leading to it: one for diners and one for hunters bringing in a steady supply of fresh meat. Customers at this and other restaurants "are mainly officials" states one journalist, who estimates that they consume 1,825 boars (which is equivalent to about 500kg of meat), 6,025 civets, and 9,125 wild tortoises per year. Such a double standard seems to favor the ethnic Vietnamese officials who own, and can afford to patronize, these restaurants; the original minority-owned restaurants truly suffer. Indeed, the enclavement of these goods, especially when they could be traced to Phong Nha-Kẻ Bàng, seems only to increase the price of the meat; when it was suggested that one proprietor's prices were too high for porcupine meat, he replied, "It's because my restaurant is located near Phong Nha-Kẻ Bàng natural heritage site."[64] This increase in price per kilogram of meat most likely induces minority hunters to continue their craft illegally, rather than to move into the more socially acceptable tourist trade.

Indeed, there is little correlation between the increase in minorities working on the tourist boats and any decrease in hunting activities. I have never seen a man operate these ferries, for example; all have been women, although they have insisted otherwise. Regardless, running a tourist boat is not a full-time job for individuals, but rather a communal affair, where multiple families have a stake in a particular vessel, its use and upkeep. The captains change from day to day; informants say they work on average of three days a week, switching duties with their fellow townspeople who, when not operating the boat, will continue their typical daily duties in the village—such as raising crops and hunting.[65]

Undoubtedly the forced closing of these minority-owned restaurants at Phong Nha-Kẻ Bàng can be viewed as a positive first step towards protecting the endemic and endangered species in the Vietnamese Central Highlands. But restaurant proprietorship double-standards aside, the government and Phong Nha-Kẻ Bàng site managers have concurrently undertaken a number of wide-spread activities that seem to call into question their true dedication to conservation, thereby promoting a narrative directly marginalizing the Montagnards.

Vietnam actually submitted Phong Nha-Kẻ Bàng three times before it was designated for this very reason. First, the land delimited by the State-Party for the World Heritage site covers too small an area to truly protect larger endangered species such as the Asian Black Bear and tigers. This was the crux of an argument made by IUCN and UNESCO when they first decided to defer a decision on declaring Phong Nha a World Heritage site in 1999. A year earlier, the Vietnamese delegation had first proposed a significantly smaller portion of land which had been known as The Phong Nha Nature Reserve, which included a total of 41,132 hectares. Rebuked, the government revised its nomination to include a significantly larger area—an impressive 147,945 hectares—and re-submitted it in 2000. At three and a half times the size of the initial proposed site, the dimension of this new proposition was deemed acceptable, however, the State-Party concurrently announced its intention of constructing the Ho Chi Minh Highway, a new major north-south highway system that followed the original Ho Chi Minh Trail from North Vietnam down through the Laotian borderland—of which Phong Nha-Kẻ Bàng is a part. Indeed, travelers today can view portions of the original Trail running alongside the mouth of the Phong Nha caves. In 2000, plans specifically called for bisecting the Nature Reserve through the construction of a roadway linking the Highway to the preexistent Route 20. A number of advisory bodies that included IUCN and Flora and Fauna International, protested, but to no avail. The Ho Chi Minh Highway system represented—and indeed, continues to represent—Vietnam's first and most significant infrastructural initiative of this century, an ambitious and symbolically charged project with great utilitarian potential. As early as 2005, it had already

been able to meet the burgeoning transportation needs of the country while lessening the impact of traffic—especially in the bottleneck areas of the Hải Vân
Pass between Huế and Đà Nẵng.[66] The State-Party and UNESCO could not
come to a compromise, and consideration of this second nomination was tabled.

The government, nevertheless, persisted in pursuing a World Heritage designation of Phong Nha-Kẻ Bàng. In May 2002, the State-Party submitted additional information to the World Heritage Center, which appeared to be much
more thoroughly researched and comprehensively planned. Among other things,
the File included more systematic plans for specific conservation projects, sustainable development programs for the Park and its management, and revised
cartography of the region, for which little geographic research had ever been
undertaken. In a particular show of compromise and dedication to conservation,
the State-Party also advised UNESCO that, in December 2001, the Prime Minister had decided to upgrade the Phong Nha-Kẻ Bàng Nature Reserve to a full
fledged National Park boasting a total of 85,754 hectares, or 59% the size of the
previous proposal. Unfortunately, the 85,754 hectares represented a "much
smaller area than the 2000 nomination," but IUCN, noting the compromise and
underscoring the potential importance of this land, pointed out that it was twice
as large as the original, and called the Ho Chi Minh Highway system "clearly
justifiable, appropriately located . . . [and] constructed with a high level of environmental responsibility," which "will provide an important benefit to the National Park in opening up views of an access to the Ke Bang Forest Area."[67]
IUCN recommended the area for nomination on the grounds of Criterion *i*, or its
universal importance for preserving and demonstrating the "earth's history and
geological features," but literally underscored in its document that the site continued to fall short of the size requirements necessary to provide for the adequate
protection of threatened species. And at the twenty-seventh World Heritage
Committee meeting in Suzhou, China from June 30 to July 5, 2003 UNESCO
finally designated Phong Nha-Kẻ Bàng a World Heritage site for its ancient
geomorphic, rather than living natural features, and extolled the Vietnamese
government to re-think the conservation of its natural resources especially in
light of the Park's total area and the negative impact of its infrastructural development.

Indeed, the creation of the connecting road between the Ho Chi Minh
Highway and Route 20 amounts to a disastrous and incredibly damaging development for the conservation of Phong Nha-Kẻ Bàng's indigenous flora and
fauna, yet in the interest of political compromise was given a pass by the World
Heritage Committee. Its very construction, which crosses the "core natural areas
of the site," represents harmful human encroachment in a place now universally
recognized for its untouched "natural" value. It is "well documented" that new

roads in protective areas damage local ecosystems, and this one, which cuts through not only strategic wildlife habitats in forests and valleys but literally through the karst rock formations for which the site was designated, surely comes at great cost to the environment that is supposed to be protected. In a letter to UNESCO on December 15, 2000, Flora and Fauna International had estimated that 4.5 tons of explosives per kilometer would be used to cut through the rock, destroying ecosystems, and creating large-scale soil erosion that would even negatively impact the "continuing evolution" of the subterranean Phong Nha cave system itself. IUCN further bemoans its aesthetic unattractiveness and "environmentally insensitive and inappropriate" character—in short, not only is it environmentally damaging, but it is a semiotically damaging human built construction that is out of place in a natural World Heritage site. Finally, its usefulness is also questioned; the roadway is thought to be used primarily for the movement of domesticated animals such as cattle, rather than for the movement of visitors or people in and out of the site. IUCN speculates that it would only help illegal loggers and poachers. This fact not only "raises the question of its [the road's] necessity," but also poses additional risk to the fragile ecosystem; the introduction of non-indigenous, domesticated animals will undoubtedly change the greater environment from the state recognized by UNESCO in its World Heritage designation.[68]

But speaking to the topic at hand, these activities can also be viewed within the narrative of a majority group marginalizing minority peoples who inhabit the World Heritage site. While both local Montagnards and the Vietnamese government in Ha Noi contribute to detrimental effects on the Phong Nha-Kẻ Bàng area, concentrated efforts to mitigate negative human impact seem to be taken only against the Montagnards, with further adverse, if unattended, consequences. It seems to have only contributed to increasing broader demand for wild game at the profit of government officials and ethnic Vietnamese, while Montagnard hunters now pursue their vocation at legal risk. Furthermore, the ostensible compromises made on the part of the State-Party seems to belie the true dedication to environmental conservation; the final size of the site, for example, was shrunk to semantically allow for most infrastructural development to occur outside of the World Heritage site's boundaries, and therefore outside the meddlesome purview of UNESCO. When infrastructure did encroach upon the site, no true compromises were offered until after the place was designated. UNESCO's allowance of these unbalanced processes further highlights the narrative celebrating modernity—revealed in the government's mastery over nature through building, blasting, and back hoeing through the environment—over that of primitivity, as represented by the Montagnards' "primitive" system of utilizing the environment, which UNESCO reveals—prejudicially or not—is more in harmony with nature. It seems to say that the Montagnards' traditional use of the environment, particularly hunting, is far less acceptable than modern infrastructural development, regardless of the differences in magnitude or detrimental impact. In this way, the narrative tacitly approved by UNESCO seems to be much more in line with the same narrative tacitly approved by the colonials of Montaigne's time—no matter how barbaric the impact of modernity is, the minorities are still more barbaric, if only because of their lack of cultural evolution.

The people living in floating villages on Hạ Long Bay face similar problematic distinctions as the Montagnards living in the mountainous Phong Nha-Kẻ Bàng. While not considered ethnic minorities, Hạ Long Bay's indigenous are nevertheless regarded as outsiders, but only for their unique sub-cultural practices. They literally live on the water. Hạ Long Bay's once-pristine ecosystem provided a wealth of seafood for subsistence, and its maze of thousands of rocky, infertile karst islands jutting like daggers into the foggy ether from the emerald sea provided an extraordinary level of protection from outsiders—both Việt and foreign. While it is not entirely clear why these people live on the water, it is seems likely that since the fish are best caught at night, and the Bay so vast and maze-like, the original fishermen may have found it easier, and safer, to remain permanently on their small fishing boats. To this day, visitors on tourist junks during daylight hours can pass several floating villages, all seemingly ghost towns: most, save a few women and children who motor up to the junk selling bananas or fish, are all sleeping.

While Vietnamese mythology celebrates both the protective nature of Hạ Long Bay and the particular bond between the Việt people and the life-giving, civilizing sea, informants have commented that their lifestyle seems exaggerated to those who live on the land. Furthermore, were one to conceptualize contemporary Vietnamese "civilization" in the same linear fashion as Modernization theorists do, these boat people seem to be primitives left behind as civilization advanced, like Darwin's first mammals, from water to land. Although they are Việt just as their brothers living on the land, these villagers were for years looked on upon as extremely backward and insular people, impoverished by their own primitive desires to live self-sufficiently on the water in dingy boats tethered together, and backwards by their self-imposed isolation among the veiled rocks of the bay. In an effort to break what the government regarded as a less-than-civilized way of life detrimental to the State, legislation was passed in the 1980s and 1990s that all but required these people to move to the land. Personal and property registration, including obtaining the obligatory identification card all citizens in the Socialist Republic had to carry, had to be done on land in the city of Hải Phòng to the south of the Bay, rather than accommodating the inhabitants of some twenty or so floating villages by placing an outpost on the water. The villages were left out of infrastructural development, such as upgrading the port in Hạ Long city, on the immediate mainland. Services, too, were nil—there was no trash collection, and children were required to attend school on the mainland during the day, which proved difficult within the people's way of life. Legally, it was as if such a community of people did not exist.

IUCN's 1994 evaluation of Hạ Long Bay—the first of two times the place was designated a World Heritage site—seems to confirm the non-existence of these boat people. Once again, IUCN provided a natural description of the Bay, as is their purview. But unlike the evaluation of Phong Nha-Kẻ Bàng, almost no reference is made to any inhabitants contemporaneously living on the water in the two-paragraph description of the place entitled "Identification." The first paragraph, which details the living, natural site, curiously seems to reference people without ever acknowledging them as such:

> Ha Long is a large bay with a multitude of limestone rocks and a limited number of earth islands formed from decayed lateritic mountains. In total, there are 1,600 islands and islets, of which 1,000 have been named. Larger islands rising to 100-200m are found in the south, interspersed with smaller islets of 5-10m height interspersed. To the east of the Bay medium size islands feature almost vertical slopes. Numerous caves and grottoes are found, with stalactites and stalagmites. The earth islands are inhabited. There is a diverse flora throughout Hạ Long, and primary tropical forest is found, mostly on the islands of Ba Mun and Cat Ba. Results from preliminary surveys indicate the presence of about 1,000 fish species. Mammals, reptiles and birds are found on the islands, especially those derived from laterite.[69]

Besides mentioning that most of the islands have already been named—by people—the authors state that the islands are also "inhabited." This is a curious choice of vocabulary. Though "inhabited" can conjure thoughts of humans creating homes, the word does not actually refer back to the human names of the islands, but to the "diverse flora" on the earthen islands. Towards the end, IUCN mentions other inhabitants: "mammals" as well as reptiles and birds also live here. For those familiar with Hạ Long Bay, this discourse is a semantic one; few, if any, indigenes ever lived on the islands themselves;[70] they are "boat people" who live in "floating villages" and any reference to inhabitation on the karst islands must not be speaking of humans. Yet interspersed between these sentences is indeed a sentence about aquatic-centered life, although the only life IUCN mentions herein is the "presence of about 1,000 fish species."

The second paragraph, however, is dedicated to discussing culture and human interaction with the site:

Numerous archaeological sites have been found and there is evidence to suggest occupation by the Hoa Binh Culture, some 10,000 years before the present. Archaeological sites at Tuan Chau, Ngoc Vung, Cai Dam, Don Naim and Cat have reveals so many artifacts that they have been grouped under the term "Hạ Long Culture," typical of the northeastern coast of Vietnam in the Neolithic Age. During prehistoric times, Hạ Long was a significant port, located on the trade routes between China, Japan and other countries in South East Asia.[71]

This description is highly problematic for two reasons. In the broad sense, such a rich history of human interface with this particularly delimited area should provide grounds for a second cultural designation. After all, there have been a great number of archaeological sites that yielded "so many artifacts" that they have been given their own designation directly related to the Bay: "Hạ Long Culture." According to IUCN's document—written, of course, at the end of the twentieth century—this culture began "some 10,000 years before the present" and ended "during prehistoric times." All reference to land use by non-prehistoric man is completely lacking. Indeed, in the aforementioned "Justification for Inscription," which is repeated below, IUCN juxtaposes the "ongoing"—or living—geological and orogenic "processes" and "biological evolution" of the natural criteria with the ossified elements of ancient human occupation that is of "archaeological" (and not anthropological) interest:

Natural property:
(iii) Outstanding examples representing significant ongoing geological processes, and biological evolution. Hạ Long's spectacular combination of seascape and islands is the direct result of orogenic processes. The area is biologically rich, especially in marine species.

Cultural property:
Criterion not specified. Hạ Long Bay area contains numerous sites of archaeological interest, indicating occupation from as long ago as 10,000 years. Hạ Long was a significant trading area in prehistoric times.[72]

The neglect of any reference to an indigenous population on the water elicits the same thought as civil legislation from this period: these people seem not to exist.

Once Hạ Long Bay gained World Heritage status, however, this began to change. Women and children from the village began seeking out the tourist junks to sell fresh prawns to the proprietors, who usually include a meal as part of both their four-hour and six-hour package tour. The boat people also began selling souvenirs to the visitors. These include postcards and small silk paintings, but, like the Montagnards, their primary stock were indigenous and endangered elements of the World Heritage site; they sold jewelry made out of pearls, karst and coral. Recognizing the negative impact this would have on the site, crackdown on this was quite swift, and admirably coordinated among four entities: UNESCO, the Vietnamese government, foreign commercial investors and members of the international tourism community. To control the sale of pearls and to contribute to sustainable management of this resource, Vietnamese jewelry companies were allowed to partner with a Japanese company—guides say it is Mikimoto—to raise cultured Akoya pearls, 80% of which are exported, but which are most visibly sold to tourists on these junks. A number of these pearl farms can be spotted behind karst islets farther out in the bay. While at first the boat company would buy a stock of pearls at a time, now it seems they directly partner with floating villagers; after picking up a woman at a newly constructed dock within the floating village, she sells her wares on the boat, and is then dropped off on the mainland to pick up the next tourist junk. The palpable markup on these wares since this new process was unofficially instituted seems to further confirm this partnership. On the mainland, a large visitor center has re-opened with large UNESCO markings all over it. In addition to selling tickets for these boat tours, they also sell cultured pearls, paintings, postcards and other typical tourist souvenirs. Even *Lonely Planet* guidebooks have gotten into the spirit, educating their readers on the origins of these natural tchotchkes and imploring their readers to "consider the virtue" of spending their dollars on postcards and silk paintings instead of coral ashtrays and key chains made of karst stalactites.[73] Finally, in 2003, the World Heritage Committee sent a formal request to the Vietnamese government to provide, for the first time, a count on the "trends in the numbers of people living inside the World Heritage area in boats" as well as the "extent of prawn culture cultivation in and around" the World Heritage site, so that the "potential impacts" of these two interrelated features of the natural site could be assessed at its next annual meeting in 2004.[74]

These initiatives grew primarily from the claims that the backwards boat people were damaging their own ecosystem in their ignorance of the site's universal value. Like the similar assertion against the Montagnards, this claim once again denies the indigenes' local environmental knowledge and appreciation for the land off of which they lived for centuries. While the introduction of tourism certainly has fostered some negative practices on the part of locals, this translated into a number of double-standards and unintended consequences that only reinforce the claims of primitivity leveled against these minority peoples. On one hand, the commercialization of pearl selling undoubtedly favors the Vietnamese jewelry companies far more than it does the local hawkers, and therefore denies to a certain extent proprietorship over the resources that belonged, for all intents and purposes, to the floating villagers. Through the companies' marketing efforts as well as the very performance of selling these pearls, awareness has been raised in the greater international community for these objects, only increasing the disparity of profits. This, in turn, seems not to have staved off the illicit sale of coral or karst jewelry as much as it has induced the minority peoples to turn to these illegal—yet plentiful—resources as a competitive source of profit; some of these jewelry hawkers have also been known to sell such wares on the tourist junks.

On the other hand, the increase in attention and interaction with those mainland entities have paradoxically done what the government had been trying to do for decades—that is, to foster a desire to civilize themselves by living as the rest of the Vietnamese do, on the mainland. Several guides have noted that the younger generation, viewing the prosperity of the jewelry growers, the tourist companies and the junk boat operators, and lured to the mainland for education or employment, wish to remain there, eschewing their traditional way of life. This could not have come at a worse time. While before the advent of tourism and Hạ Long's designation, such a culture was considered an embarrassment, today it is considered both a unique "value added" to a visitor's excursion on the Bay, as well as an endangered ecological form of the natural site. The State-Party, with help from these same outside organizations, has actually begun a concentrated effort to induce the villagers to stay by constructing both infrastructural services—such as schools and trash pickups—as well as a heritage narrative, which, while promoting the value in their particular cultural way of life, seems to condescendingly underscore the need to "educate" and "civilize" the primitives into respecting their own environment and their villages. It also promotes a double-standard favoring the mainland Vietnamese.

For example, the government has begun a campaign directed at the floating villagers to keep Hạ Long Bay clean—currently a very important topic in discourses concerning the Bay. With the introduction of mass tourism, solid waste pollution has become visible, and even tourists have embarrassingly pointed out soda cans, foodstuffs, and plastics floating by their boats. One anthropologist, working in Southeast Asia, has called Hạ Long Bay "a garbage can."[75] In response to this problem, the government has installed actual floating garbage cans on buoys. They can be seen both the outskirts and at the center of many villages, along with Vietnamese-language signs with white writing and a blue background that reads *Bao vê môi truong vịnh Hạ Long*, or "Protecting Hạ Long is everyone's duty." The gist of this tagline is repeated with similar phrasing on a number of larger signs in the same color scheme and font placed throughout the village. The most telling of these is the one that reads, *Bao vê me môi truong bao chinh minh*—"To protect the environment is to protect yourself." This public service announcement clearly places the onus of environmental protection on the villagers, whom the authorities not-so-subtly lump together with the greater natural environment. The phrase eloquently reveals the inherent notions of disorder with which conceptualizations of floating village life is imbued: Like an offense to the very notion of "culture," these people are abnormally part of nature, yet know not how to care for their own environment; through their own polluting activities, they inflict violence upon their own selves. Cursed with such illogic, it is only through the civilizing touch of culture can they be taught to care for themselves in the form of caring for their environment.

Yet paradoxically, the bulk of this trash is not generated by the floating villagers, but by the tourists[76] and the junk boat operators themselves. The signs, however, are exclusively in Vietnamese, limiting their reach. In terms of tourists polluting, ethnic Vietnamese tour guides, who frequently complain about the touristic practices of other Asians, pinpoint Koreans as the most egregious in this respect. Such an ethnocentric contention seems to stem in part from the popularity of Hạ Long Bay among this demographic; Koreans now constitute a larger percentage of tourists than Westerners do, and to accommodate their influx, the government has extraordinarily allowed the construction of Korean-managed hotels and restaurants, all conspicuously in Korean script, on the mainland. But the tour boat operators have been correctly identified as the largest polluters, based on the quantity, type and concentration of waste products dumped in the water. The increase in tourists means an increase in boats on the water—such that it is impossible today to travel on the Bay and not see another tourist junk, unlike a decade ago. This translates into a large increase in the amount of petroleum consumed—producing chemical waste in the water and in the air that can only negatively impact the broader ecosystem. Unfortunately, while some regulations are possible, this is a problem that only future technological innovation can truly solve.

But a more egregious, yet imminently resolvable, problem is the amount of solid waste dumped by the boat operators into the water. Today, much of tour boat ownership has passed from locals in the immediate vicinity to large domestic and international tour operators, mostly centered in Ha Noi and Saigon; it can be argued that, like the foreign tourists, these outsiders do not have the same ecological respect or locally oriented sensibility as the indigenous villagers or mainland citizenry do—the direct value of the vast Bay rests in touristic boat profit, not immediately on the color or the consistency of the water. To combat this, the government has admirably instated randomized "cold calls" on boat owners; periodically they are compelled to register the amount of food they carry on the junk for a particular journey, and then, upon the boat's return, they must account for the quantity of their waste. Should there be a discrepancy, the owner must pay a substantial fine. Unlike the large billboards in the floating villages, this is conveyed more subtly to the owners, such that the visitors are unaware of this process or of the potential damage they or their navigators may cause to the ecosystem. This creates, once again, an unfortunate double-standard wherein the minority group is inserted into a narrative of ignorance and disrespect, while the greater culprits are all but absolved of inclusion in this claim.

Similar to that of Phong Nha-Kẻ Bàng, the most detrimental factor affecting the site's conservation might be the government-sponsored infrastructural development itself, particularly its new cement plant in the port city of Cẩm Phả, on a portion of the Gulf of Tonkin that borders with China. It also borders Hạ Long Bay; UNESCO refers to Cẩm Phả as sitting "on the seashore of Hạ Long Bay."[77] Arguing that the placement of the plant near the famous bay is "inappropriate,"[78] UNESCO points out that the government has already destroyed 11% of its mangrove forests and have "degraded water bodies" in the buffer zone between the World Heritage site and the rest of the country, including Cẩm Phả. Troublingly, the cement plant requires an enlargement of the Cai Lan port, including the construction of a jetty four kilometers off-shore within the boundaries of Hạ Long Bay. Finally, with the enlargement of the port and the construction of the cement plant, Hạ Long Bay would be traversed, at least on its periphery, by steamers transporting clay to the plant via Bai Tu Long Bay.

Pollution is another major risk factor. The transfer of coal, cement, clinkers and other chemicals along the four-kilometer coastline would contribute greatly to air and water pollution—a problem that has been nonetheless increasing independently of the proposed cement plant. Since French times, Quang Ninh province was considered a wasteland—a coal-rich buffer zone with China where the colonials could send their political prisoners and low-paid workers to mine. With the increase in domestic prosperity, the demand for coal power has grown substantially—and the numerous coal mines around Cẩm Phả have been operating at top production. This is noticeable to outsiders as they drive through the borderland from Ha Noi to reach Hạ Long City: the greenery suddenly subsides as one enters Cẩm Phả; the whole sky is tinted brown, as if someone put on dark sunglasses. The streets are covered in soot and the buildings are blackened. One smells pungent change, and not for the better. And then it gradually subsides; the sun emerges once again as the visitor makes his way to the shore. Such a visible display of pollution could only adversely affect the unique and fragile ecosystem of this World Heritage site, and indeed, although the government denies any impact on the water quality, it does concede that "Limited pollution from coal mining wastes occurs in the buffer zone."[79]

It seemed that UNESCO and the Vietnamese government had found itself at a standstill between the effort to protect and even expand the World Heritage site, and to continue the infrastructural development necessitated by growing demand of the region—a demand that is, after all, directly related to tourism and

Hạ Long Bay's World Heritage designation. Thus, in a compromise much reminiscent of that of Phong Nha-Kẻ Bàng, direct efforts to foster conservation as well as infrastructural development at and around Hạ Long Bay continued to be focused on the boat people, rather than to those doing the developing. "The directive [given by both UNESCO and the Vietnamese government] was that both conservation and development were non-negotiable and that the Hạ Long Bay Management Department had to come up with the best possible approach to establish a way forward," writes Amareswar Galla. "Hence the launching of the Hạ Long Ecomuseum project." Reasoning that the philosophical frameworks of "ecomuseology"[80] could further foster a sense of local respect and ownership for the natural World Heritage resource—among the floating villagers—UNESCO and the official government, along with generous support from the Royal Norwegian Embassy in Ha Noi and Australia National University, devised a plan to create the first "floating" outdoor museum in July 2000. In actuality, the Hạ Long Ecomuseum is little more than the Cửa Vạn fishing village in its entirety, although UNESCO donated US$519,000 for the construction of a tangible Floating Cultural Center—a traditional museum—which was inaugurated on May 19, 2006 to some fanfare in the museum community. More importantly, the villagers of Cửa Vạn have been charged with its upkeep, so as to engage locals in the practice of protecting, not destroying, their own habitat. Writes Galla:

> Perhaps the most important element in the development of the Ecomuseum is its potential for energizing community support and conservation awareness. At present, most members of the Hạ Long community are almost completely oblivious to the global importance of the heritage of the area and the great significance of the culture and history to the nation. This lack of awareness leads to indifference to attempts to control the damaging environmental activities by means of exhortation and regulation. The Ecomuseum development has shown that, by engaging interest groups in dialogue and partnership, it is possible to bring issues of conservation to the forefront of public consciousness and have a substantial positive impact on irresponsible patterns of behavior.[81]

Galla's assertion is problematic for the same reasons cited at Phong Nha-Kẻ Bàng. Inexorably linked to the narrative of Hạ Long's "natural" designation, it assumes a measure of primitivity and ignorance that was also leveled against the Montagnards. Not only are these inhabitants of Cửa Vạn indifferent to the legislations imposed upon them from the mainland, but they are completely oblivious to the "great significance" of *their own* culture and history. And they wade in this ignorance to such an extent that they exhibit more "irresponsible patterns of behavior" towards the environment than even the industrialized ports, cement factories and coal mines do. Such a decision allows for both UNESCO and the

Vietnamese government to wash their hands, so to speak, of involvement in a lengthy battle over pollution done by mass infrastructural development and shift the blame, at least in the short-term, on the locals, as Galla seems to show. "Whilst some of the pressures on the natural environment are being effectively addressed through infrastructure improvements and better equipment, measures to mitigate damage and pollution arising from the irresponsible activities of residents, visitors and local industries are minimally effective."[82]

While one should also avoid conceptualizing these locals as Rousseauian "noble savages" who are naturally closer to the environment and therefore innately act in eco-friendly ways,[83] it is important to note that much of the worst and most conspicuous acts of pollution at Hạ Long Bay come from Cẩm Phả's coal mines, and well as from the high density of motorized tourist boats that crisscross the bay at all hours of the day and night. I have already included the quotes from UNESCO and environmental professionals attesting to this issue, but the words from several tourists who blogged on a private "World Heritage" website indicate that lay people also perceive this as a problem:

> The air pollution from the nearby coal power stations (and factories that have their own coal power) is everywhere. you can't even see the islands unless you are close to them The tour operators are ruthless in trying to take your money, and giving none back to the area which they are ruining. We went on a 2 night cruise. . . . This area should be properly protected now, its a WORLD heritage site and corrupt local officials/greedy and careless operators should not ruin it for mankind. What Halong needs is eco-tourism, ie low impact, take all your rubbish out, sail boats rather than diesel boats. If it costs more, so what. That is the price we need to pay to save these areas of outstanding natural beauty.[84]

> I have just returned from a trip to Vietnam which included 2 days on a traditional Vietnamese junk boat in Halong Bay. The site itself is breath-taking, but unfortunately, there is little respect for nature shown by those operating the tour boats. I repeatedly saw boat operators throw their garbage overboard into the waters. These are the people who survive on tourism and ought to care more about protecting the very site which is bringing the tourists to them in busloads. It was sad to see this and I hope the government forces people to clean up their act.[85]

Designating an entire village an "ecomuseum" emphasizes UNESCO's original problematic nature-culture dichotomy. By dint of its title, the Cửa Vạn village has become a museum not of cultural or current anthropological history, but that of ecology. The floating homes, the uniquely styled fishing vessels, the schools—even the trash cans—though part of an indigenous, constantly developing society with its own distinct culture, become relegated once again to just another form of primitivity, wherein the beings observed are no more greatly differentiated than the animals who also live uniquely on the bay. And they should be kept that way, insofar as they can be isolated from, or *made to want to resist*, the modernizing evolution occurring all around them.

The predominant philosophy behind this proposed shift in desires is found in "heritage economics,"—that is, the trickle-down increase in cultural awareness, employment and monetary income stemming from an embracing of the narrative of "heritage." It is the guiding principle of the heritage-scape in general. The designation of a particular town as an ecomuseum would tangibly deepen and complexify what constitutes nature and culture in the context of Hạ Long; it would also bring tourists to the expositional center, eager to view "natural" tools and the primitive lifestyle of living off of boats (as well as eat in its cafeteria and buy souvenirs). In the spirit of community-initiated eco-tourism, it is advocated that natives from the fishing village would be the primary "interpreters"—that is, assistant curators and guides. This in turn would cultivate within those interpreters a pride in the particular heritage and cultural forms they are expositing to outsiders, and raise awareness of the need for conservation among the visitors. Lastly, both self-cultural appreciation and awareness in the necessity of conservation would trickle down to the broader floating communities, as well; the end goal would be a true desire to maintain their natural state and primitive cultural activities while, at the same time, modify these same activities to be in line with modern conservation and heritage philosophy.

Conclusion

With the exception of Hội An, which will be examined at length in the following chapter, I have attempted to recount the history of the designations of Vietnam's World Heritage sites through the lens of UNESCO's natural and cultural categorizations. Viewing World Heritage sites in this way exposes UNESCO's problematic nature-culture dichotomy, which, I argue, is very much carried over from the Enlightenment-era thinking that permeates UNESCO's Constitution and its World Heritage Convention. It also elicits commentary on some of the political considerations taken by regional and national bodies during the nomination process and the sites' subsequent management. As these case studies indicate, countries may "offer up" their sites for universal valorization, yet the object of valorization is not always analogous to those whose "heritage" is associated with the indigenous owners of the site. Political marginalization of local minority communities can arise through the mere choice of a natural or cultural designation. This practice is diffuse and not simply relegated to Vietnam. Since overt marginalization is clearly contrary to the heritage-scape's guiding meta-narrative, countries working within the field of heritage production utilize preexisting categories to create subtle claims about the sites' associated populations.

I do not want to over-determine State-parties' conscious agency in this endeavor, however. Just as it is possible for a State-party to willfully contextualize its sites in a way that marginalizes one group in favor of another, it is also possible that such designations are the result of more subtle, ingrained and largely unconscious notions of the site's value and the nature of its inhabitants—in much the same way, Edward Said argues, Orientalist conceptions of "the Other" unconsciously pervade Western and colonial thinking.[86] The reverse can also be true; a State-party may balk at contextualizing their sites as "natural." This could be an unconscious occurrence, especially if the culture does not view nature and culture as separate entities. However, it can also be a conscious decision, especially by a post-colonial state reacting against Western hegemonic conceptions of its supposedly pre-modern culture. In its first few years as a signatory to the World Heritage Convention, India, for example, had six cultural properties designated and many more cultural properties on its Tentative List. IUCN noticed a pattern: India did not, however, nominate any natural sites. In an unusual on-the-record remark during the World Heritage Committee's Seventh Session in 1983, the Committee issued the following decree:

> The representative of IUCN noted that India had not yet submitted nominations of natural properties although this country had a number of sites which possibly could meet World Heritage criteria. The Committee noted that other States Parties had similarly not yet submitted natural nominations and expressed concern that appropriate balance with cultural properties be obtained on the World Heritage List. In the case of India, the Committee encouraged the Indian authorities to submit a tentative list of natural properties.[87]

It is true that these nature-culture claims are manifested in largely symbolic ways; they occur in the site's nomenclature, they are embedded in the official discourses concerning the site's designation, and they manifest themselves in the ways in which the site is managed and re-presented. Yet they nevertheless have real material outcomes. The Montagnard residents of Phong Nha-Kẻ Bàng provide an excellent illustration. Prohibitions on hunting wild game and owning restaurants, coupled with an increase in tourism, have changed traditional forms and divisions of labor. Yet the nature-culture dichotomy is not the only way a designation and subsequent management can adversely impact a site. The following chapter examines another problem that emerges from designation and management decisions concerning "living" sites: museumification.

CHAPTER SEVEN

MUSEUMIFICATION OF LOCAL CULTURES:
HẠ LONG BAY AND HỘI AN

Cửa Vạn's designation as an "ecomuseum" produces a second problem for the villagers—that of museumification. Museumification can be understood as the transition from a living city to that of an idealized re-presentation of itself, wherein everything is considered not for its use but for its value as a potential museum artifact. Such artifacts can be in varying degrees material—such as buildings, tools, industrial centers, markets and parklands—or, as Paulette Dellios points out, they can also be "abstractions such as 'ethnicity' and 'nation,' or human beings."[1] Indeed, instead of collecting, documenting, recontextualizing and exhibiting objects as a traditional museum does, the "ecomuseum" collects people and their immaterial activities. Everything becomes an artifact, and every action becomes a performance. In Hạ Long Bay, Cửa Vạn's museum is not simply the curated "Cultural Centre," with fixed and rotating exhibits, researched placards, trained guides and a sustainable management structure for processing visitors and collecting revenue from them; indeed, the term "cultural centre" was specifically chosen to differentiate itself from that. Rather, the actual "museum" is Cửa Vạn in its entirety—the sum total of all its tangible and intangible properties. By virtue of this designation, the site managers (that is, ultimately UNESCO and the Vietnamese government) authorize this shift in meaning to both outsiders and—as Galla hopes—to locals, such that the meaning of every common activity, observed or implicit, takes on an exhibitionary narrative claim.

The concept of an "ecomuseum" itself is inexorably linked to museumification. Originally the term was coined to describe the conversion of unprofitable farming centers to vast open-air nature preserves-cum-rural museums specifically for the "agri-tourist." Here, the urban vacationer can pay to learn about "traditional" ways of cultivating agriculture through viewing the tools as well as the practice of the farmers who utilized them. Often the visitor can rent a room

261

in the farmhouse, imbuing himself in the very lifestyle of the farmer, who will cook for him using the fruits of his land; some *agriturismi* as they are called in Italy, even offer the tourist a chance to till the land, harvest the grapes, or make wine in the traditional manner. In short, the farm becomes museumified, its value resting on the supposed permanence of its total culture.

Unlike inanimate objects, which are in some way concrete in form, the substance of a people's culture does not only vary from individual to individual, but is constantly changing and replicating. Thus museumification does not ossify these valued cultural forms as much as it simply creates something new. This is a dialectical re-creation, where inhabitants maintain their "traditional" or former ways of life not for the convenience of its use-value, but for its expositional qualities. They maintain a way of life frozen in heritage time only outwardly, for the expressed purpose of being seen, and consumed, by outsiders. When invited into the private living quarters of an Italian *agriturismo* or a traditional merchant's home in the World Heritage site of Hội An, for example, the tourist—coming with the expectation that locals are practicing a past way of life—may feel it strange to spy a television set or new, modern kitchen appliances; it seems not only anachronous but almost like cheating. Yet it reveals the ceaseless continuation of culture, which is always iterative.

Because of the amount of time it has enjoyed World Heritage status, as well as the sheer volume of tourists who come through the town every year, Hội An is one of the most glaring examples of museumification in the heritage-scape. Archaeological finds in the area attest to human settlement in present-day Hội An as far back as the second century B.C., where, along the banks of the Thu Bồn river, the indigenous Sa Huỳnh people established a trading center. At the epicenter of ancient Champa, Hội An (or "Fai Fo" as it was sometimes called) became one of the most important port cities in the empire—a designation that lasted even after the Vietnamese took control of the region. Indeed, the Viet-namized town flourished from the late sixteenth century to the early eighteenth century, with merchants from China, Japan, Portugal and, later, France, interact-ing as they exchanged goods. The Portuguese and French merchants introduced Christianity through Hội An, as well.[2] But the closed-door trade policies of the Nguyễn empire—which echoed those of the Chinese and Japanese—coupled with the unfortunate silting of Hội An's ancient harbor, led to sudden and gross economic stagnation. They turned mainly to fishing or farming. Though many fled the town, those who remained were impoverished and largely forgotten, eclipsed by the urban center of Đà Nẵng.

Like elsewhere in post-war Vietnam, the first "tourists" arrived in Hội An in the 1980s, and they were Soviets—mostly advisors and their families on holiday from Ha Noi or possibly Đà Nẵng, to which they were called to work. Accord-

Plate I: Angkor Wat.
Designated a UNESCO World Heritage site through extraordinary means in 1992, the Angkor Archaeological Park covers 400 km² of land and contains the archaeological remains of roughly 600 years of the Khmer empire at its height. The twelfth century Angkor Wat, constructed by Suryavarman II, is considered its quintessential embodiment of "cultural heritage."

Plate II: Ta Prohm.
With immense banyan trees and strangler fig tendrils twisting around its ruins, Jayavarman VII's twelfth century monastery Ta Prohm captivates visitors as a unique *memento mori*.

Plates III and IV: Bas reliefs of Buddhist *Bodhisattva Avalokiteshvara*s at Preah Khan from two neighboring walls.
Bodhisattva Avalokiteshvara reliefs that survived the iconoclasm following Jaya-varman VII's death.

Plates III and IV: Bas reliefs of Buddhist *Bodhisattva Avalokiteshvara*s at Preah Khan from two neighboring walls.
Empty frames previously holding bodhisattva reliefs; the figures were chiseled out during the period of iconoclasm.

Plate V: Scale model of Angkor Wat in Thailand's Grand Palace, Bangkok.
Although the Franco-Siamese Treaty of 1907 recognized Cambodian sovereignty over Angkor Wat, the site continues to be regarded as central to both Thai and Khmer cosmology and nationalism.

Plate VI: Banteay Srei.
The lithe, pink sandstone complex of Banteay Srei, part of the Angkor Archaeological Park, predates Angkor Wat.

Plate VII: Banteay Srei: "Restoration" in the Angkor Complex.
Banteay Srei can be considered a "restored" temple. Like Angkor Wat, it was cleared of the jungle's stranglehold and partially reconstructed as it was imagined to have appeared during its use by the host society. Note the lighter-colored concrete to differentiate between authentic materials (pink sandstone) and reconstructions.

Plate VIII: Tour guide discussing pre-Angkorian aesthetics on a capital at Banteay Srei.

Plate IX: Ta Prohm: "Preservation" in the Angkor Complex.
Along with Preah Khan, Ta Prohm can be considered a "preserved" temple; it was cleaned and reinforced, but has been left largely as the French discovered it, a "vestige" of cultural forms suffocated by nature. This image is of Ta Prohm's famed doorway, covered by strangler fig roots. This doorway was used in the Angelina Jolie film, *Tomb Raider*.

Plate X: Tourism at Ta Prohm.
Carnival-esque atmosphere in front of the *"Tomb Raider* door" at Ta Prohm. Locals are possibly costumed as figures from the *Rāmāyana* (known in Cambodia as the *Reamker*), while tourists jockey to take photographs at the doorway.

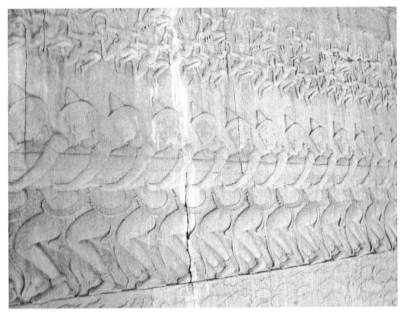

Plate XI: Churning of the Milky Sea, Angkor Wat.
Monumental bas relief on the Eastern gallery of Angkor Wat, depicting the creation myth *Churning of the Milky Sea. Asuras* and *devas* tug at Vasuki, a *naga* or sea snake, who pivots around Vishnu atop his avatar, the turtle Kurma.

Plate XII: West Gate, Angkor Thom.
West Gate of Angkor Thom, Jayavarman VII's city. At the center of the monumental gate are four of the "smiling faces of Angkor"—Bodhisattvas possibly in the likeness of the king himself. Flanking the causeway are (left) *devas* and (right) *asuras* recreating the *Churning of the Milky Sea*, pivoting around the likenesses of Jayavarman VII. Note the anchor of the *asuras* is the ten-headed *rākshasa* Rāvana, the villain of the *Rāmāyana* (or *Reamker* in Khmer).

Plate XIII: Chinese meeting house, Hội An.
The port city of Hội An was designated a World Heritage site for its tangible testimony to cultural diversity. Various Chinese communities made their homes and meeting houses here.

Plate XIV: Japanese covered bridge, Hội An.
Seamlessly coexisting among Chinese meeting houses, Vietnamese merchant quarters, and Western-style edifices is this Japanese-style covered bridge, another testament to UNESCO's meta-narrative claim, "unity in diversity."

Plate XV: Thiên Mụ Pagoda, Huế.
Gracing the Perfume River is the Thiên Mụ pagoda, or Pagoda of the Celestial Lady, named for the mythological woman in red who ordered the local lord to build a pagoda for protection against supernatural forces. It is not only the most venerated site in Huế, but considered by many to be the icon of Vietnamese cultural heritage.

Plate XVI: Tomb of Minh Mạng, Huế.
Unlike other World Heritage sites, Huế is a "complex of monuments" that includes not only the fortress-like Citadel and the imperial capital city, but also parts of the Perfume River, the Thiên Mụ Pagoda, and the tombs of the Nguyen emperors. The first tomb complex to begin restoration was that of Minh Mạng.

Plate XVII: Remains of the Imperial Purple City, Huê´.
Although Huê´ has now been appropriated as a symbol of Vietnamese strength and resilience, at the fall of the Nguyen Empire it had been considered the icon of feudalism and oppression. Much of the Emperor's city was destroyed in door-to-door combat during the 1968 Tet Offensive.

Plate XVIII: Restoration work at the Imperial Purple City, Huê´ (2006).
Years of warfare and neglect have irrevocably damaged this World Heritage site, but several local and national entities have industriously mobilized to put into effect an ambitious restoration plan. However, Phase I, the complete rebuilding of the Imperial City's galleries, calls into question the site's "authenticity."

Plate XIX: Typical Re-presentation of Mỹ Sơn.
Located near the Vietnamese city of Đà Nẵng, Mỹ Sơn was the religious center of Champa, a Shivite empire once occupying the land south of the Viet. The ways in which Mỹ Sơn is represented, both visually and textually (including the official wording of the declaration of its "universal value"), may appear to marginalize this minority group, some of whom continue to live in Vietnam today. This image is a common way of visually portraying Mỹ Sơn: crumbled, overgrown by weeds, a mere vestige of a foreign "Other."

Plate XX: Pô Klong Girai temple, Phan Rang, Vietnam.
There are a number of sites that continue to be used by the Cham people today. Recognized as a national monument, the thirteenth century Shivite temple of Pô Klong Girai continues to serve as a locus of worship and as a sacred center for Cham pilgrimage.

Plate XXI: Cham Museum, Đà Nẵng.
Until recently, Mỹ Sơn was difficult to access, with most group tours only including a visit to the Cham Museum in Đà Nẵng. Founded by the French archaeologist Henri Parmentier, the Đà Nẵng museum has preserved many of the most important artifacts from Mỹ Sơn and other Cham cities. Because of its situation in an open-air French villa, many tourists can be found touching, or even climbing atop, the artifacts.

Plate XXII: Interpretive Center at Mỹ Sơn.
With the construction of a new road leading from Đà Nẵng to Mỹ Sơn, tourism has increased to this World Heritage site. While the artifacts continue to be housed at the Cham Museum in Đà Nẵng, a new interpretive center provides hands-on instruction on Cham history, culture, and architecture through recreations and more "modern" forms of technology.

Plate XXIII: Detail of restoration work: Mỹ Sơn.
While much of the site remains overtaken by nature, several of the structures in the religious complex are undergoing restoration. Like in Banteay Srei, there is a clear delineation between the original elements and those that were added during reconstruction to maintain authenticity.

Plate XXIV: New roadway leading to the sacred mount of Mỹ Sơn (2006).

Plate XXV: "Branding" the Tower of London.
Signage is an important element in the museological interpretation of World Heritage sites, for it can serve as the initial frame contextualizing the site as a place of "universal value." The Tower of London, in the United Kingdom, is exemplary in its signage leading from the ticket office to the fortress itself.

Plate XXVI: Signage at the Angkor Archaeological Park.
In comparison to the Tower of London, initial signage at the Angkor Archaeological Park is quite different. Although both entrances are laid out the same, at Angkor there is only a small, dark sign placed a considerable distance from the ticket booth. Perhaps because of its status as an icon of Khmer nationalism, there is also no mention of its UNESCO designation.

Plate XXVII: Phong Nha-Ké Bàng, Vietnam.
Phong Nha-Ké Bàng, the complex of karst mountain caves and subterranean water-ways near the Lao-Vietnamese border, is Vietnam's second and most recently des-ignated "natural" World Heritage site. Its designation as a "natural" site, however, helps to marginalize local minority groups, frequently referred to as Montagnards, who live off of the land. Greeting visitors entering the vast park, its signage is an innovative, and striking, way of proclaiming its UNESCO status.

Plate XXVIII: Hạ Long Bay, Vietnam.
Rich in mythology, Hạ Long Bay is recognized as Vietnam's premier "natural site" for its roughly 1,600 karst islands that resemble a "dragon descending into the sea," yet the designation problematically neglects to incorporate the equally vi-brant present-day "floating village" culture.

ing to Trần Văn Nhân, Chair of the local office of the Ministry of Culture and Information, they recognized the stunning outward ossification of the town, and dubbed Hội An "old Ha Noi." Sometime around 1983, news of this old Ha Noi must have reached the Polish architect Kazim, who was working at nearby Mỹ Sơn, and one weekend he came to the town. According to Trần,

> He was so surprised to see the old buildings. For Hội Anians, it's normal. But he saw beauty, and came every weekend. He did his own study. When he came to Ha Noi, he talked with the responsible person in the Ministry and said that Hội An could be a "pearl" of Vietnam. So government officials, who knew nothing about the town [sic], came in to study it.[3]

In 1985, the Vietnamese government hosted Hội An's first domestic symposium in an expansive French villa on the outskirts of town, now the large Hội An hotel. At the symposium, experts shared their scientific and architectural assessments gathered through the past few years' study. Five years later, an international symposium was held in Đà Nẵng, which drew the participation of nearly one hundred scientists, fifty-two of whom came from abroad; experts from France, Germany, Japan, China and even the United States were said to have attended. According to Trần, this was the turning point for Hội An; the symposium sufficiently raised awareness in the academic community of this once-forgotten town.

By a stroke of good timing, less than a year earlier a man had arrived in Hội An named Daniel Robinson, a traveler affiliated with *Lonely Planet* guidebooks.[4] The backpacker-oriented travel publisher had sent him to research the country, which was on the cusp of opening up to tourism once again. His aim was to compile the first edition of a new guidebook dedicated exclusively to the three countries of former French Indochina: Vietnam, Laos and Cambodia. He had been allowed to visit Saigon and Ha Noi, but "probably with special permission,"[5] his Communist-party guides took him to Hội An. Like Kazim almost a decade before him, he was astonished by its lack of modernity and its state of preservation. Returning home to complete the book, he dedicated a full fourteen pages to this small and relatively unknown town—stunningly, the same amount he gave to Saigon and Ha Noi. This parity of pagination served its purpose, conveying the equality of value and importance of Hội An compared to Vietnam's well-known urban centers to the north and south. When the book came out in 1991, backpackers arrived in such numbers into the small town that the Ministry of Culture and Information almost immediately established a program of tourist services there.

The crush of tourism swiftly impacted the architectural bones of the small town. Hội An had already been a century into its decay, and the pressures of tourism seemed only to exacerbate the situation. Colored with expectations of a perfectly preserved town, these backpacking tourists also made "many demands" on the overseers of Hội An to improve the destination's offerings. This translated not only to cleaning and restoring the aesthetics of the place, but also to converting buildings into venues appropriate for tourists. Restaurants, bars and hostels with plumbing and electricity needed to be constructed; towards the end of 1990s, even Internet cafes were demanded. Gradually these "demands" moved from restaurants to accommodations; because there was only one small hotel in town, most had to stay in Đà Nẵng. The demand also increased for souvenir shops and tailors, presumably because most arrive in Vietnam from Hong Kong or Bangkok, two cities famous for low-cost seamstresses. The first tailor opened in 1995, and Trần believes that years of positive "word of mouth," helped Hội An become known as "a place to see, and also to shop." Tourists also brought with them different sensibilities, and interaction among the locals inevitably produced a change among the locals' understandings and expectations about the features of "modern life." Television antennae, satellite dishes and cables of all sorts began to be put up haphazardly. Especially in the early days of tourism, however, the greatest need was to reconstruct the dilapidated homes.

All of these pressures necessitated a concentrated restoration effort, but the situation was not conducive to proper preservation. At the time, the Vietnamese government had imposed a commercial logging ban; wood had to be imported from Laos. The price thus was so high that the people of Hội An could not afford it. "The people were saying, 'I can't do this. My roof will fall and it will kill my family. I'll knock it down and build another one in concrete,'" Trần recalled. Even so, tourism was seen as the primary means to support any reconstruction effort, and they knew that if the old town aesthetics were not maintained, they would lose this valuable source of revenue. After requesting help from Ha Noi, the central government sent in preservationists to restore a few exemplary edifices at no cost. To help the others, however, the Ministry of Culture and Information granted local homeowners licenses to work in the tourist sector. According to guide Pham Van Anh, non-participating locals could not help but see tourists visiting newly restored buildings, and it raised their desire to preserve their own homes in a similar fashion. Thus, the decisions private individuals made concerning their own property was, and continues to be, influenced by very public elements.

To assist the impoverished locals looking to restore their homes, in 1995 the Ministry of Culture and Information began a semi-voluntary ticket system where tourists would be strongly encouraged to pay an entrance fee. The purchase of this ticket would grant the visitor access to one museum, one Chinese meeting house, and one historic home out of a pool of three of each. At first tickets had cost only VND 50,000, or about US$4; to date, they have only increased one dollar. While twenty-five percent of the revenue would be dedicated to tourist authority's management and operation costs, such as staff payments, printing of tickets and drafting of brochures, the remainder would be put into a preservation fund to which local homeowners could apply irrespective of their engagement in the tourist sector. An application alone does not necessarily ensure funding, however; "groups of advisors" must first be sent in by the government to draw up accurate floor plans, assess the needs of the home, "suggest" a team of workers, and propose a comprehensive restoration plan. The governmental lenders will also investigate the homeowners' income, including alternative sources of funding such as family abroad with whom the homeowner continues to maintain contact. With this procedure completed, the government may then offer to pay a percentage of the total cost using revenue from the fund—it could be upwards of 80%—100%, or less than 10%. Today, most—if not all—of the homes within the historic center of Hội An have been restored in accordance to international preservation standards, and all but a few of its inhabitants are actively engaged in the tourist industry. The climate is also conducive to successfully implementing a number of public infrastructural "development" projects aimed at maintaining the old world charm of Hội An despite the growing material desires from its enriched inhabitants, such as cable television, electricity and motorcycle ownership. In particular, by 2004 all anachronistic television antennae and electrical wiring were removed from the roofs of homes, and cables were installed underground. And in 2006, the town enacted a trial program banning motorcycles within the city center a few days a week, with little adverse reaction. "We have a good community here," Trần said. "They sometimes protest but after explaining, they cooperate. It's not easy when your house is in a World Heritage site and you can or can't do things."[6]

Such success in preserving an entire village in such a pleasurable and seemingly authentic state has won public and private accolades from UNESCO officials, but it has also brought about a number of unintended problems associated with the evident museumification of the town. Problematically, museumification often presupposes that the keepers of this brand of culture are not those immediately enacting it—a point to which Trần's comment refers. Rather, they are outsiders who can further define what that "culture" is (in a problematically homogenous sense), and then dictate what is an acceptable or unacceptable performance of it. Although it seems as if Hội An's current tourist culture of heritage and dressmaking has emerged somewhat organically from a collective desire to capitalize on a ripe tourist market, in actuality, the locals have been influenced by a mix of parties often working in formal or informal conjunction with each other to determine what constitutes architectural and cultural "authenticity." Such parties include government officials, national UNESCO representatives in Ha Noi, regional UNESCO representatives in Bangkok, non-local preservation experts and even tourists; indeed, governmental tourism managers have periodically issued surveys primarily to backpackers and independent travelers, whose recommendations they seem to follow.[7]

The synergy between the local government, UNESCO officials and advisory bodies can best be revealed when examining the mayor's quest to designate Hội An a World Heritage site. Early in 1996, Richard Englehart, an American archaeologist and anthropologist who was serving as UNESCO's Regional Advisor for Culture in Asia and the Pacific, came at the behest of the mayor to Hội An. When he arrived from UNESCO's regional office in Bangkok, Trần escorted him around, along with the mayor of the town. Eager to know the official's thoughts on the village's World Heritage potential, the mayor asked him towards the end of the tour. Trần recalls that "he said no. He said the value [of the site] was good but the management was bad. And that's the most important."[8] Immediately after that encounter, the mayor personally became involved in establishing a viable tourism and conservation management plan for Hội An, which, he felt, must include instilling a better sense of industry among the local civil employees. He began a very public campaign to raise awareness, to increase productivity and a sense of ownership of the town within his local governmental office. It seems the mayor regarded his employees as exemplars to the whole community; not only must they enforce the rules regarding preservation, ticket collection, and other tourism-related efforts, but through word and deed, they should be actively encouraging locals to enjoy the same sense of pride in the town. "He met with everyone who worked for the government and whipped everyone into shape. We were a little afraid of him," Trần chuckled, "but we admired him greatly. And everything in town changed after only six months." At the end of 1996, Dr. Englehart was invited to return to Hội An. Upon his arrival, he noticed the marked improvement in the management strategy, and informed the mayor that "Hội An can think about building the File." Trần recalls:

> At 11:00 PM from the hotel, Rick called me and asked me to bring the chief to his hotel. He had printed out a list of advice—what Hội An should do and should not do. He provided much advice. Then, when he went back to Thailand, he began to send experts, like Michelle from ICOMOS, members of UNESCO Thailand, and representatives from the World Heritage Council in Paris. They build the File for us because we weren't knowledgeable about [what was required by UNESCO]. They took pictures and drew up restoration plans. It was a three year process.[9]

The entire town of Hội An was designated a World Heritage site in 1999, but the top-down approach towards directing the outward forms of the town had only just begun. By virtue of its designation, the citizens of Hội An have to live under stricter statutes and regulations that extend from their public lives into their private lives. These laws are intended to maintain the ostensible authenticity of both the physical site, as well as the way of life. Many of these laws are suggested by UNESCO, the World Heritage Committee, and its affiliates, then carried by the State-Party representative to the central government in Ha Noi, and are created by the central Ministry of Culture and Information, rather than the local mayor's office. Such regulations reveal the constructed dynamic of this particular "museumified" culture, wherein the people are compelled to make unique compromises to negotiate the fine line between living in the past and existing in the present. Some are quite straightforward and have their roots in tradition, particularly when regarding the choice of materials that must be used when restoring or making changes to the house. For example, when restoring the brick floor of their historic homes, they are only allowed to use a particular type of ceramic floor tile, rather than simply pouring cement. Others are more uniquely situated in this new cultural form. For example, those living in the city center are allowed to have air conditioning, but the unit must be hidden behind a particular type of rattan. Locals can only have cable television now; satellite dishes and antennae have all been removed. They are also allowed to have a modern toilet, but it must be constructed in a way to appear to fit in with the old building from the outside. And to maintain a more authentic public appearance, the government is slowly trying to eliminate anachronistic motorbikes from the city center, whose vibrations and pollution also contribute to the gradual deterioration of the site. The use of bicycles, which were invented at the turn of the nineteenth century, seems to remain an acceptable form of transportation; the popularity of bicycle rentals among backpackers may have contributed to this decision, as well.

Museumified culture, then, is neither a preserved or ossified state of a people's preexisting culture, nor a recovery or a restoration of their "correct" or "traditional" way of life; it is something entirely new and original that organically emerges from the ongoing iterative process. Cultivated by a heightened exhibitionary sensitivity wherein one's "culture" is specifically pinpointed, mapped and enacted for the benefit of an outside audience, although it is seemingly both semi-factual and semi-fictional, to use Timothy Luke's terminology,[10] it is at once entirely authentic and artificial—a completely organic phenomenon that stems from very contrived dynamics. It emerges from the unique interplay between the regulations imposed upon the practitioners from outside "keepers of culture" and the people's own collective interpretation of these regulations.

Thus, the impetus for an outward activity—from renovating a house to using a bathroom, from traveling down the street to shopping for food—does not emerge completely independently, but is severely enforced and sustained by those external culture makers. These outsiders then become the patrons, much the same way that kings, socialites and governments supported public art galleries and museums in the nineteenth century. Indeed, while viable cities rely on its citizenry to generate the funds necessary for the upkeep of its infrastructure in the form of taxes, commercial investments by local business owners and individual maintenance efforts on private properties, museums rely on a diversity of patronage sources for funding and maintaining its present state. And, much like museums, should the patronage which props the culture up and ensures the continuity of its trajectory cease to operate, the culture as an institution would inevitably find itself in crisis.

There are typically two kinds of patrons in a museumified society, direct and indirect, and the influence of both can be seen in Hội An. Hội An's direct patrons are political entities, primarily the Ministry of Culture and Information who is charged with shaping, contextualizing, and promoting Hội An's unique "culture." Additionally, the central government, private donors, UNESCO and its affiliates also wield considerable influence over the decisions enacted by the Ministry. All three of these entities also act as direct monetary patrons, doling out funds when it is appropriate for sustaining or furthering the development pattern of the culture. Such an activity was evident in the summer of 2006, when for a few months, many of the dusty streets of the quiet town were ripped up as contractors finalized a sweeping infrastructural development plan to bury all evidence of electricity and technology—save actual lights—underground. The Ministry of Culture and Information was responsible for financing the costly installation of electrical wires, television cables, plumbing and a modern sewage system—a privilege most towns of this size do not enjoy. In addition to tapping into the local tourist fund to invest in public or private works, the Ministry can also solicit assistance from the World Heritage Fund, especially in financing architectural or cultural research that would further contribute to shaping a more "authentic" traditional culture. The UNESCO-affiliated Fund can also be used for promotional purposes, in an effort to raise and shape awareness among the international community of what these patrons feel should be the appropriate "meaning" of the culture.

These promotional efforts are also intended to draw visitors to the site, and for good reason. Visitors constitute the museumified culture's indirect patrons, and Hội An is no exception. Unofficial estimates for 2005 place Hội An's visitor population at an average of one thousand people a day—with more visiting in high season and fewer visiting in low season. These people stay an average of about two to three days, although many do take half-day excursions to Đà Nẵng, Mỹ Sơn or down the river to "Cham Island." Of these visitors, a majority purchase one entrance fee ticket, although guides are quick to point out that about 40% of backpackers do not.[11] In 2005, a total of about 276,000 tickets sold at five dollars each. Yet, as with museums, a visitor's direct monetary contributions in the form of entrance fee purchases barely cover the basic wear-and-tear that they themselves cause, and are not a significant source of revenue.[12] Rather, museum visitors sustain the institution much more significantly through expenditures at museum gift shops, cafes and restaurants; Hội An as a museum is certainly no exception. The majority of businesses in Hội An are directly visitor-oriented—modern restaurants, cafes and gift shops selling local and regional souvenirs line the streets, seamlessly interspersed among the architectural artifacts. A good majority of the income these proprietors generate will inevitably be used to restore and update their properties in accordance with heritage regulations, without the assistance of the local fund—whose coffers can be used to assist non-tourist centered businesses. This revenue can also be used to diversify the forms of entertainment the proprietor offers to tourists; since 2004, for example, several new urban-hip restaurants have opened up in the central area to entice the younger cosmopolitan travelers, a French bakery has also been established, art galleries more closely resembling those of Saigon and Ha Noi have replaced the small souvenir-cum-gallery shops, and the chef-proprietor of one local restaurant in town offers cooking classes to groups. Yet as is the case for large-scale museums, visitor-related revenue is problematically tautological: since visitors necessarily contribute to the physical deterioration of a site, more money is needed to preserve and update the site, which can be raised by soliciting more visitors.

A common method of partially alleviating this pressure is through the hosting of blockbuster exhibitions, whose unabashed purpose is to attract larger-than-average crowds for a short time. In the museum world, this entails hosting a widely publicized temporary exhibition that is clearly differentiated from the permanent holdings. Characterized popular themes rather than esoteric ones, the blockbuster caters to the non-regular visitor and presents its material "at his present level of . . . sophistication" and is not necessarily intended to be a broadening or enhancing experience typified in the permanent collection.[13] With the blockbuster comes the hope of both short-term and long-term economic benefits: immediate and increased revenue generation from admissions in the short-term, and a more pervasive, positive publicity that could contribute to capturing a new demographic, raise awareness, and increase the institution's clout as a valuable tourist destination in the long-term. While cities have always drawn concentrated assemblies in the form of public spectacles, religious festivals and civic celebrations, these played an important role in the city's urban social script and were not typically oriented to outsiders. Hội An organizes blockbuster exhibitions not directly for the emotional benefit of the locals, but rather to capture an external audience. Like more traditional museums, Hội An's blockbusters are intended to induce former visitors to return, to attract new visitors who would not normally be interested in viewing the town's "permanent collection," and to keep the town at the forefront of tourist buzz in a globalizing world with an increasingly crowded pool of destinations from which to choose.

While there are an increasing number of unique exhibitions, shows and festivals held for the benefit of tourists in Hội An, the most well-known, repeated and beloved blockbuster is the Lantern Festival. Held on the fifteenth day of every lunar month, Hội An's Lantern Festival was intended to "bring back a night in the old days," according to Trần, who claims responsibility within the Ministry of Culture and Information for originally devising the scheme.[14] Florescent lights are turned off, and the public spaces are illuminated by strings of traditional-styled paper lanterns lining the streets. Motorcycles and even bicycles are prohibited from entering the city center. Many shops are closed, or are restricted on the wares they sell. To maintain the eighteenth-century air about the town, even television watching in private is strictly prohibited, since it not only casts an artificial glow, but its sound and images might break the suspension of disbelief hanging in the town. As one English-language Vietnamese advertisement puts it:

NO FLUORESCENT LIGHTS. NO MOTORCYCLES. NO TELEVISION.
ON THE 15TH DAY OF EACH LUNAR MONTH, THE RIVERSIDE TOWN
OF HỘI AN GIVES MODERN LIFE THE NIGHT OFF.[15]

Indeed, this festival can be understood as an intensification of the museumified culture's sense of "heritage time," which is illustrated by the basic, paper lanterns—in opposition to "modern time" which is represented by technology. Such an understanding conforms to the analytics of Western Enlightenment-era thinkers, who found it far easier to temporalize culture based on the outward signs of innovation rather than through a deeper, intangible structural analysis. Technology is denied during the Lantern Festival inasmuch as it is a symbol for "modern" contemporary life, but those intangible elements that truly define a culture—taste, philosophy, politics and language, for example—are left untouched.

When the Lantern Festival was first held on September 8, 1998, Trần contends that it was intended to simply "make a nice surprise for the visitors," to reinforce the predominant structure of Hội An's narrative claim. While foreign visitors' reactions were quite positive, the locals were less than enthusiastic at the inconvenience. The limiting of the basic amenities was an interference on an even greater, more private level than any architectural or aesthetic regulation ever had been. In addition, this imposition directly affected the primary benefit of the pseudo social contract into which they all entered: economics. Trần recalls, "At first we had a little resistance; the shopkeepers protested—no bikes, motorcycles, how can we sell? We had to convince them that next time, people will come a day or two before just for this festival, and then will stay afterwards." The Ministry held the Lantern Festival three more times, each time generating more enthusiasm; ex-pates and younger students from Đà Nẵng began visiting, and tourists were very positive about the experience in surveys. By the fourth time, it had not only received the admiration of visitors, but the local entrepreneurs were able to realize its potential to generate profits.

The Lantern Festival was created as a blockbuster that, by generating buzz among outside communities, could both draw new demographics of visitors as well as to induce tourists to remain in town longer. But since this demographic consists not of repeat visitors such as a museum's, but rather international tourists who come from afar and most likely visit the country only once or twice in their lifetimes, it was necessary to modify the way in which this particular blockbuster was conceived. Although it is an event very different from daily life, it was conceived as highly repetitive in nature—a happening that happened almost all of the time. In this way, it would be more easily correspond with an independent traveler's schedule, capturing the most tourists, while still remaining a fresh, new experience for all of these outsiders. And it seemed to have worked; travel writers began describing the festival in magazine articles and guide books; Vietnamese land operators had also begun to schedule their visitors to be in Hội An for the festival when at all possible. By 2003, the buzz had reached such venerable American institutions as the American Museum of Natural History and the Art Institute of Chicago, who were planning member tours to Vietnam. The former, in fact, was in the midst of the largest ethnographic exhibition of Vietnamese culture in the United States, which focused heavily on the viewing of videotaped festivals, and so the coupling of the trip with such a performance was optimal. And at the independent behest of the member travel planners at the Art Institute and a number of other institutions, this author planned the dates of their three-week journeys specifically correspond with the dates of the Lantern Festival.[16]

That the monthly Lantern Festival has made an indelible mark upon the business culture of Hội An was observable about five years after its inception. Previously, the numerous shops in Hội An sold a variety of wares, of which paper lanterns were a very minor part. Hội An, in fact, was not known for lanterns as it seems to be today, but rather a type of doughy noodle called *cao lầu*,[17] and a particular type of pottery named after Thanh Hà, a hamlet nearby. Capitalizing on the "traditional" narrative of the town, many of these stores dishonestly masqueraded as antique shops, selling inauthentic fragments of plates, faux opium pipes, and metal objects that were purposefully weathered to appear hundreds of years old. Of course, since many shops sold the same pieces, travelers were naturally a bit skeptical; to further convince tourists of the pieces' authenticity, a number began to place their pieces artfully behind glass, mimicking the presentation style of a museum. More "honest" proprietors stuck to selling hand-carved wood, Thanh Ha pottery, silk paintings, and tchotchkes such as chopstick holders, chess sets and statuettes, sculpted of marble from the Marble Mountains halfway between Hội An and Đà Nẵng. But about five years later, many of these same proprietors turned to making and selling silk lanterns of the type used during the Lantern Festival; they had found that the majority of tourists who experienced the festival purchased at least one lantern as a souvenir. These labor-intensive lanterns have already begun to be exported, first to Saigon and today abroad in Australia and the United States. Indeed, the buzz surrounding the festival in the international travel community has so shaped awareness of the lantern's supposedly strong connection to Hội Anese culture that travelers today seek out lanterns for purchase, irrespective of their participation in the festival. Today, the streets are literally lined with shops exhibiting lanterns of all sizes, shapes and colors; from the mercantile aspect, the streets are almost unrecognizable from what they were five years ago.

But this festival is also intended to capture a new dynamic of traveler—that of the young, mobile Vietnamese local who lives in proximity to Hội An. While for foreign visitors the Lantern Festival is billed as a spectacle illustrating most clearly the unique "heritage time" that he encounters when entering Hội An, the Lantern Festival is primarily presented as an emotional and educational romanticization of the local youths' own heritage, despite the festival's utterly contrived nature. Drawn to the candlelight, the liminal atmosphere and the placidly romantic celebration of their own heritage, "kids from Đà Nẵng come with their girlfriend or boyfriend," states Trần happily. In short, it is a perfect date event. The repetition of this event, therefore, provides almost as regular a venue for a romantic excursion as a beautiful park or lake could, and, just like these venues, can be repetitively visited without getting too trite too quickly. From that point, it is the hope that, as adults, these same people will continue to make day-trips to Hội An for shopping, eating and entertainment. "Someday they'll be addicted. We want them to be a lover of the night," Trần smiled slyly.[18]

The Lantern Festival as an educational tool is not simply directed towards domestic outsiders, but is directed inwardly as well. The repetition of this liminal event, then, can be viewed as a means of further shaping and perpetuating the museumified culture in the minds of the locals through a uniquely constructed temporality. Temporality is subtly at the forefront of this festival; not only is it intended to bring all those within its walls "back in time," it is itself a liminal period wherein daily life is suspended. Most tellingly, it is purposefully connected to the traditional lunar year, not the Westernized calendar. There is also a strong "betwixt and between" temporal status for all who enter; as discussed, some aspects of modernity are prohibited, but everyone nonetheless dresses in contemporary clothes, eats in restaurants with modern amenities, speaks English to tourists, and utilizes the monetary system of the current political regime. Furthermore, many arrive at the town with the intention of going "back in time" precisely through modern transportation such as busses, cars, and motorbikes; when they have had their fill, they depart again using the same modern vehicles.

Trần also describes the Lantern Festival in terms of filial piety, saying, "We want to say to the elder generation that the younger generation understands and appreciates" their way of life.[19] More than enacting this deep-rooted Confucian tenet, Trần reveals that the Lantern Festival also contributes to the formation of a solidarity constructed on the unique experience of living within this museumified cultural bubble—an experience that transcends generations. Despite being instituted from the outside, it punctuates the locals' calendar in the same metrical way traditional festivals and rites do. As Durkheim writes, it "expresses the rhythms of collective activity while ensuring the regularity" of the people's social life.[20] Unlike other festivals, however, this one is hyper-regular; it occurs practically all of the time, with barely a repose. Its hyper-regularity is reflective of the strong and concentrated efforts seemingly exerted on the museumified culture by outsiders, in all of their modern sensibilities, which the Lantern Festival must counteract. Contemporary Vietnamese life, as diffused through the media (television, newspapers, radio, Internet) and through interpersonal communications (via cell phones, tourist exchanges, business transactions, travel, town hall meetings with Party officials), is perceived by the external culture keepers as detrimental to heritage and the way of life they constructed for the locals. It is seen as a dangerously unceasing force pulling the people into its grasp and therefore wresting control away from the culture-keepers. The monthly Lantern Festival, with its legally imposed denial of the most technological aspects of present-day life, becomes the primary rite for collective life in the town. It is a densely concentrated form of the common experience of living in Hội An—a collective ritual illustration of the most important cultural tenet bestowed upon the townspeople by the culture-keepers.

Not only does the Lantern Festival punctuate the calendar illustratively for reinforcing the collective, but it also actively recreates temporality for the locals, who in their "between" status are constantly being pulled by modernity. The Lantern Festival allows the locals' museumified culture to organically evolve only as long as the lunar month lasts. Throughout the rest of the lunar month, locals are relatively free to immerse themselves within contemporary culture. They can sell souvenirs and contemporary art, they can sew the hippest fashions and sell the most popular brands of athletic ware. They are at liberty to move forward with the rest of society, riding on their Hondas and watching color cable television, using their indoor plumbing and their electric lights, singing along to pop music videos and watching English-language movies. They may enjoy as unfettered an access to modern ideas as is allowed in the country, pulling them along with their foreign guests, becoming one with "modern Vietnamese culture." But as if to check this so-perceived "progress," once a month all of this must be denied. Under the glow of the lantern-light, like sacramental Confession, the stains of modernity imprinted on the museumified culture are absolved through the people's active, collective rejection of this sin; the ideal state is restored once again. When the sunlight finally bathes the pastel town in its radiance, the locals emerge from this ritual cleansed—only to pick up where they left off, to catch up to their visitors' modernity that had continued on without them.

CHAPTER EIGHT

CREATING THE DRAMA OF THE DESTINATION:
MANAGING, INTERPRETING AND BRANDING
WORLD HERITAGE SITES

If "all the world's a stage," as Shakespeare so poetically contended, then the heritage-scape can be conceptualized as a grand proscenium, a playhouse of diversity and a platform from which actors of all sorts come together to muse, interact, and present their real or imagined dramas—creating, re-presenting and replicating unique meanings that change with each performative iteration. It must also be remembered that actors, in the theatrical sense, are essentially interpreters; they are guided by a script—which can either be rigorously detailed so as to leave little room for freestyle reading or open to improvisation—but in the end create a performance that is uniquely their own, and never exactly replicated. As the late father of touristic and heritage interpretation theory Freeman Tilden once remarked, "interpretation is an art" that utilizes the other arts for "provocation," stimulating the senses, and conveying information in a robust and personalized sense.[1] Informed by his work as a novelist and playwright, Tilden was outlining his "seven pillars of interpretation" for the United States' nascent National Parks Service environmental interpretation program—an aspirational set of strategies for tour guides to follow.

In addition to their guides, tourists certainly make up one set of "players" on this grand heritage stage; utilizing their own understandings of the world and their place in it to "act out," either consciously or not, their part in the immediate drama of their interaction with a destination. Chapter 4's anecdote of the Evangelical Southern gentleman in Phnom Penh is a case in point. Perceiving himself as an economically privileged American Christian in Cambodia, it was difficult to find Angkor's relevance in his own life, but when he encountered a tour guide whose family had been greatly affected by the Pol Pot genocide, he interpreted his role to be that of a potential immigration sponsor, so to "save" the young woman from the present-day difficulties of her Cambodian past.[2]

275

Indeed, as many U.S. "study abroad" institutions articulate—and many independent and group travelers likewise attest—a great number of tourists are cognizant of the fact that they "represent America in world affairs"[3] simply by touring another country; Ambassador Cynthia P. Schneider, once an instructor at Georgetown University's Villa Le Balze study abroad program in Fiesole, Italy, reflexively remarked, "I am one kind of ambassador, but all of you—and all of the students who attend your programs—also are Ambassadors. These students represent America or Canada every day. A chance encounter might leave a lifelong impression on Italians they meet."[4] Canadian backpackers, their maple-leaf flag emblazoned prominently on their belongings, employ a particularly visual way of conveying this same sense of nationalistic identity and the role they unofficially represent abroad. Many have remarked that they sewed the flag onto their clothing not out of hubris, but to differentiate themselves from U.S. citizens, whom they perceive as "ugly Americans"; I have also met a number of U.S. backpackers who have branded their belongings with Canadian flags for the very same reason. Indeed, through the choice of clothing, carry-on baggage, and equipment such as cameras and water bottles, tourists are particularly wont to dress the part; informed in some way about the climate of a place, the physicality of the terrain, and the rigorousness of the itinerary they follow—as well as their own sartorial tastes—they are costumed in a particular tourist persona.

Tourists certainly compose one set of "players" on the heritage-scape stage, but there are other, less physically animate actors—the World Heritage sites themselves. These monuments move—maybe not as locomotively as their touristic counterparts—but, as previous chapters have argued, they are seen as equal actors, motivating and constraining humans interactants, informing visitors, and adding to tourists' own lived biographies. Yet similar to stage actors, tour guides and tourists themselves, these World Heritage sites are also costumed, cosmeticized and contextualized to fit the part they are to play upon the proscenium. Historic preservation initiatives, of the sort described in the discussions of the Angkor Archaeological Park, are one type of contextualizing costuming; they are a physical enhancement to the appearance of a site for the exposition of a particular narratative interpretation.

Branding the site through titles, signage and symbolic markers—in museographic and touristic speech, these elements are subsumed under the technical term "interpretation"—is another. Such forms are visual cues that inform human actors of the narrative through which they make meaning of the site, and, ultimately, help direct the dramatic script of the interaction by prescribing the forms of approaches, activities and action they should take with their monumental counterpart. But theatrical players upon the stage are not always in the spotlight; as many a budding school-age actor bemoans, sometimes a player is directed to move to the background, to serve as set-dressing, another prop that provides an aesthetic backdrop to the main drama at front stage. In some circumstances, World Heritage sites alternatively play this role, as well. Owing to these monuments' universalized valorization, event managers and even tour operators often look upon these sites as evocative backgrounds from which to stage happenings that are tangential, or even unrelated, to UNESCO's World Heritage narrative. This chapter examines some of the ways in which UNESCO and site managers direct their World Heritage players, either when they are placed in the front-stage spotlight or relegated to the background.

Front-stage:
Branding the Physical Site, Interpreting the Heritage-scape

While I have argued that UNESCO imbues the tangible place with its meta-narrative through a ritual and museological process, this claim will contribute nothing to an individual's awareness of the heritage-scape if it is not understood simultaneously with one's physical interaction with the World Heritage site. The preservationist working at the site, the local living at or near the place, or the tourist visiting it does not automatically understand its World Heritage context on his own, but rather must be made aware of it before or, better, during these varied physical interactions. This poses a pointed problem for UNESCO and the importance conferred upon individual World Heritage sites to meet the organization's placemaking objectives. It is for this reason that UNESCO allows—and indeed, encourages—a wide variety of alternative re-presentations of these sites that can diffuse this claim and contribute to the prescribed understanding of the site's meaning. Yet again, these re-presentations are indirect and do not occur simultaneously as one interacts with the place itself. To truly live up to its epistemological and emotional potential, the World Heritage site should impart this particular narrative claim contemporarily with an individual's interactive experience with the place.

A key factor is the establishment of a narrative context that will frame all subsequent physical interactions with the site, at the inception of the experience. Most commonly, this is accomplished by assigning visual elements, such as signs and symbolic markers, to the place, which succinctly and immediately convey this meta-narrative claim. As conveyed in an earlier chapter, merely affixing the title of "World Heritage site" to a monument is an act of interpretation; it may be enough to produce a basic conceptualization of UNESCO's message, for even if one is not aware of the exact articulation of UNESCO's claim, the very title is suggestive enough to express a valorizing sense of shared heritage. Indeed, UNESCO clearly regards its signage as one of the valorizing benefits of a site's World Heritage designation, and offers this boilerplate suggestion:

> The World Heritage Committee proposes the following text as an example:
> "(Name of site) has been inscribed upon the World Heritage List of the Convention concerning the Protection of the World Cultural and Natural Heritage. Inscription on this List confirms the exceptional universal value of a cultural or natural site which deserves protection for the benefit of all humanity."
> This text could be followed by a brief description of the property.[5]

In addition to, or in lieu of, this prescribed wording, signs simply stating "UNESCO World Heritage Site" can be found at ticket booths or entranceways. Sometimes these signs are large or elaborate, conveying the sense that they were deliberately placed to capture the attention of its visitors. However, sometimes the signage is small or put to the side so as not to block the vista or panoramic view of the monument. Depending on the space available, they may not even include the words "World Heritage," but rather feature the well-known emblem of UNESCO's World Heritage program as an indication of its special designation.

UNESCO's World Heritage emblem is a thoroughly thought-out symbol deliberately designed by Belgian artist Michel Olyff to represent the interrelated components of the World Heritage convention, namely nature and culture. Adopted as the official emblem of the World Heritage Convention in 1978 along with strict guidelines for its employment, the emblem features a diamond encompassed by a circle to pictorially "represent [sic] the interdependence of the world's natural and cultural diversity." UNESCO explains: "While the central square symbolizes the results of human skill and inspiration, the circle celebrates the gifts of nature. The emblem is round, like the world, a symbol of global protection for the heritage of all humankind."[6]

The emblem is an important interpretative component at World Heritage sites for a number of reasons. Since a World Heritage site is intended to convey the same universal meaning to a diversity of people with differing levels of linguistic aptitude, education or exposure to the World Heritage project, any attempt at in-depth linguistic signage will be, to a certain extent, limited. Indeed, space constraints permit only a few languages from being represented on a sign. As with other "global" localities such as airports and urban hotels, it is far more efficient to utilize pictorial signage that can quickly and a-linguistically convey a message. Furthermore, as a standardized emblem, it is able to equally convey the sense of "unity in diversity" with immediacy from site to disparate site around the world. As an interpretative re-presentation of the heritage-scape, its likeness circulates globe. Finally, UNESCO recognizes the emblem's strong potential to valorize a site or project with which it is affiliated:

> The Emblem also has a fund-raising potential that can be used to enhance the marketing value of products with which it is associated. A balance is needed between the Emblem's use to further the aims of the convention and optimize knowledge of the Convention worldwide and the need to prevent its abuse for inaccurate, inappropriate, and unauthorized commercial or other purposes.

In a word, it is the World Heritage Convention's "brand."

While this term is ubiquitously used in commercial marketing—and indeed, UNESCO's above-cited quote seems to convey the fact that there are notable commercial benefits to a World Heritage designation—what is also important to note here is the brand's ability to serve as a stand-in, a "reproducible re-presentation" of the total heritage-scape. UNESCO's emblem, among other re-presentations, is able to stoke in the viewer's mind an awareness of this very endeavor with ease and alacrity. It is UNESCO's meta-narrative of "unity in diversity" in pictorial form, and can circulate across the heritage-scape in a way that these individual, localized sites physically cannot.

As with any proprietary brand, UNESCO actively guards its usage to dissuade potential abuses. It is protected under the World Intellectual Property Organization (WIPO) act, and its use in areas and media outside of the site itself requires expressed written permission by the World Heritage Committee. Indeed, UNESCO also urges States Parties "to make full use of their national legislation, including Trademark laws"[7] to enforce these regulations. UNESCO also provides the following guidelines for the emblem's use:

- Properties included in the World Heritage List should be marked with the emblem jointly with the UNESCO logo.
- Once a property is included on the World Heritage List, the State Party should place a plaque, whenever possible, to commemorate this inscription. These plaques are designed to inform the public of the country concerned and foreign visitors that the site visited has a particular value which has been recognized by the international community. In other words, the site is exceptional, of interest not only to one nation but also to the whole world. However, these plaques have an additional function which is to inform the general public about the World Heritage

Convention or at least about the World Heritage concept and the World Heritage List.

- The Committee has adopted the following Guidelines for the production of these plaques:
    o the plaque should be placed so that it can easily be seen by visitors, but does not spoil the view of the site;
    o the World Heritage Emblem should appear on the plaque;
    o the text should mention the property's exceptional universal value, giving a short description of the site's outstanding characteristics, if possible. States Parties may use the descriptions appearing in the various World Heritage publications or in the World Heritage exhibit, which may be obtained from the Secretariat;
    o the text should include the World Heritage Convention, the World Heritage List and the international recognition bestowed to inscription on the List (however, it is not necessary to mention at which session of the World Heritage Committee the property was inscribed).
    o It may be appropriate to provide the text in several languages for sites which receive many foreign visitors.[8]

The Tower of London, for instance, is exemplary in its signage. Designated a World Heritage site in 1988, this massive fortress construction traces its history back to William the Conqueror and, through its multifarious and often-infamous usage throughout the ages, has become a symbol of the power of the United Kingdom and its ruling aristocracy. The monument's rich history and mythology has been passed down through the ages, leading it to enjoy several diverse national, cultural and regional designations, such as a "Historic Royal Palace" of the United Kingdom.[9] Because its notoriety and popularity as a tourist attraction has preceded its World Heritage designation, there is a necessity to change the narrative context within which it is viewed, from a site of British heritage to one of World Heritage. In addition to attaching helpful links on its official websites that are specially dedicated to informing visitors of the monument's World Heritage status and offering information on the meaning behind the designation, the Tower's site managers have erected a number of impressive signs to alert visitors to this valorizing dedication before they engage in direct interaction with the site. Some of the signage resemble museum placards in that they offer a description of World Heritage and what the designation means. Ohers are simply large, clear and explicit framing devices situated at opportune places as one enters the site.

Because of the popularity of the site, the ticket booth is located some distance away from the actual building, in a vast plaza commanding a sweeping view of the Tower and its environs. Since there are frequently more visitors than the Norman structure's narrow chambers can accommodate at one time, visitors are advised to arrive early at this panoramic square to purchase tickets marked with an entry time. Cuing up to the large ticket booth, the picturesque vista of the Tower is to the potential visitor's back; what the visitor sees, in addition to the booth, is a large granite wall with only the words "World Heritage Site" etched magnificently into the stone. In this way, the narrative context is established even before the visitor can purchase his entrance ticket. Just in case the vista, troublingly large entrance fee or the frenetic masses of people effectively distract the visitor from noticing the wall, the site managers have installed another granite wall leading down from the piazza to the site itself. Although not as massive—it is a low structure that does not rise to the height of an average-sized person—its similar engraving is charmingly illuminated. Since all must pass this wall as they enter the site, it serves as a literal framing agent for the visit.

Because it is also a highly popular tourist destination, the Angkor Archaeological Park's entrance is organized in a similar fashion, but with very different signage. Immediately inside the boundary of the Park, all visitors must pass through a checkpoint-cum-ticket-booth, a ritual that immediately frames all subsequent interactions within the park. Instead of an enormous granite wall with a celebratory engraving of UNESCO's valorizing title, rising out of an embankment immediately before the turn-off is a small, dark gray sign that says in both Khmer and English, "Angkor Park." Perhaps because of the nationalistic charge this material place shares, there is no mention of UNESCO on this signage. No matter; it is so small in size and periphery in sight that many miss it, especially when the visitor is a passenger on a bus. Yet the guides, too, seem to take no notice of it either. As a test, I asked different guides and drivers to stop at the sign so that I could take a photograph of it; they passed it up every time.[10] The main focal point along the barren road is this visitor's center, which greets the tourist with a parking lot, a bus checkpoint, and a small building. Groups arriving by busses need not even get out of their seat if the guide, as is often the case, procures tickets in advance. For those who do not possess tickets, one can enter a structure to purchase them; the most popular ticket is the Angkor Pass, a laminated piece of yellow paper that is valid for three consecutive days and features the visitor's photograph. It also features an image of Angkor Wat juxtaposed with UNESCO's ubiquitous symbol. The title "UNESCO World Heritage site" also appears on the permit. Given the layout of this entranceway, the choice to prominently feature UNESCO's symbol and honorific title on the ticket is a wise one; valid for multiple days and required to be shown to ticket-checkers at every major stop within the park, it continues to raise awareness of the site's World Heritage designation in the mind of its holder as he repeats the performance of flashing the pass to guards when entering a new temple.

Although these signs and symbols are often featured prominently at World Heritage sites, effectively shaping the awareness of the site's value in accordance with the heritage-scape's unifying claims, there are many possible instances where these may not be effective. People who are unaware of the existence of UNESCO or its work, as well as people who do not recognize the symbol, will find that these signs provide no extra meaning to subsequent interactions with the site. While these signs are often written in multiple languages—at least in some of the five official languages of UNESCO, but also according to visitor demographics—they would provide no meaning to tourists who are illiterate or do not understand those languages. This may not merely be an oversight, but rather a concerted effort on the part of the site manager to allow the visitor to construct his or her own meaningful interpretation of the place, as members of the British National Trust point out.

There is also the possibility that a visitor will simply not notice, or care to read, the signage. Indeed, it is one thing to distribute tickets with UNESCO's seal on it to Angkor's visitors; it is another to ensure that these symbolic references are properly consumed by them. World Heritage site managers are not alone in this problem; directors of museums and other institutions that rely on signage to provide meaning or context for object-based epistemology frequently debate this topic[11]—especially when their goal is to reach large and diverse demographics. At one end of the spectrum, the institution must take into consideration the varying abilities of the audience to comprehend the narrative claim it wishes to promote through the tangibles on display—their previous level of awareness, their education and language abilities, and their interest in the material. At the other end of the spectrum, the narrative must "speak" to the audience in ways that go beyond simple linguistics. It must take into consideration the type or level of awareness, the remembered narrative claims that are already attributed to the place or object, and any cultural or ideological perspectives that may be associated with them. This assures that the narrative would be given proper attention and not fall upon deaf or incredulous ears. Thus, it is one thing to offer a title or blanket statement framing an Angkorian tourist's interactions with a site, but it is another thing to convince him of this status when his awareness of the site may already have been shaped by other, possibly contentious ideologies.

Conceptual narratively may diverge even farther from UNESCO's heritage claims as these sites are co-opted by the for-profit sector eager to capitalize on these sites for their own commercial interests. The travel industry is especially eager to shape sites' narratives to make them more appealing to certain demographics of clients. Narratives predicated once again on binary opposition abound, especially for post-colonial nations in Southeast Asia, Latin America or Africa—as travel articles such as "Ruins By Day, Luxury By Night" convey.[12] Orientalist claims contextualize these sites as places for exciting exploration, interaction with supposedly backwards natives, encounters with untamed nature, or locations affording unabashed purchasing power. Hotels, restaurants and souvenir shops also offer their own claims in an attempt to link an awareness of their own commercial enterprises with that of the site for profit. Although Siem Reap is filled with hotels of all qualities, an inordinate amount are four- to five-star luxury properties, which, through their design, aim to perpetuate an Orientalist, Old *Indochine* ambiance; it seems the country's well-known colonial history and the people's poverty are both conducive to this commercial end.

One of the most venerable and historic of these hotels, despite having dedicated significant funds to positive development and historic preservation efforts, nevertheless engages in such a practice, as well. Upon checking into its luxurious silk-adorned rooms, the visitor is offered a bedtime story: an excerpt from Henri Mouhot's journal, beautifully printed on high-quality card stock, describing the strangeness of the natives and the thrill of discovering the vestiges of a lost civilization in the Kampuchean jungles. Through this story, the hotel attempts to contextualize the entire experience of visiting Angkor through the company's own colonial narrative; it is a not-untrue narrative of luxury, set in a thrilling time of discovery, where the White visitor supposedly lived like a king—or, better still, like a colonist, who, through his enlightened culture, considered himself more advanced than the backward native rules.[13] This bedtime story, however contained within the chamber room it may seem to be, may nevertheless damage the overall Angkorian experience the heritage-scape would wish on its visitors. As the visitor most often checks into the hotel before exploring the Angkorian ruins, this narrative colors the tourist's awareness of the value of the monuments; it frames all the other claims he may encounter—including the subsequently conveyed World Heritage claim. Angkor is re-presented once again, this time as a site of playful colonial exploration.

As indicated by these examples of alternate re-presentations, the sight of a World Heritage title etched upon a wall, the mere presence of UNESCO's emblem on a ticket stub, or even an explanatory note posted like a museum placard near the site may not suffice against the glut of enticing or more ideologically forceful re-presentations. Museums and site managers must be aware of the presence of these alternative narratives simultaneously vying for the visitor's attention, because they could be recalled as he interacts with the physical site. They must try to make their narrative attractive and convincing; they must make their location speak to each individual group on their own terms. In this way, they can assure that the heritage-scape's meta-narrative claim is appropriately conveyed. Offering a more personalized approach to contextualizing these experiences may best render the site essentially "all things for all people,"[14] when the phrase "all people" includes an enormous range of prior knowledge, prior expectations, and learning abilities. Because this type of learning is a sociocultural "dialogue between the individual and his or her environment through time" that is a "contextually driven effort to make meaning,"[15] as John Falk and Lynn Dierking contend, such an approach must be extremely interactive. This interactive approach must measure a visitor or group of visitors' awareness level, ideological understandings, and expectations of the experience, and then tailor the contextualizing narrative to fit best with these variables.

Digital and satellite-based technology is providing one answer to the constructivist interpretation dilemma, as Brian Bath reveals in a particularly illuminating essay on the proposed use of new technologies at Stonehenge. Designated in 1986, Stonehenge and its related prehistoric henge at Avebury are arguably "among the most famous groups of megaliths in the world," as UNESCO states.[16] Like Angkor, the recognition of their value extends to the earliest days of heritage conceptualizations. Also like Angkor, since the 1860s Stonehenge had been endangered by touristic pressures and looting associated with unregulated visitation.[17] Unlike Angkor, however, the present management answered these problems by limiting direct interaction with the monument, constraining visitors to gaze at the structure from a distance. As Bath states, "One of the major problems all such sites face is that everyone wants to see it and be there, even though they would prefer that all other visitors were not there as well to spoil the view and the atmosphere. The temporary solution has been to rope off the henge to give everyone a clear view."[18] Bath diplomatically attributes this solution to providing an equal tourist experience for all, rather than arguing that this was a conservation-based decision, for a particular reason: he reveals a number of ways that tourists, through the use of new technologies, can interact more closely with the World Heritage site without the erection of damaging interpretative signage that would adversely affect the historic environment's "sensitive setting."

One innovation currently being considered is the introduction of "video wands," which Bath describes as "small, hand-held computers that provide audio information, as well as having a small screen that can provide graphics, texts and images." Upon the purchase of a ticket to the site, visitors would individually program their wands by completing a computerized questionnaire on their interests, knowledge of the site, and expectations. Coupled with satellite-based technology, these wands could detect the spatial location of a tourist within the World Heritage site and offer geographically-exact information. "You simply link a Global Positioning System (GPS) to an audio tour and every visitor can be told exactly where they are, and where everything else is, at any point on the landscape."[19] He muses that "such a device would have the benefit, not only of fully interpreting the landscape, but would, as it could at Stonehenge, help spread the visitor load at peak times."[20] That is, based on the information provided by the tourist, these wands could suggest visiting the other henges and related sites within the geographically diffuse "Stonehenge, Avebury and Related Sties" World Heritage site, thereby reducing the load of tourists at any given time. Such a solution would also be of great benefit at the Angkor Archaeological Park, which, like Stonehenge, Avebury and Related Sites similarly boasts a great number of temples but where tourists are concentrated in only a limited number of these fragile constructions. "This is an example of satellite technology helping to rid the landscape of unsightly signs and helping to conserve the landscape by allowing (or even encouraging) visitors to take different paths through the landscape in order to reduce wear and tear on the fragile downland."[21]

While sometime in the future computers or other forms of information and communication technologies may be able to appropriately effect this level of interactivity,[22] today tour guides and docents can fulfill this task if they are trained properly and sensitive to different groups' particular needs, preconceptions and experiences. Since learning can be successful through sociocultural interactions with the place, employing the proper guide is one way that could alleviate the gap between how the site, through its preservation, curation and management, speaks to the visitor and address his or her requirements.[23] While the architectural and decorative elements of the site often remain fixed, as do the content in any informational placards added, guides are not. They are fluid; they can gauge interest and prior knowledge; they can actively interact with the varied visitors to meet their level of understanding and method of learning.

Tour guiding is "interpretation" in its most embodied sense. As Freeman Tilden wrote, interpretation is "an educational activity which aims to reveal meanings and relationships through the use of original objects, by first-hand experience and by illustrative media, rather than simply to communicate factual information"[24] —in short, that it is mediatory in its own right, a way to provide the object of visitation a meaningful voice to the visitor. In its embodied sense, it is a performative re-presentation, a method of teasing out those qualities of the monument and its narrative script that resonates with the particularities of a group. It is the pivoting capacity of face-to-face interpretation, or tour guiding, that led Tilden to contend it is "the highest and best form of interaction, and the

. . . best use of visitors' time," as Margi Bryant notes.[25] Written for the United States National Parks Service in 1957, Tilden's classic text, *Interpreting Our Heritage*, outlines six fundamentals of interpretation; noteworthy are their highly performative, re-presentational qualities:

1. Any interpretation that does not somehow relate what is being displayed or described to something within the personality or experience of the visitor will be sterile.
2. Information, as such, is not Interpretation. Interpretation is revelation based on information. But they are entirely different things. However, all interpretation includes information.
3. Interpretation is an art, which combines many arts, whether the materials presented are scientific, historical, or architectural. Any art is to some degree teachable.
4. The chief aim of Interpretation is not instruction, but provocation.
5. Interpretation should aim to present a whole rather than a part, and must address itself to the whole person rather than any phase.
6. Interpretation addressed to children (say, up to the age of twelve) should not be a dilution of the presentation to adults, but should follow a fundamentally different approach. To be at its best it will require a separate program.[26]

Tilden's argument was seminal, not solely for heritage management in America, but also in Europe.[27]

As Tim Copeland reveals, such an approach is subsumed under the "Constructivist" theory of education, whereby "the interpreter(s) construct(s) a view of the site but from the perspective of a wider maturity of experience. In mediating the interpretation to a public, that maturity of experience is often hidden and a more didactic account is presented."[28] Though the guide's knowledge of the "facts"—the history, dates, personalities, aesthetic styles, and so forth—is still of utmost importance, the ability to "interpret" the material—that is, to select and convey this knowledge through his or her personality, speech and actions—is just as important. Guides work on a microcosmic level the way that ICOMOS and UNESCO work at the macro level by teasing out bits of a locality's total life history to create a World Heritage site whose meaning is in line with the heritage-scape's meta-narrative claim. Indeed, the U.S. National Parks Service offers an anecdotal reference to archaeologist Dale King's 1940 exhortation of guides to focus not on sterile facts, but emotional significance. King's advice predates Tilden's arguments, yet captures perfectly the linkage between heritage interpretation and UNESCO's own endeavor to tease out and convey its meta-narrative claim of unity in diversity:

Let us try to analyze our monuments in terms of their real meaning and importance. Let us attempt to stress those parts of their story which have some lasting value and significance. We can't expect John Q. Public to go away and remember forever that the compound wall is 219 feet, six inches long, or that the thumb print is to the right of the little door in Room No. 24. We can try to make the people of that vanished historic or prehistoric period live again in his mind. Give him some insight into their troubles and joys, show him that they were human, and underline their differences from us as well as their likenesses to us. In other words, build understanding, and, eventually, tolerance.[29]

Just as the preservationists re-present the place's narrative in the heritage-scape's context, so too can the guide filter these same bits and pieces of the place's narrative once again, this time in accordance with the expectations and abilities of the individual groups. In the constructivist view, "The interpreter uses the selection of evidence to make a construction that will either involve fitting the evidence into already available mental schemas (assimilation) or producing new ones to accommodate the selection (accommodation)."[30] This is not always an easy task; because of the almost infinite combinations of understandings, personalities and skill sets that a tour escort must negotiate and master, an excellent guide for one group does not necessarily make an excellent guide for another group. As Copeland points out, "A new mental schema is likely to result from cognitive dissonance or cognitive conflict. This occurs when the new evidence does not fit the interpreter's present experience or when the generally accepted interpretation is viewed through a new viewpoint."[31]

Tamar Katriel reveals this in her monograph examining tour guides at Israeli kibbutzim; she relates a particularly poignant story of an older, seasoned guide who took a group of Holocaust survivors who settled on a kibbutz not far from the one in which she had lived. Normally effective and charming, the guide "Sara" excitedly treated these former pioneering "old-timers" as peers, only to find that she could not sustain their attention:

[D]espite her obvious delight in taking on this group, the audience's obvious familiarity with the pioneering world depicted in the display, her highly personalized style, and her expressed feelings of solidarity with her audience, a good many of the visitors left the guided tour in the middle and began to roam around the museum and in its garden on their own. Even the few who stayed throughout the tour did not seem to resonate with the story to the extent that both the guide and I had expected. It was clear that she was more invested in telling the story than they were interested in hearing it out. They had to be coaxed into attending to the guide's account with repeated requests for silence or attention. . . . Noting the elderly visitors drop one out after another, I followed the shrunken group to the end of the tour route, inwardly cringing at the guide's unaccustomed entreaties for silence and attention and wondering what had gone wrong. . . .

Reflecting on this tour, I realized that the pathos-filled discourse of the guide, which most visitors either resonate with or take in their stride, did not go down well with that group. For them, it seems to me, the drama of Jewish pioneering—which his the drama of the New Jew as an active, future-oriented maker of history—with its themes of personal sacrifice, collective struggle, and national revival, was eclipsed by the story of the destruction of Jewish life in Europe and the indelible personal and collective loss it entailed for them personally. . . . They could not wholeheartedly or even indifferently participate in this celebration of the pioneering spirit without hearing in it the echoes of the cultural vindication, and even disapprobation, that greeted many Holocaust survivors who arrived in Israel as refuges in the late 1940s and early 1950s.[32]

As this anecdote reveals, differences in perspective, approaches and life experiences may lead to ineffective moments of interpretation. I have observed this frequently at a number of World Heritage sites in Italy and in Southeast Asia. There is sometimes a generational or class gap; I noticed this occur once between a group and a tour guide in a popular Tuscan village. One of the most sought-after (and expensive) guides in the town is a knowledgeable tri-lingual woman who speaks frankly and casually, and, belying her somewhat advanced age, whose dress is as spunky as her strong personality. Often this resonates effectively with visitors, who are attracted to her down-to-earth style, youthful nature, and ostensible love of shopping. However, extremely wealthy groups formed a pattern of distaste for this guide; one client of noble lineage, who sponsored a number of tours that involved this Tuscan guide, seemed to convey the sense that she was too cartoonish, not proper enough, and nouveau-riche.

Sometimes competition within an ethnicity can be the cause of ineffectiveness. An extremely famous client from the United Kingdom who has led a number of American groups expressed a strong abhorrence for another guide in a different Tuscan city. Unlike the first guide, this one was not an Italian but a transplant—she shared the same ethnicity as the client—and spoke with a very proper-sounding accent that often conveyed to her American guests a type of authoritative gravitas. She was extremely passionate, and very knowledgeable about the history and culture of the city in which she interpreted. The normally passive and amicable client was an expert in the itinerary's particular theme, and it became clear after a number of group tours that both subtly jockeyed for epistemological supremacy in the eyes of their groups.

Ethnic differences may also lead to ineffectiveness, as was the case with a very popular (Catholic) Vietnamese guide who led a tour of Jewish Americans through Saigon's historic Chinatown district, Cholon. At one ethnically Chinese temple, the guide began to list his very Vietnamese prejudices against the Chinese, likening them to stereotypes of American Jews. This immediately prompted an outcry among the travelers. Despite his recognizable mastery of Vietnamese history and culture, personable nature, first-hand experience, and even his efforts to apologetically correct his unfortunate slippage, it was very difficult to regain the group's attention or trust for the remainder of the tour.

Just as a linguistic interpreter is most effective when translating for an audience who shares his mother tongue, a guide who shares similar life experiences, interests or personality traits with his clients might be better suited than one who "speaks" in another set of cultural metaphors, expressions or concerns. It therefore becomes incumbent for the site manager to have multiple official guides that can be selected to accompany a range of groups, in order to effectively convey the proper narrative context to the physical interactions at the World Heritage site.

The Material Site as a "Background Re-Presentation"

Despite the valorization they enjoy, World Heritage sites are sometimes re-presented not as the central focus of interaction, but rather as mere setting for other activities. In these surprisingly common occurrences, they serve as backstage "set dressing" for a variety of staged performances. The monument or site is not the focus of one's attention or primary interaction, but rather is used as a container that visually contextualizes some other object or interaction. It becomes something's "ambiance" or "background." Here, the physical interactivity is indirect; that is, all of the social aspects of place—such as physical interactions, cultural manifestations and interpersonal exchanges—happen in the site's shadow but are not linked to it. While the site is thought to impact these social performances, either by imbuing value or coloring the overall decisions one makes, these activities would be performed almost completely regardless of whether the site was actually there or not. Like other types of re-presentations featuring the authentic site itself, the place is valued for its unique link to the past, and is thought to color the performances it frames with this added value. Thus, the heritage narrative is most often left intact, celebrated as a unique drawing point for the event. Since the heritage-scape's meta-narrative claim broadly appeals to audiences on a "universal" basis, it often is preferred over those locations that enjoy a more limited appeal. Depending on the characteristics of the particular World Heritage site, coupled with the narrative claim intended to be espoused by its site managers, different articulations of this theme emerge, from literal "background re-presentations" to looser, more ambiental re-presentations.

Almost since their inception in the 1970s, World Heritage sites have been featured as literal "background re-presentations," either formally or informally playing the role of a "set dressing" or performative setting to special events such as concerts, stage plays, special lectures, feats of oratory, or private receptions. This trend, however, extends much farther back through history, as the ancient peoples throughout the world have consistently chosen to perform in venues to which they already had attributed greater value. It was their hope that the place's separate valorizing narrative would imbue their own special event with extra value. Early people from the East to the West have constructed religious edifices upon what they considered as special loci of veneration or spiritual transcendence; temples were constructed at the site of an oracle, *torii* atop a sacred mount, rune stones marking an important vista, and basilicas above a saint's body. Many secular performances were also held in the shadow of these more value-laden places; the ancient Greeks and Romans are especially renowned for having constructed immense and elaborate theatrical spaces. These theaters were beautiful in and of themselves but, more importantly, were many times located in the choicest of valorized locales throughout the Ancient Western World. This was especially the case in the fascinating provinces outside of Rome, such as Libya, Gaul and Sicily. While all amphitheaters are constructed to be framing agents themselves, Taormina's Hellenistic Teatro Greco was specifically built to incorporate the outside environment into the background. The action on the stage was intended to be further framed by stunning vistas of Mt. Etna and the expansive Mediterranean Sea peeking through the large open archways behind the rostrum. Today, as an archaeological vestige, a historic monument, and a millennia-old theatre whose acoustics remain optimum, it provides a wondrous venue for concerts and cultural events.

Although Taormina's Greek Theater is not yet a World Heritage site—it is mentioned on Italy's Tentative List as a potential Natural-Cultural "Mixed Site," however—there are indeed Roman theaters that enjoy UNESCO's valorizing designation themselves, such as Arausio, located in Orange, southern France. Considered "the best preserved of all great Roman theatres" by UNESCO—one online tour operator has written, "it's 20 centuries later and the acoustics can't be beat"[33]—it provides a unique and value-added setting for a number of unamplified performances, including the famed lyric festival *Les Chorégies d'Orange*, held every summer since 1860. Considering Greece's recognition as the founder of the performing arts in Western culture, it is understandable that this country also boasts a number of World Heritage theaters. And the Greeks continue to utilize many as such, demonstrating an unbroken link between the country's tangible and intangible cultural properties. Among these is the Archaeological Site of Epidaurus, a "sprawling" theater complex constructed around the fourth century B.C. in a small valley in the Peloponnesus about two hours from Athens. Considered to be "one of the purest masterpieces of Greek architecture" by UNESCO when the organization designated the theater in 1988,[34] it also provides the stage to the performance of ancient and modern theatrical masterpieces; the fifty-five-row, 14,000-seat property is home to an annual theater festival and hosts Greek National Opera performances. Closer to the symbolic heart of ancient Hellenic culture, a widely attended annual festival of Greek theater is held in the Odeon of Herodes Atticus, an amphitheater built at the base of the UNESCO-designated Acropolis in the first century AD. Known as "the Herodeion," it also provides a background for contemporary concerts and ballets, including a blockbuster spectacle held by Greece's own New Age artist, Yanni.

While these particular World Heritage sites were specifically constructed as theaters, there are also World Heritage sites that were originally constructed for unrelated purposes but are now employed as backdrops or containers for theatrical spectacles. Many times these re-presented sites are embraced because they are considered to share a narrative with the particular performance, adding more historic value to it. Made famous by Shakespeare as the site of mythical Hamlet's Elsinore, Denmark's Kronborg Castle was designated a World Heritage site in 2000 and has served as the venue for a highly regarded, annual Shakespeare festival. This popular festival is held not inside the castle, but rather in an open-air theater some distance from the World Heritage site, so that the vista of the castle literally serves as an immutable background. The performances framed by Kronborg not only draw an international audience, but important stage actors the world over vie for the privilege of playing the fictitious prince in the shadow of his "authentic" palace. Among others, Richard Burton played Hamlet here in 1954. Derek Jacobi and Kenneth Branagh are also counted among the list of Shakespearian players drawn to the power of the World Heritage site to imbue their own craft with added universal value and authenticity; they performed here in 1979 and 1988 respectively.

Perhaps the most spectacular example of this phenomenon is Yanni's famed 1994 concert, *Yanni Live at the Acropolis*. Performing at the 2,000-year-old Herodeion in the shadow of the Parthenon, arguably his motherland's most renowned World Heritage Site, the contemporary pianist offered a blockbuster audio presentation to a standing-room-only crowd that he billed as "a stunning spectacle of sight and sound."[35] Many audience members agreed, and the album has sold well over seven million albums worldwide, reached more than half a billion television viewers in 65 nations, and, at the time, its video recording became the third best-selling music video in history.[36] On one online books and music distributor's website, www.amazon.com, fans indicated that, even when simply listening to the audio recording, understanding that it was recorded in such a universally valued site imbued the music with added value. One wrote, "It is a double-feast for I could feel not only the music but also the beautiful [sic] scenes of the structures from Acropolis appropriately picturized for the song." The backdrop also seemed to have succeeded in imbuing the heritage-scape's universalizing narrative to the music; the same blogger wrote, "I think Yanni envisioned this album for all kinds of people."[37] And indeed, three years later, Yanni produced a second album and video entitled *Tribute*, a compilation of concerts held at other World Heritage sites, such as India's Taj Mahal and China's Great Wall. This, too, was 1998's first multi-platinum seller according to the Recording Industry Association of America.[38] One cannot know for certain if Yanni would have enjoyed the same success if these same live performances were recorded at traditional concert venues. It is doubtful, considering *Live at the Acropolis* and *Tribute* quickly became the Greek artist's best-selling and most enduring albums—outselling his subsequent live recording at the Royal Albert Hall, a London theater.

Such "once-in-a-lifetime" performances at World Heritage sites can be considered blockbuster events. Blockbusters are important for a variety of reasons; they not only contribute to the commercial interests of the performer, but also can positively contribute to raising awareness of the site itself. In an era of movie blockbusters, instantaneous flows of information, and more selective audiences, museums and tourist destinations alike constantly need to differentiate themselves from one another by innovating their presentation styles in order to keep audiences returning and to capture new segments of the population.[39] As the description of Hội An showed, there is a trickle-down effect for blockbusters that induce the participation of co-sponsors, who share site managers' hopes for short-term economic profit and a positive, long-term image branding through its association with World Heritage.

The Cambodian government partnered with the Singapore-based Raffles Group, the owners of Siem Reap's historic Grand Hotel d'Angkor, to produce a spectacular and much-lauded benefit concert by famed tenor José Carreras at the Angkor Archaeological Park. This gala "evening unlike anything in the 900-year history of the monument" featured 150 dancers, 32,000 flowers, 20 life-size ice carvings, 4 elephants, 70 chefs and a coterie of "magnificent" orange-robed monks stationed at various positions at the monument.[40] Commenting on the monks, journalist Seth Mydans accurately states,

It was their robes that were being used to enhance the evening, though, not their religion, here in Cambodia's most venerated Buddhist shrine. The temple, it turns out, is a stage manager's dream, with its five looming towers, its grand porticos and its layered rows of pillars."[41]

Performing in the shadow of an illuminated Angkor Wat in December 2002, which one nonprofit organization also called "an impressive stage for this prestigious concert,"[42] Carreras raised US$160,000 for four aid organizations—the Cambodian Red Cross, Veterans International for Landmine Victims, WildAid and SOS Children's Villages.[43] But funding was not the only thing raised. In addition to the thousand international guests who joined the Cambodian Prime Minister Hun Sen and his Cabinet in attendance, over one hundred members of the world media, including journalists from *The New York Times*, CNN, Associated Press, Reuters, the *Bangkok Post* and Danish Broadcasting also attended the gala outdoor dinner and concert, which featured speeches by government officials and video clips prepared by each nonprofit organization. Tickets were as expensive as $1,500.00 per person.[44] No doubt most of these dignitaries and high-end visitors chose the luxurious Grand Hotel d'Angkor for their accommodations, whose rooms begin at about US$150.00 per night. Thus, the spectacular fusion of Angkor and Carreras served to raise funds for the Cambodian government, nonprofit humanitarian organizations and for-profit companies such as Raffles; it also raised equally varied levels of awareness—for the World Heritage site, for the plight of the Cambodian people and the aid organizations actively working to alleviate it, and for the universal valor of charity which underlies the heritage-scape's claim of "unity in diversity." Though Angkor was relegated to the background, coupling the great intangible musical patrimony of the West with such a prominent heritage site of the East seems to further underscore UNESCO's message.

Blockbusters are not the only instances when World Heritage sites serve as background re-presentations. Many World Heritage sites also play the backdrop to less publicized, specially organized cultural events on a smaller scale. High-end group tours often offer special performances, lectures, art exhibitions or cocktail receptions within a site for a particular group. In this case, the site provides a picturesque and unique backdrop, valorizing the often unrelated action taking place at center stage. Yet sometimes, too, these experiences can complement well the overall tourist interaction with the tangible heritage site by inserting an added dynamic—intangible culture. In Cambodia, tour operators and site managers often fuse the two to illustrate the breadth of Khmer culture by inserting an Apsara dance recital within the touring itinerary. A sinuous classical dance that has been associated with the royal Cambodian court for over a millennium, the Apsara would be performed to mark important religious and royal observances, and images of these lithe performers in their uniquely contorted positions adorn many a bas relief in Angkorian temples; the pink sandstone Banteay Srei boasts especially beautiful depictions. Like the Western-style ballet, it is an expository form of movement that utilizes a codified system of gestures that takes years to master, and each performance re-tells a classical myth or a religious story. The Apsara dance is believed to be as old as Khmer people themselves, and is a symbol of refinement, respect and spirituality—three virtues the culture holds in particular esteem. Indeed, accompanied by sacred music played by an orchestra and a female chorus providing the narration, the dancers were traditionally considered the king's messengers to the Gods and the ancestors.[45] Unfortunately, the Khmer Rouge genocide imposed a massive cultural forgetting of this unique cultural expression; they disbanded the king's Royal Ballet, sent its patrons into the rice paddies, and killed many of the performers, whom they considered symbols of courtly refinement and of education. According to UNESCO, today only a very few master dancers remain who are able to pass on the intricate system of movements properly. Because of the dance's historical and cultural value, coupled with its precarious status in the cultural memory of the people, UNESCO declared the Apsara dance to be a Masterpiece of Oral and Intangible Culture in 2003, and devised an "action plan" for regenerating the Apsara dance. This plan calls for training new students, funding public and private troupes, reinforcing legal protection for the performers, and researching the ancient rites with an eye to expanding the current institutional repertoire. It also calls for promoting the dance among the Khmers and outsider visitors; while one of the dangers it faces is denegration into a "mere tourist attraction,"[46] "dance festivals" are specifically mentioned as a means of "enhancing public awareness and appreciation of the Royal Ballet."[47]

Some preservation societies have partnered with performing arts schools to offer an experience at the Angkor Archaeological Park that fuses the grand, tangible cultural properties of the park with that of the sublime, intangible performances. Exclusive Apsara dances can be arranged with special permission through the World Monuments Fund in the temple of Preah Khan. The New York-based preservation organization offers selected guests a performance by young students of the Enfants D'Asie (ASPECA) orphanage; guests can enjoy this show at a candle-lit cocktail reception within the grounds of the ancient Khmer temple. These arrangements mutually benefit the two non-profit organizations, as they generate both funding and awareness of the activities of each. The World Monuments Fund does not arrange this spectacle casually—the minimum donation alone is $7500.00 as of 2008—but is dedicated to effectively conveying the heritage-scape's meta-narrative claim through a complete visitation experience. Taking appropriate means to be "all things to all people," an organization representative, often the Project Manager in Siem Reap, will conduct a brief lecture about the organization, the temple and its restoration, as well as the background of the dance and the orphaned performers.

Although World Monuments Fund officials are thankfully tenacious in ensuring the integrity of the heritage-scape's meta-narrative claim even while representing their site as a background venue, there are other instances where commercial businesses perform their own ideological claims even as they reference the dance's valorized status. Restaurants and hotels catering to the tourist crowd have made a niche market for what can only be called Apsara "dinner theater." At the most commercial of outfits are the buffet, where the space is large, the crowd rowdy, and the food and performances are poor. One look at the locale can swiftly reveal the restaurant's priority—such venues more closely resemble beer gardens than performance spaces, with guests coming and going as they please; their layouts are not even conducive to viewing the show. It is possible in some locations that guests, seated without a direct view of the performance and engulfed in a babbling din of inattentive tourists talking among themselves, may not even realize a performance is taking place. The Grand Hotel d'Angkor does its part to promote the Apsara dance in a more central way, though nevertheless more for entertainment purposes than for epistemological ones; it is famous among the high-end tourist population in Siem Reap for offering an elaborate dinner theater feast on its property. Guests who have reserved their space sometimes days in advance arrive at sundown to a partitioned section of the hotel's yard, where, after checking off their names, they are granted entry into an open-air barbeque. It is a feast for the senses, with bountiful buffet tables offering Western, Chinese, Japanese, Thai, Vietnamese and Cambodian fare. After filling their plates, guests sit communally on picnic benches, eating, drinking and talking. At some point in the evening, young, school-age performers take the stage and perform their dances. The guests' attention is initially captured, thanks to the sound system and the light show that introduces the ballet, but often this attention is only sustained for a few dances before the chatting begins again. After all, this is the entertainment for the night. It is not an ideal situation, but better than those found at the other restaurants in town.

When an entire city, town, or *centro storico*[48] is designated a World Heritage site, however, the commercialism associated with background representations sites inadvertently reaches its fullness. Tourist cities such as Rome, Florence, Venice, or Hội An and Huế, play background not only to performances of the monotony of daily life, but to the commercial interests of the tourist sector. When a city or town is inscribed in its entirety as a World

Heritage site, not only its temples and museums are elevated in valor, but implicitly, so are its restaurants and hotels, hostels and brothels, bazaars and shops. The designation does not stop at the façade, but extends to that which is contained within. ICOMOS clearly set this precedent when it advocated on behalf of Venice, stating, "the least palazzetto, which in Venice seems only a minor construction, would constitute the glory of many historic cities."[49] ICOMOS makes it clear that World Heritage status does not stop at the grand *palazzi* such as St. Mark's Basilica, the Doges' Palace, Peggy Guggenheim's villa and the Rialto bridge, but includes even those mere and overlooked edifices: the one-star *pensioni*, or traditional Italian motels; the stagnant canal water; the graffitied walls in the university district; the ubiquitous tourist shop and hotels are all, in fact, equally re-preventative of the heritage-scape. In addition, palaces make excellent converts to restaurant and hotels—where the more historic, universally appealing, and valorized of heritage re-presentations fare the best. They are valued for either their ambience or for the stories connected with their total life histories; both are considered conducive to facilitating a tourist's literal retreat into their fantasies of living in another time and social situation.

As the heritage movement becomes more diffuse, reclaimed hotels in particular are rising in popularity, both among hoteliers and among discriminating guests. Half-timbered farmhouses, which, at the time of their construction were the humble residences of the lower classes, are being converted into four and five star luxury hotels; their value rests not on the sumptuousness of the constructions but on the quaintness or traditional nature of their "historic settings." Mid-level European aristocracy, the ubiquitous counts and countesses who litter the English or Italian countryside, with little more than a title and an old villa or palazzo are finding it increasingly lucrative to convert their crumbling abode into a historic hotel. Often, as in the case of Venice or Hội An, they are forced into this situation, since maintaining a property in a city deemed a World Heritage site puts stringent and costly constraints on how they are maintained and modernized. And to increase their value and reach, many are joining associations of historic properties such as the *Abitare la Storia* consortium in Italy. The consortium, whose name means "Live the history," is a network of independent villa and palace owners who have converted their estates into luxury properties. Counted among the mix are palaces, ancient farmhouses, and even a few very small, one-street towns that were converted as multi-edifice hotel complexes.

Overnighting in a place with a heritage narrative may also be an attempt to imitate the lives and tastes of the rich, the famous, or the valued. I have noticed that many travelers choose to stay in hotels with celebrity associations, and often these hotels will advertise the famous people who had slept there. Copenhagen's Hotel d'Angliterre boasts large bronze plaques in its foyer listing a litany of important people who stayed there—politicians, movie stars, celebrities, corporate executives—as if its picturesque location on the historic Kongens Nytorv square and its large guest rooms were not enough of a draw. The same is true for Ha Noi's Sofitel Metropole, which boasts in every media outlet that Graham Greene supposedly wrote *The Quiet American* there, instead of pushing its excellent Vietnamese restaurant or centralized location steps from the beautiful Hoàn Kiếm Lake, a major attraction for both locals and visitors. The life history factor is also an assurance of the quality of the accommodations; if it was good enough for the celebrity, it can be good enough for the American middle-class tourist. Of course, this reasoning neglects to consider the changes that can occur in the onward movement of the years: preferences, tastes, styles, managers, chefs, and amenities are frequently different. Higher end tour groups, for example, are often interested in staying in one of Saigon's famous four-star hotels, such as the Continental, the Grand or the Rex. All of these hotels boast their one-time prominence as the preferred properties for the French Colonial and 1970s American elite; unfortunately, they have not been upgraded since that era. Nevertheless, these properties simultaneously flaunt and push to the background their World Heritage status, their commercial interests and needs taking center stage.

Fortunately, as newer World Heritage sites are designated, UNESCO and its site managers are taking steps to stave off this type of commodifying re-presentationality as best they can. At the time of Hội An's conversion from a sleepy port town to a World Heritage site, it was both small enough and relatively untouched to allow the preemptive drafting of plans aimed at limiting this problem. Consequently, there are very few hotels that exist within the small town's historic center; to accommodate the glut of tourists who flock to the town either in search of an "authentic Vietnamese experience," sprawling new resort-hotels are currently being erected on the outskirts of the town. Similar in concept to those in Siem Reap, Cambodia, they are veritable oases of lush gardens, immense teak rooms and luxurious textiles, all constructed in an idealized colonial style—with the whole World Heritage site literally sit in the background.

Finally, monuments can be turned into background re-presentations even when they are technically forbidden to be rendered as such; a visitor with enough cache or funds may very well convince site managers to use a site as a venue for private visits or receptions. These monuments can be privately opened for "extra-special visitors"; the normally prescribed rules of visitation can be stretched or outright broken under such supposedly "extraordinary circumstances." Luxury tour operators separate themselves from run-of-the-mill travel agents by designing tours laden with "private visits," "specially-arranged cocktail receptions" or "behind the scenes tours" in historic homes, monuments or temples. The Old World aristocrats who do not own a villa large enough to be converted into a bed and breakfast or hotel can still rent out their historic locale for cocktail receptions or as a venue for the increasingly more common "destination wedding." Venice's St. Mark's Basilica, in all of its gilded Byzantine splendor, never looks better than when opened secretly at night for tour groups—a private visit this author had provided many times to his groups. Like the Doges of old who constructed the immense church for their own private use, tourists can enact their fantasies (and, sometimes, their belief) of being better than the throng of commoners who line up for hours just to be jammed into the church during normal visiting hours. Likewise, the Vatican opens the Sistine Chapel and the rest of its rich museum holdings, allowing, for a hefty price, visitors to liken themselves to Pope Sixtus, rather than to line up for literally hours only to be quickly herded through Michelangelo's masterpiece like cattle.

A State visit is another common instance of utilizing background re-presentations. Because of their universality, intransience and valorized status, politicians often prefer to utilize World Heritage sites as backgrounds to imbue their visits, speeches, and even their own biographies, with added value and appeal. The Presidential transplant to Texas, George W. Bush, in a well-conceived plan to be seen as a "real American" cowboy, eschewed his family's New England refuge for his Texas ranch, where he was frequently available for photo opportunities while cleaning brush or digging ditches. Presidents and politicians hoping to be connected with the Conservation movement have given speeches at the Grand Canyon, Old Faithful, or other natural heritage sites. The fascist dictator Benito Mussolini preferred to address crowds from the balcony of the Palazzo Venezia, located in the historic center of Rome—the Roman forums and the Coliseum in the background. More contemporary occurrences include a 1999 State Visit by then-President Bill Clinton and his family to China. Images were projected around the world of the First Family alone amid the famed clay statues of Emperor Qin in Xian, which were designated a World Heritage site in 1987; this event followed images taken the day before of the Presidential family enjoying a specially-arranged cultural performance "extravaganza" by "scores of dancers in elaborate silk robes," according to CNN correspondents. When used as a venue for a concert, a performance, a wedding reception, a Presidential photo op, a restaurant or a hotel—wherein these actions take center stage—World Heritage sites become background re-presentations.

Conclusion

In the spirit of chapter 1, this section has examined World Heritage sites as monumental mediators—social actors in their own rights, who contain, coerce and constrain particular forms of human interaction. However, this chapter has attempted to show that these life stories are not intrinsically conveyed to the visitor. Rather, human actors—particularly site managers and tour guides—are equally able to dictate the particular manner in which their monumental subjects interact with tourists through the ways in which they position these sites within visitors' experiential place. This is largely an immaterial process of narrative contextualization that exits in apart from, yet in tandem with, the similarly immaterial act of recontextualization exercised in the politically charged field of heritage production. Through both of these acts, the site becomes a Hegelian re-presentation of itself within the touristic social system. Although specific recourse was made to the technical activity of "interpretation"—that is, the ways in which visitors are guided verbally, pictorially and literarily through the place—it should be noted that here, *every action is an interpretation*, whether it is an overt act on the part of site managers or historic preservationists, or in the subsequent interaction by tourists themselves. And every interpretation likewise produces a re-presentation of the place. It is in this inherently dialectical process that discourses concerning the value of World Heritage sites and the meaning of heritage-scape, often unintended by UNESCO or site managers, often arise. The following chapter will explore the ways that well-intentioned historic preservationists, though even more immanently constrained by the dictates of the World Heritage Convention, are nevertheless engaged in an act of interpretation—and thus re-present in a very material way—World Heritage sites and the heritage-scape.

CHAPTER NINE

PRESERVING THE PAST:
THE HERITAGE-SCAPE AND HISTORIC PRESERVATION

> *Outstanding universal value means cultural and/or natural significance which
> is so exceptional as to transcend national boundaries and to be of common im-
> portance for present and future generations of all humanity. As such, the per-
> manent protection of this heritage is of the highest importance to the interna-
> tional community as a whole.*
>
> —UNESCO, *Operational Guidelines for the Implementation
> of the World Heritage Convention*[1]

Value and the Emotional Efficacy of World Heritage Sites

Citing Georg Simmel, Appadurai shows that value "is never an inherent property of objects, but rather a judgment made about them by subjects."[2] Robert
Hewison and others similarly note the decidedly social origins of World Heritage sites' value:

> UNESCO is concerned with a variety of material objects which are deemed to
> have 'outstanding universal value.' It is the valorization of these material ob-
> jects which distinguishes them from all the others that constitute the physical
> world. These objects are from the past, and hold value because they represent
> the past in the present.[3]

Precisely because of their durability—their resistance to the destructive
flow of time—World Heritage sites are often comprehended not as objects with
life stories but as vestiges, authentic remnants calcified in a particular time and
space despite the ceaseless evolution of the world surrounding it. They provide,
as Barbara Kirshenblatt-Gimblett states, a simultaneous sensation of "then and
now,"[4] or, rather, then *in* now. Indeed, monuments are often conceived as liminal spaces[5] that transport the present viewer into the past—not an entirely fac-

tual past, but rather into the imagined past fossilized in time and rewritten by the narrative to which it corresponds. A recent statement by UNESCO's Director underscores this sentiment: "To value heritage in all its dimensions, to care for it as a treasure bequeathed to us by our ancestors, to recognize it is our duty to transmit it intact to our children, is a sign of wisdom."[6]

As LeFebvre states, "By building in monumental terms, we attempt the physical embodiment of an eternal and imperishable social order, denying change and transmuting the fear of the passage of time, and anxiety about death, into splendor."[7] Thus, the value of World Heritage sites is decidedly social in origin, and can emerge from personal, emotional interactions with the place itself, as Peter Fowler points out when he writes that "these value-laden attributes" in World Heritage sites "come not from what has happened in or survived from the past; they come solely from our contemporary minds or, perhaps more precisely for we are not dealing with the wholly rational, from that human ability to react which we identify in ourselves as an emotional response."[8]

The efficacy of these World Heritage sites lies in their emotional manipulation of memory's reflexive and processual dynamics by provoking feelings of what Stephen Greenblatt calls "resonance and wonder."[9] According to Greenblatt, *resonance* is the power of the object or site to strike a chord in the present viewer, to "reach out beyond its formal boundaries to a larger world, to evoke in the view the complex, dynamic cultural forces from which it has emerged and for which it may be taken by a viewer to stand." Operating on the reflexive aspect of memory, resonance is that quality which enables an individual to apply preexisting, culturally historicized understandings of the world in such a way that it brings to light some of the features most important to the narrative. In terms of historically global flows of tourism and their relationship to place, resonance was the impetus for early Grand Tour goers, who traveled from their contemporary eighteenth-century habitats in Northern Europe to experience first-hand their intellectual roots in Roman and Renaissance Italy. There, the monuments of antiquity could "teach"—or, rather frame—their current understandings of world history through imaginarily transporting them back to the past. They achieved an understanding of the glories of Rome by *being* there—not eighteenth-century Rome, where tumbled columns stripped of their majesty lay moss-covered and buried in silt, but almost literally "there" in antiquity, where they could see in their minds the great amphitheatres, bustling fora, and sumptuous baths in lively vivacity. This usage of monumentality and memory, as classicist Susan Alcock points out, is not limited to the Grand Tour; it hearkens back to the Romans themselves, who talked of the practice of *ars memorae*. Drawing on material mnemonic techniques linking places (*loci*) and mental images (*imagines*) "like dancers hand in hand," Roman orators embraced this "art of memory," conducting imaginary walks through the streets in order to think clearly and accurately. With great admiration, the thinkers of the Grand Tour era embraced this idea, as Yates eloquently expresses:

> The word "mnemotechnics" hardly conveys what the artificial memory of Cicero may have been like, as it moved among the buildings of ancient Rome, seeing the places, seeing the images stored on the places, with piercing inner vision which immediately brought to his lips the thoughts and words of his speech.[10]

The emotional response of resonance was that quality which allowed the French explorers, and, later, the lay-people back in France, to understand and make meaning of these strange new temples. Previous to the formation of colonial Indochina, the French missionary Charles-Emile Bouillevaux published the first detailed, though relatively overlooked, article on Angkor's temples, which he said resonated with his own religion's towering cathedrals. Centuries later, H. G. Quaritch Wales would publish an entire book detailing the correspondences between the ruins of Angkor and those of Rome.[11] More recently, scholars such as Michael Coe and Bennett Bronson have noted such resonant similarities between the Incan ruins at Machu Pichu with Angkor Wat that they have put forth comparative geographic theories concerning possible cultural linkages.[12]

Existent in binary opposition to resonance, *wonder* plays on the processual aspect of memory, introducing a new narrative claim to an individual's consciousness. Unexpectedly capturing the imagination with its "arresting sense of uniqueness," it is that quality which resists conforming to the visitor's expectations. It is the cause of the phenomena of "swooning" or weeping in front of paintings, which has been often documented throughout history, from the ancient Greeks onwards.[13] Today, wonder is often seen as the primary impetus for "post-modern" tourists who wish to "experience a culture which is thought to possess something that the tourist's culture has lost, [be it] a sense of community, spirituality, or being closer to nature."[14] Just as resonance powerfully alters memory and identity by transporting one's mind in space and time, wonder also powerfully shapes memory and identity. Noting the strangeness or uniqueness of a monumental form expands the mind and broadens horizons, allowing one to arrive at a more complete picture of the workings of diverse cultures and lands. Greenblatt excerpts a passage from Albrecht Dürer's famous journal entry describing his impressions of Mexican objects that Cortes brought back to Charles V's court to illustrate this sensation:

> I saw things which have been brought to the King from the new golden land:
> . . . all kinds of wonderful objects of various uses, much more beautiful to be-

hold than prodigies. . . . All the days of my life I have seen nothing that has gladdened my heart so much as these things, for I saw amongst them wonderful works of art, and I marveled at the subtle ingenia of men in foreign lands. Indeed, I cannot express all that I thought there.[15]

For Dürer, the feeling of wonder opened his eyes not only to new aesthetic representations, but also to the awe-inspiring diversity of mankind and its pantheon of unknown cultures. Likening his arrestingly unexpected find to suddenly coming upon "a verdant oasis in a sandy desert," Henri Mouhot clearly was taken by this sensation of wonder when he "discovered" the Angkorian monuments:

> I shall commence with the temple of Ongcor, the most beautiful and best preserved of all the remains, and which is also the first which presents itself to the eye of the traveler, making him forget all the fatigues of the journey, filling him with admiration and delight, such as would be experienced on finding a verdant oasis in the sandy desert. Suddenly, and as if by enchantment, he seems to be transported from barbarism to civilization, from profound darkness to light . . .[16]

Along with the inherent permanence of the site, which elicits such powerful emotions as resonance and wonder, comes an equally sensitive emotional awareness of its structural opposite—the monument's physical transience, which Freud may have described best as "the proneness to decay of all that is beautiful and perfect."[17] As LeFebvre points out, humans are constructive, attempting to thwart time, which is destructive. Monuments are edifices intended to endure the ravages of time, so as to spark memories of the past in the present and future minds of its viewers. The creation of these structures is thus "a demand of immortality [which] is a product of our wishes too unmistakable to lay claim to reality."[18] Yet although a place may endure after the builders have perished, it too is tangible and thus subject to the innumerous dangers of destruction that time, coupled with the material world, can impose. The acute sensation of the site's inevitable and impending destruction only adds to its desirability, its impact and its value.[19] Suffice one remark from ICOMOS' nomination file on Hadrian's Wall, which would eventually become the transnational site, "Frontiers of the Roman Empire":

> Hadrian's Wall has been respected by time. The only damage of note occurred during the second Jacobite revolt, when in 1745 General Wade had some portions of the Roman fortifications destroyed in order to establish a strategic road. Today the wall offers an incomparable ensemble of defensive constructions and settlements in an archaeological zone that is no doubt the largest in the United

Kingdom. ICOMOS wishes to emphasize the exemplary character of the nomination with respect to the Hadrian's Wall Military Zone.[20]

Hadrian's Wall, like Time itself, is regarded here as animate, almost anthropomorphic. The Wall is not a passive relic, nor does it merely continue to exist. It seems to be an actor "respected" by another actor, Time. The term *respect* is exceptionally significant. It carries the connotations of deferential regard, esteem, honor and appreciation.[21] In addition, since the term stems from the Lain *respectus*—"to look back" or assess—it is clear that a spatially situated Time plays a central role in this conception. Hadrian's Wall, like other World Heritage sites, are to be valued by Man because it has done what no Man can do—it has resisted the materially destructive movement time, thus earning the respect of Time itself.

It is no wonder, then, that UNESCO has positioned itself as the world's "preeminent legal tool for conservation," states Francesco Bandarin, the Director of the World Heritage Centre in Paris.[22] The concept of preservation is inherently tied to staving off transience; it can be defined as "the act of protecting something from loss or danger,"[23] whose goal, in this context, is to "prolong the existence of cultural property."[24] "Ensuring World Heritage sites sustain the universal value for which they have been designated,"[25] preservation is integral to the survival of the very heritage-scape. As a unique material manifestation of the heritage-scape's diversity, united and equal in importance to all of the other unique manifestations, one site's eradication would effectively de-complexify the overall heritage-scape, re-covering that which the heritage-scape had previously uncovered, and simplifying one's understanding of "unity in diversity."

Heritage and conservation are also historically linked, especially in the case of Southeast Asia's monuments. As Penny Edwards reveals, the terms *monument historique* ("historic monument") and *patrimoine* ("patrimony"—a term still used by UNESCO's World Heritage program, or *Patrimoine Mondial*) appeared in France as early as 1790, when a compendium of "national antiquities" was created to "determine, illustrate and clarify national history." *Patrimoine Française* appeared forty years later when historian François Pierre Guizot created the Inspectorate of Historic Monuments. In a particularly telling statement, Edwards argues that Guizot's Inspectorate "had a dual mandate of recovering antiquity and discovering the modern French nation," and indeed, though the Inspectorate and its heir, the 1836 Commission of Historic Monuments, were "earnestly committed to conserving past heritage, these groups often elaborated new pasts for their locality, region and nation." The formal linkage of heritage ideas to the conservation of these authentic relics also was a product of the time, as fears of "degeneration and decadence" swept through Europe at the turn of the century.[26] Indeed, this was also the era of the birth of sociology, anthropology and psychology—Comtian "social sciences" that concerned themselves with empirically pinpointing origins and evolution. Though many today consider him a naturalist, Charles Darwin was certainly a social scientist, ultimately concerned with the origins of socio-biological life. His 1871 work, *Descent of Man*, posits that humans are fundamentally social, and many of the capacities civilized races possess are the results of social evolution; he warns that, while Civilized Man is more intelligent than Savages, his instinct naturally has degenerated.[27] In fin de siécle France, Emile Durkheim, the father of sociology and, ultimately, of anthropology, discusses the differences between Primitives and Civilized in much of the same light. And, of course the aforementioned statement made by Sigmund Freud, working at roughly the same time as Durkheim, best connects heritage conservation with these socio-cultural fears of degeneration in his discussion of transience: Man's attempt to conserve heritage is a manifestation of his psychological desire to stave off his own biological degeneration.

As LeFebvre and by extension, Freud, have noted, there is a direct correlation between Western society's view of death and the struggle to preserve monumental constructions. In the Western perception of transience, death permanently halts the capacity for meaningful action—the very thing that these inspirational World Heritage sites strive to create. In this context, a decomposing monument is regarded not as changing from one form to another, or as reflecting the onward movement of time and culture, but rather as teetering dangerously on the fringes of oblivion. Conceptualized as a portal to another time and place, which produces a unifying effect with all those who come into contact with it, the inevitable destruction of a monument translates into a gradual slide into its irrelevance. As the monument is altered from the state to which its heritage value has been attributed—by looting, violent destruction or natural decomposition—the portal that it symbolizes is perceived to be irreversibly closing. And thus with the death of the monument comes the death of its contextualizing narrative; the stones that once spoke are regarded as being converted into silent gravel, rather than into stones that speak a new language.

Yet there is much scholarly literature today contending that the notion of equating death with silence and inaction is innately a "modern" Western cultural phenomenon. This is certainly the case in "Eastern" traditions informed by notions of *samsara*, wherein the body is an impermanent shell caught in cyclical regeneration within a larger reality. Yet even before the twentieth century, death was consciously understood by Westerners to be a natural part of life, something that literally touched all, present in daily life. Especially in Medieval Catholic Europe, which Mary Carruthers calls a "memorial culture" for its reliance on the instructive and action-inducing qualities of memory,[28] diffuse were the images of skeletons or bodies in advanced states of decay, aptly named *memento mori*. Espousing such a narrative claim—"memento mori" is loosely translated to mean "remember thy death"—these tangible macabre images, which were often carried on the person, were thought to inspire proper moral action as they symbolically urged Europeans simultaneously to be conscious of the transience of all life, and the omnipresence of death in life itself. Yet during the push to universally "modernize" cultures, coupled with the destructive forces of the World Wars that also contributed to the foundation of UNESCO itself, death was pushed to the fringes of Western consciousness and out of everyday life. Stringent mourning requirements for widows, such as wearing black for many years, were relaxed.[29] As Joanne Tippett points out, ladies' home journals, among other popular magazines, bemoaned the barbaric practice of holding wakes inside the house, where friends and family could "keep watch" over the decomposing body as devout Jewish-American tradition still dictates. In an overt effort to remove death from the wakeful consciousness, parlors were replaced by "living rooms"—no longer spaces to hold the deceased, but places to embrace the living. The dead were sent to special parlors—funeral parlors—whose sole profession was, and is to this day, a form of historic preservation, whereby the body is literally preserved in embalming fluid and even reconstructed in the image of the family's favorite photograph of the deceased. Such an institutionalized procedure prevents the living, when paying their final respects to the deceased, from ever committing the contemporary state of the dead body to memory.

Citing Metcalf and Huntington, Tippett asserts that this modern procedure also "prevents the necessity of a confrontation between mourners and 'the process of putrescence in the corpse' (in American society),"[30] thus separating the living from having to deal with death. As this example illustrates, for the Westerner death and the dying process is also considered a divisive phenomenon, one that irrevocably separates the living from the non-living. Increasingly in the West, the sick are placed in hospitals, the elderly in separate "retirement communities," and the dead in funeral parlors before being interred out of sight below ground or in the thick, sanitized, marbled walls of modern-day mausoleums. Gone is the time when, as Mediterranean tradition from southern Europe and the Middle East dictated, the bones of the dead were dug up, cleaned in the presence of witnesses, and permanently exposed behind the glass of a chapel altar or the trellised gate of a family mausoleum. Jennifer Hockey summarizes studies of death among British society by concluding that "the living are seen to have no direct relationship with death. It stands apart, separated off by boundaries . . . medical, social and conceptual."[31] Coupled with the narrative claim of "memento mori" as omnipresent in life, the perspective that death is divisive translates into a very problematic narrative for the heritage-scape's unifying claims.

Despite diversity—despite the bounded separation of cultures—a peaceful life can emerge only through unified action, not destructive separation. Such action, furthermore, is impelled by encounters with World Heritage sites, places universally valued for the emotion produced by their outward appearance, and the narrative that such aesthetics convey. And to ensure the emotional efficacy of these tangible sites, they must be left integral and intact. They must be preserved whole, authentic, and in a specific aesthetic manner that tangibly illustrates UNESCO's narrative claim.

Yet in present-day Southeast Asia, whose cultures are thoroughly embracing Western "modernity," such a separation between life and death may not be as pronounced; death and decomposition remains a part of traditional daily life. Whether Catholic or Buddhist, for example, death is integrated within the living space. Private shrines to the dead can be found near the entrance to residences, shops, museums, hotels and restaurants, regardless of whether these locales cater to locals or foreigners. Such forms of ancestor memorialization inside places designated for living activity serve not only as reminders of specific departed ancestors, but as types of "memento mori" in their own right. Subtly reconfirming such blurred lines between life and death, and between growth and decomposition, food offerings of fruit, tea or alcohol are often found on the shrine. Should tourists neglect to notice these often understated sites of veneration, they are often taken to large Buddhist temples in Cholon—Saigon's "Chinatown"— and to the World Heritage site of Hoi An. In these religious sites, deities are impressively honored by the burning of immense spiral rings of incense hanging from every inch of the ceiling. From the air, thick with the smell of burning sandalwood, snowfalls of ash drop onto the visitor as he watches worshipers leave offerings of food. The decomposition symbolized by the smoldering sandalwood embers quite literally touches the living as smoke is inhaled and ember dust falls upon the head and shoulders. Perhaps in a conscious effort to put on the most "modern" of faces, the Vietnamese tour operator and guide often contextualize such a visit as an example of the unique traditions of Chinese minorities in southern Vietnam.

Even if the Vietnamese attempt to convincingly distance themselves from the beautiful ritual melding of life and death in front of their insulated tourist clients, their food also belies this cultural propensity. The object of increasing anthropological study, food can be considered a primary manifestation of one's culture for its important semiotic elements. Like the experience of a place, the experience of food is at once individual and collective; it communes directly with the consumer but is produced through complex and ritualized social action.[32] It also mimics the universal human life cycle, for the basic ingredients in any food—meat, vegetables, grains and spices—are germinated, born, grown, and killed or harvested. Most importantly, food is bodily consumed, physically becoming one with the person in a way that even a World Heritage site cannot. Along with such consumption is the issue of taste, which can be considered not only a chemical and physiological phenomenon at work inside one's mouth, but also the manifested preference one has for the sensation. Like an experience of place, this preference is both individualized and socially mediated; and, based on the meaning one makes of it in the memory, taste is used discriminately. One smells, one tastes, and one ingests food—and he determines whether he likes it or not.

In Vietnam and other areas of Asia, most notably Korea with its famed *kimchi*—a form of fermented cabbage—the food includes strong elements of decomposition. While their contemporaries in the West shun the consumption of decaying food as sickness inducing—and indeed, Americans especially inject inordinate amounts of preservatives in most regularly consumed, packaged foodstuffs[33]—Vietnamese and Thai utilize *nước mắm* as a foundational ingredient in almost all of its dishes. Literally translated as "fish sauce," nước mắm is, put indelicately, the oil extracted from barrels of salted, rotting fish.[34] Western travelers to Vietnam, especially when visiting the Mekong Delta, which is renowned for its superior nước mắm and which prepares inordinate amounts for export around the world, are often struck by its pungent smell, repulsed by what they consider the sickening odor of dead fish.[35] Yet for the Vietnamese, this distinctive smell of decomposition, and its accompanying taste, are akin to ambrosia—truly the taste of the Gods. Chef Mai Pham cites an old Vietnamese proverb, "Without good fish sauce, the father's daughter will not shine" to illustrate this point, writing:

> I have always been struck by the above saying. On one level, it points to the Vietnamese view of the universe and how everything is seen from the family's perspective. The implied pronoun—in this case "she"—is replaced with the "father's daughter." On another level, it suggest that without good fish sauce, the quintessential sauce of Vietnamese cuisine, *food can never taste good*, no matter how talented the cook. While the saying about fish sauce may sound a bit exaggerated, it really isn't.[36]

As Pham conveys through this proverb, the chemical taste of, essentially, decomposition, is not only preferred by the Vietnamese, but is fundamental to their cuisine—and, indeed, to their very worldview. It is put in soups and sauces, consumed cooked or cold with chilies. Here in another instance, death and decomposition is certainly not shunned, reduced or eliminated, but is truly a welcomed building block of life.

Although this discourse on divergent conceptions of death touches on themes that do not directly deal with historic preservation, it is nevertheless relevant to the topic at hand. All of these examples provide valuable insight into differences between Western and Southeast Asian worldviews, indicating the particular ways in which these cultures regard decomposing structures, their reuse, and the perceived need to "preserve" or prolong their current forms. In Vietnam, for example, travelers are often amazed by the prevalence of recycling old parts and seemingly useless structures, many of which were left behind by the Americans during the war. On popular cyclo tours through Ha Noi's Old Quarter, where tourists ride past thirty-six specialized streets called the *36 Phố Phường*, each one named after a merchant's guild. While some streets are filled with shops selling modern merchandise, fruit, spices and even gravestones, others represent mechanics' shops, where often specialists repairing motorcycles can be seen ingeniously replacing parts with cans and even old scrap metal from abandoned United States machinery. In another instance some years ago before the reconstruction boom at Huế's Forbidden Purple City, visitors frequently could encounter locals living in the bombed-out ruins and tilling the open space where once stood vast royal plazas and opulent imperial edifices.[37] No doubt the sight of these farmers unearthing richly decorated ceramic tiles—which once beautified the forbidden interiors of the royal palace—only to pulverize them with hoes and till the remains under, would be upsetting to the historic preservationist. Such actions seem especially troubling in light of the fact that they had been officially considered of heritage value to the Vietnamese people by the governing authorities since the time of French colonial rule, and adequate open space remains along vast stretches of the fertile Perfume River that winds in front of the site. Chalking these instances up to either examples of Vietnamese ingenuity or of abject poverty, visitors often neglect to note the very different conception of what constitutes value in objects that have lost the capacity for use in their originally intended manners.

Such examples of structural reuse at heritage sites are not limited to Vietnam, either. Visitors and travel guides to the Angkor Archaeological Park often note instances of competing uses when visiting the World Heritage site, where visitors come to photograph a supposedly "abandoned" city and instead find its structures living loci of veneration. Indeed, unlike Catholic churches in the West, which are ceremoniously de-sanctified when abandoned or destroyed, a temple in Cambodia does not necessarily lose its religious value even when reduced to rubble or overgrown with thick banyan trees. Nor do the headless statues of the Buddha Avalokishvara or a cracked Shiva-*linga* lose their religious significance, even when they are placed on exhibition in a museum; locals dress them in saffron robes or drape them in orange cloth, offering fruit and incense.

In the National Museum of Phnom Penh, devotees give offerings of money or sweet-smelling jasmine flowers to statues on display, and pressure visitors to do the same. A curator once remarked that it must be a curious sight to visitors, but it is one that is tolerated, for it is better to engage the locals for the sake of "educating the Cambodian people about appreciating Khmer art. They find them in streams, old temples, and other places—and now they bring them to us."[38]

Even during the era in which Westerners thought these Angkorian religious locales had been "lost" to the jungle, these temples and monasteries nevertheless had continually been reused for private worship. Today, local worshipers burn incense and dress priceless broken statuary in fresh orange linens amongst the ruins of Angkor, much to the amazement of the World Heritage site's paying visitors, who scramble to photograph such a seemingly intriguing sight. Like the intrepid Vietnamese, who frequently utilize existing portions of destroyed structures in novel ways, so too do some present-day Cambodians treat the ruins of their sites. Since a sacred site does not easily lose its religious import regardless of its aesthetic or structural states, Cambodians have been seen taking small pieces from ancient religious ruins and utilizing them in the construction or maintenance of their home, in order to imbue their living quarters with the sacred.[39] Clearly the sacredness of the decomposing place and its independent pieces trumps the notions of historic or "heritage" value these pieces could have should the site be left intact or reconstructed. Again with these examples, the blurring between the living and the dead translates into an alternative perception of value inherent in heritage sites.

The concept of "World Heritage" itself is also problematic in Cambodia, a land that has suffered under the ultra-nationalist paranoia of Pol Pot. Gerd Albrecht, a German archaeology instructor training Cambodians, attests that his university students "have no concept of 'World Heritage.'" On the contrary, he states that the Khmer Rouge regime had utilized notions of "heritage" in a way completely antithetical to the heritage-scape. In this era, "heritage" became a tool for divisive ethnocentrism:

> Even during Pol Pot times, at the forced commune meetings in the evenings (the only social events which took place), people were told to respect the Angkor heritage, which was said to be absolutely outstanding in the world—but only the specific Angkor civilisation, no other heritage like pagodas, prehistoric sites etc.. This might be the reason, that Khmer believe in Cambodia as the absolute centre of the world and in Cambodians as highest standing people. The result of this: It is hard to find villagers to destroy an Angkorian temple—they respect antiquities of that time—but very easy, for only few money, they will destroy e.g. a cemetery to look for goodies or a colonial palace, just for fun. For

the Angkorian temples the looters and antiquity sellers use the Cambodian police or army.[40]

In their reeducating communes, it is clear that the Khmer Rouge used notions of heritage in a way that could unify their people through defining what
they were not. Such a method is an extreme illustration of Benedict Anderson's
fundamental notion of an "imagined community" as a group, though disparate,
that can rally together behind tangible imagery contextualized in a narrative
claim that defines itself in binary opposition to others. According to Dr.
Albrecht's assessment, Cambodians as a society value the temples and monuments of Angkor, and thus will tailor their actions to preserve it or, at the least,
to not contribute to its destruction. Yet in this archaeologist's experience, it is
clear that monuments to whose life histories is attributed another narrative—one
that does not focus on Cambodian society, and indeed, seen in opposition to it—
do not hold value and are thus dispensable. Their value lies, rather, in the economic gain or even base pleasure attained through the harvesting or destruction
of its parts. Lacking in this example, then, is the perception that these Cambodian and non-Cambodian sites can be of "universal value," that they are not only
able to emotionally affect either foreigners or Cambodian nationals, but rather
can speak to all the peoples of the world with the same unifying claim.

Universal Responsibility and the World Heritage Fund

UNESCO's narrative claim, which centers on the universal value of these designated sites, is therefore important for imparting a sense of shared responsibility
for their protection. If a site is universally valued, then it is universally desired.
The right to use these monuments in their integral forms, if only to visit them for
the memory-triggering emotional experiences of resonance and wonder, is a
right for all. Thus, the silencing of these stones through the destructive forces of
man or nature would conversely be a loss to all. Bandarin emphasizes the shared
ownership for each individual monument in the heritage-scape, which produces
this unified responsibility for the protection of every World Heritage site:

> In ratifying the Convention, States Parties commit to protect and maintain des-
> ignated sites on their territory and acknowledge that it is the obligation of the
> world community to protect all sites on the list, no matter where they happen to
> be located.[41]

Universal responsibility is a guiding force of UNESCO's preservation movement, which relies on the combined efforts of all nations for conservation causes. Indeed, although the World Heritage Convention establishing the designation of World Heritage sites was signed in 1972, UNESCO in its press documents continually trace its origins back to an extraordinary event in 1959, when it launched an international campaign to "save" the Abu Simbel temples in the Nile Valley, which were in direct line with floodwaters from Egypt's High Dam. In response to an appeal for international support, UNESCO initiated a successful worldwide campaign to raise funds for their removal and reinstallation on higher grounds, an arduous project that began in 1963 and eventually cost over 36 million dollars. From this international initiative, UNESCO actually raised 80 million dollars—44 million dollars in excess—from fifty countries and numerous private philanthropists and from large companies, which indicated the willingness of private individuals and nation-states alike to donate their resources to pressing preservation issues.

With the help of ICOMOS, UNESCO also produced a draft of a convention on the protection of cultural heritage. This document was converted into a 1962 encyclical entitled *Recommendations on the Safeguarding of the Beauty and Character of Landscapes and Sites*, outlining best practices for the preservation and restoration of natural and man-made sites having cultural or aesthetic interest.[42] In this document, not only is aesthetics valorized, but the problem of its destruction universalized; the document argues that

> at all periods men have sometimes subjected the beauty and character of landscapes and sites forming part of their natural environment to damage which has impoverished the cultural, aesthetic and even vital heritage of whole regions in all parts of the world. . . . [O]n account of their beauty and character, the safeguarding of landscapes and sites, as defined in this recommendation, is necessary to the life of men for whom they represent a powerful physical, moral and spiritual regenerating influence, while at the same time contributing to the artistic and cultural life of peoples, as innumerable and universally known examples bear witness.[43]

Issued on December 11, 1962, this document was seminal because it dealt not only with monuments or other artifactual sites, but also extended its reach to encompass contemporary urban centers, which at the time UNESCO and several European countries considered "most threatened" by the push to modernize infrastructure and public works. It called for "measures to be taken for construction of all types of public and private buildings . . . to be designed . . . to meet certain aesthetic requirements, [and] while avoiding facile imitation of . . . traditional and picturesque forms, should be in harmony with the general atmosphere which it desired to safeguard."[44] This conception would eventually afford the recognition of entire living cities such as Vietnam's Hoi An or Huế as coherent, integrated World Heritage sites. Soon after this document was issued, an exclusive conference was held in the White House, where delegates agreed to call for a "World Heritage Trust" to kindle worldwide cooperation to conserve "the world's superb natural and scenic areas and historic sites for the present and the future of the entire world citizenry."[45]

In 1966, less than a year after the White House conference, the Italian maritime city of Venice was inundated by a series of disastrous floods that prompted UNESCO to once again spearhead an international campaign to raise funds to "Save Venice." This campaign was integral to the cause of international historic preservation, for it created a number of American non-profit organizations, such as the World Monuments Fund, who has been incredibly active today at Angkor in the last few years. The World Monuments Fund, in fact, spun off its original Venetian operations some years ago into the Save Venice Fund, which is still active today. From the Venetian episode, IUCN developed a proposal similar to the World Heritage Trust for its members. Recognizing the enthusiastic cooperation among individual donors as well as the similarities in the preservation mission statements of these NGOs during the *United Nations Conference on the Human Environment* in Stockholm, Sweden in the summer of 1972, UNESCO convened its World Heritage Convention that November. Officially entitled *The Convention Concerning the Protection of World Cultural and Natural Heritage*, it combined all of the proposals of IUCN, ICOMOS and UNESCO and focused on not only the designation of World Heritage sites, but also on ensuring that these places "of universal value" could be universally protected.

Such collective responsibility to protect cultural and natural sites is not in name only; it does not simply stem from individual States-Parties' signatures on the official World Heritage Convention document, but rather UNESCO ensures tangible, yet "amorphous" action. In the most general of collective actions, all countries essentially pay for all UNESCO-funded activities. Those nations who sign the World Heritage Convention and thus are eligible for World Heritage designations in their home territories are obligated to contribute at least one percent of their annual UNESCO dues for a collective trust fund administered by the Convention in Paris. The product of Washington DC's 1965 White House Conference, the "World Heritage Fund" is aptly named *A Fund for the Protection of the World Cultural and Natural Heritage of Outstanding Universal Value*. This long, official title mirrors that of the World Heritage Convention itself, yet it specifically adds the heritage-scape's valorizing meta-narrative claim. The fund protects worldwide places of heritage, and it underscores the value-laden qualities they possess.

Although these "compulsory" annual dues are a "requirement for the States Parties to be able to present themselves for election in the World Heritage Committee and for receiving technical cooperation and preparatory assistance,"[46] they are not earmarked for a specific endeavor in the home country from which the money came, nor are these countries ever obligated to benefit from these funds. Rather, individual State-Parties must submit an official request to the World Heritage Committee, indicating the type and amount required. Such requests can be met with rejection. A bi-annual budget meeting assesses the amount of compulsory and voluntary donations the Fund received and then determines the beneficiaries, type and amount of its "international assistance." International assistance can take five forms and is up to the individual States Parties to request the type and amount required:

FORMS OF INTERNATIONAL ASSISTANCE
FROM THE WORLD HERITAGE FUND[47]

1.) Preparatory Assistance: With a budgetary ceiling fixed at US$ 30,000 per request, this type of assistance can be provided for the preparation of tentative lists of properties suitable for inclusion on the World Heritage List as well as for the preparation of training courses or large-scale technical assistance projects.

2.) Technical Cooperation: This is assistance for the conservation and management of sites inscribed on the World Heritage List through:
a)   studies concerning the artistic, scientific and technical problems raised by the protection, conservation, presentation and rehabilitation of the cultural and natural heritage, as defined in paragraphs 2 and 4 of article 11 of the Convention;
b)   provision of experts, technicians and skilled labor to ensure that the approved work is correctly carried out;
c)   supply of equipment which the State concerned does not possess or is not in a position to acquire;
d)   low-interest or interest-free loans which might be repayable on a long-term basis;
e)   the granting, in exceptional cases and for special reasons, of non-repayable subsidies.

3.) Training: Assistance can be provided for the training of staff and specialists at all levels in the field of identification, protection, conservation, presentation and rehabilitation of the cultural and natural heritage.
N.B.: The Committee is limiting individual training to short-term modernization programmes or experience exchanges, and gives the highest priority to regional *group training*, preferably in national or regional institutions.

4.) Emergency Assistance: Emergency assistance can be provided for the preparation of urgent nominations, to draw up "emergency plans" or to take emergency measures for the safeguarding of properties *inscribed* on or *nominated* to the World Heritage List.

5.) Assistance for Educational, Information and Promotional Activities can be provided, up to $US 5,000, for activities which:
a)   help to create interest in the Convention within the countries of a given region;
b)   create a greater awareness of the different issues related to the implementation of the Convention to promote more active involvement in its application;
c)   can be a means of exchanging experiences;
d)   stimulate joint education, information and promotional programmes and activities, especially when they involve the participation of young people for the benefit of World Heritage conservation.

As this synopsis indicates, financial assistance from the World Heritage Fund comes in a diversity of forms, and does not center solely on physical conservation procedures at individual World Heritage sites. Preparatory Assistance, which is capped thirty million dollars, is intended for States Parties to prepare their Tentative Lists—those "wish lists" of sites the nation-state considers to nominate. Such assistance, therefore, pertains to the gathering of information, the documentation, and the inspection of a variety of locales in order to prepare a conglomerate listing of places. Furthermore, these places are not yet designated as World Heritage sites, and may never be. Rather, such assistance funds the representatives from States Parties in their efforts to create both their Tentative Lists and their individual Files—the isolating action of UNESCO's ritual recontextualization process. It also funds the inspection tours ICOMOS or IUCN will eventually make to the potential site. Both of these do not guarantee that the individual locality will even become a valorized World Heritage site whose preservation is understood to be the collective responsibility of the world. A secondary function of this type of assistance focuses on preparatory measures pertaining to educational endeavors; here, funding is provided for laying the groundwork for holding eventual training courses or for the drawing-up of long-term conservation plans, both of which are taken into consideration by ICOMOS and ICCROM before they make their official recommendation to the World Heritage Committee. Again, while the State-Party is required to submit strategic plans for ensuring a potential World Heritage site would be adequately conserved, maintained and managed, the World Heritage Committee is not obliged to designate it a World Heritage site.

Although the second type of assistance provided by the World Heritage Fund does indeed pertain to individual places that are already designated as World Heritage sites, only in "exceptional cases and for special reasons" can moneys be applied directly to an individual site's physical preservation activities; even the provision of equipment is predicated on such extreme circumstances wherein "the State concerned . . . is not in a position to acquire." Rather, these funds represent "Technical Cooperation"—a performance of sorts that demonstrates the ongoing collaborative efforts between UNESCO and the States Parties. While the term "cooperation" indicates mutual benefit—and indeed, in the long run a States Party certainly profits from any assistance it can get—most of these funds symbolically benefit UNESCO and the heritage-scape. Materially, UNESCO profits by providing low-interest loans to States Parties that necessitate funds to carry out their own preservation activities. Even when these are interest-free, which is an exceptionally good deal, the act of lending and repaying is another performance of power, for it positions UNESCO as a benevolent sovereign with monetary might in juxtaposition with a needy State-Party as a sort-of vassal entity.

Indeed, funds earmarked for "Technical Cooperation" provide the World Heritage Commission with methods of enacting subtle performances of power over the State-Party—integral when considering UNESCO's overall placemaking strategy of reordering identities so they are not predicated on traditional territorial perceptions. A majority of its proposed monetary actions is dedicated to the funding of outside experts—most probably ICCROM or perhaps independent non-profit organizations such as the World Monuments Fund—to "oversee" the local efforts underway, and also to collaborate with local site managers in producing "studies concerning the artistic, scientific and technical problems raised by the protection, presentation or rehabilitation of the site."[48] Both of these are essentially quality control issues, which underscore the power of UNESCO to contextualize and control the ways an individual World Heritage site's designation is materially manifested. The former conveys UNESCO's power and authority performatatively, by financially enabling itself, through its collaborators, to manage the technical details of preservation activities, ensuring that the process runs smoothly, in a timely fashion, and in the prescribed manner. The latter is more important for the integrity of the heritage-scape itself, for it enables these same UNESCO-designated collaborators to analyze the aesthetic and presentational elements of the site and its associated museums, publications and surrounding landscape. Such analysis ensures that the meta-narrative claim of the heritage-scape is materially manifested in the World Heritage site—a growing concern as the interpretative parameters of what constitutes "universal value" and the monuments that can espouse such claims broadens and complexifies. In a later chapter, a similar type of analysis will be carried out utilizing the Angkor Archaeological Park as a case study.

While the first type of assistance could be used to prepare local authorities for conducting training courses, the third type of assistance provided by the World Heritage Fund centers squarely on implementing such endeavors on a limited basis. Once again, however, such funds do not usually pertain to a specific site, but rather to broadly conceived educational endeavors such as a "workshop on mosaic conservation" or a "Regional Seminar on the Conservation of Earthen Architecture"[49] that can be applied to places of local or universal interest. A majority of the "seminars" the World Heritage Fund finances, furthermore, focus on instructing State-Party representatives on correct methods of monitoring their World Heritage sites on behalf of the Convention, how to properly prepare Tentative Lists, or how to deal with consequences and implications resulting from a country's Periodic Reports.[50] While these actions once again perform a certain exhibition of power on behalf of UNESCO, such activities also are intended to once again further UNESCO's deterritorializing placemaking strategy by diffusing universal methodologies and facilitating broad interactions that extend beyond the site and into the greater heritage-scape. Indeed, many are termed "experience exchanges," manifested either as "study trips" for local managers at foreign World Heritage sites, or as "regional networking events" that can gather diverse managers and experts together. Indeed, UNESCO hastens to add that these training "seminars" should not be localized, but rather "regional group training, preferably in national or regional institutions" is given "the highest priority."[51] These activities contribute to the cohesiveness of the heritage-scape and its meta-narrative claim, but also underscores its fundamental assertion that these monuments do not belong to the State-Party itself, but to all; as such, it is the responsibility of all nations to conserve each World Heritage site, at least as mediated by the World Heritage Fund.

The shared responsibility for preserving sites deemed to be of universal value is most prominently illustrated in the World Heritage Fund's fourth provision of assistance. Here, the World Heritage Fund sets aside moneys to be utilized for Emergency Assistance, that is, when a place that is already on either the Tentative List or the World Heritage List itself is in dire or impending danger. Certainly a result of the watershed emergency conservation activities in Egypt and Venice from which the World Heritage Convention traces its origins, this is an important and material performance demonstrating international understanding of the shared responsibility that comes with membership to the Convention. Such assistance comes in a variety of forms, many of which center around strategic planning for the short-term and long-term. First, the World Heritage Fund can support the "preparation of urgent nominations." As UNESCO makes clear, a site must already be at least in the first stages of its ritual transformation from a space of local use into a site of universal value; it must be in the midst of its isolating process. This is an important dynamic when considering that UNESCO intends to solicit international cooperation for preserving a specific national monument. Regardless of whether or not the monument will pass the nomination process and become a veritable World Heritage site, in order to justify the material expenditures stemming from a collective international response, the monument must be isolated from its previous local context. It must stand alone, like a museum object, its value and particular structural state able to be assessed by foreign decision-makers who are called upon to support this emergency funding.

The List of World Heritage in Danger

The isolation of this monument also allows it to be placed on another inventory, and not just a nation-state's Tentative List. This is called the *List of World Heritage in Danger*, one of the most important and selective lists the World Heritage Convention possesses in its conservation arsenal. Under Article II of the 1972 World Heritage Convention:

> The Committee shall establish, keep up to date and publish, whenever circumstances shall so require, under the title of "List of World Heritage in Danger", a list of the property appearing in the World Heritage List for the conservation of which major operations are necessary and for which assistance has been requested under this Convention. This list shall contain an estimate of the cost of such operations. The list may include only such property forming part of the cultural and natural heritage as is threatened by serious and specific dangers, such as the threat of disappearance caused by accelerated deterioration, large-scale public or private projects or rapid urban or tourist development projects; destruction caused by changes in the use or ownership of the land; major alterations due to unknown causes; abandonment for any reason whatsoever; the outbreak or the threat of an armed conflict; calamities and cataclysms; serious fires, earthquakes, landslides; volcanic eruptions; changes in water level, floods and tidal waves. The Committee may at any time, in case of urgent need, make a new entry in the List of World Heritage in Danger and publicize such entry immediately.[52]

The Emergency Assistance to which the World Heritage Fund references is extraordinary in nature. Unlike other forms of assistance, immediate funds can be allocated directly pertaining to restorative activities at the individual site. Although the Committee ultimately determines inscription, ostensibly with or without the direct behest of a State-Party, the UNESCO's more contemporary documents state such extraordinary assistance must be requested first by the State-Party. This most likely is the case because such an inscription also grants greater authority to UNESCO and its subsidiaries to control the efforts, and thus usurps the managerial power of the nation-state. Inscription on the List "requires" the World Heritage Committee, "in consultation" but not in collaboration with the State-Party, to "develop and adopt . . . a programme for corrective measures, and subsequently to monitor the situation of the site. All efforts must be made to restore the site's values in order to enable its removal from the List of World Heritage in Danger as soon as possible."[53]

While it can be argued that a great many potential World Heritage sites are "in danger" of succumbing to the destructive forces of time—after all, they are all transient structures—the World Heritage in Danger list specifically addresses situations wherein a particular monument may be in immediate risk of loosing its proven or soon-to-be-proven "World Heritage values." The definition of danger varies; sometimes it pertains to world events, and sometimes it pertains to direct development plans by the nation-state. It ranges from wars and landmines to unbridled poaching and uncontrolled urbanization. It also may pertain to "unchecked tourist development," which may be interpreted as either dangerously high wear-and-tear that stems from mismanaging tourist flows and security, or an incongruous recontextualization of the individual monument's narrative that would change the sites' illustration of the heritage-scape's "unity in diversity" claim. The latter could be a result of excessive commoditization, either at the site or in terms of how the monument is portrayed in the media—especially a problem for recognizable monuments in developing countries, such as Ta Prohm in Cambodia's Angkor Archaeological Park.

Cambodian authorities frequently "sell" Angkor to bring in much-needed funds. José Carreras held a benefit concert in 2002 at Angkor Wat to raise money for its conservation, and the World Monuments Fund, which is very active at Angkor and oversees the monastery Preah Khan, arranges Apsara dances and expensive candlelight cocktail receptions to select donors and tour operators within the Buddhist structure. However, sometimes UNESCO or preservation authorities take recourse to a particular function when they determine that it might not portray the World Heritage site in accordance with the heritage-scape's meta-narrative claims. This was the case when the APSARA organization that oversees the Angkor Archaeological Park agreed, for a hefty fee of $18,000.00 a day for three months, to allow a Hollywood studio film the Angelina Jolie blockbuster *Tomb Raider* at Angkor Wat and Ta Prohm. Although the fictional film left the latter monument as an anonymous Khmer structure, rather than specifically mentioning which site Jolie's character, Lara Croft, was supposed to be "raiding," it grossly misrepresented the aesthetic features of the edifice. Huge Buddhist-inspired statues come to life, with Lara Croft and her tomb raiding associates compelled to destroy these figures by any means possible. UNESCO may have still been able to suspend its disbelief, if not for the very premise of the movie—a theme that romanticizes pillaging and destroying World Heritage sites for personal profit. Fundamental to the heritage-scape's meta-narrative is that its World Heritage sites are owned by all, and thus discourages performances of possession such as those the film conveyed. It also holds that it is the collective responsibility of all people to ensure the structural integrity of the monument, not to desecrate it. Allowing such a message to be affixed to a World Heritage site, which is juxtaposed in the heritage-scape with all others, would be akin to allowing this message to be affixed to all.

To make matters worse, Angkor had already been inscribed on the World Heritage in Danger list precisely because of the danger of destruction by unexploded landmines left over from the Khmer Rouge era, and, more disturbingly, because of the inordinately high instances of unbridled tomb raiding—often by Cambodians affiliated with local governmental authorities—running rampant at the site. APSARA and the site managers were severely reprimanded by UNESCO, who threatened to take away its World Heritage status should such a damaging recontextualization ever be permitted at the Angkor Archaeological Park. Fortunately, this is an instance that was not permanent, is relatively fixable, and which did not require Emergency Funding. However, it underscores the idea of what constitutes "danger" for a site, and how it impacts all others. Since the heritage-scape draws its own authority, illustratively and value from the juxtaposition of each individual site, should a present or eventual World Heritage site lose—through material or expository destruction—those qualities that fosters "peace in the minds of men" through the understanding of "unity in diversity," it would damage the entire coherency and potency of the heritage-scape itself.

The List of World Heritage Sites in Danger operates in the same way as the World Heritage List. Not only does the list valorize a site by singling it out as a place worthy of extraordinary collective assistance, but it also conversely singles it out as a place that dangles precipitously on the threshold of substantial loss. Such attention is meant to spur the international community to action must more quickly than usual. It is also a tool for pressuring a negligent host country; when the World Heritage Committee condemned Dresden's plans to build a bridge over the Elbe, it placed the World Heritage site on this list and summarily issued press releases explaining why it did so. But a few days later, Germany scrapped the plan. Juxtaposing the site with other places threatened by extreme cases of war, natural disaster or unbridled plundering, it similarly draws an imagined link between the specific and unrelated problems and weaknesses of one country to that of this particular country. For example, as of 2006, thirty-one out of 830 World Heritage properties were inscribed on the List, which includes sites such as Afghanistan's Bamiyan Buddhas and the whole of Jerusalem, both of which are associated with social strife, religious persecution, terrorism and cultural aggression. Afghanistan's Cultural Landscape and Archaeological Remains of the Bamiyan Valley, which was dynamited by the Taliban in an internationally publicized act of religious persecution and cultural aggression, was inscribed on the list in 2003 and reconfirmed in 2005, according to UNESCO, because of its

> fragile state of conservation considering that it has suffered from abandonment, military action and dynamite explosions. The major dangers include: risk of imminent collapse of the Buddha niches with the remaining fragments of the statues, further deterioration of still existing mural paintings in the caves, looting and illicit excavation. Parts of the site are inaccessible due to the presence of antipersonnel mines.[54]

Today, antipersonnel mines remain at the site and across Afghanistan, which is still wracked with war, cultural upheaval and terrorist activity. Such ongoing political strife threatens the very future of the site, since it "threatens the use or ownership of the land," as Article II of the Convention specifies. Because of the instability of Afghanistan's political situation, there still remains the possibility of further symbolic destructive action or a change in the individual narrative claim concerning the site.

Jerusalem poses a similarly extraordinary danger, for territorial possession and management of this living body of structures has been in flux for decades. The city itself is at the epicenter of an extremely combustible and ideologically changed tug-of-war that constantly threatens both the integrity of the structures, as well as the perception of them. While the Taliban's destruction of the Bamiyan Buddhas and their housing of terrorists are considered reprehensible by the international community, the same community as a whole has not come to an agreement on how support—or even conceptualize—the city. Yet it is precisely the diversity of significances that makes Jerusalem one of the most expository sites of UNESCO's universalizing meta-narrative. Divisive worldwide politics is interwoven at the site as well; Iranians and other Middle Easterners have founded an annual "Jerusalem Day," held on the last Friday of Ramadan, where Shi'ite Muslims are urged—or even required—to march in symbolic solidarity against the State of Israel and the United States of America, which is generally seen as supporting the Israelis.[55] Of Jerusalem's precariousness UNESCO states:

The situation of Jerusalem is an exceptional one in that there is no general political agreement as to the status of the city, certain states declaring that they abided by the situation defined in the 1947 United Nations partition plan which considered Jerusalem as a corpus separatum located neither in Israel, nor in Jordan.

The site of Jerusalem was nominated in 1981 by Jordan, it being agreed at the time that inscription should in no way be regarded as a means for registering political or sovereignty claims by any State. Its subsequent inscription on the List of World Heritage in Danger in 1982 was a recognition by the Committee of the danger to religious properties, threats of destruction following uncontrolled urban development and of the general deterioration of the state of conservation of the city's monuments due to the disastrous impact of tourism and to lack of maintenance.

The safeguarding of the monumental, religious and cultural heritage of the Holy City of Jerusalem has been one of UNESCO's main concerns since 1967. To this end, the Executive Board and the General Conference have repeatedly requested the application of internationally recognised principles, especially the UNESCO Convention for the Protection of Cultural Property in the Event of Armed Conflict (the Hague, 1954), the 1956 New Delhi Recommendation on International Principles Applicable to Archaeological Excavations and the 1972 World Heritage Convention. In conformity with UNESCO's resolutions, financial aid for heritage restoration projects in Jerusalem has been requested from Member States. Favourable responses to these appeals have enabled UNESCO to finance the restoration and conservation of a number of monuments and religious and cultural properties in this city.[56]

The dangers posed to these sites are extraordinary, and are directly linked with the very precarious social situations in which these nation-states and their citizens are involved. Inevitably imbued in such understandings is the inability of governing bodies to keep peace and to ensure safety. It often reflects negatively on States Parties, begging the question of how a government can ensure safety to its living, interacting people if it cannot even ensure the safety of an inanimate structure. This is also underscored with the inscription of a number of sites which are threatened with natural disaster—uncontrollable calamities even by the most powerful countries in the world. Iran's City of Bam, which is considered a World Heritage site for the continual importance of its "cultural landscape" from antiquity to the present-day, stood at the epicenter of a December 2003 earthquake that decimated its historical structures and claimed the lives of over 26,000 people. Caused by the uncontrollably volatile clash of ideologies, or the powerful activities of nature, all of these dangers are "cataclysmic," to use the terminology of Article II. Through their juxtaposition on the list, one cannot but connect other listed sites with such negative and fear-inspiring activities, even if the danger associated with them is completely unrelated, such as the United States' World Heritage site of the Everglades National Park. According to UNESCO, the Everglades was listed in 1993

> after the park's Superintendent informed the Committee of extensive damage to Everglades' ecology due to a number of causes including nearby urban growth, pollution from fertilizers, mercury poisoning of fish and wildlife, and a fall in water levels caused by flood protection measures. In addition, on 24 August 1992, Hurricane Andrew altered much of Florida Bay and its ecological systems and destroyed the park's visitor centre.[57]

As this description illustrates, the inscription of the Everglades is not predicated on one singular cataclysmic act of God or nature, nor is it indicative of extraordinary social strife. Nevertheless, the Committee rightly decided that the problems facing Florida's unique biosphere warrants swift and extraordinary international activity. Yet juxtaposed with these other sites, it nevertheless places a particular and authoritative judgment on the State-Party's ability to handle the situation on its own. Indeed, in its recent informational packet, UNESCO astutely points out that

> Inscription on the List of World Heritage in Danger is not perceived in the same way by all parties concerned. Some countries apply for the inscription of a site to focus international attention on its problems and to obtain expert assistance in solving them. Others however, wish to avoid an inscription, which they perceive as a dishonour. The listing of a site as World Heritage in Danger should in any case not be considered as a sanction, but as a system established to respond to specific conservation needs in an efficient manner.[58]

UNESCO's wording here is important, for it underscores the visibility that comes with being placed on such a List. This visibility is vitally important to all of UNESCO's ongoing conservation activities, and was proven to be effective from the time of Egypt's Abu Simbel and Venice's deluges to the present day. Because the World Heritage Fund's preservation activities rely greatly upon sentiments of collective responsibility within the international community and also by private donors and nonprofit organizations, one of the primary benefits of this List is to raise awareness of a site's precarious nature. Article II establishing the List of World Heritage in Danger specifically mentions "publicizing such an entry immediately" as one of its primary methods of conservation.

In fact, the final type of monetary aid available from the World Heritage Fund is described as Assistance for Educational, Information and Promotional Activities. All three of these activities can be considered forms of raising awareness—generating and disseminating information about UNESCO's globalizing idea to the greater public. It is, after all, this public that is to benefit not only from the heritage-scape's message, but also from its subsequent conservationist appeal. There are two different types of "awareness" to which these funds refer, although it should be noted that they are two sides to a whole, much like the Structuralist claim of "unity in diversity"; both messages, both understandings, serve to deepen the meaning of the other. One message pertains to the material structure's efficacy and value when whole, while the other pertains to the transient nature of this materiality and the need to conserve it. Through these funds, then, UNESCO promotes activities that will educate the public and the States Parties' delegations about World Heritage, its "universal value," the specifics of each individual site, and even how to help nominate a site. Without such information on the value of these monuments, there would be no international impetus to conserve them. On the flip side, UNESCO also raises awareness of the very transient nature of the site through politicking, publishing articles on preservation, and maintaining the World Heritage in Danger list. This creates the perceived need to preserve these sites of "universal value" for future generations. Without this understanding, it is probable that these unique, value-laden monuments will fall to the harsh winds of time and war.

So-called "developing nations" are not the only ones requiring awareness-raising endeavors. Asserting that "Italians are surrounded by so much art that many of them take it for granted," NPR journalist Sylvia Poggioli quotes a Roman tour guide who mused, "I often saw people every day going to work not seeing the Colosseum and suddenly realizing when they have some people visiting them that there is the Colosseum."[59] Such conceptual non-recognition, the article seems to state, translates into a lack of willingness by taxpayers to contribute to basic upkeep; the Italian Ministry of Culture's 2005 budget only includes half as much money as needed to preserve the country's wealth of monuments and artistic heritage pieces. In an effort to raise awareness of Italians' cultural properties, and the transience they face, an Italian nonprofit organization, the *CittáItalia* Foundation, has begun to run television and print ads that feature doctored images of famous destinations without the monuments that made them so renowned: Pisa without the Leaning Tower, Rome without the Colosseum, and Venice without its idyllic Bridge of Sighs. Alongside the slogan, "Without your help, Italy could lose something," one print ad features Michelangelo's David as an amputee.[60]

In addition, the publicized need to conserve these transient built structures serves to articulate UNESCO's valorizing meta-narrative claim. Heritage claims are fundamentally predicated on the understanding that the site in question is an authentic carry-over from the past, and as it is understood in this context, that the value of the heritage monuments rests in the emotional efficacy an interactive experience with such uniquely time-resistant structures; to paraphrase Freud, the inherent value of transience is "scarcity value in time."[61] Thus, there is an unspoken understanding that, if there were never the need for these structures to be preserved—if they never could be destroyed—then they would not be as valuable. It would therefore be acceptable to take these sites for granted, thus lessening the impact of the heritage-scape and its claim. By publicizing the tangible, site-specific dangers these monuments face, UNESCO ensures that these monuments are perceived as extraordinarily valuable. It is in this way that the heritage-scape's meta-narrative claim of "unity in diversity" can truly foster the cohesive sense of collective responsibility for historic preservation.

Raising awareness for preservation needs has proven effective for UNESCO ever since it launched its watershed push to save Ramses II's tombs from Egypt's High Dam floods. Mainly through disseminating information about the importance of the monuments and their plight, UNESCO succeeded in not only raising millions of dollars, but in convincing organizations to physically reposition the enormous temples to higher ground. One 1963 *Time* magazine article nicely captures the sense of horror not at the prospect of flooding the Aswan basin, but of the international community's lack of mobilization:

> [F]or all its magnificence, the Temple of Abu Simbel is apparently doomed. For lack of $22 million, the cost of a few bombers or missiles, it will soon be submerged under 200 ft. of muddy water backed up by the High Dam being built at Aswan 180 miles downstream. . . . The dam would probably cost $80 million . . . [but the] lifting would cost $42 million plus $24 million for finishing the job.
>
> But even $42 million is not available. Last week UNESCO Secretary-General René Maheu added up what had been gathered by passing the international hat. Egypt pledged $11.5 million. West Germany gave $1,845,000, Italy $1,800,000. India $714,000, Cuba $160.000. In all. 37 countries contributed, including Bolivia and Nepal, each of which gave $1,000, but the total is more than $22 million short.
>
> Three of the world's richest nations, the U.S., the U.S.S.R. and Britain, have thus far given nothing. The Russians claim that their money is already helping Egypt to build the High Dam; someone else, they say, should take care of Abu Simbel. The U.S. apparently believes that attempts to raise the temple would destroy it. and anyway. $42 million would only begin to cover the cost of jacking it up.
>
> As they discuss the final fate of threatened Abu Simbel, the U.S. and other countries still show no sense of urgency. Even if the water starts rising on schedule in 1964. there will be time left for some kind of action. A simple,

cheap cofferdam can protect the temple temporarily while last-minute efforts are made to save it.[62]

By simply raising awareness of the plight of Ramses II's monuments, UNESCO literally moved mountains. While this in itself was a watershed feat, UNESCO's awareness-raising endeavor and the subsequent mobilization of forces to conserve Abu Simbel truly paved the way for the World Heritage Convention itself. It revealed the strong emotional relationship that such heritage monuments—and the prospect of their impending transience—exert upon the international community, irrespective of national origins; this activity literally performed "unity in diversity" almost a decade before the Convention was ever drafted. Though it went unrecognized at the time, saving Abu Simbel was a portentous act. Remembering that Ramses II was one of the earliest heritage conservationists, who had preserved and restored Old Kingdom pyramids that had lain fallow for over a millennium, it seems fitting that one of his own temples in the Upper Nile would be the earliest, and most paradigmatic, effort of UNESCO's World Heritage Convention.

The World Heritage Fund benefits from several flows of money, in addition to the obligatory contributions by its member-states. Individual philanthropists are directly and indirectly solicited; one can even donate through the official website of UNESCO's World Heritage Centre, www.whc.unesco.org—which calls itself an "Elegant site from UNESCO explaining the choice of certain buildings and sites as World Heritage. [It also includes the official] List with pictures and information available on each." A September 2007 posting on its homepage advertises:

> <u>Donate Online to Support World Heritage Conservation</u>
> It's easier than ever to participate in the preservation of World Heritage sites by making an online donation on the UNESCO World Heritage Centre website. With a few clicks you can make a donation in any amount and 100% of it will be used to help protect the most spectacular sites in the world.
> To make a donation:
> http://whc.unesco.org/en/donation/[63]

There are also several different organizations that often contribute to preservation activities in general. These range from UNESCO-affiliated nongovernmental organizations such as IUCN, ICOMOS and ICCROM to foreign-based non-profit preservation societies, such as New York's World Monuments Fund. The benefits of engaging these disparate organizations are two-fold. First and more materially important, these organizations represent specific epistemic communities who are socially accepted brokers of practical and academic knowledge concerning the best practices of historic preservation. While the World Heritage Convention is regarded as authoritatively sanctioned to determine which sites are uniquely expository of the "unity in diversity" claim, these epistemic communities are regarded as exclusively capable of carrying out the most reliable of conservation activities. In the end, it would not be wise to employ politicians as preservationists. Yet there is also a second benefit to engaging the efforts of these non-profit organizations—these communities represent a different segment of the world's population. While UNESCO and States Parties officials may have strong links to local and regional governments, they may not be in the best position to cultivate the same relationships with individual benefactors, intellectuals or professionals. As socially accepted epistemic communities, as well as communities dedicated specifically to one particular theme—that of historic preservation—these non-profit organizations convincingly call upon the various expertise and support of a host of related groups and individuals, often reaching out across borders to do so. As organizations uniquely dedicated to historic preservation or natural conservation, they are able to speak to individual benefactors who are equally passionate and dedicated to the topic even though he or she might not possess the appropriate professional knowledge. However, as discriminating and knowing participants, they are able to support the endeavors of these communities monetarily, through the media, or even emotionally. Not only can they donate voluntary monetary contributions to assist various preservation activities, but many can also can lobby government representatives to provide case-specific aid beyond simply that which they give to the collective World Heritage Fund. In the best-case scenario their lobbying efforts could help place diplomatic pressure on other countries to do the same. They can also entreat local research and professional communities, such as universities, and private architectural and preservation firms and associations, to donate their time and resources to the same end. Thus, drawing on such disparate and far-reaching organizations, groups, communities and individuals, UNESCO's fostering of shared responsibility is exponentially furthered.

Unifying Under a Preservation Imperative:
The International Community and Angkor's Inscription

While the material results of this sense of shared responsibility are revealed in hundreds of post-World Heritage Convention "success stories" similar to UNESCO's efforts to save Egypt's Abu Simbel temples, one particularly salient example is referenced here. The case of the Angkor Archaeological Park is noted for its hitherto unprecedented mobilization of international diplomacy and expertise for the purposes of historic preservation. Following the Khmer Rouge's retreat and eventual defeat at the beginning of the 1990s,[64] the temples in Angkor were in particular disarray, threatened with destruction by unexploded landmines buried by the Khmer Rouge, and subject to intense looting by poverty-stricken locals engaged with profiteering foreign collectors. The entire Kingdom of Cambodia, occupied for a time by the Vietnamese army who had ultimately halted the Khmer Rouge's systematic genocide and cultural destruction, was finally placed under the United Nation's watch, whose aim was to foster infrastructural development as well as the country's re-integration into the greater global community. Almost immediately upon brokering its 1991 peace agreement between Khmer nationalists (some previously allied with the Khmer Rouge) and Vietnam, the United Nations and its affiliated departments realized the precarious state of the Angkor monuments, and UNESCO embarked on a fervid and emotional appeal to the international community to help preserve these sites. Since Cambodia had neither the diplomatic nor the economic resources to sign the World Heritage Convention, however, these historic structures could not officially be inscribed on the List of World Heritage in Danger, let alone on UNESCO's valorizing World Heritage List. Thus, the entire designation process was fast-tracked to provide immediate protection to the temples; UNESCO forewent the usual lengthy ritualized inscription process, which takes about a decade if done thoroughly.

If strict adherence to the nomination procedures established by the World Heritage Convention in 1972 was a solid requisite for designation, as UNESCO purported it to be, then the cause of Angkor would have been in grave peril. But Angkor was given a pass; almost every prerequisite was unfulfilled. First and foremost, Cambodia was not a signatory to the World Heritage Convention, and thus technically should not benefit from any World Heritage activities. More importantly, the nation was at the threshold of a political transition. Cambodia was devastated by a series of wars, which stemmed from the mid-twentieth century when France struggled for and ultimately lost control of its Protectorates after the Viet Minh victory at Điện Biên Phủ. Conflict continued with increasing ferocity during the (American) Vietnam War, which saw increased U.S. bombings despite Cambodia's purported neutrality, as well as a *coup d'etat* that sent the king into exile in China, where he supported Pol Pot's movement to throw off the American-supported military government of Lon Nol. Phnom Penh fell on April 1, 1975; the King returned and was summarily placed under a sort-of "palace arrest," and Pol Pot proceed to empty the city of its inhabitants in an effort to create a solely agrarian society based on "traditional" values. The imposition of his version of traditional values required the decimation of millions of Cambodians suspected of being educated, urban, espousing "modern" Western views or sentiments, or disagreeing with the Communist ideology. When the Khmer Rouge began slaughtering ethnic Vietnamese in the borderlands between the two countries, the Vietnamese army invaded Cambodia and eventually forced the Khmer Rouge to retreat northward into the jungles, where they remained with intermittent strength until the early 1990s. With the end of the Cold War and the collapse of the Soviet Union, who had materially supported the Vietnamese government, Vietnam could not afford to keep its troops in Cambodia. Control over the land was ceded to the United Nations in 1991, which created the United Nations Transitional Authority (UNTAC). Bringing together diverse factions within Cambodia, the UNTAC constructed an interim democratic government under the leadership of the Supreme National Council (SNC). It was amid this turmoil that the World Heritage Convention turned to Angkor's designation.

Occupied with forming a more permanent, cohesive government, Cambodia was not in a position to join the World Heritage Convention, prepare its Tentative List, or compile a detailed File on Angkor. Indeed, there was not even a detailed zoning of what a World Heritage site at Angkor would include, although it was understood that an eventual World Heritage site would be composed of more than just Angkor Wat. With the collaboration of the UNTAC, ICOMOS and ICCROM began to conduct site inspections to ascertain the state of the monuments' preservation, its authenticity, and the mechanisms in place for managing Angkor's upkeep, preservation and eventual tourism. In all of these areas, too, the outlook was bleak. Commenting that the "monuments of the Angkor ensemble face a number of conservation problems," ICOMOS provided a detailed assessment of the proposed site's structural status, which extended beyond the obvious "damage of human interaction" such as plundering and extended warfare. The "fundamental" problem was natural—vegetation grew in and around the unmortared building blocks, contributing to a captivating aesthetic but also to extreme damage. More problematically, the ancient Khmer irrigation systems, which archaeologists today are heralding as extraordinary for the time period for their lasting efficacy, were finally succumbing to centuries of abandonment, allowing the regular monsoon rainfall to significantly weaken the sandy subsoil upon which the monuments stood. Furthermore, "by capillary action" this rainwater was damaging the very structures themselves, exacerbated by "thermal shock" and the invasive "growth of mosses and lichens." There was also no preservation plan in place by the government to address these issues—one of the prerequisites for designation.[65]

Second, authenticity is also a fundamental requirement for designation, and one of the main reasons ICOMOS is called in to assess each potential World

Heritage site. Despite worldwide, historical understanding of the importance and duration of Angkor's temples and monuments, especially during the French Indochinese period, ICOMOS noted that the previous conservation and restoration efforts of the last century had damaged the monuments' structure and authenticity. Commenting that warfare was "mercifully" not the major cause of damage, ICOMOS stated that "more damage has been caused inadvertently by the use of certain restoration techniques, especially the introduction of reinforced concrete and over-abrasive water cleaning."[66] Indeed, the introduction of unrelated, non-traditional materials effectively changes the very structure of the monument; it tangibly converts it into something materially different. It causes it to lose authenticity. ICOMOS explains,

> Much of the conservation work carried out at Angkor since 1931 does not accord fully with ICOMOS doctrine, as set out in the Venice Charter and subsequent documents. It is essential that any future work should rigidly eschew the extensive use of concrete and that stone-cleaning treatments should take into account the special characteristics of both the stone itself and the environmental conditions. A vital prerequisite in drawing up the conservation policy for the Angkor complex is the establishment of standards and approved methodologies.[67]

The third requisite for designation is the capacity for self-sufficient maintenance on the part of the State-Party and its appointed site managers. These plans extend beyond architectural or preservation strategies and into the management of the site as a tourist destination. ICOMOS underscores the importance of such a plan, another prerequisite for designation:

> One of the most serious potential threats to the Angkor monuments is the probability that, once the political problems have been resolved, tourism will become a major source of revenue for Cambodia. the impact of increased tourist facilities (hotels. restaurants. shops, an extended airport, car parks, etc) around the monuments could be catastrophic if they are allowed to encroach too closely. This factor must be given the highest priority in defining eventual buffer zones and the constraints that apply within them, so as to avoid irreparable damage to the setting of the monuments. Already a restaurant has been built into the south bank of the Eastern Baray, whilst houses are remorselessly creeping northwards from Siem Reap towards the monuments.[68]

Along with these plans, UNESCO also requires that the nation-state demonstrate a dedication to educating and effectively training local preservationists, scholars, managers and guides. Once again, nothing of the sort was present at Angkor. ICOMOS points out that

Degree courses in archaeology and architecture are currently being taught at the Universite des Beaux Arts in Phnom Penh, but the Faculty of Archaeology is grossly understaffed and under-resourced. Short field training courses in excavation and conservation methods are provided regularly at Angkor by Sophia University (Tokyo), but the first group of graduates will inevitably be of only limited value in their initial years. It is essential therefore that international collaboration in training and field operations, as well as infrastructural projects (inventory, general administration, procurement, logistics) should be made available to the NHPAC in its early years through multilateral and bilateral agreements.[69]

Yet education alone cannot ensure a World Heritage site's protection, especially when threatened by severe looting as was the case of Angkor. UNESCO always requires the State-Party to demonstrate that legal procedures are put into place to ensure the site's survival. Citing a "complete lack of antiquities legislation, or of a properly constituted professional heritage protection authority or agency,"[70] ICOMOS reveals that UNESCO employed the services of M. Ridha Fraou, an international lawyer, to create a draft Resolution on the Protection of Cultural Property for the area. Not only was the Resolution intended to cover "basic elements such as the protection, registration, and classification of monumental cultural property, trade in cultural property, chance discoveries, and the regulation of archaeological excavations," but it also established a so-called National Heritage Protection Authority of Cambodia (NHPAC) as "the competent authority for the implementation of the Resolution." Even at that point, in November of 1992, the Resolution was only in the process of being "considered" by the Supreme National Council governing the nation, and was not implemented, as the World Heritage Convention requires.[71]

Although not every requirement, save the existence of the monument itself, had been fully met, the World Heritage Committee in December of that same year designated Angkor a World Heritage site, with the reasoning that it met the first four cultural criteria as articulated by ICOMOS in its assessment:

Criterion i: The Angkor complex represents the entire range of Khmer art from the 9th to the 14th centuries, and includes a number of indisputable artistic masterpieces (eg Angkor Vat, the Bayon, Banteay Srei).

Criterion ii: The influence of Khmer art, as developed at Angkor. was a profound one over much of south-east Asia and played a fundamental role in its distinctive evolution.

Criterion iii: The Khmer Empire of the 9th-14th centuries encompassed much of south-east Asia and played a formative role in the political and cultural development of the region. All that remains of that civilization is its rich heritage of cult structures in brick and stone.

Criterion iv: Khmer architecture evolved largely from that of the Indian sub-continent, from which it soon became clearly distinct as it developed its own special characteristics, some independently evolved and others acquired from neighbouring cultural traditions. The result was a new artistic horizon in oriental art and architecture.[72]

The Committee announced the designation this with the following statement:

> The Committee took note of the report presented by Mr. A Beschaouch [Azedine Beschaouch, the outgoing chairman of the Committee]. Given the unique situation in Cambodia, which, in accordance with the Paris Accords, has been placed under the temporary administration of the United Nations since July 1991, the Committee has decided to waive some conditions required under the Operational Guidelines and, on the basis of criteria (i), (ii), (iii) and (iv), has inscribed the Angkor site, together with its monuments and its archeological zones as described in the "Périmètre de Protection" accompanying the ICO-MOS report, on the World Heritage List.[73]

Simultaneously inscribing Angkor on the World Heritage List and the List of World Heritage in Danger, the Committee, at the behest of the United States and other representatives, also underscored the unique nature of this endeavor, taking great pains to assert that this was not to be considered a precedent for similar action in the future:

> The Committee stressed that this action was not to be taken as setting a precedent for the inscription procedure. Therefore, in order to guarantee protection of the site for a three year period (1993–1995), the Committee has decided that a special in-depth study will be made of the Angkor site, and that reports will be presented to the Bureau and the Committee on the status of the monuments and the protective perimeter; the first report is to be presented at the June 1993 session of the Bureau to be followed by a report to the Committee during its seventeenth session in December 1993.[74]

Indeed, the United States' representative to the World Heritage Convention requested the following statement to be appended:

> The Representative of the United States of America presented a statement explaining his Government's position on the Committee action. He noted

that, although the United States has voted in the Bureau to inscribe the site only subject to the conditions identified by ICOMOS, that position was now to support the compromise consensus to inscribe Angkor immediately.

He noted, however, the United States hope that inscription would in fact lead to stronger protection of this site of unquestioned international value, and the United States concern that the Committee be willing and able to deal with future problems at the site should circumstances not improve.

He noted the position of the United States that this inscription not be understood as a precedent, and congratulated ICOMOS for the integrity of their position and advice to the Committee.[75]

Just under a year after Angkor's designation, UNESCO took unprecedented action in resolving the legal and institutional impediments to such a designation. Meeting in Tokyo, Japan, delegates from thirty countries in Europe, Asia, the Middle East and the Americans, as well as representatives from the European Union, the Asian Development Bank, the Southern Asian Ministers of Education Organization Regional Centre for Archaeology and Fine Arts (SEAMEO/ SPAFA), ICCROM, and a number of United Nations affiliates such as UNESCO, the United Nations Development Program (UNDP), and the United Nations Volunteers Program (UNV), held a two-day Intergovernmental Conference on the Safeguarding and Development of the Historic Site of Angkor to specifically identify and construct a systematic plan to conserve Angkor and to shepherd it through the World Heritage Convention's designation process. The resulting *Declaration of Tokyo*, passed on October 13, 1993, "defined the means of ensuring coordination of effort and providing the framework within which the work of each country and organization should be carried out."[76]

The Declaration of Tokyo was a particularly evocative exposition of UNESCO's "unity in diversity" meta-narrative. Given the importance of Angkor for national reconstruction, and the tenuous hold on power the nascent government seemed to have had, the bulk of the Declaration urged all countries currently undertaking restoration efforts to unite under the King, the head of this newly reconstituted kingdom. It first recognized Angkor's mediatory role on both the national level and in the heritage-scape, and ceded "sovereignty" over the temples to the people—something quite unusual given that State-Parties supposedly offer up their sites "without prejudice to national sovereignty or ownership."[77]

1. We recognize that the Angkor monuments are one of the world's most valuable cultural heritages in Asia as well as the national symbol of Cambodia and its people, and that international co-operation for the safeguarding and

development of the Angkor region, including the Angkor monuments, is of particular importance for national reconstruction.

2. We recognize that the people of Cambodia have sovereignty over and primary responsibility for the safeguarding and development of the historic area of Angkor. Based on this recognition, we will support the Cambodian people's efforts to bring about and pursue this task. We pay tribute to His Majesty Samdech Preah Norodom Sihanouk, King of Cambodia, for His actions in favors of national reconciliation; His personal commitment has been the essential factor in the mobilization of the international community for the site and region of Angkor. We welcome the establishment of the new Government of the Kingdom of Cambodia as a result of free and fair elections, permitting the reinforcement of international co-operation for the site of Angkor and the surrounding region. We also welcome the announcement but the Government of the Kingdom of Cambodia of the introduction of organizational and legal measures to protect the site, prevent looting, and ensure the maintenance of security of the region as well as to facilitate efficient operations of preservation, restrain and development.[78]

The Declaration then recognized the urgent need for the international community to continue its preservation work:

3. . . . We recognize the urgent need for international assistance to prevent the Angkor monuments from further decay and destruction. These international efforts should be carried out in a coordinated manner for the safeguarding and preservation of the monuments and historical area taking into account their cultural, socio-economic and ecological dimensions.

4. We hold this conference for the purpose of mobilizing such international efforts. . . .[79]

Lastly, after praising the numerous nations and non-profit organizations for their work, the Declaration urged them to "support" the Kingdom and unite under a common coordinating body:

5. We declare our deep appreciation of UNESCO's action for safeguarding of the Angkor monuments to date, as well as for the recognition of the site as a common heritage of mankind. This deep appreciation is also extended to the countries, organizations and foundations which, despite difficult conditions, took and are taking measures for preventing decay and launching restoration works on the site of Angkor. . . .

6. We also declare our deep appreciation for the role of international and national non-governmental organizations as well as community based organizations in preserving the site and hope that they will continue and increase their efforts.

7. We recognize that each country and organization has its own ways and means of co-operation in accordance with its circumstances to decide what would be done in order to best mobilize international support.

8. We appeal to the international community for its support to the Government of the Kingdom of Cambodia in its actions against the looting and illicit traffic of cultural property which continue to plague the heritage of Cambodia.[80]

While most of the document consisted of a unified articulation of international support to the "Cambodian government," as embodied by the King, to help draft a master zoning plan of the site and a program of "rehabilitation and promotion," it did perform one important feature. The *Declaration of Tokyo* created an International Coordinating Committee for the Safeguarding and Development of the Historic Site of Angkor (ICC).[81] Co-chaired by France and Japan with UNESCO as acting secretariat, the ICC is responsible for coordinating the various localized projects spearheaded by different foreign countries and historic preservation organizations. By sanctioning and coordinating these international efforts, the ICC essentially placed all decision-making of the Angkorian restoration and management in the hands of foreigners. These decisions do not center solely on the macrocosm. Even technical plans must be vetted through the ICC's Technical Sub-committee, which meets biannually in either Siem Reap or Phnom Penh.

Per UNESCO's designation of the Angkor Archaeological Park as a World Heritage site, the Cambodian government, with the help of the ICC, created a national management office. Aptly named the Authority for the Protection and Safeguarding of the Angkor Region—its acronym, APSARA, is not so coincidentally also the name of Cambodia's renowned traditional dance—this organization was established by Royal Decree to "act, with the Ministries concerned, as an umbrella organization over the establishments responsible for the administration and management" of the World Heritage site. According to this Royal Decree, APSARA oversees:

- The *Angkor Conservation Office*, responsible for the preservation, maintenance and restoration of the site of Angkor, in cooperation with the Ministry of Culture and Fine Arts;

- The *Tourism Development Agency* of Angkor, responsible for developing and coordinating the tourist network of the region, in cooperation with the Ministry of the Environment, the Ministry of Tourism, and the provincial sub-committee for Territorial Management, Urban Planning, and Construction;

- The *Urban Development Agency*, responsible for the conception and realization of tourism infrastructures and superstructures in the region, under the direct control of APSARA and in cooperation with the Governor of the province of Siem Reap and the provincial sub-committee for Territorial Management, Urban Planning and Construction;

- The *Institute of Khmer Culture*, in charge of the training of the historians, archaeologists and conservators responsible for the administration and maintenance of the site of Angkor, the purpose of which is to further the knowledge of Khmer culture and civilization in cooperaion with the Ministry of Culture and Fine Arts;

- A *Cultural Heritage Police Corps* specialized in the protection of the heritage, coming under the Ministry of the Interior, and carrying out its duties in the region of Angkor, in cooperation with the provincial authorities of Siem Reap.[82]

However, APSARA works in coordination with the ICC, and not above it. In fact, the ICC's Technical Committee voted in 1997 to create an Ad Hoc Committee of experts charged with advising APSARA in both specific cases—such as when Angkor Wat's western moat step collapsed—and in broader conservation issues. This effectively ensured the ICC's presence in all matters pertaining to the Angkor Archaeological Park. Indeed, "reconfirming" APSARA's charge in a Second Royal Decree in 1999, the King directly articulates the subordinate nature of APSARA and Cambodian governmental authority regarding the World Heritage site:

> The Royal Government of Kampuchea has the obligation to respect and protect the Angkor site which has been classified as a World Heritage Site and agrees to ensure the safeguarding and preservation of the said site. Hence, *any provisions or authorizations granted by national authorities or local authorities at all levels which are contrary to the international obligations shall be considered null and void.*[83]

The case of Angkor's World Heritage designation, and subsequent conservation, is an extraordinary illustration of the power of the heritage-scape's metanarrative claim to both impart an understanding of universal responsibility for the protection of foreign monuments, and also to inspire meaningful activities surrounding them. Indeed, almost immediately after these unprecedented actions, foreign governments, nonprofit organizations, and private individuals swiftly became engaged in an enormous international process of excavation and conservation. The World Monuments Fund has been the most visible nonprofit organization operating at Angkor. With a regional headquarters in Siem Reap itself, the WMF raises international awareness for the preservation of these Cambodian monuments through fundraisers, dissemination of its own "watch

list" of World Heritage in danger, and publications—including a hardcover picture book entitled *Vanishing Histories: 100 Endangered Sites from the World
Monuments Watch*, which was

> dedicated to the memory of all the vanished monuments of the world. The fra-
> gility of our monuments was highlighted by the destruction in 2001 of the giant
> Buddhas of Bamiyan in Afghanistan. Intolerance, war and politics can be as
> much the enemies of humanity's inheritance as natural disasters and the pas-
> sage of time. Nothing is sacred and we must be eternally vigilant.[84]

More materially, the WMF has also completed one of the most successful
and intricate conservation efforts at Jayavarman VII's Preah Khan, where its
experts were able to preserve both the original monastic structure and the subsequent picturesque foliage growing throughout it. The World Monuments Fund
also exercises inordinate authority over this particular temple, controlling the
tourist flow, privately opening the site to academic lectures, and hosting dance
recitals and receptions within its walls.

Agencies supported directly by foreign governments comprise a majority of
the entities at work in the Angkor Archaeological Park, an incredible feat considering the amount of World Heritage sites around the world in need of assistance and the undesirability of creating a precedence for actively participating in
all of their needs. Perhaps because Japan co-chairs the ICC, but most probably
an indication of Japan's dedication to preservation—the country makes up the
biggest single donor to the World Heritage Fund—it is also the most active in
terms of projects undertaken. The Japanese Government Team for Safeguarding
Angkor has been working in Angkor Thom, restoring concurrently its towers of
Suor Prat, as well as the immensely important Bayon temple. It has also begun
to work on Angkor Wat's Northern Library. Tokyo's private Sophia University
is also extremely active at the World Heritage site, having created an "Angkor
Mission" under the auspices of its Sophia Asia Center for Research and Human
Development Projects, which has worked on preserving Angkor Wat's main
causeway. Meanwhile, the Japanese International Cooperation Agency Cambodia (JICA), another Japanese-government-funded organization, works on related
development issues, advising Cambodia's health ministries, educating the youth,
demobilizing soldiers and installing electricity.

Even developing countries, whose World Heritage sites are numerous and
often in need of their own intensive restoration work, are committed to preserving Angkor. The Chinese Government Team for Safeguarding Angkor (CSA) is
actively at work at the ancient temple of Chau Say Thevoda. And recently the
Indian government has agreed to take on the immense responsibility of preserv-

ing the famed monastic complex of Ta Prohm, second only to Angkor Wat itself in popularity with tourists. Like the World Monuments Fund's efforts at Preah Khan, Ta Prohm requires meticulous strategic planning, as well as a great deal of monetary and technical resources, to maintain its unique fusion of nature and culture.

European governments have also offered much assistance. Funded by Switzerland's Foreign Ministry, the Swiss Agency for Development and Cooperation has undertaken the Banteay Srei Conservation Project (BSCP), an immensely important preservation effort at one of Angkor's most fragile and unique temples. Echoing its historical activities of the last centuries, France's state-funded Ecole Francaise d'Extreme-Orient (EFEO) is also active, working at the Bauphim, one of Angkor's oldest and most damaged sites. Germany's cultural department, along with the University of Cologne, embarked on a successful and intensive restoration effort at Angkor Wat itself. Called the "German Apsara Conservation Project" (GACP), it currently focuses on restoring Angkor Wat's plentiful and historically important bas-reliefs, as well as preserving the well-known temple of Preah Ko.[85] Like Japan, Germany is also active in the educational sector, instructing the German language to school children in two different programs in Phnom Penh, and also sponsoring exchange programs. The German Academic Exchange Service (DAAD) facilitates cultural and educational exchange by financing German professors' teaching missions to Cambodia, as well as by arranging scholarships for Cambodians to study in Germany. Both visiting professorships and scholarships are offered on a short and long-term basis. Founded in 1994, the Cambodian-German Association (KDV), the Phnom Penh chapter of the German Cultural Association, also receives funding from the German Foreign Ministry. The association has approximately ninety members, mostly former students of the German Democratic Republic. Finally, the German government has been active in promoting and supporting sports for the handicapped in Cambodia. It established a special National Volleyball League for the Handicapped and funds one of its teams.

As this partial list of activities demonstrates, the benefits of a World Heritage designation can be extensive. It infuses the site with valorizing claims of "unity in diversity," which in turn contribute to imparting a sense of shared responsibility for the preservation of these universally valuable, emotionally evocative sites. Raising awareness to the plight of these tangible structures only furthers substantive and meaningful activity, which, though beginning with material conservation efforts, can, as the case of Angkor demonstrates, extend into more infrastructural development endeavors. In the past decade, not only have many sites been satisfactorily restored, but they are also being studied, marketed and visited in increasing numbers. American universities have seen an increase in graduate students engaging in fieldwork at Angkor, and many, like the University of Chicago, have extended their operations into this previously understudied region. Most importantly, these activities demonstrate stabilization and regulation in the region. Looting, at least within the UNESCO-designated confines of Angkor Archaeological Park, has been staved. New temples outside the Park are beginning to be explored, researched and restored. Electric lights have been installed on the major thoroughfares leading to and from Siem Reap. Youths are being educated. As a result in increased tourism, not only have more funds that can be used for a greater quantity of infrastructural development projects entered the country, but qualitative cross-cultural communication has also increased. And symbolically reflecting these normalizing developments within the socio-economic environment of the country as a whole, in late 2004, the Angkor Archaeological Park was removed from the World Heritage in Danger List.

CHAPTER TEN

PROBLEMATICS OF PRESERVATION:
NARRATIVE AND PRACTICE
AT THE ANGKOR ARCHAEOLOGICAL PARK

While each World Heritage site is impacted by the heritage-scape differently, the Angkor Archaeological Park can be considered an optimal case study for an examination of the heritage-scape's effects at the local level for many reasons. Perhaps more so than most other countries that take part in UNESCO's global experiment, the post-colonial and post-Khmer Rouge Kingdom of Cambodia has wholeheartedly embraced the concept of "World Heritage" as a viable means of reconstructing a new society with a global identity. While it is not true that Angkor had been 'lost' to all society until Westerners discovered it, Nicholas Tarling eloquently points out that

> The appropriation of Angkor by modern Khmers as an important part of their history is based upon relatively recent reconstructions of the past. Between the days of Angkor and the twentieth century were generations of Khmers for whom Angkor, if not unknown, was nonetheless without the significance now attached to it. Unlike the case of the Viets . . . the Khmer world offered options that did not require the retention of Angkor. Exercising the option to relocate the Khmer polity, both geographically and culturally, offered the possibility of leaving behind a particular historical experience. That this experience should be retrieved in modern times reflects a case of shrinking options. In a world of multiplying predators, the Khmers have begun to need Angkor.[1]

Yet as Penny Edwards shows, this is not the first era in which the Khmer have appropriated Angkor to construct a valorized nation-state on the world stage; Angkor was also integral to the perception of Khmer-ness during the period of the Protectorate. Thanks to the efforts of the EFEO and its related Commission of Antiquities, which was created in 1905 by Jules Morel, the monuments "gradually but steadily" began to be "imbue[d] with national significance" in the eyes of the French-educated Khmer literati.[2] Edwards points out that the meaning of these intransient ruins shifted in their minds, from serving as "evidence of the Buddhist law of impermanence (*anitcang*)" to "material proof of the imported idea of linear historical development centered on the nation state."[3]

It is worth noting that Angkor continued to play a role in valorizing Khmer identity even through the terrible reign of the Khmer Rouge, whose radical form of placemaking entailed forcibly "forgetting" much of the colonial concept of place that became ingrained in Cambodian identity during its inclusion in French Indochina.[4] Despite embracing a vision of a secular and completely agrarian Communist society at "year zero," they did not harm the Angkorian structures as the Taliban has done to the Buddhist monuments in the Bamiyan Valley. Indeed, the Khmer Rouge even preserved the basic image of Angkor Wat on its flag—a tradition that began in the times of the French Protectorate, was replicated during the American-supported government of Lon Nol ("Khmer Republic" from 1970-1975) and the post-Khmer Rouge occupations of Vietnam ("People's Republic of Kampuchia" from 1979 to 1989 and, after an agreement between Hun Sen and King Norodom Sihanouk, the "State of Cambodia" from 1989 to 1991) and the United Nations.[5] To date, Cambodia is the only country in the world with a World Heritage site on its flag. Angkor Wat is also featured on its banknotes and even on the cans of the popular local beer. The importance of UNESCO and its globalizing endeavor is evident even in the selection of Cambodia's new King Norodom Sihamoni, who was the country's official ambassador to UNESCO until he took the throne in October 2004.

Though Angkor is a semiotic icon of the Cambodian nation-state, the site itself very much remains a product of the international community, notwithstanding its alternative contextualization in the heritage-scape. Just as the École Françes d'Estrême Orient was responsible for excavating, preserving and producing knowledge concerning the ruins within the Angkor Archaeological Park during the period of the Protectorate, so too are coteries of international experts engaged in a similar endeavor today. Indeed, Angkor is a hub where, informed by disparate cultural understandings, the activities of Eastern and Western governments, non-profit organizations and academic institutions conjoin, ostensibly under the administrative umbrella of the governmental APSARA organization—which itself was a product of UNESCO's World Heritage program.

It is precisely this "structure of the conjuncture," in the words of Marshall Sahlins,[6] that problematically produces competing claims at Angkor. Sahlins' famed concept is exceptionally appropriate in the context of the heritage-scape's Angkor Archaeological Park. For Sahlins, the "structure of the conjuncture" is the "practical realization of the cultural categories in a specific historical context, as expressed in the interested action of the historical agents, *including the microsociology* of their interaction."[7] In other words, it is the localized "system of relationships"[8] that is created, in a particular place and time, by the intersection of diverse cultural agents who may carry with them their own cosmologies, histories, motivations, and cultural categories. Cultural agents may be meta-social actors or micro-social actors—both groups and individuals. The decisions and actions of particular individuals can indeed change the course of history.[9]

Sahlins' concept builds on Anthony Giddens' belief in the "duality of structure"—that is, the structure is simultaneously a preexisting concept (which includes the "intended consequences of people in power") and the unintended consequences which arise.[10] This is, I believe, what is occurring at the Angkor Archaeological Park. The APSARA organization, as a dualistic mediator both of the government and, to a certain extent, UNESCO's World Heritage Committee itself, coordinates disparate efforts at preserving the physical monuments and disseminating particular forms of knowledge about them across the heritage-scape. The intended consequences are to valorize the Khmer people and, simultaneously, to contribute to the heritage-scape's broader meta-narrative claim of "unity in diversity." But the very participation (and non-participation) by particular agents produce outcomes that are quite unintended. This is not a product of ill-intended or self-serving individuals or groups; on the contrary, it is a specific product of the structure of the conjuncture of preservation activities at the Angkor Archaeological Park. The following pages detail two specific components that create competing narrative claims: The first are the two classes of forms these monuments take: "preserved" ruins or "restored" monuments. These are historically situated; they are largely colored by the decisions made by the EFEO a century ago. The second is the practice of contemporary preservation itself, at Angkor. It, too, is historically situated, but from a different period. Because of the actions of the Khmer Rouge, UNESCO has taken an unprecedented hand in determining the management of the site, as I have shown in the previous chapter. Combined with the unfortunate lack of indigenous Khmer who have the proper epistemic abilities and skills to lead conservation efforts, this management program perpetuates a subtle performance of neo-colonialism.

Competing Narrative Claims at Angkor Archaeological Park

Though the heritage-scape extends across the globe ostensibly without regard for national sovereignty, standardizing diversity and imbuing each individual site with UNESCO's meta-narrative, its numerous individual applications translate into an equal number of variations. The amorphous nature of the heritage-scape, coupled with a rather flexible meta-narrative, allows for each World Heritage site to negotiate and frame the narrative it espouses in uniquely singular ways. At the local level, James Wertsch's assertion becomes hauntingly clear: what one culture deems a usable narrative claim is often quite different from what another one requires.[11]

The Tourist Encounter

Left to Cambodian guides and tour operators,[12] a typical itinerary through the Angkor Archaeological Park usually follows the same course. The tour bus, or *tuk tuk* motorized cyclo for the more independent "adventure" traveler, departs from the hotel, passing a myriad of new accommodations sprawling on either side of the freshly paved Charles De Gaulle Boulevard. Buildings bearing names synonymous for luxury pass like a "who's who" list in Condé Nast: Raffles, Le Meridian, Sofitel, Shangri-la, and others. The road itself is freshly paved; reddish-brown clay laid down by the pavers still line each side, a dusty shoulder perhaps awaiting new tiles to make a picturesque walkway. On the right, a half-finished building dominates a prominent intersection. A hulking structure of concrete and steel, this will be the new Angkor National Museum, whose ill-conceived English-language tagline urges passers-by to "See Angkor and not die yet!" Despite this quizzical mistranslation, this museum will be a large and more fitting home for the many statues currently stored up in the Angkor Conservation Unit, only a part of which is open to visitors through special arrangements. A little farther down on the left side the road, past a luxury hotel constructed out of an old Cambodian prison, a mass of people will invariably be seen gathering outside a rambling complex with neatly manicured lawns and freshly painted gates. This is the Children's Hospital, a well-respected institution in a country currently without adequate health services; for injuries as minor as a broken bone, tourists must be flown first-class to Bangkok to receive treatment.[13] The Children's Hospital is the brainchild of a Swiss doctor, Beat Richner, who goes by the Italian-esque stage name of "Beatocello" (or little Beat); his name is also a play on words, for "beato" means "blessed" (and thus "beatocello" is a "blessed little one"). The institution doubles as a weekly concert forum for the medic-flautist, who holds one-man shows as a fundraising/awareness-raising device to help the poor rural children.

The coach stops at the checkpoint, essentially a large parking lot and a small administration building, where a foreign-owned company collects visiting fees. One travel writer has likened it to "a rest stop on the New Jersey Turnpike" for its uninspiring aesthetic.[14] With his group's yellow Angkor Passes in hand, the guide swiftly jumps off and on the bus to get approval for entry. Forty United States dollars buys an official looking three-day pass, complete with a laminated passport photo on an image of Angkor Wat or another famous temple from the park. Approval granted, the bus rumbles onward, into what seems to be a jungle, thick with dipterocarp, smooth-trunked trees the locals call *chuuteal*. The hopeful tourist strains to catch a glimpse of traditional homes amid these native trees—the indigenous population surely does not live in the town's multitudinous five-star paradises—but only infrequently is he contented with the sight of these stilted structures of wood, aluminum and palm leaves. Since the Angkor Archaeological Park was turned into a World Heritage site, regulations have stripped the land from all residential zoning, although towns do exist in the hinter-regions of the park near the temple of Banteay Srei. Only the grandfathers are grandfathered in, so to speak; those who built houses on the land before the UNESCO designation are allowed to stay with their families, but the right does not carry onto their children once this older generation passes away. Mostly, however, visitors can feed some ornery monkeys who wait in increasing numbers for tourists who disembark at the West Gate of Angkor Thom.

It is an imposing structure, crowned by three immense stone heads, each sculpted in the likeness of the king who commissioned it. Adding to this allure is an impressive causeway leading up to the gate, flanked on each side by equally imposing regiments of gods and demons frozen in an eternal tug-of-war to churn the milky cosmos. Although Khmer architectural cosmology dictates that this would be Angkor Thom's exit, its proportion, state of preservation and general orientation at the beginning of the park has rendered it a fitting introduction to the magic and mystery that has greeted visitors since the time of the first Portuguese and French explorers "discovered" the jungle-choked temples in the eighteenth century. To prevent any more damage by local chauffeurs attempting to squeeze increasingly bigger busses through the entrance, the government now requires tourists to disembark before passing through, and making the trip across Angkor Thom by foot. It is worth the physical exertion. Angkor Thom was the great capital city of King Jayavarman VII, under whose 40-year reign the Khmer empire expanded to its greatest extent, and under whose patronage Khmer architecture flourished. Aside from the older Angkor Wat, Jayavarman's constructions are some of the most important, monumental, and enduring of Khmer sites in Southeast Asia; in the Angkor Archaeological Park alone, Angkor Thom, Preah Khan, and Ta Prohm are his—and each tell a different aspect of his story. While the latter two are monastic complexes dedicated to his parents—linking his lineage to the gods—Angkor Thom, or "Great City," is his embodiment.

After an in-depth examination of the vast ruins of Angkor Thom and its central Bayon temple, renowned throughout the world for its famed smiling faces, the landscape becomes a blend of yellowed grasses burnt from the Southeast Asian sun, dotted with tall coconut palms. There is a saying in Cambodia about these trees, which picturesquely pepper photographs of the great Angkor Wat; *the nation extends as far as the coconut palm grows*. The Khmer Rouge evoked this phrase when attempting to grab land from Vietnam, where these trees grow in the Mekong Delta and in the old Cham-influenced central and southern provinces. The bus can meet tourists here again for the next stop. Driving across a bumpy road through the cleared fields, one is suddenly greeted to the left by a tall and broken laterite wall containing what looks like a forest behind, and a continuation of a clearing on the right, brimming with makeshift cabins exhibiting "traditional" Cambodian handicrafts. The sight is as striking as it is mysterious—a dense thicket of green rising up unexpectedly from the clearing, a jumble of rocks still held captive in its vegetative tentacles. It is Ta Prohm, and a visit here amongst the twisting trees and collapsed constructions allows visitors the chance to indulge the Indiana Jones or Lara Croft in each of them. While this sentiment is best enjoyed when the site is empty of tourists, parts of this rambling structure invariably become congested with visitors vying with and locals dressed in "native" costumes to photograph themselves before a distorted doorway featured in *Tomb Raider*. Perhaps in moving from one site to the other, the visitor may also catch a glimpse of foreign archaeologists and preservationists busy at work in the hot Cambodian sun. What is certain is that Cambodian children selling t-shirts or postcards will approach the traveler at almost every stop; even some police officers keeping watch over the tourists have been known to offer their badges as souvenirs for a few dollars.[15]

Following lunch back in the hotel or at a restaurant catering to Siem Reap's foreign visitors, the traveler can enjoy a half-day tour of immense Angkor Wat, where each passing bas relief, sacred niche, and stunning building are all humbling in their size, cosmological layout and aesthetic beauty. In contrast to Ta Prohm, which has been preserved as it looked to the French explorers, Angkor Wat has been restored to more closely resemble how the temple appeared during the height of its use. The grass is neatly manicured; the moat is filled with water. No fallen, lichen-covered piles of bricks can be seen, and little vegetation can be spotted growing between the walls. This is not a jungle atmosphere, and no wild trees grow, save the important coconut palm. After soaking in this culture, the visitor is granted access to climb the rooftop of Angkor Wat—certainly not something the local Khmers at the time of the temple's use were able to do with ease, but an opportunity not unlike that of exploring Ta Prohm. Luckily for those less flexible visitors for whom a climb up the narrow and crumbled steps is difficult, there is serious talk of installing an elevator in the ruins.

Spectacular views are to be had at the Angkor Archaeological Park, thanks to a number of durable "mountain temples" built in the heyday of the Khmer empire, whose elevation afford breathtaking panoramas of the park to those whose physical strength allow it. Another less taxing way to take in a birds-eye view of the park is by a dirigible. The giant, yellow Angkor Balloon, tethered one kilometer away from the park but marring the landscape nonetheless, costs a little over ten dollars per person and flies about 30 times regularly between dawn and dusk. Sunrise and sunset, however, are the most common times for getting a "unique" or "not-to-be-missed" view of Angkor Wat, and while the great temple is best viewed at sunrise from within its outer walls, many make the pilgrimage up a select few mountain temples for an aerial view of it as the sun sets. The most popular place for this is Phnom Bakheng, one of the earliest mountain temples in the park. Despite its historic and archaeological importance to academics, it is clear that the never-restored temple's importance to tourist is limited to its ideal position to collectively view Angkor Wat: during the rest of the day it is almost completely vacant, but as the heat begins to subside and the shadows grow longer, it quickly becomes the most popular monument in the park. Indeed, an experience at Phnom Bakheng at sunset is an experience of a multicultural festival. Local vendors congregate first, readying their wares in anticipation of the foreign crowds. Most of the elephant jockeys, who are positioned at a few locations within the park during the day, congregate at the foot of the hill as well; fifteen dollars is all it takes a group of four to bypass the precariously steep and crumbled steps and ascend to the top of the mount (it is only an additional ten dollars for the easier trip back down). Young independent travelers arrive on foot and by *tuk tuk*, their huge packs tethered to their back. Cars and taxis drop off older independent travelers as the tour busses arrive with groups, who tumble out unaware of the steep climb ahead. Through all of the confusion and noise, the guides point to the way up and remain below with the drivers and the vendors. Atop the mountain, the actual experience is a bit anticlimactic, for the humidity that emerges as the hot air dissipates tends to mar the sunset's spectacular splashes of color over a tiny Angkor Wat in the distance. But the descent is once again a memorable group experience; while visitors climb up the mountain at staggered times during dusk, a mass exodus occurs after the sun has slipped below the horizon. Somehow, amidst the mass of elephants, vendors and the dusty travelers jockeying for space down the mountain, the guide always tend to spot his clients before they see him, and he whisks them off to Siem Reap.

Back in town a banquet awaits, complete with an "Apsara dance performance" by young orphans from the French-run Enfants D'Asie ASPECA Orphanage, and a buffet of "traditional" culinary delicacies. "Traditional" is a term used loosely here, as the long smorgasbord tables are filled with a variety of vaguely "Oriental" stir-fried fare sufficiently Westernized for the tourist palate. One guide shrugged when asked which food was his favorite in the buffet, stating, "You wouldn't like what we [really] eat at home."[16] The din of tired yet excited discussions flows over the backdrop of music, lights and clanking plates, as visitors trade stories of their discovery of Cambodian culture, already committing them to memory and interpreting their experiences against the remembered experiences of their compatriots. Retiring to their rooms at a prominent five-star hotel, each visitor is greeted not with a goodnight mint on the pillow, but rather with an elegantly typed "bedtime story"—an excerpted passage from Henri Mouhot's famed diary, detailing the wonder and excitement he felt when he first "discovered" the lost kingdom of Angkor in the eighteenth century. Drifting off to sleep, memories of one's own discovery resonate with the story, and he is eager to return to the park to relive the adventure all over again.

Conveying Competing Claims through Preservation

As the "ideal type" of group tour to the Angkor Archaeological Park illustrates, the visitor to Cambodia's only World Heritage site is forced to negotiate a series of competing and conflicting narratives, each one framing in a different way the heritage-scape's conceptually amorphous meta-narrative. In this way, it can be conceived of as a series of concentric circles, a matryoshka of frames, each one nested within and interacting with one another. Recalling Parker Pearson and Richards' assertion that even the "cultural artifact of a name" creates a specially delimited place,[17] the very title of the Angkor Archaeological Park elicits a host of competing claims. While "archaeological" suggests a learned, academic pursuit of uncovering the vestiges of a culture buried under the sands of time, "park" suggests a setting for vibrant and enjoyable leisure activities. Similarly, the former suggests an educational endeavor—perhaps uncovering Khmer material cultural remains; the latter encourages an active indulgence in recreation—perhaps imagining oneself as Henri Mouhot or Lara Croft.

ICOMOS' justification for Angkor's designation also subtly includes contradictory messages. At first glance, it appears that the temples of Angkor frame UNESCO's "unity in diversity" narrative by serving as an idealized material manifestation of the former Khmer empire and its multicultural connections; notably absent is any direct mention of French influence or of the harmonious illustration of nature blending with culture. Yet examined more critically, a subtle and contradictory commentary about Western superiority emerges, as illustrated by the last sentence tacked onto Criteria iii—that "all that remains of that civili-

zation is its rich heritage of cult structures." Angkor is certainly not unique in
this respect; many of the over eight hundred World Heritage sites are no longer
occupied places, yet such a statement rarely is included in their justifications for
inscription. Indeed, this sort of commentary is already referenced in the title
"World Heritage site" itself; the very concept of a *site* seems to designate a
Processualist notion of isolated cultural remains rigidly frozen in time, ready to
be unearthed.[18] The presence of Criteria *iii*'s statement amid a historicized description of the past legacy of the Khmer, however, frames Angkor in the narrative of Western valorization, suggesting that only empty vessels of Khmer culture remain—vessels that must be protected lest the civilization be swept from
the world's memory, just as they seemed to have been swept from the material
world itself. Such a claim produces a marked imbalance in the perceived ownership of the site, leading to problems of perceived social inequity currently faced
in Cambodia today. Indeed, as one delves deeper into the complex frames of this
vast World Heritage site, it becomes clear that two narrative claims feed off of
and compete with one another, coloring individuals' interpretation of what constitutes the "universal value" of these heritage places. These narrative claims can
be distilled into two categories, which have their roots in diverse historical periods within the greater life history of the monuments: *valorization of Khmer culture,* and *valorization of Western culture.*[19]

The first claim—*valorization of Khmer culture*—can be found in a variety
of monuments within the Angkor Archaeological Park that were restored in
what preservationists feel best resembled the form at the time of their initial
construction. Often a project such as this requires clearing the many trees that
have grown in and around the structure, excavation, replacing broken stones,
and rebuilding entire sections. Such a practice, while widespread, is often contentious, considering that conservators are actively denying a part of the structure's more recent total life history in an effort to re-create the physical structure
as it is imagined to have originally appeared. This, then, serves to re-present one
particular set of narrative claims, those thought to have been initially conveyed
at the point in time to which the preservationists are "restoring" the monument.
Such legitimizing claims to grandeur is a source of pride for Cambodians, as illustrated by re-presentations of Angkor Wat on the nation's currency and flag.

For this particular World Heritage site, many of these monuments represent
the original Khmer kings' claims to legitimacy and valorization for which the
monuments were created during the Angkorian era. Indeed, many of the structures typically visited were created by a single king, Jayavarman VII (1125-
1215), who, after a life of dubious merit to his countrymen—marked by voluntary exile among the Khmer's enemies, lost love, religious conversion, his father's short reign, a tragic coup toppling his Khmer predecessor, and idle wit-

nessing of the greatest defeat of the Khmers in history—took the crown at a late age and proved to be "arguably not only the greatest of all the Khmer kings but also the greatest personage in Cambodian history,"[20] a sentiment no doubt passed down generations with the help of an unprecedented array of evocative, monumental structures he created. Jayavarman VII's constructions, which broke from the past century's tradition of building smaller structures in wood, demonstrated various claims of power, which probably was conveyed by stirring a collective sense of wonder. Hearkening to Pierre Bourdieu's claim that architecture can be read as a materialization of social relationships, and Giddens' assertion that architecture can help to direct human activities and serve as a "major prerogative for those who are in power," Michael Kolb believes "often this increase in monumental grandeur is accompanied by shifts in elite ostentation and elaboration . . . and the iconography of ritual begins to depict human elites' controlling natural or divine forces of the universe."[21] The ability to provide for rich adornments and to mobilize a large workforce over a lengthy period of time certainly attest to some form of power, be it economic, religious or purely physical. Ta Prohm, for example, includes two large courtyards and intricate series of long, low buildings connected by narrow passages and concentric galleries—all contained within 7,536,457 square feet of laterite walls[22] and a moat. Although exaggeration is always a possibility in formal inscriptions, Ta Prohm's stelae maintains that the monastery boasted a wealth of gold, silver and precious jewels in its coffers, owned 3,140 villages, employed 12,640 people, and was supported by the labor of 79,365 men.[23] These land holdings may also demonstrate claims to power over nature, claims which may have been necessary to make considering that the devastating Cham victory ten years prior demonstrated rival Champa's mastery over the Mekong Delta and Tonle Sap River, an unexpected feat never attempted before. Like the gardens of Babylon, Persia, China, Japan and Europe, the presence of large tracts of fertile courtyards within the monastery's thick walls may also symbolize an internalization, and hence, control, over nature.[24]

Besides simply articulating claims to legitimacy through a Bourdieuian display of power, the architectonics, aesthetics and arrangement of these temples embodied these claims through the use of mythological and religious frames of reference. Jayavarman VII was a Buddhist monarch whose two wives were instrumental in his conversion from Hinduism. Coe notes that he was a "major patron of the Sangha, the community of monks, and at Angkor he built three cities in miniature for them."[25] In an effort to garner legitimacy for his religion, he melded Mahāyāna adornments and practices with long-entrenched Hindu motifs—such as those seen in the architecture of the great Angkor Wat, itself a temple dedicated to the Hindu god Vishnu.[26] Replicating prior architectural

forms that would resonate with Cambodian collective memories, while introducing new religious adornments and practices, would serve, as Connerton states,
"to ensure that these [new] forms are intelligible at all."[27]

In addition, seen in relation to one another, Ta Prohm, Preah Khan and the
Bayon also served to frame Jayavarman VII's personal claims to legitimacy in a
religious and mythological light by mapping his kinship onto a sacred geography of his own creation. One of the first complexes the king constructed was Ta
Prohm,[28] which he dedicated to his mother, Queen Sri Jayarajacudamani. It was
from her line he could trace his lineage to the mythological rulers of the pre-
empire period, Soma/Kaundinya and Mera/Kambu, whose names and narratives
were already inscribed in Cambodian collective memory.[29] Ta Prohm included a
monumental statue of the king's mother in the form of Prajnaparamita, the
mother of Buddha. Although the statue clearly linked Jayavarman VII's mother
to that of the Buddha, it aesthetically drew on preexistent religious motifs such
that it was called by locals "Ta Prohm," or "ancestor Brahma." In *trimurti* Hinduism, Brahma is the Creator (with Vishnu as the Sustainer of *dharma* and
Shiva as the purgative Destroyer); Brahma is the "grandfather" god who creates
the earth, the deities, Man and nature. In Vaishnavism (a somewhat monotheistic
Hinduism that posits Vishnu as the incarnation of the primordial energy *Brah-
man*, and therefore as the ultimate generator of all) to which Angkor Wat's
Suryavarman II likely was devoted, Brahma is himself merely a part of
Vishnu.[30]

While Ta Prohm and its central statue was intended to represent his mother
in the form of Prajnaparamita, Preah Khan, constructed some years later, featured a central devotional statue of Jayavarman VII's father in the likeness of the
bodhisattva Lokeshvara. This, too, was integral to Jayavarman's personal valorization claims. Although his father, Dharanindravarman II, was installed by the
powerful Suryavarman II, he reigned no more than a decade; his death set into
motion a period of coups that so destabilized the empire's power structure that
the Cham king Jaya Indravarman—who himself had usurped the Cham
throne[31]—invaded, sacked and briefly annexed Angkor. It seems that Jayavarman VII, in addition to lauding his ultimate victory over Jaya Indravarman four
years later, would wish to depict himself not only as a restorer to the throne, but
as the legitimate heir to the last true king, who ruled before the storm. In Cambodia, Lokeshvara, which literally means "lord of the world" (-*ishvara* means
"lord" in Sanskrit), is not simply understood as an Avalokiteshvara, or compassionate lord "who looks down" with sympathy on his fellow man (as denoted by
the Sanskrit -*shvara*), but rather the embodiment of the supreme principle of the
world as incarnated in the ruler[32]—in much the same way as Vishnu (and therefore Suryavarman II) was conceptualized. Indeed, despite being a monastery and

proto-university for the Buddhist *sangha*, Preah Khan architecturally was also a religiously transitional space. While Ta Prohm's central statue seemed to have called upon preexistent Hindu tropes, at Preah Khan, the entire monastery more clearly posited a syncretistic cosmology that fused Hindu and Buddhist motifs. At Preah Khan, the outer sectors were dedicated to different sects of Hinduism—the north was Shivite (as Banteay Srei was), while the west was Vaisnavite (as Angkor Wat was); the south was dedicated to ancestor worship.[33] Its core, however, was Buddhist, and culminated in a statue of Dharanindravarman II as Lokeshvara. Supposedly constructed on the spot at which Jayavarman VII defeated the Chams, this structure was called "Preah Khan," which means "sacred sword;" it fuses two strengths integral to Jayavarman VII's kingly authority: the ascribed legitimacy that comes from his sacred kinship, and his acquired authority that comes from his own heroic actions.

Geographically placed between the two of these temples is Angkor Thom,[34] Jayavarman VII's "Great City," where at its very center rises the wondrous Bayon temple with two hundred enigmatically smiling faces believed to be Jayavarman VII's face in the form of the bodhisattva Avalokiteshvara.[35] Though the iconography of these famed faces as the bodhisattva Avalokiteshvara is speculative, it is a sound one. The bodhisattva Avalokiteshvara is the central figure in Mahāyāna Buddhism—to which Jayavarman VII ascribed—and, from the 10th century onward, represents that transcendent personage[36] who has achieved Enlightenment, but out of compassion has chosen to remain a presence for humankind to help all in their path to Nirvana. As Rooney points out, though the Khmers did not have the caste system as in India, the king was nevertheless considered the highest entity on the social scale and the protectors of all; the ubiquitous suffix of Khmer kings, -*varman*, which originally meant "armor," had come to mean "protection" or "protector."[37] Yet Jayavarman seemed to take this to another level; he protected by the sword and by devotion (*bhakti*),[38] as Preah Khan so aptly illustrates and as the *Bhagavad Gītā* prescribes for the noble warrior-caste, the *kshatriya*s, but he also wanted to be remembered as having done so with great compassion.[39] Indeed, Jayavarman VII greatly facilitated devotional travel to Angkor by constructing a complex network of laterite roadways dotted with 121 rest houses[40]—not unlike the Western pilgrimage routes of Santiago de Compostela[41] or the via Francigena. Jayavarman also created the earliest known hospitals in Southeast Asia; from inscriptions there are said to have been as many as one hundred and two,[42] arranged in a four-tier hierarchy. According to archaeologist Alan Kolata, who is currently conducting excavations of some of them, the highest status hospitals were placed just outside of the main gates of Angkor Thom; some scholars also believe Ta Prohm to have also served as a hospital.[43]

Like Ta Prohm and Preah Khan, Angkor Thom fuses Hindu and Buddhist tropes: in addition to boasting a hospital, the West Gate entrance to the city is endowed with a lengthy causeway flanked by *devas* and *asuras* pulling on a water snake (*naga*) in a divine tug-of-war. While the sight of these is impressive in and of itself—especially the frightening power-hungry *asuras,* whose anchor is the ten-headed Rāvana, the immoral counterpart to Rāma in the Rāmāyana. This structure is extremely evocative of preexisting religious motifs on a number of levels. First, the tug-of-war is a sculptural representation of a prominent Hindu creation myth, the Churning of the Milky Sea. This myth is featured in the Hindu epic poem, the *Māhabharata,* the tale which frames the divinely revealed[44] *Bhagavad Gītā.* This creation story was prominently featured as the bas relief *tour de force* on the East Gallery of Angkor Wat, and depicts Vishnu—standing upon his turtle avatar, Kurma—as the pivot around which the devas and asuras tug. There is a pivot around which the sculpted devas and asuras of Angkor Thom revolve, too: the West Gate itself, which is topped with four smiling faces of Jayavarman in the likeness of the Buddha Avalokiteshvara. Thus, its presence at the entrance of Angkor Thom serves to also link Angkor Wat, Suryavarman II's "city that is a temple"[45] with Jayavarman VII's new capital city, but in a way that subtly transitions it from Hinduism to Buddhism, and from mythology to biography. The presence of Rāvana in this depiction further serves to further call upon a beloved and commonly understood myth, the Rāmāyana (or in Khmer, the *Reamker*), to effect this transition. In Vaisnavism, Rāma is one of most important of the avatars of Vishnu (the other most prominent being Krishna, the central character of the *Bhagavad Gītā*). It therefore makes sense that his story would be depicted on the Western Gallery of Angkor Wat.[46] Save Rāvana, there is no prominent depiction of the Rāmāyana at Angkor Thom; rather, Vishnu's counterpart is the Jayavarman VII, presumably a bottisattva Avalokiteshvara. Today, the seventeenth-century Khmer adaptation of the Rāmāyana, the Reamker, uses Rāma (called Preah Ream) to illustrate Buddhist tenets and ideals.

The presence of Rāvana, however, also served to insert the biography of Jayavarman VII into the mythology of the Khmers. In one inscription, Jayavarman VII likens his Cham rival, Jaya Indravarman to the mythological arch-enemy: "Jaya Indravarman, the king of the Chams, presumptuous as Rāvana, transporting his army in chariots, when to fight the country of Kambu, like to heaven."[47] What is important in this inscription is that it fuses historical information that was lived and remembered by his contemporary Khmer audience with both the mythologies of the Rāmāyana (Rāvana) and that of Jayavarman's lineage (Kambu). The presence of Rāvana at the West Gate served to underscore the historical as well as the mythological, which congealed into the biographical in both these inscriptions and in the depictions of Jayavarman VII and his deeds.[48] Indeed, just as Rāma defeated Rāvana with the help of outsiders (the monkey general Hanuman and his army), in the Bayon's East Gallery Jayavarman VII clearly depicts his re-conquest of Angkor from the Chams as aided by outsiders (Chinese, who are portrayed with exotic headdresses and goatees, in contrast to their Khmer counterparts—depicted in an upper level of the relief—who wear their hair short and without any headdresses Thus, Jayavarman VII was adept at visually and textually fusing both of these to create a rich biography of himself that could—and indeed would—resist the transience of time. Indeed, as the celebrated French epigrapher George Coedès once argued, Jayavarman VII departed from the "usual mythological bombast to release precise biographical facts" in his inscriptions that creates his character with immediate "concreteness that makes it possible to trace a living portrait"[49]—no matter how factually true it was.[50]

At the center of Angkor Thom is Jayavarman VII's main temple, the Bayon. While Ta Prohm represented Jayavarman's mother as Prajnaparamita and Preah Khan his father as Lokesvara, the Bayon represents Jayavarman himself as the Lord Buddha, or "Buddharaja,"[51] for at the geographic center of the Bayon's central shrine stood an immense image of the Buddha.[52] Coedès goes on to argue that "this statue was not only a Buddhist substitute for the Shivite Devaraja [in the form of a golden lingam, which was often placed at the geographic center of a (Shivite) Hindu city], but also a statue of apotheosis of the founder king, whose features are undoubtedly also to be seen on the upper parts of the towers in the form of the Bodhisattva Lokeshvara Samantamukha, 'who has faces in all directions.'"[53] These three figures—Buddha, Bodhisattva Lokesvara and Prajnaparamita—are the "Buddhist trinity" evoked at the start of Jayavarman VII's inscriptions and often found together on numerous small votive tablets or in sculptures. Taken together, the architectural trifecta of Ta Prohm, Preah Khan and Bayon temples served to emphasize not only spiritual unity but also the powerfully religious mandate the king enjoyed.

Perhaps because the second narrative claim at work—*valorization of Western culture*—operates in a number of more subtle ways, at least to Western viewers, it can be considered even more contentious. This narrative began as early as the first colonial conservators at Angkor, well-intentioned individuals from the École Frances d'Estrême Orient who, beginning formal restoration work in 1901, purposely left Ta Prohm and other structures as they found them—monuments to the destructive forces of time. This was as much a testament to history and archaeology as it was an overt colonial claim of superiority; they clearly wanted to leave evidence of some structures for posterity as they appeared before the Westerners' material interference. Yet the French did inter-

fere with the linear trajectory of the monuments' life histories, and the very juxtaposition of sites "restored" to how the conservators imagined they were intended to appear with those simply "preserved" as they were found at the inception of the colonial era—frozen in time—only seems to underscore the transience of the first narrative claim. Indeed, such juxtapositional activity can also
be read as the paragon of Orientalism as Edward Said defined it:

> *Orientalism* [is] a way of coming to terms with the Orient that is based on the
> Orient's special place in European Western experience. The Orient is . . . the
> place of Europe's greatest and richest and oldest colonies, the source of its civi-
> lizations and languages, its cultural contestant, and one of its deepest and most
> recurring images of the Other. In addition, the Orient has helped to define
> Europe (or the West) as its contrasting image, idea, personality, experience. Yet
> none of this Orient is merely imaginative. The Orient is an integral part of
> European material civilization and culture. Orientalism expresses and repre-
> sents that part culturally and even ideologically as a mode of discourse with
> supporting institutions, vocabulary, scholarship, imagery, doctrines, even colo-
> nial bureaucracies and colonial styles. . . . Orientalism is a style of thought
> based upon an ontological and epistemological distinction made between "the
> Orient" and (most of the time) "the Occident."[54]

For Said, however, though the Orient is a Western cultural construction and "not
an inert fact of nature,"[55] Orientalism is not simply an overt political discourse,
nor a "structure of lies or of myths which, truth be told, would simply blow
away."[56] Though it is not "automatically nonpolitical," it is, rather, a subtle and
pervasive narrative of difference which works its way into the collective imagi-
nations of all walks of Western life. Academics, such as those at the École Françes d'Estrême Orient, are not immune, despite their good intentions and their ostensible objectivity. Just as Sahlins would contend that all people work the Other
into their cosmologies despite ignorance of the Other's existence,[57] Said remarks:

> If it is true that no production of knowledge in the human sciences can ever ig-
> nore or disclaim its author's involvement as a human subject in his own cir-
> cumstances, then it must also be true that for a European or American studying
> the Orient there can be no disclaiming the main circumstances of his actuality:
> that he comes up against the Orient as a European or American first, as an indi-
> vidual second. And to be a European or American in such a situation is by no
> means an inert fact. It meant and means being aware, however dimly, that one
> belongs to a power with definite interests in the Orient, and more important,
> that one belongs to a part of the earth with a definite history of involvement in
> the Orient almost since the time of Homer.[58]

Thus, Orientalism is a way of seeing not only the Other, but really oneself. It is a way of positioning oneself in his culture's cosmology, a way of understanding the reality of lived experiences. While political, it is not necessarily conscious, and many an objective academic, artist, or social worker—Said contends—will almost unknowingly fall into Orientalist tropes as he situates himself in relation to what he has come to know as the Orient:

> Orientalism is not a mere political subject matter or field that is reflected passively by culture, scholarship or institutions; nor is it a large and diffuse collection of texts about the Orient; nor is it representative and expressive of some nefarious "Western" imperialist plot to hold down the "Oriental" world. It is rather a distribution of geopolitical awareness into aesthetic, scholarly, economic, sociological, historical and philological texts; it is an elaboration not only of a base geographical distinction (the world is made up of two unequal halves, Orient and Occident) but also a whole series of "interests" which, by such means as scholarly discovery, philological reconstruction, psychological analysis, landscape and sociological description, it not only creates but also maintains; it is, rather than expresses, a certain will or intention to understand, in some cases to control, manipulate, even incorporate, what is a manifestly different (or alternative and novel) world; it is, above all, a discourse that is by no means in direct, corresponding relationship with political power in the raw, but rather is produced and exists in an uneven exchange with various kinds of power, shaped to a degree by the exchange with power political (as with a colonial or imperial establishment), power intellectual (as with reigning sciences like comparative linguists or anatomy, or any of the modern policy sciences), power cultural (as with orthodoxies and canons of tastes, texts, values), power moral (as with ideas about what "we" do and what "they" cannot do or understand as "we" do). Indeed, my real argument is that Orientalism is—and does not simply represent—considerable dimension of modern political-intellectual culture, and as such as less to do with the Orient than it does with "our" world.

Indeed, just as it is now at Angkor, nature was central to the Orientalist narrative claim that the industrialized and cultured French used to shape the memory of the people of Cambodia. Nature—personified as the Earth Goddess of the pagan animists and certain sects of Hinduism—was at once destructive and continuous, ordered by chaos; like Kalī herself, it seemed to be the guardian of the cycles of birth and death. Nature thus revealed both the collapse of a civilization as well as the continuity of "primitive" Cambodians:

> Everywhere around you, you see Nature in its dual role of destroyer and consolidator, strangling on the one hand, and healing on the other; no sooner splitting the carved stones asunder than she dresses their wounds with cool, velvety

mosses, and binds them with her most delicate tendrils; a conflict of moods so contradictory and feminine as to prove once more—if proof were needed—how well "Dame" nature merits her female title![59]

Though the French dedicated much effort to clearing away the dense growth strangling the Angkor structures, they purposely left Ta Prohm as an example of the state in which they found the monuments. The emphasis on remembering the ruin of Ta Prohm at the hands of nature naturally led to the "forgetting" of the monastery's previous life history. Clearly ignoring the original significance of the site, the French deemphasized its original importance as a structure and underscored the subsequent significance of conquering nature. Ta Prohm, collapsed by the strong tendrils of a deadly natural world, became the anonymous metaphor for the collapse of a once-great civilization and for the weakness of the Cambodians. Pierre Loti's sentiments, excerpted from his famous 1912 book, *A Pilgrim in Angkor*, reveal this attitude:

> Palaces once stood here; here kings once lived a life of prodigious luxury, kings of whom we now know nothing, who have sunk into oblivion *without leaving so much as name engraved on a stone or in the memory of men*. These tall rocks now blending with the forest, enveloped and clasped by a myriad roots like the tentacles of an octopus, are the work of human hands. For there is as stubborn will to destruction even in the world of plants. The Prince of Death, whom the Brahmans call Shiva, he who created for each beast that special enemy by which it is devoured, for each creature the gnawing microbes that leach its essence, seems, form the dawn of time, *to have foreseen that men would endeavor to prolong their own lives by building things that last*. So, to annihilate their work, he thought up, among a thousand other agents of destruction, these plants that grow on walls, and in particular the strangler fig that obliterates everything. It is this fig tree that is lord of Angkor today.[60]

The unique and wonder-filled sight of monuments in Ta Prohm's state also resonated with other remembered images of the Romantic era, whose popular panoramas portraying Roman ruins and moss-covered cathedrals reinforced the notion that civilization had left its seat in antiquity and now graces the people of Northern Europe. These ruined Khmer temples became the ideal, physical embodiment of this Romantic-era colonialist narrative, best described in a nostalgic comment by Bouillevaux that was published in Mouhot's popular diary: "There are few things that can stir such melancholy feelings as the sight of places that were once the scene of some glorious or pleasurable event, but which are now deserted."[61] The title of H. W. Ponder's famed 1936 book, *Cambodian Glory: The Mystery of the Deserted Khmer Cities and their Vanquished Splendour; and a Description of Life in Cambodia Today*, also quite explicitly conveys this colonial claim—there is a clear separation between today's Cambodian culture and the once-splendorous, yet defeated and heretofore absent, Khmer culture. As a container for measuring civilization, Angkor was once full, but now empty; civilization has evolved, gone from the primitives currently occupying the site. These places bound in the grasp of nature represented the vestiges of the Orientalist phrase *Lux ex Oriente*—"light from the East." The torch was passed; Middle East, Southeast Asia, Africa, the Pacific islands, and even Southern Italy were seen as the calcified remains of Civilization, which has made its way up the continent to Northern Europe. Even after initial treatises linking Angkor's creators with more "civilized" people like Alexander the Great, the Roman emperor Trajan, or, in one case, Chinese Jews, were refuted, this only served to give greater credence to such Orientalist colonial notions. H. G. Qudritch Wales' famous comparative history entitled *Angkor and Rome* brings this example to the extreme, allowing anecdotes about Angkor to resonate with the collective memory of the Roman experience.[62] Just as Northern Europeans saw themselves as heirs of the Roman Empire—the backwards city-states of Southern Italy, alternatively passing from French to Spanish colonial rule, certainly were not considered as "civilized" as ancient Rome was remembered—so too did they see themselves as the heirs and saviors to these unknown civilizations laying pathetically captive to nature. Indeed, upon visiting the "heathen" Angkor, the governor of French Cochinchina (south Vietnam, including Saigon), Admiral Bonard, remarked that clearly it was no longer possible "to deny that the pitiful Cambodia of today once nurtured and can still nurture a great nation, a nation both artistic and industrious." It was the very duty of the colonials to rescue the vestiges of ancient civilization, rightfully internalize them in their own collective narrative, and restore a nation to its past grandeur.[63] Thus, this narrative claim actually relies on and feeds off of the former claim, actively working to frame narrative of Khmer legitimacy, within the broader evolutionary narrative of Western superiority.

As more sites are cleared from the jungle and restored today, effectively pushing nature to the background, these certain ruins stand out even more, providing an even greater emphasis on this Orientalist narrative claim. Indeed, sites such as Ta Prohm and Preah Khan are the most photographed and widely-discussed places in the whole Angkor Archaeological Park, for it is here that one can experience the wonder of "discovering" these hidden ruins in a controlled environment. Such experiences are garnered most prominently though the ruins' architectonics. While the architectural, decorative and architectonic features of the original Khmer constructions performed mighty expressions of power through their rigid control of the flow of people, today the Western claim is performed in the opposite manner in almost every temple including Angkor Wat, where one can clamor up the towers and over the rooftops in a manner impossible to most Angkor-era citizens. Ruined sites such as Ta Prohm and Preah Khan provide the ultimate experience. Its thick walls collapsed, the destruction and disarray of Ta Prohm's network of narrow causeways allowed for the movement of people over, under and through previously erected barriers. Scrambling atop the crumbled stones of Ta Prohm, visitors literally were able to "walk all over" Khmer culture. Like Henri Mouhot or Louis Delaporte—or Indiana Jones or Lara Croft in today's pop cultural collective memory—one can easily re-experience the colonials' power over primitivity, and travelogues from the 1920s to today have extolled the wonder of discovery, the freedom of control over the ruins, and the liberation of communing with nature and primitivism. One tourist book, written by an academic art historian, states:

> From that point, visiting Ta Prohm is really going wherever your instincts lead you, to enjoy the wonder of making new discoveries, of finding hidden passages or obstructed reliefs, of climbing over fallen stones, and of experiencing the harmony between man and nature. There are many pleasant spots to simply sit and enjoy the tranquil surroundings.[64]

Though John Sanday—the former head of World Monuments Fund Siem Reap, which conducted the admirable restoration effort at Preah Khan—astutely states, "when you are dealing with historic buildings, you have no right to decide what period you should return to; history began yesterday,"[65] the concept of "historic preservation" —which I had deconstructed as "restoration" and "preservation" in chapter 1—takes the site back to an idealized, historicized period which never actually existed. Denying the monument's total life history, "preservation" can only conserve one set of many narratives embodied in the structure in a point in time. The inherent subjectivity of the restorers, based on the narrative claim to which they adhere, will inevitably frame any of their decisions, as David Lowenthal cautions when he writes, "the tangible vividness of these remnants tempts us to ignore our own influence on them—to forget that our own acts, reflecting our own changing concerns, continually alter our understanding of their history."[66] No matter how good the intention, preservation and restoration justify a certain amount of destruction. Like Zerubavel's act of remembering, the practices themselves inexorably involves a certain level of forgetting—whether it is forgetting the structure's grandeur 800 years ago, nature's effects of the past four hundred years on Preah Khan, or simply the effects of tourists last week at Angkor Wat. Even as World Monuments Fund attempts to bridge this gap by restoring segments of the partially ruined site only inasmuch as it structurally—rather then aesthetically—requires, the imprint of the preservationists' intervention can be seen, effectively changing the place's meaning and course of its life. Even so, though architecturally and even ethically Sanday's assertion is most prudent, one must also remember that the site exists not in isolation but in the deeply contextual realm of the heritage-scape, where it is juxtaposed, compared and understood against other monumental forms in authoritative ways. As Jan Assman states, "the present is 'haunted' by the past and the past is modeled, invented, reinvented and reconstructed by the present."[67] Any place is understood in the context of past narratives—individual or collective—and are constantly being written and revised as more narratives are added.

As it is conducted today, over ten countries and international organizations work separately and with relative autonomy to preserve separate sites, and some like the World Monuments Fund regulate visitors' experiences at the particular structures in varying degrees. Not only do they lack close consultation with each other, but they also manage 'their' sites relatively independent from Cambodian experts. While, as Winter points out, "such an organizational culture was undoubtedly justifiable in the early 1990s when the priority was emergency conservation,"[68] the complexity of Angkor's narrative structures, coupled with the World Heritage site's prominent place in the heritage-scape, demands greater continuity and coordination among the various participating parties. Such a coordinating body already exists in the form of Cambodian-led APSARA organization, which was founded concurrent to Angkor's World Heritage designation. To ensure narratives that are complementary rather than conflicting, APSARA as an oversight organization should change its focus from strictly conserving individual monuments to understanding the implications of their juxtaposition against each other and against other World Heritage sites in the heritage-scape.

Performing Colonialism:
The Act of Preservation in Vietnam and Cambodia

The examination of the Angkor Archaeological Park's competing narrative frames illustrates that Angkor is dynamic, processual and, above all, contextual. But since the sites are imbedded in a larger social milieu, memory is also conditioned by the interactive *experiences* of place in its material form, whereby the narrative is not only presented but also contextually articulated. "Places are created, imbued with meaning, argued over, changed, remembered and forgotten, but to see them simply in terms of ideas is to miss their critical phenomenological and material dimensions," writes anthropologist Kathleen Morrison.[69] Indeed, the practice of World Heritage—through preservation, tourism management, and cultural education—also fundamentally determines how individuals understand the "universal value" of each World Heritage site. Michael Parker Pearson and Colin Richards best articulate this fundamental point when they state that "Space is practice (our everyday actions); it is also a symbol, and we might conceive of architecture as symbolic technology."[70]

The practice of preservation at Angkor is itself a performance of Western claims of valorization, as it currently includes very few native Cambodians in the process.[71] Though more research needs to be conducted, it does not seem that the lack of native Cambodian participation in restoration efforts is cultural; on the contrary, an understanding of their beliefs about the sacred may point to the opposite tendency. A temple does not lose its religious import even when in disarray or destroyed; the temples and monasteries of Angkor have continually been loci of small-scale private worship, and, consequently, upkeep, even when supposedly lost to the jungle. Researchers at the Center for Khmer Studies in Phnom Penh have also noted the local preservation practice of brickfacing wooden pagodas during the beginning of the French colonial period. Several domestic practices also point to a tendency towards preservation. Researching domestic architecture for the Center, Dr. Hok Sokol points out that the home and the land upon which it is built is believed to be sacrosanct,[72] and Daena Funashashi notes that Cambodians will even take a few bricks and stones from fallen temples and use them when building their own homes in an attempt to further imbue their domicile with the sacred.[73] While this anecdotal evidence does not confirm a Khmer tendency towards historic preservation *per se*, it does illustrate a Cambodian regard for edifices after they have outlived their primary use.

Cambodians should therefore be included at all levels of the restoration process, for ownership is performed most noticeably in the social act of preservation. Given the original necessity for swift and complex conservation efforts, it was judicious in the 1990s to employ experienced professionals. From its beginnings in the last decade, preservation management also required autonomy, self-regulation and standardization in order to complete their tasks in an effective and timely manner. Because of the unfortunate lack of local scholars, combined with an education system that understandably was insufficient for such technically specific needs, the majority of Cambodians do not meet the necessary standards set forth by the foreign organizations, and are therefore excluded from most processes except the menial ones. Though Deputy Prime Minister Sok An states that the impressively successful international collaborative movement is "a model of cooperation—more than ten countries and international organizations coming together in a spirit of solidarity for the work of preserving cultural heritage,"[74] and it certainly is a symbol of unity and cross-cultural ownership that the heritage-scape wishes to foster, this unity seems to be solely between the professionals in developed countries to the exclusion of native Cambodians. Stating that it "would literally be committing a moral sin in the profession" if preservationists represent anything historically and spatially "inaccurate" during the process, a representative from an American historic preservation firm underscores that necessity of making decisions that are "decided upon in conjunction with *local input.*"[75] Yet at Angkor, "The French have their way, the Japanese have their way, the Americans and so on. But who is asking the Cambodians?" remarks Philippe Paycam, the director of Siem Reap's Center for Khmer Studies. In a nod to apparent neo-colonialism, he continues, "We are back in the 19th century, with the games of the big political parties."[76]

This is not a problem localized exclusively at the Angkor Archaeological Park; Vietnamese sites that valorize minority cultures seem to share the same dynamic. Mỹ Sơn in particular resembles the Angkor Archaeological Park, in that the exclusive preservation activities of foreign countries are eminently visible in the World Heritage site. While local preservationists are active in restoration activities at Hội An and Huế—sites valorizing the Việt—Mỹ Sơn seems to be left completely for the foreigners to restore. Large billboards advertising and explaining individual restoration projects and their principal donors, are erected near the monuments; walking on the paths connecting the various groupings of temples, one notices that Italian, French, Japanese, American and Polish teams all seem to be active here, and in multiple locations, although unlike at Angkor or Huế, one is hard pressed to see anyone actually present and working. In addition, there seems to be little cohesiveness in the broader conservation effort of the World Heritage site; there does not appear to be any cross-collaborative efforts between teams, the temples claimed by each team are scattered throughout the site, and they vary in size, importance and structural integrity. For this reason, it seems to the outside observer that the countries are more interested in staking claims to various locations than actually accomplishing a highly successful, systematic preservation project.

The billboards seem not only to explicitly convey this narrative of Western valorization, but it seems to manifest the colonialism behind such a claim. Although the Western nations have ceased the colonial scramble of the eighteenth and nineteenth centuries, they seem to be continuing it here. This time, the billboards serve as their flags, as each country stakes their claim to a particular monument. Indeed, at one site visit to what used to be E1, which had been one of the most important temples before a U.S. B-52 bomb leveled it, a hastily erected corrugated tin roof and some wooden props were noticed above a minute tower behind it. It was the smallest of the group and relatively intact. It was also not the oldest or most significant. A sign was staked next to it, advertising that it was the work of an Italian team. Standing at the site of the destroyed E1 and looking at the spectacle before us, one Vietnamese curator accompanying this author shook his head. "Why do they do this?" he asked rhetorically about the Italians. "They are already working on a temple; they should focus on that one! They picked the easiest one on purpose . . . so that others can't work on it. They do it to claim their territory! If they work on one in a group, other countries won't touch it. Japan, U.S., Italy all do it. We need to be learning from international groups, not separate." The era of colonialism seemed not to have passed; it just moved to the monuments of Mỹ Sơn.[77]

The active participation of locals is especially important when considering the heritage-scape's goal of creating a universal sentiment of ownership across cultures, not simply within one culture. A vastly unbalanced preservation effort essentially reverses the paradigm in which Cambodians exercised cultural ownership over the site, to the exclusion of others in the international community; now, it seems, Westerners quite literally hold the monuments' very materiality in the palms of their hands. While Ang Choulean, the director of APSARA, states that Cambodians currently "tolerate" such "problems" because "we want to see this preserved as a living site,"[78] the time is ripe for Cambodians to be more integrated into the processes; the situation has stabilized, and Angkor was taken off of UNESCO's *World Heritage in Danger List* on July 4, 2004. Most guides in both Vietnam and Cambodia attest to locals' desire to participate as well; relegation to the sidelines seems only to exacerbate a feeling of alienation. Indeed, a deepening gulf in perceived ownership will only exacerbate social tensions. At the worst, alienated locals, having lost ownership of the sites, could contribute to their destruction through symbolic acts of black market looting.

As chapter 1 argued, the act of plundering is not simply a means to secure "valuable" economic commodities, but is central to imperialism. The *linga* Jayavarman VII carried home from his successful battles in Champa were subsequently taken by the Thais to their capital when they sacked Angkor; these same *linga* were then transported to Mandalay when the Burmese then conquered the Thai. Likewise, French explorers such as Louis Delaporte and the avant-garde writer Andre Malraux plundered the temples of Angkor on behalf of the French government and, in the case of Malraux, for his own benefit. Before Angkor's inscription, and, to a lesser extent today, the black market thrived on such looting. Through plunder, not only does one symbolically and politically gain possession of the civilization that was the Khmer empire, but he quite tangibly possesses the material vestiges of that very culture. The subsequent placement of these artifacts in a museum, which Carol Duncan calls a "producer of potent symbolic meanings"[79] can also serve to frame the same evolutionist narrative through both its choice in classification and its architectonics, as people are often physically moved from "primitive" to "contemporary" art, connoting the progression of civilization that itself moved from the hallowed forums of antiquity, up to the public chambers of developed Western countries. UNESCO anticipated such a potential risk at the original World Heritage Convention, writing "the cultural heritage and the natural heritage are increasingly threatened with destruction not only by the traditional causes of decay, but also by changing social and economic conditions which aggravate the situation with even more formidable phenomena of damage or destruction."[80] Calling this "the problem of two ends," Ang implores, "Cambodia cannot fight this alone." He cites the need for collaborative educational efforts between locals and Westerners to "raise consciousness," creating an equal sense of ownership among both the impoverished Cambodians who steal the statues to feed their families, and among collectors in developed countries who sustain the market.[81]

Just as foreign professionals should be conscious of the heritage-scape in which they are working, so too should local Cambodians understand the broader context in which the Angkorian monuments lie. With the exception of guides and "very educated people," most Cambodians do not have a sense of "World Heritage" and are not aware of Angkor's status, states Gerd Albrecht, a German archaeologist who has instructed archaeology to Cambodians for the last decade. Even his archaeology students are not familiar with other World Heritage sites outside of Angkor.[82] Because of the need to instruct Cambodians in basic subjects such as reading, writing and simple mathematics during their primary and secondary education, "nearly nothing is taught about environment, ecology, heritage, world culture," the archaeologist states. "High school graduates come to study archaeology without having the slightest idea about history, archaeology, civilizations."[83] Knowledge of Cambodian history or of the world is not only important on the practical level, but is crucial to conveying the narrative claims of unity that form a community. As Mr. Sok remarked, "Experience shows that national unity [is achieved when] an education [is] offered to children in understanding and love for their own culture. In this way, they have preserved and developed their cultures wisely and sustainably."[84]

Finally, it follows that more attention should be paid to local involvement in the Cambodian tourism industry and, through education, to offering viable alternatives that would provide more equitable social exchanges between Cambodian citizens and foreigners. The most visible phenomenon in Cambodia, tourism is not only enticingly lucrative, but also offers a wide range of opportunities for meaningful educational interaction. While difficult standards exclude locals in the preservation process, the standards in the tourism sector are much more varied and favor local involvement. Urry's theory of the "tourist gaze" emphasizes the fact that tourism is a specific type of interaction that combines the experiential and the material, pre-formed conceptions and in situ encounters. In search of both authenticity and reminders that they can bring home—be they souvenirs, photographs or simply notable memories—tourists' standards are easier to meet, even for those with low levels of education. Tourism also creates opportunities for the marginally skilled. Yet few opportunities exist even for those with an amount of specialization, and most must revert back to the only commodity they have—the "authenticity" of being Cambodian. The result is a commodification of cultural resources, of re-presenting themselves and their material culture for consumption, as shown in some cases of the foreign-run art and dance schools.

Noting, as Marshall Sahlins and Jean Baudrillard do, that consumption itself is an exchange of meanings, a discourse that emphasizes specific power relations,[85] these paradigms exhibit a similar social imbalance for both the skilled and the unskilled, wherein once again Cambodian culture is "enacted" and subordinated for the benefit of foreigners. As a particular social phenomenon, the commodification of culture seems to suggest that "culture" can be pinpointed, exchanged and even owned by outsiders, such that locals are impoverished of the one thing they are entitled to possess. As Louise Erdrich remarks, "dollar bills cause the memory to vanish."[86] While tourism can provide a valuable opportunity for the flow of cross-cultural exchanges central to the mission of the heritage-scape, without opportunities for equitable interaction, tourism can also create meanings antithetical to UNESCO's narrative claim. An imbalance in social relations would exacerbate, rather than bridge, the perceived gulf between foreign and Cambodian cultures. Instead of celebrating the "universal value" of all cultures interacting in Cambodia's portion of the heritage-scape, the marginalization of Cambodian culture serves to perpetuate a distrust of foreigners and a disdain for the perceived negative influences of cultural diversity—a disdain that seems to be brewing as His Excellency Sok An seems to suggest in this passage:

> We have to find strategies to cope with the negative effects of globalization of cultures, which seriously affects Khmer society. We have to be brave enough to accept the positive sides of foreign cultures in order to complement Cambodia culture. We must recognize that any culture in the world, in small or big nations, cannot be perfect, and, will thus, always have some deficiencies. Therefore, the cross-cultural influence is an unpreventable phenomenon. Please bear in mind that culture-rich Cambodia in previous time was influenced by foreign cultures, namely from India and France. We all know that no single individual can understand everything in this world, a world full of uncountable great knowledge. Because human need is unlimited, each individual has to be necessarily interdependent as so do individual cultures.[87]

After all, cultivating such a consciousness, which understands and celebrates global cultural diversity, is the cornerstone of the heritage-scape.

CHAPTER ELEVEN:

RAISING AWARENESS,
RE-PRESENTING THE HERITAGE-SCAPE:
FRAGMENTARY AND REPRODUCIBLE RE-PRESENTATIONS

The case of Angkor Archaeological Park illustrates the heritage-scape's extraordinary authority to produce meaningful and multidimensional action through the valorization of a particular World Heritage site. It is this valorization, and the global recognition that stems from it, which induces nation-states to voluntarily offer up their sovereign space to the heritage-scape:

> The prestige that comes from being a State Party to the Convention and having sites inscribed on the World Heritage List often serves as a catalyst to raising awareness for heritage preservation on the part of governments and citizens alike. Heightened awareness, in turn, leads to greater consideration and general rise in the level of protection and conservation afforded to heritage properties. A State Party may receive both financial assistance and expert advice from the World Heritage Committee as support for the promotional activities for the preservation of its sites as well as for developing educational materials.[1]

Although this excerpt expressly deals with the issue of historic preservation, it posits that the fundamental benefit of a World Heritage designation is fostering a "heightened awareness," which leads to "greater consideration" of the property by the general public. After all, monuments do not get preserved simply upon joining the Convention, nor by simply by inscribing them on the List of World Heritage in Danger; they are preserved when people are aware that they exist, and that they have value worth preserving. Likewise, these monuments become tourist destinations not by merely inscribing them on a World Heritage List, nor through preservation efforts, no matter how massive or multinational these may be. Rather, they are visited in this context *en masse* when these lists are disseminated, affording groups the opportunity to know about the existence of these monuments, and to recognize their value to enlighten and

367

educate. World Heritage sites are preserved and visited precisely because there is an audience who is aware of both their existence as well as their value.

Awareness is a notably imprecise term often used when considering the issue of cognition by psychologists and philosophers. Yet as UNESCO's decades-old document attests, it need not be relegated only to the realms of vagaries; it also serves as an idiom to explain deep social and individual impetuses for action. Awareness can therefore be described as the effect, or personal understanding, produced by the processes of memory as outlined by sociologists such as Halbwachs and Connerton. The state of being informed or cognizant of something, awareness is created and cultivated by the remembering of a particular narrative claim that is always subjective, selective and ever changing. Always relative, always perceived individually, this recognition is intensely subjective and constantly evolving through memory's iterative process; it is dependent upon the meaning made from remembering an experience, and re-remembering it processually as it becomes framed and re-framed by subsequent interactions, experiences and narrative claims. Awareness does not necessarily imply a complete or precise understanding, but rather, a mindfulness or recognition of the existence of something. It imbues individuals with an often ineffable and inexplicable understanding of "what something is like"—a type of vague remembrance of the existence of something, regardless of how precise that understanding or knowledge is. Its opposite, therefore, is oblivion—the complete physical, memorial and narrative inexistence of something in one's mind. It is no wonder that awareness factors heavily on issues of historic preservation and World Heritage sites, for these are sites that are intended to resist oblivion; they should always remain integral, effective and expository—but most importantly, they must never submit to the destructive sands of time. They must continue always to exist, at least in the minds of men.

Like Benjamin's "aura," awareness circulates apart from a World Heritage site's physical locality and from a tourist's particular situated experience with the place because it exists within the "minds of men." It is the means through which the heritage-scape is diffused throughout the world—rendering UNESCO's new social system pervasive, amorphous and non-localized—yet immanently real. It allows the heritage-scape to transcend geopolitical borders and inspire meaningful action despite a tourist's reintegration into his daily life.

As I have argued, awareness is most effectively achieved through embodied processes of re-presentation that stem from physical interactions with place as it is re-presented in the heritage-scape. In this case, World Heritage sites act as tangible mediators between the heritage-scape and individuals. However, alternative re-presentations of World Heritage sites provide enhanced opportunities for raising awareness and diffusing the heritage-scape without necessitating direct touristic interaction with the place. As outlined in chapter 1, I have categorized these as *fragmentary re-presentations* and *reproducible re-presentations*. Both uniquely create new ways for individuals to interact with, and experience, the sites and the heritage-scape in general. Fragmentary re-presentations differ from reproducible re-presentations in that they are physical pieces of the authentic monumental mediator, and thus uniquely exist in a particular instance in space and time. They are most often contained in museums, tourist spaces in their own right, which therefore act as surrogate World Heritage sites; their physical form prescribe a particular method of embodied interaction with the World Heritage site. When World Heritage sites occur as reproducible re-presentations, however, they exist as secondary mediations and thus are subject to additional frames of interpretation that are even more difficult for UNESCO to police. Though they lack the spark of authenticity, they benefit from the ability to be replicated and disseminated in multiple times and spaces simultaneously. Consequently, while reproducible re-presentations are integral for diffusing the heritage-scape, they may produce claims that greatly conflict with the its narrative of "unity in diversity." Without attempting to be exhaustive in enumerating the varieties of fragmentary and reproducible re-presentations, this chapter discusses the nature of such forms, revealing both their importance to, and their inexorably problematic relationship with, the heritage-scape.

Fragmentary Re-presentations

Museums are inherently re-presentational places. Whether they are instructive institutions utilizing object-based epistemology, temples offering transcendence, treasure chests of value-laden booty, or simply storehouses for the stuff collected by an individual or group over time, they are all physical arenas that frame, contextualize and present objects. They are the stage, the proscenium, upon which objects are presented in a new light, to espouse the specific narrative claims of the institution's leaders. Much like the theatre, museums are the destination to which people travel—but they are not often intended to be the primary object of attention. Rather, these travelers, with only a few notable exceptions, visit specific museums with the precise understanding that they will commune and interact with the objects housed within the place, rather than with the place itself. It is unlikely, for example, that the masses who line up daily to visit Florence's Accademia would be doing so if Michelangelo's *David* were not present. It may also be unlikely that long lines would continue to form outside the Uffizi should Botticelli's *Birth of Venus* and *Primavera* be removed from the famed museum. Should every one of its objects be removed, visitors would be less likely still to explore the Uffizi, despite the embeddedness of its name in the Western psyche. And even when tourists visit museums to simply attest that they have been there, as this author has observed with the Guggenheim's architectural gems in Bilbao and Venice, countless are the instances that these visitors exhibit a post-facto dissatisfaction with the experience because the objects contained within did not meet expectations.

Museum visitors are thus tourists visiting foreign lands, similar to Grand Tour-goers across nineteenth-century Indochina or today's group travelers across the heritage-scape. But rather than interacting with a complete location as tourists do, museum visitors interact with fragments taken from them and housed in new places. Museums are coherent places in and of themselves, places that compel physical interaction and have meaning. Like the tourist destination, museums are inherently re-presentational; the objects selected for their expositional, metaphoric properties are their primary resource[2] for providing meaning and coherence to the place. Speaking about Mankind in one representational way,[3] the social institution of a museum imbues its disparate and fragmented objects in an over-arching narrative claim just as the heritage-scape imbues each World Heritage site within its meta-narrative. These objects are re-contextualized and thus are presented not in terms of their total life story, or in terms of the meaning that was intended when they were constructed or last utilized, but rather in a novel way that creates a tangible coherent script for the institution's narrative claim. When the heritage-scape's unique narrative is employed for this contextualization, the museum and its objects can also serve as important re-presentational forms with great potential to raise and shapes individuals' awareness of the heritage-scape. This is because the museum object, at least in its "purest" form, possesses three traits conducive to fostering re-presentations of the heritage-scape in accordance with UNESCO's prescribed methods.

First, the museum object is understood to be *authentic* in the same way as a World Heritage site. Chapter 1 defined authenticity as the secular sacredness of an artifact that is based on the object's temporary permanence. That is, when one is communing with it, he understands that it is a genuine fragment constructed in the past and exists in a somewhat unadulterated state in the present. Since this inanimate object possesses a life history that can be traced from its creation to its present state before the gaze of the museum patron, it is not unusual for the visitor to perceive the object as having its own soul, or *hau*, to use Bronislow Malinowski's oft-cited Trobriander term. Rather than being inactive and inanimate, the soulful object is invested with life, with individuality. Like a true native, it seems to always seek a return to "its place of origin" or to produce on behalf of the native soil from which it came, an equivalent to replace it.[4]

Referencing its place of origin that is distanced from its present position within the museum, a fragmentary re-presentation can also be perceived as possessing such a *hau*. In this case, the *hau* is its kernel of authenticity predicated on the object's unbroken participation in the chain of existence. While often the object, like the World Heritage site, is touched up, physically rebuilt and restored, or even completely reconstructed, people travel to physically interact with it precisely because they recognize this value of the past.[5] It holds value because, like a portal to another time and place, it allows the individual to interact with the "then" in the "now." Most importantly, since this value is a quality attributed to the object externally from a subjective actor and is not an intrinsic natural quality, it cannot be reduced or fragmented even when the object is split from something larger; the object possesses the same amount of authenticity as its place of origin, and can preserve this authenticity even if the original structure from which it was taken has succored to oblivion, as Durkheim has argued.[6]

Despite its understood authenticity, what makes the museum object so conducive to re-presenting the heritage-scape is that it is necessarily *incomplete*. While World Heritage sites are often consumed as totalities in of themselves, these objects are necessarily understood to be fragments: comprising a greater collection, they are considered unique parts of a disembodied whole, and they are unified by a particular narrative offered by the institution within the museum context. In the words of the revolutionary museum director Sir Henry Flower, museum objects are considered "illustrative specimens,"[7] each object is presented for individual consideration, but nevertheless re-presenting its own articulation of some greater concept. Just as World Heritage sites index the greater heritage-scape, these objects contribute as pieces of a puzzle to the museum's unique exposition of what constitutes Man and his place in the world. When these two narrative claims intersect through World Heritage fragments, each museum is rendered a tangible illustration of the heritage-scape.

Finally, because these objects are physically fragmentary, they are also *portable*. They are able to be transported from their original site, or disassembled and re-assembled while still maintaining both their structural integrity and epistemic authenticity. Just because they are removed from their original locations—and indeed, many come from World Heritage sites or other historic places recognized for their heritage value—their value or their emotional effects are not often dampened. They are still recognized as authentic portals to another time and place, just as their parent World Heritage sites are. But in this case, they are portable portals; they afford individuals who otherwise could not have the opportunity to travel long distances to commune with the total place itself. While the heritage-scape "imports visitors to consume goods and services locally", as theorists such as Barbara Kirshenblatt-Gimblett point out,[8] the portability of these objects allows for the very same valorized site to be physically exported for consumption abroad, thus providing an alternate dynamic for the diffusion of the heritage-scape and its meta-narrative claim. For some, it may be that communion with this sliver of World Heritage may suffice, and for others, this limited physical interactivity may whet the appetite for more concentrated interaction with the place itself. Touching a larger audience, these objects are able to raise awareness in a very emotionally effective and perceivably authentic way. An experience with a fragmentary re-presentation is therefore not only a temporal interaction with "then" in "now," but also with "there" in "here."

Itself the tourist destination, the museum space is important in its own right; it serves as an immanently physical frame within which visitors' activities are rigorously prescribed. As Carol Duncan points out, the birth of the public art museum—especially the Louvre—was not only tied to the goal of producing narrative claims about the nation-state through the recontextualization of these fragmentary re-presentations, but also a means for "civilizing" the general populous. The museum space was therefore conceived of as a ritualized theater, offering forth not only a narrative script, but providing a performative stage for visitors to become perfect citizen actors.[9] She writes,

> The museum setting is not only itself a structure; it also constructs its dramatis personae. These are, ideally, individuals who are perfectly pre-disposed socially, psychologically, and culturally to enact the museum ritual.[10]

Interacting with fragmentary re-presentations certainly may have the same sort of transformative, even transcendent, effect as World Heritage sites do *in situ*, but within the space of the public museum, they were thus employed to produce a moral effect, as well; they instructed visitors on proper taste and proper comportment. They were liminal spaces where one interacts with place and with neighbors in a way that differed from quotidian "vulgar flux of life" outside the museum.[11] Traces of this can be found to this day; museum visitors are instructed to look not touch; to whisper not shout (or talk on cell phones); to sketch not photograph (at least, to not use a flash—even when the photographer wishes to capture a sculpture or object that is not harmed by the bright light). Inside the museum, one is to "contemplate" rather than impulsively act.[12]

When transferred to the discourse of the heritage-scape, the museum containing fragmentary re-presentations of World Heritage sites therefore serves not only to transport visitors to another place and time, but to imbue them with a strong sense of respect, contemplation and reverence for these sites—activities that are often greatly divergent from those allowed at many World Heritage sites. The aforementioned case of Ta Prohm is exemplary. While a Buddhist object from the Angkorian monastery is silently and reverently gazed at within the confines of a museum, the site itself is loudly clambered over, photographed and touched in a circus-like atmosphere where locals are dressed in costumes and visitors jostle with each other to pay for their pictures.

Another notable example of this dichotomy can be found at the Đà Nẵng Museum of Cham Sculpture, most commonly called the "Cham Museum" (Bao Tang Cham) by local and foreign guides. Boasting a graceful architectural style fusing the French colonial structural design with idealized indigenous Cham motifs, this semi-open-air museum serves as both a center of conservation of artifacts from the nearby sacred mount of Mỹ Sơn, and a site where visitors exhibit the respect that should be accorded to these holy objects. Like Ta Prohm, visitors to the World Heritage site of Mỹ Sơn are free to walk over and through the constructions, touch the crumbling structures and carry on conversations about mundane life. Within the museum space in Đà Nẵng, however, there is a notable air of reverence, with guides often quieting visiting groups when they get too loud, and even admonishing brash tourists who frequently attempt to climb atop the monumental sculptures of elephants for a jocular photo.[13]

The Cham Museum is also a notable example of how the museum object's form of re-presentationality can contribute to raising awareness of the heritage-scape and the physical World Heritage site itself. From its construction in 1915 until recent infrastructural improvements were made at Mỹ Sơn—including paving a road to the holy citadel and erecting a new interpretative museum at the base of the mountain—the museum was the primary place where groups could interact with any part of the World Heritage site. Indeed, its very genesis can be tied to this idea. In 1892, Charles Lemire brought his collection of about fifty sculptures to the Tourane Garden for public display. The number soon grew to about ninety, and by 1894 he had published an acclaimed article on the Cham temples of Trà Kiêu and Binh Dinh in the journal *Le Tour du Monde*, in which he painted a delicious description of sacred relics strewn like seed across nutty fields and sandstone sculptures half-buried in the ground in the journal—no doubt whetting many an archaeologist's and Grand Tour-goer's appetite for discovery and collection. Later, a French postal worker in Đà Nẵng discovered the remains of Cham towers in plantations around the city, from which he collected a number of sculptures in order to save them from destruction. By the turn of the century, the French government had determined that these two collections of relics were indeed valuably representative of an ancient indigenous heritage, and in 1902 decided to transport them to their capital, Ha Noi. Also recognizing the value of these objects, local public figures refused, and by 1908 Henri Parmentier published a scathing report decrying the disunity and neglect of the collection, which was scattered in private residences, public parks, and jumbled in the Saigon police headquarters. According to the official catalogue of the museum,[14] Parmentier's report featured three principles that to this day guide the institution's mission—principles predicated on preservation, respect for the objects' former use, and attention to the way in which the life histories of the objects and the monuments from which they came were re-presented:

1) Any object found away from its original site must without fail be taken to the Museum. The same holds for individual sculptures when the original building has disappeared, provided they are of sufficient archaeological interest and not under active worship, and for inscribed stelae unless they are part of a surviving monument.

2) Items found in excavations which are part of a recognizable building, the study of which can help to interpret the building, should be left where they are, unless they are in a condition or of a nature which does not allow them to be conserved at the find-spot, for example, the carved tympana of Mỹ Sơn which are broken into numerous fragments.

3) The worship of certain items should be respected, as farmers believe they can intercede effectively in times of drought.[15]

While at times the semiotic elements of the museum's display are problematic, it should be lauded not only for saving these important relics from certain destruction during the ensuing wars—when Mỹ Sơn was used by North Vietnamese troops as an ammunition depot and was heavily bombed by the Americans—but also because of its focus on raising awareness of the Cham people coupled with stringent attention to the objects' re-presentationality. The museum is roughly divided into four large semi-open-air rooms, each named after an ancient Cham city from which its artifacts came. Thus, there is the Mỹ Sơn room, the Tra Kieu Room, the Dong Duong Room and the Thap Mam Room. Within these rooms, attention is given to the orientation of the display, especially when re-presenting various Hindu altars, which Guillon states are the "essential link between the deity and the shrine," or, to put it into placemaking terms, between the ephemeral and conceptual (heavens), and the tangible and social (the site itself). While most of the museum's objects are fragments of otherwise destroyed altars, the place also features examples in their complete forms, disassembled from their original locations, re-assembled in the museum and restored where necessary. Dating from the eighth to ninth centuries, the Mỹ Sơn altar in particular is beautifully ornate and immense in size, stretching from floor to ceiling and jutting out from the wall a considerable distance. Equally immense color photographs of the surrounding landscape of Mỹ Sơn enhance the experience, providing a more complete understanding of the place from which it was removed.

In addition to their epistemological value, which undoubtedly provides more visual information for understanding the altar's narrative, these photographs, which reveal the disarray of the World Heritage site, also unwittingly underscores the reality of Mỹ Sơn and the contemporary necessity of this museum located in Đà Nẵng. Mỹ Sơn has unfortunately been eclipsed by its neighboring World Heritage sites, Hội An and Huế, which are in better states of restoration and boast a diversified series of attractions. Benefiting from flourishing commercial centers, the local governments of Huế and Hội An are also better positioned to spend lavishly on promotions—from unique cultural events to publishing advertisements in travel magazines to offering FAMs to travel industry professionals who will subsequently create their Vietnamese itineraries. Although Mỹ Sơn falls within the same province as Hội An, and thus theoretically benefits equally from marketing endeavors by the provincial tourist board, it is not a living city with multifaceted commercial entities willing to devote a portion of their own budgets on mutually beneficial awareness-raising endeavors or capital improvement projects. Such improvement projects are strategically responsible for directly connecting Hội An to its larger, more industrial city Đà Nẵng, by a short road. But until 2005, arriving at Mỹ Sơn was quite difficult—leading most tour operators to eschew the 80 km trip from Hội An in favor of a two-hour visit to the museum in downtown Đà Nẵng. Indeed, guides like to describe the experiences of adventurous travelers they accompanied; jeeps would be stuck in thick mud, makeshift bridges leading to the site would be inaccessible, and the mere hike up to the mountaintop site would take most of the day.

The difficulties these travelers faced were finally mitigated in 2005, when Quảng Nam Province inaugurated a new tourist-friendly Mỹ Sơn. Thanks to Japanese financing, a 1-kilometer access road was ceremoniously opened on March 25, 2005, along with an impressive new museum at the base of the mountain. Unlike the Cham Museum in Đà Nẵng, this museum is a modern and airy structure, embracing the contemporary aesthetics of glass and steel, and equipped with multi-media facilities. Relics from Mỹ Sơn are few—as they continue to be housed in Đà Nẵng or in a handful of temples that have been turned into gated repositories up at the site itself. Following the lead of many "site museums" at World Heritage sites whose objects have been dispersed across the heritage-scape, this museum functions as an "interpretative center" rather than a repository of fragmentary re-presentations. Unlike Đà Nẵng's museum, it was constructed explicitly to frame a visitor's *in situ* experience at Mỹ Sơn, not to serve as a surrogate experience in lieu of a tourist's visit to the destination. Thus, emphasis is given to the site itself, especially regarding the ethnohistory of the Chams, their religious traditions believed to have been enacted here, and the sordid history of its 'discovery,' wartime destruction, and conservation.

Despite the improvements in access and facilities, interviews with guides and tour operators after 2005 reveal that Mỹ Sơn remains on the periphery of the tourist track, though this seems to be changing gradually. As it stands now, it appears that the image of a costly, time-consuming and uncomfortable visit to the World Heritage site remains. Thus, Đà Nẵng's Cham Museum continues to serve two important purposes. First, it continues to be an expository storehouse for Cham material culture; the interpretative center at Mỹ Sơn complements—not precludes—a visit to Đà Nẵng's Cham Museum. And second, thanks to the portability of these authentic fragmentary re-presentations, the museum is able to raise appropriate awareness of UNESCO's enterprise by bringing Mỹ Sơn to a wider audience. It seems to defy the fixity of the physical place by decrying, "if people will not come to Mỹ Sơn, then Mỹ Sơn will come to them."

Reproducible Re-presentations

Arguably the most popular tools for raising and shaping awareness of World Heritage sites today are *reproducible re-presentations*. These are all portable in ways similar to fragmentary re-productions, but they differ from museum objects in that they have no direct, tangible link with material sites themselves. This varied category of re-presentations include, among others, textual descriptions, models, maps, and a diversity of visual, photographic, cinematographic and virtual images. While reproductions such as travel literature, paintings, panoramas, maps and sculpture have since antiquity been commissioned to instruct or otherwise raise awareness of people, places and objects, reproducible re-presentations are products of what Walter Benjamin has famously called today's era of mechanical reproduction. That is, through the use of technology, exact copies of the depiction can be copied and disseminated with alacrity, precision, and detail that begs a reconsideration of the hegemony of authenticity for being the exclusive authoritative voice of truthful re-presentation. Because the effectiveness of any awareness-raising effort can be measured by the number of people who recognize the subject by sight, narrative or title—regardless of how the subject had been initially presented to them—these reproducible re-presentations are uniquely potent methods for raising and shaping awareness across the world in equitable intervals at lightening speeds.

The defining characteristic of the reproducible re-presentation is its extremely low level of physical interactivity with the subject it signifies; unlike the museum object, which is at best a complete original work and at the least is a fragment from the greater site, this genre of re-presentation boasts no direct link to its subject in the same way an "authentic" fragmentary re-presentation does. Such depictions nevertheless inspire much of the same kind of action as the original. People are moved to action by a photograph, a newsreel, a film, a live or "live on tape" interview; they induce laughter, tears, pleasure and fear; they set a mood; they inspire love and hatred. Many Americans attest that they feel like they know a celebrity personally not because they have ever interacted with them on a real and tangible level, but because they have interacted with highly re-contextualized—yet life-like—images of them in the media. Among the inanimate community of varied places in the world, World Heritage sites are the celebrities; they also enjoy an abundance of re-presentations in books and newspapers, published in magazines and journals, displayed in art galleries and museums, and beamed into offices, living rooms, movie theatres, and internet cafes on print, video, film and digital media. And these re-presentations inspire action.

This is not merely attributable to an audience's suspension of disbelief, but rather a shift in the perception of what constitutes authentic. In today's Benjaminian era of mechanical reproduction, there is a heightened level of trust attributed to the abilities of technology to create accurate and objective physical depictions of a subject in ways that human artists have never been able to enjoy. Although a reproducible image's removal from any physical linkage to its subject allows for greater manipulation, it is nevertheless considered more a form of ethnographic reportage than art; the technology itself is often viewed as the ethnographer, as objective, descriptive and able as possible to produce not authenticity, but *accuracy* in its re-presentation of the subject.

The perception that these images are accurate re-presentations may stem from the fact that they are created and mediated by technology believed to be capable of capturing the minute details of the subject, in perfect proportion and to an exceptionally precise degree. These details can be captured from, and within, a single moment in time and space. Even when portraying a supposedly solitary moment, traditional forms of visual and textual re-presentations all take significantly more time to execute. Whether the reproduction is a painting, a sketch, a map, a model, a sculpture or a work of literature, it is not wholly created in a single instant, but is formed over some amount of time. With the inevitable onward movement of time, however, this reproduction necessarily becomes idealized; neither the subject nor the memory of that subject in any given moment will be exactly the same as it is intended to be portrayed. While to the naked eye the subject might remain the same, with each proceeding second it changes both physiologically and interiorly, albeit slightly. Transient, it inevitably grows physically older. It also grows older in history, understanding and meaning; each second brings another second's worth of memory and, in the case of animate creatures, another re-framing of one's understanding. Yet advances in photographic and digital technology have freed the artist from this tradition; photography and cinematography are supposedly able to immediately capture a subject exactly as it looked in a particular moment.

For these reasons, the perceived accuracy of the reproducible re-presentation stems from social distinctions of subjectivity and objectivity, which are attributed to technology; the image is often considered accurate because the mediating instrument is not Man, but machine. Machines, as inanimate products of science, are often thought to be incapable of subjectivity. The camera has nothing to gain by portraying Angkor Wat or Hạ Long Bay one way and not another. Thus, many would not consider a Tahitian landscape painted by Gauguin to be an accurate depiction—although it would be considered an authentic Gauguin—but a photograph of the same landscape would be considered accurate precisely because its creator can be traced back to the objective machine that captured that image. Of course, however, for every piece of technology, there is still someone behind it. In this case, therefore, a mechanical reproduction is actually removed by at least two degrees from the physical object itself. The artist remains, but instead of serving as an intermediary between the subject and the re-presentation, he pits the technology between the two and stands as an intermediary between the subject and the technology. Others, who edit the work after it is captured, can also stand between the technology and the final product. Thus, albeit believed to be more accurate, this form of re-presentation is just as subjectively manipulated, if not more.

Despite the trust many give in the accuracy of the representation, the fact that it is not physically linked to any site necessarily means they are open to manipulation that goes beyond merely the contextual. A *naga* head culled from an Angkorian temple may mean one thing in a World Heritage site, another in a museum, and another in a private gallery, but it will still look the same, have the same physical properties and be composed of the same material. But a photograph of that same *naga* can be manipulated in color and clarity through filters or lenses the photographer has selected; parts can be left out or emphasized disproportionately through angles he has chosen. In post-production, the photographer can further change the very appearance of the object; details in and around the subject that he perceives as blemishes or unbecoming of the narrative he is creating can be touched up, changed, or erased. The size of the finished product—the photograph itself—can be increased or decreased, such that the viewer does not readily know the true dimensions of the subject; when viewing Leonardo da Vinci's *Mona Lisa*, for example, many tourists have attested that it is smaller in real life than they thought. Finally, the context in which it is placed adds another discursive frame to the re-presentation. Frames and matting add aesthetic embellishments, drawing out particular color schemes in the photograph. The choices in their quality and quantity—whether it is double matted, whether it is in an elaborate hand-carved wooden frame or in an inexpensive metal one—may subtly speak to the value the owner or artist feels his re-presentation possesses. The image can be placed not simply in a museum, but in shrunken form in an art book, magazine, or in poster form on the wall of a college dormitory. Indeed, being able to be manipulated in size and volume allows it to be placed in a number of media venues with their own narrative contexts; art books, gossip magazines, Internet sites, blogs, television shows, cinematographic backgrounds all bestow different narrative claims on the re-presentation that will inexorably affect the meaning one makes of the subject depicted. Presented anew in such a form, the subject can be manipulated in many different ways, often unbeknownst to the viewer.

Like the modern museum is to tangible objects, the Internet today can be considered the storehouse and exhibition space for these digital, reproducible re-presentations of World Heritage sites. While the museum is fixed in one tangible location, however, the Internet is spread across space in much the same way the heritage-scape is. While it is often considered a "virtual" realm—a Gibsonian *cyber*space (as opposed to an earthly or embodied space)—as chapter 1 points out, it nevertheless impacts the world in real, material ways. Gibson's neologism is nevertheless helpful because it underscores the alternative and ephemeral spatiality the Internet seems to create through reordering traditional temporal and physical boundaries in much the same way the heritage-scape does. While many variations on the definitions of Internet or cyberspace exist, a number reflect this decidedly placemaking bent; one British website design firm defined it very much as "the total interconnectedness of human beings through computers and telecommunication without regard to physical geography."[16] This sounds very similar to the heritage-scape and its meta-narrative claim. And indeed, without strong geographic, social or economic constraints placed on anyone accessing the Internet, it can be considered the new great equalizer,[17] an alternative democratizing movement that, like the heritage-scape purports to do in theory, foregoes traditional geopolitical constraints to link the disparate peoples of the world in one community under a narrative of "unity in diversity."[18]

Spreading across the world irrespective of geopolitical boundaries,[19] and with relative cost-effectiveness, the Internet is a powerful tool. It can re-present a place in any context and to any constituency around the world, simply in as much time as it takes one to connect to it. And with Internet cafes springing up in towns and cities in every country, no matter what their socio-economic or geopolitical status, it is reasonable to state that everyone has the potential to access it. Since today a number of websites providing free or low-cost e-mail and weblog hosting, as well as a number of "chat" forums, not only can anyone with an Internet access point link up, but they can literally disseminate their own thoughts, messages, and re-presentations instantaneously across the globe. Indeed, academics conducting research, professionals contacting each other across the world, and "armchair travelers" seeking a quick, immediate and temporary escape from real life into a "virtual" reality all turn to the Internet for its simultaneously multifaceted simulacra. With great alacrity, a cacophonous babble of words and a mosaiced kaleidoscope of images are accessed almost immediately in conjunction with each other from potentially all points in the world, deepening, cross-referencing and complexifying awareness and understanding of virtually any subject. Voices, today translated with ease but with inexactness are carried forth, expanding the audience for word-of-mouth recommendations.

The Internet is also considered a great equalizer because its very re-presentationality can theoretically assure all an equal voice, and equal access to each voice. Small businesses benefit from equal space on the Internet as large companies do; a mom-and-pop business operating out of the home can nevertheless have an equally effective virtual storefront as a large retail store. An anthropology student can post his freshman paper alongside a doctoral candidate's dissertation and a veteran professor's published article. The student filmmaker and the amateur photographer may have equal room to exhibit their work as a Hollywood-employed or gallery-sponsored artist would. As every country has their own nomenclature, the government of the smallest country in the world may take up as much space as the largest; the country with the smallest population can have as much voice as the country with the largest. Most importantly for the heritage-scape, regardless of the remoteness, popularity, visitability, size or state of preservation, every World Heritage site can be equally presented and re-presented to audiences around the world.

Despite the altruistic exultations of the Internet's power to foster parity, there are drawbacks to this system. As composed entirely of digital reproductions, the images and messages, as well as the identity of the person sending them, can of course be manipulated. Without that basic "spark," or traditional authenticity that the original possesses, there are no assurances that these re-presentations are accurate depictions except for the trust the viewer puts in the source's motives. Unlike print publications, which are costly and time-consuming to produce and even more costly to recall, the Internet allows for anyone to post any impression, regardless of its accuracy or the underlying ideological perspective. Yet coupled with powerful democratization, mechanical reproduction produces relative anonymity on the Internet; an Internet user can easily disguise his identity or simply neglect to provide information on it, undermining the traditional methods for establishing and testing socially sanctioned information brokers.

Underscoring both the democratizing element of the Internet, as well as its often-problematic fostering of discursive equality, is the weblog, commonly referred to as a "blog." On the surface, these seemingly personal online ruminations and diary entries might seem obtuse, petty or too exclusive to really warrant being placed online, in public for all strangers to read. Nevertheless, people post—and read—blogs rather religiously, and for a variety of reasons. In the summer of 2006, I informally asked a number of travelers who posted blogs the simple question of why they spent time writing public postings about their trip. They gave several answers, mostly centered on the medium's facility and immediacy; they can write more detailed messages than a postcard's space affords, they can post images to supplement the writing, it saves the writer time by not having to type individual messages and eliminates the risk that comes with sending a mass e-mail of either inadvertently leaving someone out or having the message relegated to someone's "junk mail" box and the information can be accessed as soon as its posted by audience members at their leisure, without putting undue pressure on them to respond. Thus, one reason for posting "travelblogs" is sheer simplicity—in the past, someone returns from a trip with a box of photographs or a reel of slides to show friends and family; with blogs, those curious acquaintances can access the same information individually when it is convenient for them. The same seems to go for those non-travelers who increasingly are turning to the medium as a way to indirectly communicate with friends, co-workers and family members they may not speak with on a regular basis. Blogging provides a one-to-many mode of communication that allows the blogger to narrowcast his story.[20]

Yet others are drawn to blogging for the sense of empowerment that the anonymity alacrity and ubiquity of the medium affords them, and travelers are but one constituency. Travelers who feel particularly passionate about a positive or negative experience can take to the keyboard and place his criticism or complement for all to read. Yet they also provide a megaphonic means of safely expressing a view that might otherwise be stifled. Blogs are inherently a back-channel means of communication. They circumvent and supplement the official message, whether it be from a state-controlled press or simply a commercially sidelined one. War zone blogging from Iraq, Afghanistan, and Darfur picked up where the mainstream media left off, providing the world with information and perspectives previously unthinkable, just as "travelblogs" supplement traditional tour books and travel agents with current, personal, unmediated and first-hand information about a destination. In early 2006, for example, the official message from the White House was that war-torn Iraq was steadily being pacified, and that the "outlook was not as gloomy as some opponents of the war proclaim." Owing to the extreme danger of the region, size and terrain of the country, lack of journalists and stringent military restrictions on the information that can be published, neither of these claims was particularly easy to assess. Yet from Baghdad came local bloggers who would otherwise have no voice were able to announce to the world what they saw. In a *Los Angeles Times* article, Max Boot, senior fellow at the Council on Foreign Relations, points to a "pro-democracy Iraqi blogger named Alaa" at messopotamian.blogspot.com, who reveals, "The situation in Baghdad is deteriorating from day to day. . . . Very soon, if this situation continues like this, the city is going to be brought to a complete stand-still and paralysis. . . . Whole sections of the city have virtually fallen to gangs and terrorists." He also cites Omar Fadhil, "another pro-democracy resident of Baghdad" blogging at iraqthemodel.blogspot.com, who pleads for security forces to do more to bring the capital under control.[21] These entries represent blogs' capacity as informative alternative information sources on what is "really happening" on the ground. Yet the writers' anonymity and subjectivity should also be noted; these pseudonymous writers are "pro-democracy Iraqis"—their own interests, as universal as they may be, show through. Conversely, security analysts attest that jihadists combating Western troops are particularly adept and active bloggers, using the same medium to offer alternatives to the Western media's portrayal of the war, disseminate their own messages, and recruit followers.[22]

Blogs are re-presentative in nature, and like other such reproducible media, can manipulate the subject or, at the very least, compellingly include inaccuracies in their narratives, unbeknownst to readers. Critics often bemoan the lack of editorial oversight on the "blogosphere." Without the supervision of an institution, the argument goes, lone-wolf authors are free to spread lies, misinformation, or just plain boring material across the web. An oft-cited example of this is the case of Elena Filatova, who posted pictures from her motorcycle rides through the "dead zone" of Chernobyl using the pseudonym KiddOfSpeed. Stunning photographs of abandoned buildings and roads accompanied a travelogue with a rich narrative, along with a little melodrama:

At first glance, Ghost Town seems like a normal town. There is a taxi stop, a grocery store, someone's wash hangs from the balcony and the windows are open. But then I see a slogan on a building that says, "The Party of Lenin Will Lead Us To The Triumph Of Communism" . . . and I realize that those windows were opened to the spring [sic] air of April of 1986.[23]

The blog became immensely popular after receiving a mention on the popular content aggregator site Slashdot.org, and by mid-March of 2004, Filatova's site was averaging tens of thousands of unique visitors each day. There have been many accounts of the Chernobyl catastrophe and its aftermath, but Filatova's site provided readers with a personal perspective previously unavailable. By late-March, however, strong criticism of her site began appearing around the Internet; it seems that Filatova had taken more than a little license with her story. She likely had not actually traveled through the secure sections of Chernobyl by motorcycle, but rather had ridden through in a car as part of an organized tour. In addition, it seems that even outside the restricted area, she was not a "lone woman on a motorcycle" as she would have her readers believe, but instead was traveling with her husband and a friend. By mid-April, the site had been edited to remove most of the text describing her solitary travels and instead leaving her observations and ruminations on the communist state. By the summer, Elena had shut down her website, but it quickly went up again, and is ostensibly maintained by an unaffiliated website manager. The website's current manager, who claims to have "nothing to do with the project other than donating the bandwidth to allow the world to see it," provides an impassioned response to these allegations in much the same way James Fray defended himself against his similar fictionalizations:

How ironic that although they would label her a hoax and a fraud, she was able to achieve what they could not even dream of achieving. Bringing this issue the world wide attention it deserves. As the only email contact, I have seen each of the moving emails that were directed to "Elena." Her words have definitely made the world think about this piece of forgotten history. . . . Did she do it for fame or notoriety or even money? Or did she do it in order to bring attention to a forgotten region. Read her words and decide for yourself.[24]

This anecdote is recounted not to elucidate the potential deviousness of some bloggers or website owners. Although Filatova added romanticized embellishments that seem a bit disingenuous given the context and the moral message she conveys, it does not seem that she did this with any concertedly malicious intent, other than, perhaps, attempting to make herself famous; her commentator seems to convey Filatova's desire to create a more interesting back-story that would ultimately help circulate her important (and authentic) observations. Rather, this story is told here to illustrate the other side of the coin: Just as the Internet's qualities allow—and even foster—inaccuracies, disingenuousness, and even the dissemination of blatant misrepresentations or falsehoods, so too does it have inherently self-correcting mechanisms. Readers, observers, interpreters and experts are as equally tuned into the same accounts as the uninformed and the downright devious. They can speak in equal volume and authority to offer counter-positions, and, it is presumed, that if provoked or impassioned enough by the inaccuracy, they will be moved to write, inundating the blogosphere with their competing (and more accurate) viewpoint.

Blogs and other interactive forms of Internet-mediated "Social Media" are not merely re-presentative, but dialogical; readers are not constrained with passivity by the medium in the same way as with traditional re-presentational media forms, but can interact—not only with the re-presentation, but with each other—to foster new re-presentations and new discourses. There are multiple interactions, embodied and "virtual," in Filatova's story. At first the Russian motorcyclist mediated between Chernobyl and the viewers, re-presenting the place in a highly reproducible fashion. The reproducible re-presentation of Chernobyl in the form of descriptive blog entries was disseminated across space and time simultaneously and immediately. Readers—acting in much the same way as those who poured over the printed travelogues of Mouhot and Loti—consumed these re-presentations, filtered and manipulated as they were through the author's lens. Yet the readers were able to do something that their colonial predecessors could not: they could comment on her account to the author and to each other directly, immediately, and just as diffusely. Some readers jumped in to point out the flaws in Filatova's descriptions, questioning its authenticity directly to the other readers in her blog and in other linked websites. Debased and disgraced by these comments, Filatova changed her descriptions, excising those fictionalized bits before eventually removing her story altogether—further modifications of Chernobyl's re-presentative presence in the digital world. These modifications came about swiftly and directly through the blog's dialogical dynamic. Later, one passionate reader responds to these changes by hosting the site again, by re-presenting Filatova's original, problematic re-presentation—citing the numerous positive e-mails and comments the description elicited. But in his iteration, the heretofore authentic Filatovan re-presentation of Chernobyl is modified again, as this back story of fictionalization, dialogue and modification—a vital component of the re-presentation's life history, is indexed. Indeed, it serves to not only index, but also to construct, further re-presentations in the digital and print (such as this paragraph) realms.

There is great potential, therefore, for blogs and other forms of interactive Internet media to contribute to the diffusion of the heritage-scape and the fostering of its meta-narrative of "unity in diversity" in the re-presentational "virtual" world. This potential has not gone unrecognized by UNESCO's Scientific arm, which deals exclusively with science and technology, and its Cultural arm—which, in addition to overseeing the World Heritage program, also has positioned itself as a leader in the realm of international copyright and intellectual property discourses. Indeed, as early as 1948, UNESCO passed an "Agreement for Facilitating the International Circulation of Visual and Auditory Materials of an Educational, Scientific and Cultural Character" at its third general meeting in Beirut.[25] As the Agreement's title conveys, this document was intended to contribute to the circulation of expressive "materials." Just as the *World Heritage Convention* defines potential places in such broad categories such as "monuments," "groups of buildings" and "sites," so too does this *Agreement* intend to identify "visual and auditory materials . . . deemed to be of educational, scientific and cultural character"[26] such as film, sound recordings, glass slides, maps and models—those aforementioned reproducible re-presentations that are of a Benjaminian nature, which are employed as "accurate" forms of documentation (despite their ability to be manipulated) in placemaking endeavors such as the heritage-scape. The ability to be manipulated is also addressed; the materials must be deemed "representative, authentic, and accurate."[27]

Indeed, the document's legacy can certainly be traced to the employment of these re-presentational placemaking forms in the Western colonial era; the Agreement applies to those materials whose "primary purpose or effect is to instruct or inform through the development of a subject or aspect of a subject, or when their content is such as to maintain, increase or diffuse knowledge," just as the maps and models of Angkor did during the Indochinese period. Yet UNESCO couples this with its meta-narrative objective; these materials' purpose must also "augment international understanding and goodwill." Indeed, the Agreement begins tellingly:

> [UNESCO's] Constitution states as one of the functions of the United Nations Educational, Scientific and Cultural Organization that it will "collaborate in the work of advancing the mutual knowledge and understanding of peoples through all means of mass communication and, to that end, recommend such international agreements as may be necessary to promote the free flow of ideas by word and image . . .[28]

Notably absent from the 1948 Agreement's categories of reproducible re-presentations are those so-called traditional media forms, such as "books and works of art" which were described alongside "monuments of history" in UNESCO's Constitution as "objects of artistic and scientific interest." [29] Noting two years later in Florence that "the free exchange of ideas and knowledge. . . is accomplished primarily by means of books, publications and educational, scientific and cultural materials," an Annex to the original Agreement was passed on June 17, 1950.[30] Another two years later, the important *Universal Copyright Convention* was passed in Geneva,[31] and in 1958 a series of Conventions concerning the circulation of publications (both governmental and private) was signed.[32] October 1971 saw the passage of a revised *Universal Copyright Convention*, which included all of these diverse forms. Signed in Paris, the new Convention agreed that each signatory "undertakes to provide for the adequate and effective protection of the rights of authors and other copyright proprietors in literary, scientific and artistic works, including writings, musical, dramatic and cinematographic works, and paintings, engravings and sculpture."[33]

As this was the height of Cold War period's push for space-age technological innovation, in 1974 UNESCO sought to regulate the dissemination of "Programme-Carrying Signals Transmitted by Satellites" to constituencies for whom the programs were not intended. Though this seems like a barrier to the free circulation of expression, UNESCO states the 1974 *Convention Relating to the Distribution of Programme-Carrying Signals Transmitted by Satellite* was preempting possible censorship to free expression in forms that could be disseminated through satellite, such as television programs. "Recognizing, in this respect, the importance of the interests of authors, performers, producers of phonograms and broadcasting organizations," the Convention notes that "this lack [of regulation] is likely to hamper the use of satellite communications."[34] In effect, this Convention attempted to force an agreement among major powers that freedom of expression is foundational for a global society, and so it should not be tampered with through the dissemination of propaganda and other politically manipulated forms of re-presentation. Another document, drafted a few years later, prohibited the double taxation of copyrighted materials; this was an attempt to maintain the sovereignty of the nation-state to tax materials while preventing it from becoming an undue burden to creativity and free expression.[35] These documents all paved the way for UNESCO to take a comprehensive stance on the use of Internet technology to contribute to the diffusion of diverse forms of re-presentational expression.

UNESCO also does an admirable job in positioning itself as an authoritative voice in the competitive cacophony of often ideological discourses about these places. Its website is easy to locate; it has a straightforward name—www.unesco.org—and website search engines bring up the site quickly. The website itself is clear, easy to navigate and accessible. It provides access to many of its documents, links to individual State-Party websites, and even a map of the heritage-scape, although it does not call it as such. Yet re-presentations of World Heritage sites themselves must nevertheless compete with these other, sometimes conflicting, re-presentations; a quick search for "Angkor Wat," for example, brings up no UNESCO-sanctioned website in the first ten listed.[36] Rather, it produces a website that sells images of Angkor Wat and other "places of peace and power" (this site comes up second); an entry in *Wikipedia*, a free online encyclopedia written collaboratively by users and not experts (in third); a private website on "Forgotten Wonders" in fourth place,[37] a "selection of 100 slides" of Angkor with limited commentary provided by Leiden University in the Netherlands in fifth; a translation of "Maurice Glaize's popular and definitive 1944 guide to the Angkor Monuments for free" in sixth; and a number of travel agency sites, including a particularly disingenuous one called Angkor.com, which provides information and news about Cambodia and Thailand but is owned by a presumably Thai hotel-booking agency (in seventh). In first place, however, is a website that does not have any direct epistemological linkage to the World Heritage site, but rather is the portal for a private organization of U.S.-educated Cambodians whose self-stated "sole purpose for making this homepage is to bond and unite Cambodians (Khmers) from around the globe." In their introduction page, the webmasters illustrate the national heritage narrative with which they imbue Angkor Wat:

> In our efforts, we have been faced with the huge challenge of how to go about preserving our culture for future generations. Our heritage and culture is a unique one that has stood the test of time. We have made it this far and have escaped from the realm of our darkened past. Despite this, it is quickly vanishing at an alarming speed and we must put our efforts into maintaining a tight hold in it as we once had before. It is our hope that this homepage will create active participation on the part of our people to retain their rich traditions, great values, and gentle memories. . . . We, as Khmers, will continue to stand tall and look to the future.[38]

One way to increase UNESCO's online visibility is to create separate web presences for each World Heritage site. A number of these currently exist. Like the World Heritage sites themselves, however, the responsibility to create the re-presentation, contextualize it and manage the site rests with the local site managers. This puts developing countries like Cambodia in a trifold predicament. First, there are already less local managers and employees at the sites themselves; foreign companies are responsible for much of the ticket-taking, international preservationists lead preservation projects, and NGOs like World Monuments Fund often care for the site's daily upkeep—sometimes autonomously controlling a particular section. The additional responsibility of maintaining a well-conceived and attractive web presence may provide a significant strain on preexisting resources, which are scarce.

Second, many developing countries, and Cambodia counts among them, do not have as vibrant a computer culture; computers are not in every home, and most schools do not instruct computer science, although there are a number of NGOs specifically dedicated to placing used computers in rural schools. Once again, the dearth of professional webmasters poses a problem for the maintenance of the official website.

Third, stemming from this dynamic, local web designers on par with their international counterparts are also scarce. This is an important consideration. The above test of websites produced through a simple Google search saliently reveals this fact. At the time of the survey, Google enjoyed the moniker of one of the world's most widely used search engines,[39] and was recently granted access to operate in China, the world's most populous country, in a controversial rights deal.[40] Its popularly stems from a system whereby the results of a search are ordered by amount of web traffic a site with the search terms receive, rather than the most authoritative site. This is rapidly creating a popularity contest, where the "best" site—visited for its visual style, navigability, or desirability of its product or narrative wins. And the best site is not always the official site, as the aforementioned survey reveals; indeed, often the state party must compete against a number of commercial sites run by travel agencies or hotels, who can afford highly skilled webmasters from Europe, Australia, America, Japan or Korea. Outside experts would undoubtedly need to be brought in, although UNESCO as an institution has begun to take initiatives for ameliorating this digital divide in developing countries; under the auspices of its Education sector, UNESCO has conducted academic conferences on best practices for Information and Communication Technologies education, held computer training workshops in developing countries such as Afghanistan, and youth exchanges towards this end. This is not specific, however, to the current problem at hand; creating and maintaining a captivating and compelling website that can compete on the global level requires specific knowledge, a concerted effort, design experts, and, most of all, a continual source of funding.

To help shape its online presence, the World Heritage Fund—which earmarks the bulk of its annual distributions for promotional endeavors—should finance the construction of highly navigable and visible websites for all of its World Heritage properties. In addition, it should ensure that a link to the World Heritage Convention's official website is included on not only every official site of each World Heritage property, but on governmental and ambassadorial websites, commercial websites dealing with travel, and possibly selected private websites and blogs that fit into UNESCO's context.

Just as a World Heritage site can physically serve as a background re-presentation, its image or description can also be relegated to the background, as the Filatova anecdote also reveals. Her friend's message conveys the frustration they encountered when her scandalous "back-story" suddenly seemed to be at center stage, given more importance that the description of the site itself. Chernobyl is not a World Heritage site, although certainly there could be arguments for its expository qualities concerning science, technology, Man's ambition and the treatment of minority groups within a nation-state (it is not a World Heritage site for the contentious aspects within these very reasons). Regardless, World Heritage sites encounter the same difficulties in personal travel blogs, commercial websites, novels and film. The aforementioned study of the first ten websites that emerged when searching the words "Angkor Wat" also reveals this. Hotel and travel agencies use images and descriptions to draw interested visitors in, appealing to their interests, curiosity or yearnings for a visit. Yet the primary focus of the site, and the subsequent action it facilitates, does not concern the World Heritage site; the webpage becomes a venue to research and book hotels, excursions and guides. Suddenly Angkor Wat is literally nothing but a pretty background or a banner at the top of the page, if it continues to be re-presented at all. The same can be seen in the overseas Khmer community website, which emerged in first place among the thousands of web pages that were produced through the simple search. The search brought up a link that provides a trove of data about Angkor Wat, the history of the Khmer people, and even travel information; however it is contextualized, Angkor, at this point, is at front stage. Yet clicking on one of the headings at the top of the page, such as "About Us," brings one to the host site, the pages of the overseas Khmer community. Now, Angkor has slid from the foreground to the background, the common setting underlying the actions and activities of this virtual community.

Background re-presentations also occur quite frequently in travel literature, online and in print. In July 2005, a search for "Halong Bay"[41] and "World Heritage site" brought a curious blog, since removed, into the top ten results. It was a travelogue of a young American male backpacking Vietnam around Christmastime.[42] After an unsatisfactory experience at a "local" hotel, where apparently he was uncomfortably hot, overcharged and could not make himself understood by the non-English-speaking staff, he left with great anticipation for Hạ Long Bay, which he did identify in passing as a World Heritage site. Alongside his commentary were some nice digital photographs he took of the Bay, but the majority of his text concerned his disappointment about the experience during the standard three-hour luncheon boat ride. Particular time and emotional effort were devoted to a literary rant about how he was overcharged for a beer during the meal. He then turned self-reflective at the end of the online journal entry. Realizing that although the experience of being overcharged was unsavory and humiliating, the price was still affordable by American standards, and he said he attempted to enjoy the scenery, which he then briefly describes. Although the World Heritage site was intended to be the primary focus of both his *in situ* experience and the journal entry, it clearly took a back seat to the action during the meal. The story seemed not about the interaction with the Bay, but with his interactions with the boat's staff, as well as with himself. The Bay, then, experienced a dialectical transformation as it served as both the set dressing for more "important" or "relevant" action at center stage, and, at the same time, became contextualized by this very activity; it became imbued in a narrative of cheating, anger and humiliation—certainly not one of "unity in diversity."

Such is standard procedure for a majority of travel articles, which tend to focus more on the particular experiences of a writer inside the destination, rather than to provide a center-stage description of the site of interest. A perfect example of this can be found in a September 2001 *Travel + Leisure* column entitled "The Next Hotspot," written before the terrorist attacks on America. It is an extensive and well-researched piece, with able literary descriptions complemented by artistic color photographs. Yet from the very first line, it becomes clear that this destination has been deemed a new "hotspot" for its pleasure-inducing vacationland luxury, wherein the temples of Angkor rest backstage like the faux Bavarian castle of the Magic Kingdom. Indeed, the author devotes only the last two pages of his seven-page article to any description of the temples; the majority focuses paradoxically on the harshness of Cambodian minefields and post-Pol Pot life, and the indulgences provided by the burgeoning tourist infrastructure— from five star hotels to three-Michelin-star meals. The temples add value and diversity, but seem not to the primary focus of the touristic experience. The article begins with the following introduction:

> Freckled and tan and thin as a gecko, Nan Kempner is slouching around the pool of the Grand Hotel d'Angkor. "Isn't this delicious?" asks the best-dressed-list recidivist as she drags on a bummed cigarette. "Just delicious," Mrs. Thomas Kempner of New York and the gossip columns repeats herself. "Just being here and breaking all the rules."
> What exactly are the rules? No smoking and no sun. Those, and a temple a day. Claude Lévi-Strauss was right when he predicted that the modern traveler would spend his leisure chasing the "vestiges of a vanished reality." But he didn't anticipate tourists like Mrs. Thomas Kempner and me.

It's not that we're jaded. We're just taking a pass on the ruins today. Mrs. Kempner is sitting out a World Monuments Fund day trip to Angkor Thom; I'm nursing an allergy to force-fed awe with a cold chicken salad and an icy beer. If the customary reaction to the mythical worlds of Disney is a giddiness so severe as to induce vertigo, one typical response to the mythical world of Angkor Wat is a solemnity that can make your head ache. Yet it might surprise you to know that the charms of the two places are not so different.[43]

According to the *Lonely Planet*'s guide to effective travel writing, which in the industry is dubbed "travelese," the genre is not solely about the destination, but the experiences the author enjoys there:

> What makes a wonderful travel story? In one word, it is place. Successful travel stories bring a particular place to life through a combination of factual information and vividly rendered descriptive details and anecdotes, characters and dialogue. Such stories transport the reader and convey a rich sense of the author's experience in that place. The best travel stories also set the destination and experience in some larger context, creating rings of resonance in the reader.[44]

As this citation conveys, while the place is obviously integral to the story, it is contextualized through anecdotes, characters and dialogue. The medium need not focus as much on describing the places encountered *per se*, but the resonant human experiences one may have during the entire travel process. The entire focus of the description, which is ostensibly intended to inform the reader about the site through fostering a literary re-presentation of it, shifts from the re-presented to the re-presenter. It becomes more overtly about the experience of the particular writer, colored by his or her previous understandings, as well as his taste, than about any ostensibly "objective" view in which the site stands alone. Each article becomes a mini ethnographic account of one's particular experience traveling through the broader heritage-scape at a particular point in time and space. Regardless of whether he shares a similar interaction with a destination, the reader must connect with the writer's experience during travel—the anxieties, miscommunications, resonance with a place despite foreignness, wonder encountered in unexpected places, and, importantly, a renewed understanding of self. In this way, the young American blogger in Hạ Long Bay speaks travelese well—he recounts a story of a person in a foreign land, who, embroiled in miscommunications as he bears witness to wondrous sights, learns about himself, his reactions and his level of tolerance. For the travel writer at Angkor, he learns that chasing after "mythical worlds" gives him a headache, as well as a craving for his Western comfort-food of choice, cold chicken salad and beer. Where is the site in all of this, as the couple lounges around their five-star hotel some ten kilometers away from Angkor? Where is Hạ Long Bay, as the boy broods over his beer inside the boat? Both Angkor and Hạ Long lie in the background, giving the stories character and depth as they quietly emanate their own narratives. Yet the primary narrative of the travel writer is also transmitted into the background, mingling with that of the site, and inexorably changing it. For the audience of this re-presentation of Hạ Long Bay, bad hotels and bad sailors combine with emerald water and overpriced beer to produce a singular meaning of what it is to be the Bay, just as the luxury and comfort of the five-star hotels at the "mythical world of Angkor Wat" can protect travelers from the harshness of reality—be it cancer, overwork, vertigo, heat or Cambodian landmines.

Travelese is also a language of superlatives. If it is to be seen at all, if it is to draw travelers over great distances to commune with it, a site must always be described as not only unique but exceptional. Travelese describes everything with the understanding that wondrous diversity abounds, but within a seemingly infinite number of destination choices, this particular site is not-to-be-missed. A site can therefore be portrayed as the oldest, the most beautiful, the most characteristic, the most innovative, or the most revealing. And multiple sites, even within the same destination, use these very same epithets. The astute reader may therefore question the veracity of such statements as provided above; after all, only one thing can be "the oldest" in a list. But travelese does not lie; rather, it is able to fashion these superlatives into an often subtly subjective narrative. Something is rarely portrayed as the oldest structure in the world, for example, but it can be qualified by referring to it as the oldest structure in a town, or a region or a country. The shrewd travel writer can further manipulate this superlative as "the oldest surviving structure in a town," and build upon this as "the oldest surviving structure of a particular style in a town," and so forth. Travelese can find a superlative for any site, and, in doing so, may create a grotesquely disproportionate—if quite complementary—literary portrait of the place.

That these sites can be manipulated in such reproducible background representations is common and perhaps unavoidable. Like Gauguin's depictions of Tahiti, the place, whether at center stage or pushed to the wings, is filtered through the author's particular and utterly singular lens. Unlike Gauguin, however, who is allowed through the conventions of his medium to take aesthetic and descriptive liberty when visually realizing his feelings about the place, travel writers have a "moral obligation" to present a destination "with accuracy." Morality aside, the obvious reason for this tenet, of course, is that a reader is drawn to a particular travel article because of their knowledge or interest in the place itself; they want to gather some reliable details on the destination that can be used when preparing to travel there themselves one day. This includes knowing the names, locations and proximities of hotels, restaurants and places of interest; they frequently yearn to know more about what sort of feelings they will encounter if they were in the author's shoes traipsing about in all of this foreignness. Travel writing—whether in the form of guidebooks or, more so, travel articles—creates precise, hierarchical and, above all, subjective discourses concerning the emotional worth of each place. It is concerned more with creating an exacting expectation of one's potential personal experience with the site rather than the site itself—a point Daniel Boorstin famously bemoans as "pseudo-events."[45] Thus, as a container for actual yet immeasurable emotions the visitor might likely encounter, the destination must itself be measurably accurate in its portrayal; a glaring inaccuracy in the description of the background itself might translate into the inauthenticity of the raconteur's so-called experience. Even so the place can be manipulated in its immeasurable dimensions. A few verified facts provide the authenticating skeleton on the canvas of this literary impressionism; they can be thrown out to prove the reliability of the author before he begins adding his own embellishments to the place. For the American gossip columnist and the travel writer, lounging about the poolside resort, Angkor Wat—and Cambodia in general—was a medieval and untamed country, from which the bastion of refuge that was their hotel selflessly shielded them. For them, the comfortable five-star hotel was an oasis of sanctity and safety in an otherwise infernal and oppressive country requiring enormous effort to touristically tame its heat, physically taxing terrain, and its very foreignness. It was such a refuge that it even protected them from the harmful practices—smoking, drinking, sun-tanning—that they brought with them from home. Yet these very same emotions—the very same brushstrokes with which the Angkor Archaeological Park is painted in the piece—connects with the writer's audience, eliciting from them their own singular recollections of similar emotional experiences such that, despite the dearth of description about the site itself in the first half of the article, they are able to paint their own picture of Angkor that is "accurate" in its rootedness in the very human pantheon of emotions.

Yet these settings often contribute to raising awareness in the minds of the viewers. Frances Mayes' 1996 book, *Under the Tuscan Sun*, and the subsequent 2003 film based on it, can be seen as one of the best examples of this. Based on the author's factual experience of fixing up and living in an old Tuscan farmhouse she rather impulsively purchased,[46] *Under the Tuscan Sun* re-presents the Tuscan countryside and the small medieval town of Cortona, previously unknown to the tourist circuit, as a idealized paradise of quirky yet kindly citizens, idyllic vistas, and sumptuous food—the recipes of which Mayes includes in her books. Although featured in the title, the countryside and the town are nevertheless backdrops to the story's true theme: one woman's journey of self-discovery and adventure. Italy, the Italian culture, customs and cuisine—and Tuscany in particular—are beautifully re-presented through the author's own Anglo-American filter as a cosmopolitan outsider in a land full of rural, if not outright quaintly primitive, natives. These natives know how to build with rocks, negotiate and barter rather than abide by rules and hard prices, and even grow their own food. What they do not grow, they buy fresh daily in a market to which they must make a pilgrimage from the countryside. A particularly innovative and successful element of the book—and one that could not be portrayed cinematically—was Mayes' inclusion of "traditional" recipes, taught to her from the food-loving Italian locals, which she learned to master. Through this exceptionally effective device, Mayes allows the readers not only to identify with her experience through the act of reading, but through the practice of cooking—and of eating. The book has the potential to become a complete emotional and sensory experience; readers' emotions resonating with her account, they can relive and re-present Cortona through sight, touch, taste, sound and smell in their own kitchens far away from Tuscany. And, their awareness raised, many decide to fully relive Mayes' experience. Indeed, this presentation of Tuscany strongly appealed to her cosmopolitan, Anglo-American audience, who continue to flock in record numbers to Tuscany. Now, Cortona and the Tuscan countryside have become destinations in and of themselves, not simply the view one sees from a car or train window passing through *en route* from Rome to Florence.

For those who may still doubt the significance of this particular author's re-presentation to raise and shape awareness, one last example can be offered. When the book was made into a feature film, its marketing materials utilized the image of a zigzagging road of cypress trees, which has become so widely publicized that it has become the quintessential visual re-presentation of Tuscany as Mayes describes it. This image is featured on postcards found all across Italy, on photo calendars and websites. It is an icon, in the American imagination at least, for the idyllic land that is "Tuscany." While many think that this road must be located in the vicinity of the north-eastern Tuscan city of Cortona, it is in actuality found within the property line of Villa La Foce, located some 30 miles away, near Montepulciano, the famous winemaking town in Southeast Tuscany's Val d'Orcia. One must literally drive down the winding roads of eastern Tuscany for almost an hour to arrive at the villa. It is a lovely drive past a kaleidoscope of changing landforms—from the Apennine foothills of Cortona, through the barren, clay-filled hills of the Crete region, and through the vineyards of Montepulciano and Pienza—and one that renders evident the disconnect between the real Cortona and that which was presented by images of La Foce.[47]

Because of these re-presentations, the villa has become a tourist site in its own right; that the magnificent Italianate gardens were designed by famed British designer Cecil Pinsent provides a solid "educational" basis for visiting the site. It continues to be owned by the family of deceased Anglo-American author Iris Origo, who wrote a largely unknown, but nevertheless moving, account of being an ex-pat in Tuscany during World War II[48]—a considerably different background re-presentation of Tuscany although the theme of independent, female self-discovery is largely similar to Mayes'. Tour operators and travel writers, with the help of Origo's daughters, publicized this villa, turning it into a now-obligatory stop of the Tuscan countryside tourist circuit, despite its distance from Cortona and Siena. Now, the once private villa features private garden tours led by Origo's daughters, and is open one day a week to the general public. In a testament to the power of visual re-presentations to shape awareness, while independent travelers may prefer to reenact *Under the Tuscan Sun*'s experience by spending the night in a Cortona hotel, many group travelers eschew the more complicated daytrip to Cortona for a stop-over or drive-through of La Foce. In my own experience a tour operator, 90% of my Tuscan countryside tours from 2001 to 2005 visited La Foce, while only 80% visited Cortona.

And finally, in 2005, UNESCO named the Val d'Orcia, the valley in which La Foce is found, a World Heritage site for the natural beauty of its craggy clay hill formations, its Renaissance-era management system, and its inclusion on the medieval Via Franchigina pilgrimage trail.[49] And although the Tuscan valley is officially described as "the agricultural hinterland of Siena," a town located about an hour and a half north-east from the Val d'Orcia, its official webpage on UNESCO's website features the same zigzagging image of privately owned La Foce[50]—perhaps in deference to its true re-presentational quality. Indeed, ICOMOS most likely had La Foce in mind when it recommended the Val d'Orcia for its "associative quality" as being a "landscape as an icon."[51]

There are many literary-cinematic fusions presenting a World Heritage site as a background, which have successfully raised awareness. Although, for example, *Memoirs of a Geisha* is concerned with a particularly skewed and not altogether complementary representation of the traditional geisha culture in Japan's World Heritage city of Kyoto, many travelers cited the book and recently released cinematic adaptation as an impetus for visiting Kyoto.[52] Half-day "Geisha tours" are planned in the Gion section of Kyoto by the national tour operator conglomerate, JTB, which ends with a performance at the Miyako Odori. Guests are herded into the tourist theater in large groups, made to sit at long tables and participate in a hastily prepared demonstration of a tea ceremony. While a real tea ceremony is a complex affair, marked by slow and deliberate movements by the hosts and individual guests seated on the *tatami* floor, this is more a performance, with the host onstage and waiters distributing cups of tea and a sweet glob of glutinous rice. The group is then ushered into the main theatrical space to watch a variety show highlighting the different forms of traditional Japanese theatre, including Noh and Kabuki—two types of opera that can last upwards of six hours each in their complete forms.

Real-life landscapes can also be re-presented as entirely fictional places. Peter Jackson's *Lord of the Rings* trilogy was especially powerful in raising awareness for the natural beauty of New Zealand, whose sweeping panoramas he used as the setting for J.R.R. Tolkien's mystical fantasyland of Middle Earth. Upon the completion of the series, the New Zealand tourist board erected billboards in Australia, enticing its neighbors to relive the narrative of magic and mystery with the simple, tongue-in-cheek phrase: "We haven't taken down the set yet."[53]

The highly manipulated re-presentations of place as a cinematic background is one reason why films like *Tomb Raider* seem so insidious, and why it elicited such a harsh reaction from UNESCO: On the one hand, it was drawing on the life history of the monument and its valorized status, but on the other end it twisted this life history to suit its own, competing means. The makers of *Tomb Raider* did this in a number of ways, not the least of which was combining the theme of international black-market looting with re-presentations of Angkor—a site which had been so plagued by this very problem that unprecedented diplomatic action was necessary to stop it.[54] However, perhaps even more insidious that that was the fact that the cinematographers seamlessly melded accurate depictions of the site itself with completely fictitious sets, thereby drastically changing the way the place looked and the meaning that it would have. The awareness it undoubtedly raised—and it did generate an increase in tourism for the Kingdom—would be colored by the inaccuracy of the reproduction. Two scenes stand out. In one scene, Angkor Wat was used as a backdrop to a false Cambodian "village," awash in hanging clothes and dirty sepia tones, which the movie producers erected especially for this film. Their awareness raised by this portrayal, visitors would be quite surprised to view Angkor as it really stands— amid a vast parkland, surrounded by low grasses and, in the distance, other temples—a good guide, of course, can proudly point out where exactly this scene was shot. This was not, however, the focus of UNESCO authorities' objections. The portrayal of Ta Prohm was much more manipulated, and gave a highly skewed impression of Khmer architecture and statuary. They utilized a highly stylized, but still relatively accurate, shot of a crumbled doorway in Ta Prohm that is partially obscured by strangler fig tendrils. This offered forth an understanding of a temple deep in the thick of a jungle—and not standing somewhat anachronistically verdant and wild amid an otherwise clearing of this highly controlled Park. This is not the problem either.

What was problematic is the way the fictitious interior allows the temple to slide from the foreground to the background as the characters and their destructive tomb raiding adventure takes celebratory center stage. Yet this manipulated "Khmer" temple would not stay silent in the background, but would subtly slide back into the foreground, and into the adventurous plot, as its statues—imaginative hybridizations of "Oriental" Buddhist styles, which do not exist in such a state in reality—come to life as a threatening force necessitating the various feuding factions of tomb raiders to join together to defeat a common enemy. As dangerous as Lara Croft and her unethical adversaries are to each other, these primitive anthropomorphic relics—including a giant Buddha—are more menacing. And so side by side they fight, destroying the false temple and its magical stone statues with explosions and machine-gun fire. One by one, the threatening statues are felled—some by bullets, some by fire, and some by collapsing columns and roofs. In the end, the Western raiders are of course victorious; not only would they survive the onslaught, but they would succeed in stealing the fictitious artifact the statues were protecting. Despite the animosity between the two groups of avaricious tomb raiders, they could still share the common bond of Western modernity to defeat the threatening backwardness of these barely known, and misunderstood, Oriental vestiges. Echoes of the French missions of Louis Delaporte faintly ring, though he brought these fragments to be "conserved" museums such as the Guimet. But in this film, the tomb is not simply raided, but destroyed—a more frightening prospect were it to happen in reality.

THE FUTURE OF THE HERITAGE-SCAPE

Since wars begin in the minds of men, it is in the minds of men that the defenses of peace must be constructed. . . . A peace based exclusively upon the political and economic arrangements of governments would not be a peace which could secure the unanimous, lasting and sincere support of the peoples of the world. . . . The peace must therefore be founded, if it is not to fail, upon the intellectual and moral solidarity of mankind.
— UNESCO, *Constitution of the United Nations Educational Scientific and Cultural Organization*

Breaking Boundaries, Creating Peace in the Minds of Men

The purpose of this book is, broadly, to analyze UNESCO's World Heritage program in socio-cultural terms, and, more specifically, to describe how it fits into UNESCO's overarching mission of fostering "peace in the minds of men" through its designation process, through related preservation and awareness-raising activities, and through global flows of tourism. As I hope this book has revealed, UNESCO's ambitious and impassioned heritage discourse is not meant to be an empty monologue—full of sound and fury but signifying nothing, in the cynical words of Macbeth—but is actively employed to create a very real, a very material, and a very novel system that touches individuals the world over, regardless of their affiliations, status, identity or ethos. It is a complex and multi-faceted global placemaking endeavor, which calls upon a variety of stakeholders from all levels of global life, and co-opts a number of situated and non-situated social structures to effect its objective.

The collectivity of these interrelated social systems I have termed the heritage-scape, so as to convey both the totalization of temporal, spatial and cultural forces that UNESCO wishes to foster, as well as the amorphous and continually changeable nature of its imagined boundaries.[1] Its charter, the World Heritage

Convention, establishes its structural interconnectivity: The World Heritage program engages governments to cede resources—of both the monetary and material cultural types—to disparate individuals who may not initially identify with the monument's country of origin, as well as to global flows of tourists, preservationists, academics and "armchair" information consumers. Thus, individuals fuse with collectivities, institutions fuse with bureaucracies, local modalities fuse with global infrastructures, narrative fuses with dialogue, culture fuses with politics. Mediating all of these procedures are monumental structures—the World Heritage sites themselves—which act as primary nodes on this intangible heritage-scape, providing materiality, context and localization to an otherwise immaterial, de-contextualized and de-localized global phenomenon.

As awareness of UNESCO's World Heritage program grows, as heritage discourses become more prominent the world over, and as tourism finally begins to be taken seriously as a "social fact" in its own right and not merely as a commercial sidebar, a number of eminent scholars and experienced professionals—more worthy than I—have attempted a related undertaking. Yet I have found that their admirable products tend towards one of two poles: either thematically general or ethnographically specific. This statement is certainly not a criticism, either on generality or specificity. Indeed, with regards to the former, some of the most thought-provoking, groundbreaking and insightful essays have necessarily been of a generalized nature, and, as readers have undoubtedly noticed, a number of them have been extensively employed here as theoretical foundations upon which the heritage-scape could be analyzed.[2] Likewise, the intentionally broad arguments made in this book could not have been effectively substantiated had it not been for those highly ethnographic pieces, especially with regards to the history and society of Cambodia and Vietnam, whose World Heritage sites are used as primary—though not exclusive—exemplars.[3] Indeed, the anthropological practice of ethnography has always been a microcosmic pursuit, at least in theory. As Emile Durkheim and Bronislaw Malinowski argued in the early days of socio-cultural inquiry, anthropology's goal is to obtain a detailed, synoptic view of an otherwise imponderable native life,[4] and must be rigorously "objective, specific and methodological."[5] To these early ethnographers and many others in the present day, this translates into "living among the natives," of "observing them in all areas and at all times of the day"[6]—in short, in conducting fieldwork among neatly delimited societies within a geopolitically bounded area. This notion has changed somewhat, especially as 'global ethnography' has emerged onto the academic stage, but to make any sense at all of the "real life of social fabric," the *imponderabilia* of actual life, and a culture's *corpus inscriptionum* (or "native spirit"),[7] practitioners of global ethnography still must be situated for some time in a specific place.

Early on in the writing process, I made the decision to broaden the focus of this book, specifically in the kinds and the manner in which ethnographic data would be utilized. This book is about the heritage-scape as a global social system that boasts as much materiality—and as much intangibility—as any traditional one; it enables and constrains individuals in similar ways and through similar means; it creates as many re-presentations of itself and compels as many to significant action. Most importantly, through the utilization of juxtaposed monumental media that strike directly at the individual "minds of men," it possesses as much potential to create identity and solidarity as any other traditionally conceived society. Social and cultural theorists from Durkheim to Sahlins have revealed that, while society is individually perceived such that it can only live in and by means of their individual members,[8] it is more than the sum of its parts; it is, rather, the system formed by their association,[9] and its culture is a process of totalizing those individual differences in ways that are easily comprehendible and inspire collectively comprehendible action.[10] The heritage-scape, composed as it is of diverse monuments and diffused by divergent forms of touristic interactants and re-presentations they create, is no different.

I decided, then, that the only fitting way of organizationally approaching UNESCO's World Heritage program in any substantive manner is to juxtapose the systems, institutions and, especially, the monuments themselves—to extend beyond an in-depth discussion of a particularity to call upon elements that, outside of the heritage-scape, may seem unrelated, but which impact the totality of this global social realm. It would, of course, be impossible to describe in great ethnographic detail every one of the nearly one thousand natural, cultural and "mixed" properties in the heritage-scape, but it would be equally inadequate to describe only a few without making reference to their monumental brethren, who, despite being geographically, structurally and temporally removed from each other, all impact each monument equally within the context of the heritage-scape. That is, taking Angkor alone as illustrative of the kind of monumental mediator that composes the heritage-scape, for example, is insufficient. What I have tried to show, and what I think differs from other monographs on this particular place, is that Angkor cannot be understood adequately *as a World Heritage site* without understanding something about Hạ Long Bay and the Bamiyan Buddhas, Phong Nha-Kẻ Bàng and the Acropolis, Hội An and Stonehenge, Hiroshima and Venice. Within a system that totalizes even aesthetic differences, each individual member—in this case, Angkor the site itself—systematically is impacted by, and assumes qualities of, other members that are removed from it in space and time. Likewise, the human society that exists within the heritage-scape is composed of and enacted by individuals (primarily tourists), but takes on a discrete life of its own as these diverse touristic individuals interact at the same nodes within the heritage-scape.

It is in this vein that UNESCO and the heritage-scape are approached. Just as UNESCO is composed of representatives from the world's nation-states, but is something greater than the aggregate of its individual members when they are working together, so too is the heritage-scape composed of individual World Heritage mediators that create something more when juxtaposed together. UNESCO's place in this is to change each monument's narrativity and object of employment—from a local to global, divisive to unifying—by totalizing all of its differences, rendering them equal in value and equally apprehensible to all human individuals who come into contact with them. It must also be noted that UNESCO is itself complex and multifaceted; though its ultimate aim is to contribute to the United Nation's mission of fostering a lasting, worldwide peace through intergovernmentality, the organization is not relegated to simply one task. Though I have used "UNESCO" somewhat interchangeably with its World Heritage program in this book, it must be noted that UNESCO operates many more programs that just the World Heritage Convention. UNESCO is focused on promoting a broad range of programs and activities that are intended to significantly impact individuals and their societies; as its name suggests, these activities fall into the categories of education, science and culture—and, in this highly mobile and networked era of globalization, it has expanded to deal with a wide range of issues concerned with information, communication, sustainable development and intellectual property. Though not directly connected to the interworkings of UNESCO's World Heritage program, they, too, play a vital role in the totality of this intergovernmental organization, impacting the ultimate decisions it makes within the field of heritage production, and must be discussed. At the very least, in most cases an individual diplomat (as a representative of the same state-party) will be the decision-maker in multiple UNESCO programs.

Indeed, it is this juxtapositional nature of UNESCO's field of heritage production that ultimately bestows each World Heritage site its narrative of "unity in diversity," its authoritative air of universality. A local place simply cannot be made into a World Heritage site without global consent—that is, the unifying coming-together of diversity. Member-states who have no national claim to the monument are made to actively deliberate and agree upon a property's universal value. This protracted process of positioning and position-taking during the often years-long nomination period actively performs the narrative of "unity in diversity" in its most basic sense: there is a physical confluence of locals, governmental representatives, NGOs, and UNESCO representatives, whose specific aim and ultimate outcome is the *creation* (rather than mere identification) of a monument of universal value. These properties, therefore, are direct products of negotiation, and hence, of cross-cultural dialogue. They become universalized monumental media, mediating now between a grand, unified social body composed of smaller societies, and individuals who will come into contact with it.

This last point is most important for fulfilling UNESCO's ultimate goal of creating world peace. By analyzing documentary and ethnographic evidence in light of anthropological theory, I have reasoned that the heritage-scape's ultimate objective is to foster "peace in the minds of men" by co-opting and inverting a common process of identity formation that traditionally employs monumental mediators to delineate boundaries predicated on conflictual narratives of difference. UNESCO's Constitution seems to echo Fredrik Barth when its Preamble asserts that a group often defines itself by what it is not, rather than what it is. In other, more localized venues, monuments serve as material manifestations of narrative cultural distinctions, which are defined, maintained and then practiced by those individuals who identify with these claims.[11] UNESCO's World Heritage program attempts to invert this by re-contextualizing these sites and their narrative claims, so that they do not illustrate any boundaries; rather, they each re-present a borderless world, since each can be viewed as part of any individual's global identity as a member of earth's humanity. If wars are fought over boundaries that are themselves imaginative constructions but gain materiality through monuments, peace can likewise be created by erasing these boundaries in the minds of men through the designation of World Heritage sites, which are the agreed-upon products of an ostensibly willing, multicultural group of world representatives.

To effectively construct a group identity, however, boundaries cannot merely be imposed upon individuals. Rather, Barth argues, boundaries—and the social (as well as physical) categories they demarcate—must be accepted, maintained and enforced by the individuals themselves, even when the categories are general or stereotyped. Thus, to use a rather banal and anecdotal example, in a multicultural milieu that characterizes Italians (or "Italian-Americans") as "pizza eaters,"[12] Italians must not only be ascribed but accept the stereotype (albeit begrudgingly), and through their actions and discourses of authenticity they will determine who lies inside and outside of this stereotypical categorization. This example reveals that identity—formed by ascription to categories and remembered in the minds of individuals both inside and outside the boundary—is contextualized by a narrative ("to be Italian, you must eat pizza") and concretized in an observable thing (the authentically "Italian" pizza) or a tangible activity (regularly eating this pizza, remembering the position of pizza in one's upbringing, or knowing the proper recipe or ritual to create its authentic "taste") to which the narrative refers.

Monuments, as Alcock puts it, are deliberately designed or designated to be the concretization of a narrative that serves to create such boundaries and the categories they demarcate. They mediate between the society who constructs the narrative and the individuals who receive it. To use the Cambodian example, Angkor Thom and the Bayon were constructed by the Khmer leader Jayavarman VII and adorned with storytelling stelae, sculptures and bas reliefs that evoke, replicate and symbolize narratives important to "Khmer" cosmological categories as the king saw them to be: Categories represented range from a unique religious fusion of Hinduism and Buddhism to mythological kinship origins; from political struggles with Champa and collaboration with China to everyday economic rituals of hunting, fishing and cookery.[13] Owing to French colonial endeavors, post-colonial conceptualizations of the nation-state and UNESCO's World Heritage program, these same temples today alternate between espousing narratives valorizing Khmer cultural history and Orientalist claims of Western civilization's safeguarding against natural decadence which they saw illustrated in contemporary Kampuchean life. Interaction with these monuments sediment narratives of boundaries and categories into individuals' minds, as it must have done for Khmer individuals in the twelfth century. It also constructs a mediatory affinity between the two; in one interaction with these monuments, the life-history of the site and the life-history of the individual interactant join together, affording the possibility for the individual to identify with it, should the narrative context be appropriate. The subsequent iconoclastic defacement of Jayavarman's Buddhist imagery in some of his temples reveal that many individuals, while still identifying with many of the monuments' symbols, did not agree with their new Buddhist categorization. They were the subjects of contestation almost from their creation.

Monuments serve to create conflict when these categorizations are not accepted by an outside group, or when the terms of the categories shift without the consent of the society—such as when it is appropriated by another collectivity like the Thai. Unlike the French some centuries later, the Thai utilized the Angkorian temples—especially Angkor Wat—as a marker of Siamese-ness; they physically brought the temples into their political borders and narratively brought Angkor Wat into the fold of national mythos. The Thai had brought fragmentary re-presentations in the form of statuary and linga back to Ayutthaya, and later created reproducible re-presentations at Bangkok in the form of scale models of the temple, which they placed in public view. When such appropriations occur, the categories thus are either shared, blurred or conflict with the previously instated categories. Contestation between Cambodia and Thailand surrounding Angkor's monuments extend to the present, and conflicts have flared up as recently as 2004, when Cambodians set fire to Thailand's embassy in Phnom Penh after a Thai actress publicly claimed cultural possession of the site for her country.

An even more recent, and perhaps more explosive, conflict erupted in the summer of 2008 when Cambodia succeeded in designating the temple-hermitage of Preah Vihear as a World Heritage site, over several years of Thailand's veto. While Preah Vihear may not yet elicit much reaction from international tourists—certainly not the kind of emotions associated with Angkor Wat—for Thais and Cambodians it is considered an "emotive issue"[14] that is embroiled in over a century of border disputes and internal political wrangling. Straddling a Thai-Cambodian boundary whose lines were drawn by the French in the Franco-Siamese Treaty of 1907, Preah Vihear (or "Khao Phra Wihan" in Thai[15]) is strategically situated on a breathtaking promontory in the Dangrek Mountains, towering 600 meters above the plain of Cambodia. Thailand had disputed this demarcation, and in 1962 the case was brought before the International Court of Justice in The Hague. The court ruled in Cambodia's favor, deciding that the hermitage's structure was located a few hundred feet in Cambodia's territory. This decision was based, in part, on post-colonial arguments of Khmer heritage. From the Thai point of view, this did not settle the dispute; they questioned the French-drawn map and pointed to Thai settlements in the area. Thai citizens had repeatedly donated money to help finance "the country's push to defend the temple in the international court."[16] It remains a "painful memory" of "national trauma and shame," according to one commentary.[17]

Positionality was at the forefront of UNESCO's designation, as well. Preah Vihear was elevated to World Heritage status not only for its historical importance during the Khmer period and for its unique architectural and aesthetic features, but for its very location; UNESCO's designation begins thusly: "The Sacred Site of the Temple of Preah Vihear is distinguished by its exceptional natural environment, and the close relationship with its setting."[18] Complicating matters is the way in which political geography is performed at Preah Vihear by visitors and locals: One enters the site through Thailand's Si Saket province, for the plateau on which the temple is positioned begins in Thailand and is not readily accessible through the Cambodian jungle below, which one of the last strongholds of the Khmer Rouge and is thought to still contain unexploded landmines. Furthermore, while the main temple may lie on the Cambodian side of the border, its monumental *naga*-lined staircase and its traditionally Khmer-styled reservoir (*baray*) are on the Thai side. Indeed, when tensions surrounding the site have caused Cambodia to close the border (literally by locking the large gate at the top of the steps), visitors often could still approach the site to peer in at what one Thai operator called "mysterious artwork . . . along a narrow Cliff-side path which leads down towards Cambodia on the East side of the cliff and is blocked by a large gate about 50 feet down." This is of particular interest to Thai claims of sovereignty, for as the operator states, "The origin and type of characters depicted has been speculated on greatly since they do not seem to match known Khmer or Buddhist styles."[19]

Cambodia officially began the nomination procedure as early as 1992—the year of Angkor's designation—and its File was first considered by the World Heritage Committee's twenty-fifth meeting in Helsinki, Finland in December 2001. Thailand was serving on the Committee that year, and blocked the designation amid fears that it would threaten its continued claim over the disputed territory.[20] Cambodia offered Preah Vihear for nomination every year hence, and Thailand vetoed it every year,[21] though these proceedings were kept off of UNESCO's public "Decisions Adopted by the World Heritage Committee" meeting records.[22] The situation changed in 2007, when Thailand's government supposedly agreed to a mediation of the dispute during the thirty-first meeting in Christchurch, New Zealand.[23] Unofficial talks were held in Koh Kong, Cambodia between Thai Foreign Minister Noppadon Pattama and Deputy Prime Minister Sok An on 14 May 2008. This was followed by formal negotiations at UNESCO's Paris headquarters on May 22, 2008 between a Thai delegation—including Noppadon, the Deputy Permanent Secretary for Foreign Affairs and other Ministry officials, and the Thai ambassador to France—and a Cambodian delegation represented by Sok An and other Cambodian government officials; it was mediated by "high-ranking" UNESCO officials led by Ms. Francoise Riviere, Assistant Director General for Culture.[24]

The joint communiqué signed by Thailand and Cambodia seemed to be steeped with mutual understanding and respect for the site: Thailand gave its support to Cambodia, provided that Cambodia would submit only the temple itself—and not the staircase or secondary monuments that fall on the Thai border, so as not to claim physical objects within Thailand's internationally recognized territory. Cambodia would include an amended map in the file that would only refer to the temple and not to the greater region, so as not to reinforce broader territorial claims; this new map would "supersede the maps and all the other geographic references."[25] On June 17, the Thai cabinet endorsed the map.[26] Finally, Thailand and Cambodia both agreed that the designation of Preah Vihear would have no legal effect on broader claims of territoriality; rather,

> The nomination of the Temple of Preah Vihear proper as World Heritage Site will be without prejudice to the rights of both Thailand and Cambodia on their overlapping territorial claims over the areas adjacent to the Temple. Neither Thailand nor Cambodia loses their rights from this agreement and Thailand would preserve its full sovereignty and territorial integrity.[27]

A 61-page White Paper defended this agreement by stating that

> Thailand was only concerned that if Thailand and Cambodia have not agreed in
> principle o how to systematically manage the overlapping zones around the
> area, the preservation and conservation of Preah Vihear in practical terms could
> not be embarked without obstacles or could not be implemented at all despite
> being listed as a World Heritage site." [28]

Unfortunately, domestic politics between the unpopular People's Power
Party (formed by deposed members of Thaksin Shinawatra's Thai Rak Thai
party) and the opposition People's Alliance for Democracy (PAD) created a
crisis that has marred the UNESCO proceedings[29] as well as public understanding of UNESCO's World Heritage endeavor. Arguing that the government had
sold out the Thai people to Cambodia by "losing" Preah Vihear, the PAD organized large protests in Bangkok and Si Saket called for the ouster of party officials; a petition with upwards of 20,000 signatures was submitted to the government, [30] prompting a Constitutional Court hearing which eventually ruled in
favor of the joint communiqué.[31] Cambodia deployed riot police in Phnom Penh
to protect Thai businesses from Cambodian counter-protests. On June 28, Cambodia closed the border at Preah Vihear as 20 activist groups organized by the
Patriotic E-San Network rallied at the entrance of the temple to urge Thai authorities to expel ethnic Khmers from Si Saket;[32] this did not prevent some
young locals from crossing the border in protest. Thailand also deployed troops,
and the Prime Minister made a publicized visit to them that supposedly "won the
hearts of the troops when he cooked up a big pot of 'khao na kai', rice with
stewed chicken, and then served them personally while visiting Pha Mor E-
daeng near the disputed border with Cambodia", according to a front-page news
article in the English-language *Bangkok Post*.[33] Cambodian celebrities also
showed their solidarity by distributing food to their soldiers. Thailand's representatives to UNESCO also had to assuage erroneous rumors that the decision
regarding Preah Vihear would impact the country's other World Heritage sites
such as Ayutthaya and Sukhothai, both located well within the border.[34]

Relations have begun to normalize, and though the border remains closed as
of this writing, troop levels on both sides are being reduced.[35] Cambodia and
Thailand have issued statements reinforcing mutual friendship and cooperation,
and their mutual belief that this designation will ultimately contribute to positive
developmental outcomes on both sides of the border—particularly through an
increase in tourism and in international grants. Although media focus has shifted
to Thai trepidation concerning sovereignty over other Khmer temples along the
disputed border—such as Surin province's Ta Moan Thom temple, the topic of a

Bangkok Post article entitled, "Show us Your Proof, Say Tour Guides: Thais on the border reject Phnom Penh's latest claims to temples in disputed territory as Preah Vihear struggle spreads to new areas"[36]—conversations I held with Thais in August 2008 convey an understanding that fatiguing and instable governmental politics, held behind closed doors and without popular consent, have exacerbated the situation more than the designation itself. "They are so secret about everything," one guide exclaimed; "if they were honest with the people from the beginning, this could have been avoided."[37]

While it seems that the designation of Preah Vihear may have created more conflict than unity, this experience pointedly illustrates my contention in chapter 6 that nation-states often embark on World Heritage endeavors, and appropriate valorizing World Heritage status, for political motives that may be in disharmony with UNESCO's objectives, both between nation-states and within a nation's domestic politics. It also underscores the continuing need to raise awareness of the heritage-scape and World Heritage sites' unique meta-narrative claim of "unity in diversity," as well as the need for transparency in its proceedings. Indeed, boundary wars often occur, states UNESCO, when categories and stereotypes collide and when they are not agreed upon by insiders and outsiders; both sides will struggle for discursive—if not physical—dominance over the structure so as to claim the authority to make and attribute its exhibitional categories. Recognizing this, UNESCO appropriates these monuments once again, but seeks to expand the narrative and widen the boundaries, claiming that all people equally share the categories, all people can identify with them, and all can accept each Other as having equal share in the now-universalized category of membership. Though each State-party may have different—and often immanently visceral—reasons for engaging with the World Heritage Convention, the field of heritage production forces all nation-states—whether those involved in a particular discursive or physical struggle over a monument, or completely outside this milieu—to agree upon the terms of the categories.

The problem remains, however, in how to effectively broaden the reach of these local, yet universalized, properties, so that they truly interact with a diversity of peoples. The problem is solved, at least theoretically, by calling upon tourism. In this age, tourism touches a vast number of people around the world—people who serve as both hosts and guests at various stages of their life. Though it does not touch everyone (at least in the present), tourism is the largest and largest-growing industry, moving well over eight hundred million people annually at a yearly increase of nearly 5%. It is also global, with low barriers for participation; its structure is such that it can be applied anywhere and to anyone.

On the social end of the spectrum, tourism is a particularly perspectival form of interaction with place that can be applied without prejudice across the globe; an individual can visit sites at both ends of the earth equally, with little change in his preparation, level of knowledge or skill set. As simply a way of seeing, and not necessarily a form of movement, locals who may not have the means to participate can still engage in the touristic process at home. On the physical end of the spectrum, tourism has become particularly homogenizing in its demand for certain types of infrastructure that renders touring conducive. While many correctly bemoan this aspect of tourism as creating a number of negative outcomes—both intended and unintended—infrastructural improvements often benefit the host population when done properly; that is, when locals are not excluded from the total process. Infrastructural improvements often bring tangible resources, enable communication and increase commerce. And especially when tourism is involved, they enable cross-cultural interaction. Aided by shared identification with World Heritage sites, such interaction may contribute to the process of boundary eradication by fostering mutual recognition of unity in diversity.

My phenomenological argument that tourism can foster the kind of "unity in diversity" sensation that UNESCO wishes to create follows a line of reasoning based on Victor Turner's argument that the ultimate goal of a pilgrimage is to foster *communitas*—"the direct, immediate and total confrontation of human identities",[38] a "relationship between leveled and equal total and individuated human beings, stripped of structural attributes."[39] Communitas is different from "community"; Turner asserts that the latter "refers to a geographical area of common living"[40]—and, I would add, it often integrates some forms of social structure (including legal processes, terrestrial rites of passage, economic exchanges, political factionalism, etc.). If one conceptualizes community as crystallizing around tangible sites, the *communitas* formed at World Heritage sites through the "secular pilgrimage" that is tourism is indeed the anti-structure that Turner calls it. Standing in dialectical opposition with social structure, individuals experiencing *communitas* create a type of "society" that is "homogeneous . . . [and] whose boundaries are ideally coterminous with those of the human species."[41] Boundaries may still exist, but in that transcendental interaction, all participants recognize their similarities. They tease out from their identities those qualities they share with others: "seeking oneness is not . . . to withdraw from multiplicity," Turner writes, "it is to eliminate divisiveness, to realize nonduality."[42] In short, *communitas* creates a "culture of cultures,"[43] totalizing differences as it transcends traditional territorial or status distinctions.

Tourism intersects with, and is employed by, the heritage-scape for ultimately diffusing and individually instantiating UNESCO's meta-narrative claim. But although tourism can be conceived as a social system itself—with certain homogenizing properties and common structures—its "culture" (as a totalization of differences) cannot be neatly pinpointed; there are as many touristic cultures as there are individual and groups of tourists on any given day throughout the world. Yet when attempting to understand tourism's connection with a World Heritage site, I believe it would be similarly ineffective to merely study its properties in a localized fashion. A tourist at Angkor who has not interacted with another, disparate World Heritage site is a relatively rare occurrence—especially if he is counted among the mobile Western tourists followed in this book. Just as those diplomats who ultimately decide the narrative claim of one particular World Heritage site also actively determine the narrative of another World Heritage property, those individuals who materially impact the structure and infrastructure of one World Heritage site—such as historic preservationists, site managers, tour operators and global hoteliers—are often informed by, if not also engaged with, other World Heritage sites. UNESCO, for its part, enables this through the disbursement of its World Heritage Fund to support cross-cultural educational and professional exchange programs. Site managers' work cannot be seen decontextualized from the global fields of heritage and touristic production. Thus, *in the context of the heritage-scape*, touristic interaction in the Tuscan Val d'Orcia, in the Japanese city of Kyoto, or in the sacred Cham mountain site of Mỹ Sơn, should not be neglected; they should also play a part in the analysis of tourism at Angkor.

Touristic individuals may come from far and wide, espousing differences in both beliefs and practices, but when traveling across this heritage-scape of World Heritage monuments—interacting with its diversity of forms and imbibing its meta-narrative of "unity in diversity" that collectively these monuments espouse—they too become one with the heritage-scape's sociality and form a uniquely universalized identity. It is this identity—constructed and continually revised in a dialectical fashion as they amass ever-the-more interactive experiences in each additional touristic itinerary they pursue throughout their lives, and with each interaction they have with the heritage-scape's multifarious representations—that grants individual actors a deeper understanding of "unity in diversity." When one's identity can effectively totalize diversity, when it can not only apprehend and appreciate diversity but rather come to see it as fundamental to itself—peace can be constructed.

"Does it Work?"—Material Effects of the Heritage-scape

This book has attempted to systematically argue that UNESCO's World Heritage program is not merely a designatory process, but a global, monumental placemaking endeavor whose essential creation is the heritage-scape, which is a diffuse socio-spatial system that totalizes worldwide differences in the minds of men. By analyzing documentary and ethnographic evidence in light of current anthropological theory, I hope I have also made the case that this program can, indeed, induce significant positive action—to the point of fostering worldwide peace. Readers, however, might still ask, "But does it work?" Peace, after all, has certainly not been achieved around the world, and the protection of cultural heritage is not always a priority.[44]

Even more problematically for my argument, much of my ethnographic data has centered on the "unintended consequences" that arise through UNESCO's very processes. Because UNESCO is an intergovernmental organization—that is, it derives its fairly limited power from the political cooperation and participation of States-parties—the World Heritage Convention is designed to empower nation-states to voluntarily "offer up" a property for designation. If it were evident that UNESCO is creating an alternative global order, it seems unlikely that nation-states would participate in this lengthy and costly enterprise. Yet the valorization of the country that comes from designation, I argued, induces the nation-state to participate. Coupled with the control a country continues to exert over the management of a World Heritage property within its borders, a State-party is positioned to contextualize a property that not only furthers its own national interest, but may compete with the heritage-scape's meta-narrative of "unity in diversity." Some of my ethnographic examples, especially those concerning Vietnam and Cambodia, reveal the complexity of competing discourses and practices surrounding a UNESCO-designated property. The previous chapter has also shown that the cacophony of contradictory narratives only increases as World Heritage sites become re-presented by diverse communities. Museums, "interpretative centers," travelogues, guidebooks, photography, cinematography, blogs and other Internet-related reproducible re-presentations all recontextualized the site, imposing upon it yet another, oft-competing, claim. Guided by a "non-conflictual" policy, and dependent upon nation-states for effecting material change, UNESCO has relatively few tools to combat this phenomenon.

Perhaps a more aptly phrased question is "*Will* it work?" Indeed, I have investigated past and present "social facts," but have thus far not engaged in discourse of a predictive quality. Since the heritage-scape has an intrinsic future orientation, it is necessary to step back from the theory and view some of the practical trends that have appeared since UNESCO's World Heritage Convention was enacted in 1972.

The process of producing peace in the minds of men is intended to be a slow one, marked by gradual changes in perception and self-identification. These are culture changes, and just as it takes many habituated years for an immigrant to view the world through his adopted culture's lens and for others to view him as one of their own (if ever at all),[45] it will also take a great number of years—generations perhaps—for individuals to identify themselves, and each other, through the heritage-scape's cultural meta-narrative. Indeed, the process of "acculturation" into the heritage-scape would involve individuals' participation in a number of short- and medium-term processes that do not affect each other causally, but dialectically. There are three short-term and medium-term efforts in which the heritage-scape engages, which theoretically contribute to creating "peace in the minds of men": awareness-raising, preservation and cultural tourism.

The first is raising awareness. Awareness-raising has been discussed at length in the final chapter, and with good reason. The awareness-raising effort of re-presenting World Heritage sites across the heritage-scape is indexical, performative and constitutive. In its most basic sense, it is an indexical endeavor; that is, it draws attention to UNESCO's World Heritage program. It references the facts of "what is out there"—what this program is and what it has done. UNESCO achieves this primarily through the publication of its ever-lengthening World Heritage Lists in a variety of print and online media. Currently, UNESCO's World Heritage Centre in Paris publicizes three Lists: the *List of World Heritage* sites, the *List of Intangible Heritage*, and the *List of World Heritage in Danger*. The first two can be considered an inventory of the World Heritage Convention's designatory accomplishments since 1972—a means of quickly and efficiently indexing the many sites that have passed through the ritualized field of heritage production, of literally raising awareness in the minds of its readers of which places are supposed to be understood as possessing "universal value" and which should be approached, interacted with and conserved as such. The third list, that of World Heritage in Danger, a subset of the first. It is more pointedly geared towards raising awareness of those sites that are in material peril of losing the qualities that render it universally valorized; such dangers may include inadequate management techniques, endeavors by the host nation that directly impact the social and material context surrounding the physical site, or disasters (natural or political) that threaten the site's very existence.

The Lists are arranged in a particular, standardized order. World Heritage properties, including those ephemeral cultural forms on the Intangible Heritage List, are catalogued under the State-party (or parties) who initially "offered it up" to the heritage-scape and under whose tutelage the individual monument falls. The date of the property's inscription is also mentioned. Tangible World Heritage sites in the first and third Lists are additionally categorized by type— that is, whether they fall primarily under the category of "cultural site," "natural site" or "mixed site." On UNESCO's interactive website, http://whc.unesco.org, one can sort through the list by any of these three categories—host country, date of inscription, type of monument, or a mixture of the three. Such an arrangement affords individuals ways of conceptualizing the totality of the heritage-scape, of comprehending the necessary interrelationship between sites.

As with any attempt at categorization, the ways of listing these sites are not without their problems. Cataloguing sites by the political nation-state under which it is geographically located seems to belie the unstated premise of the boundary-less heritage-scape, as it fractures the heritage-scape back into the traditional geopolitical divisions. The converse of this—that is, not listing it in this readily understandable means—may hinder an individual's (especially a tourist's) apprehension of where the site is located in the world; to date, few lay people are able to think in terms of latitude and longitude, though UNESCO does identify individual sites by this method in other venues. The alternative to this problem proposed by UNESCO is to categorize World Heritage sites by their type, thereby erasing political boundaries while still providing a means of digesting the lengthy List. As chapter 6 argues, however, "cultural" and "natural" are misleading hermeneutics, for by the very recognition of the category "natural," one is necessarily imposing a cultural construction.

Listing a site by nation-state also aids the country in employing World Heritage discourses as a means of promoting its own narrative claims; a look at almost any national tourist promotional material or even any official Embassy website will often reveal explicit references to the country's World Heritage sites—often in areas that seem unrelated to culture. Under the "Foreign Policy" section of the Turkish Embassy's website, for example, is a page on "Navigational Risks" in Turkish waterways. Here is how the Embassy describes the Strait of Istanbul:

> The length of the Strait of Istanbul is approximately 17 NM with a width varying from 700 meters to 1500 meters and is characterized by several sharp turns. The ships are bound to alter course in this Strait at least 12 times up to 80 degrees. . . . The dangers of navigation for a large tanker around these sharp turns are very well known by the whole maritime community. Even medium size ships encounter difficulties while navigating in the dangerous sections of the Strait of Istanbul. *The Strait of Istanbul is also unique as it runs right through the city of Istanbul, declared as a "World Heritage" by UNESCO, with more than 12 million inhabitants.* The shorelines of Istanbul are densely populated. The vessels carrying dangerous cargo regularly approach as close as 50 meters to these inhabited areas.[46]

The inclusion of this unrelated fact conveys cautionary note to seafarers (there are universally valued properties as well as 12 million inhabitants), but it also subtly aims to raise awareness of the value of Istanbul and Turkey proper.

Listing sites by nation-states is inherently constitutive—that is, it also aids in the nation-state's attempts to construct a valorizing narrative about itself. This narrative always revolves around claims of "universal value," and often the number of World Heritage sites a country boasts will show up on national promotional materials. This is an inherently relational act, possibly fostering competition among nation-states, similar in form to what Appadurai has called "tournaments of value." Tournaments of value are

> complex periodic events that are removed in some culturally well-defined way from the routines of economic life. Participation in them is likely to be both a privilege of those in power and an instrument of status contests between them. . . . [W]hat is at issue in such tournaments is not just status, rank, fame or reputation of actors, but the disposition of the central token of value in the society in question.[47]

The annual cycle of designating properties as World Heritage sites is certainly a "complex periodic event" that engages those "privileged" power elites—that is, nation-states—to both exert power claims over local properties, as well as to negotiate value-laden claims among themselves.

This has far-ranging effects on both the domestic and the international sphere, and reveal that such awareness-raising mechanisms are not only indexical, but both performative and constitutive. Within the nation-state, for example, the push to include more places on the List provides a compelling rationale for majority groups to exert influence over ethnic minorities. Chapter 6 details, for example, some of the ways in which the Vietnamese nation-state stakes claim to indigenous places through its push to designate Phong Nha-Kẻ Bàng, Hạ Long Bay and even Hội An as World Heritage sites; through its discourses and its management strategies, locals are constrained, often against their will, to adopt practices that are contrary to their culturally specific daily life processes; at Phong Nha-Kẻ Bàng, this includes forbidding the consumption of certain traditional foods, while at Hội An, this includes the prohibition of the use of "modern" technology such as electricity and automobiles.

Internationally, this may become a veritable competition, as nation-states compare the numbers of their properties with those of other countries. In a particularly salient ethnographic moment, a researcher working at one of China's proposed World Heritage sites explained to me the government's feeling that it is marginalized by Westerners by invoking World Heritage discourse. "China has 35 World Heritage sites, but Italy has over 100," she remarked in full confidence. Factually, her statement was only partially correct; as of July 2007, when this conversation occurred, Italy counted only 41 World Heritage sites to China's 35. Though she truly believed her numbers to be correct, this error was not important; what is important in our discussion was that, in her experience, the Chinese *felt* significantly marginalized in the World Heritage Convention— they felt that they needed a much greater representation within the heritage-scape to accurately reveal their competitive cultural value was on par with those Western nation-states on the world stage.

According to UNESCO, the publication of these Lists, and the subsequent diffusion of the heritage-scape's meta-narrative claims, aids in another important outcome that contributes to the creation of "peace in the minds of men"—that of historic preservation initiatives. UNESCO references this tellingly in one informational pamphlet where it asserts that "[t]he prestige that comes from being a member of the Convention and having sites inscribed on the World Heritage List often serves as a catalyst to raising awareness for heritage preservation."[48] Conservation is not an indexical action in the way that composing World Heritage Lists is. Rather, it is a constitutive and performative endeavor that operates on a number of levels. At its core, it constructs (or re-constructs) the physical site itself; that is, it is a process that modifies the tangible World Heritage property for the objective of further resisting the naturally destructive flow of time. Through the act of preservation, its practitioners perform that Freudian desire to transcend transience by creating a surrogate entity that will testify to their impact on the environment long after they have left this world. Yet as chapters 9 and 10 argued, preservation is not merely a "staving off" initiative, but rather an effort to re-make a monumental mediator in correspondence to the practitioners' narrative claims. Thus, after undergoing conservation activities, the properties in the Angkor Archaeological Park are made to illustrate two competing narrative claims which are subtly articulated in the World Heritage site's official designation: one valorizes the Khmer empire, and another valorizes pervasive Orientalist claims concerned with civilizational decadence in Southeast Asia. Now made tangible, these narratives serve to inform touristic interactants of the ways in which they should make meaning of UNESCO's "unity in diversity" claims— and, in the meantime, possibly reinforce preexisting conceptions of the place of the Other in their own cosmologies. Importantly, these touristic interactants are not passive receptors of such a claim, but also become stakeholders in the site's well being.

Yet preservation has other material outcomes, as well, which directly aid in creating the sense of peace that UNESCO so fervently desires; the act of preserving a World Heritage site performs a stakeholder's understanding of the site's "universal value" and both creates and performs *communitas* that extends beyond local boundaries. As chapter 8 argued, the conservation of historic properties is a guiding principle in the heritage-scape for this very reason; it is able to emotionally and physically mobilize a variety of actors ranging from individual philanthropists to epistemic communities of archaeologists and preservationists, from local communities to nation-states, who are joined together in a common cause. Such mobilization of non-state actors is central to UNESCO's endeavor; peaceful activities cannot be achieved through the mediation of the nation-state alone, its Preamble states. Gabriella Barbieri, an archaeologist in Tuscany's Department of Archaeological Heritage (*Soprintendenza per i Beni Archeologici*), echoes UNESCO's sentiment when she declared "The more [individual] citizens are concerned, the more they can help us...The state can't be everywhere at once."[49] When engaged in this common cause, these stakeholders actively perform the heritage-scape meta-narrative claim of "unity in diversity"—that is, they are united in a communal recognition of a site's universal value, and dedicate their resources towards preserving it for the future. While many World Heritage sites benefit from international cooperative conservation endeavors, such collaborative efforts were institutionalized at the Angkor Archaeological Park shortly after its designation. On October 13, 1993, less than a year after Angkor was Listed in December 1992, a joint agreement was signed in Tokyo between France, Japan and UNESCO that created the International Coordinating Committee on the Safeguarding and Development of the Historic Site of Angkor (ICC). The ICC's first meeting was convened in Cambodia that December—a year after Angkor's designation—with France and Japan as cochairs, UNESCO acting as secretariat, and over twenty countries participating; it was "the first high-level international discussions on Angkor ever to be held in Cambodia itself," according to the APSARA organization.[50] In addition to creating a legal agreement among the international community, the December meeting created a sub-committee responsible for debating management plans and "making decisions on technical issues regarding Angkor;" this Technical Committee continues to meet twice a year either in Phnom Penh or Siem Reap; all national and international plans for work at Angkor must be submitted to the ICC. In 1997, the Committee further expanded its reach and diversified the number of actors engaged at Angkor by creating an ad hoc group of preservation experts who are responsible for advising APSARA—the Cambodian government's management structure, on "technical solutions to precise problems (such as the collapse of Angkor Vat's western moat step) as well as broad questions related to the safeguarding of Angkor."[51]

Finally, on November 15, 2003—just over 31 years since the signing of the World Heritage Convention—UNESCO passed the *Paris Declaration on Safeguarding and Preserving Angkor* at the Second Intergovernmental Conference for the Safeguarding and Sustainable Development of the Historic Site of Angkor and of its Region. The *Paris Declaration* was notable for bringing together signatories from thirty-six countries (including the United States and Cambo-

dia's Southeast Asian neighbors such as Laos, Vietnam and Thailand); represen-
tatives from intergovernmental bodies such as UNESCO, the World Bank, the
Asian Development Bank, the Food and Agriculture Organization of the United
Nations (FAO), the International Monetary Fund (IMF), the Southeast Asian
Ministers of Education Organization Regional Centre for Archaeology and Fine
Arts (SEAMEO/SPAFA), the United Nations Development Program (UNDP),
and the World Tourism Organization (UNWTO); and experts from NGOs such
as the World Monuments Fund (WMF), ICOMOS, ICCROM, and the International Council of Museums (ICOM). They also agreed to hold a third conference, at a "suitable" yet unspecified time, to "examine the progress made and to
determine the need for new action." Next time, they allowed, the conference
could possibly be held in Cambodia itself.[52]

Declarations such as these created and performed "unity in diversity" discursively; they also paved the way for material performances of preservation
that are visible even to Angkor's lay visitors. A tourist to Angkor can see this
multicultural *communitas* at work as he moves from site to site in the Angkor
Archaeological Park. The Japanese Team for the Safeguarding of Angkor is
actively engaged in work at the Bayon, at Angkor Wat's northern library, and at
the temple of Suor Prat, while a Japanese contingent from Sophia University is
currently in the midst of rebuilding Angkor Wat's causeway, across which most
visitors pass when entering the monumental temple. German preservationists,
under the auspices of the German Apsara Conservation Project (GACP) are also
at work at Angkor Wat. A visit to Ta Prohm reveals experts from India working
in conjunction with the Kingdom of Cambodia in an effort to preserve the site's
evocative fusion of nature and culture by reinforcing the structures against further damage by strangler figs and banyan trees, and by constructing slightly elevated wooden walkways that crisscross the ruins, ensuring safe passage to visitors and mitigating damage done by foot-traffic. A sign announcing the presence
of Chinese preservationists can be seen at Chau Say Tevoda, while the Swiss
Agency for Development and Cooperation heads the Banteay Srei Conservation
Project (BSCP), whose workers can be seen toiling at the pink sandstone structure. The École Frances d'Estrême Orient is still active at Angkor, both in its
preservation work at the ancient Baphoun and in joint excavation work with the
University of Chicago, which has uncovered a number of Jayavarman VII's
famed hospitals.

Awareness-raising endeavors—such as the distribution of UNESCO's
World Heritage Lists by UNESCO and reproducible re-presentations circulated
by past visitors, artists, preservation societies and tourism promoters—therefore
impel people and organizations to action. This seems to be quite literally the
case when considering tourism to the Angkor Archaeological Park, which was

given "priority status" for developing the country by the Cambodian government shortly after Angkor was designated a World Heritage site in 1992. As I mentioned in previous chapters, tourism to Angkor was significant in the French era, and it increased even during the height of regional hostilities, from 21,180 visitors in 1963 to 46,706 visitors in 1969—the majority of which were American, European and Japanese.[53] Twenty years of warfare associated with the Khmer Rouge effectively eradicated Cambodia from the tourist track. As a testament to Westerners' negative associations with the country, only 5,194 tourists visited Angkor in post-war Cambodia in 1990, and most of them were Thai, Taiwanese and Japanese. This number represents 30.6% of the total number of visitors counted as "tourists" in the country, who presumably mixed business and aid work and were localized in Phnom Penh or other regions of the country that year.[54] This number remained stable until the year of Angkor's designation, when the number doubled to 10,530;[55] roughly 23% of these were from Japan, 17% from America, and 15% from France, and less than 6% from Thailand.

From the statistical perspective, one can speculate with relative certainty that Angkor's positioning as a prominent World Heritage site greatly factored into the country's stunning increase in tourism. In the first year after Angkor's designation, tourism increased by 26%, and by 1998 tourism had increased by 46%. While in 1992 only 30% of Cambodian tourism was localized at Angkor, by 1998 a full 85% was situated at the World Heritage site.[56] By 2004, the total number of tourists to Cambodia surpassed one million, with 560,940 (nearly 55% of the total) visiting Angkor. Also in this period between 2000 and 2004, Cambodia topped the World Tourism Organization's list of Emerging Tourist Destinations in Asia whose growth rate was above the world's average.[57] By the first half of 2007, tourists to Angkor already numbered 678,422—or 60.65% of the total 1,118,649 who visited Cambodia—a further increase of 50.17% from those who visited Angkor in the first half of 2006. While tourism has certainly contributed to a number of positive and negative material effects at Angkor, these numbers indicate that over a half million people each year have interacted with the heritage-scape in this one location alone.

The Future of the Heritage-scape:
UNESCO's Global Strategy and its Outcomes

Implicit in the previous section's discussion is the notion that each discreet World Heritage site uniquely engages a diversity of actors with their own distinctive abilities and predispositions, who come together to produce a locally instantiated yet globally oriented culture at each node of the heritage-scape.

Some of these actors are exclusively concerned with a particular World Heritage property and not with others—for example, Italian preservationists are active in Mỹ Sơn but not at Angkor, while those in the German Apsara Conservation Project (GACP) are concerned with Angkor Wat but not with Mỹ Sơn or even with Ta Prohm; likewise, a tourist with a desire to visit Southeast Asia may never visit Afghanistan's Bamiyan Buddhas or the World Heritage site of Tiwakanu in Bolivia (designated in 2000), while a Jewish "birthright" tourist may be interested in visiting Masada but not Angkor Wat. Yet there are also substantial overlaps between actors at each of these sites; Japanese preservation experts are engaged in activities at Angkor and at Mỹ Sơn, the head of UNESCO's regional office in Thailand coordinates World Heritage programs in the whole Southeast Asian region, and the head of the University of Chicago-run excavations at Angkor and Preah Vihear continues to be engaged in his life-long archaeological activities at Tiwakanu. Similarly, there is also substantial overlap in the tourist sector. On a typical tourist itinerary to Southeast Asia, for example, tourists will visit World Heritage sites such as Angkor, Mỹ Sơn and Hạ Long Bay; in addition, I have noted a number of "repeat travelers" on museum-sponsored trips to Southeast Asia who had previously traveled with their institution to other World Heritage sites in Africa, Europe and Asia.

Such overlapping naturally fosters formal and informal exchanges of experiences that further raises awareness of the many instantiations of "universal value" to create a more nuanced understanding of "unity in diversity." Formal exchanges may occur in the preservation sector, as experts employ, and convey to their teams, the knowledge and technical methods they previously utilized at other sites. They also occur within the field of touristic production, as tour operators, sponsoring organizations and other professionals apply their knowledge of touristic infrastructures and group management across a wide range of diverse destinations. Informal exchanges are also particularly prevalent in the touristic sector, as tourists swap stories of their previous visits to other World Heritage destinations in group gatherings such as Welcome Dinners, bus transfers, and long waits at airports. Such intersections and "cross-overs" of actors within these discretely localized cultural communities constitute the heritage-scape as a global social structure, a "culture of cultures" as Marshall Sahlins once so elegantly described.

The introduction of new and diverse sites that push the boundaries of what can be interpreted as a World Heritage site would expand the reach of the heritage-scape, not merely in the geographic but also in the experiential sense. New World Heritage sites produce new opportunities to engage new locals, new nations, new experts and new visitors. They also pave the way for even more novel ways of ascertaining the "universal value" of cultural forms, and of designating sites that would never have been considered for World Heritage designation at the original signing of the Convention.

This reasoning guides the implementation of UNESCO's 1994 *Global Strategy for a Balanced, Representative and Credible World Heritage List*, which was born of a UNESCO-sponsored study that found certain "over-representations" of primarily Western categories of what constituted "universal value." The Committee's record of this is telling:

> A number of gaps and imbalances were already discernible on the World Heritage List:
> - Europe was over-represented in relation to the rest of the world;
> - historic towns and religious buildings were over-represented in relation to other types of property;
> - Christianity was over-represented in relation to other religions and beliefs;
> - historical periods were over-represented in relation to prehistory and the 20th century;
> - "elitist" architecture was over-represented in relation to vernacular architecture;
> - in more general terms, all living cultures—and especially the "traditional" ones—, with their depth, their wealth, their complexity, and their diverse relationships with their environment, figured very little on the List. Even traditional settlements were only included on the List in terms of their "architectural" value, taking no account of their many economic, social, symbolic, and philosophical dimensions or of their many continuing interactions with their natural environment in all its diversity. This impoverishment of the cultural expression of human societies was also due to an over-simplified division between cultural and natural properties which took no account of the fact that in most human societies the land-scape, which was created or at all events inhabited by human beings, was representative and an expression of the lives of the people who live in it and so was in this sense equally culturally meaningful.[58]

Couched in terms of making the List more "balanced, representative and credible," the Global Strategy was, on the surface, concerned with the spatial distribution of World Heritage sites. Thus, it endeavored to create a heritage-scape that has equal reach across the world, and that provides opportunities for all peoples to come into contact with world heritage discourses. This is achieved not by simply designating more sites in different areas, but by veritably pushing the boundaries of what is considered to be of "universal value:"

> In order to ensure for the future a World Heritage List that was at the same time representative, balanced, and credible, the expert group considered it

> to be necessary not only to increase the number of types, regions, and pe-
> riods of cultural property that are under-represented in the coming years,
> but also *to take into account the new concepts of the idea of cultural heri-
> tage* that had been developed over the past twenty years.[59]

Previously, the over-representation of monumental Western edifices was not an entirely unconscious decision. For example, over a decade after the World Heritage Convention was signed, UNESCO continued to reject sites that were too "vernacular," such as Bulgaria's "Ancient City of Plovdiv." Plovdiv boasts well-preserved structures dating from the prehistoric, Thracian, Hellenic and Roman periods, as well as buildings from the Ottoman period. The post-Ottoman National Revival period in the eighteenth and nineteenth centuries is particularly unique and well-represented in this historic city. Interspersed are post-Nazi Communist buildings and monuments, as well. But after a roll-call of accepted designations during the 1983 Committee meeting in Florence, these comments were added:

> The Committee also decided not to include the Ancient City of Plovdiv nomi-
> nated by Bulgaria on the World Heritage List. The Committee considered that
> it was difficult at this stage to include urban sites on the list for their vernacular
> architecture and that the problems concerning the types of towns characteristic
> of the different regions of the World would first have to be clarified.[60]

After that Committee meeting, which designated Bulgaria's Srebarna Nature Reserve, Bulgaria had only one more designation—a monumental Thracian tomb found near the town of Sveshtari, uniquely decorated and dating from the 3rd century BC. It was only in 2004 that Bulgaria added Plovdiv back onto its Tentative List, after other urban centers with "vernacular" architecture were designated. Perhaps it will see success now that the *Global Strategy* is in effect.

The *Global Strategy* was actualized by dividing the world into regions, implementing tactics for inducing nation-states in underrepresented areas of the world—namely developing countries in Africa and the Pacific Islands—to join the World Heritage Convention and to work closely with the Advisory Bodies to nominate their properties, and, in the last few years, employing an ad-hoc quota system among World Heritage Committee members to designate more properties from these underrepresented regions.

In this vein, the *Global Strategy* seems to be fairly effective. Since 1994, thirty-nine new countries—most from Eastern Europe, Africa, the Middle East and small Pacific Island states—have ratified the Convention, raising the total number of nations engaged in the heritage-scape from 139 to 185. UNESCO's promotion of "new categories" for understanding what constitutes World Heri tage—such as deserts, marine heritage, "itineraries," railways, "industrial heritage" and the problematic "cultural landscapes"—has enabled a striking increase in the number of new signatory countries who have submitted Tentative Lists; while previously merely thirty-three state-parties (mostly from Western Europe and East Asia) actually submitted Tentative Lists, today over 145 nations from around the world have done so. Coupled with the new quota system, one can project a higher increase of future designations from under-represented nations for the years to come.

The *Global Strategy*'s conflation of space means that one has more opportunities to encounter World Heritage sites, and therefore encounters the whole of the heritage-scape in two ways. On one hand, the designation of, and subsequent awareness-raising activities for, World Heritage sites in "underrepresented" regions may provide an increase in visitation from Western and Asian tourists who currently comprise a majority of international travelers. Just as a museum promotes new acquisitions and utilizes innovatively conceived "blockbuster" expositions to both capture new demographics of visitors and encourage repeat visitation among one-time visitors, so too does expanding the diversity of sites within the heritage-scape provide opportunities for new and potentially repeat travelers to interact with the heritage-scape. And as this set of tourists encounters these utterly new cultural and natural forms, UNESCO's meta-narrative of "unity in diversity" can become more nuanced and complexified in their minds. On the other hand, the more even distribution of sites throughout these underrepresented areas also provides opportunities for new local populations, and potential tourists who have not previously had the means of traveling long distances, to encounter World Heritage sites in closer proximity to home. If they are effectively contextualized in UNESCO's meta-narrative claim, the "lure of the local" can become for this demographic a veritable "lure of the universal."

The heritage-scape also conflates the concept of time. As I have argued throughout this text, the very concept of "heritage" is constructed around a decidedly future-oriented understanding of an object's ability to mediate temporally between a static conception of the past and the on-going touristic present, a way of tangibly inserting a narratively defined *then* in the individually understood *now*. The "restored" Angkorian sites of Banteay Srei, the Bayon and Angkor Wat, for example, afford the tourist an imaginative encounter with the Khmer past that is perceived to have resisted 800 years of time's transient flow, while the "preserved" sites of Ta Prohm and Preah Khan provide the same tourist with a fantasy of colonial exploration in a way that is nearly impossible in the present. When this concept is expanded to the whole of the List, which includes sites whose temporal narrative claims range from the prehistoric to the modern, a tourist moving across the heritage-scape can construct an imaginative itinerary encompassing millennia of time travel.

The *Global Strategy*'s categorical re-positioning of what can be interpreted as World *Heritage* has thus, in the past decade, not only expanded an understanding of *where* these universally valorized sites should be located, and *what* could be considered a site of universal value, but also the concept of *when* these places can be found. The early years of the World Heritage Convention focused primarily on sites from the more remote past, such as Eastern and Western antiquity, the Middle Ages, the pre-contact Mesoamerican empires, and Renaissance and Baroque periods. There were, of course, a few extraordinary exceptions to this, such as the "negative" sites of Auschwitz and Hiroshima. Possibly because of the temporal precedent set by these negative sites—whose valued "heritage time," it should be remembered, occurred in the lifetime of many presently living people—the years since the signing of UNESCO's Global Strategy has seen a marked increase in the designation of sites that were originally constructed in the very recent past. In particular, sites identified as illustrating the world's colonial and "industrial heritage"—the very indicator of "modernity"— have been designated. Coal mines in Eastern Europe, railways in India, and even "ideal cities" for factory workers have worked their way into the List.

One such industrial World Heritage site is the village of Saltaire, located just north of the center of the Victorian industrial city of Bradford, United Kingdom. Conceived by the philanthropist-cum-industrialist Sir Titus Salt, and constructed between 1851 and 1879, Saltaire was intended to provide a self-contained living and working place for the employees who staffed his wool mills. While Salt wanted his new town to be a positive alternative to the "dark and satanic" industrial counterparts in Leeds and Bradford,[61] it was notably heavily controlled; foremen were lodged in "nobles' houses"—taller townhouses dotting each street corner—while smaller row-houses for factor workers and their families lined the spaces between. Flowered terraces, detailed architectural elements and tall churches uniquely punctuate the blocks of habitations, built in Neo-Italianate style of honey colored stones. Named after members of Salt's family, British royalty, and the architects Lockwood and Mawson, the village's twenty-two streets are laid out in a rigid grid pattern containing 850 homes and 45 Alms Houses. Although it is still a living community, much of the town remains as it was upon Salt's death in 1876.[62]

According to a Saltaire official who was integral to the site's 2001 designation, the World Heritage property is a "key site" in an international initiative called the European Industrial Heritage Route,[63] a "network of the most important industrial heritage sites in Europe" that stretches from Germany, Luxemburg, Holland, Belgium and Great Britain.[64] Its justification for inscription lay in the town's "completeness" and "authenticity"; it is the largest "model village" still in use, and boasts a number of innovative design principles for the time period. Most importantly, the official said, UNESCO considered Saltaire a testament to the "place in history in terms of development of this kind of industrial site. . . . They did [nominated] three industrial heritage sites, and this was the newest, occurring at the end of the Industrial [Revolution]."[65] The official's statement was telling, for she indicated that UNESCO found a "place in history" that needed to be represented, and that place was the underrepresented time of the nascent "modern" age.

This is not to say that all of these sites have been met without skepticism from those who still espouse a traditional conception of what constitutes "heritage," however. A private conversation I had with another top municipal official from a city near Saltaire elicited this very response. Clad in heavy 18-karat gold chains that marked his position as a political representative of the Yorkshire region, this official had just completed an impassioned speech about the value and tour-worthiness of Victorian England and the Yorkshire region when I approached him for his impressions of Saltaire as a World Heritage site. Given the talk he had just completed on the beauty of his own Italianate-Victorian industrial city, his response was a bit startling. He stated that he was unsure why Saltaire was nominated a World Heritage site; "certainly it may not be as beautiful as others."[66] The "others" he then discussed were more traditionally conceived sites of heritage—such as Stonehenge and Venice—disparate sites of widely varying aesthetics that belied the true intention of his statement: the living village of Saltaire was not as "old" or of traditionally conceived "historic value" as these other World Heritage sites.

Such responses to these "newer" World Heritage sites, whose designations were certainly products of the Global Strategy, seems at first to lend credence to the famous contention by former chairman of the British National Heritage Memorial Fund, Lord Charteris, that, essentially, heritage can mean "anything you want"[67]—that anything, if it successfully weathers the field of heritage production, can be a World Heritage site. This contention is most tellingly illustrated in the rather unprecedented designation of the Sydney Opera House during the 2007 meeting of the World Heritage Convention. Unlike the industrial sites of Saltaire, the Mountain Railways of India, or Essen's Zollverein Coal Mine, the Sydney Opera House does not trace its narrative to the past colonial or industrial age, but is a work of the twentieth century. Yet unlike the few other properties dating from the twentieth century—the "negative" World Heritage sites of Auschwitz and Hiroshima, which were designated for the extra-ordinary events that occurred there—Sydney's Opera House was added to the World Heritage List precisely for its aesthetic qualities. The expressionist-modernist style of architecture for which it was designated, furthermore, continues to be used to-day; the Opera House as a site of heritage does not espouse an architectural style of the *past*, but a style still used in the *present*. In addition, the main architects who designed and constructed the structure are still living. UNESCO words its designation as such:

> Inaugurated in 1973, the Sydney Opera House is listed as a great architectural work of the 20th century that brings together multiple strands of creativity and innovation, both in architectural form and structural design. A great urban sculpture set in a remarkable waterscape, at the tip a peninsula projecting into Sydney Harbour, the building has had an enduring influence on architecture. . . . In 1957, when the project of the Sydney opera was attributed by an international jury to the then almost unknown Danish architect Jørn Utzon, it marked a radically new and collaborative approach to construction. In listing the building, the Sydney Opera House is recognized as a great artistic monument accessible to society at large.[68]

The long nomination process the Sydney Opera House underwent reveals the ways in which the *Global Strategy* has challenged, and changed, UNESCO's temporal conceptualization of "heritage time." According to ICOMOS' official nomination file, the Australian government originally proposed the Sydney Opera House in 1980 as a type of "mixed site" under criterion *i* (as a "masterpiece of human genius") that included not only the modernist architectural form, but also the natural environment of Sydney Harbor and the promontory on which the construction stands. *The Sydney Opera House in its Setting*, as the state-party proposed it should be called, would include the Sydney Harbour Bridge and the surrounding waterways of Sydney Harbour from Bradley's Head to McMahon's Pointe. When ICOMOS was charged with analyzing the site, which at the time had only been operation for about six years, the Advisory Body expressed strong reservations, calling it "part of a series of experiments in 'sculptural architecture.'" In April 1981, ICOMOS recommended that the nomination be deferred with the further statement concerning the second criterion:

> ICOMOS also considered that as a question of the work of a living architect, inaugurated less than ten years ago at that time, ICOMOS did not feel itself competent to express an opinion on the eventual admissibility based on criterion ii. The inscription was recommended to be deferred until its exemplary character or its role as model appears more clearly attributable to the creation of Jørn Utzon.[69]

Criterion *ii*, it should be remembered, states that a site should "exhibit an important interchange of human values, over a span of time or within a cultural area of the world, on developments in architecture or technology." While certainly this new "experiment in sculptural architecture" represented a development in both architecture and technology, it would be doubtful that it exhibited a clear "interchange" of time or cultures; the original architect, while not Australian, was still Western, and his design was clearly born of the post-World War II period.

Unstated, yet implicit, in this second argument was also the issue of the site's authenticity in relationship to its albeit short, yet sordid, history. Although created from the award-winning 1956 design of Utzon, the architect had, in fact, a brief and contentious role in its construction. After the "podium," or terraced base, was built between 1958 and 1961, skyrocketing costs, an unachievable construction timeframe, and severe problems with the famous shelled roofing forced Utzon out of the job; when Robert Askin was elected Premier of New South Wales in 1965, his new Minister of Work, Davis Hughes, questioned Utzon's design and eventually stopped payments to the Danish architect. In February 1966, Utzon fled the country, never to return. Architect Peter Hall, whom ICOMOS later contended was "in conversation" with Utzon for over a year after the Dane's departure, took over the project in conjunction with Australian architects Lionel Todd and David Littlemore, and then-New South Wales government architect Ted Farmer. Based on Utzon's design, this group completed the technologically daunting task of the famed roofing structure, and created the interior performance spaces. However, the interior spaces were modified to cut costs and finish the work quickly.[70] According to one expert at Sydney's University of Technology, they modified Utzon's original design and positioning for the two stages; although operas such as *Aida* would necessitate a large main-stage and backstage area, they problematically relegated it to the Minor Hall, while the Major Hall was re-created for symphonic concerts despite problematic acoustics.[71] When Queen Elizabeth II inaugurated the finished product on October 20, 1973, Utzon was not invited.

Such modifications called into question both the "authenticity" of the monumental opera house in relationship to its original design, especially if criterion *i*'s category of "human genius" implicitly referred to Utzon and his original design. ICOMOS requested the State-Party to provide a more detailed analysis of the material role Utzon and the other architects played in the construction of the edifice. Furthermore, these unfortunate political interactions necessitated a far stronger argument by the State-Party for the relevance of criterion *ii*. Marked with very public expositions of political power struggles and exclusionary activities, it seemed as though the Opera House could not provide a positive, universalized narrative of an "important interchange of human values." Indeed, when famed architect Frank Gehry awarded Utzon the Pritzker Prize for Architecture in 2003, he found it necessary to discuss not only the Dane's technological and architectural achievement, but Utzon's "persever[ance] through extraordinary malicious publicity and negative criticism to build a building that changed the image of an entire country."[72]

In the late 1990s, when UNESCO's *Global Strategy* was in full force and the Opera House was nearing its twenty-fifth anniversary celebrations, the monument's managers worked to address these core issues blocking the site's designation. Between 1998 and 1999 architects created a "revitalised performance space for the presentation of innovative music and performing arts" as well as an assembly area for the orchestra.[73] Sydney architect Richard Johnson was also hired as an advisor on future development of the property, and spearheaded an initiative by the Sydney Opera House Trust to "reconcile" and "re-engage" with Utzon. In 1999, the Danish architect accepted a personal invitation from New South Wales' Premier Bob Carr to serve "in an advisory capacity" by formally articulating his original design principles that "outline[d] his vision for the building and explain[ed] the principles behind his design."[74] Though Jørn Utzon never returned to Sydney, his son and business partner, Jan Utzon, worked with him and Johnson to improve the Concert Hall acoustics, construct a western loggia, and rebuild the interior of the Opera Hall. But just months before the site's World Heritage designation, media reports circulated that Jørn Utzon was suffering a degenerative eyesight condition which constrained his ability to effectively advise on restoration work, and that "his name is being used to push through substandard work."[75]

These significant changes to the material site could be understood in World Heritage terms as a type of "restoration" work. It was an unprecedented conceptualization of what constitutes "restoration," however. While many sites are materially conserved before they are nominated for World Heritage status, such "preservation" or "restoration" endeavors are attempts at re-creating the physical place as it was imagined to have materially appeared during its UNESCO-created life-historical narrative. Conversely, what was restored in the Sydney Opera House was not its original appearance, but rather the site's original—and heretofore un-manifested—design. Yet despite the engagement of the original architect and his original "design principles," the Sydney Opera House as it stands today is still not a reconstruction—for both technical and social reasons—and one cannot consider it to now appear as it would have, had Utzon never left Sydney midway through the initial construction.

The Sydney Opera House was finally designated a World Heritage site at the thirty-first session of the World Heritage Committee in Christchurch, New

Zealand on July 2007, along with a wide spatial range of places from Europe, Asia, the Americas and Africa. Juxtaposing sites from the Stone Age petroglyphs of Twyfelfontein in Namibia and Korea's Jeju Volcanic Island, to the ancient city of Samarra in Iraq and Sydney's Opera House, the 2007 World Heritage meeting also illustrated the heritage-scape's wide temporal range—a detail which UNESCO pointedly referenced in its official newsletter, the *Courier*, shortly after the meeting's conclusion:

> Six thousand years separate the Sydney Opera House from Twyfelfontein. These two sites just inscribed on the World Heritage List add to its extraordinary richness, which the UNESCO Courier aims to illustrate. Among the twenty-two new sites, the Courier focuses on five that reflect the diversity of world heritage down through the ages.[76]

James Wertsch argues that "what constitutes a usable past in one sociocultural setting is often quite different from what is needed in another."[77] In juxtaposing sites of such temporally disparate magnitudes as Twyfelfontein's 6,000-year-old petroglyphs and the late twentieth-century Sydney Opera House, UNESCO makes it clear that any past—remote or recent, is usable. And in many ways, it well should be. The World Heritage Convention is ultimately concerned with creating monumental mediators that can bridge boundaries and fuse categories, properties that conflate space and time; what is important is not that a monumental complex preexists in a society's mythos—as Angkor or the Acropolis may have—but that it can be integrated into the ever-expanding cosmology of the heritage-scape. The Sydney Opera House is an extraordinary example of the way in which UNESCO's Global Initiative conflates—and even inverts—heritage time to create a "useful" narrative that conjoins peoples of differing cultures and cosmologies. UNESCO's official narrative for the World Heritage site makes this explicit:

> Criterion (i): The Sydney Opera House is a great architectural work of the 20th century. It represents multiple strands of creativity, both in architectural form and structural design, a great urban sculpture carefully set in a remarkable waterscape and a world famous iconic building.
>
> All elements necessary to express the values of the Sydney Opera House are included within the boundaries of the nominated area and buffer zone. This ensures the complete representation of its significance as an architectural object of great beauty in its waterscape setting. The Sydney Opera House continues to perform its function as a world-class performing arts centre. The Conservation Plan specifies the need to balance the roles of the building as an architectural monument and as a state of the art performing centre, thus retaining its authen-

ticity of use and function. Attention given to retaining the building's authenticity culminated with the Conservation Plan and the Utzon Design Principles.[78]

As this citation reveals, in designating the Sydney Opera House, UNESCO designated not only the material building, but its very conceptualization—a conceptualization that was neither fully realized nor strictly material. In addition, this immaterial conception is not crystallized into "heritage time;" it is ongoing and active in the minds of its site managers. As a World Heritage site, therefore, the Sydney Opera House not only espouses the *then in now*, but the *now in now*. And for future generations, furthermore, it may also stand for the *now in then*. As its "restoration" work is still in process, the site will most likely continue to "evolve" beyond the time frame localized in its narrative. While no World Heritage site is materially or conceptually static despite its associated narrative claims, UNESCO builds not only the past, but the future, into the Sydney Opera House's World Heritage narrative. A World Heritage site now may mediate between not only what *was*, but also what *will be*. Though highly unlikely, this may even open up the possibility of designating a site before it is ever created; perhaps someday a monument may even be made to the heritage-scape.

A World Heritage site dedicated explicitly to World Heritage itself may never be constructed, but the future orientation of UNESCO's World Heritage endeavor—which was always latently present in its long-term objective to create "peace in the minds of men"—has taken now a new form. This new form may certainly pave the way for more innovative concepts that would, in turn, provide future opportunities for new groups of people to enjoy formative interactions in the heritage-scape. And with the ongoing integration of new forms of "universal value," the heritage-scape will continue to expand, complexifying participants' conceptualizations of their position with others in history and in the world—their very heritage—linking them with disparate times and places, and orienting them towards meaningful future activity. What constitutes meaningful activity may continue to be re-interpreted in the short term, but ultimately, UNESCO hopes, it will be a lasting, worldwide peace based on the "intellectual and moral solidarity of mankind."

NOTES

Introduction

1. A note on Vietnamese placenames in this book: With the exception of the cities most commonly recognizable in the West (Ha Noi and Saigon, the latter being the former name of present-day Ho Chi Minh City) and the name of the country itself, I decided to spell Vietnamese dynasties and placenames in *chữ quốc ngữ* format ("script of the national language"—that is, as they are "officially" written with diacritics). Although some readers may find my rather selective usage of quốc ngữ (the "national written language") distracting and others—especially those who read Vietnamese—may find it applied unevenly, I do this for a specific purpose.

    Placenames, as I stress multiple times in this book, are exceptionally important in providing a contextual frame to each locale. It imbues the place with meaning. Writing these place names as the State-party does is a small (and rather deferential) act, on my part, to maintain the nationalized socio-political aspects of the site while still arguing that the site is part of something greater, something global. It recognizes the necessary role of the State-party as a co-constructor of the heritage-scape, despite any ignorance it may have regarding the heritage-scape's geopolitical reordering of the world. It is also ethnographically salient to note who spells a place in quốc ngữ and who spells it in the more Anglicized version (or in limited accent marks, as is sometimes the case). In particular, Vietnamese websites that leave out the diacritics have likely made a conscious decision to do so, so as to appeal to a more global demographic of web surfers. One will also note Anglicized spellings of these places in several documents by UNESCO and its Advisory Bodies. On the practical level, some of the places are not exceptionally well-known or would be undifferentiated from other sites without their markings; a traveler (both embodied and the armchair Internet surfer) may wish to have the official Vietnamese spelling of the site on hand.

    Though I did not utilize diacritics for the names "Ha Noi," I have maintained its syllabic separation (rather than writing "Hanoi"). However, I have maintained the Americanized spelling of "Vietnam" (instead of Việt Nam) and "Saigon" (Sài Gòn), the city now presently known as Ho Chi Minh City.

2. John McCain toured his cell in the "Hanoi Hilton" on April 26, 2000 with one of his sons; a plaque across the street from the prison now commemorates the visit. Bill Clinton made a Presidential trip to Vietnam on November 7, 2000; and Colin Powell visited Hanoi on July 26, 2001.

3. Washington, DC's Meridian International Center hosted what can be considered the first true traveling gallery exhibition of contemporary Vietnamese art in the United States in 1997. Entitled "A Winding River," the exhibition began in Washington, DC and traveled across the Midwest and California. From March 2003–March 2004, New York's American Museum of Natural History produced the blockbuster ethnographic exhibition, "Vietnam: Journeys of Mind, Body and Spirit" featuring a mix of multimedia and artifacts such as Hanoi water puppets from contemporary Vietnam. It was considered the first important exhibition dedicated solely to Vietnam in a major United States museum. High-end group tours to Vietnam were offered to its members during the run of the exhibition, as well.

4. I have averaged the annual growth rate from 2002–2007. In 2002 and 2003, the growth rate stagnated around 3% (Hospitality Net 2003) amid SARS and the Iraq war (UNWTO 2005b). In 2004 tourism rose to a "staggering" rate of 11% from the year before, the highest and only two-digit growth rate since 1980. The UNWTO points out that this represents 73 million new tourist arrivals, "representing a volume equivalent to a new 'destination' of virtually the size of France, the world's top destination in terms of tourist arrivals" (UNWTO 2005b:1). In 2005 it dipped to 4.1%;(UNWTO 2006); in 2007 it rose to 5.4% (UNWTO 2007). Finally, it should be noted that these figures are all positive growth rates; the last year that saw a negative reduction in the amount of tourism was in 2001, which experienced a rate of -0.5% (Hospitality Net 2003).

5. UNWTO 2005a
6. See, for example Global News Wire Asia 2006
7. Appadurai 1996
8. See, for example, Tucker 1978:32, 172
9. Tucker 1978:172-173
10. Nash 1981:465, 467
11. Nash 1989:38
12. Pratt 2002:6-7
13. Sahlins 1987:147
14. Boorstin 1994
15. MacCannell 1976:98, Bruner 2004
16. This draws on Smith 1989; Graburn 1983 and 1989; and Urry 2002.
17. Bourdieu 1993
18. Anderson 2003
19. Appadurai 1996
20. In particular, Anderson 2003
21. In particular Halbwachs 1992 and Connerton 1989
22. Kirshenblatt-Gimblett 1998:151
23. See, for example, Boorstin 1994 and MacCannell 1999
24. Graburn 1983, 1989 [1977].
25. Bennett 1995:59
26. UNESCO 2000a
27. Geertz 2000:429

28. Geertz 2000:4-5
29. See, for example, Asad 1993:27-54
30. See, for example, Knorr-Cetina 2000
31. Sahlins 2000:488
32. Nelson Graburn famously calls tourism a "secular pilgrimage" (Graburn 1989)—a term that, in the context of Angkor, finds its roots in the famous book by Pierre Loti, *Un Pélerin d'Angkor* (A Pilgrimage to Angkor), published in 1912 (Loti 1996). Loti, who—having penned over thirty novels recounting his journeys in Southern Europe, North Africa and, of course, Indochina, is regarded as France's "leading exotic novelist and travel writer" at the time, according to Penny Edwards—claimed to have caught the tourism bug while perusing "a faded colonial revue [of Angkor] in Provence in the 1860s" as a young man (Edwards 2007:29-30).
33. Dagens 1995:34
34. Indeed, one of Mouhot's contemporaries, Adolf Bastian, would publish his monograph, A Journey in Cambodia and Cochin-China, in 1864.
35. Edwards 2007:36
36. Edwards 2007:36
37. Dagens 1995:86
38. Though published in 1912, about 5 years after Angkor was ceded to Cambodia, the English version printed a year later would simply title Loti's monograph Siam.
39. Seton 1938

Chapter 1

1. Alcock 2002:28
2. Mazzarella 2004:346
3. Mazzarella 2004:345
4. Spitulnik 1993:293
5. Anderson 2003
6. Anderson 2003:13
7. By this statement, I am also calling upon Bourdieu's critical definition of "life history" in his brief essay, "The Biographical Illusion." He states, "To produce a life history or to consider life as a history, that is, as a coherent narrative of a significant and directed sequence of events, is perhaps to conform to a rhetorical illusion, to the common representation of existence that a whole literary tradition has always and still continues to reinforce" (1987:2).
8. Underscoring its hidden dimension of selectivity, Bourdieu describes "the narrative" as a discourse of events that "tend or pretend to get organized into sequences linked to each other on the basis of intelligible relationships," rather than chronological order. The biographical enterprise, as revealed in autobiographical narrative, "is always at least partially motivated by a concern to give meaning, to rationalize, to show the inherent logic, both for the past and for the future, to make consistent and constant, through the creation of intelligible relationships, like that of the cause

(immediate or final) and effect between successive states, which are thus turned into steps of a necessary development" (1987:2 emphasis in original).

9. LeFebvre 1991:143
10. Geertz 2000:429
11. Halbwachs 1992:200-201. Monumentality, heritage and memory theory will be discussed in greater detail in chapter 3 of this book.
12. Benjamin 1968:220
13. Benjamin 1968:221
14. Benjamin 1968, qtd. Mazzarella 2003:53
15. Benjamin 1968:220
16. Benjamin 1968:221
17. Augustine 1958:525; Mauss 2000:13
18. Benjamin 1968:223
19. Benjamin 1968:221
20. qtd. Mazzarella 2003:53
21. Mannikka 1996:9.
22. The Cham king mounted a daring attack by sailing through the Mekong Delta and up the Tonle Sap River—an unprecedented military feat. He slew the king and sacked Angkor, burning its mostly wooden structures to the ground. Unpublished archaeological research by the French art historian Bernard Groslier confirms the presence of immense, charred timbers underneath Angkor Thom.
23. Coe 2003:98
24. Kolata 2007
25. Coe speculates that the coordination of this iconoclasm had to have been the work of a king (Coe 2003:128).
26. Coe 2003:128
27. Appropriate in this context is Susan Alcock's contention that, especially in empires, the reworking of social memory is at its height during periods of extreme social transformation (2001:324).
28. Coe 2003:128
29. The Khmer conversion of Theravāda Buddhism from Hinduism was, of course, a slow process likely stemming from repeated contact with the Thais from the thirteenth century onward. The conversion of the monuments into Theravāda Buddhist (albeit Khmer) sites was enacted by the Khmer kings between the fourteenth and fifteenth century, during this period of increased interaction and conflict with the Thais.
30. Keyes 1977:70. This is also qtd. in Bentley 1986:294.
31. Qtd. Davis 1997:74
32. Durkheim 1995:230-231, emphasis added
33. As recently as January 29, 2003, rumors circulated in Phnom Penh that Thai actress Suwanan Kongying supposedly made an off-the-cuff remark that Angkor Wat belonged to neighboring Thailand, an assertion that the actress later denied saying. Perpetuated by the powerful former Khmer Rouge member-turned-Prime Minister, Hun Sen, who said the Thai actress was "not even worth a few blades of grass" that

grow around Angkor's temples, mobs took to the street, burning the Thai embassy, the ambassador's residence and Thai-owned businesses such as the Royal Phnom Penh Hotel in the Cambodian capital, causing flight cancellations, a temporary de-normalization of relations between the two countries, a disruption in tourism, and an estimated $46.8 million dollars in damage. Although less violent, mobs took to the Bangkok streets in reaction, protesting in front of the Cambodian embassy, burning Cambodian flags and stomping on pictures of the Cambodian king, prompting Suthichai Yoon to write in *The Nation*, "Until that dark ugly night of January 29, the Thai psyche simply refused to absorb the hard, cold fact that we were considered a new breed of imperialist. . . . We thought since they use our mobile phone service, watch our TV soap operas and consume our instant noodles, they must really love all things Thai" (Yoon 2003).

34. Tarling 1999:98-99. See also Vickery 1979.
35. Dagens 1995:23
36. Qtd. Dagens 1995:35
37. "Resonance" and "wonder" are identified by Stephen Greenblatt as the two emotional responses to aesthetics. See Greenblatt 1991:42-56.
38. This phrase can be found in Latin, Greek and Hebrew—representing the three cultures from which the Light came—on the University of Chicago's Haskell Hall, the original site of the famed Oriental Institute and now the seat of the Department of Anthropology.
39. Duncan 2004:25, see also Bennett 1994
40. Fogelson 1991:75
41. A central element in Edward Said's theory of Orientalism is that it is subtle and pervasive, often unintentionally informing one's understanding and portrayal of the Oriental Other (Said 1994).
42. Said 1994:12
43. UNESCO 1972:1
44. UNESCO 1945:1
45. Durkheim 1984:204
46. Matsura 2002a:3
47. UNESCO 2005:2
48. UNESCO 2002a:6
49. Sahlins 2000:488
50. Sahlins 2000:489
51. Matsura 2001:11
52. Matsura 2002b:3
53. Bourdieu 1993:34
54. Becker 1976:703 Qtd. in Bourdieu 1993:34-35. See also Becker 1982.
55. Bourdieu 1993:43
56. Bourdieu 1993:35
57. Bourdieu 1993:35
58. UNESCO 2005d:9
59. Turner 1986:45

60. UNESCO 2005c:5
61. UNESCO 1999:2
62. Bourdieu 1993:72
63. ICOMOS 1992:8
64. Ang et al. 1998:165; cited. as "UNESCO 1996" in Winter 2002:324, the article from which I was made aware of this quote.
65. One can compare the title (revelatory of its content) of H. W. Ponder's famed 1936 book, *Cambodian Glory: The Mystery of the Deserted Khmer Cities and their Vanquished Splendour; and a Description of Life in Cambodia Today with a citation concerning Ta Prohm* from Dawn Rooney's contemporary travel manual (2003:224).
66. To date, UNESCO keeps three lists of global heritage—tangible heritage, natural heritage, and, most recently, intangible heritage. Though it is not discussed here, the intangible heritage list, the criteria of which was finalized in 2001 after several decades of debate and fine-tuning, is quite interesting and illustrates once again how UNESCO changes something of previously local use, such as mythology and folklore, into something of global import. Barbara Kirshenblatt-Gimblett discusses intangible heritage in her essay "World Heritage and Cultural Economics" (Kirshenblatt-Gimblett 2007).
67. Appadurai 1996:46
68. Incidentally, it is not as physically impossible as one might think. The World Heritage Programme actually was born when UNESCO coordinated the physical relocation of Egypt's massive Temple of Ramses II to the top of an artificial hill to avoid being submerged during the building of President Nasser's Aswan Dam in the 1960s.
69. UNWTO 2005 qtd. in Berno and Ward 2005:594
70. Weber 1992, Mintz 1985, Sahlins 1985
71. Kirshenblatt-Gimblett 1998:153
72. There is not one kind of "tourist culture" but a multiplicity of tourist cultures produced in the touristic field of production. However, this book argues that there is only one heritage-scape produced from the work of UNESCO's World Heritage Convention.
73. That is, each operator is equally known and tested (or unknown and untested) in the eyes of the client, and each itinerary is relatively similar. Institution clients have mentioned the amount and quality of color images, overall design of the proposal, and even the quality of the paper stock as elements affecting their perception of the proposed tour and of the professionalism of the tour operator.
74. Leite 2007
75. For example, I organized two Tuscany tours for a prominent Chicago-area garden in 2002 and 2003. The first was a very expensive tour for high donors, which was marketed as a luxurious Tuscan sojourn. It proved to be so popular that the institution offered it again to its general membership the following year. Keeping the exact same itinerary and private visits (but featuring a four-star "country hotel" and less meals at the private homes), the second was marketed with a narrative of

exploration of the authentic countryside. This is not an isolated occurrence, but is a practice throughout the industry.

76. Norindr 1996
77. In chapter 4, I break the category of "group travelers" into generalized sub-categories. My categorization is based on the way the tourism industry considers group travelers. While wealthy travelers comprise the highest echelons of "group travelers," there are also those who are willing to pay extraordinary amounts for a pre-planned tour for themselves or for a small group of their friends or families. They are not considered group travelers, but FITs, or "free and independent travelers." Certain tour operators, such as Abercrombie and Kent or Butterfield and Robinson, cater to these luxury FITs, and market individual package tours complete with private guides, porters and even security details.
78. Snape 2007:5
79. Snape 2007:5; Snape's translation. The original text can be fond in Gomaa 173.
80. Snape states that these inscriptions provide "the most substantial documentary evidence of ancient Egyptians looking back on their own distant past" (Snape 2007:1).
81. Snape 2007:2
82. Snape 2007:2
83. Snape 2007:3
84. Snape 2007:3; translation is Snape's own.
85. Snape 2007:4
86. Snape 2007:4; translation adapted by Snape from Kitchen 1892.
87. Urry 2002. Appropriately, Snape also makes reference to this concept in his introduction (Snape 2007:1).
88. Owen 1990:294, 308
89. Daniel 2007
90. There are many English-language translations of this poem by authors ranging from Burton Watson to Octavio Paz. One excellent book is Weinberger and Paz 1987. The particular interpretation included here, however, is my own.
91. Especially in Zen Buddhist art, this is often referred to by the Japanese terms *wabi* and *sabi*—the former meaning "loneliness" or emptiness, while the latter can be roughly translated to beauty that comes from transience or scarcity.
92. Dagens 1995:86
93. Edwards 2007:137
94. Edwards 2007:137
95. Dagens 1995:84
96. Dagens 1995:86
97. An image can be found in Dagens 1995:88
98. A copy of a poster advertising guided tours can also be found in Dagnes 1995:98
99. Dagens 1995:100
100. Edwards 2007:36

101. Tourism theorist Edward Bruner (2004), in fact, points out that all tourist sites are essentially liminal "border zones" where both visitors and locals perform divergent roles from their everyday identities.
102. Meyer et al. 1997:145-6
103. The phrase "World Heritage Convention" is UNESCO's official terminology for what can alternatively be described as its "World Heritage Programme." That is, it is not a one-time convention, but rather self-perpetuating program aimed to promote, solidify and continue the endeavor outlined (and agreed upon by representatives of nation-states) in the physical, written text entitled the World Heritage Convention. That is, the "World Heritage Convention" both stands for the establishing document itself, as well as the ongoing process of nominating, designating and preserving World Heritage sites in the new social structure this book calls the heritage-scape. However, for the sake of clarity, this book will often use terms such as "World Heritage Programme" or generally, "World Heritage endeavor" rather than the phrase "World Heritage Convention."
104. A list of sites can be found at the website www.nps.gov/history/worldheritage.
105. Statistics provided by IATA: www.iata.org/about/mission.htm. Accessed on September 24, 2007.
106. Until recently, there were famous signs erected at the periphery of the Angkor Archaeological Park which said "Danger! Landmines" in English and Khmer, complete with a skull and crossbones. Another curious one, found in a women's restroom near Angkor Wat, showed an "X" marked over a picture of a woman squatting above a western style toilet. No text accompanied this etiquette message, and it is unclear whether it was directed exclusively to locals who may have not had experience with western-style toilets, or to tourists from all over the world.
107. Orbitz 2007:1.
108. Smith 1989:2, Graburn 1983:11, MacCannell 1999:7, Cohen 1979:182
109. UNESCO 2005c:9; UNESCO 2008a:1.
110. Kirshenblatt-Gimblett 1998:151
111. Dagens 1995:14-17
112. Dagens 1995:28-29
113. Dagens 1995:22-23
114. Dagens 1995:36-37
115. Edwards 2007:19. In her chapter on the depictions of "colonial fantasy" of the Temple Complex, Edwards makes the case that early colonials were primarily concerned with depicting an abandoned Angkor to reveal the void of Khmer memory in the present population. When Mouhot's journals were serialized in *Tour du Monde*, she states that prominent engravers "excised" people from his drawing to depict this fact. However, this author would make the case that Mouhot, as a naturalist (who was primarily interested in researching the flora and fauna of this region) operating at the dawn of the social sciences that saw primitives as more closely aligned with animals (see, for example, Darwin 2005:739-823), his decision to portray the natives may have been informed by his overall desire to portray the various forms of "natural" (as opposed to simply "cultural") life.

116. Dagens 1995:36
117. Edwards 2007:20
118. Edwards 2007:20
119. Both advertisements are mentioned in Dagens 1995:111
120. Norindr 1996:4
121. This is according to several Khmer sources in the country's tourism industry. Fieldnotes August 9, 2006.
122. Winter 2002
123. Qtd. Sassoon 2004:186
124. Berger 1980:291; qtd. Sassoon 191
125. Sassoon 2004:190
126. Sassoon 2004:194
127. Wallach 1998:52
128. Agre 1999
129. Wilson and Peterson 2002:451, 455; see also Miller and Slater 2001:5
130. Wilson and Peterson 2002:451
131. Miller and Slater 2001:10-11
132. Sassoon 2004:194
133. http://images.google.com/images?svnum=10&hl=en&gbv=2&q=Angkor+Watt Accessed on May 14, 2007.
134. http://images.google.com/images?hl=en&q=Angkor+Wat&gbv=2 Accessed on May 14, 2007.
135. This website was www.toddadams.net
136. Masco 2005:488
137. www.toddadams.net/images/wallpaper/hires/Sunset%20over%20Angkor%20Wat. jpg. Accessed on May 14, 2007.
138. Digitally editing a photo utilizing the computer program Photoshop.

Chapter 2

1. At two recent Chicago art fairs, one in Hyde Park and another in Old Town in the spring of 2005, a number of unrelated art stalls were selling beautiful photographic and artistic works of Angkor Wat, Cambodia and Vietnam.
2. At the Angkor Archaeological Park alone, Asian countries such as India and Japan, and European countries such as Germany, Italy and France are currently working on independent, multi-million dollar restoration projects. Prominent American nonprofits, such as World Monuments Fund, have been working in the area since Angkor's designation as a World Heritage site. Finally, the recent tabloid news has been abuzz with stories of actors, musicians and philanthropists raising awareness for the cause; José Carreras held a concert in front of Angkor Wat to raise money for its preservation, and Angelina Jolie, the star of the problematically titled *Tomb Raider*, shot at Ta Prohm, has adopted a Cambodian orphan, established a residence

in the country, donated the land for a Cambodian national nature preserve, and recently received Cambodian citizenship.

3. Halbwachs 1992:200
4. Connerton 1989:6
5. Pearson and Richards 1997:5
6. Wagoner 2000:311
7. Geertz 2000:429
8. To date, UNESCO keeps three lists of global heritage—tangible heritage, natural heritage, and, most recently, intangible heritage. Though it is not discussed here, the intangible heritage list, the criteria of which was finalized in 2001 after several decades of debate and fine-tuning, is quite interesting and illustrates once again how UNESCO changes something of previously local use, such as mythology and folklore, into something of global import. Barbara Kirshenblatt-Gimblett (2007) discusses intangible heritage in her essay "World Heritage and Cultural Economics."
9. Burawoy 2000:338
10. Robertson 1992:8
11. http://portal.unesco.org/en/ev.php-URL_ID=6207&URL_DO=DO_TOPIC&URL_ SECTION=201.html downloaded on September 22, 2005
12. http://portal.unesco.org/en/ev.php-URL_ID=6207&URL_DO=DO_TOPIC&URL_SECTION=201.html   downloaded on September 22, 2005
13. UNESCO 1972:1
14. UNESCO 1945:1
15. In its lengthy "brochure" on the history of educational initiatives, UNESCO states, "In the early post-war years, UNESCO's action (1) consisted of providing aid to the war-ravaged countries of Europe and Asia, in particular in assessing needs for the material rebuilding of educational and cultural institutions destroyed or damaged by the war and for the moral rebuilding of education systems." (UNESCO 1997:42).
16. It increased short-term literacy from 3% to 9% (UNESCO 1961, qtd. in UNESCO 1998:76).
17. UN 1948
18. Sané 2001:1
19. Pierre 2001:1
20. UNESCO 1972:2
21. UNESCO 1972:2
22. Anderson 2003:13. Although Anderson primarily discusses "cultural facts" such as common-language newspapers and other media sources, the same definition can be applied to this discussion of monuments.
23. Anderson 2003:14
24. Anderson 2003:129
25. Anderson 2003:15
26. Italy's admittance to the United Nations was very much tied to its post-war reconstruction and dubious political stance. Both Monarchists and Communists were vying for control of the Republic, against the wishes of America and its allies. In

addition, it was only in 1954, when portions of Mussolini-conquered Balkans were ceded to Yugoslavia, that Italy's territorial integrity was formally established.

27. I borrow this term from Mary Carruthers, who stated that the European Middle Ages was a "memorial culture" (Carruthers 1992:8).

28. Despite diffusion in the media (including videotapes of children speaking to the Virgin Mary), which continues to bring pilgrims to Garabandal, Monsignor José Vilaplaua, the Bishop of the diocese of Santander, issued a written statement on Oct. 11, 1996 citing no documentation as to the "supernatural validity" of the Marian sightings. This statement can be found at the website, www.ewtn.com/library/ BISHOPS/GARABAND.HTM (downloaded on September 29, 2005). Similarly, Medugorje is one of the most popular twentieth-century loci of pilgrimages, despite the fact that the Vatican, short of denying the spiritual validity, will not approve its supernatural import.

29. Fieldnotes, September 19, 2005. Because of a surge in tourism stemming from the recent sainthood of St. Padre Pio of Pietrelcina, a small town on the outskirts of the provincial capital of Benevento, the city has been in the midst of an ambitious restoration and reconstruction plan. The Duomo, behind which stands the aforementioned structure, was hastily rebuilt, unadorned, after the American bombing raids in 1944, but is currently being gutted and restored to its pre-World War II state. Furthermore, Corso Garibaldi, the main thoroughfare passing in front of the Duomo and this bombed out building, is being turned into a pedestrianized zone and adorned in cobblestones artistically arranged in the form of a dragon. Yet no plans are in place for removing or renovating this anachronistic building.

30. UNESCO 2000b:5

31. See, for example, Zerubavel 1995 or Abu El-Haj 2001.

32. ICOMOS 2001:137-138. See also Zerubavel 1995:60-62.

33. Zerubavel 1995:62-63

34. Zerubavel 1995:63

35. Zerubavel 1995:63

36. Zerubavel 1995:64

37. Katriel 1997:29

38. Katriel 1997:29

39. The following excerpts are taken from UNESCO's justification for Masada's inscription as a World Heritage site, and although are not placed all together, they represent the complete criteria cited for its designation. UNESCO 2001b:43

40. UNESCO 1972:3

41. ICOMOS 1999a:116

42. Television antennae were actually a source of much frustration for Hội An's cultural authorities, and were subsequently removed by 2004. In 2005, the town began a complex multi-year traditionalization project to remove all visible antennae, cables and wires; along with installing modern sewage systems, they are burying these cables underground. For a discussion on Hội An's "museumification" as a result of such traditionalization projects, see chapter 10.

43. That is, dedicated to the worship of Vishnu and his avatars as the supreme Triune god as depicted in the *Bhagavad Gītā*.
44. Valmīki's version of the *Rāmāyana*, as well as many others, reveal the righteous king Rāma to be an avatar of Vishnu (see especially Book I and Book VI). In some Buddhist cultures, such as in Laos where the *Rāmāyana* is known as *Phra Lak Phra Lam*, Rāma is considered an incarnation of the Buddha. Nevertheless, there are deep implications for a king—whether Vaishnavist such as Suryavarman II or Mahayana Buddhist as Jayavarman VII—to associate himself with Rāma.
45. Dagens 1995:28
46. This is the description of the Angkor Archaeological Park found on UNESCO's webpage dedicated to this World Heritage site:http://whc.unesco.org/en/list/668. Downloaded on November 15, 2006.
47. Pearson and Richards 1994:5
48. Hewison 1989:15. The well-connected Charteris was known for his fundraising ability, and this statement should be read in light of his desire to appeal to a wide range of potential donors to the Trust. One obituary recalls, "A veteran at dealing with obdurate Whitehall mandarins, he [Charteris] was able to extract far more money for the reconstituted fund than the Treasury had originally promised" (Tomlinson 1999:2).
49. The Vietnamese name of Hạ Long Bay—*Vịnh Hạ Long*—literally means "Dragon Descending into the Sea." It applies a Vietnamese creation myth to the Bay's landscape of immutable karst mountains that jut up from the emerald waters, which are thought to resemble the spiked back of a large, sleeping dragon.
50. Anderson 2003:24
51. Despite their similarities, the heritage-scape as presented here differs slightly from Appadurai's neologisms. Appadurai lists five dimensions of global cultural flows to which he affixes the suffix *–scape: ethnoscapes, mediascapes, technoscapes, financescapes and ideascapes,* which overlap each other and exist simultaneously (Appadurai 1996:33-35). Critics of this concept contend that these idioms may seem too general, too lacking of a conception power distribution, too methodologically unspecified, and above all, too fluid to warrant a special term such as a *-scape*. The *heritage-scape* can be seen as a more concrete model than Appadurai's neologisms, a map of UNESCO's newly ordered global sphere that encompasses his more general -scapes in a specific manner. This particular version also incorporates a clear idea of power distribution; the heritage-scape is firmly constructed by a specific chain of institutions incorporating UNESCO, nation-states, various monuments recontextualized in similar ways, and various types of individuals. Furthermore, this paper specifically delineates the way in which the heritage-scape is bound together with the individuals contained within, an important dynamic that seems unclear in Appadurai's conceptualization. Through the interaction of individuals and mediated by memory, UNESCO's narrative claim infuses with place to create an increasingly delineated deterritorialized *–scape.*
52. Appadurai 1996:32

53. By this, of course, I am also referring to Walter Benjamin's famed essay, "The Work of Art in the Age of Mechanical Reproduction" (Benjamin 1968).

54. Qtd. in Kirshenblatt-Gimblett 1998:133

55. www.usps.com/communications/news/stamps/2004/sr04_062.htm.

56. Weber 1992:56

57. Weber 1963:398

58. www.virtualmuseum.ca/Exhibitions/Landscapes/e-e.html.   Downloaded   on September 28, 2005.

59. Barris 2005

60. Galitz 2005:1

61. Qtd. in Galitz 2005:1

62. www.nga.gov/education/american/landscape.shtm. Downloaded on September 28, 2005.

63. Hobhouse 2002:8

64. Field Operations Design Firm 2001:3. Emphasis in the original.

65. Field Operations Design Firm 2001:3.

66. Incidentally, evoking notions of an idealized -scape, "Distant Horizons" is the name of a cultural tour operator that specializes in "exotic" travel to the more unknown destinations, whose governments particularly use the heritage-scape for valorization.

67. Appadurai 1996:46

68. As of this writing there are 878 properties inscribed on the World Heritage List of tangible and natural sites; 679 of which are honored as "cultural," 174 "natural" and 25 as "mixed." The heritage-scape encompasses 145 nations (with 40 other nations who are signatories to the World Heritage Convention but do not yet have any sites designated). In the past 10 years (as of this writing), an average of 30 sites have been inscribed per year: 30 in 1998; 48 in 1999; 61 in 2000; 31 in 2001; 9 in 2002 (reflecting the downturn of tourism and related endeavors post-9/11 terrorist attacks; UNESCO was also occupied with drafting and promoting the *Universal Declaration of Cultural Diversity*); 24 in 2003; 34 in 2004; 24 in 2005; 18 in 2006; 22 in 2007; and 26 in 2008.

69. UNESCO 2004b:1

70. Appadurai 1996:46

71. See Benedict Anderson's discussion of homogeneous empty time and news media in the construction of community (Anderson 2003:33-36).

72. Winter 2003:63

73. UNESCO 2006e:1. A modified version of this quote can be found in UNESCO 2006d:112. An elaborate timeline of the decision-making process specific to Dresden's inscription on the World Heritage in Danger List can be found in UNESCO 2006a:197-201.

74. AP 2007a:1

75. UNESCO 2007a:37

76. UNESCO 2007a:37

77. According to an official tourism site, the Darjeeling Railway represents "a marvel . . . of non-engineering," for it "utilized neither rack mechanism nor cable as other

mountain railways do, but moves only on adhesion. It was the genius and vision of Franklin Prestage, which conceived of such a mechanism and executed it to perfection." The Nilgiri Railway was a bit diverse. According to the same informative site,

> The main feature of this line is the unique rack system and the equally unique and complicated locomotives. To quote from Sir Guilford L. Molesworth's report of 1886: "The locomotive used for working on the Abt System has two distinct functions: first, that of traction by adhesion as in an ordinary loco and second, that of traction by pinions acting upon the rack bars. "The brakes are four in number- two hand brakes action by friction and two acting by preventing the free escape of air from cylinder and thus using compressed air in retarding the progress of the engine. The former are used for shunting whilst the latter for descending steep gradients. One of the hand brakes acts on the tyres of the wheels in the ordinary manner and the second acts on grooved surfaces of the pinion axle but can be used in those places where the rack is laid. Even after hundred years, the brake system on Nilgiri locomotives is as intricate and cumbersome as it was in 1886."

This citation is from the website, www.hill-stations-india.com. Individual quotes came from two of its pages, www.hill-stations-india.com/hill-trains-india/the-darjeeling-railways.html and www.hill-stations-india.com/hill-trains-india/nilgiri-mountain-railway.html, both downloaded on October 5, 2005.

78. From the website, www.hill-states-india.com. Individual quotes came from two of its pages, www.hill-stations-india.com/hill-trains-india/the-darjeeling-railways.html and www.hill-stations-india.com/hill-trains-india/nilgiri-mountain-railway.html, both downloaded on October 5, 2005.
79. Lowenthal 1998:156
80. www.hadrians-wall.org/template.asp?ID=541&parentID=539&refID=578&ref parent=539 Accessed on September 27, 2005.
81. ICOMOS 1987:3
82. http://whc.unesco.org/en/list/430. Downloaded on September 27, 2005
83. See, for example, the websites of British and German cultural offices: www.culture. gov.uk/global/press_notices/archive_2005/dcms095_05.htm, downloaded on September 27, 2005; and www.limes-in-deutschland.de, downloaded on September 27, 2005.
84. http://portal.unesco.org/culture/en/ev.php-URL_ID%3D1549&URL_DO%3DDO_T OPIC&URL_SECTION%3D201.html. Downloaded on March 23, 2006.
85. UNESCO 2005c:15
86. UNESCO 1972:14
87. Yoon 2003:1
88. UNESCO 2003d:86
89. UNESCO 2005b:1
90. UNESCO 2005b:1
91. UNESCO 1972:2 (emphasis added)
92. UNESCO 1972:2 (emphasis added)

93. Peter Fowler states that, although sites were categorized as either cultural or natural sites, "from early on" the designation of mixed sites was "encouraged" (Fowler 2003:17). In practice, a mixed site was determined through a "straightforward numerical, almost formulaic equation along the lines of '2 natural criteria + 2 cultural criteria = a World Heritage 'mixed site'" (Fowler 2003:18).

94. Fowler 2003:22

95. Fowler 2003:22

96. Fowler 2003:17

97. While I argue here that intangible cultural heritage adds a critical dimension to the heritage-scape, I do not treat it fully in this book because this text is more concerned with the ways in which tourists interact with material culture (particularly in monumental form). The concept of intangible cultural heritage is continuing to evolve, as are the procedures for nominating and "proclaiming" these masterpieces (for example, the Committee meets every two years; the criteria are different, etc.). As one can see from just the nomenclature, the Intangible Heritage Convention very much intends to speak to the World Heritage Convention, while at the same time, it appears to be a separate entity. More time must pass, and more research must be conducted to truly understand the dialogue between tangible cultural heritage discourses and intangible cultural heritage discourses. In the meantime, in addition to Kirshenblatt-Gimblett 2004 and 2006, I suggest Hafstein 2004.

98. UNESCO 2003a:2

99. Kirshenblatt-Gimblett 2004:53

100. See, for example, a summer 2001 article on his visit to the San Remo Pizzafest on the website: www.pizza.it/curiosita/attualita/varie/ministro-a-sanremo.htm, downloaded on October 5, 2005. While holding the position of Italian Agricultural Minister, Scanio was ultimately successful in obtaining a new type of designation for pizza, akin to the certification of Italian wines as DOC and olive oils as DOP. This indication, called the *Specialita' tipica garantita* (STG), is akin to World Heritage designations insofar as it simultaneously celebrates the type of food, and reifies some articulations of the type over the others. His success has led him to crusade for other designations in an effort to reinforce Italian identity and preserve it against the numerous copies it has spawned. He stated in April 2004:

> Il riconoscimento della pizza napoletana come specialità tipica garantita è una vittoria molto importante, attraverso la quale sarà possibile tutelare un rinomato prodotto tipico e l'intera identità territoriale di Napoli e della Campania. . . Furono migliaia i prodotti tipici che censimmo, viste le grandi tradizioni italiane e i numerosissimi prodotti tipici nostrani, ed è per questo che l'Italia è la principale vittima della agropirateria e delle contraffazioni alimentari in ogni parte del pianeta, fenomeno contro il quale bisogna intensificare al massimo gli sforzi. . . .

> [The recognition of Neapolitan Pizza as a guaranteed specialty (Sgt) is a very important victory, through which traditional products, and indeed the whole identity of Naples and the Campania region, will be celebrated anew. . . . There were thousands of typical products that we Italians celebrate, given our great culinary

traditions and the copies it produced throughout every part of the planet, phenomena against which we must intensify our fight with maximum force . . .]

Another example can also be offered. Animal rights activists are often critical of the process by which *fois gras*, or fatty goose liver, is created. Farms—80% of which are in France—forcefully tube-feed partially cooked corn twice a day to expand the size of their livers up to ten times their normal size. In reaction to the political strides these activists have made in attempting to ban the production and consumption of this food—Israel and California have banned it, as did the city of Chicago until the interdict was overturned in 2008—in September 2005, French lawmakers unanimously passed a declaration pronouncing *fois gras* a masterpiece of cultural heritage (Johnson 2005:1).

101. Quoted in Kirshenblatt-Gimblett 2004:56
102. UNESCO 1996:165, qtd. Winter 2002:324
103. Giddens 1990:21
104. Luke 2002:14
105. Fisher 1991:18

Chapter 3

1. LeFebvre 1991:230
2. Geertz 2000:8
3. Geertz 2000:429
4. Anderson 2003
5. Halbwachs 1992:200-201
6. Wertsch 2002:56
7. MacIntyre 1984:216
8. Pearson and Richards 1997:5
9. Wertsch 2002:56
10. Connerton 1989:6
11. Johnson 1992:xi.
12. Geary 1994:160
13. Zerubavel 1995:214
14. Indeed, built into the official designation of the first "negative World Heritage site," Auschwitz since UNESCO's reasons could apply equally to the numerous other Nazi concentration camps in Europe: "The Committee decided to enter Auschwitz concentration camp on the List as a unique site and to restrict the inscription of other sites of a similar nature" (UNESCO 1979:11).
15. Though there has been talk of reconstructing the Buddhas to frame the heritage-scape's narrative based on the past Buddhist culture in the region instead of the

horrific act of intolerance, it is most probable that they will remain as negative spaces to memorialize the effects of cultural intolerance.

16. UNESCO 2001a:1, 3
17. ICOMOS 1978:2
18. ICOMOS 1995:115
19. ICOMOS 1995:117
20. UNESCO 1997b
21. Sasaki was inspired by the myth of *senbazuru*, which states that if one folds 1000 origami cranes (literally "*senbazuru*"), the gods would grant her a wish. She only completed about two-thirds before succumbing to cancer at age ten—eight years after the bomb was dropped.
22. UNESCO 2006a
23. UNESCO 2007b:1
24. UNESCO 1999:17
25. ICOMOS 1993:128
26. ICOMOS 1992:8
27. See, for example, Darwin 2005:774-775.
28. Morgan 1877
29. Robertson 1992:62
30. Weber 1992:xvii and 20
31. ICOMOS 1999b:176
32. UNESCO 1999b:18
33. According to George Stocking, one of the great authorities on Franz Boas, the anthropologist engaged in a lengthy and protracted debate with these two evolutionist ethnologists over the evolutionist notion of "independent invention"— that is, in human culture, "like causes produce like events" (Stocking 1974:2). This argument posits that all cultures within a given environmental and historical context will inevitably change in the same way. There is thus one cultural trajectory, at least for a particular geographic region at a particular point in time, and each culture finds itself in an inescapable, almost predestined, evolutionary trajectory.
34. Stocking 1974:96
35. Stocking 1974:96
36. Stocking 1974:4-5
37. Stocking 1974:96, emphasis added.
38. See, for example, Lévy-Bruhl 1923:431-433, 442.
39. UNESCO 2000b:2
40. Butcher 2003:85
41. Geertz 2000:8
42. Turner 1967:20
43. Geertz 2000:429
44. UNESCO 1972:1
45. In a speech at Doha in December, Matsura explicitly states that UNESCO was "the first United Nations body, through its General Conference, to reject this pernicious vision of how cultures and civilizations interact" (Matsura 2001a:3).

46. Matsura 2001b
47. UNESCO 2001c:13
48. Appadurai 1996:12
49. Appadurai 1996:12
50. UNESCO 1972:4
51. In addition to memory theory as outlined earlier, I am specifically referencing Edgar Dale's classic model of learning, the "Cone of Experience" (Dale 1946), which states that memories will be most effectively sedimented through active interactions. His model has become a rule of thumb in the heritage and tourism industries (see, for example, Bryant 2006:184) and especially in the information technology discipline—perhaps because of its supposed clear-cut quantification of learning apprehension: 10% learn what they hear, 30 percent of what they read, 50% of what they see and 90% of what they read. However, Dale never gave percentages, and, according to Dr. Michael Molenda, thought of these categories as fluid, rather than rigid (Molenda 2003). Nevertheless, the "10-30-50-90" rule, as it is often called, is a guiding force in the heritage and tourism industries. In another link to my concept of the heritage-scape, Davis asserted that the mutual sharing of experience between people optimizes the learning process (Dale 1953). As I will show in the next chapter, tourism is both an embodied and perspectival interaction with place, and a ritual that allows participants to share a common experience over time and space.

Chapter 4

1. Valene Smith defines a tourist as "a temporarily leisured person who voluntarily visits a place away from home for the purpose of experiencing a change." She further states that the "foundation of tourism rests on three key elements (all must be operative) which form an equation: Tourism = leisure time + discretionary income + positive local sanctions" (Smith 1989:1). While Smith's statement is one of the earliest, comprehensive definitions of tourism in the modern anthropological field of tourism studies, and indeed, this book agrees with her definition of a tourist, when it comes to her second statement, Smith seems to be defining only a segment of the panoply of touristic cultures—that is, those tourists who must translocate to tour. As this chapter will argue, tourism is also perspectival; a way of contextually approaching a site, and does not necessarily require discretionary income or the bodily movement of people.
2. Graburn 1983:11
3. Field notes 8/1/2007
4. Turner 1974:305
5. Victor Turner's model of pilgrimage, of course, is the primary model on which early tourism researchers (such as Graburn) based their analyses. As he builds on the work of van Gennep—who modeled his theory of (social) rites of passage on what he

called territorial passages (1960:15)—Turner's definition of pilgrimage is also linked to territorial movement:

> What seems to be common to pilgrimages in several of the great historical religions (Christianity, Islam, Judaism, Hinduism, Buddhism, Shintoism in Japan) an some others, is the notion that when one goes on pilgrimage one is not only moving from profane to sacred space and time, getting closer to one's religious roots as a member of a specific culture or civilization, moving from ideas about God or the supernatural world, to an experience or hopefully, a foretaste of the divine or spiritual order—a few days in the City of God; but one is also moving away from a social life in which one has an institutionalized social status, plays a set of expected roles, and belongs to such social groups as family, neighbourhood, ward, political party, parish, faction, village, town, club, business, labour union, fraternal associations and so on. One is moving into a different kind of social atmosphere, one in principle (if not always in practice) stripped of status, role-playing attributes, corporate group affiliations, and the like (Turner 1974:306-307).

6. www.tourism.govt.nz/quicklinks/ql-glossary.html. Accessed on June 1, 2006.
7. www.tourism.govt.nz/quicklinks/ql-glossary.html. Accessed on June 1, 2006.
8. The full title of MacCannell's text is *The Tourist: A New Theory of the Leisure Class*.
9. MacCannell 1999:7
10. MacCannell 1999:13. In his original version (published in 1976), he calls tourism a byproduct of modernity. However, in the preface to his later edition, he adjusts his thinking, issuing statements such as the one cited above to illustrate the very "postmodern" nature of tourist interactivity.
11. Middleton 1991:viii
12. Abbink 2000:1-3
13. Kirshenblatt-Gimblett 1998:141
14. Kirshenblatt-Gimblett 1998:153
15. Kirshenblatt-Gimblett describes this image on her book's back cover with the citation: "The Warrior for Gringostroika, character from the project The Year of the White Bear, by Guillermo Gómex-Peña and Coco Fusco. Walker Art Center, Minneapolis, 1992. Photo by Glenn Halveston, courtesy of the Walker Art Center."
16. UN 2003:5
17. Cabrini 2006
18. Further development was supported in part by the World Bank's International Finance Corporation (IFC), project number 21363, originally disclosed in October 29, 2003. It took effect in January 28, 2005. Details can be found on the webpage, http://ifcln001.worldbank.org/IFCExt/spiwebsite1.nsf/2bc34f011b50ff6e85256a550 073ff1c/63ea373e2378da6385256dce006ebb91?OpenDocument as of May 5, 2006.
19. In the years leading up to 2005, tour guides would invariably mention that the number of tourists was projected to reach one million in 2005; now that this benchmark is achieved, guides and officials seem now to mention this as a prophecy fulfilled.

20. Homepage of the Embassy of the Kingdom of Cambodia, www.embassy.org/cambodia/, Accessed on June 18, 2006. Emphasis in the original.
21. GNWA 2006:1
22. MacCannell 1999
23. Alpers 1991:29
24. Urry 2002
25. Lippard 1998, Lippard 2000
26. van Gennep 1960; Turner 1967; Turner and Turner 1978
27. Graburn 1983:12-14
28. van Gennep 1960:10
29. "Rite of Passage" 2006:1
30. For an excellent anthropological study of the museological reuse of Israeli kibbutzim for fostering ethnic pride, see Katriel 1997.
31. www.birthrightisrael.com/bin/en.jsp?enPage=BlankPage&enDisplay=view&enDispWhat=Zone&enDispWho=TheTrip&enZone=Faqs&&channel=TheTrip#40
32. I have certainly observed this while attending (and in some way participating in) study abroad programs sponsored by a number of accredited colleges and universities (both American and foreign) between 1992 and 1999.
33. He has since retired, but informants at the university attest that the program has maintained this unique quality.
34. Morrill, Laura and Timms, Theresa (private communications)
35. Graburn 1983:12
36. Graburn 1983:15
37. Smith 1989:2
38. Fulton 2002:66-67
39. Shafer 2003:26
40. Boym 2001:8
41. Cohen 1979:182
42. Turner 1967:45
43. Turner 1974b:201
44. Turner 1974b:202
45. Turner 1974b:201; here he is partially quoting Robert Merton's definition of "social structure."
46. Turner 1973:217
47. Turner 1974a:217
48. Interestingly, Erik Cohen feels that the only true, authentic tourist experience is one in which the person actually eschews his previous life and permanently adopts the lifestyle of the culture he is touring. He calls this the "existential mode" of tourism, wherein he "is fully committed to an 'elective' spiritual centre, i.e. one external to the mainstream of his native society and culture. The acceptance of such a centre comes phenomenologically closest to a religious conversion, to 'switching worlds,' in Berger and Luckmann's (1966:144) terminology, though the content of the symbols and values so accepted need not be 'religious' in the narrow sense of the term." This is an acceptance of the narrative claim imbued in the site. Thus, the

existential tourist who visited Hoi An need not feel Vietnamese, but he could truly understand "unity in diversity" if that was the narrative claim with which he was approaching the site (Cohen 1979:189-190).

49. Bourdieu 1984:56
50. Many erroneously think this stands for "Foreign Independent Traveler." Writing in 1961, Boorstin, for one, states that American Express divides individual travelers into FITs and DITs—Foreign and Domestic (1994:93). However, the common usage now is "Free and Independent Traveler."
51. www.abercrombiekent.com. Accessed on June 20, 2006
52. www.butterfield.com/index.asp?navid=5160. Accessed on June 20, 2006.
53. Barbara Kirshenblatt-Gimblett seems to assert this when she writes:

> Standardization is part and parcel of the economies of scale that high-volume tourism requires. First, vertical integration in the tourism system places much of the infrastructure in the hands of a few national and multinational corporations: the biggest earners are international airlines, followed by hotels. Airlines often own interests in hotels. Not surprisingly, tourists spend much of their time in the grips of the industry, in the planes, hotels, buses and restaurants. Second, the industry requires a reliable product that meets universal standards, despite the dispersal of that product across many widely separated locations. Third, the very interchangeability of generic products suits the industry, which can quickly shift destinations if one paradise or another is booked solid or hit by a typhoon, political unrest, or currency fluctuations. For this and other reasons, the discourse of tourism marketing is so consistent that only the insertion of place names tells you which getaway or which natural wonder you are being sold (Kirshenblatt-Gimblett 1998:152-153).

54. This demographic was my primary clientele during the years of 2001-2005.
55. Gray 2006:70
56. Wilkening 2006b:1
57. Wilkening 2006a:1
58. Clarkson 2006. See also Wilkening 2006d:1
59. http://leisure.travelocity.com/Promotions/0,,TRAVELOCITY|2989|pkg_main,00.html. Downloaded on 5/30/06.
60. MacCannell 1999:101-102
61. Wilkinson 2005:198
62. Edutainment 2006. Children's programming is a prime example of edutainment; for an interesting examination of Walt Disney World as a form of edutainment, see Fjellman 1992.
63. Harris Poll www.harrisinteractive.com/harris_poll/index.asp?PID=526 December 8, 2004. Accessed 1/10/05.
64. Boorstin 1994:79-80
65. MacCannell 1999:91-107
66. MacCannell 1999:98
67. MacCannell 1999:101

68. Kirshenblatt-Gimblett 1998:153
69. Fieldnotes, 9/14/2005
70. Loti 1996:55-56
71. Or, as Graburn describes it, "travel away from home" (Graburn 1983:12).
72. Fulton 2002:73 emphasis added.
73. Turner 1967:44
74. Graburn writes, "The period between entry into and departure from the ritual was characterized as "sacred . . . a period when the individuals in the non-ordinary state drew closer to the core beings of their religion in order to make contact with the supernatural, which would perform extraordinary feats, cures, or miracles for the benefit of the participants. (How remarkably analogous to the claimed benefits of tourism!)" (1983:12).
75. van Gennep 1960:12-13
76. www.cannon-beach.net/cbhaystack.html. Accessed on 23 June 2006
77. Florence and Storey 2001:243
78. Asia News/Scmp 2006
79. de Botton 2002:11-13. Emphasis in the original.
80. *Washington Post* travel blogger K.C. Summers reveals the existence of an expectation gap concerning hotels and their amenities when analyzing hotel ratings on the popular user-generated website TripAdvisor.com. While she had "two really nice stays at two wonderful hotels" that were centrally located in Paris and Madrid, she was appalled by the "rants and raves by people whose judgment seems questionable at best and downright loony much of the time." By this she means that the lay writers chose not to focus on the hotels' "character," "palpable sense of history," "perfect location," "charming architectural details," or "helpful staff," but rather ranted about the "dodgy" plumbing, "street noise" or "non-fluffy towels." She begins: "I've just had two really nice stays at two wonderful hotels, Hotel D'Angleterre in Paris and Hotel de las Letras in Madrid. The first is charming and old-fashioned, the second edgy and hip, and both more than lived up to my expectations. But you sure wouldn't know it from reading the citizen reviews on TripAdvisor.com." Summers' opening paragraph reveals not only the intense feelings that hotels elicit when they do not live up to expectations, but the more general discrepancy between what one traveler finds acceptable is not an empirical fact, but widely varied. Expectations, as she reveals, are subjective and changeable. Some respondents, such as one writing under the pseudonym "NAJ" also describe their "expectations" of hotels and how they attempt to mediate them. NAJ consults TripAdvisor only for chain hotels where he has a "current expectation" so that he can "see if it meets the criteria that I have in mind. I also look at the dates of the comments to see if they are outdated and may not reflect any improvements that may have been made." Another writer, "Richard," gives his take on evaluating the differences between his expectations and those of TripAdvisor readers: "I did an interesting experiment on Trip Advisor. I looked at the reviews for a very nice hotel in our area and a really seedy, scary highway motel. The reviews were about even with a mix of pros and cons, 5 stars and 1 stars, germophobes and fans. This tells me

that Trip Advisor is totally worthless. It provides no useful information. . . Before you rely on Trip Advisor try this experiment: Look up the best hotel in your area and the worst. See if you can figure out a difference in the Trip Advisor review" (Summers 2007). While Richard chalks this up to a general "worthlessness" of the travel review website, he nevertheless provides an interesting ethnographic methodology for interpreting the differences in expectations one has: reviewers of 5-star hotels have fundamentally different expectations than those reviewing 1-star hotels, both of which are prey to an exceedingly varied elicitation of responses.

81. One female tour manager recounted a story of an elderly woman who was irate at the standard of the group's hotel, and in particular of her room. Speaking to the angry traveler from her own hotel-room doorway, the manager told her that unfortunately it was not possible to change her room or upgrade her because the hotel was full. The manager recounts that the passenger, looking her square in the eye and then down at her hand grasping the frame of the doorway, grabbed the door and flung it closed on her fingers.

82. Fieldnotes 10/22/2001
83. Richman 2005:3
84. Loti 1996:11
85. Loti 1996:15
86. Loti 1996:19
87. Loti 1996:29
88. Loti 1996:9-10. Loti's brother, 15 years senior, was posted as a naval doctor in Cochin-China in 1892. He contracted dysentery in 1895, and departed for France, but passed away at sea a week later.
89. Loti 1996:42
90. Loti 1996:45
91. Loti 1996:46
92. Loti 1996:51-53. Emphasis added.

Chapter 5

1. Kirshenblatt-Gimblett 1998:52
2. Conn 1998:4
3. Conn 1998:4
4. Qtd. in Conn 1998:3-4
5. Bennett 1995:24 cites Key 1973:86.
6. Greenblatt 1990:172-73
7. Duncan 2004:16
8. See, for example, Bucher 2003.
9. Duncan 2004:10
10. She states, "[E]verything in a museum is put under the pressure of a way of seeing" (Alpers 1991:29).
11. Duncan 2004:24
12. Duncan 2004:25
13. Bann 1984. Hooper-Greenhill 1989

14. Bennett 1995:39
15. Low 2004:30 (emphasis added).
16. Flower 1898:18. qtd in Bennett 1995:42
17. Knorr-Cetina 1999
18. In describing international policy coordination, Peter Haas (1992) has popularized the term "epistemic communities," which he considers a "network" of specifically "policy-oriented" professionals (3) sharing the same worldview (27). In Haas' conceptualization, they may come from different disciplines (3) but are bound together in common beliefs concerning governance and share intersubjective notions of "validity," or internally defined knowledge of weighing and considering the deployment of certain kinds of knowledge. For the context of the heritage-scape, I prefer Knorr-Cetina's concept of an "epistemic culture," for it eschews the network-oriented connotations of Haas' concept and focuses instead on the intangible and dynamic elements that traditionally mark "culture." It also can draw upon semiotics and collective memory theory; epistemic cultures can very well identify with their own symbols and, as I touched upon in chapter 4, even have their own linguistic markers to differentiate those inside the culture and those outside (for example, travel professionals call travelers "pax," "FITs," etc.).
19. Bennett 1995:40
20. Katriel 1997:74
21. Knorr-Cetina 1999
22. See the IAU's website at www.iau.org.
23. Inman 2006:1
24. The popular social networking website Facebook (www.facebook.com) lists over 500 groups with this theme. Boasting nearly 1,250,000 worldwide members in January 2008, the largest group is named, "When I was your age, Pluto was a planet."
25. Barbara Kirshenblatt-Gimblett states, "Heritage is created through metacultural operations that extend museological values and methods (collection, documentation, preservation, presentation, evaluation and interpretation) to living persons, their knowledge, practices, artifacts, social worlds, and life spaces" (Kirshenblatt-Gimblett 2004:52).
26. Turner has often likened rituals to dramas. See, for example, Turner 1974b.
27. Turner 1967:45
28. Greenblatt 1991:44
29. UNESCO 2000b:4
30. Blumer 1969:80
31. Cuno 2004:52-53. Emphasis in original
32. ICOMOS 1986:1
33. Meyer 1997:145.
34. UNESCO 1983:2
35. UNESCO 2005a:14
36. Urry 2002:6
37. The components of the tourist gaze are made explicit in Urry 2002:1-3.

38. Alpers 1991:27
39. Kirshenblatt-Gimblett 1998:132
40. UNESCO 2000B:5
41. UNESCO 2004a:41
42. UNESCO 2004a:25-26
43. UNESCO 2004a:38
44. UNESCO 2004a:17
45. UNESCO 2004a:19
46. UNESCO 2004:38
47. ICOMOS 1986:2
48. ICOMOS 1992:7
49. UNESCO 2005c:13

Chapter 6

1.   A British website listing profiles of various Cultural Ministries provides an excellent
     list of the many branches of the Vietnamese Ministry of Culture and Information at
     the following link: www.culturalprofiles.org.uk/viet_nam/Units/2356.html. Down-
     loaded on 13 October 2006.
2.   This perspective was provided by two informants, one in Đà Nẵng and one in Huế.
3.   ICOMOS 1993:127
4.   Interview with Mr. Phan Thuận An, Huế, 8/19/2006
5.   Interview with Mr. Phan Thuận An, Huế, 8/19/2006
6.   Tucker 1978:53
7.   ICOMOS 1993:126
8.   ICOMOS 1993:127
9.   Florence and Storey 2001:319
10. ICOMOS' recommendation document states: "An ICOMOS expert mission visited
     Hue in March 1993 and spent three days visiting the monuments and discussing the
     nomination with Vietnamese officials. The mission was impressed by the dedication
     and high professional competence of the staff of the Service for the Management of
     Historical and Cultural Monuments . . . " (ICOMOS 1993:128)
11. ICOMOS 1993:128
12. See, for example, Kolb 1994. The archaeologist Michael Kolb attempts to calculate
     the strength of pre-contact Hawaiian religious authorities through an analysis of the
     amount of labor they most likely mobilized to construct their edifices.
13. ICOMOS 1993:124
14. Huế is considered a "cultural landscape" in many of UNESCO's publications,
     including the office of UNESCO's Regional Advisor for Culture in Bangkok (Box
     1999:138-139).
15. All World Heritage sites have buffer zones, but these usually fall within preexisting
     property borders.
16. ICOMOS 1993:127

17. ICOMOS 1993:127
18. Phan Thuân An used the term "re-created" when he mentioned this. Fieldnotes 8/19/2006.
19. Fieldnotes 8/19/2006
20. Dharma 2001:16
21. Private communication 8/19/2006
22. As at Angkor, there are bas reliefs depicting Rāma and episodes of the *Rāmayana*. In Book III.1.15 of Vālmikī's version, the king is "the fourth part of Indra himself and the protector of his subjects"—the "guardian of righteousness and glorious refuge of his people . . . a guru who wields the staff of punishment" (Vālmikī 2006:39). But he is also often likened to the "equal of great Indra" (cf. Vālmikī 2006:271). Indeed, as Pollock states in his introductory note, the god-king also incorporates aspects of *Trimurti* Hinduism; that is, he possesses characteristics of the triune God: Vishnu (the preserver), Brahma (the creator) and Shiva (the destroyer). For example, the ascetic rākshasa Marícha tells Rāvana, Rāma's kingly rākshasa counterpart, "The power of kings is infinite, they are able to take on any of five different forms: They can be hot like Agni, god of fire, bold like Indra or mild like the Moon; they can extract punishment like Yama, or be gracious like Váruna" (Vālmikī 2006:227). According to Pollock, this is a "very prevalent tenet of Indian political theology" (Pollock 2008:79). A "preternatural" being, the "terrestrial" king "literally becomes the one or the other god" (Pollock 2008:79-80).
23. Dharma 2001:19
24. Dharma states that there are about 80,000 who live in Binh Thuân and Ninh Thuân provinces and 15,000 others living in the Chau Doc region and Saigon (Dharma 2001:27).
25. Fieldnotes 8/19/2006
26. Dharma 2001:27
27. This is the title of a sweeping monograph by George Coedes (1968).
28. Guillion 2001:12
29. Ngô 2005:17
30. Florence and Storey 1991:351
31. Trần 2004:18
32. Trần 2004:24. I have corrected the spelling of "ensure" (from "insure") in Trần's citation.
33. Trần 2004:25
34. Ngô 2004:11
35. www.lerici.polimi.it/chi_siamo/index.html. Accessed on March 20, 2008.
36. That is, the predominant worship of Shiva.
37. In "Hinduism," goddesses highly resemble the dualistic qualities of the earth: fertility and beneficence, and uncontrollable destruction. In writing "Dame Nature," I am also referring to a quote by Ponder (1936:305) that discusses nature in terms of both the creator and the destroyer at Ta Prohm; chapter 10 cites the full quote.
38. As of December 2006, these photographs can be found at http://whc.unesco.org/en/list/949.

39. Võ 2002:cover
40. UNESCO 1972:3 (emphasis added)
41. UNESCO 1972:3 (emphasis added)
42. Pearson and Richards 1997:5
43. Kant 1998:158-159
44. In their original context, Parker Pearson and Richards also refer to space somewhat interchangeably with place. While Kant says there is only one endless type of space, for these archaeologists, there exist multiple spaces. Nevertheless, their main point is that all earthly spaces/places have a human phenomenological dimension, even if they are simply recognized and named from afar. They become social spaces—able to be excavated and studied, whether natural or cultural—from an infinite unknown Space when they are tinged in some way by the social. Kant's definition of space, then, serves to clarify this discussion by setting up two distinct terms: *space* becomes the undifferentiated conceptual container wherein the multiplicity of known, and therefore social, *places* exist. Coupled with this Kantian understanding of space, therefore, their assertion works well within the present discourse.
45. UNESCO 2005a:19-20
46. IUCN 1992:88. When designating the site, UNESCO simply referred to IUCN's wording of criteria *iii* (UNESCO 1994b:44-55).
47. IUCN 1992:88
48. IUCN 1992:87
49. Agence France Presse 2006:1
50. Galla 2002:65
51. IUCN 1999:119
52. UNESCO 2003c:103
53. Montaigne 2003:232-233 Emphasis added.
54. See, for example Smalley 1954:217. In this page, Smalley states that the French call the minority groups of the mountainous inland areas "Moi, Montagnards, Köho or Péimsiens," the latter being an type of "portmanteau" acronym "derived by Rene de Berval from the initials *of Les Populations Montagnardes du Sud-Indochinois.*"
55. I asked one Vietnamese-American informant about the use of the term, to which she replied "FYI never use "moi" for minority. It's a racial slur. You would say "nguoi thiểu số" . . . No one knew what I was talking about because it is so derogatory." Private e-mail communication, 5/14/2008.
56. There are many variations to this legend; but the major tropes remain the same.
57. www.unep-wcmc.org/sites/wh/Phong_nha.html. Accessed on October 1, 2006.
58. Sterling, Hurley and Bain 2003:1
59. For a contemporary account of muntjak hunting in the region, see Wikramanayake 1999.
60. Current versions of the film call it either *Kliou the Killer* or *Kliou the Tiger*, although the latter is used by the venerable *Internet Movie Database*, or *IMDB* as it is known to hoards of American college students. According to IMDB, the film, thought for many years to be lost, enjoys three special recognitions. Not only is it the first known cinematic footage of French Indochina, but it was also the last

Hollywood silent film known to have been shot, as well as the last to be released in two-strip Technicolor, a process that was discontinued a year earlier. Downloaded from www.imdb.com/title/tt0431202/ on 18 October 2006.

61. SGGP 2005:1
62. Fieldnotes 8/20/2006
63. SGGP 2005:1
64. SGGP 2005:1
65. Fieldnotes 8/20/2006
66. On June 25, 2005, a tunnel was opened to lessen the traffic on the Pass. As the longest tunnel in Southeast Asia, it also was the only project outside the United States to win a coveted award by the American Construction Management Association (Hai 2007).
67. IUCN 2003:57
68. IUCN 2003:58
69. IUCN 1992:87
70. One family from a floating village has recently erected a lovely villa along a small, sandy beach on a karst island, but this seems more recent, and exceptional.
71. IUCN 1992:87
72. IUCN 1992:88
73. Florence and Storey 1991:243. Chapter 4 included the full quote and a more complete discussion of the role of souvenirs and pillaging Hạ Long Bay.
74. This was decree 27COM7B.13 (UNESCO 2003c:36-38).
75. Lempert, David. Private communication, 7/27/06.
76. Ethnic Vietnamese tour guides, who frequently complain about the touristic practices of other Asians, accuse Korean tourists as the largest polluters in the area.
77. UNESCO 2006a:42
78. Vietnam News Briefs 2006:2
79. UNESCO 2006a:41
80. Galla 2002:67
81. Galla 2002:69
82. Galla 2002:68
83. There are many documented cases of indigenous groups perceived to be living off the land in "less-developed" ways have acted contrary to environmental interests. The insightful works of Mohan and Stokke 2000, T. Turner 1995, Conklin and Graham 1995, and Kane 1993 provide compelling examples which caution against applying a "noble savage" stereotype.
84. Anonymous posting on www.worldheritagesite.org/sites/halongbay.html. Accessed on 5/23/2008.
85. "Deborah (USA)." From www.worldheritagesite.org/sites/halongbay.html. Accessed on 5/23/2008.
86. Said 1994. Said's conception of Orientalism is discussed in chapter 10.
87. UNESCO 1983:4

Chapter 7

1. Dellios 2002:1
2. ICOMOS 1999a:114
3. Interview with Trần Văn Nhân and guide Pham Van Anh, Hội An, 8/18/2006. The following story was recounted by Trần Văn Nhân and guide Pham Van Anh, locals who both attested to have been witnesses throughout these developments.
4. A biography for Robinson can be found on Lonely Planet's website, http://shop.lone lyplanet.com/authors.jsp?CONTENT%3C%3Ecnt_id=10134198673231416. Accessed on March 9, 2008.
5. Fieldnotes 8/18/2006
6. Fieldnotes 8/18/2006
7. The tour guide Pham Van Anh, who works with higher-end tourists, bemoans this. He joins other local professionals in pointing out that the group and high-end tourists spend more money in Hội An; not only do they tend to stay in more expensive hotels, but they purchase entrance tickets and donate funds to the town. Backpackers, on the other hand, do not even buy the semi-obligatory tickets.
8. Fieldnotes 8/18/2006
9. Fieldnotes 8/18/2006
10. Luke 2002:10. Luke uses this terminology to describe the recontextualization of museum objects.
11. Fieldnotes 8/17/2006
12. Indeed, many state museums, especially in Europe, do not charge entrance fees to their citizens, and the Smithsonian-operated museums of Washington, DC are completely free to all visitors—domestic or foreign.
13. Philippe de Montebello bemoans the lack of mission that is inherent when one throws a blockbuster exhibition. He talks of the "regrettable . . . interesting paradox, namely, that when the visitor, as opposed to the work of art, occupies center stage, he is likely to be less well served, not better served. As the museum strives to attract [the non-regular visitor] and please him, he will, inevitably, be catered to. That is, to ensure that he is counted at the gate, he will not be challenged. Instead, most likely he will be greeted, through the programs that are offered, at his present level of artistic sophistication. By definition that is not a broadening or enhancing experience of the kind that we [museum professionals] are obligated by mission to provide" (Cuno 2004:157-158).
14. Fieldnotes 8/18/2006
15. www.vietnamtourism.com/e_pages/heritage/Hoian.asp. Accessed October 29, 2006.
16. I worked with several prominent art museums in the United States to plan tours to Vietnam, a process that was actually made more complicated because of the insistence of this correspondence between the dates of the Lantern Festival and the dates the groups had to be in Hội An. Primarily because of the Lantern Festival's schedule and the schedules of the museum and its accompanying curator, one of the trips actually departed two years later (I began the tour planning in 2003; it finally departed in 2005).

17. Unlike traditional Vietnamese vermicelli (mỳ), which is made from rice flower, cao lầu is made from rice flower soaked in ash-filled water; the ash must be produced by burned wood taken from Cham Island (Nguyễn 2000:101-102).
18. Fieldnotes 8/18/2006
19. Fieldnotes 8/18/2006
20. Durkheim 1995:10

Chapter 8

1. Tilden 1957:9
2. See chapter 4.
3. From a description of the U.S. State Department's Thomas R. Pickering Foreign Affairs Fellowship for Undergraduates. Among other places, this can be accessed at www.cau.edu/acad_prog/stud_abroad/stud_scholarship.html.
4. Schneider 2000
5. UNESCO 2007c:1
6. UNESCO 2007c:1
7. UNESCO 2007c:1
8. UNESCO 2007c:1
9. www.hrp.org.uk/webcode/tower_home.asp
10. Fieldnotes 8/9/2006; 8/10/2006, 8/11/2006
11. See, for example, Kotler and Kotler 2004, and Copeland 2006.
12. Landler 2000:1
13. For one of the more egregious examples of this colonial attitude towards native kings, see Georg Hegel's discussion of Africa in his "Introduction" to The Philosophy of History (Hegel 1956:91-99).
14. Kotler and Kotler 2004:165-186
15. Falk and Dierking 2004:140
16. http://whc.unesco.org/en/list/373. Accessed on September 11, 2007.
17. Rago 2007
18. Bath 2007:164
19. Bath 2007:164
20. Bath 2007:165
21. Bath 2007:164
22. For an exceptional overview of proposed uses of mobile technology at Stonehenge World Heritage site, see Bath 2006.
23. Falk and Dierking 2004:142
24. Tilden 1957:9
25. Bryant 2006:184
26. Tilden 1957:9
27. Bryant 2006:173
28. Brooks and Brooks 1993, referenced in Copeland 2007:83

29. King 1940 qtd. in "NPS Archaeology Program: Interpretation for Archaeologists" www.nps.gov/archeology/IforA/whatIs_2.htm. Accessed on September 7, 2007.
30. Copeland 2007:86
31. Copeland 2007:86
32. Katriel 1997:111-114
33. www.theculturedtraveler.com/Heritage/Archives/Arausio.htm. Downloaded on December 20, 2005.
34. http://whc.unesco.org/en/list/491. Downloaded on July 19, 2006.
35. www.yanni.com/media/video_acropolis.asp. Downloaded December 20, 2005.
36. Entertainment Wire 1997:1
37. http://www.amazon.com/gp/product/6305781427/103-21740120205400?v=glance& n=130. Downloaded on December 20, 2005.
38. www.riaa.com/news/newsletter/press1998/032898.asp. Downloaded on December 20, 2005.
39. Barbara Kirshenblatt-Gimblett states, "To compete for tourists, a location must become a destination. To compete with each other, destinations must be distinguishable, which is why the tourism industry requires the production of difference" (Kirshenblatt-Gimblett 1998:152).
40. Mydans 2002:1
41. Mydans 2002:1
42. SOS 2005:1
43. www.raffles.com/raffles/retreats/partner_special_detail.asp?id=434
44. Mydans 2002:1
45. www.unesco.org/culture/intangible-heritage/masterpiece.php?id=64&lg=en Downloaded on July 23, 2006.
46. UNESCO 2006c:25
47. www.unesco.org/culture/intangible-heritage/masterpiece.php?id=64&lg=en. Downloaded on July 23, 2006.
48. *Centro storico* is the Italian term for "historic center," ubiquitous on signage in Italy.
49. ICOMOS 1986:2

Chapter 9

1. UNESCO 2005a:14
2. Appadurai 1988:3
3. Hewison 1989:17
4. Kirshenblatt-Gimblett 1998:197
5. LeFebvre alludes to this when he writes, "buildings are to monuments as everyday life is to festival" (1991:223).
6. UNESCO 2002a:8
7. LeFebvre 1991:221
8. Fowler 1989:60
9. Greenblatt 1991:42-56

10. Alcock (2002:21-22). She cites Quintilian's *Institutio Oratoria* 11.2.21 for the quote "linked one to the other like dancers hand in hand." On page 21 she notes that "*ars memorae*" can be traced to the Archaic poet Simonides, though Cicero and Quintilian's later descriptions are the most well known and most often cited during the Romantic era. In a footnote, Alcock provides a valuable list of citations from this Grand Tour era.

11. There are many texts that metaphorically note the resonant similarities between Rome and the Khmer ruins, including a number of contemporary travel sources, but a formative early text is H. G. Quaritch Wales' *Angkor and Rome*, written at the end of the French colonial era. This will be discussed in greater detail in the next chapter.

12. See, for example Coe 2003:11-12. Attempts linking Angkor to the Incan monuments previous to Angkor's inscription on the World Heritage List include Coe 1967, Coe 1957, Heine-Geldern 1966:284-291, Bronson 1978.

13. For an interesting and detailed account of this, see Elkins 2001.

14. Butcher 2003:84

15. Qtd. in Greenblatt 1991:52

16. Qtd. in Dagens 1995:139

17. Freud 1950:35

18. Freud 1950:35

19. As Freud points out, the value of transience is "scarcity value in time" (Freud 1950:35).

20. ICOMOS 1987:2

21. See, for example, Merriam-Webster Online Dictionary's entry for "respect' at www. merriam-webster.com/dictionary/respect. Downloaded on March 10, 2008.

22. UNESCO 2002a:12

23. From *Wordnet*, Princeton University, 8/2003, http://dictionary.reference.com/search ?q=preservation. Downloaded on May 1, 2005.

24. From *Definitions of Conservation Terminology*, Stanford University. http://aic.stan-ford.edu/geninfo/defin.html. Downloaded on May 1, 2005.

25. UNESCO 2002a:13

26. Edwards 2006:27

27. Darwin 764

28. Carruthers 1992:8

29. Metcalf and Huntington 1991; cited in Tippett 2004:3

30. Quoted in Tippett 2004:3

31. Hockey 1990:27; also quoted in Tippett 2004. Hockey is summarizing arguments concerning death and mourning by Geoffrey Gorer (1965) and concerning the medicalization of British society as discussed by Ivan Illich (1975).

32. See, for example, Dietler 2001. Lévi-Strauss' classic essay, "The Culinary Triangle" also conveys this point (Lévi-Strauss 1997).

33. This anecdote is intended solely as an illustration of divergent conceptions between many Western tourists and local Vietnamese of the ingestion of foods understood as decomposing. Of course, notable exceptions can be brought to mind that illustrate

Westerners' own ingestions of foods that could be considered decomposing, although it also should be noted that the following examples are strictly regulated, ostensibly for health reasons (although no doubt for economic, moral and social class reasons as well). Alcoholic drinks, especially wine and beer, as well as vinegars, are fermented foodstuffs and many may make the case that the "acquired taste" of such liquors is really an acquired taste of decomposition. However, Westerners conceptualize these in just the opposite fashion, as a method of preserving other foods and staving off decomposition. Cheeses can also be considered a form of rancid milk, although once again Westerners believe it is a way of staving off the transience of milk. Furthermore, strict regulations are placed on all of these ingestible. America in particular limits or forbids certain types of cheeses, that have living cultures. Guarantees are also applied to wines, cheeses and vinegars, such as the Italian wine gradations of "Denominazione di Origine Controllata" (DOC), "Denominazione di Origine Controllata e Garantita" (DOCG), and "Indicazione Geographica Tipica" (IGT), which attest to the authenticity of their origins and the acceptability of their highly regulated production practices.

34. The recipe for *nước mắm* is simple: Place a layer of fish or shrimp in a clay pot or barrel and cover with three layers of sea salt. Replace this with another layer of fish and three of salt. The juice that emerges is the "first press" and is highly valuable. Subsequent presses are exported commercially. In Phan Thiết, a seaside town renowned for its *nước mắm*, this first press is then fermented again for six months.
35. Fieldnotes 1/15/2003
36. Pham 2001:24 (emphasis added).
37. I observed some of these residents in May 2001. By January 2003 they were gone; I suspect they had been removed.
38. Fieldnotes 8/11/2006
39. Daena Funahashi, private communication 2005
40. Gerd Albrecht, private communication 2005
41. UNESCO 2002a:12
42. UNESCO 1962
43. UNESCO 1962:139
44. Yang and Pharès 2002:10
45. Quoted in UNESCO 2005b:6
46. UNESCO 1972:10
47. This was outlined in Article 22 of the World Heritage Convention (UNESCO 1972:12)
48. UNESCO 1972:12
49. UNESCO 2001b:65
50. UNESCO 2001b:65
51. UNESCO 1972:12
52. UNESCO 1972:8
53. UNESCO 2005b:17
54. http://whc.unesco.org/en/list/208

55. See, for example, www.israelnationalnews.com/news.php3?id=91940. In October 2005, Jerusalem Day was marked in Iran by a top official calling for Israel to be "wiped off the map," a statement condemned by its non-Middle Eastern allies such as Russia. Despite Iranian diplomatic efforts to diffuse the situation, most top officials still attended the prescribed rally in central Tehran. http://news.xinhuanet.com/english/2005-10/29/content_3699641.htm. In Beirut, the typical anti-American sentiments expressed against US support for Israel was converted into a large anti-American rally protesting American support of a United Nations declaration condemning Hezbollah and the Syrian influence on Lebanon. www.arabmonitor.info/news/dettaglio.php?idnews=11780&lang=en. Downloaded on July 23, 2006.
56. http://whc.unesco.org/en/list/148
57. http://whc.unesco.org/en/list/76
58. UNESCO 2005b:17
59. Poggioli 2005:1
60. Poggioli 2005:1
61. Freud 1950:35
62. Time 1963:1-2
63. http://whc.unesco.org/en/news/377. Accessed on September 28, 2007. In the online version, the underlined passages are hyperlinked to the webpage featuring UNESCO's World Heritage List.
64. The Khmer Rouge reigned from 1975 to 1979, at which point a Vietnamese invasion drove its leaders from power and installed a puppet head of state. Resettled in the western regions of Cambodia, the Khmer Rouge allied itself with other nationalist organizations opposed to Vietnamese control, and waged guerilla warfare through the material aid of China, though its grip over the country slowly ebbed. While most nationalists subscribed to the United Nations-brokered peace agreement in 1991, the Khmer Rouge continued warfare into the 1990s; Pol Pot officially dissolved the movement in 1995—almost three years after Angkor was declared a World Heritage site—and is believed to have died, perhaps imprisoned by his men, in 1998.
65. ICOMOS 1992:6
66. ICOMOS 1992:6
67. ICOMOS 1992:7
68. ICOMOS 1992:7
69. ICOMOS 1992:4
70. ICOMOS 1992:4
71. ICOMOS 1992:4
72. ICOMOS 1992:8
73. UNESCO 1992:35
74. UNESCO 1992:35
75. UNESCO 1992:78-79 (Annex V)
76. APSARA 1993:1
77. UNESCO 2005c:4
78. UNESCO 1993b
79. UNESCO 1993b

80. UNESCO 1993b
81. This is in the latter half of the Declaration; points 10 and 11 (UNESCO 1993b).
82. Sihanouk 1995
83. Sihanouk 1998
84. Amery 2001
85. www.phnom-penh.diplo.de/en/06/Bilaterale__Kulturbeziehungen/Bilaterale__ Kulturbeziehunge. html

Chapter 10

1. Tarling 1999:163
2. Edwards 2007:38
3. Pelaggi 2002:4 qtd. in Edwards 2007:38.
4. This forced forgetting seemed to begin to work, as a guide in Phnom Penh illustrated. Remembering an outbreak of a curable disease that almost claimed her life, her family had neither the medicine nor the expertise to help her, but had to rely on traditional remedies that was passed down orally from generation to generation (field journal 1/18/03).
5. The United Nations used two flags interchangeably: one resembled the royal red-and-blue flag with the image of Angkor, and another featured the outline of the country on a baby-blue background, the color of the United Nations' own flag.
6. Sahlins 1987:152-154
7. Sahlins 1987:xiv; emphasis added
8. Sahlins 1987:139
9. Sahlins employed the concept of the "structure of the conjuncture" to show why Captain Cook, on his return trip to Hawai'i where he had formerly been considered a god, had to be killed by the inhabitants. The course of history was altered when Cook was slain. This was an unintended consequence of Cook's repeated interaction with Hawaiians, and it was only the direct result of the intersection of discordant cultural understandings (the macro-social), but also of the decisions of particular individuals operating within these conflicting cultural categories (the micro-social).
10. Sahlins 1987:152
11. Wertsch 2002:43-45
12. Of course, visitors have a certain level of flexibility in deciding where they would like to be taken, but if left to Cambodian travel companies or guides, this is an average (if very full) itinerary.
13. I was a tour director when this happened to one of my passengers in 2004.
14. Trebay 2001:260
15. A number of articles (cf. Paddock 2004) corroborate my own experience at being offered police badges by the guards.
16. Fieldnotes 2/17/04
17. Pearson and Richards 1994:5
18. See, for example, Wiley and Phillips 1958

19. The term "Western culture" is used here in an effort to emphasize the historical continuity of the colonial claims popular throughout nineteenth-century Europe, which were imbedded in several monuments during the French colonial restoration process. Such a term is, of course, a somewhat problematic generalization, not the least of which because several non-Western cultures, including Japan and India, are extremely active in numerous important conservation projects currently underway in the Angkor Archaeological Park.

20. Coe 2003:122

21. Kolb believes that labor investment in constructing monuments can be calculated and interpreted as to the extent of power exerted (Kolb 1994:521).

22. Rooney 2003:221

23. Coedes 1963:104

24. Most garden historians tend to make this point. For an excellent overview, see Hobhouse (2002). Indeed, the temple's proximity to adjacent East Baray reservoir, coupled with its utilization of the irrigation system would most likely render these courtyards fertile and vibrant with controlled vegetative growth.

25. Coe 2003:125

26. Coe also states that Angkor Wat's founder was a "thoroughgoing devotee of Vishnu: on his death around 1150 he received the posthumous name of Paramavishnuloka, 'who has rejoined the realm of the supreme Vishnu'" (Coe 2003:116).

27. Connerton 1989:6

28. According to inscriptions, Ta Prohm was called Rajavihara. "Ta Prohm" actually refers to one of its statues that the locals called "ancestor Brahma." Often called "grandfather," Brahma was the Hindu god who created this earthly existence, the pantheon of lesser gods, and Manu, the first man.

29. According to Trudy Jacobsen, the former was a member of the Vyadhapura people residing southeast of the Tonle Sap lake, while the latter was a Khmer from the northeast of the Tonle Sap; together these figures represented the first rulers of a unified Cambodian race (2003:361).

30. In chapter 9, lines 4-5 of the *Bhagavad Gītā*, Krishna, as the avatar of Vishnu, states that "All this world is strung on me in the form of the Unmanifest; all creatures exist in me, but I do not exit in them" (van Buitenen 1981:105).

31. Coe 2003:122

32. Schuhmacher and Woerner 1994:205

33. Rooney 2003:182

34. Angkor Thom is positioned southwest of Preah Khan and northwest of Ta Prohm; it can also be seen as the apex of a triangle pointing westward.

35. Scholars debate the iconography of these faces; many believe that the majority of them represent the Bodhisattva Avalokiteshvara, while the four larger, central faces pointing in the four cardinal directions represent Jayavarman VII surveying all directions of his empire (Rooney 2003:162). While in Cambodia the Avalokeshevara is "better known as Lokeshvara" (Tarling 1999:296), most distinguish between the depiction of Dharanindravarman II in Preah Khan as "Lokeshvara" and Jayavarman VII's supposed depiction of himself as Avalokiteshvara.

36. Schuhmacher and Woerner 1994:396
37. Rooney 2003:53
38. See the *Bhagavad Gītā*, chapters 7-12 (which corresponds to van Buitenen 1981:99-121). Van Buitenen also describes bhakti as "a form of religiosity specifically Hindu in that it allows a religious man to create out of a social polytheism a personal monotheism" (1981:25); I would argue that this also allows Jayavarman VII even more flexibility in creating a specifically Khmer syncretism in both religiosity and in aesthetic depictions.
39. In an unpublished talk, Alan Kolata (2007) makes a strong case for Jayavarman VII's "compassionate kingship" based on Kolata's own excavations of some of these hospitals.
40. Tarling 1999:162
41. One can also compare the presence of rest houses on the Iberian peninsula associated with the Camino, too: there are about eighty approved "rest stops" with hospices for pilgrims who make the pilgrimage on foot (there are more if one counts the entire pilgrimage route from France, which according to Pope Calixtus II's *Codex* authorizing the pilgrimage, could officially begin as far away as Arles, Tours (another French pilgrimage site), Vézelay or Le Puy or even from the Cistercian abbey of Cluny). This is important, as only those who obtain a stamp in their pilgrimage passport were allowed to stay at these houses and could receive a plenary indulgence upon arriving in the town of Santiago de Compostela. In addition to designating the town of Santiago de Compostela a World Heritage site, UNESCO lists the Route of Santiago de Compostela as a separate World Heritage "itinerary."
42. Coedès 1968:173, Tarling 1999:162
43. Personal communication 6/26/2008
44. Although the *Mahābhārata*, which contains the *Bhagavad Gītā*, is considered *smerti*—a text based on remembered tradition—because the Gita is pronounced by Krishna, it is often considered along with the Vedas as "divinely revealed" (*shruti*) and thus authorized by the divine.
45. Rooney 2003:125
46. The Western Gallery prominently features the Battle of Lanka, in which Rāma, aided by the Hanuman's monkey troops, defeats Rāvana and rescues his wife, Sītā.
47. Coedès 1968:165
48. Many guides will point this out, but see also a description in Rooney 2003:170-172.
49. Coedès 1968:xix
50. See, for example, Bourdieu's essay, "The Biographical Illusion" (1987) and my discussion of it in chapter 1, footnote 7.
51. Coedès 1968:175
52. In a shaft underneath this central shrine, archaeologists have uncovered fragmented remains of a large Buddha, which, Hingham points out, also is telling of the iconoclasm which occurred after Jayavarman's death (Hingham 2001:121).
53. Coedès 1968:175

54. In a shaft underneath this central shrine, archaeologists have uncovered the fragmented remains of a large Buddha, which, Higham points out, also is telling of the iconoclasm which occurred after Jayavarman's death (2001:121).
55. Said 1994:1-2 (emphasis in the original)
56. 1994:4
57. 1994:6
58. Sahlins 2000:489
59. Said 1994:11
60. Ponder 1936:305. See also footnote 37 in chapter 6.
61. Qtd. and translated by Dagens 1995:148 (emphasis added)
62. Qtd Dagens 1995:35
63. Emphasizing the parallels between the two civilizations, Wales places the founding of Rome at BC 475 and the mythological founding of Angkor at AD 475; his diagrams of the Italian peninsula and the Indochinese peninsula are strikingly similar, and even likens the Carthaginians to the Javanese.
64. Dagens 1995:47
65. Rooney 2003:224. Further underscoring this point, it should be mentioned that this book, illegally copied and sold local Cambodians within the Angkor Archaeological Park, are the most popular guides purchased by tourists visiting Angkor.
66. Qtd. in Paddock 2004. Although Preah Khan has been restored in a fashion that maintains the air of nature fused with culture, WMF Siem Reap does a very admirable job in contextualizing the life-story of Preah Khan through the use of on-site lectures with representatives from the organization, often with Sanday himself. This was made possible when WMF regulated the flow of visitors to "its" monastery in a much more selective fashion; when WMF was actively working at the site, permission had to be granted beforehand. Performed this way, Sanday's assertion that a historic structure should be preserved the way in which it is found carries adequate weight. Unfortunately there are not the same possibilities to contextualize similarly preserved sites that are open to the public, such as Ta Prohm.
67. Lowenthal 2004:26, 114
68. Assman 1997:9
69. Winter 2003:63
70. Morrison (n.d.):5
71. Pearson and Richards 1997:5
72. Gerd Albrecht, an archaeologist training Cambodians outside the Angkor Archaeological Park, comments that although foreign groups employ educated Cambodians to act as translators, and sometimes local laborers to assist, there is little to no local participation in the technical or decision-making aspects of preservation, even when official documents attest to it (personal communication). Winter also noted the difficulty of obtaining statistics on Cambodian participation, but that any involvement by locals is quite small (personal communication).
73. "In the house," he said, "beings—humans and animals, spirits, the god of the stairhead, the house spirit, which is the main column, and others—live together in tolerance and in harmony under the same roof above ground." Quoted Vachon 2003.

74. Funahashi, Daena. Private communication 4/6/05.
75. Quoted in Paddock 2004:1
76. England, Hildreth. Private communication 5/4/05 (emphasis in original).
77. Paddock 2004
78. Fieldnotes 8/18/2006
79. Paddock 2004:1
80. Duncan 2004:25. See also Bennett 1995.
81. UNESCO 1972:2
82. Quoted in McCarthy 2005:1. Experts in the area point out the difference between looting the Angkorian temples, which are recognized as symbols of the Khmer people and are thus regarded with great reverence, and cemeteries, pagodas or colonial palaces. One remarked, "It is hard to find villagers to destroy an Angkorian temple—they respect antiquities of that time—but very easy, for only few money, they will destroy a cemetery to look for [objects] . . . or a colonial palace, just for fun" (personal communication).
83. Personal communication 4/11/05
84. Albrecht, personal communication, 4/11/05
85. Sok 2004:1
86. Sahlins 1976:177; see also Baudrillard 1998
87. Quoted in Berlo 1995:7
88. Sok 2004:2

Chapter 11

1. UNESCO 2000b:6
2. Cuno 2004:52-53
3. Bennett 1995:39
4. Mauss 2000:13
5. Perhaps because authenticity is endowed with such early anthropological notions of primitivity that post-modernists such as Dean MacCannell regard travel as "a quest of authenticity," as Erik Cohen points out. "Since modern society is inauthentic, those modern seekers who desire to overcome the opposition between their authenticity-seeking self and society have to look elsewhere for authentic life. The quest for authenticity thus becomes a prominent motif of modern tourism, as MacCannell (1973, 1976) so incisively showed." But, perhaps because an object is considered authentic in the Malinowskian sense as possessing an irreducible *hau* that was more evident in simpler times, MacCannell and others confuse the notion as a "primitive concept." Cohen discusses this when he synthesizes MacCannell's post-modernist, Marxist position: "The alienated modern tourist in quest of authenticity hence looks for the pristine, the primitive, the natural, that which is as yet untouched by modernity. He hopes to find it in other times and other places (MacCannell 1976:160). This, as Cohen rightly points out, is a serious confusion of the "philosophical concept" of authenticity with that of a subjective "criterion of

evaluation used by the modern tourist as observer" (Cohen 2004:103). Note: MacCannell 1976 is cited in this book as MacCannell 1999; as I have mentioned in chapter 4, MacCannell 1999 includes a "post-modern" update to the original work.

6. Durkheim 1995:230-231. Emphasis added.
7. Bennett 1995:42
8. Stating that "Heritage Produces the Local for Export," Kirshenblatt-Gimblett writes, "tourism is an export industry and one of the world's largest. Unlike other export industries, however, tourism does not export goods for consumption elsewhere. Rather, it imports visitors to consume goods and services locally" (1998:153).
9. Duncan 2004:12
10. Duncan 2004:13
11. Duncan 2004:14-15. Citing museum historian Niels von Holst, Duncan quotes an eighteenth century museum visitor Wilhelm Wackenroder who in 1797 said that interacting with art removed the museum patron from the "vulgar flux of life" and engaged him in an experience akin to that which one has in a church or temple (von Holst 1967:216 in Duncan 2004:15).
12. Duncan quotes an English critic who writes in 1819 that inside the museum,

> The business of the world at large, and even its pleasures, appear like a vanity and impertinence. What signify the hubbub, the shifting scenery, the fantoccini figures, the folly, the idle fashions without, when compared with the solitude, the silence, the speaking looks, the unfading forms within? Here is the mind's true home. The contemplation of truth and beauty is the proper object for which we were created, which calls forth the most intense desires of the soul, and of which it never tires (Hazlitt 1824:2-4 qtd. Duncan 2004:15).

There is, however, a relationship between contemplation and action. Though the museum prescribes a contemplative disposition, such a civilized temperament was supposed to be carried over into the "real world." In *Bodyworlds*, a contemporary traveling anatomical exhibition of plastinated human cadavers, proper action regarding reverence to the body is supposed to be carried over into the real world; after visitors examine lung cancer victims, for example, the exhibit managers offer a chance for smokers to deposit their cigarette packs and sign a cease-smoking pledge.

13. Fieldnotes 8/19/2006
14. First published in Paris in 1997, Emmanuel Guillon's book, *Hindu-Buddhist Art of Vietnam: Treasures from Champa* is recognized as the first comprehensive catalogue of the Museum's collections since Henri Parmentier's publication in 1919, although it was not necessarily intended to serve in this capacity. Indeed, it was not sponsored by the Museum, but rather by Guillon's charitable organization, the French Association of Friends of the Orient (AFAO). As such, it was at first only available to members and not for commercial resale. However, the AFAO donated many copies to the Cham Museum, allowing them to legally sell photocopies, royalty-free, as a catalogue to visitors wishing to obtain a more in-depth understanding of the collection. In April 2001, a paperback version was published for commercial use, and can be purchased in bookstores and online, although

museum visitors can still purchase bound photocopies of the earlier, trilingual version (English, Vietnamese and French) at the museum for considerably less.

15. Guillon 2001:10
16. www.creotec.com/index.php?page=e-business_terms. Other definitions of the term "cyberspace" often refer to placemaking directly. For example, Hawaii's Public *School's E-handbook* defines cyberspace as "a nebulous place where humans interact over computer networks." From www.k12.hi.us/~ehandboo/glossary.html. Accessed on January 13, 2006.
17. www.webpronews.com/ebusiness/seo/wpn-420040422NaturalSearchTheGreatEqual izer.html Accessed on January 13, 2006. One website states that it is the "new great equalizer since the Colt pistol arrived in the West" (www.lionhrtpub.com/ee/ee-spring98/erp.html Accessed January 13, 2006).
18. Just as the heritage-scape has yet to touch all individuals the world over, so too is the Internet geo-socially constrained; it remains unevenly distributed and controlled. As I argued at the close of chapter 1 and again later in this chapter, the eco-politics of web design and management also contribute to uneven representation of users.
19. There was talk of regulating the Internet country by country, and the largest search engine, Google, agreed to China's request to block websites the communist government deems offensive or subversive (cf. BBC Online 2002).
20. Robert Pennoyer, personal communication
21. Boot 2006:1
22. Complementing the work of international intelligence communities, freelance International Terrorism Consultant Evan Kohlman systematically tracks these blogs on his website, www.globalterroralert.com.
23. Accessible at www.kiddofspeed.com
24. www.kiddofspeed.com, Accessed September 27, 2006
25. UNESCO 1948
26. UNESCO 1948:113
27. UNESCO 1948:114
28. UNESCO 1948:113
29. This can be found in Article I.c (UNESCO 1945:3)
30. UNESCO 1950
31. UNESCO 1952
32. UNESCO 1958a, 1958b
33. UNESCO 1971:1
34. UNESCO 1974:1
35. UNESCO 1979a
36. Search conducted on September 27, 2006 on Google.com.
37. The webmaster does, however, provide links to UNESCO.
38. http://camweb.org/index.php?module=NukeWrapper&file=aboutus/aboutus.html Accessed on September 27, 2006.
39. This moniker has been used since the first half of the twenty-first century. For this term used with respect to the Chinese market, see, for example, China 2002
40. See, for example, Lyman 2004 or Kirkpatrick 2006.

41. Although this book uses diacritics on the Vietnamese proper names, the search used the more common, anglicized version to cast a wider net; to a certain extent, it also presupposed the emergence of websites by Westerners.
42. I also referred to this blog in chapter 4.
43. Trebay 2001:260
44. George 2005:65
45. Boorstin 1987
46. Mayes 1996. The film has changed a number of elements, including how impulsively Mayes supposedly chose this farmhouse. In the book, Mayes and her husband, both professors in San Francisco, decide to look into purchasing a farmhouse after visiting Tuscany for the first time on holiday. The film, however, portrays a single Mayes who, in the midst of a mid-life crisis and on a group tour to Tuscany, one day impulsively purchases a run-down home.
47. By "Tuscan countryside" I am differentiating between those tours that only stop at Florence or Pisa. Such tours are not only thematically different, but the cities themselves are located quite a distance away from both Cortona and the Val d'Orcia. Furthermore, my terminology excludes the "whirlwind tours" of Italy that visit only Rome, Florence and Venice (with perhaps an occasional stop *en route* elsewhere).
48. Origo 1995
49. UNESCO 2004a 45-46
50. http://whc.unesco.org/en/list/1026. Accessed on January 13, 2006.
51. ICOMOS 2003:132
52. This assertion is based on my personal experiences operating large group tours to Japan, where I spoke with travelers about the book. Many had brought the book with them or had just finished reading it. Additionally, some sponsoring organizations requested we build the tours in with walking tours to Gion—Kyoto's geisha district—and feature a dinner served by geishas. My personal communications with members of the Japan National Tourist Organization in New York, and with Japanese guides, also corroborate this.
53. Fieldnotes 4/18/2003
54. See Winter 2002 (reprinted, with slight variations, in Winter 2003) for a thoughtful and in-depth discussion of *Tomb Raider* and Angkor.

Conclusion

1. Appadurai 1996
2. For a general theory on heritage, I owe much to Kirshenblatt-Gimblett 1988, who discusses heritage sites as museum forms; for tourism I have used Graburn's concept of a "secular ritual" (Graburn 1983, Graburn 1989), in addition to the works of Cohen 1979, MacCannell 1999, Nash 1989, and Urry 2002. For community formation I have relied on Anderson 2003; background theory on memory and monumentality are based on Alcock 2002's general introduction, and fuse collective memory theories from Halbwachs 1992, Connerton 1989, Wertsch 2002. Most

importantly, the concept of the *–scape* is based on the globalization theory articulated by Appadurai 1996.

3. I supplemented my own ethnographic research in the field with the following particularly helpful works detailing Angkor's history and Khmer culture, both past and present: Norindr 1999, Tarling 1999, Winter 2002, Coe 2003, Edwards 2007.
4. Malinowski 1984:3-8
5. Durkheim 1982:35
6. Malinowski 1984:6-7
7. Malinowski 1984:19
8. Durkheim 1995:223
9. Durkheim 1982:129
10. Sahlins 2000:488, Durkheim 1984:38-9
11. Barth 1969:13, 29
12. See, for example, chapter 2's mention of Alfonso Pecoraro Scanio's endeavor to declare pizza a masterpiece of Italian heritage. The linkage between this and Intangible Heritage was made by Barbara Kirshenblatt-Gimblett 2004:56.
13. To review, the Bayon, Ta Prohm and Preah Khan housed monumental statues of the Buddha in the likenesses of Jayavarman VII, his mother and his father; inscriptions contextualized the statuary as such. Furthermore, the Bayon and other monuments were endowed with elaborate bas reliefs depicting Cham, Khmer and Chinese warriors in battle, as well as daily life processes such as cooking, fishing and hunting. These were further contextualized through their juxtaposition with other reliefs depicting mythological tropes taken from such foundational cultural and religious works such as the *Rāmayana* and the *Mahābhārata*.
14. Kazmi 2008
15. One Thai tour operator reacted to my calling the site Preah Vihear by calling the site Khao Prah Wihan and then providing the following unsolicited explanation:

> Khao Prah Wihan and Prasat Preah Vihear are exactly the same place, the differences in the names arise from three sources, mainly the difficulty in translating Thai or Cambodian into English, secondly the differences in the name in either Thai or Khmer, and thirdly the difference between the physical name and the proper religious name. Khao Phra Wihan is the place here the Temple is located, and is Thai-based. Prasat Preah Vihear is the Temple itself and is Khmer-based" (personal communication, 4/23/2008).

This reveals how overlapping claims on the temple between Thailand and Cambodia are negotiated by locals within the field of touristic production.
16. AP-Worldstream 2008
17. Thai Press Reports 2008b
18. UNESCO 2008b:16
19. Personal communication, 4/23/2008
20. AP 2008
21. Deutsche Presse-Agentur 2008; AP 2008

22. Cf. UNESCO 2001b, UNESCO 2002b, UNESCO 2003c, UNESCO 2004a, UNESCO 2005c, UNESCO 2006d, UNESCO 2007a
23. This is based on a public statement by Thailand's Foreign Minister Noppadon Pattama during a Constitutional Court hearing on July 4, 2008. Attempting to defer criticism on his government's agreement with Cambodia in May 2008, he contended that the military-installed government, which ousted Thaksin Shinawatra in September 2006 and represented Thailand at the thirty-first Committee meeting in New Zealand, made the pledge (BBC Monitoring Reports 2008)
24. Ministry of Foreign Affairs 2008
25. Ministry of Foreign Affairs 2008
26. Thai Press Reports 2008a
27. Ministry of Foreign Affairs 2008
28. BBC Monitoring Reports 2008
29. The day that Preah Vihear was designated was called by the international media "the most contentious of its 8-day meeting" (cf. Deutsche Presse-Agentur 2008b).
30. This number is probably inflated; some news sources claim 3,000, others 40,000.
31. Thai Press Reports 2008c
32. Thai Press Reports 2008e
33. Wassana 2008:1
34. Thai Press Reports 2008d. Indeed, Ayutthaya is a short trip north from Bangkok, and Sukhothai is further north, en route to Chiang Mai. These are both World Heritage sites for their history as Thai capitals, rather than as Khmer settlements.
35. When Prime Minister Samak visited his troops on August 19, 2008, there were 300 troops positioned on the Thai side and 500 on the Cambodian side.
36. Onnucha 2008:4
37. Fieldnotes 8/16/2008
38. Turner 1969:131
39. Turner 1974b:202
40. Turner 1974b:201
41. Turner 1969:131
42. Turner 1974a:217
43. Sahlins 2000:488
44. These two elements are intertwined in the war-torn countries of Afghanistan and Iraq—the former has seen the purposeful destruction of immense Buddhist statuary by the Taliban shortly before the regime was toppled in 2001, and the latter has been ravaged by extensive looting of museums and archaeological sites immediately following the 2003 American invasion.
45. By this, I am thinking about Barth 1969, Bateson 1972 and Clifford 2002. For a variety of acculturation perspectives germane to this discussion, see Redfield, Linton and Herskovits 1936; Herskovits 1958; Lycett 2002; Silliman 2005.
46. www.turkishembassy.org/index.php?option=com_content&task=view&id=511&Ite mid=489. Downloaded on October 23, 2007. Emphasis added.
47. Appadurai 2005:21
48. UNESCO 2005:9

49. Qtd. in the informational website of the NGO Saving Antiquities for Everyone (SAFE): www.savingantiquities.org/aboutusmission.php. Accessed July 24, 2008.
50. www.autoriteapsara.org/en/apsara/about_apsara/history_organization.html. Accessed on September 23, 2007.
51. www.autoriteapsara.org/en/apsara/about_apsara/history_organization.html. Accessed on September 23, 2007.
52. UNESCO 2003b
53. Soubert and Hay 1995:2
54. Soubert and Hay counts 16,993 tourists in Cambodia, with only 5,194 visiting Siem Reap; they state that "the number of Thai and Taiwanese tourists was high" and accounted for some 70% of the total number of visitors. Representing over 10% of the total tourists, the Japanese were the largest group of visitors in the ethnic categories considered (1995:6-7).
55. This number, however, represents only a 12% of the total foreign visitors to Cambodia, which totaled 87,720—a 246% increase over the previous year. Angkor was officially designated as a World Heritage site at the end of that year.
56. These percentages are total tourist numbers for Cambodia, calculated from the following data:1992:87,720 (Soubert and Hay 1995:3); 1993:118,183; 1996:218,843 (Source: Immigration Department, Ministry of the Interior, Kingdom of Cambodia. Accessed from the Royal Cambodian Embassy's website, www.embassy.org/cambodia/toursim/tour.htm#STATISTICS on October 23, 2007).
57. In the period of 2000-2004, Cambodia had the highest growth rate in the UNWTO's Asia and Pacific category with an average increase of 22.1%, and placed sixth in the world, following Kyrgyzstan (61.2%), Armenia (55.5%), Angola (39.7%), Yemen (39.2%), and Uganda (27.6%). (UNWTO 2005:1)
58. UNESCO 1994a
59. UNESCO 1994a. Emphasis added.
60. UNESCO 1983:8
61. From Saltaire's website, www.saltaire-village.co.uk/saltaire-info.html. Accessed on October 23, 2007.
62. "Saltaire" from ICOMOS' website, http://icomos-uk.org/whs/saltaire. Accessed on October 23, 2007.
63. Private conversation 7/21/2007
64. European Industrial Heritage Route. http://en.erih.net. Accessed October 23, 2007.
65. Private conversation 7/21/2007
66. Private conversation 7/19/2007
67. Qtd. in Hewison 1989:15
68. From UNESCO's webpage dedicated to the Sydney Opera House: http://whc.unesco.org/en/list/166. Accessed on July 31, 2007.
69. ICOMOS 2007:89
70. AP 2007b:1
71. Personal communication 7/20/2007
72. AP 2007b:1
73. ICOMOS 2007:89

74. ICOMOS 2007:89-90
75. AP 2007b:1
76. Šopova 2007:1
77. Wertsch 2002:45
78. UNESCO 2007a:160

Bibliography

Abbink, Jon
  2000 "Tourism and its Discontents. Suri-Tourist Encounters in Southern Ethiopia." *Social Anthropology* Vol. 8 No. 2, pp. 1–17.
Abu El-Haj, Nadia
  2001 *Facts on the Ground*. Chicago: University of Chicago Press.
Agence France Presse—English
  2006 "UN Questions Vietnam About Cement Plant Near Protected Halong Bay." July 12, 2006. Accessed through Lexis Nexis on July 13, 2006.
Alcock, Susan E.
  2001 "The Reconfiguration of Memory in the Eastern Roman Empire." In *Empires: Perspectives from Archaeology and History*. Alcock, Susan, ed. Cambridge: Cambridge University Press, 2001, pp. 323–350.
  2002 *Archaeologies of Greek Past*. Cambridge: Cambridge University Press.
Alpers, Svetlana
  1991 "The Museum as a Way of Seeing." In *Exhibiting Cultures: The Poetics and Politics of Museum Display*, edited by Ivan Karp and Steven D. Lavine. Washington, DC: Smithsonian Institution Press, pp 25–32.
Amery, Colin
  2001 *Vanishing Histories: 100 Endangered Sites from the World Monuments Watch*. New York: Harry N. Abrams, Inc.
Anderson, Benedict
  2003 *Imagined Communities*. NY: Verso.
Ang, Chouléan; Eric Prenowitz and Ashley Thompson
  1998 *Angkor—Past, Present and Future*. Phnom Penh: APSARA.
AP (Associated Press)
  2007a "Court Gives Go-Ahead to Disputed Dresden Bridge, Despite Worries over Bats." *International Herald Tribune*. November 14, 2007. www.iht.com/bin/printfriendly.php?id=8330711. Accessed on November 15, 2007.
  2007b "Sydney Opera House Saga Plays On As Visionary Architect's Sight Dims." *International Herald Tribune*—Asia-Pacific online edition. March 28, 2007. www.iht.com/articles/ap/2007/03/29/asia/AS-GEN-Australia-Opera-House-Drama.php. Accessed on October 23, 2007.

2008   "Temple on Disputed Cambodia Border a Heritage Site." Associated Press, July 8, 2008. Accessed through Lexus Nexis on July 8, 2008.

AP-Worldstream
   2008   "900-Year-Old Temple on Disputed Thai-Cambodia border Named World Heritage Site." Associated Press, July 8, 2008. Accessed through Lexus Nexis on July 8, 2008.

Appadurai, Arjun
   1996   *Modernity at Large.* Minneapolis: University of Minnesota Press.
   2005   *The Social Life of Things: Commodities in Cultural Perspective.* Cambridge: Cambridge University Press.

APSARA
   2006   "Declaration of Tokyo." October 13, 1993. www.autoriteapsara.org/en/apsara/about_apsara/history_organization/tokyo_declaration.html. Accessed on June 23, 2006.

Asad, Talal
   1993   *Genealogies of Religion: Discipline and Reasons of Power in Christianity and Islam.* Baltimore, MD: Johns Hopkins University Press.

Asia News/Scmp
   2006   "Only Tourists Can Kiss, But Not Passionately." April 6, 2006. www.asianews.it/index.php?l=en&art=5854#. Accessed on April 6, 2006.

Assman, Jan
   1997   *Moses the Egyptian: the Memory of Egypt in Western Monotheism.* Cambridge: Harvard University Press.

Augustine of Hippo
   1958   *The City of God.* Translated by Gerald Walsh, Demetrius Zema, Grace Monahan and Daniel Honan. New York: NY: Doubleday.

Bann, Stephen
   1984   *The Clothing of Clio: A Study of the Representation of History in Nineteenth-Century Britain and France.* Cambridge: Cambridge University Press.

Barris, Roann
   2005   "Course Materials: Nonwestern Art." Charleston, Ill: Eastern Illinois State College, 2005. www.ux1.eiu.edu/~cfrb/chineselandscape.htm. Accessed on October 4, 2005.

Barth, Fredrik
   1969   "Introduction." In *Ethnic Groups and Boundaries.* Boston: Little, Brown and Co., pp. 9–38.

Bateson, Gregory
   1972   "Culture Contact and Schismogenesis." In *Steps to an Ecology of Mind.* NY: Ballantine Books, pp. 61–72.

Bath, Brian
   2006   "The Use of New Technology in the Interpretation of Historic Landscapes." In Hems, Alison and Marion Blockley, eds. *Heritage Interpretation.* New York: Routledge, 2006.

Baudrillard, Jean
   1998   *The Consumer Society.* London: Sage.

BBC Monitoring Reports
  2008   "Thai Minister Blames Last Government for Supporting Cambodia's Temple
         Claim." Bangkok: *Bangkok Post*, July 5, 2008.
BBC Online
  2002   "China Blocking Google," September 2, 2002. http://news.bbc.co.uk/2/hi/tech-
         nology/2231101.stm. Accessed on September 27, 2006.
Becker, Howard S.
  1976   "Art Worlds and Social Types." *American Behavioral Scientist.* Vol 19, No. 6,
         pp. 703–719.
  1982   *Art Worlds.* Berkeley: University of California Press.
Benjamin, Walter
  1968   "The Work of Art in the Age of Mechanical Reproduction." In *Illuminations*,
         trans. Harry Zohn. New York: Schocken Books, pp 217–251.
Bennett, Tony
  1995   *The Birth of the Museum.* London: Routledge.
Bentley, B. Charles
  1986   "Indigenous States of Southeast Asia." *Annual Review of Anthropology.* Vol.
         15, pp. 275–305.
Berlo, Janet Catherine and Ruth B. Phillips
  1995   "The Problematics of Collecting and Display, Part 1." *Art Bulletin* LXXXVII
         no. 1, March 1995, pp. 6–24.
Berno, Tracy and Colleen Ward
  2005 "Innocence Abroad." *American Psychologist.* Vol. 60, No. 6, September 2005,
         pp. 593–600.
Blumer, Herbert
  1969   *Symbolic Interactionism: Perspective and Method.* Englewood Cliffs, NJ: Pren-
         tice Hall.
Boorstin, Daniel J.
  1994   *The Image: A Guide to Pseudo-Events in America.* New York: Vintage Books.
Boot, Max
  2006   "Securing Baghdad is a Numbers Game" *Los Angeles Times*, May 24, 2006.
Bourdieu, Pierre
  1977   *Outline of a Theory of Practice.* Translated by Richard Nice. New York: Cam-
         bridge University Press.
  1987 "The Biographical Illusion." Translated by Yves Winkin and Wendy Leeds-
         Hurwitz. In *Working Papers and Proceedings of the Center for Psychosocial
         Studies.* No.14.
  1984   *Distinction: A Social Critique of the Judgment of Taste.* Translated by Richard
         Nice. Cambridge: Harvard University Press.
  1993   *The Field of Cultural Production.* New York: Columbia University Press.
Box, Paul
  1999   *GIS and Cultural Resource Management: A Manual for Heritage Managers.*
         Bangkok: UNESCO Principal Regional Office for Asia and the Pacific.
Boym, Svetlana
  2001   *The Future of Nostalgia.* New York: Basic Books.

Bronson, Bennet
   1978   "Angkor, Anuradhapura, Prambanan, Tikal: Maya Subsistence in an Asian Per-
           spective." in *Pre-Hispanic Maya Agriculture*, ed. P.D. Harrison and B.L.
           Turner. Albuquerque: University of New Mexico Press.

Brooks, J. G. and Brooks, M.
   1993   *In Search of Understanding: The Case for Constructivist Classrooms*. Alexan-
           dria, VA: Association for Supervision and Curriculum Development.

Bruner, Edward M.
   2004   *Culture on Tour: Ethnographies on Travel.* Chicago: University of Chicago
           Press.

Bryant, Margi
   2006   "Tilden's Children: Interpretation in Britain's National Parks." In *Heritage In-
           terpretation*. Hems, Alison and Marion Blockley, eds. London: Routledge.

Burawoy, Michael, ed.
   2000   *Global Ethnography*. Berkeley: University of California Press.

Butcher, Jim
   2003   *The Moralisation of Tourism: Sun, Sand. . . . And Saving the World?* London:
           Rutledge.

Cabrini, Luigi
   2006   "Conclusions." Remarks given at the *UNWTO Conference on "Impact of Euro-
           pean Union Enlargement on tourism development in Europe"* held in Vilnius,
           Lithuania, March 1–2, 2006. http://www.world-tourism.org/regional/europe/
           menu.htm. Accessed on March 10, 2006.

Candee, H. Churchill
   1925   *Angkor, The Magnificent, The Wonder City of Ancient Cambodia.* London:
           H. F. & G Witherby.

Carruthers, Mary
   1992   *The Book of Memory: A Study of Memory in Medieval Culture.* Cambridge:
           Cambridge University Press.

Central Intelligence Agency
   2005   "Cambodia." *CIA World Fact Book*, www.cia.gov/cia/publications/factbook/
           geos/cb.html. Accessed on November 1, 2005.

Chappel, Eliot D. and Carlton S. Coon
   1942   *Principles of Anthropology*. New York: Holt.

Clarkson, Diane
   2006   "U.S. Travel Consumer Survey 2006" JupiterResearch. Accessed May 2, 2006.

Clifford, James
   2002   *The Predicament of Culture: Twentieth-Century Ethnography, Literature and
           Art*. Cambridge: Harvard University Press.

Coe, Michael
   1957   "The Khmer Settlement Pattern: A Possible Analogy with that of the Maya."
           American Antiquity 22, no. 4.
   1961   "Social Typology and the Tropical Forest Civilizations." *Comparative Studies
           in Society and History* 4, no. 1, 1961.
   2003   *Angkor and the Khmer Civilization.* London: Thames and Hudson.

Coedès, George
    1963   *Angkor: An Introduction.* Translated by Emily Floyd Gardiner. London: Oxford University Press.
    1968   *The Indianized States of Southeast Asia.* Translated by Sue Brown Cowing. Walter F. Vella, ed. Honolulu: University of Hawai'i Press.

Cohen, Erik
    1979   "A Phenomenology of Tourist Experiences." *Sociology.* Volume 13, Number 2, 1979: 179–201.
    2004   *Contemporary Tourism: Diversity and Change.* New York: Elsevier.

Conklin, Beth and Laura Graham
    1995   "The Shifting Middle Ground: Amazonian Indians and Eco-Politics." *American Anthropologist.* Vol. 97, No. 4, pp. 695–710.

Conn, Steven
    1998   *Museums and American Intellectual Life.* Chicago: University of Chicago Press.

Connerton, Paul
    1989   *How Societies Remember.* New York: Cambridge University Press.

Copeland, Tim
    2006   "Constructing Pasts: Interpreting the Historic Environment," in Hems, Alison and Marion Blockley, eds. *Heritage Interpretation.* New York: Routledge.

Cox, Christopher
    2004   "Monumental Dilemma." *Travel + Leisure,* December 2004. www.travelandleisure.com/invoke.cfm?ObjectID=AB4CF9B3-7AD5-4C93-83CC5C396BC37091. Accessed on April 8, 2005.

Cuno, James, ed.
    2004   *Whose Muse? Art Museums and the Public Trust.* Princeton: Princeton University Press.

Dagens, Bruno
    1995   *Angkor: Heart of an Asian Empire.* New York: Harry N. Abrams, Inc.

Dale, Edgar
    1946   "The Cone of Experience." In *Audio-Visual Methods in Teaching.* NY: Dryden Press, pp. 37–51.
    1953   "What Does it Mean to Communicate?" *AV Communication Review,* Washington, DC: National Education Association. Vol. 1, No. 1, pp. 3–5.

Daniel, Glyn Edmund
    2007   "Schliemann, Heinrich." *Encyclopædia Britannica.* Encyclopædia Britannica Online. http://search.eb.com/eb/article-6488. Accessed on September 25, 2007.

Darwin, Charles
    2005   *The Darwin Compendium.* New York: Barnes and Noble Publishing, Inc.

Davis, Richard H.
    1997   *Lives of Indian Images.* Princeton: Princeton University Press.

de Botton, Alain
    2002   *The Art of Travel.* New York: Vintage Books.

Dellios, Paulette
    2002   "The Museumification of the Village: Cultural Subversion in the 21st Century." Paper prepared for *The Third IIDS (International Institute for Development*

Studies) Conference, Bhubaneswar, Orissa, India, January 3–6, 2002.

Deutsche Presse-Agentur

2008a "Analyst: UN Listing of Hindu Temple Adds to Thai Political Crisis." Deutsche Presse-Agentur, July 8, 2008. Accessed on Lexus Nexis July 8, 2008.

2008b "Cambodia's Disputed Hindu Temple Joins Heritage List." Deutsche Presse-Agentur, July 7, 2008. Accessed through Lexus Nexis on July 8, 2008.

Dharma, Po

2001   "The History of Champa" in *Hindu-Buddhist Art of Viet Nam*, Emmanuel Guillon, ed. Trumbull, CT: Weatherhill, Inc.

Dietler, Michael

2001   "Digesting the Feast." In M. Dietler and B. Hayden, eds. *Feasts: Archaeological and Ethnographic Perspectives on Food, Politics and Power.* Washington, DC: Smithsonian Press.

Duncan, Carol

2004   *Civilizing Rituals: Inside Public Art Museums.* New York: Routledge.

Durkheim, Emile

1982   *The Rules of Sociological Method.* New York: The Free Press.

1984   *The Division of Labor in Society.* New York, NY: The Free Press.

1995   *The Elementary Forms of Religious Life.* New York: The Free Press.

Edwards, Penny

2007   *Camboge: The Cultivation of a Nation, 1860–1945.* Honolulu: University of Hawai'i Press.

Elkins, James

2001   *Pictures & Tears.* New York: Rutledge.

Embassy of Cambodia

2005   "Tourism in the Kingdom of Cambodia." www.embassy.org/cambodia/toursim/tour.htm. Accessed on April 8, 2005.

Entertainment Wire

1997   "Yanni 'Tribute' Album, TV Special and Concert Dates Set New Records in Mexico and North America." November 25, 1997. www.serve.com/gregl7/entwire.htm. Accessed on December 20, 2005.

Falk, John H. and Lynn D. Dierking

2004   "The Contextual Model of Learning." In *Reinventing the Museum: Historical and Contemporary Perspectives on the Paradigm Shirt*, edited by Gail Anderson. Walnut Creek, CA: AltaMira Press, pp. 139–142.

Field Operations Design Firm

2001   "Lifescape: Fresh Kills Landfill to Landscape Design Competition." Pamphlet. New York: *Field Operations Design Firm.*

Fisher, Philip

1991   *Making and Effacing Art: Modern American Art in a Culture of Museums.* Cambridge: Harvard University Press.

Fjellman, Stephen M.

1992   *Vinyl Leaves: Walt Disney World and America.* Boulder: Westview Press.

Florence, Mason and Robert Storey

2001   *Vietnam.* Oakland, CA: Lonely Planet Publications.

Flower, Sir William Henry
  1898 *Essays on Museums and Other Subjects Connected with Natural History*. London: Macmillan and Company.

Fogelson, Raymond D.
  1991 "The Red Man in the White City." In D.H. Thomas, ed. *Columbian Consequences*. Vol. 3. Smithsonian Institution, pp. 73–90.

Fowler, Peter
  1989 "Heritage: A Post-Modernist Perspective" in Uzzell, David, ed. *Heritage Interpretation*. London: Belhaven Press.
  2003 *World Heritage Cultural Landscapes 1992–2002*. Paris: UNESCO World Heritage Series.

Frangialli, Francesco
  2001 "Address by Francesco Frangialli Secretary-General of the World Tourism Organization to the Third UN Conference on the Least Developed Countries." Brussels: World Tourism Organization, May 17, 2001.

Freud, Sigmund
  1950 *The Standard Edition of the Complete Psychological Works of Sigmund Freud. Volume XIV* (tr. James Strachey). London: The Hogarth Press.

Fulton, Rachel
  2002 *From Judgment to Passion: Devotion to Christ and the Virgin Mary, 800–1200*. New York: Columbia University Press.

Galitz, Kathryn Calley
  2005 "Romanticism" from *Metropolitan Museum of Art Presents a Timeline of Art History* website. NY: Metropolitan Museum of Art. www.metmuseum.org/toah/hd/roma/hd_roma.htm. Accessed on October 4, 2005.

Galla, Amareswar
  2002 "Culture and Heritage in Development: Ha Long Ecomuseum, A Case Study from Vietnam." *Humanities Research*. Vol. IX, No. 1, pp. 63–76.

Geary, Patrick
  1994 *Phantoms of Remembrance: Memory and Oblivion at the End of the First Millennium*. Princeton: Princeton University Press.

Geertz, Clifford
  2000 *The Interpretation of Cultures*. New York: Basic Books.

George, Don
  2005 *Travel Writing*. Oakland, CA: Lonely Planet.

Giddens, Anthony
  1990 *The Consequences of Modernity*. Stanford: Stanford University Press.
  1991 *Modernity and Self-Identity*. Cambridge: Polity Press.

GLNWA (Global News Wire Asia Pulse Pty Limited)
  2006 "Thailand Eastern Provinces to Promote Trade and Tourism with Cambodia." *Financial Times Information*. Accessed on March 9, 2006.

Graburn, Nelson
  1983 "The Anthropology of Tourism." *Annals of Tourism Research*. Vol. 10, 1983, pp. 9–33.

1989	"Tourism: The Sacred Journey" in Smith, Valene (ed.) *Hosts and Guests: The Anthropology of Tourism*. Philadelphia: The University of Pennsylvania Press.

Gray, PJ
2006	"(Family) Cruising." *Pink*. Spring 2006.

Greenblatt, Stephen
1990	*Learning to Curse: Essays in Modern Culture*. New York: Routledge.
1991	"Resonance and Wonder," In Karp, Ivan and Steven D. Lavine, eds. *Exhibiting Cultures*. Washington, DC: Smithsonian Press, pp 42–56.

Groslier, Bernard
1966	*Angkor: Art and Civilization*. Translated by Eric Ernshaw Smith. New York: Frederick A. Praeger, Inc.

Guillon, Emmanuel ed.
2001	"History of the Museum." In *Hindu-Buddhist Art of Viet Nam*, Emmanuel Guillon, ed. Trumbull, CT: Weatherhill, Inc., pp. 10–13.

Haas, Peter M.
1992	"Introduction: Epistemic Communities and International Policy Coordination." *International Organization* Vol 46, No. 1, Winter 1992.

Hafstein, Vladimar Tr.
2004	"The Making of Intangible Cultural Heritage: Tradition and Authenticity, Community and Humanity." Ph.D. Dissertation. Berkeley: University of California. In *ProQuest Digital Dissertations* [database online]; Available on www.proquest.com (publication number AAT 3165395).

Hai, Chau
2007	"U.S. Association Awards Hai Van Tunnel." *VietNamNet*. January 24, 2007. http://english.vietnamnet.vn/biz/2007/01/657251. Accessed on Feb. 13, 2008.

Halbwachs, Maurice
1992	*On Collective Memory*. Chicago: University of Chicago Press.

Harris Poll
2005	www.harrisinteractive.com/harris_poll/index.asp?PID=526. December 8, 2004. Accessed on January 10, 2005.

Harvey, David
1990	*The Condition of Post-Modernity*. Malden, MA: Blackwell Publishers.
1996	*Justice, Nature, & the Geography of Difference* Oxford: Blackwell.

Hegel, Georg Wilhelm Friedrich
1956	*The Philosophy of History*. Translated by J. Sibree. New York: Dover Publications, Inc.

Heine-Geldern, Robert
1966	"The Problem of Transpacific Influences in Mesoamerica." in *Handbook of Middle American Indians*, Vol 4. ed. Gordon F. Ekholm and Gordon R. Willey. Austin: University of Texas Press.

Herskovits, Melville J.
1958	*Acculturation: The Study of Cultural Contact*. Gloucester, MA: Peter Smith.

Hewison, Robert
1989	"Heritage: An Interpretation." In Uzzell, David ed. *Heritage Interpretation Volume I*. London: Belhaven Press, pp. 15–23.

Higham, Charles
    2001 *The Civilization of Angkor.* Berkeley: University of California Press.
Hobhouse, Penelope
    2002 *The Story of Gardening.* London: Dorling Kindersley.
Hockey, Jennifer
    1990 *Experiences of Death: An Anthropological Account.* Edinburgh, UK: Edinburgh University Press.
Homans, Peter
    2004 Class Handout "Rewriting the Past." February 13, 2004.
Hood, Marilyn G.
    2004 "Staying Away: Why People Choose Not to Visit Museums." In *Reinventing the Museum: Historical and Contemporary Perspectives on the Paradigm Shirt,* edited by Gail Anderson. Walnut Creek, CA: AltaMira Press, pp. 150–157.
Hooper-Greenhill, Eileen
    1989 "The Museum in the Disciplinary Society." In Pearce, Susan ed. *Museum Studies in Material Culture.* Leicester: Leicester University Press.
    1992 *Museums and the Shaping of Knowledge.* London, United Kingdom: Routledge
Hospitality Net
    2003 "'WTO Tourism Highlights, Edition 2003': Changes in Market Behavior and Weak World Economy Dictate Tourism Trends." Press Release. October 14, 2003. www.hospitalitynet.org/news/4017359.print. Accessed January 27, 2006.
ICOMOS (International Council on Monuments and Sites)
    1978 "World Heritage List No. 31." Paris: World Heritage Center, June 6, 1978.
    1987 "Hadrian's Wall Military Zone. No. 430." Paris: World Heritage Center, December 23, 1986 (Submitted May 1987).
    1986 "World Heritage List No. 394." Paris: World Heritage Center, April 22, 1986.
    1992 "World Heritage List 667." Paris: World Heritage Center, September 22, 1992.
    1993 "Hue. World Heritage List No. 678" Paris: World Heritage Center, September 29, 1993.
    1995 "Hiroshima. World Heritage List No. 773" Paris: World Heritage Center, September 28, 1995.
    1999a "Hoi An" No. 948. Paris: World Heritage Center, July 28, 1998 (Submitted September 1999).
    1999b "My Son" No. 949. Paris: World Heritage Center, July 28, 1998 (Submitted September 1999).
    2001 "Masada (Israel)" No. 1040. Paris: World Heritage Center, June 30, 2001.
    2003 "Val D'Orcia (Italy) No. 1026 REV." Paris: World Heritage Center, January 30, 2003.
    2007 "Sydney Opera House No. 166 REV." Paris: World Heritage Center, January 21, 2007.
Inman, Mason
    2006 "Pluto Not a Planet" *National Geographic Online,* http://news.nationalgeographic.com/news/2006/08/060824-pluto-planet.html. Accessed on September 29, 2006.

IUCN (International Union for the Conservation of Nature and Natural Resources)
  1992   "Ha Long Bay: IUCN Technical Evaluation 671" Paris: World Heritage Centre.
  1999   "Ha Long Bay: IUCN Technical Evaluation Renomination." Paris: World Heritage Centre.
  2003   "Phong Nha-Ke Bang—IUCN Technical Evaluation No. 951 Rev" Paris: World Heritage Centre.
Jacobsen, Trudy
  2003   "Autonomous Queenship in Cambodia—1st to 9th Centuries AD." *Journal of the Royal Asiatic Society, Series 3*. London: Royal Asiatic Society. Vol. 13, No. 3, pp. 357–375.
Jessup, Helen and Thierry Zephir
  1997   *Millennium of Glory: Sculpture of Angkor and Ancient Cambodia.* Washington, DC: National Gallery of Art.
Johnson, Anna
  2005   "Chicago Gets Worked Up Over Fois Gras" *Associate Press Release.* http://news.yahoo.com/s/ap/20051110/ap_on_re_us/foie_gras_feud. Accessed on November 10, 2005.
Johnson, George
  1992   *In the Palaces of Memory: How We Build the Worlds Inside Our Heads.* New York: Vintage Books.
Kane, Joe
  1993   "With Spears from all Sides." *The New Yorker*, September: pp. 54–79.
Kant, Emmanuel
  1998   *Critique of Pure Reason.* CambridgeCambridge University Press.
Katriel, Tamar
  1997   *Performing the Past: A Study of Israeli Settlement Museums.* Mahwah, NJ: Lawrence Erlbaum Associates, Publisher.
Kazmi, Kristina
  2008   "Thai Government Suspends Endorsement of Cambodian Temple Listing." World Markets Research Limited, July 2, 2008. Accessed through Lexus Nexis on July 8, 2008.
Key, Archie F.
  1973   *Beyond Four Walls: The Origins and Development of Canadian Museums.* Toronto: McClelland and Stewart, Ltd.
Keyes, Charles F.
  1995   *The Golden Peninsula: Culture and Adaptation in Mainland Southeast Asia.* Honolulu: University of Hawai'i Press.
King, Dale
  1940   "Scope and Function of the Interpretation Program of the Southwestern National Monuments." *Report of Meeting of Custodians, Southwestern National Monuments.* Washington, DC: National Park Service, History Division, February 14–16, 1940.
Kitchen, Kenneth A.
  1982   *Pharaoh Triumphant: The Life and Times of Ramesses II.* Missisuaga, Ontario: Benben Publications.

Kirkpatrick, David
  2006   "Google Founder Defends China Portal." *CNNMoney.com*. January 25, 2006. http://money.cnn.com/2006/01/25/news/international/davos_fortune/. Accessed June 23, 2006.

Kirshenblatt-Gimblett, Barbara
  1998   *Destination Culture*. Berkeley: University of California Press, 1998.
  2004   "Intangible Heritage as a Metacultural Production." In *Museum International*, Vol 56, Issue 1–2, June 24, 2004.
  2007   "World Heritage and Cultural Economics." In *Museum Frictions: Public Cultures/Global Transformations*. Ivan Karp and Corinne Kratz, eds. Durham, NC: Duke University Press.

Knorr-Centina, Karin
  1999. *Epistemic Cultures: How the Sciences Make Knowledge*. Cambridge: Harvard University Press.
  2000   "How Are Global Markets Global? The Architecture of a Flow World." In *The Sociology of Financial Markets*, edited by Karin Knorr-Cetina and Alex Preda. Oxford: Oxford University Press.

Kolata, Alan
  2007   "Kingship and Compassion: The Hospitals of Jayavarman VII," Paper presented at the Interdisciplinary Archaeology Workshop, University of Chicago, May 2008.

Kolb, Michael
  1994   "Monumentality and the Rise of Religious Authority in Precontact Hawai'i" *Current Anthropology* 24, no. 5, December.

Kotler, Neil and Philip Kotler
  2004   "Can Museums Be All Things to All People? Missions, Goals and Marketing's Role." In *Reinventing the Museum: Historical and Contemporary Perspectives on the Paradigm Shirt*, edited by Gail Anderson. Walnut Creek, CA: AltaMira Press, pp. 167–186.

Landler, Mark
  2000   "Ruins by Day, Luxury by Night." *New York Times*. http://query.nytimes.com/gst/fullpage.html?res=9E06E1DF163AF935A15752C1A9669C8B63. Accessed on June 25, 2006.

Lash, Scott and John Urry
  1994   *Economies of Signs and Space*. London: Sage.

LeFebvre, Henri
  1991   *The Production of Space*. Translated by Donald Nicholson-Smith. Cambridge: Blackwell Publishers.

Leite, Naomi
  2007   "Materializing Absence: Tourists, Surrogates, and the Making of 'Jewish Portugal'" Conference Proceedings from *Things That Move: The Material World of Tourism and Travel*. Leeds, UK: Centre for Tourism and Cultural Change.

Lévi-Strauss, Claude
  1997   "The Culinary Triangle." In *Food and Culture: A Reader*. Counihan, Carole and Penny van Esterik. New York: Routledge, pp.36–54.

Lévy-Bruhl, Lucian
    1923   Translated by Lilian A. Clare. *Primitive Mentality*. New York: Macmillan Company.

Lippard, Lucy
    1998   *The Lure of the Local*. New York: The New Press.
    2000   *On the Beaten Track*. New York: The New Press.

Loti, Pierre
    1996   *A Pilgrimage to Angkor*. Translated by W. P. Baines and Michael Smithies. Chiang Mai, Thailand: Silkworm Books.

Low, Theodore
    2004   "What Is a Museum?" In *Reinventing the Museum: Historical and Contemporary Perspectives on the Paradigm Shirt*, edited by Gail Anderson. Walnut Creek, CA: AltaMira Press, pp. 30–43.

Lowenthal, David
    2004   *The Heritage Crusade and the Spoils of History*. London: Cambridge University Press.

Luke, Timothy
    2002   *Museum Politics*. Minneapolis: University of Minnesota Press.

Lury, Celia
    1997   "The Objects of Travel." In Rojek, Chris and John Urry. *Touring Cultures: Transformations of Travel and Theory*. London: Routledge.

Lycett, Mark T.
    2002   "Transformations of Place: Occupational History and Differential Persistence in 17th Century New Mexico." In Preucel, P.W., ed., *Archaeologies of the Pueblo Revolt*. Albuquerque, NM: University of New Mexico Press, pp. 61–74.

Lyman, Jay
    2004   "Google's China Filtering Draws Fire." *Technewsworld*. December 1, 2004. www.technewsworld.com/story/38573.html?wlc=1223135723. Downloaded on June 23, 2006.

MacAloon, John
    1981   *This Great Symbol: Pierre de Courbertin and the Origins of the Modern Olympics Games*. Chicago: University of Chicago Press.

MacCannell, Dean
    1999   *The Tourist: A New Theory of the Leisure Class*. Berkeley: University of California Press.

MacIntyre, Alisdair
    1984   *After Virtue: A Study in Moral Theory*. Notre, Dame: Indiana: University of Notre Dame Press.

Malinowski, Bronislaw
    1984   *Argonauts of the Western Pacific*. Long Grove, IL: Waveland Press, Inc.

Mangold, Tom and John Penycate
    1986   *The Tunnels of Cu Chi*. New York: Berkley Books.

Mannikka, Eleanor
    1996   *Angkor Wat: Time, Space, and Kingship*. Honolulu: University of Hawai'i Press.

Masco, Joseph
  2005   "The Billboard Campaign: The Lost Alamos Study Group and the Nuclear Pub-
         lic Sphere" in *Public Culture* vol. 17, no. 3, pp. 487–96.
Matsura, Koïchiro
  2001a "Address of Mr. Koichiro Matsura, Director General of UNESCO, on the Oc-
         casion of the Third Session of the Islamic Conference of Cultural Ministers."
         Islamic Conference of Cultural Ministers, Doha, December 29, 2001.
  2001b "The Cultural Wealth of the World is Diversity in Dialogue." In *Universal
         Declaration of Cultural Diversity* official packet. UNESCO. Paris: Thirty-first
         Session of UNESCO General Congress, November 2, 2001, pg. 11.
Mauss, Marcel
  2000   *The Gift*. New York: W. W. Norton and Company, Inc.
Mayes, Frances
  1997   *Under the Tuscan Sun: At Home in Italy*. New York: Broadway Books.
  2000   *Bella Tuscany: The Sweet Life in Italy*. New York: Broadway Books.
Mazzarella, William
  2003   *Shoveling Smoke: Advertising and Globalization in Contemporary India*. Dur-
         ham, NC: Duke University Press.
  2004   "Culture, Globalization, Mediation." *Annual Review of Anthropology*. Vol. 33,
         October 2004, pp. 369–392.
McCarthy, Terry
  2000   "Reclaiming History" *Time Magazine—Asia*. August 21, 2000.
Metcalf, Peter and Richard Huntington
  1991   *Celebrations of Death, the Anthropology of Mortuary Ritual*. Cambridge,
         United Kingdom: Cambridge University Press.
Meyer, John W., John Boli, George Thomas, Franciso O. Ramirez
  1997   "World Society and the Nation-State." *The American Journal of Sociology*,
         Volume 103, No. 1: July 1, 1997.
Middleton, John
  1991   *The World of the Swahili: An African Mercantile Civilization*. New Haven:
         Yale University Press.
Miller, Daniel and Don Slater
  2001   *The Internet: An Ethnographic Approach*. New York: Berg.
Ministry of Foreign Affairs
  2008   "The Results of Consultation between Thailand and Cambodia concerning the
         Inscription of the Temple of Preah Vihear on World Heritage List." Bangkok:
         Ministry of Foreign Affairs, Kingdom of Thailand. Downloaded from
         www.mfa.go.th/web/2654.php?id=19992 on July 1, 2008.
Mintz, Sidney
  1985   *Sweetness and Power: The Place of Sugar in Modern History*. New York: Pen-
         guin Books.
Mohan, Giles and Kristian Stokke
  2000   "Participatory Development and Empowerment: The Dangers of Localism."
         Third World Quarterly. Vol. 21, No. 2, pp. 247–268.
Molenda, Michael

2003 "Cone of Experience." In *Educational Technology: An Encyclopedia.* Koval-
      chick, Anne & Kara Dawson, eds. Santa Barbara, CA: ABC-Clio.

Montaigne, Michel de
2003 *Complete Essays.* New York: Penguin Books.

Morgan, Lewis Henry
1877 *Ancient Society: or Researches in the Line of Human Progress from Savagery
      through Barbarism to Civilization.* Chicago: C.H. Kerr.

Morphy, Howard
1993 "Colonialism, History and the Construction of Place: The Politics of Landscape
      in Northern Australia." In Bender, Barbara, ed. *Landscape: Politics and Per-
      spectives,* Oxford: Berg, pp. 205–243.

Morrison, Kathleen D.
n.d.   *Oceans of Dharma: A Political Ecology of Reservoirs, Farming and Food in
      South India.* Seattle: University of Washington Press.

Mydens, Seth
2002 "Gala at Angkor: 'Cue the Monks,' Then the Tenor." New York Times. De-
      cember 7, 2002. http://query.nytimes.com/gst/fullpage.html?res=9F06E4D8103
      BF934A35751C1A9649C8B63. Accessed on June 25, 2006.

Nash, Dennison
1981 "Tourism as an Anthropological Subject." *Current Anthropology.* Volume 22,
      No. 5, October 1981, pp. 461–481.

1989 "Tourism as a Form of Imperialism" in Smith, Valene (ed.) *Hosts and Guests:
      The Anthropology of Tourism.* Philadelphia: University of Pennsylvania Press.

New Zealand Ministry of Tourism
2006 "Glossary of Tourism Terms" www.tourism.govt.nz/quicklinks/ql-glossary.
      html. Accessed on June 1, 2006.

Ngô Van Doanh
2005 *Mỹ Sơn Relics.* Ha Noi: Thế Giói Publishers.

Nguyễn, Văn Xuân
2000 *Hội An.* Đà Nẵng: Danang Publishing House.

Noriendr, Panivong
1996 *Phantasmatic Indochina.* Durham, NC: Duke University Press.

Novogrod, Nancy
2004 "Editor's Note." *Travel + Leisure.* April 2004. NY: Travel + Leisure. www.
      travelandleisure.com/articles/editors-note-april-2004. Accessed on July 27,
      2006.

Orbitz.com
2007 "Save $50 Instantly and Try Our New Traveler Community Feature." E-mail to
      subscribers, October 8, 2007.

Origo, Iris and Denis Mack Smith
1995 *War in the Val D'Orcia.* Boston, Massachusetts: David R. Godine Publisher.

Owen, Stephen
1990 "Poetry in the Chinese Tradition." *Heritage of China: Contemporary Perspec-
      tives on Chinese Civilization.* Paul S. Ropp, ed. Berkeley: University of Cali-
      fornia Press.

Paddock, Richard
2004 "Spirit Reset in Stone" Los Angeles: *Los Angeles Times,* April 26, 2004: A1.
Pearson, Michael Parker and Colin Richards
1997 *Architecture and Order: Approaches to Social Space.* New York: Routledge.
Peleggi, Maurizio
2002 *The Politics of Ruins and the Business of Nostalgia.* Bangkok: White Lotus Press.
Pham, Mai
2001 *Pleasures of the Vietnamese Table: Recipes and Reminiscences from Vietnam's Best Market Kitchens, Street Cafes and Home Cooks.* New York: HarperCollins Publishers.
Phan Thuận An
2002 *Kién Trúc Co Dô Hué / Monuments of Hue.* Hué, Viet Nam: Thuân Hóa Publishing House.
Poggioli, Sylvia
2005 "A Provocative Campaign to Save Italy's Artworks." *NPR Morning Edition.* October 26, 2005. www.npr.org/templates/story/story.phpstoryId=4975049&ft =1&f=1004 Accessed on October 28, 2005.
Pollack, Sheldon
2008 "Introduction." *Rāmāyana Book III: The Forest.* NY: Clay Sanskrit Library and NYU Press. www.claysanskritlibrary.org/excerpts/aranya/aranya-introduction. php. Accessed on February 11, 2008.
Ponder, H. W.
1936 *Cambodian Glory: The Mystery of the Deserted Khmer Cities and their Vanquished Splendour: and a Description of Life in Cambodia Today.* London: Thornton Butterworth.
Pratt, Mary Louise
1992 *Imperial Eyes: Travel Writing and Transculturation.* New York: Routledge.
Rago, J. Lyndsey
2007 "Touching the Old Stones: Souvenirs, Stonehenge and Victorian Tourism." In *Conference Proceeding from Things That Move: The Material World of Tourism and Travel.* Leeds, UK: Centre for Tourism and Cultural Change.
Redfield, Robert; Ralph Linton and Melvin Herskovits
1936 "Memorandum for the Study of Acculturation." *American Anthropologist.* New Series. Vol. 38, No. 1, January–March 1936, pp. 149–152.
Richie, Donald
2004 "Filling in the Template for a Changing Cambodia" *Japan Times* Mar. 28, 2004
Richman, Alan
2005 "Victual Reality: What do America's favorite take-out cuisines—Chinese, Thai, and Vietnamese—Taste Like in Situ?" *Condé Nast Traveler,* Dec. 2005.
"Rite of Passage"
2006 In *Encyclopaedia Brittanica.* Downloaded on June 20, 2006 from Encyclopaedia Brittanica Premium Service: www.britannica.com/eb/article?tocId=66339.
Robertson, Roland
1992 *Globalization. Social Theory and Global Culture.* London: Sage.

Rooney, Dawn
  2003 *Angkor: An Introduction to the Temples.* New York: W.W. Norton and Company, Revised Edition.
Royal Embassy of Cambodia website
  2005 "Tourism in the Kingdom of Cambodia" www.embassy.org/cambodia/toursim/tour.htm. Accessed on April 8, 2005.
Sahlins, Marshall
  1976 "La Pensée Bourgeoise" from *Culture and Practical Reason.* Chicago: University of Chicago Press.
  1987 *Islands of History.* Chicago: University of Chicago Press.
  2000 "Goodbye to Tristes Tropes." In *Culture and Practice: Selected Essays.* New York, NY: Zone Books.
Said, Edward
  1994 *Orientalism.* New York: Vintage Books.
Sané, Pierre
  2001 "Address by Mr. Pierre Sane, Head of the UNESCO Delegation to WCAR and Assistant Director-General for Social and Human Sciences to the World Conference Against Racism." Durban, South Africa: UNESCO World Conference Against Racism, April 2001.
Sassoon, Joanna
  2004 "Photographic Materiality in the Age of Digital Reproduction" in Elizabeth Edwards and Janice Hart, ed.s. *Photographs Objects Histories: On the Materiality of Images.* New York: Routledge.
Schneider, Cynthia P.
  2000 "Art, Culture and Diplomacy: Three Links on the Chain of Greater Understanding." *Educating in Paradise Symposium.* Florence: Palazzo Vecchio Salone dei Cinquecento, October 5, 2000.
Schuhmacher, Stephan and Gert Woerner, ed.s
  1994 *The Encyclopedia of Eastern Philosophy and Religion.* Boston: Shambhala Press.
Seton, Grace Gallatin
  1938 *Poison Arrows: Strange Journey with an Opium Dream through Annam, Cambodia, Siam and the Lotus Isle of Bali, illustrated with maps and many photographs taken by the author.* London: Travel Book Club.
SGGP (Sai Gòn Gió Phong Online News Service)
  2005 "Phong Nha-Ke Bang: Wild Animals Cry for Help." *Vietnam Net.* October 24, 2005. http://english.vietnamnet.vn/service/printversion.vnn?article_id=72212. Accessed on October 20, 2006.
Shafer, Roy
  2003 *Bad Feelings.* New York: The Other Press.
Sihanouk, Norodom
  1995 *Royal Decree establishing a National Authority for the Protection and Management of Angkor and the Region of Siem Reap, named APSARA.* February 19, 1995. Phnom Penh: APSARA. www.autoriteapsara.org/en/apsara/about_apsara/legal_texts/decree1_text.html. Accessed on June 28, 2006.

1999   *Royal Decree NS/RKT/0199/18*. January 22, 1999. Phnom Penh: APSARA. www.autoriteapsara.org/en/apsara/about_apsara/legal_texts/decree2_text.html. Accessed on June 28, 2006.

Silliman, Stephen W.
2005   "Culture Contact or Colonialism? Challenges in the Archaeology of Native North America." *American Antiquity*. Vol. 70, No. 1, pp. 55–74.

Smalley, William A.
1954   "Srê Phonemes and Syllables." *Journal of the American Oriental Society*. Vol. 74, No. 4 (October—December 1954), pp. 217–222.

Smith, Stacey Vanek
2000   "Asian Beauty Restored" in *Time Europe*, Volume 157 No. 4. www.time.com/time/europe/magazine/2001/0129/guimet.html. Accessed on October 24, 2005.

Smith, Valene, ed.
1989   *Hosts and Guests: The Anthropology of Tourism*. Philadelphia: University of Pennsylvania Press.

Snape, Steven
2007   "Walking in Memphis: Tourism in Ancient Egypt." In *Conference Proceeding from Things That Move: The Material World of Tourism and Travel*. Leeds, UK: Centre for Tourism and Cultural Change.

Sok An
2004   "Speech by His Excellency Mr. Sok An, Senior Minister, Minister in Charge of the Office of the Council of Ministers at the 22nd World Tourism Day." Phnom Penh, Cambodia: September 27, 2001. www.camnet.com.kh/ocm/government/041023_1.pdf. Downloaded on March 6, 2005.

Šopova, Jasmina
2007   "From Herders to Architects: Man's Imprint on World Heritage." *The UNESCO Courier*, Vol. 2007 No. 6. June 29, 2007.

SOS Children International
2005   "José Carreras Gives Benefit Concert in Cambodia" www.soschildrensvillages.org/cgibin/sos/jsp/retrieve.do?cat=/514_news_archives&ll=37588&lang=en&nav=5.1&quart=38198&site=ZZ. Accessed on December 20, 2005.

Soubert, Son and Suong Leang Hay
1995   "Case Study on the Effects of Tourism on Culture and the Environment: Cambodia." Bangkok, Thailand: UNESCO Regional Office for Asia and the Pacific.

Spitulnik, Debra
1993   "Anthropology and Mass Media." *Annual Review of Anthropology*. Vol. 22, pp. 293–315.

Sterling, Eleanor J., Martha M. Hurley and Raoul H. Bain
2003   "Vietnam's Secret Life" *Natural History Magazine*, March 2003. www.naturalhistory-mag.com/master.html?http://www.naturalhistorymag.com/0303/0303_feature.html. Accessed on November 11, 2006.

Stocking, George
1989   *A Franz Boas Reader: The Shaping of American Anthropology, 1883–1911*. Chicago: University of Chicago Press.

Summers, K. C.

2007   "The Trouble With Trip Advisor" in "Travel Log," a blog for the Washington
        Post's online Arts and Living / Travel section. http://blog.washingtonpost.com/
        travellog/2007/02/the_trouble_with_trip_advisor.html#comments. Accessed on
        February 27, 2007.

Tarling, Nicholas
1999   *The Cambridge History of Southeast Asia, Vol. 1, Part 2.* Cambridge: Cam-
        bridge University Press, 1999.

Tilden, Freeman
1957   *Interpreting Our Heritage.* Chapel Hill: University of North Carolina Press.

Time
1963   "The Pharoah and the Flood." *Time Magazine* Online Archives. www.time.com
        /time/magazine/article/0,9171,828111,00.html. Accessed September 29, 2006.

Tippett, Joanne
n.d.   "Death, Sex and Gardening: Conceptions of Death, Illness and Health and the
        Medicalization of Western Society." www.holocene.net/sustainability/essays%
        20and%20e.g.s/meaning-symbols-gardening.htm. Accessed on November 11,
        2005.

Tomlinson, Richard
1999   "Obituary: Lord Charteris of Amisfield." *The Independent.* London. http://find
        articles.com/p/articles/mi_qn4158/is_19991227/ai_n14272530/print. Accessed
        on February 7, 2008.

Trần Kỳ Phương
2004   *Vestiges of Champa Civilization.* Ha Noi: Thế Giới Publishers.

TravelMole Presswire
2006   "Online Travel Packages up to 40%." May 29, 2006. www.travelmole.com/
        stories/108955.php?mpnlog=1. Accessed on May 30, 2006.

Trebay, Guy
2001   "The Next Hot Spot" *Travel+Leisure*, September: pp. 259–262; 279–282.

Tucker, Robert ed.
1978   *The Marx-Engels Reader.* New York: W.W. Norton and Company.

Turner, Terrence
1995   "An Indigenous People's Struggle for Socially Equitable and Ecologically Sus-
        tainable Production: The Kayapo Revolt against Extractivism." *Journal of
        Latin American Anthropology.* Vol. 1, No. 1, pp. 9–121.

Turner, Victor
1967   *The Forest of Symbols: Aspects of Ndembu Ritual.* Ithaca and London: Cornell
        University Press.
1969   *The Ritual Process: Structure and Antistructure.* London: Routledge and Kegan
        Paul.
1973   "The Center Out There: Pilgrim's Goal." *History of Religions.* Vol. 12, pp.
        191–230.
1974a   "Pilgrimage and Communitas." *Studia Missionalia.* Vol. 23, pp. 305–307.
1974b   "Pilgrimages as Social Processes." In *Dramas, Fields and Metaphors: Symbolic
        Action in Human Society.* Ithaca: Cornell University Press, pp.166–229.

Turner, Victor and Edith Turner

1978 *Image and Pilgrimage in Christian Culture.* New York: Columbia University Press.

Turntian, Jan

2000. *Globalising Heritage.* Paris: UNESCO SCORE Rapportserie.

UN (United Nations)

1948 *Universal Declaration of Human Rights,* December 10, 1948.

2003 "Poverty Alleviation through Sustainable Tourism Development." www.unes cap.org/publications/detail.asp?id=1020. New York: United Nations Economic and Social Commission for Asia and the Pacific. Accessed on June 1, 2006.

UNESCO (United Nations Education Scientific and Cultural Organization)

1945 *Constitution of the United Nations Educational, Scientific and Cultural Organization* London: UNESCO 1st General Conference, November 16, 1945.

1948 "Agreement For Facilitating the International Circulation of Visual and Auditory Materials of an Educational, Scientific and Cultural character with Protocol of Signature and model form of certificate provided for in Article IV of the above-mentioned Agreement." In *Records of the General Conference of UNESCO, 3rd Session.* Beirut, December 10, 1948, pp. 113–114.

1950 *Agreement on the Importation of Educational, Scientific and Cultural Materials, with Annexes A to E and Protocol annexed.* Florence, 17 June 1950

1952 *Universal Copyright Convention, with Appendix Declaration relating to Articles XVII and Resolution concerning Article XI.* Geneva, 6 September 1952.

1958a *Convention Concerning the Exchange of Official Publications and Government Documents between States.* Paris, December 3, 1958.

1958b *Convention Concerning the International Exchange of Publications.* Paris, December 3, 1958.

1961 "Thirty-Five States Sign the 'Addis Ababa Plan' For Vast Expansion of Education in Africa." Paris: *The UNESCO Courier,* July/August 1961.

1962 "Recommendations on the Safeguarding of the Beauty and Character of Landscapes and Sites" in *Records of the General Conference, Twelfth Session.* Paris, pp. 139–144.

1971 *Universal Copyright Convention as revised at Paris on 24 July 1971, with Appendix Declaration relating to Article XVII and Resolution concerning Article XI.* Paris, July 24, 1971.

1972 *Convention Concerning the Protection of the World Cultural and Natural Heritage,* Article 1. Paris: World Heritage Centre, UNESCO, November 16, 1972.

1974 *Convention Relating to the Distribution of Programme-Carrying Signals Transmitted by Satellite.* Brussels, Belgium, May 21, 1974.

1979a *Multilateral Convention for the Avoidance of Double Taxation of Copyright Royalties, with model bilateral agreement and additional Protocol.* Madrid, December 13, 1979.

1979b "Report of the World Heritage Committee Third Session." Cairo, Egypt, October 22–26, 1979.

1983 "Report of the World Heritage Committee Seventh Session." Florence, Italy. December 5–9, 1983.

1992   "Report of the World Heritage Committee Sixteenth Session." Santa Fe, New Mexico. December 7–14, 1992.

1993a   "Report of the World Heritage Committee Seventeenth Session." Cartagena, Colombia, December 6–11, 1993.

1993b   *Tokyo Declaration*. Tokyo, Japan. October 13, 1993.

1994a   "Expert Meeting on the "Global Strategy" and thematic studies for a representative World Heritage List" Addendum to the "Report of the World Heritage Committee Seventeenth Session." Phuket, Thailand. Dec. 12–17, 1994.

1994b   "Report of the World Heritage Committee Eighteenth Session." Phuket, Thailand. December 12–17, 1994.

1996   "Report of the World Heritage Committee Twentieth Session." Merida, Mexico, December 2–7, 1996.

1997a   "50 Years of Education." Paris: UNESCO.

1997b   "Report of the World Heritage Committee Twenty-First Session." Naples, Italy. December 1–6, 1997.

1998   *50 Years for Education*. (CD-Rom) Paris: UNESCO.

1999a   "Item 6 of the Provisional Agenda: Progress report on the implementation of the regional actions described in the Global Strategy Action Plan adopted by the Committee at its twenty-second session." Paris: World Heritage Centre; October 21, 1999.

1999b   "Report of the World Heritage Committee Twenty-Third Session." Marrakesh, Morocco, November 29–December 4, 1999.

2000a   "Cairns Decision." In "Report of the World Heritage Committee Twenty-Fourth Session." Cairns, Australia, November 27–December 2, 2000, pp.9–13.

2000b   "Mission Statement" Paris: World Heritage Centre, UNESCO.

2001a   "31C/46 Acts Constituting Crimes against Common Heritage of Humanity." Item 5.5 of the Provisional Agenda. Paris, France: General Conference, Thirty-Fifth Session, September 12, 2001.

2001b   "Report of the World Heritage Committee Twenty-Fifth Session." Helsinki, Finland, December 11–16, 2001.

2001c   *Universal Declaration of Cultural Diversity*. Paris: Thirty-first Session of UNESCO General Congress, November 2, 2001.

2002   *World Heritage 2002: Shared Legacy, Common Responsibility*. Paris: World Heritage Centre.

2003a   *Convention for the Safeguarding of Intangible Cultural Heritage*. Paris: UNESCO, October 17, 2003.

2003b   *Paris Declaration for the Safeguarding and Development of Angkor*. Paris: Second Intergovernmental Conference for the Safeguarding and Sustainable Development of the Historic Site of Angkor and of its Region. November 14–15, 2003.

2003c   "Report of the World Heritage Committee Twenty-Seventh Session." Paris: UNESCO Headquarters. June 30–July 5, 2003.

2003d   *The State of World Heritage in the Asia-Pacific Region*. Paris: UNESCO.

2003e   *UNESCO: What it is, What it does* information packet. Paris: World Heritage Centre.

2004a "Report of the World Heritage Committee Twenty-Eighth Session." Suzhou, China, June 28–July 7, 2005.

2004b "World Heritage." UNESCO information website, http://portal.unesco.org/culture/en/. Accessed on December 4, 2004.

2005a *Operational Guidelines for the Implementation of the World Heritage Conventions*. Paris: World Heritage Centre. Accessed on February 2, 2005.

2005b Paper Series No. 12: *The State of World Heritage in the Asia-Pacific Region* (2003)." Press Release. Paris: World Heritage Centre. April 2005. http://whc.unesco.org/en/news/117. Accessed on February 2, 2005.

2005c "Report of the World Heritage Committee Twenty-Ninth Session." Durban, South Africa, July 10–17, 2006.

2005d "World Heritage Information Kit" Paris: World Heritage Center.

2005e "World Heritage List." UNESCO information website, http://whc.unesco.org/pg.cfm?cid=31. Accessed on January 12, 2005.

2006a "30COM/7B elaboration." Thirtieth Meeting of the World Heritage Committee. Vilnius, Lithuania: UNESCO July 8–16, 2006.

2006b "30COM/8B (Auschwitz Concentration Camp)" Addendum to the *Report of the World Heritage Committee Thirtieth session*. Vilnius, Lithuania: UNESCO July 8–16, 2006.

2006c *Masterpieces of the Oral and Intangible Heritage of Humanity: Proclamations 2001, 2003 and 2005*. Paris: World Heritage Centre.

2006d "Report of the World Heritage Committee Thirtieth Session." Vilnius, Lithuania: UNESCO July 8–16, 2006.

2006e "World Heritage Committee threatens to remove Dresden Elbe Valley (Germany) from World Heritage List" *Press Release*. Paris: World Heritage Centre, July 11, 2006.

2007a "Report of the World Heritage Committee Thirty First Session." Christchurch, New Zealand, June 23–July 2, 2007.

2007b "World Heritage Committee Approves Auschwitz Name Change." Press Release. Paris, France: UNESCO, June 28, 2007.

2007c "World Heritage Emblem." Paris, France: World Heritage Centre website, http://whc.unesco.org/en/emblem/ Accessed on September 19, 2007.

2008 "Benefits of Ratification." UNESCO information website, http://whc.unesco.org/en/164. Accessed on March 4, 2008.

UNWTO (United Nations World Tourism Organization)

2005a "Tourism Highlights" www.world-tourism.org/facts/menu.html. Accessed on November 1, 2006.

2005b "World's Top Emerging Tourism Destinations in the period 1995–2004." www.world-tourism.org/facts/menu.html. Accessed on November 1, 2006.

2006 "Tourism Highlights, 2006 Edition." www.world-tourism.org/facts/menu.html Accessed on June 28, 2007.

2007 "Tourism Highlights, 2007 Edition." www.world-tourism.org/facts/menu.html. Accessed on March 4, 2008.

Urry, John

2002 *The Tourist Gaze*. London: Sage.

Vachon, Michelle
   2003   "Our House: Why Traditional Khmer Houses are Disappearing." *The Cambodia Daily*, WEEKEND Saturday, February 1–2, 2003.

Vālmīki
   2006   Translated by Sheldon Pollock. *Rāmāyana. Book III: The Forest.* New York: Clay Sanskrit Library and New York University Press.

van Buitenen, J. A. B., translator and editor
   1981   *The* Bhagavadgitā *in the* Mahābhārata. Chicago: University of Chicago Press.

van Gennep, Arnold
   1960   *Rites of Passage.* Chicago: University of Chicago Press.

Vickery, Michael
   1979   "The Composition and Transition of the Ayudhya and Cambodian Chronicles." *Perceptions of the Past in Southeast Asia.* A.J.S. Reid and David Marr, eds. Singapore: Heinemann Educational Books. Published for the Asian Studies Association of Australia.

Vietnam National Administration of Tourism
   2006   "Phong Nha-Ke Bang National Park, World Heritage." Hanoi. www.vietnam tourism.com/e_pages/heritage/phongnha.asp. Accessed on October 20, 2006.

Vietnam News Briefs
   2006   "UNESCO Asks for Pollution Assessment in Ha Long Bay." July 12, 2006.

Võ Văn Dáng, ed.
   2002   *Những Di Sản Thế Giới ở Việt Nam: World Heritage in Vietnam.* Da Nang: Nhà Xuất Bản Đa Nẵng.

Wagoner, Phillip L.
   2000   "Epilogue: Each Particular Place: Culture and Geography." In *Cultural Encounters with the Environment. Enduring and Evolving Geographic Themes.* Murphy, Alexander B. and Douglas Johnson, eds. New York: Rowman and Littlefield, pp. 311–322.

Wales, H.G. Quaritch
   1965   *Angkor and Rome: A Historical Comparison.* London: B. Quaritch.

Wallach, Alan
   1998   *Exhibiting Contradiction.* Boston: University of Massachusetts Press.

Ward, Coleen A., Stephen Bochner and Adrian Furnham
   2001   *The Psychology of Culture Shock.* Philadelphia: Taylor and Francis, Inc.

Weber, Max
   1963   "Objectivity in Social Science and Science Policy." In M. Nathanson, ed. *Philosophy of the Social Sciences.* New York: Random House, pp. 365–418.
   1992   *The Protestant Ethic and the Spirit of Capitalism.* New York: Routledge, Chapman and Hall.

Weinberger, Eliot and Octavio Paz
   1987   *19 Ways of Looking at Wang Wei: How a Chinese Poem is Translated.* Kingston, RI: Asphodel Press.

Wertsch, James
   2002   *Voices of Collective Remembering.* London: Cambridge University Press.

Wikipedia
    2006   "Edutainment." http://en.wikipedia.org/wiki/Edutainment. Accessed June 1,
            2006.
Wikramanayake, Eric
    1999   "Muntjaks and Rice Wine." *ZooGoer*. Washington, DC: Smithsonian Institu-
            tion, January / February 2006 edition. http://nationalzoo.si.edu/Publications/
            ZooGoer/1999/1/munjaksricewine.cfm. Accessed on November 1, 2006.
Wilkening, David
    2006a   "Christian Cruise Line Finds Heavenly New Niche." London, United Kingdom:
            Travelmole online, September 12, 2006. www.travelmole.com/stories/110712.p
            hp?mpnlog=1 Accessed on September 12, 2006.
    2006b   "Gays and Lesbians Invited to a Wedding" *Travelmole News* 5 June 2006.
            www.travelmole.com/stories/109083.php. Accessed on June 6, 2006.
    2006c   "Internet Continues to Revolutionize Travel." *Travelmole News* (November 16,
            2006. www.travelmole.com/stories/1114013.php?mpnlog=1 Accessed on No-
            vember 16, 2006.
    2006d   "Online Travel Packages up to 40%." *TravelMole Presswire*. May 29, 2006.
            www.travelmole.com/stories/108955.php?mpnlog=1. Accessed on May 30,
            2006.
Wilkinson, Brooke
    2005   "The Fabulous 50" *Condé Nast Traveler,* December 2005.
Willey, Gordon R. and Phillip Phillips
    1958   *Method and Theory in American Archaeology*. University of Chicago Press,
            Chicago.
Wilson, Sam and Leighton Peterson
    2002   "The Anthropology of Online Communities," in *The Annual Review of Anthro-
            pology,* Vol. 31, pp. 449–467.
Winter, Tim
    2002   "Angkor Meets Tomb Raider—Setting the Scene." *International Journal of
            Heritage Studies*, Vol. 8, No. 4, 2002, pp. 323–336.
    2003   "Tomb Raiding Angkor: A Clash of Cultures." *Indonesia and the Malay
            World*, Vol. 31, No. 89, March 2003:58, 60.
Yang, Minja and Jehanne Pharès
    2002.   "Safeguarding and Development of World Heritage Cities" in Proceedings
            from the Conference, *Partnerships for World Heritage Cities: Culture as a
            Vector for Sustainable Urban Development*. Urbino-Pesaro, Italy: UNESCO
            World Heritage Centre and the Istituto Universitario di Architettura di Venezia,
            November 11–12, 2002.
Yoon, Suthichai
    2003   "In Search of Deeper Answers to Cambodia" *The Nation*, February 6, 2003.
            www.nationmultimedia.com/page.arcview.php3?clid=11&id=73559&usrsess=
            1. Accessed on December 12, 2005.
Zerubavel, Yael
    1995   *Recovered Roots*. Chicago: University of Chicago Press.

INDEX

Abercrombie & Kent 158–159
Abitare la Storia hotels 296
A-Bomb Dome. *See* Hiroshima
Abu Simbel 313, 324, 326–328
Accademia Museum 325, 369
Acropolis 199, 291
Addis Ababa Plan 73
Advisory Bodies 9, 38, 45, 55–56, 198-199, 205, 206, 208–209
Aeneid 51
Afghanistan 388
airlines 4, 61, 146, 158, 169–170, 182; and Frequent Flyer programs 170
airports 4, 56, 148, 175, 182–185, 278; and global infrastructures 278; in Phnom Penh 148, 149; in Siem Reap 148, 175; as sites of touristic reaggregation 182–185, 419; in Vietnam 175
Alpers, Svetlana 149, 449n23
Altiers for the Conservation of Cultural Properties of Poland (PKZ) 219, 230 *See also* Kwiatkowski, Kazimier
Amatibo, Amadu 219
American Museum of Natural History 4, 271, 432n3
American War. *See* Vietnam, War
amorphism. *See* heritage-scape
Anderson, Benedict 9, 10, 77–79, 93, 119, 440n22
Angkor Archaeological Park 5, 87, 95, 111, 116, 199–201, 367, 393, 401, 404–406, 415, 419, 422, 428; and authenticity 330–331, 422; as background 276, 281, 285, 292–294, 390–392, 393, 439n2; as blockbuster venue 292–294, 439n2; designation of 328–340, 406, 416–419; designation text 40, 88–89; and economic development 148; "discovery" of 18–19, 31, 60, 304, 345, 348, 356, 359; and EFEO 19–20, 53–54, 354; and Khmer Rouge 311; and locals 311, 345, 362, 363–365; and looting 311–312, 306, 322, 329–330, 332, 335–336; and Machu Picchu 303, 461n12; and mediation 28–33, 53; narratives of 40–41, 310–311, 341–344, 348–360, 415; and nature 357–359, 343, 348, 350–351, 355–356; as a park 40; preservation of 41, 314, 318, 328–340, 354, 359, 361–362; touristic pressures on 284; as ruins 40; re-presentations of 14, 61, 65, 66–67, 320–321; and ancient Rome 19, 31, 303, 358, 461n10, 467n63; and signage 281–282; universal value of 134; and valorization of Khmer identity 351–354; and valorization of Western culture 354–360; visitation of 41–42, 344–348, 410, 417–418; and World

ABOUT THE AUTHOR

Michael A. Di Giovine is an anthropologist and former tour operator currently completing his Ph.D. in the Department of Anthropology at the University of Chicago. Working in both Southeast Asia (Cambodia and Vietnam) and Europe (Italy), his research focuses on tourism and pilgrimage, heritage and place-making, development and revitalization movements, historic preservation and museums, and religion and popular piety. He is also a Lecturer in the University of Chicago's Graham School, where he teaches courses on the landmark texts that have influenced Southeast Asia, including the *Rāmāyana*, *Mahābhārata* and *Bhagavad Gītā*, as well as Western religious and social scientific classics. Possessing nearly a decade of experience with the travel sector, Michael is also a consultant and a research associate for Slover-Linett Strategies, an audience research and planning firm specializing in museums and arts organizations. A dual Italian and United States citizen, Michael is currently conducting ethnographic research in Southern Italy, where he is examining urban and cultural revitalization associated with religious tourism at the birthplace of the newly sainted Padre Pio of Pietrelcina.

Michael earned a B.S. *cum laude* in Foreign Service from Georgetown University's School of Foreign Service, and an A.M. in the Social Sciences from the University of Chicago. He is a member of Phi Alpha Theta International History Honor Society, Theta Alpha Kappa International Theology and Religious Studies Honor Society, Delta Phi Epsilon Professional Foreign Service Fraternity, The International Commission for Ethnological Food Research, The Society of the Anthropology of Religion, the Society for the Anthropology of Europe, and the American Anthropological Association.